HIDDEN SCHOLARS

HIDDEN

SCHOLARS

Women Anthropologists and
the Native American Southwest

NANCY J. PAREZO,

EDITOR

Foreword by Nathalie F. S. and Richard B. Woodbury

University of New Mexico Press / Albuquerque

Library of Congress Cataloging-in-Publication Data

Hidden scholars: women anthropologists and the
    Native American Southwest / Nancy J. Parezo,
    editor. — 1st ed.
            p.   cm.
Based on a conference held Mar. 1986 in Tucson,
    Ariz.
Includes bibliographical references (p.   ) and
    index.
ISBN 0–8263–1428–7 (cloth)
1. Women anthropologists—Southwest,
    New—Biography.   2. Anthropology—
    Southwest, New—History.   3. Indians of
    North America—Southwest, New—Study
    and teaching.   I. Parezo, Nancy J.
GN20.H53   1993
301'.092'2—dc20
93–9994
CIP

Designed by B. Williams & Associates

To

Lita Osmundsen

who stretched our vision

and to

all future Southwesternists

CONTENTS

FOREWORD

The southwestern scholars presented in this volume have perhaps not been so much hidden as taken for granted, merging with the shadows like the pines in a forest where the oaks are more prized for their timber. We have had the advantage of knowing many of these women personally as teachers, friends, or colleagues and have learned about others from the comments of men and women who knew them. These portraits seem wonderfully true and sympathetic. Yet, although the existence of these women was certainly acknowledged and their work respected, they were too often a part of the background of southwestern studies, and they rarely achieved positions of leadership as timbers in the profession's structure. As time has passed their roles and their contributions have become ever less familiar to the new generation. *Hidden Scholars* corrects this neglect and brings the women into the prominence they deserve alongside their male contemporaries.

But this is not just a volume celebrating the role of women in anthropology. It adds up to a comprehensive survey of southwestern anthropology, offering historic depth and critical comment that extend beyond the geographic area and contribute substantially to the history of anthropology in the United States.

This book reflects Nancy Parezo's long interest in the Southwest (her book on Navajo sandpainting has recently been reprinted) and in the history of anthropology, a topic that in the last couple of decades has claimed increasing attention from many anthropologists. We now have, for example, not only the *History of Anthropology Newsletter* but the recently begun *Bulletin of the History of Archaeology*. George W. Stocking, Jr., began his History of Anthropology series in 1983, and it has continued on an annual basis. Historical insights are also provided by the growing wealth of biographies as diverse as those of W.H.R. Rivers, Edward Sapir, and Mortimer Wheeler, to name only three of many.

For some, *Hidden Scholars* may be mistaken for a feminist tract, but it avoids the shrillness and bias of many such works. What Parezo and other contributors have assembled is foremost a history of an important area in anthropology and the roles of some of its leading practitioners. The chapters are thoughtful, clearly written and edited portraits, warmly presented. We enjoyed these visits with old friends and earlier scholars, which will now be available to the coming generations. And in the process of presenting these women anthropologists, the "Daughters of the Desert," the book also gives us many valuable glimpses of some of the "Sons of the Desert."

NATHALIE F. S. WOODBURY

RICHARD B. WOODBURY

PREFACE

Several years ago, Barbara Babcock and I were sitting at a dining room table talking about our recent fieldwork experiences. Barbara was working with a remarkable Cochiti woman who made storyteller figurines, while I was completing a survey with numerous Navajo sand painters. At some point we began to discuss the women anthropologists who had worked before us. As often happens we had been thinking about the same thing. Barbara mentioned that she could not have begun her work at Cochiti without the enabling influence—both intellectually and practically—of Elsie Clews Parsons, Ruth Benedict, and Esther Goldfrank. I mentioned that my work would not have been possible had it not been for the remarkable scholarship of Gladys Reichard, Maude Oakes, Mary Wheelwright, Franc Newcomb, and others who had spent their lives collecting sand paintings and analyzing Navajo religion. Barbara had been thinking for quite some time about the quality of the contributions of Parsons, Benedict, Goldfrank, Ruth Bunzel, and Matilda Coxe Stevenson, who had dedicated their lives to understanding Puebloan culture. In fact, she felt overwhelmed by the sheer body of their work and wondered why so few people cited it today. We asked ourselves, Was it because they were women?

As we discussed the rich body of literature on southwestern Native American cultures and identified individuals who had produced it, we became intrigued. We wanted to learn more about these women to discover why they were invisible. As we brainstormed that evening and during the weeks and months that followed, we thought about the history of the discipline. How many women anthropologists had worked in the Southwest with Native Americans and had made significant contributions to anthropology? Why had

we never read about them in the books dealing with the history of anthropology?

One possibility, of course, was that there were no worthy female scholars. Historians, as we had been led to believe during our school years from kindergarten through graduate school, do not write about things that do not exist or about individuals too unimportant to merit remembrance. Were there no women anthropologists? Were women not mentioned because they had done so little? Were their contributions so negligible that they should not, and did not, need to be remembered? Or were there other systemic reasons for this displacement, reasons having to do with the structure of the discipline, the subject matter of anthropology, the politics and reward structure of academe, or the nature of society that excluded women, relegated them to secondary roles, and hid their contributions? Was the lack of power and the lower status of women in the professions, especially science, at the root of this obfuscation?

Thus began a project and a quest: to discover women scholars, re-place them in the history of anthropology, and discover the reasons for the disciplinary silence. This tall order could quickly get out of hand and take several lifetimes to complete. To develop a more focused research project, we decided to concentrate on one culture area, the Greater Southwest. We began with questions: Who were the women who worked in the Southwest? When, why, what, and with whom did they study? What were their contributions?

As we compiled more and more names we felt the necessity to further limit the study to a consideration of those who worked with Native Americans. Although this concentration unfortunately eliminated those who worked with Hispanic-, Anglo-, and African-Americans as well as other populations (although many of the women who worked with Native Americans also worked with Hispanic communities), we felt that any larger study needed to wait for more information on ethnicity and ethnic relations. Our focus on the Native American Southwest made sense for three reasons: (1) this was our specialty; (2) the large number of societies present in the region meant that there would be possibilities for comparison; and (3) the great historical depth of research meant we should be able to see changes over time, if there were any to be seen.

The Greater Southwest has always been one of anthropology's premier research areas. Robert Lowie noted in 1934 that it was the most studied region in the world. He stated, based on the distribution of articles in the *American Anthropologist,* that "the most important single ethnographic area, both in terms of the amount and the significance of research, was probably the southwestern United States" (quoted in Stocking 1976:12).[1] It was likely, then, that many women would have worked in this area and that the research produced by at least some of these women should have been important and worthy of remembrance in the history of anthropology.

To answer our questions we first had to discount the possibility that no suitable women scholars existed. After constructing an initial list of individuals whom we thought were key women, we discussed the list with several colleagues, who added more and more names. Next came a great deal of tedious library investigation in which we "discovered" women by revealing the results of their research—publications, theses, dissertations.[2] We found the first glimpses of many more women, and men, than we had anticipated. From the resulting thousands of file cards we compiled a list of over 3,500 men and 1,600 women who had worked with and published articles and books on Native Americans of the Greater Southwest. More female scholars trained in U.S. institutions, especially before the explosion of anthropology in the 1960s, had come to

the Southwest than we had ever anticipated. We definitely had found women anthropologists, and we had defined a core group of women whom we and others thought were significant scholars.

Although we have had neither the time nor the funds to conduct a similar search for other culture areas of the world, it was our intuitive feeling that more women had come to the Greater Southwest (and probably men as well) than to other culture areas. We tentatively concluded that there was something about the Southwest as a place, as an idea, and as a locale for anthropological research that attracted women. Because of Barbara's literary interests, she posed an additional research question: How did the Southwest as a place and as an idea affect the writing of these women? The harsh terrain of the Greater Southwest was frequently described as "no place for a lady" (Babcock and Parezo 1988:1). What were all the ladies doing there? Was it a place where they could thrive and create new identities for themselves as they served as students and interpreters of the region's past and present cultures? Or was there something about the peoples who lived in the Southwest and the nature of anthropological questions that made this an ideal place for research?

Because of my interest in the history of the discipline, we began to raise further questions: If we can take as a given that the Greater Southwest was the most studied region of the world—the place where people encountered anthropology and learned how to do anthropology—what effect have the writings of this group of women had on the theoretical and methodological development of the discipline? Who in the Southwest were studied (Native Americans, Anglo-Americans, or Spanish-Americans), and did this change through time—i.e., were Hispanic peoples studied only for their folklore and stories before World War II? Were Native Americans studied first because they could be made to fit neatly into Morgan's evolutionary scheme? Were only certain groups, for example, the Zuni but not the Huichol, studied by women? Did patterns change through time? Were the settled, "peaceful" Puebloans studied before the wandering, "fierce" Apaches?

Was it as an archaeologist, linguist, physical anthropologist, folklorist, cultural anthropologist, ethnomusicologist, or generalist that each woman came to the Southwest? Were these women regionalists, dedicated to living in the region, or individuals who came from the East on summer expeditions and who later went to other locales?

What were the backgrounds and personalities of these women, and what were their goals? Were they scientists who, as Matilda Coxe Stevenson once wrote to John Wesley Powell (NAA: MCS/ JWP 5/23/00), wished "to erect a foundation upon which students may build . . . and do the most for science in this way?" Were they romanticists like poet and novelist Mary Austin, who "wrote eloquently and endlessly about the 'transactions' that took place between her spirit and the spirit of the land and its ancient people" (Babcock and Parezo 1988:1)? Were the women rebels who sought the freedom of the West? Were they unconventional individuals who did not feel comfortable in their own culture? Were they activists who went to help conquered peoples and in the process reinvented themselves and changed government policies? Were they schoolteachers and wives like Franc Newcomb and Laura Armer who wanted to share their lives with others? Were they trained anthropologists like Ruth Benedict who came with a problem to solve, or were they amateurs like Dama Smith who were dedicated to popularizing anthropology? Who was an anthropologist? How did male and female anthropologists differ in background and outlook?

Our list of questions and ideas grew and grew, but we forced ourselves to return to our original proposition. Obviously women anthropologists had worked in the Greater Southwest, at least 1,600 of them, for, of course, we missed many by relying on published sources to locate individuals. The amount of work they had produced was staggering—thousands upon thousands of published books and articles and hundreds of unpublished manuscripts. Like the anthropological literature produced by men, some of these contributions were good, some bad. But as a corpus it was, and remains, impressive. There is no question that much of it was worthy of notice. For who has not been influenced by Benedict's *Patterns of Culture,* the most widely read book in all of anthropology? Who can work in the Southwest and not refer to at least one site report or ethnography by a woman anthropologist?

Some individuals have been recognized, those whose books have been used and reviewed in the discipline's major journals: Benedict, Bunzel, Ellis, Irwin-Williams, Parsons, Reichard, Shepardson, Stevenson, and Underhill. The list could go on and on, and no matter who we include, any reader will think of others. But with the exception of Ruth Benedict, these women are invisible in the history of the discipline. This, although disturbing, came as no surprise. Social historians have noted for several years that women are conspicuously absent from almost every kind of history.

Our goals again expanded and became more complex: (1) to make the invisible visible; (2) to discover why women were hidden; (3) to find out what it was about anthropology as a discipline that encouraged this behavior and whether anthropology was similar to or different from other sciences; (4) to analyze how women fared in anthropology as a discipline—to identify the roadblocks they encountered and the strategies they used to succeed (or fail) in a male-dominated and controlled endeavor; and (5) to discover women's voices to determine whether they had special perspectives and genres for discourse and whether these voices were discredited and ignored in the discipline.

We could have proceeded in many directions from this point. Having roughly mapped out our universe—those individuals who had worked in one region with one subgroup of peoples—we decided to focus on individuals rather than co-horts and to use a modified case history approach. We realized that given the state of anthropologi-cal records it would be impossible to discover enough comparable information on cohorts to make meaningful generalizations. Our method-ology was not intended to be either chronologic or synchronic, although there are sketches of lives at individual points in time. Contextualization was also important. Lives were embedded in time, and careers were influenced by the changes taking place in anthropology, in academe, and in Anglo-American and Native American societies. The closing of the frontier, the inaugurations of the women's movements, World Wars I and II, the Great Depression, McCarthyism, the G.I. Bill, the shift from teaching to research in Ameri-can universities, feminism, and the civil rights movement all affected women's place in the disci-pline and the work they accomplished in the Southwest.

It was also quite evident that we had to place temporal limits on the study, just as we had made spatial, ethnic, and cultural limits. We decided to include individuals who had come to the South-west to systematically conduct research with Na-tive Americans from the mid 1870s to roughly the end of World War II. We focused, therefore, on people who had begun their careers between 1880 and 1945. However, this is a very loose re-striction, since many of the women who had be-gun in the 1930s have continued to be active and prolific. We often implicitly and explicitly chose to compare individuals who had worked in the 1930s with those who worked in the 1970s and 1980s. We readily recognized that a few individ-uals such as Mary Shepardson who are members of our senior age grade did not begin their illus-trious careers until they had grey hair. Many of these individuals have continued to work into the 1980s.

With the increasing complexity of our ques-tions came the realization that we had tapped into an unexplored area in the history of science, aca-demic institutions, southwestern studies, Native American history, western history, the history of universities, and women's studies. We quickly re-alized that we had enough questions for a lifetime of research for each of us, even if we had the help of at least twenty colleagues. We concluded that we needed those twenty colleagues as well as the women themselves to make visible their contri-butions and the issues of being a woman anthro-pologist. We decided that a conference and a se-ries of oral interviews would be the best forum to isolate these issues.

We contacted Lita Osmundsen, president of the Wenner-Gren Foundation for Anthropologi-cal Research, and provided her with a preliminary proposal for a conference of scholars and senior women. Lita took our ideas and expanded them into a series of subprojects—a scholarly confer-ence, a public conference and celebration, an ex-hibit, an exhibit catalogue, an oral history proj-ect, and a videodocumentary. The exhibit and documentary traveled to public institutions for five years, and the exhibit catalogue is in its sec-ond printing (Babcock and Parezo 1988). The oral history project was designed to provide much of the data for the other subprojects and to allow senior women to present a statement to the pro-fession that future anthropologists could consult and analyze. Our project thus fit into the larger agenda of the Wenner-Gren Foundation to docu-ment the history of anthropology with taped oral interviews and videotapes of senior anthropolo-gists, a project that the current president, Sydel Silverman, has expanded to include other aspects of the documentation of anthropology. (The oral history tapes and the videodocumentary are avail-able through the Wenner-Gren Foundation for classroom and scholarly use.)

Funding allowed us to interview twenty women. How were we to choose? We decided to focus on what we called key and representative women. To be included in this all-too-small sample, a woman had to have conducted origi-nal ethnographic, linguistic, or archaeological research with Native American cultures in the Southwest, have published on this research, and be at least 70 years old. For representative women we chose individuals who had worked in various capacities in universities and museums, in government service, and in trading posts; chosen different career paths; written popular as well as scholarly books; and devoted their lives to service and teaching as well as research. We did not want only individuals who had worked or graduated from Columbia University and then taught at elite institutions such as Harvard University, the University of California at Berkeley, or the University of Chicago, nor only those whom everyone liked or whom everyone agreed was "the most important person to have worked in the Southwest." Our final list was also limited by practical considerations such as the present locations of the women (for example, we could not afford to go to Hawaii to interview Florence Voegelin) and their health (Florence Kluckhohn, for example, was too ill to see us and died just as we began the project). We interviewed the following senior women: Katharine Bartlett, Ruth Bunzel, Bertha Dutton, Florence Hawley Ellis, Frances Gillmor, Esther Goldfrank, Katherine Spencer Halpern, Kate Peck Kent, Dorothy Keur, Marjorie Lambert, Dorothea Leighton, Alice Marriott, Mary Shepardson, Rosamond Spicer, Clara Lee Tanner, Laura Thompson, Sallie Wagner, Nathalie Woodbury, and H. Marie Wormington. This project was timely because Bunzel, Ellis, Kent, Keur, Leighton, and Marriott have since passed away.

Our graduate research assistant, Jennifer Fox, interviewed these women in 1985 and 1986 using a detailed yet open-ended interview schedule that Barbara and I constructed. Some of the interviews required two consecutive days because of the problems of format and recall. On the first day Jenny conducted a semistructured audio interview in the form of a conversation. Although there was a prearranged ordering to the questions, Jenny was instructed to let the women's responses determine the order of the discussion and the top-

ics to some extent, as well as the amount of time spent in each area. The women, of course, also introduced topics of their own. In ten cases, on the second day, the same questions were repeated but the conversation was videotaped in a living room to produce a relaxed atmosphere. The desired effect was an intimate conversation. From these interviews we gained rich personal perspectives, reminiscences, autobiographical accounts of productive individuals, information on their teachers, colleagues, friends, and students, and reflections on anthropology as a discipline in the 1930s, 1940s, and 1980s.

The interviews were conceptualized and designed both to answer our questions and to serve as personal statements to future generations of anthropologists, especially young women. We asked these women to look back over their careers and reflect on the key people who had helped them. We were particularly interested in how and why they had become anthropologists; the influences on their intellectual and professional development, including familial attitudes toward professional career goals; the role of mentors; their career development both in college and after completion of their education; professional subdisciplinary choices; the relationship between their personal and professional lives; analyses of their contributions; and why they had chosen to work in the Southwest. As all dialogues were undertaken without referring to personal papers, there is selective remembering and selective forgetting. In some cases time has homogenized the memory and led to the suppression of negative situations. Interestingly, weeks after the formal interviews we would receive letters or telephone calls with more specific information on problems the women had faced. Fox's paper in this volume contains a summary and analysis of some of the information gleaned from these interviews. We also distributed notes, transcripts, and copies of tapes to conference participants for use in the papers in this volume.

The interviews provided the raw footage for

the videodocumentary and quotes for the museum exhibit and exhibit catalogue (Babcock and Parezo 1988). In addition, we utilized other texts—published works, reviews, and unpublished field notes, letters, and journals—in the manner described by Nancy Lutkehaus (1990: 313), who used Wedgewood's personal papers for her own research project as a means of "becoming the other." For us they were crucial to understanding the anthropologists who worked in the Southwest. The resulting data from the interviews and archival sources is primarily qualitative and sometimes impressionistic but of a quality and richness not duplicated by other methodologies.

The public conference, held in Tucson, Arizona, in March 1986, and the exhibit were designed to honor these key women and the countless others who worked in the Southwest. The goal was to document the range and depth of their contributions, to demonstrate that many women anthropologists were or are scholars who cannot be ignored. Wenner-Gren provided travel funds to the women who were physically able to attend the conference, and for two days they again shared their lives and focused on what it was like to work in the Southwest. Several of their Native American consultants also attended the public celebration. Our keynote speaker, Louise Lamphere, delivered an excellent summary of their work in light of feminist research; she later refocused this discussion for her American Ethnological Society distinguished lecture on Elsie Clews Parsons (Lamphere 1989).

The scholarly conference that followed the public conference was not a celebration. Instead, it was developed to identify and analyze the problems of being a female scholar working in the Native American Southwest and an anthropologist trying to gain access to and acceptance in academe. Scholars were asked to write about those women who have dealt with issues, cultures, and subfields in which the scholars worked. We felt that a scholar who had conducted fieldwork in an area would bring a different and deeper set of understandings to the analysis of the life and efforts of these older women than would one who had never known what living with a Navajo family or working in a field school at Chaco Canyon was like. They would thus have a sense of the whole, a sense of the limits, a sense of the tensions, and an understanding of the triumphs, however small, and thereby give an informed ordering to the immutable texts and choices that make up an anthropological career.

Participants at the conference included (in addition to Barbara Babcock, Lita Osmundsen, and myself) Linda Cordell, Deborah Gordon, Margaret Hardin, Katherine Spencer Halpern, Joyce Herold, Louis Hieb, Curtis Hinsley, Leanne Hinton, Louise Lamphere, Charles Lange, Kay Sands, and Marta Weigle. Our discussants were David Aberle, Fred Eggan, Eleanor Leacock, Sidney Mintz, and Joan Mark. Our rappateur was Jennifer Fox. Unfortunately, several other participants, including all three of our Native American scholars, informed us at the last minute that they were unable to participate. We sorely missed their insights and perspectives.

We looked at aspects of ourselves, our own lives, the lives of our intellectual ancestors, and the social structure of our discipline by focusing on individual case studies and surveys of particular subgroups, such as archaeologists, linguists, and those who worked in museums. This was often painful and brought to light some aspects of anthropology that we did not like to think existed—prejudice, elitism, sexism. Discussions were rich and fruitful, but it was often difficult to pull back and analyze, to try to figure out why some behaviors occurred and, unfortunately, continue to occur.

A brief example will highlight the problem we faced. I do not think I will ever forget sitting at the conference, outlining why I thought popularizing was so suspect to university anthropologists and wanting to discuss whether I was on a productive track. After presenting my partially formed ideas, I was met with stony silence. After a few minutes the conversation turned to a non-threatening topic—the images we help create of other cultures. The Other was safe to analyze, while our treatment of ourselves, the knowledge that we create castes within our discipline, that we exclude many people from our prestige structure, was not. We could distance ourselves from the images of others because although the issue dealt partially with us, it really dealt with others, not ourselves. There are still some topics about which we are not yet ready to be self-reflexive. For the rest of the afternoon, the topics I raised were ignored. In effect, I was briefly ostracized. I talked with Lita Osmundsen about this exchange later. Because she has had a lifetime of experience with group interaction, she had not been surprised by the episode. In half an hour I had matter-of-factly, and unthinkingly, broached and begun to analyze taboo subjects and questioned long-held, and believed in, myths. It took two days of informal discussions at dinner before anyone would (or could?) mention some of these issues again in the formal (i.e., taped) conference setting.

There were other topics that we skirted, never formally acknowledged and thus never came to grips with—sex, sexuality, how sex is used against women, sexual harassment, lesbianism, religious prejudice, anti-Semitism, racism, the role of gossip in establishing and ruining reputations. There was a good reason for this; the public discussion of sexuality can be damaging to a career in academia. Listening to corridor talk quickly teaches one that women speaking of sex does little for one's career. Just as the women we interviewed could not talk about issues such as sexual harassment, marginalization, or pay discrimination (for fear of being ejected from the profession as a troublemaker), for us, fear of retaliation and rejection was still strong. As Florence Hawley Ellis (1985) noted, gender discrimination "is, of course, discouraging when you stop to think of it. So you just don't dare stop to think of it. All you do is just see what you can do to get

around the situation at the moment and go ahead with your work."

So we must go ahead with our work but acknowledge that we are not ready to bare our souls too much, to overcome the double taboo of women openly discussing sexuality, or to acknowledge that our profession and the people who espoused the ideas we believe in have not always behaved ethically either by our standards or by those of their own period. There is still a definite dichotomy between what can be published and spoken of in a professional forum and what can be said off the record. Nor could the women we interviewed talk about these issues or in some cases even discuss their marriages because of the ingrained fear of the consequences for their careers and reputations. The myths remain. Many topics are sub rosa and still need to be discussed. They must wait for another study, one probably not based on life history and case study materials. To acknowledge the need for sensitivity to the interests and aspirations of women, to make the invisible visible, to find those who have been hidden and uncover the reasons for their placement in the shadows, and to challenge the political and intellectual culture of the discipline has proven more difficult than expected.

The papers that follow are generally based on presentations made at the Wenner-Gren conference and the topics we felt we could discuss. In addition, the volume has been enhanced by the contributions of Susan McGreevy, Jennifer Fox, and Shelby Tisdale. The organization of the papers is similar to that of the conference. As such, it is somewhat flexible, since different papers work toward different understandings. Many analyze and document ways in which women have become anthropologists, have striven to remain in the field, or have made contributions against great odds. Some of the papers are intellectual and biographical histories of our key women—Stevenson, Parsons, Underhill, Reichard, Bunzel, Benedict—focusing on documenting the range of contributions and specific methodologies. Lange's discussion of Goldfrank is a very personal account, semiautobiographical in character. Authors place these individuals in the history of southwestern anthropology; this is especially evident in the papers by Babcock on Benedict, Hieb on Parsons, Lange on Goldfrank, and Parezo on Stevenson. Other papers are representative assessments of the contributions made by women to the anthropology of a particular group, in a particular genre, or a particular subfield: Sands, for example, looks specifically at work with the Yaqui; Cordell analyzes the careers of several archaeologists; and Lamphere, although focusing on the work of Gladys Reichard, compares Reichard's contributions to the scholarship of others on the Navajo. Likewise, Hinton presents a brief essay on the history of women linguists in the Southwest but concentrates primarily on the unusual genealogy of women who worked with the Yumans. Gordon analyses women who wrote biographies of Native American women. Still other authors deal with women who worked in marginal institutions and with the contributions of unofficial anthropologists—wives, philanthropists, popular writers, photographers, librarians, curators, traders, and Indian rights activists. Parezo and Hardin look at the careers of women who worked in museums, McGreevy investigates those individuals who had the power and money to found institutions, while Tisdale analyzes the women who taught and popularized anthropology.

Several themes crosscut and interlace these papers, including the influence of gender in determining what women studied and what they wrote and questions of ethnographic authority. This is especially evident in Babcock's, Gordon's, and Sand's papers, which deal with gender inflection in an anthropological perspective and pose inferences about the theories women scholars espoused and developed. Other themes are mentoring, the influence of intellectual ancestors on the work of women and their access to jobs and resources, and the impact of these women in turn on American anthropological theory, subsequent southwestern

research, and the careers of other women. The consequences of male bias and male support of women's research, careers, publications, and subsequent assessments is also evident in many papers. Others focus on problems of appropriation, erasure, disparagement, and invisibility in the profession, in academic and nonacademic institutions, and in historical discourse. The introduction sets the stage by asking "Why are women hidden or invisible in the history of anthropology?" and the concluding chapter reiterates some of these themes by drawing on the rich discussion of the conference and the insights of the women themselves.

All the papers have been revised, but no editorial attempt has been made to impose a unified theoretical approach on them. Nor do I necessarily agree with certain readings and conclusions posed by some contributors. In some cases, for example Cordell and McGreevy, contributors disagree in their assessments of individuals' contributions. Each paper stands as an individual contribution to a subject that is only just beginning to emerge, in which an increasing number of anthropologists have become seriously interested. As will be readily apparent, a rich dialectical tension exists in the book that can be summed up in the current debates on the role of feminism in anthropology and the epistemological underpinnings of anthropology as both a scientific and a humanistic discipline. Underlying several of the papers is the contention that the central problem of anthropology is that it has been conceptualized as a science that utilizes a male model of the world to which women anthropologists brought the insights of the humanities. This debate deals with the scientific ethos as defined by Merton (1957) and Barber (1962) and the consequences this ethos has had for anthropologists and the peoples they study (James 1973). The model of science as a concept and process embedded in a puzzle-solving paradigm that is absent in the humanities and as a depersonalized, linear, and mechanistic pursuit that cannot be divorced from colonialism is seen as a barrier that has kept women out of anthropology. The authors whose papers follow this critique concentrate on semiotics and demonstrate that interactions are reproduced as knowledge, as analytic categories, as field notes, and as anthropological products. They give attention to the gendered discourse of the enterprise and demonstrate that gender is woven into the connection between experience and the production and dissemination of knowledge.

Just as women are defined as occupying a gendered place in cultures, women anthropologists appear in the discipline and the academy in particular ways that change through time. Several papers take the generalizability and comparability approaches of the scientist and attempt to see how women have fared in anthropology as it has followed its professional course. Still others treat their subject matter as would the historian, focusing on events, individuals, and places. Some of these contributions are intentionally descriptive and documentary, others are intentionally theoretical, still others reflexive. As a mix, they present several perspectives on the role of women in southwestern anthropology.

It should be noted in closing that this volume is but a first step. We have not exhaustively answered our questions. Indeed, in many ways, we are only at the stage of discovering what are the important questions. In this book of varied types of analyses and case studies, there are inevitably holes, and the results are neither congratulatory nor comforting. Many readers will be frustrated because we have not included a favorite individual. Barbara and I have discovered that reviews for *Daughters of the Desert* tend to focus on this issue—one reviewer even took us to task for forgetting his grandmother (who incidentally had never published anything on southwestern Native American peoples) and another for not including Georgia O'Keefe, who was never an anthropologist or even especially interested in native peoples! We freely acknowledge that we have neither included everyone nor given equal weight to each individual or to all pertinent issues. That would have been impossible. All projects require that choices be made, and we have made ours based on sound theoretical, methodological, and practical reasons to focus our study as much as possible.

Understanding is an evolving process. A goal of this volume is to engender dialogue and further study that will advance research and practice. We hope that readers will take as a challenge to themselves the areas we have not covered and will begin to rediscover more hidden scholars and isolate more reasons for their invisibility. This will benefit anthropology as a theoretical endeavor and as an occupation.

NOTES

1. Bibliographic references are located at the end of the volume.

2. This compilation was done as part of a bibliographic project with funding from the National Endowment for the Humanities (Parezo et al. 1991).

ACKNOWLEDGMENTS

A multifaceted project such as this is indebted to more individuals than I can possibly ever thank. On behalf of Barbara and myself, I would like to thank the contributors to the volume as well as those who participated in the conference but were unable to finalize their papers for inclusion here. They have continued to work in the area through other outlets. I would also like to thank the many, many individuals who have listened over the years and helped us find the women who have worked in the Southwest. We could not have completed this project without scholars such as Nathalie Woodbury, Richard Woodbury, Katherine Spencer Halpern, Raymond Thompson, R. Gwinn Vivian, Nancy Lurie, Richard Ford, J. J. Brody, June Helms, Susan Bender, Anabel Ford, Joan Gero, Patty Jo Watson, Laurie Webster, Jerrold Levy, David Aberle, Fred Eggan, Curtis Hinsley, Carol Kramer, Eleanor Leacock, Karen Sacks, Joan Marks, Don Fowler, Catherine Fowler, Watson Smith, Carol Kramer, Robert Netting, Molly Thompson, Mary Greene, Lynn Teague, Ruth Perry, Marta Weigle, and Sydel Silverman, to name but a few, who shared data and provided innumerable insights. Indeed, their patience and interest was much appreciated. Each author also has many individuals to thank for assistance on their papers. But on behalf of all I would also like to thank the archivists and librarians from the many institutions that have saved the papers and field notes of the women who have worked in the Southwest and granted us permission to use them.

Without the generous support of the Wenner-Gren Foundation for Anthropological Research this project would not have been attempted. I cannot thank Lita Osmundsen and Sydel Silverman enough for their financial support and encouragement over the years. Whenever things went wrong, like when the computer caught on fire and destroyed several files, they were there with encouragement that the project could be finished. I would also like to thank the Southwest Institute for Research on Women, the Arizona State Museum, the Department of Anthropology, and the Southwest Center at the University of Arizona for cosponsoring this project. Most especially we would like to thank Myra Dinnerstein, Janice Monk, Karen Anderson, Raymond Thompson, Joseph Wilder, William Stini, and R. Gwinn Vivian for providing the necessary logistical support. Sue Ruiz spent many, many hours transcribing the audio tapes and helping to ensure that several of the papers were presentable. I would also like to thank the staff of the Wenner-Gren Foundation who spent many hours copying tapes and setting up an archive to save this important information for anthropology.

Many young women have helped us along the way and made this book possible. I would especially like to thank our research and editorial assistants Mary Walker, Martha Brace, Jennifer Fox, Kelley Hays, Sue Wolfe, Barbara Slivac, and Jay Cox, who have now embarked on careers of their own. We hope their work will be enriched by having met and known the women in this book as their dedication and assistance has contributed to our endeavors. I would especially like to thank Shelby Tisdale, a valued friend and colleague. Without her assistance I have no doubt that this volume would not have been completed. While I was serving as a system administrator, commuting to Phoenix and trying to deal with the inevitable daily crises that are now all too common in higher education, Shelby helped edit the papers and order photographs, standardized the individual contributions, and made sure that papers were not lost in the computer.

Without the dedication and intelligence of 1,600 women this book would have been impossible. Thanks go to the women whose books we have read and been influenced by, but whom we have not been able to meet. I would especially like to thank the women whom we interviewed, who allowed us to come into their homes and share with us and others in the profession their lives, careers, and ideas, their failures and their accomplishments. Our professional careers have all been enriched by the opportunity to work with these strong women, who have always believed that women and women's lives were of equal importance as men and men's lives. They have incorporated into their philosophies a commitment to achieving equality for all women in anthropology and the academe. And not least of all, they have extended their friendship and provided us with examples of their dedication to anthropology.

I would especially like to thank Elizabeth Hadas, director of the University of New Mexico Press, who convinced us that it was essential to publish both this work and *Daughters of the Desert*. Under her direction the University of New Mexico Press has demonstrated a commitment to furthering our understanding of the Southwest, of anthropology, and of native peoples. I would also like to thank Andrea Otañez and Sally Bennett for their excellent editorial assistance. Needless to say, I also want to thank the staff of the press for their excellent production work.

Of course it goes without saying that I want to thank my husband, Richard Ahlstrom. He has done journeyman's duty on this project, from picking up people at the airport to running errands, helping with tentative organization, being a sounding board for ideas, being enthusiastic even when he was tired, listening, and above all, caring. A supportive husband makes it all possible.

Finally, I would like to thank Lita Osmundsen, without whose vision we would never have attempted anything this large and complex.

NANCY PAREZO

HIDDEN SCHOLARS

ANTHROPOLOGY:
THE WELCOMING SCIENCE

Nancy J. Parezo

The search for what happened is out there, but we are the subject in here. We ourselves are there even as we look at them, the others in the past.

Sheila Rowbotham (1973:xviii)

We have been invisible even to each other— at least until now.

Florence Howe (1984:41)

O F ALL the sciences anthropology has the reputation for being most open to women scholars. One scholar notes, "Anthropology, in comparison to the other social sciences, has attracted many women who have been successful as members of that profession" (Nader 1986:113). As Margaret Mead (1960:5) reflected,

Anthropology, a new science, welcomed the stranger. As a science which accepted the psychic unity of mankind, anthropology was kinder to women, to those who came from distant disciplines, to members of minority groups in general (with American Indians assuming a special position as both the victims of injustice and the carriers of a precious and vanishing knowledge), to the "over-mature," the idiosyncratic, and the capriciously gifted or experienced, to refugees from political or religious oppression. Elsie Clews Parsons, a woman of wealth who pioneered in new investigations on the effect of culture on women, could be herself and drop the pseudonym of John Main under which, as a sociologist, she had written about ceremonial chastity.

Openness has a long history in the discipline. Scholars in the nineteenth century realized that anthropology, as a fieldwork endeavor, could not be successfully undertaken without women. When Professor Edward B. Tylor of Oxford University addressed the Anthropological Society of Washington in 1884 he stated,

It was interesting at Zuni to follow the way in which Col and Mrs. Stevenson were working the pueblo, trading for specimens, and bringing together all that was most valuable and interesting in tracing the history of that remarkable people. Both managed to identify themselves with the Indian life. And one thing I particularly noticed was this, that to get at the confidence of a tribe, the man of the house, though he can do a great deal, cannot do it all. If his wife sympathizes with his work, and is able to do it, really half the work of investigation seems to me to fall to her, so much is to be learned through the women of the tribe, which the men will not readily disclose. The experience seemed to me a lesson to anthropologists not to sound the "bull-roarer," and warn the ladies off from their proceedings, but rather to avail themselves thankfully of their help (Tylor 1884:550).

One hundred years later Ruth Bunzel (1985) reiterated this generally accepted view with regard to accessibility: "Fieldwork requires both men and women to really get a whole picture of culture." Women were needed to gather information from non-Western peoples that was inaccessible to male researchers due to sexual divisions of labor, gender roles, and secrecy rules. Parsons believed that women helped ethnology, for "a woman student [had] many opportunities for observing the life of women and children that male ethnographers have lacked." Likewise, ethnology was good for women because "ethnology opens your eyes to what is under your nose" (Parsons quoted in Rosenberg 1982:166). According to Dorothea Leighton (1985),

I don't think women are described by men half as effectively as women [are] described by women, and the same way with men. I think it really makes a big difference. . . . I think you don't get a full picture unless you have both men and women represented. It seems to me that the male and the female view on all kinds of things are different.

As a result of this widely held view, women have had a long tradition of studying about, and working with, women in other societies.

Other scholars have gone further in rationalizing why women are needed in anthropology. They have considered women to be better at obtaining information on special subjects, such as the role of gossip, that were felt to be associated with women, reflecting the notion of categorical unity of the researcher and the subject (Nader 1986: 114). Women have been said to be especially good at focusing on the emotional aspects of research regardless of the sex of the informant because they are more open to emotional communication than are men (Codere 1986; Whitehead and Conaway 1986). As Keller (1985) has remarked, science has been identified with rationality, objectivity, cognition, and the mistrust of emotion—traits associated with men in our society. Women have been identified with irrationality, subjectivity, eroticism, and emotion, areas that men, if they are to be proper scientists, cannot acknowledge because it will contaminate their work. Women researchers, even empirical scientists, are not tainted by studying feelings. Women thus have access to topics and methodologies unavailable to men.

A few scholars (e.g., Douglas 1979; Keller 1985) contend that women are crucial to anthropology and sociology because they are better fieldworkers than men in all circumstances. They base their conclusions on the roles and stereotypes of white, middle-class women in Western societies, which categorize women as natural nurturers, communicators, and sexual objects. "It is almost a truism of interview research, for example, that in most situations women will be able to achieve more 'rapport' with respondents because of their less threatening quality and better communication skills" (Warren 1988:44); men by definition are more threatening (Angrosino 1986). Women are sociability specialists because they are low-key; they are thus better at opening up fieldwork situations and smoothing the path for male members of fieldwork teams (Douglas 1979:214). Women are flexible and adaptable in the field because these skills are required of women in our culture. Women succeed in anthropological and sociological fieldwork, therefore, because they are person-oriented. Following this chain of reasoning, participant observation is consonant with the roles of white, middle-class women.

Warren (1988:43) has called this extreme scenario "the mythology of women's particular contributions to the fieldwork enterprise." Like many folk explanations there is some truth to the idea that women, at least in Western cultures, are "better able to relate to people than men" (Nader 1986:114). And the division between men's and women's social worlds is so sharply drawn in many societies that women studying women and men studying men is necessary. But "if it really took one to know one, the entire field of anthropology would be an aberration" (Shapiro 1981:125).

Regardless of its truth content, the belief that women are crucial to fieldwork has affected anthropology and the place of women within the discipline in ways that are not evident in laboratory sciences. I, like many other women, chose anthropology partly because it had the reputation of being less sexist than other social, natural, or physical sciences. Anthropology could not afford to ignore or exclude women. But this need for women fieldworkers created a dilemma for the discipline. Anthropology as a fieldwork science that dealt with people living in societies could not, and can never be, a male-only science as could physics, chemistry, or zoology, theoretically. While anthropology was still developing, these later sciences were the established, prestigious disciplines. The need for women made anthropology suspect in the academy during its professionalization period in the early 1900s when anthropologists were trying to establish that it was a scientific discipline rather than the home of dilettantes. Could anthropology be accepted by the academic community as a serious science if it needed women?

Anthropology, like other social sciences, however, was a male-dominated and male-oriented field from its infancy, and this fact has affected women's welcome. By definition and general perception, the academy assumes that male scholars are the model for all scholars and that the male world is the only academic world (Rossiter 1982; Warren 1988). Although rarely acknowledged and studied, even by "sociologists of science" (Delamont 1987), the gender of a scientist has always been an issue because of the normative expectation that women be passive and retiring in our society. Even as women's educational levels rose and their occupational opportunities outside the family expanded, women were seen as capable of undertaking only a narrow range of womanly activities. This stereotype limited women to soft,

delicate, emotional, noncompetitive, and nurturing kinds of behavior. At the same time, the stereotype of science was the opposite: tough, rigorous, impersonal, competitive, rational, and unemotional. In this idealization a woman scientist was a contradiction in terms; she was thought to be unnatural in some way. Women scientists were caught between two mutually exclusive stereotypes: as scientists they were atypical and would not be listened to or respected because they were emotional and as women they were unusual because their lives did not revolve around the home and they were cold and rational. And the no-win situation did not necessarily ease over time; in some cases it became worse, especially in periods when increasing numbers of women employees threatened the perceived prestige of an institution and a discipline. As Marie Wormington (1985) pointed out when describing her work situation and the attitude of the director of the Denver Museum of Natural History, "He didn't feel there was a place for either a woman or an archaeologist in a science museum. . . . I always published under my initials, H. M. Wormington. The director of the museum felt nobody would read a book written by a woman."

If women were marginal to the world of science by definition and anthropology had to have women in order to develop, how was anthropology to be taken seriously in the university and not be a marginal discipline? One way was to rigorously limit women's participation, both consciously and unconsciously. Anthropology needed women but only as fieldworkers and gatherers of data. It did not need them as analysts, interpreters, or translators, as senior principal investigators or project directors, as the holders of endowed chairs, as full professors (or even assistant professors), or as theoreticians. A topical and methodological division of labor developed; research areas were defined as male or female. Since women were thought not to be good with numbers, quantitative work became the domain of men and gained more prestige than interpretive work.

Since physical anthropology required extensive use of statistics and numerical measurements, few women were encouraged to work in that field.

Thus there were limits to women's participation in the field, despite the welcome. Mead in the Introduction to *The Golden Age of Anthropology* (1960:5) noted that anthropology's stance of liberality was not complete and that there were many instances of professionals discouraging individuals from participating because they were poor, secretaries, Jewish, or women. Mead attributes this to professional jealousy by mediocre individuals. While feminist scholars and women in other disciplines have regarded anthropology as far less sexist than their own fields (Sanjek 1982: 846), those within the field have been ambivalent. Professors of anthropology gave women students mixed messages, as Katherine Spencer Halpern (1985) remembered when she described her decision to become an anthropologist:

In anthropology there were a number of women from a very early date and I think I sensed that they were welcome. . . . But I can remember my first interview with linguist Harry Hoijer. He met me and said, "But there's no place for women in anthropology." It wasn't quite in those words, but he was trying to discourage students, especially women, who thought they could earn a living in anthropology. This was the fall of 1936, in the depression. There was no assurance that anyone would get jobs, especially women. Later when I had him as a professor I didn't get any sense [that he thought] women were intellectually incapable. But I had to stand up for what I wanted to do.

Years later Eleanor Leacock (1981:9) had a similar experience:

I had no women teachers at the time: the Harvard anthropology faculty that taught Radcliffe students (though classes were still sex-segregated) was all male. I remember sniffing to myself with a certain stubborn complacency when a gentleman of the old school, Alfred Tozzer, bluntly told his Radcliffe class that women were not welcome in anthropology. He warned them that they should not plan careers in the

field unless they were independently wealthy since there were no jobs for them.

Ironically, anthropology has long been noted for its prominent women scholars. The most famous anthropologist to those outside the discipline is Margaret Mead. The most widely read anthropology book was written by Ruth Benedict. But "the underside of the achievement of women in anthropology has been the long struggle for professional equality with male anthropologists" (Sanjek 1982:848), and, I would add, for recognition and visibility within the field. For if female anthropologists were necessary to the discipline, where are they? Why do we know so little about them? Why, when we tell people how many women have worked in the Greater Southwest, are we met with looks of disbelief? Why are women not in our history of anthropology books? Why are they not cited in theoretical discussions? Why, with the exception of Benedict and Mead, are women anthropologists hidden, seen only in the shadow of men or at the margins of the field? Is anthropology really a good discipline for women? Are women hidden because women's contributions had to be made invisible, shown to be handmaidenly or less important than those of male theoreticians, for anthropology to be accepted as a science?

Those few women who are mentioned are obfuscated and belittled through a series of leveling mechanisms that hide their contributions. This treatment of women in the history of anthropology (and science) should come as no surprise, since disciplinary historians work within the university structure. There are systemic reasons for the displacement of women in disciplinary history. The structure and organization of the workplace in higher education and related institutions such as museums has fostered the marginalization of women anthropologists and their contributions (as it has women scholars in all disciplines, even those dedicated to "women's subjects") by creating barriers that women scholars have encountered on their career paths. This contextualization is designed to demonstrate that the frustrations and problems met by the women discussed in this book are not of their own making; individual personalities cannot explain the collective experiences of women anthropologists who have worked in the Southwest.

INVISIBILITY

In 1973 British historian Sheila Rowbotham published *Hidden From History,* a book made necessary by her realization that women were not included in official history texts. Although there were records of Great Men, there were no records of Great Women and certainly none of common women or men. Anthropology is the same. We have our Great Men and Culture Heroes (Morgan, Spencer, Tylor, Boas, Kroeber, Kidder, Leakey, Lévi-Strauss, Sapir, Linton, Lowie, Radin, Kardiner, Durkheim, Malinowski, Radcliffe-Brown, White, Steward, Evans-Pritchard, Geertz, Redfield) and Great Women (Mead and Benedict). The same list of characters appears in every book that provides the grand scheme for the discipline and every compilation of the greatest essays ever written (e.g., Bohannan and Glazer 1973).[1] We use the Great Men even to define anthropology's periods of development: "The first two decades of the 20th century in American anthropology might be called the Age of Boas, so completely did that giant dominate the field" (Bunzel 1960: 400). By comparison, we know almost nothing about the women (and many of the men) who, by their equally important endeavors and insights, have enabled anthropologists to undertake work in the 1970s, 1980s, and 1990s.

This pattern of nonacknowledgment is quite common in the sciences. Rossiter (1982:xi) discovered that most women scientists "bordered, for a variety of reasons, on the 'invisible.'" One reason for this invisibility is that scholarly contributions and scientific discoveries have been viewed both as the "massive achievements of certain giant male figures" (Crutchfield and Krech 1962:25) and as the logical outcome of particular stages of development (Kuhn 1962). As Curtis Hinsley (1986b) has remarked, "We have been taught that the history of science and anthropology is the history of individuals' ideas," but only those of certain types of individuals.[2]

The definition of what is a contribution varies by field. All disciplines have generalized norms regarding the quality and quantity of contributions that constitute high-level performance, are meritorious, and deserve remembrance. One of these norms is that the contribution should be made by a professional rather than an amateur and by a theoretician rather than an experimenter or data gatherer. Another is that a person's ideas merit remembrance based on their value (truth, elegance, usefulness) alone. It is part of the ethos of science that scientific merit should be evaluated independently from the personal or social qualities of the individual. The scientist is expected to evaluate new knowledge critically and objectively; to use his or her findings in a disinterested, nonsecretive fashion; to maintain an attitude of emotional neutrality toward his or her work and that of others; and to judge the merit of an idea without reference to the individual (Barber 1962; Hagstrom 1965; Merton 1957; Storer 1966).

The growth of scientific knowledge has not exhibited this rational, logical, or continuous process, however. Scientific assertions and humanistic interpretations are not accepted on the basis of logical reasoning alone but also on how well the study fits into a set of implicit and explicit assumptions that are not empirically testable (Dolby 1971). As one scholar has noted,

Great Men with revolutionary ideas not only develop these ideas over long years; they also convince others of the validity of these ideas and develop an institutional and social structure for their implementation. Most often, they do so self-consciously, fully aware of the possibility of failure (Darnell 1972:85).

Science is a group product (Kuhn 1962). Scientific communities—loose groups of scholars who are recruited as students and collaborators and through citation—concentrate on particular sets of problems at any one time, and these subjects change quickly (Crane 1972:99). In these communities, scientific behavior consists of an exchange of information for recognition and reputation (Hagstrom 1965). Scientists must compete for recognition, since very few individuals and their work are remembered for longer than ten years (Price 1965), due to a high emphasis on originality and criticism.

Scientific merit has never been gender-free: "Eminence in and leadership of the world's affairs of whatever sort will inevitably belong oftener to men. They will oftener deserve it" (Thorndike 1914:188). Given the harsh race for status and prestige in the academic world, those in power gain by eliminating potential competition. Individuals who control work and how it is evaluated and rewarded in professions also control its official histories. Science, anthropology, the research establishment, and the university are upper- and middle-class, male-dominated and -controlled worlds. Consequently, men's definitions of learning and scholarship and how these activities should be remembered prevail (Hinsley 1986b). In the Western world of knowledge, men are held to be the natural scholars, because the occupations associated with the generation of new knowledge are prestigious and carry access to scarce resources. This idea is so ingrained that women can easily be forgotten. For example, Murphy (1976: 4) when speaking of anthropology's fallow period during World War II attributes the lack of research to the fact that "the Universities had been stripped of all students at both the graduate and undergraduate levels, and most younger professional anthropologists were either members of the military or assigned to government agencies directly connected with the war effort." This ignores, of course, the fact that some female students continued working in North America, even if their overseas efforts were curtailed.

The typical member of the academic community is a white, middle-class male. Freed from primary household, child-care, and community responsibilities, he has the time to think, conduct research, and impart his knowledge to worthy students. Women, when they enter this world, are categorized in terms of the prevailing sexual division of labor in which women are subordinate helpers. They are quickly assigned to the invisible proletariate:

Women in organizations have traditionally been file clerks, secretaries, and more, recently, data processors and computer workers. . . . The social place of women in Western society has traditionally been to stand behind men, out of their sight: as mothers, wives, nurses, secretaries, and servants (Warren 1988:18).

Women become, by definition, deviant or discordant when they try to enter the world of knowledge makers as equals. Women are perceived to be engaged in unimportant work and to have low productivity because it is assumed that (1) women do not take themselves as seriously as men; (2) they will stop their career trajectory to have babies; (3) they do not need money to survive because their husbands will support them; and (4) they lack ambition and ability. Because they are considered "by nature passive," women will not have the drive to publish and bring fame upon themselves and their academic departments (Howe 1984:39). To this can be added the stereotype that

women, because of biological or natural differences from men, do not have the same commitment to their profession as do men. Outside interests such as home, husband, and children naturally take first place in their lives. Their primary satisfactions come from aspects of their lives outside their professional work while, for men, the primary satisfactions are found in their professional work (Abramson 1975:73).

Since a majority of academicians are male, there is the normative expectation that suppressing the role of women "is as it should be."

Because of this, women have been a "muted group" (Moore 1988) under the influence of the dominant groups in society, which generate and control the dominant modes of expression. Although women have spoken, they have not always been heard. One of the tasks of feminism is continually to insist upon recognition. Muted groups, especially helpers, are silenced by the structures of domains; if they wish to express themselves, they must do so through dominant modes of expression and ideologies. They are also silenced by the attitudes of colleagues:

Many women, especially when they are still in the lower ranks, exhibit exasperation at the unwillingness of male colleagues to hold serious discussions. They are often treated with condescension or their ideas are treated as a form of entertainment for which the appropriate response seems to fall into the category of cocktail party repartee. Or through politeness or dependence on the good will of male colleagues for future employment they may submit to long and simplistic explanations of material they already know because their male colleagues assume they know nothing (Abramson 1975:89).

Moreover, works written by women are viewed as less serious than those penned by men, while the critiques of their materials are harsher. The correctness, value, and importance of a statement, fact, or study is evaluated on one scale for men and another for women (Lovano-Kerr and Fuchs 1983). This dual standard is used by both men and women for publication and manuscript reviews and grant proposal evaluations, not to mention promotion reviews (Lutz 1990). People assume that the work of men is more worthy of respect than that of women. Because of this differentiation, many women have been reluctant to voice their opinions strongly or to express their disapproval of discriminatory practices resulting from stereotyping or the dual system (Astin 1969).[3] Those who are silent or who do not speak forcefully are rarely remembered.

As Rowbotham discovered, in historical research there are individuals whom one cites as the source of ideas and those whom one does not. She wrote, "In those days it was not the thing to put Marx in your footnotes even if he had started the whole thing off in the first place" (Rowbotham 1973:xi). Lutz (1990) has demonstrated that women are not cited as often as men, even though they produce and publish at a rate similar to their proportional representation in anthropology. The same is true for acknowledgments (Ben-Ari 1987). In all fields women have been overlooked as the source of ideas, methods, and models.[4] As one scholar argues,

The citation is a central part of all academic writing and is one of the most important ways in which academics evaluate the written works of others. To engage in scholarship is to involve oneself with the ideas of others, to attempt to support, amend, or overturn them, but first of all to take them under consideration. The citation is an index of a judgement, made by the author of the article in which the citation appears, that the person cited has been taken seriously. Citations also, therefore, implicate relations of power, including gender relations as well as race relations (Delgado [1984] quoted in Lutz 1990:627).

A citation is thus more than an index of the quality of a work; it also reflects social networks, for it is one of the ways in which scholars attach (or try to attach) themselves to those who are powerful in the field. Citations are used to demonstrate that one works in the mainstream of a field and that one has a position within an intellectual elite (Burton and Kebler 1960; Cole 1979; Crane 1972; Ferber 1986; Lutz 1990; Price 1965). Authors ignore those who are not seen to have prestige and power—or the ability to secure a position for an author. Thus, members of elite departments cite others in elite departments rather than scholars in less prestigious universities or colleges (Cole 1970:400).

Citations are gendered and serve as a measure of the lower status of women. Women cite other women much more often than men cite women. Women's works are devalued and hence not cited. Women's topics are considered less important than men's topics, which are categorized as mainstream. Even when women study core topics at specific historical moments, their work is deemed less meritorious. This fact has been widely recognized in anthropology as in the other sciences. As Ellis (1985) told us,

The general tendency is, as far as anthropologists go, if a woman produces something she gets about half the credit that she might get if a man had produced the same thing. . . . If you have thought of something new, you are not looked up to nearly as much as if you were a male and did something new.

In this, historians of anthropology have behaved similarly to other historians (Schmidt and Schmidt 1976). Those whose work is devalued are invisible, for they have less access to legitimization. Citations are thus the "symbolic capital" (Lutz 1990) of scholarly reputations, and historians of a discipline remember only those individuals who are cited frequently.

Taken all together, it is no wonder that few women have achieved fame, let alone been remembered for their contributions and discoveries. Rarely are women (and most men) mentioned in the histories of science or higher education. Except for a truly brilliant individual like Madame Marie Curie (who cannot be ignored but can be said to be the exception), the contributions of those who do much of the work in science are not recognized. And when women have been mentioned, they have been historically subordinated in the histories of science in a number of very specific ways.

The History of Anthropology: Pretending Women Are Not There

The history of anthropology has neglected women most often by pretending they have not been there. This is seen most clearly in conscious omission. If one reads a history of linguistics, archaeology, or physical anthropology, one gains the impression that there has never been a woman in the field. Sociocultural anthropology is somewhat better, but even there women and their contributions are underrepresented. For example, Parsons published almost 30 articles in the *American An-*thropologist between 1916 and 1945 (the most prolific writer in the profession); yet Stocking (1976) in his anthology of the period makes almost no mention of her, as Hieb points out in his chapter in this volume, except to note that "at critical moments in the 1920s [ethnographic work] was sustained by the *ad hoc* benefactions of Elsie Clews Parsons" (Stocking 1976:12). Likewise, Hoebel's (1954) assessment in "Major Contributions of Southwestern Studies to Anthropological Theory," in addition to being only a partial historical record, glaringly omits women. Although Ruth Benedict's works are mentioned and analyzed, those of Dorothy Eggan, Esther Goldfrank, and Florence Hawley Ellis are referred to only in relation to Benedict's papers and the debate she sparked. Matilda Coxe Stevenson is part of the initial "flurry" of anthropologists who are not discussed further; Barbara Freire-Marreco, the first woman from Britain to work in the United States, is mentioned for a "limited contribution" (to what is never mentioned). Hoebel (1954:722) credits Morris Opler with the first theoretical statement about Southern Athabascan kinship systems, ignoring the fact that Gladys Reichard published a monograph on Navajo kinship seven years before Opler's contribution.

One would hope that the situation has changed, especially since the advent of feminist criticism. Our history texts and memories are proving to be highly resistant, however. For example, Willey (1988) has recently published an autobiographical memoir in the form of remembrances of 16 influential anthropologists. Willey chronicles his career by presenting a series of sketches of the men who influenced his life, whom he considers to have been the most influential individuals in American anthropology. The choices for inclusion are very individualistic—"a personal gallery of portraits" (Willey 1988:117)—and, as such, cannot be questioned. But the exclusions also speak loudly. Willey met no women who influenced his career or his thinking. His lack of attention to women scholars echoes and brings to the surface the nature of the prestige hierarchy in archaeology and anthropology's marginalization of women. Portrayed are those who were powerful or influential, those who controlled jobs, resources, and access to excavation sites—that is, men. Women exist in the background as wives, mothers, and unpaid helpers.

Women are also conspicuously absent from annotated volumes. For example, Manners and Kaplan (1968) selected articles by only 3 women (one of whom is a sociologist) out of 53 entries as works that represented the best theoretical statements in anthropology. Likewise, Murphy (1976) chose the work of 1 woman and 21 men for his *Selected Papers from the American Anthropologist, 1946–1970* from a total of 1,006 possibilities. Although the articles may have been representative of prominent authors, disciplinary subfields, and theoretical perspectives, they were not representative of the gender composition of the field. This problem, Murphy (1976:5–6) posits, reflects the small number of women in the field. After World War II, he argues, women

found themselves squeezed out of graduate schools and jobs by returning veterans. It was not until the late 1960s that women would return with renewed vitality into academic life. This decline of female involvement is manifest in the authorship of *American Anthropologist* articles. I did a count of sex of all authors during the 1946–70 period. The total number of authors was 1,219—a number greater than the total number of articles, due to co-authorship—of whom 1,060 were men and 158 women. For the entire period, 13% of the authors were female. The male-female ratio of authorship was further broken down by five-year periods, yielding the following percentages of women authors: 1966–70—12%; 1961–65—13%; 1956–60—10%; 1951–55—13%; 1946–50—22%. By themselves, these figures might be straws in the wind, but they follow the pattern already documented by careful studies of women in the academic profession.

Although this is a perceptive analysis that other authors have not even advanced, nevertheless under 5% of the papers in Murphy's volume were authored by women.

I do not want to be unfair; a historian, compiler, editor, or biographer must always make choices, because one cannot include everyone. In general, historical discussions of specific topics such as ethics, applied anthropology, political controversies, philanthropy, and relations with native peoples include women as active participants (see Goldschmidt 1979; Helm 1966, 1985). Nancy Lurie (1966) also produced the outstanding essay "Women in Early Anthropology" in part to demonstrate women's participation. We can read dominant texts in the field (e.g., Bidney 1953; Brew 1968; M. Harris 1968; Hatch 1973; Hodgen 1964; Leaf 1979; Malefijt 1974; Stocking, ed. 1976) and sometimes find a few women, often in footnotes. There is almost always mention of Benedict (the exception to the rule) and Mead ("the ultimate honorary male anthropologist," Warren 1988:59)—the mavericks no one quite knows what to do with. Paradoxically, early histories of anthropology mention women more often than do those written after World War II. Lowie, for example, repeatedly recognizes Parsons as a significant theoretician and ethnographer, especially in the realms of kinship and religion and as a "leader who recognized the deficiency of current monographs [in 1922]" and led the way to rectify the matter (Lowie 1937:275). Parsons does not merit a separate chapter, however. Conversely, texts penned after World War II occasionally mention that a pioneer woman, often Alice Fletcher or Zelia Nuttall, lived and did some fieldwork. These summary texts tell us that women anthropologists existed and that they can be placed in the anthropological genealogy, but little else.

Histories of anthropology also speak to how women and their contributions are viewed in the discipline by the types of reviews in which they are mentioned. By and large, regional or culture-specific reviews represent women more prominently than do disciplinary or subdisciplinary reviews, partly because the former tend to be more field-oriented; it is acceptable for women to be fieldworkers and data gatherers. Spicer's (1948) analysis of Pueblo ethnologies focuses on the works of Benedict, Bunzel, Parsons, and Bandelier. He analyzes each individual's contributions in perspective as he contends that the corpus of work fits together into a whole that has increased our knowledge of Pueblo societies. Spicer follows the tenet that science does not exist in the abstract but that scientists are influenced by and influence the world around them. When he mentions personal characteristics or background information, he does so to emphasize the researcher's methodological techniques and approaches. For example, he writes, "Parsons' feeling for the dynamic of Pueblo culture arose out of her own long and intimate contact with Pueblo life. She attempted no synthesis until after she herself had visited, talked, and lived in most of the villages for varying lengths of time during a period of more than twenty-five years" (Spicer 1948:82).

Likewise, Basso (1973) lists and analyzes the work of Parsons, Goldfrank, Underhill, Benedict, Kurath, and Shepardson along with Eggan, Kroeber, Opler, White, Kluckhohn, and Lowie; he mentions the work of more men than women, but the ratio is approximately that of the percentage of men to women in the area (3 to 1). Commendably, Basso (1973:229) explicitly recognizes the value of data gathering. For example, he notes,

Mary Shepardson and Blodwen Hammond have completed the only full-length ethnography of a Navajo community to appear within the last decade. Largely descriptive and guided by what the authors themselves imply may be an out-dated form of "structural-functional analysis," it is nonetheless a valuable and informative study which presents large amounts of carefully collected data on a wide range of topics.

Also unusual is Basso's acknowledgment of several team efforts, including husband-and-wife initiatives by James and Dolores Gunnerson, Stanley and Ruth Freed, Ross and Lynn Crumrine, Jane and Kenneth Hill, George and Felicia Trager, and the father-daughter team of William Holden and Jane Holden Kelley.[5] Women are thus found in regional assessments that stress knowledge about individual societies and their intersection with general theory rather than in books that focus on abstract or mid-range theory.

Anthropology's Techniques of Marginalization

Historians and anthropologists downplay and marginalize women's contributions in historical texts. As a result, women are remembered in narrow, specific ways. For example, women, along with a few men, are most frequently identified as the students or the teachers of prominent figures in the field; this is the primary manner in which Ruth Bunzel, Beth Dillingham, Lucy Mair, Audrey Richards, Ruth Underhill, and Gene Weltfish are placed in history or theory texts (e.g., Malefijt 1974).[6] Today, even such an important figure as Parsons is mentioned usually because of her influence on Benedict or as the enabling source of funds for Boas or White (see Mead 1974; Mintz 1981).

Women are also considered important or unimportant depending on how the critic views a few key charismatic figures in anthropology.[7] For this volume, because it deals with American anthropology rather than British, German, or French anthropology, the most important key figure is, of course, Boas. Women scholars become disciples or fictive daughters in the social hierarchy of ethnology (and occasionally archaeology), loyal children and followers in anthropology's often-feuding families. Boas' "daughters" are held to be either intellectually correct or incorrect depending on the author's view of Boas; rarely are women assessed in terms of their own contributions as independent thinkers. For example, when Marvin Harris (1968:305) analyzed one of Boas' contentions, he mentioned Reichard (one of two brief references in the entire book) in the following manner:

On the basis of this one drastically deficient case, there gradually diffused out of Schermerhorn Hall at Columbia, through lecture, word of mouth, article, and text, the unquestioned dogma that Boas had proved that it was just as likely that patrilineality succeeded matrilineality as the reverse. When the case was cited in the general textbook that Boas had edited, Gladys Reichard (1938:425) referred to it as "more convincing" than the other possible instances among the Trobrianders (also highly dubious, however) because "the details of its course are more positive."

The inference, of course, is that Reichard's inability to analyze critically and recognize empirical deficiencies or logical flaws stemmed from her blind devotion to Boas and his cause. By being a dutiful daughter, Reichard could not be an adult scholar. Thus, all her work was questionable and could be ignored. Nor is Harris alone in his use of this marginalization technique. Leaf (1979: 211–24) subsumes Benedict's contribution under a section entitled "Reinterpreting Boas" and then contends that her work "represents a similar distortion of Boas' idea that culture was in some fundamental sense an elaboration of basic ideas" (Leaf 1979:221). Even if she used Boas' idea, therefore, she failed to get it right.

Conversely, women students could be intellectually correct because they adhered to the research agenda and ideas of the charismatic leader. Using Boas again as an example, Lowie demonstrates his own ambiguity toward women anthropologists as well as how Boas' agenda enabled women to work in the field, how Boas recognized the need for women in anthropology, and how his "stimulation" empowered women to make their greatest contributions to the field:

The same urge to see aboriginal mentality in all its phases has made Boas encourage work by trained women. Since primitive peoples often draw a sharp line between the sexes socially, a male observer is automatically shut off from the native wife's or mother's activities. A woman anthropologist, on the other hand, may naturally share in feminine occupations that would expose a man to ridicule. Women have made important contributions independently of Boas, but probably nowhere have they achieved so much work as under the stimulation of the Columbian atmosphere—witness the publications of Drs. Elsie Clews Parsons, Ruth Benedict, Ruth Bunzel, Gladys

Reichard, Erna Gunther, Margaret Mead, Gene Weltfish, Ruth Underhill (Lowie 1937:134).

So ingrained and almost unconscious has the association between male father figure/mentor and female student/daughter become that for a woman not to follow the male lead is considered worthy of note. Voget (1975:38) has found evidence that Benedict did not carry out Boas' research agenda. He concludes, however, that "this theoretical turn in contradiction to 'Papa' Boas is curious," a proposition that is not noted for any of Boas' male students, such as Kroeber.

One gains the impression from reading summary texts, the histories of the discipline, and citation indexes that use these marginalization techniques that women did not have independent thoughts or their own research agendas, that they did not (or could not) develop the crucial core idea, or that the authors are not quite sure what to do with women scholars. There is no problem, however, with noting that women expanded on the work of Great Men. Honigmann (1976:202–3) presents Benedict's intellectual contributions in such a way that they appear to have stemmed from the ideas of Kroeber, Lowie, and Boas rather than her own insight even though he later refers to her as "a sensitive, insightful and intelligent woman" (Honigmann 1976:207). Voget (1975:334) uses the same intellectual source and finds that Goldenweiser's work served as a prototype for Benedict's. Rarely are women said to be the source of ideas for male scholars. As the articles in this volume argue, to view women as only the recipients of the master's ideas, whether rightly or wrongly interpreted, is one-sided and makes women seem incapable of creative, original thought. Ample evidence exists to combat this view.

Historians also marginalized women scholars by portraying them as sidekicks or individuals who happened to be in the right place at the right time. Hoebel (1954) mentions Parsons because she was at Zuni at the same time as Kroeber and Lowie and could "reasonably balance" the theoretical claims regarding kinship nomenclature of the two Great Men—i.e., she gathered data to test their ideas, served as a field assistant, and ultimately became a mediator.[8] This type of helping behavior is apparently appropriate for women and worthy of remembrance. Historians also note other instances of assistance to the profession. They often remember women who saved or edited the work of important or overlooked men, emphasizing women's role as preservers of knowledge. Fred Eggan (1986) felt that Parsons had made one of her greatest contributions to anthropology in buying and editing Alexander Stephen's diaries on the Hopi. Historians recall other women, such as Helen Codere, because of their documentation of a Great Man's (usually Boas') contribution, for their critiques of his work, or because they served as his chroniclers, even though they were intimately involved in fieldwork and the production of their own texts. Marvin Harris (1968:266), for example, relegates Reichard to the role of "keeper of knowledge about Boas," as the one to whom the Great Man related his first field experiences with the Eskimo. From this type of positioning one can gain no insight into Codere's or Reichard's contributions. They become simply sources of information, like the peoples that anthropologists study, no longer researchers themselves.

Finally, when women are remembered they are spoken of with less enthusiasm than men. For example, Harris considers White's fieldwork among the Keresan Pueblos to be "vigorous" (Harris 1968:723), but he does not so categorize the work of women who also worked with the Rio Grande Pueblos; they merit no descriptive adjectives, even when the corpus of work was more extensive and intensive. When Willey (1988) mentions a woman professional, he adopts a belittling tone. For example, when speaking of his undergraduate days at the University of Arizona he stated, "I began my archaeological studies with just a single introductory course that would be offered by a comely young lady seated at [Dean Byron Cummings] side, a Miss Fraps" (Willey

1988:10). The attractive Miss Fraps, the sidekick, is Clara Lee Tanner, who is effectively sidelined as unimportant. This tendency harkens back to the point made earlier that women either are criticized more extensively and harshly than men or are not taken seriously.

When You Can't Ignore Women Find a Leveling Mechanism

A few women—Mead and Benedict—have been impossible to marginalize in the ways just mentioned. Everyone agrees that Benedict was one of this century's truly outstanding anthropologists, yet authors view this recognition as that of an exceptional individual. Exceptions to the rule, whether they are men or women, have long proven to be a problem for American scholars, including historians of anthropology. As Babcock observes in her article in this volume (p. 126), Benedict displayed that which "could not be denied and a courage to carry on regardless, challenging conventional boundaries between disciplines and reorganizing our ways of making sense of the world." Many historians have recognized these intellectual contributions: Stocking (1976) presents a balanced assessment of her work, and Lowie (1937) analyzes her ideas and places her contributions firmly within the period in which she wrote, seeing her as an heir to a rich intellectual tradition. Even when he disagrees with her conclusions, he takes her and her work seriously. But others have approached Benedict differently. One scholar noted, "Like most of Ruth Benedict's students, I looked up to her with a mixture of veneration and bewilderment" (Barnouw 1949:241). This ambivalence, which stems from an inability to easily understand or pigeonhole Benedict, has led to a series of sympathetic and unsympathetic portraits that depict either a deeply disturbed personality searching for peace in the anthropological endeavor (see Babcock and Parezo 1990) or a romantic, idealistic poetess, as Babcock notes in her article (see also Mintz 1981; Modell 1983). Benedict's work and life are seen as the result of an unhappy childhood. She has also been, as Babcock documents, the subject of contempt and hostility, as are all important individuals who earn public recognition. One is not neutral when speaking of Benedict, just as one is not neutral about anthropology's other charismatic leaders, such as Boas, Mead, or Malinowski.

More than for any other figure in anthropology (with the exception of Mead and possibly Malinowski), discussions of Benedict and her contributions have focused on personal characteristics—her shyness, melancholy, deafness, generosity, and aloofness. Her personality is seen as the basis for her ideas (when she is credited for having had ideas). There are advantages to this concentration, which reveals the inseparability of the intellectual and the personal, of observer and observed, of ideas and their contexts, of public and private, and of knowing and feeling. Historians of anthropology have uncovered an important dimension for women anthropologists, at least. Benedict, like many other women anthropologists, did not separate her professional from her private life. Her anthropology was a compelling focus for her. Whether the same is true for male anthropologists we do not know; the question has never been addressed. Historians keep men's professional and private lives rigidly distinct. Unfortunately, this holistic analysis all too often becomes a leveling mechanism that downplays Benedict's (and other women's) contributions—if Benedict was melancholy, could she have done adequate fieldwork to support her work, was she really able to be objective? Scholars base this type of critique or analysis on Anglo-American societal concepts about male and female natures, which presuppose that women's identities are located in the body and the emotions while men's are located in the mind (Aisenberg and Harrington 1988). As the exception to the preconceived rules about women scholars, the history of anthropology has treated Benedict exceptionally. As an exception she can be conceptualized as deviant and theoretically dismissed. When this happens her ideas can be appropriated by others.

I am not suggesting that personality traits,

psychological profiles, past life events, alcoholism or drug addiction, physical disabilities, or even psychological problems are unimportant or that they have not influenced individuals' conceptualization of the world and choice of research problems and hence affected the development of anthropology. Information of this kind and the insights it can bring have a place in the history of anthropology. As will be seen throughout this book, personality looms large; it has affected the fields individuals have chosen, the types of research situations and theoretical problems anthropologists have felt comfortable tackling, and anthropologists' ability to complete projects. Individuals and their relationships are central to understanding the development of theories as well as the theories themselves. But scholars too often view women's accomplishments as a form of pathology: thus, we have criticism of Mead's "domineering ways" (Toulmin 1984). In addition, an unspoken assumption exists in cultural anthropology that an insensitive individual is incapable of being a sensitive fieldworker. This assumption, however, has an unacknowledged gendered corollary; females should naturally be more sensitive than males. When we discover the same types of individual temperament—melancholy/joyful, nice/not nice, shy/boisterous, retiring/flamboyant—in women as in men we tend to dismiss the work of insensitive women more quickly than that of insensitive men. For it is still a truism that "the eccentric brilliant man is a culturally recognized and endearing role; Gregory Bateson's iconoclasm was a key to his status as a countercult figure. The eccentric brilliant woman is still a bag lady" (Tannen 1986:202).[9]

I also do not want to suggest that personality arguments are reserved only for women. Historians have also used leveling mechanisms against men about whom the profession is ambivalent or feels are too successful, i.e., those who are exceptionally arrogant, nonconformist, flamboyant, successful, have "gone native," or have done an outstanding job of advancing themselves. They have suffered the same fate as women when their works have been assessed. Malinowski is a prime example of an anthropologist who was intent on depicting himself in the role of "fieldworker as hero" (Kuper 1985; Stocking 1983), a fatal flaw in terms of remembrance. For example,

The furor over the publication of Malinowski's *Diary* (1967) represents a low point in the discipline's degree of sophistication. In the inflamed political atmosphere of the 1960s, Malinowski was attacked because of his private diary, which records his tribulations and miseries as he did his magnificent field work. A Polish word, which he used for the Trobrianders when he was most emphatically fed up with them, was translated as "nigger." The increase in self-evaluation and puzzled, troubled exposure of difficulties in the field has not been accompanied, as it might have been, with greater charity or detachment. Anthropologists have continued to be highly personal, unskilled in separating their own affects from their material, polemic, given to *ad hominen* arguments and, as if they were all members of one giant extended family, personal rather than relevant nit-picking (Mead 1973:5–6).

Cultural heros, especially our often romanticized pioneers, are certainly referred to and evaluated with regard to their personal lives: age, physical appearance, shyness, outspokenness, marriages, temperament, wealth, and political connections.

Personality as an interpretive tool has never been adequately dealt with in the history of science, as Joan Mark noted at the conference.[10] Notably, it is these types of analyses—the idea that a theory was formulated as the catharsis for a personality flaw or that a theory can be dismissed because the author was not a likeable individual—that are leveled at women more often than men. "It is peculiar that reviewers avoid the same kinds of information in reviews of the work of men" (Abramson 1975:91). Overwhelmingly, the reviews of men about other men focus on the work, not on the individual. As a result, much of the history of women in science has not been "worked out simply in the realm of objective reality, of what specific women could or did do, but co-

vertly, in the psychic land of images and sexual stereotypes, which had a logic of 'its own' " (Rossiter 1982:xv).

Finally, the oral folklore of fieldwork and anthropology (our unofficial histories) is used differentially with regard to men and women and harkens back to our double standards of personal behavior. Although the literature is silent on this matter, "corridor talk" accounts of anthropologists will often say that "she got her ideas from sleeping with anthropologist X," or "she got her ideas from sleeping with a native." Accounts of culturally legitimate sexual participation have been made by male but not female fieldworkers (Warren 1988:34–35) and have not been used against men in academic gossip.[11] Our cultural sex and gender norms are used to delimit and assess the value of women's but not men's anthropological work. And this, of course, relates back to power; such denigrations are used in historical assessment, in evaluation, in criticism, indeed in many areas of life to equalize those who are seen to be threatening.

In one sense, members of the discipline ratify views of the past shown in disciplinary histories (Darnell 1972). Women anthropologists in the official texts have thus been devalued, trivialized, demeaned, ignored, dismissed, made less important, and hidden from view. Their contributions, perspectives, and accomplishments have been marginalized. When they have been referred to they have been categorized as foils, helpers, data collectors, and the keepers of the knowledge. Rarely have they been portrayed as individuals with the ideas, perspectives, insights, or visions that have pushed anthropology intellectually or caused paradigm shifts. This portrayal endorses and rationalizes the structure of anthropology and its host institution, the university, which have erected implicit and explicit barriers to women that have limited or had a negative impact on their productivity and have hidden them from view.

A LIFETIME OF BARRIERS

Occupations defined as male provide a social context uncomfortable for women because they are regarded as deviants. As a result, few women attempt to enter such fields, and those who do often face negative social sanctions that bar full access to the profession's rights and privileges (Epstein 1970:967). One such arena is higher education and its resident disciplines. At successive key points of advancement within the academic world women have met roadblocks, walls, concrete ceilings, closed doors, and padlocked gates that discouraged or effectively eliminated their participation. At every juncture, women have been more likely than men to exit the path to a senior academic position, regardless of discipline or time period (Menges and Exum 1983:127). And because of this, fewer women have been remembered than men.

Barrier 1: The Structure of Anthropology and the Academy

The social structure and dynamics of scientific communities affect the growth of knowledge (Crane 1972; Merton 1957; Rogers 1962); science is an organized social process situated in historical and social contexts. Whether and when a new idea or theory is accepted partly depends on the value of the idea, the scholar's position within the discipline, the discipline's organizational history, the number of people with whom a scientist has personal and regular contacts, and the prestige of the employing institution. These factors, in turn, help account for which individuals are remembered in a discipline for generating crucial knowledge and theories.

Although there is still much to be learned about how scientific communities are structured and function, we can conceptualize them as an organized social activity functioning with a social system. The system is composed of social circles, schools, or groups that study particular research areas (Cole and Cole 1973). As Storer (1966) conceptualized it, a discipline such as anthropology works as an organized social activity of individuals concerned with extending empirical knowledge and generating theories, guided by shared norms and a set of techniques and methods, which change over time. Part of the complex social structure of the discipline is based on gender relations, just as part is based on age, class, race, ethnic, political, religious, and economic relations. Thus, to be an anthropologist is to be a gendered anthropologist in the same sense that all knowledge is political because it reflects power relations (Foucault 1978). Gender, power, and knowledge are interconnected. In addition, all disciplines are embedded in other organizations—universities, research centers, museums, foundations, government—and this factor adds another dimension to its organization.

A high degree of informality characterizes interaction in professions and their institutional homes, especially in the top echelons (which function like an exclusive club). Clubs have a high degree of social solidarity with a characteristically strong dependence on colleagues for opinions and judgements (Hughes 1973:124–25). Individuals in the top echelon or the most exclusive social circle are most visible. It is very difficult for new individuals, both men and women, to break into this circle without an active mentoring relationship or an introduction by a prestigious member. As will be evident throughout this book, mentoring and sponsorship have been necessary for women to break into anthropology's club.

Visibility in a profession can be defined in terms of the extent to which others are familiar with a scholar's work. Contributions must be observed and commented upon to be noted, and they must be made visible by the activity of senior men who belong to the club who promote them (Epstein 1970; Zuckerman 1967). Under the leadership of one or two scholars, who are usually located at prestigious universities, key gatekeepers formally and informally recruit new members, socialize them, and give them a sense of commitment. From these invisible colleges develop schools of research (Mullins 1968). Needless to say, women are rarely, if ever, listed as leaders of invisible colleges; they are seen as followers if they are noted as members at all (Kaduschin 1968; Kohlstedt 1978). One investigator of this process has discovered that

ideas are more likely to be accepted if they are promoted or mentioned by eminent sponsors, or if they are the product of joint authorship with a well-known professional, or derive from a well-known laboratory or university. Whether a woman is 'sponsored' in these ways will partially determine who reads her work, listens to her reports, or even offers friendly comments on the draft of a paper (White 1970:414).

Unfortunately, women are sponsored less often than men and thus miss out on the informal signs of belonging and recognition that pave the way to recognition in histories of a discipline. Women in science, therefore, have not been given credit for their contributions because they have not been promoted; nor have they been in positions where such sponsorship can be seen. Cole and Cole (1968) discovered that those whose work had been frequently cited were known to almost all scholars in a profession regardless of their specialty. These individuals became the giants of the field, and, they noted, were almost always men in all disciplines.

Barrier 2: Education

Roadblocks become evident from the time of acceptance into the university at the undergraduate level. Women who could attend elite women's colleges such as Barnard, Smith, and Vassar have done well in science (Oates and Williamson 1978), but these schools cost a great deal of money.[12] Although these were the schools of choice for undergraduate women before World War II, the lack of funds in the Great Depression meant that many women went to smaller urban schools, such as the University of Denver, or land grant colleges. Ellis told us,

We were in the middle of the deep depression. We were darn lucky to be in school at all, so many of the people were dropping out of school. . . . We worked hard and did our Masters in one year because we were worrying about jobs anyway, especially the girls (Ellis 1985).

These coeducational colleges were preoccupied with the needs of their male students (Tidball 1974:52). In undergraduate settings it was difficult for women to major in science because of professors' preconceptions. Tanner (1985) recounted that on her first biology field trip in the mid 1920s, the instructor was "shocked that a woman could wash her face in cold water. He had always considered fieldwork beyond the abilities of women because of their delicate natures." Ellis (1985) likewise noted, "When I was young it was almost impossible for a woman to go on a field expedition." Yet these undergraduate research experiences were a crucial rite of passage for acceptance into the scientific community, as Cordell analyzes in her article in this volume. Not being able to major in anthropology or an equivalent science meant that women were at a disadvantage when they applied to graduate school.

The process continued in graduate school, where women found numerous barriers to acquiring advanced training. Many women were not allowed to attend the school of their choice. As Thompson (1985) stated, "At Harvard there was tremendous prejudice against women. . . . I had to sit in the hall while the men attended classes." As late as the 1960s, women were required to have higher I.Q.'s, better grades, and better credentials than men to be admitted to graduate school (Bernard 1964:80; Roby 1973). As a result, women in doctoral programs tended to be exceptionally able (Carnegie 1973:88).

One scholar has noted the result for women.

Not excluding academic qualifications, sex is probably the most discriminatory factor applied in the decision whether to admit an applicant to graduate school. . . . Several department chairs volunteered the information that women are purposely screened out as Ph.D. prospects (Heiss 1970:93).

Lander (1972:8) found that half of the women in anthropology felt that their sex had been a negative factor in their graduate school career. Opportunities for securing financial aid, teaching, and research assistantships were limited for women (D'Andrade 1975). As early as 1906, women had fewer opportunities to pay for their educations than men: "Columbia offered twelve university fellowships each year, valued at $650, but none was open to women, and of the thirty-two scholarships offered to cover the $150 tuition, women could apply for only four" (Rosenberg 1982:87). As a result, although 160 women a year between 1899 and 1906 were enrolled at Columbia in advanced philosophy, psychology, sociology, and anthropology courses, only 2 (Elsie Clews Parsons, 1899, and Naomi Norsworthy, 1904) were awarded Ph.D.'s. Professors told women, then and later, that their education would be a waste of time because they would get married; men were more productive since they would not stop to have babies (Abramson 1975: 76; Howe 1984:19).[13] And due to the lack of day care, having small children to care for did take its toll. Many women quit when they were ABD because of family responsibilities. For example, Rosamond Spicer (1985) said of her decision not to complete her doctorate, "I never made that tremendous sacrifice to give up children in order to do the Ph.D. because I knew it would mean another year of fieldwork and how could I?" Instead she raised three children and supported her husband's career.

The atmosphere of graduate school also did not promote success, as Elizabeth Colson (1970: 1188) discovered for women students at the University of California at Berkeley:

There is evidence that women doctorates are more likely to have received NO teaching assistantships and also more likely to have received NO support of any kind. The overall percentage of men who received no support as a teaching assistant is 33 percent, the corresponding percentage for women is 44 percent, which is 11 percentage points worse. The percentage who receive no support of any type is 9 percent for men and 15 percent for women, a large difference.

When women did obtain research assistantships, they were disproportionately required to perform menial tasks to prove their seriousness. In anthropology this meant cleaning the lab, sorting pot sherds, and filling in forms, activities that reinforced the notion of women students as helpers. Even after the completion of an education, double standards were used for predoctoral and postdoctoral fellowships and internships, especially if one was married. Dorothea Leighton, for example, early encountered the problem of the dual-career family. When she and her husband Alexander applied simultaneously for internships and residencies at Johns Hopkins University, he was given a position but she was not because of rules against nepotism. Dorothea was made a research assistant. The lack of a residency meant that she had to wait several extra years before she could practice medicine and psychiatry.

Subtle but very powerful prejudice in the form of double standards also lowered the completion rate for women. "Qualified" meant something very different for men than for women, a distinction that continued throughout professional careers. Women were continually scrutinized for ability and motivation; they were not allowed to make mistakes. As Freeman notes (1970:998), "In conversations with male faculty members [at the University of Chicago] one is given the impression that qualified for a woman means only the best in the field" and women's "continued presence" in school and later in the field "may be contingent upon passing certain loyalty tests, including ignoring derogatory remarks or allowing her gender to provide a source of humor for the group" (Gurney 1985:44). Women students (including myself in the 1970s) have been told they were smart for girls, too cute to want to be a professor, and not expected to be brilliant, and they have been urged to take the easiest courses (Harris

1970:285). They have not been encouraged to build images of themselves as scholars. Women have been excluded from the informal networks of communication among male faculty and their students through which much of the information necessary for professional socialization and admittance to the club is passed. Male professors have encouraged male students and have given them the support that in reality determined the course of an academic career. The lowered expectations for women and the lack of support affected women's performance.

As a result of these conscious and unconscious barriers, preconceptions, and double standards, women students took longer to receive their Ph.D.'s and had a higher attrition rate than men (Kramer and Stark 1988). Many stopped at the M.A. level or before completing their Ph.D. in a period when Ph.D.'s were increasingly required for entry level positions. Although this did not preclude women from succeeding in academia it did make the "ideal" career path more difficult to follow:

I didn't finish my Ph.D. thesis, so I'm completely naked. And they didn't give M.A.'s in those days. The M.A. was a terminal degree, and I was considered quite bright and promising, as a matter of fact. So I have gone through life without a degree, and I don't see that it's made any difference except I would have made a little more money in each place. . . . Probably if I hadn't been married, I would have completed the dissertation when I was at Barnard as a teacher, but I ran into a feeling that because my husband taught in the department at Columbia it would not be suitable; and this was not just *ad homina* because there was the same problem with a woman in political science (Woodbury 1985).

The ones who made it, with or without their degrees, were exceptional people and would have succeeded in anything they attempted.

Barrier 3: Finding a Job

There is a growing body of literature and solid statistical data indicating that the last hundred years have seen an increase in women's opportunities to obtain an advanced degree. But at the same time, American society has been unwilling to employ them. One scholar has observed, "Higher degrees in science did not necessarily lead to desirable jobs—often they led only to unemployment; nor did good work or major publications frequently lead to advancement or better working conditions, as they often do for upwardly mobile men" (Rossiter 1982:xvi). Nevertheless, brilliant, determined women did earn their credentials, enter the market, and secure professional positions in academia. But they remained a numerically small group, located in lower-level positions, concentrated in "women's" professions, and underrepresented at prestigious institutions. Few attained full professorships in most disciplines.

For women scientists this pattern of sex-segregated employment was firmly established by 1910. Women were frozen out of jobs in academia by administrators using as justification

an essentially conservative rhetoric that women had "special skills" or "unique talents" for certain fields or kinds of work. The phenomenon basically seems to have been an economic one whose origin and perpetration were the result of three forces: (1) the rise of a new supply of women seeking employment in science, including the first female college graduates; (2) strong resistance to this female work force's entering traditional kinds of scientific employment (such as university teaching or government employment); and (3) the changing structure of scientific work in the 1880s and after which provided new roles and fields for these entrants (Rossiter 1982:51).

Unfortunately, this pattern has continued. Few gains have been made over the years, although there has been some cyclical variation and periods of movement toward equity (Cole 1979). Historical trends are difficult to assess in detail because of insufficient data on the distribution of women within universities and because numbers vary according to data source. Nevertheless, a few examples provide evidence of the underrepresentation of women and the lack of progress toward equality. This employment history helps explain why women are invisible in disciplinary histories.

Over a century ago college faculties were reported to be well over half female; many women taught in women's colleges, normal schools, and the new coeducational land-grant agricultural colleges. By 1890 the proportion of women educators had dropped to one-quarter of that of men (Hornig 1980:116). As higher education became institutionalized and more important in the political and economic life of the United States, women students and educators were increasingly displaced by men. By 1910, 20% of faculty were women: of these, 10% were professors, 5% associate professors, 10% assistant professors, and 73% instructors (Handschin 1912:55). Above the ranks of instructor, women were found almost exclusively in the professions of domestic science/ home economics, English, music, and modern languages.

In 1921, when 145 colleges and universities with 4,760 faculty were surveyed, 4% of the full professors and 23% of the instructors were women (Caldwell 1921:24−25). Although half of the institutions had women on their academic faculties, Caldwell found that women were hired only when it was discovered that they could "handle some subject better than a man" (1921: 22). Women also attained higher ranks in certain types of institutions: 45% of the full professorships in women's colleges were held by women, but no women held such a rank in men's colleges.[14]

By the mid 1920s, women were earning 12.3% of the doctorates in the sciences and even a few in engineering; in the social and behavioral sciences, women were receiving 17.1% of all doctorates (Vetter 1987:2). These numbers helped account for the increasing number of women found in the universities in the 1920s. The proportions of women as faculty, however, remained stable. Of the 680 women university teachers identified at 70 universities in a 1924 American Association of University Professors survey, 4% were professors, 5% associate professors, 19% assistant professors, and 72% instructors. Women were still concentrated in English, home economics, and the Romance languages but were also found as tokens in almost all disciplines (Lonn 1924:6). Jonathan Cole (1979:223) reasoned that "attempts to achieve equity" were high in this period because "feminist activity in the 1920s [reduced] discrimination on the basis of sex at least in the high prestige academic departments." Lonn (1924: 10), however, came to a different conclusion: "Chairmen do not desire women except in departments other than their own and except in positions lower than professor" because of "lack of scholarship, broad viewpoint, aggressiveness and vigor in teaching methods, mental freedom, mastery of subject matter, and world-mindedness." An associate professorship was the highest rank to which most women could realistically aspire. Women social scientists had more opportunities for employment in clinical or social work than in the universities (Hutchinson 1929:203).

Nevertheless, gains were made throughout the 1920s, for this decade was critical for educated women. During this 10-year period, women achieved their highest proportions of the undergraduate population, of doctoral recipients, and of faculty positions. Using U.S. Bureau of Census materials, Epstein (1970:967) discovered that the percentage of women college professors, administrators, and instructors reached a high of 32% in 1930. But when the impact of the women's suffrage movement began to fade, women's representation also began to decline—a decline that did not reverse until the 1960s.[15] This was first seen in the percentage of women earning doctorates during the 1930s, which dwindled from 11.0% in the 1930s to 8.9% in the 1940s (Vetter 1987:2). The social and behavioral sciences' proportions of women faculty also declined, from 15.8% in the 1930s to 14.5% in the 1940s and 11.0% in the 1950s. Economic, political, and societal changes were the keys to this decline. In the Great Depression, administrators emphasized the employment of men; women were laid off and men given their positions.[16] By 1939, 27% of the scholars working in higher education were women. Even during World War II, when there was a marked shortage of men in industry and women took over many positions, there was no comparable increase in the number of women university teachers. In fact, the percentage decreased (Moore 1946:150) because universities did not expand and most male professors were too old for military service. "In anthropology, sociology, and history the percentages of women who received Ph.D.'s during the lowest periods [1940–41] of women doctorate production still were more than twice as large as the percentage of women full professors" (Morlock 1973:263).[17] Thus there was no labor shortage in academe into which women could move. (As Halpern will demonstrate in her chapter in this volume, this was not the case in government work, however.)

The postwar period also was not advantageous for women in academia, even though it was a period of expansion for higher education. The most rapidly expanding fields in the 1940s and 1950s were the "men's" fields of science, engineering, and business administration, fields in which women earned the fewest doctorates. The emergence of the research university as the model for higher education, the flowering of the sciences, and the greater financial rewards for university professors created a climate unfavorable to women because of their traditional concentration on teaching (Graham 1978). The G.I. Bill filled the nation's colleges to overflowing. Although men were able to take advantage of these openings, women's opportunities were curtailed. Higher admission standards for women than for men were established to make room for male veterans, and many elite universities established quotas for women that eliminated many of those who met the higher standards (Hornig 1984). Concomitantly, the idea that a Ph.D. was a pre-

requisite for teaching positions at all four-year institutions grew. The baby boom further hampered the participation of women in higher education. Domestic help became harder to obtain and more costly; women with small children stayed home. In 1955 only 22% of the nation's faculty were women (Eells 1958).

By 1960, the percentage of all women college professors, administrators, and instructors (19%) equaled the 1910 percentage (Epstein 1970:967). Women held only 3% of professorships, excluding home economics and library science (Parrish 1962:102), and only 2% of social science professorships in research universities (Pollard 1977:268). The University of Chicago, for example, reflected this pattern; the percentage of women on the faculty dropped from 8% at the end of the nineteenth century to 2% in the mid 1960s (Howe 1984:19). Even though the 1960s was a decade characterized by an explosive growth in higher education, women lost ground proportionately as regular faculty in all four-year institutions.

In absolute terms women shared in the educational boom. The number of doctorates awarded to women in the sciences grew from 107 in 1920 to almost 4,000 by 1970 (Vetter 1987:2). And women slowly entered the marketplace as well. Although 40,000 women served as faculty in higher education in 1939–1940, by 1963–64 their number had almost tripled to 110,000. But in relative terms women lost ground (Roby 1973:37), remaining below their 1920 representations in all levels. The decline was most notable at the associate professor level (21.7% in 1959 to 14.6% in 1971); only as instructors (29.3% to 39.4%) did women gain ground (Carnegie 1973:110). Women were simply not being given tenure.

The 1960s did mark the revitalization of the women's movement. Societal changes that necessitated the return of women to the workplace brought increasing numbers of women to the sciences. Thus women's opportunities grew slightly in the latter part of the decade, but in 1969 there were still fewer women even on the faculties of women's colleges than there had been in the mid 1930s (Howe 1984:19). In anthropology the number of women faculty in sociocultural anthropology grew from 11% to 30% between 1962 and 1983, if instructors and lecturers are included (Lutz 1990). Women constituted more than 20% of the field in 1971 (and have maintained that level). That is, the percentage of women in anthropology receded to its 1920 national average. "In anthropology, as in microbiology, physics, and political science, the proportion of women full professors is one fourth to one third their percentage as instructors and lecturers" (Morlock 1973:216). This placed women into the full professor level at a proportion of only one-third of their availability, as measured by the Ph.D. pool.

The 1970s and 1980s witnessed increases as universities initiated affirmative action programs and as more women earned doctorates and professional degrees (Chamberlain 1988); women were awarded 14% of science doctorates in the 1970s and 24.8% in the 1980s. Even greater gains appeared in the social and behavioral sciences— 24.2% in the 1970s and 37.9% in the 1980s (Vetter 1987:2). Women still were concentrated in the humanities.[18] The figures cited in this period for the proportion of women nationally on college and university faculties ranged between 18% and 27%; most were 20% to 23% (Carnegie 1973:111; Howe 1984:41; Robinson 1973; Wandersee 1988). Women's representation in different disciplines varied from a high of 37% in modern languages to a low of 3% in physics (Morlock 1973:258). Individual schools demonstrated even greater variation—between 2% and 35%. According to a study released in 1973 by the American Council on Education, women accounted for 20% of the faculty members on American college and university campuses in the 1972–73 academic year. Women made up 40% of the instructional employees in junior and community colleges but less than 10% of the instructional employees in the prestige universities

(Weal 1970:310). In the top 25 institutions, women were seven times more likely to be instructors or lecturers than were men (Wandersee 1988:116). Women were least represented on the faculties of elite schools (Robinson 1973: 204), and relatively few women were in the senior ranks of faculties in research universities (Carnegie 1973:30). Sanjek (1978) noted a declining proportion of women in the top departments and a total lack of women in half of the 22 departments he surveyed for the American Anthropological Association. Exactly the same pattern holds for sociology (Deegan 1978). By 1983, women accounted for 26% of full-time college faculties at four-year colleges, but differences in rank were again striking; only 1 in 3 instructors, 1 in 3 assistant professors, 1 in 5 associate professors, and 1 in 10 full professors were women (Anonymous 1981; Lovano-Kerr and Fuchs 1983; Menges and Exum 1983; Ransom 1989; Vetter and Babco 1978). By 1988, women constituted 27% of all full-time regular faculty in higher education, but less than 10% of tenured faculty (Anonymous 1988a:6). These figures led Vetter (1987:6) to conclude that "although their opportunities for participation have increased substantially—by almost any statistical parameters—over the past decade, [women] have not yet reached equality with men having similar credentials."

Barrier 4: Low Status and Nontenured Positions

One overriding theme of women in academia is their underrepresentation in relation to their male colleagues. Another is the divergent career tracks that have resulted in a two-tier system of responsibility and rewards. This can be seen first in a lack of job security. Women are concentrated in "soft-money," irregular, nonladder, exceptional, fringe, or part-time positions, that is, the lowest positions in the highly stratified world of academia. Academia has a small elite and a large underprivileged stratum at the bottom and the sides.[19] Nationally, the number of part-time faculty positions has tripled since 1960, and between 25% and 33% of faculty members at four-year institutions teach part-time. Close to 40% of these part-time faculty members are women, a significant difference from the 27% of women who are full-time faculty members (Anonymous 1988b). Women, more vulnerable because of their lack of seniority, have tended to be concentrated in the "hidden professorate" because of differential treatment in the areas of instruction, hiring, evaluation, promotion, pay, and other forms of institutional recognition and reward.[20]

Since jobs went to men first, this pattern of women only securing institutionally peripheral jobs has a long history, as does the difficulty of moving from special and part-time positions to full-time, tenure-track positions. Bunzel, for example, only had soft-money jobs throughout her long and productive career. She said,

I came in at a time when things were opening up for women. There was no difficulty in fieldwork . . . [but] women had a tough time in getting appointments in anthropology. There were no jobs and they didn't go to women when they did turn up. . . . There was a time when I wanted to have a stable position but it wasn't in the cards. I had no illusions. I knew as a woman it would be difficult (Bunzel 1985).

Other women discussed in this book also had "permanent temporary" positions; women in anthropology were more than twice as likely to be hired in nonladder positions than were men (Lander 1972). The situation in the 1930s was so bleak that Boas transformed the field's lack of jobs into what one scholar describes as a

noble, self-sacrificing cause of great appeal to affluent individuals. Yet as many anthropologists discovered later, the highly romanticized sacrifices required in a field like anthropology were not shared equally, and most of the actual jobs in the field in the 1930s went to men, while the women made do on short-term grants and fellowships (Rossiter 1982:39).

The wealthy Parsons never held a permanent position in academe although she occasionally taught at Columbia University and the New School for Social Research. "She remained a patron of anthropology rather than one who could directly shape its future through the intellectual training of students" (Lamphere 1989:525). Other women remained isolated, for as Benedict (1940d) remarked, throughout the 1930s there were few enough teaching jobs in anthropology and practically none for women. Actually, anthropology may have been a bit worse in this respect than the other sciences:

Anthropology presents an extreme case of this dependency on foundations and fellowships during the 1920s and 1930s. Since it was a small field and had few teaching positions available, most of its younger women did important work and built whole careers on little more than a series of temporary fellowships from the NRC and SSRC. In fact, there seems to have been a tendency, in this field at least, to give the fellowships to women to "tide them over" while the few jobs available went to men (Rossiter 1982:272).

The women interviewed for this study support this interpretation. All felt that they had obtained ample research fellowships for their work.

Women anthropologists in general have been overrepresented in part-time positions and underrepresented in tenured positions and administrative posts (Fried 1971:7).[21] Discrimination in hiring has long been noted: there has been "a consistent pattern of discrimination in the hiring and promotion of female anthropologists with qualifications equal to male anthropologists" (Ad Hoc Committee 1979:1). Moreover, Lutkehaus (1990:313) argues,

It is tempting to attribute the receptivity of anthropology to women to the nature of the subject matter and its practitioners, individuals who were inherently interested in marginal groups and minorities. But the "feminization" of an academic field was characteristic of disciplines with slow growth rates and a general lack of employment prospects. . . . As with other fields of science, although women might enter anthropology in almost equal numbers to men, they were less likely to get jobs in academic departments, especially in co-educational universities.

Study after study have also shown that of the number of women in the academy, only a small proportion are tenured and promoted, and that women are hired in at lower ranks, so they have further to advance (Robinson 1973). Men also tend to gain tenure at an earlier age than do women despite equal productivity (Carnegie 1973:114; Howe 1984:19; Simon et al. 1967). Women in anthropology, as in all disciplines, are less likely than men to achieve promotion (Vance 1970). For example, it took Clara Lee Tanner almost 50 years after she was hired as an instructor to be promoted to full professor. Kate Peck Kent, who served for years as department chair at the University of Denver, was never awarded tenure or promoted to full professor. Benedict also waited years for advancement:

Ruth Benedict became a lecturer at Columbia in 1923 and continued on one-year appointments until 1931, when Franz Boas was able to secure for her an untenured assistant professorship. In 1936, Boas retired, and Benedict became acting chair. In the spring of 1936, Howard Lee McBain, who was then Dean of the Graduate School planned to name Ruth Benedict chairman of the Department of Anthropology. He remarked that some university was going to have to make a woman chairman of a graduate department and that Columbia ought to be the first to do so. But Dean McBain died of a heart attack on May 7, 1936. . . . Benedict never became chair. Under Mc-Bain's successor, Ralph Linton received that position. In 1937 Benedict was appointed associate professor. In 1948—after 25 years at Columbia, after publishing four books, and after being elected president of the AAA—she became a full professor (Sanjek 1982:848).

Women professors are subject to the same threats as men and, in addition, face the jeopardy of violating rules applicable only to women. For example, women are more readily labeled as troublemakers than are men, even if they have legitimate complaints; women faculty have family obligations that men do not; women are less likely to be awarded funds for travel to professional meetings than men. As French (1979: 136) notes, "The rules employed against women are unwritten, and those administering and interpreting rules regarding their employment often do not make decisions in a consistent fashion."

Despite equal productivity, academic women (both married and single) attain lower academic rank than do men (Simon et al. 1967); when men and women of comparable education and experience are employed, women's rates of promotion are significantly inferior to men's (Howe 1984: 19). In sociology, for example, men tend to begin their academic careers as assistant professors, and are quickly advanced to the associate professor level once they have published sufficiently. As Alice Rossi (1970) discovered the academic ladder is a two-step hierarchy for men but a three-step hierarchy for women. While men begin their careers as assistant professors, women begin as instructors. While men are advanced as soon as they show promise and are accredited by significant publications, women remain in rank over twice as long and are required to have a greater number of significant publications before they are advanced. Men spend the greatest proportion of their careers as full professors, women at lower ranks. "The independent bright women may be tolerated as instructors or lecturers, but they are kept off the male turf that begins with the assistant professorship" (Rossi 1970:7–8).

It is no wonder that women do not move up the ladder as quickly as men. Trying to overcome this hidden and unacknowledged class structure is difficult, so it should come as no surprise that women anthropologists who worked in the days before affirmative action provide example after example of underemployment and of being passed over for promotion by mediocre or less qualified males. Since women are disproportionately concentrated in the lower ranks, they have little autonomy and fewer options than men. And individuals without permanent tenured jobs tend not to be remembered; histories of anthropology have focused on individuals who have worked within universities and occasionally museums. Only recently have the lives and ideas of anthropologists who have worked outside academe been recognized.

Barrier 5: Jobs in Nonprestigious Departments and Institutions

Inside the university, women had to hold certain kinds of jobs to be remembered; full professorships at universities with large student populations were crucial, for it is graduate students who remember and cite their teachers, especially their thesis and dissertation advisors. A professor's ideas and orientation toward the field are likely to leave their mark upon the student's perception of the field, for it is during the internalization of the great ideas of a discipline that one learns the unspoken values of the field. As Hymes (1962:81) has stated,

Our revered elder men have often transmitted [stories of our origin, nature, and destiny] to us in that part of the initiation known as the course on History and Theory. . . . And there is also the esoteric lore that elders sometimes impart to us, as a badge of their status and sign of favor, orally in little groups.

Thus, those who are remembered must be more than college teachers; they must be what Bernard (1964) has termed "men-of-knowledge." Men-of-knowledge are originators and innovators who generate knowledge in a theoretical form. Professorships in elite universities are focal centers that have attracted scholars and students. To the holders of these positions accrue editorships of prestigious journals, board memberships, invitations to speak at professional meetings and to serve as symposia discussants, consultancies to government agencies, foundation grants, and communication with others at similar institutions. They influence resources for research, govern tenure committees, and control publication outlets.

"To be recognized as influential requires in addition to ability and perseverance, access to professional networks, admittance to research laboratories, and affiliation with prestigious universities" (Denmark 1980:1059). Not surprisingly, women are less likely than men to be affiliated with large prestigious institutions (Dunham et al. 1964:64–65). As Lamphere notes in her chapter in this volume, Reichard had a full-time position and became a full professor, but at an undergraduate college. Women in all disciplines are more likely to teach in colleges without graduate programs and in two-year institutions. Unfortunately, women tend not to be employed by elite coeducational comprehensive or research universities. For example, sociology departments with graduate schools had women as 12% of its faculty in 1972 (Hughes 1973:10) compared to 33% in colleges with only undergraduate departments. Although women were as likely as men to have Ph.D. degrees from elite departments, they were unlikely to be given permanent or tenured positions in these same departments (Vance 1970:5). Like those in sociology, women in anthropology departments at all colleges held 7% of the full professorships in 1970, but they accounted for only 2% in the elite private schools. Rossi (1970:6) found an inverse relationship between the prestige standing of the university and the proportion of women on the full-time faculty at each of the top three ranks in the academic hierarchy.

Barrier 6: Teaching Assignments

To be a man-of-knowledge, one needs time to conduct research, think, and write. This is usually translated as a teaching load of six to nine hours of class instruction per week. As Astin (1969) observed, women Ph.D.'s have spent significantly more time than men teaching (50% to 31% respectively) and less time in research (25% to 41% respectively). Women who were fortunate enough to be employed by elite universities had heavier teaching and advising loads than men (Abramson 1975). Teaching loads in all course types, especially large survey courses, are heavier for women.

In addition, women serve on almost twice as many college committees as do men (Lovano-Kerr and Fuchs 1983).[22] Workloads have had a real impact on professional development. Universities have had different expectations of men and women regarding how they allocate their time and what their responsibilities are. These expectations parallel the cultural stereotypes of women as caretakers, nurturers, and natural teachers.

The type of classes a professional teaches also influences whether he or she is remembered. One must teach graduate courses in theory, methodology, and advanced seminars (as well as serve on dissertation committees) rather than introductory surveys of the field. Women are more likely to teach undergraduates. Women in sociology graduate departments, for example, are twice as likely to teach only undergraduates and half as likely as men to teach only graduate students (Rossi 1970: 6). In Astin and Bayer's study (1973), more than two-thirds of the female faculty, but fewer than half of the male faculty, exclusively taught undergraduate courses. Women carry a disproportionate share of teaching loads at introductory levels; in the 1960s, 28% of women faculty taught 13 hours or more weekly, but only 15% of the men carried this load (Hornig 1980:121). The percentage of women among the teaching faculty declines as the course level rises (Howe 1984:40). And this can have adverse results on promotion:

A woman political scientist was denied tenure because she had not qualified for the graduate faculty. Earlier, when she expressed a desire to teach at the graduate level, she had been told that students had more confidence in male professors. Further, she was informed that the chairperson felt that women did their best teaching to freshmen and sophomores who needed a little "mothering" to help them establish good study habits (French 1979:137).

Women serve as thesis and dissertation advisors significantly less often than men (Khasket et al. 1974:491). Women, who have been confined to the lower-status survey and lower division courses, thus have not been remembered in historical texts even though they may have been crucial in shaping students' decisions to enter a field.

Barrier 7: Publishing, Obtaining Resources, and Equal Pay

This situation leaves little time to publish, although it does not mean that women are unproductive. Astin (1969) found that 75% of women had published at least one article since beginning their teaching careers, and more than 50% had four publications. Heavy teaching loads mean that women have less contact with fellow scientists than do men; they are less likely to attend professional meetings and thereby miss an important part of the communication network (Bernard 1964:152). Researchers are able to advance most effectively through quantity rather than quality of publications early in their careers (McGrath and Altman 1966:87). (This has led to an emphasis on methodological rigor and substantive fact rather than theory and synthesis.) Heavy teaching loads and self-expressed commitments to teaching, however, has meant fewer publications. And this, in turn, means there are fewer items for people to cite. As Dorothy Keur (1985) perceptively pointed out, when speaking of her colleague Elsie Steedman, whom she considered an influential anthropologist: "You don't hear of her because she put her whole emphasis on building anthropology at Hunter College." Steedman's commitment to undergraduate education and her decision to ignore the notion of the superiority of research over teaching has meant that she will be absent from any history of anthropology text.

One other way in which membership in the proletariate plays against individuals can be found in access to research grants and publishing outlets. A simple rule of thumb exists in gaining research support: the less secure your academic position, the lower your chances for gaining such support. The more support you have and the better your reputation for gaining support, the easier it is to gain funding in the future. Women have been at a disadvantage in this regard. They have been less successful than men in marshalling support to conduct their research, and when they have succeeded they have been given lower dollar awards. Indeed,

department chairmen and research directors on campuses have been known to require that younger women, especially untenured ones, not use their own names as principal investigators on research proposals. . . . Women have been denied even a shared principal investigator status and forced to take a subordinate role, even though they originated the research idea. Yet most universities view principal investigator status as a clear indication of productive research (Abramson 1975:88–89).

As Kramer and Stark (1988) and Plattner et al. (1987) have shown, funding has been influenced by sexist assumptions and personal networks. And individuals who have not secured their own research funds rarely are asked to serve as reviewers of those seeking funds. Thus, until recently, most reviewers have been men, and powerful male reviewers have led to the marginalization of women's voices (Spender 1981).

Research grants and publications are important for negotiating salary raises and higher status. Lower status, for whatever reason, is reflected in low salaries (Loeb and Ferber 1971). Throughout the literature there is ample and irrefutable evidence that men are paid more than women for performing the same jobs. For example, Dutton (1985a) noted, "Because I am a woman, I have never received more than $12,000 a year for all that I've done." A study of 50 land-grant colleges in 1927–28 revealed that median salaries of women faculty were $860 less than men (Anonymous 1938). The same situation existed 40 years later. Women in anthropology at the beginnings of their careers were at an 8.5% disadvantage relative to men with regard to salaries; after 30 years in the field the discrepancy widened, their salaries were 28% below men's. The same differential holds for mathematics and chemistry (Johnson and Stafford 1979). Starting salaries for women are consistently below men's, and the differential

increases with rank; this pattern holds true even when levels of educational attainment, productivity, rank, and years of service are controlled (Carnegie 1973; Epstein 1970; Khasket et al. 1974). Pezzullo and Brittingham (1979) found that the sex differential varies directly with length of university service, discipline, and university type. Salary differences by gender are greater in research universities and in the biological and physical sciences.

Lack of visibility enters another arena as well. One standard of status is how often individuals are invited to participate in prestigious extramural events—present lectures or consult outside their home institution, receive invitations to review, write a chapter or a book, serve on a panel to review grant applications or on an editorial board, serve as a discussant, organize plenary sessions or deliver a keynote address at professional meetings, or hold the editorship of important journals. These are all very visible positions. Women microbiologists, for example, are invited for all these activities less often than men (Khasket et al. 1974:491). A number of factors influence invitations to prestigious events: the status of the individual's home institution, friendships and personal networks, perceptions of the centrality of the individual's research to the discipline, and the ability of the individual to evaluate and synthesize, to see the "big picture." Lutz (1990) discovered that in anthropology men are asked to serve as discussants almost twice as often as are women. Even presenting papers at a meeting is affected by gender: male-organized panels have a female participation rate of half that of female-organized panels (Lutz 1990).

Thus, anthropology as a whole has not been hospitable to women outside the fieldwork situation. It may be that anthropology is relatively more accessible to women than many other professions, but there has always been a problem of parity, partly because anthropology is situated in universities. There have been periods of relative welcome. Anthropology had in the 1920s, 1930s, and 1940s the reputation of attracting marginal people, including women (Kuper 1985), which was a self-fulfilling preconception. Mavericks go to a profession that defines itself as nonelitist. As one scholar points out,

There is an acceptance of a certain very general pattern of social organization in the larger society which embodies formal hierarchy, the cultivation of esoteric specializations, and elitism. There is an alternative that deplores all of these things and asserts that a counterculture can be built on opposite principles (Fried 1972:231).

Two opposing forces were working in anthropology. Like other professions and communities, anthropology has tended toward homogeneity as it aged (Goode 1957), which has meant the exclusion of women and minorities. One must question, therefore, whether anthropology has ever valued internally the diversity it studies.

Opportunities for the women anthropologists discussed in this volume, like all women scholars in higher education, were limited. Women academicians have worked under a multiple bind with regard to professional recognition: to be well known and have status, one has to have been a theoretician, a full professor in a graduate department, hold seminars at prestigious universities, not have a heavy teaching load in order to have time to write, be able to find jobs for aspiring professionals, be seen as an aggressive leader, and by almost all counts be male in order to be well-known and hold status. No wonder women are conspicuously omitted from histories of science. Women were acceptable only if they were overachievers, brilliant, and willing to work for low wages, and if no qualified men were available.

THE REDISCOVERY OF MARGINAL WORLDS: DEFINING AND FINDING HIDDEN SCHOLARS

The rediscovery of women scholars is a critique of the history of anthropology and a call for a reexamination of anthropology, academia, and society. It is in many ways the discovery of the history of a marginalized group without a recognized voice.

This theme has been acknowledged since the 1970s and was increasingly important in the 1980s as the study of women was embedded in the context of power, social production, and work. Feminist scholars have focused on the discovery of the female heritage, gender attribution, gender ideologies, the role of women in other cultures, general relations, and gender asymmetry. They have examined the interpretation of women based on preconceptions in old explanations, added women's contributions and achievements to the canons of several disciplines, and analyzed gender as both a symbolic construction and a social relationship (Moore 1988). Added to this is the study of how economics affects female status, how control over production intersects with women's place in the work force (Lamphere 1986; Sacks and Remy 1984). Still to be undertaken is an in-depth study of gender in anthropological history using ethnographic techniques. Some scholars are beginning to reverse this omission, however (see Gacs et al. 1988 for an excellent example), for we now recognize that we can trace a long tradition of thoughtful and articulate women, if only we begin the search for them.

Contemporary feminist anthropologists/historians are interested both in the careers of their predecessors and in the non-Western "women's worlds" into which female fieldworkers have traditionally gained access (Warren 1988:10). Within the discipline a significant body of work has come from the archaeological and ethnographic study of gender and the influence of gender on theory and methodology. We know much more about status and about how gender influences research, writing, and employment in elite occupations. However, we still lack an adequate study of women scientists embedded in this literature on feminism and work, an analysis of how the history of the distribution of academic power can be seen under the critical eye of feminism (see Keller 1985). Following feminist scholars, we are aiming for an assessment of female status, roles, and achievements contextualized within a discipline but with values that may be counter to the established definition of the subject. This is a difficult task; study after study shows the obstacles to characterizing female status in a multiethnic class society (Kessler and McKenna 1978; Mukhopadhyay and Higgins 1988).

The message of feminist anthropology and history is more than just the acceptance of the fact that women have been ignored and need to be incorporated into disciplinary texts. Just as feminist discourse analysis has questioned the taken-for-granted androcentric features of scientific writing, categories, research questions, and approaches (Conkey and Spector 1984; Farnham 1987; Gero 1988; Haraway 1986; Keller 1985; Sampson 1978, 1981; Shapiro 1981; Strathern 1984), so must we question the taken-for-granted features of academe and anthropology. As Deborah Gordon (1988) contends, science is phallocentric in intent and outcome; thus nongendered and nonreflexive models in history and the history of anthropology do not permit satisfactory explanations of women's experiences or women's writing. Even works consciously dealing with narrative conventions in the framing and writing of research and theoretical discourse, such as that of Clifford and Marcus (1986), do not deal effectively with gender and how androcentric biases enter into the construction and the practice of ethnography (Moore 1988). It is necessary to question and reconstruct traditional models of anthropology and its careers, structure, and enterprise to make them amicable to the study of women scholars (Howe 1977). For some authors in this volume, this process is seen as a disjunction in discourse. The world presented by a discipline is one discourse; to express the world as women practitioners experience it requires developing a new discourse. As Menges and Exum (1983:134–35) argue,

In the social sciences particularly, the dominant paradigm has been naturalistic and ahistorical. It seeks conclusions that are absolute and universal. This dominant paradigm, which Sampson (1978) calls

"Paradigm I," emerged from a male subculture and reflects male values, including individualism, achievement, mastery, and detachment. The alternative, "Paradigm II," seeks conclusions that are historical, context-bound, concrete, and particularistic . . . Paradigm II by definition challenges dominant values.

Also needed are studies that question the fundamental constructs of academe and disciplinary organization in much the same vein as Collier and Yanagisako (1987) questioned the categories of kinship, Hartman (1981) the household, and Gailey (1985) the state. This questioning for anthropology must be done both within the university as an occupational setting and within the field. If we agree with Mukhopadhyay and Higgins (1988:481) that "scholarship, by examining context, must determine how gender acquires meaning through concrete social interactions," then what is needed in the history of anthropology are life histories and biographies, embedded in time and space, that analyze the personal investment of becoming and being an anthropologist. One of the most critical essays and books to begin this quest for women in anthropology was written by Nancy Lurie (1966); her work laid the foundation for this volume.

There is the beginning of a rich literature that deals with issues of gender in fieldwork in anthologies such as *Women in the Field* (Golde, ed. 1986) and individual autobiographies or biographies (Bowen 1954; Goldfrank 1978; Laird 1975; Langness and Frank 1981; Mark 1980a, 1988; Mead 1959a, 1972; Powdermaker 1967; Shepardson 1986a; Silverman 1981). Lange's chapter on Goldfrank is in this mold and draws heavily on both biographical and autobiographical information. Personal and retrospective, these works are concerned with the production of identity by women scholars. Several of the papers in this volume have as a subtheme the search for identity and place.

Ironically, there is considerably more information on women than men in the fieldwork literature, reflecting the emphasis on women in methodological situations. As Warren (1988:8) notes,

I suspect that this methodological 'feminocentrism' (which contrasts with the 'androcentrism' of substantive and theoretical concerns) arises from the paradoxical situation of women field researchers. From the moment of their entrance into fieldwork in anthropology and sociology in the earliest twentieth century, women scholars did their research against the background of taken-for-granted androcentric assumptions about social life.

Thus, we need to make women no longer the marked category that requires special explanation or consideration. To do so we need to analyze their theoretical contributions and learn more about their disciplinary lives and careers, because our knowledge is still so meager. We need to locate the scholars first and then go beyond the compensatory and congratulatory quest. We need to understand how gender has worked in anthropology and in academe in all its dimensions. This involves more than one kind of history; it requires new ways of looking, new definitions, and multiple paradigms. Just as Gero and Conkey (1991) call for archaeology to be engendered, so we call for the history of anthropology to be engendered through a discussion of ideology, barriers, roles, relations, and discourse as these relate to social and professional lives. Needed is a feminist history written under the theoretical rubric of the sociology of knowledge.

To find the invisible and hidden is not to displace what is known but to add a new dimension and discourse to the dominant framework. Although we must be remedial to a degree because the history of anthropology has a great deal of remedial work to undertake where women are concerned, we do not want to discuss only those women whose work approximated that of the Great Men or to evaluate their contributions based on a preconceived and unacknowledged model. We want to look for distinctive qualities and expressions of women as well as those that are

similar to or different from those of men to insure that we do not fall into the trap of "a stereotyped characterization of women's roles in terms of the cliche of male dominance" (Leacock 1977:17).

The more one learns to read between the lines of official discourse and accepted history, the more one discovers how much women have contributed to our understanding of anthropology. As we highlighted in *Daughters of the Desert* (Babcock and Parezo 1988), the deeper one probes the more one is impressed by the sheer breadth, sensitivity, and quality of the research accomplished by women who have worked in the Native American Southwest. And here we speak both of individuals who have been formally recognized as anthropologists and those who will never make it into official discourse—unofficial anthropologists, the avocational amateurs and those who made contributions while pursuing other professions as photographers, novelists and essayists, philanthropists, authors of children's books, wives, government employees, teachers, and traders. As McGreevy, Halpern, and Tisdale document in their papers, neither the Southwest as we conceptualize it nor anthropology as a discipline would be what it is today without the vision of these women. Amateurs are the most invisible anthropologists.

There have been two ways to define an anthropologist. This definitional problem has plagued the discipline since McGee and Boas argued over who could become a member of the American Anthropological Association. One could define it narrowly as those who have been trained in a university department and have obtained advanced degrees, preferably a Ph.D., and who actively conduct research or teach in a limited set of institutions (academia, museums, and government service) as did Boas and Tozzer. The advantage of this definition is the presence of measurable and easily identifiable criteria for being an anthropologist—the fact that one has passed a rite of passage, been certified as a professional by a faculty at an accredited institution, and been accepted as a practicing professional in that one earns a living from that practice and produces (i.e., publishes) regularly. It neatly delimits individuals so that a hierarchy can be established, a status ranking professional anthropologists above amateurs. The association could have fellows—as an elite to which one must be nominated by another fellow—as well as regular and associate members. This definition grew in a period when professionalization and exclusion were deemed necessary to establish the discipline as a legitimate science. It stopped short, however, of accreditation and professional exams, which provide the ultimate quality control.

The problem with this definition, of course, is that it excludes those without steady employment and those who relate their knowledge to nonprofessionals by teaching, exhibiting, consulting, and reporting—areas in which many women and men have devoted much time. In fact, this restrictive definition would eliminate most ethnologists from 1900 to 1940 (Frantz 1985), for it limits the field to those who could secure jobs in certain institutions that carry high prestige. Given that men have traditionally acquired academic and research positions to the exclusion of women, a narrow definition eliminates many of the women who have contributed to our knowledge of southwestern Native Americans. Finally, most individuals, even those meeting educational and employment requirements, are rarely highly productive. As Price (1971) discovered, most professional scientists have produced only one or two papers in their entire careers.

Anthropology can be defined more broadly as "a way of life"—a way of looking at the world. As Keur (1985) stated, "Anthropology colors your life, your personality, your relationships to other people." Thus, an anthropologist is one who is dedicated to an anthropological view and method (Firth 1963). This definition allows individuals who have learned by experience rather than through advanced university training and who hold one of a wide range of jobs to be con-

sidered anthropologists by avocation, perspective, and practice. As Frantz (1972:61) observes, although one can be considered an anthropologist when one has a Ph.D. and has authored a piece based on original research in a scholarly journal, it is more meaningful to consider an individual a practicing anthropologist "when he [or she] undertakes a deliberate project of research which focuses on some problem or area that interests other scholars in the discipline." This includes research in libraries, museums, laboratories, and in our own and distant cultures.

The first categorization scheme is narrow and eliminates, while the second is encompassing. Thus, the second definitional approach frames this volume. To use the first definition would have eliminated almost all women who worked in the Southwest, because few women have been able to secure official academic positions. We have defined an anthropologist as a person who conducted research in the field (for field experience is the principal initiation rite and methodological base of the profession), in the museum, or in archives and then shared the results of these pursuits with others through scholarly and popular publications. Fieldwork, especially if conducted repeatedly and for a long period of time, affords a way for one without a Ph.D. to become an anthropologist. This alternate route to acceptance as a "real" anthropologist has been used successfully by men and women. "Anthropological rank is achieved through field work, and at times the rougher the field situation, the greater the rank" (Nader 1986:114)—what we might call the Indiana Jones success index. "Anthropologists often characterize themselves as mavericks and individualists, holding an 'I did it my way' attitude about fieldwork" (Sanjek 1990:92). Individualists roughing it in exotic situations are more easily conceptualized as men than women. But as we know, "the lone ethnographer designing, conducting, and writing up his or her own fieldwork adventure is mainly Malinowskian myth and post-1960 individual grant practice" (Sanjek

1990:329). Thus, we broadened our definition to include primary and secondary research in mundane as well as exotic situations to offer the greatest number of avenues for participation.

To find the universe of anthropologists who worked in the Native American Southwest I looked for individuals who had conducted research in the area and had published the results in a public outlet (monographs, books, journals, proceedings, annals, memoirs, transactions, reports, leaflets, magazines, pamphlets, dissertations, theses), as noted in the preface. We have not been able to deal with consultants, public lecturers, and teachers who have conducted independent research and shared their results with others in verbal form, nor have we been able to obtain information on women who earned a degree, published one work and then seemed to disappear, an all-too-common phenomenon. This flaw we could not avoid; there were no readily obtainable means of securing information—no guides, listings, or finding aides that could be the basis of a compilation. We did not consider this an overwhelming limitation, since in anthropology, writing and publishing remain the most valued way to convey understandings and knowledge newly obtained through independent and group research.

With our encompassing definition of an anthropologist, we had to develop limits to ensure a reasonably controlled endeavor. We have taken the time-honored idea of the culture area and focused on the Greater Southwest as the most studied area in the world and concentrated on those who worked with native peoples. We have also followed Rossiter (1982) by focusing primarily, but not exclusively, on individuals who began to work before World War II. Even with a limited locale and time period, it was difficult to learn about women scholars' work and lives. They are effectively hidden. One of the problems with dealing with some of the women in this book was that they were brought up and worked in a positivistic age where personal impressions were viewed as less important than facts. This meant that authors' views were eliminated from texts. Thus, we had to acquire information from letters to friends and colleagues as well as from our interviews; though some evidence is housed in libraries and archives, much is not. Unfortunately, the letters and papers of many anthropologists, including most women, have not been deemed worthy of saving.

CONCLUSION

This historical analysis of a discipline belongs to the present as much as to the past. Since "history, like myth, provides a charter for behavior, we believe that this evocation of the past can be useful in the present" (Goldschmidt 1979:1). To understand anthropology today requires understanding the behaviors, social structures, and customs of the past, going beyond a recitation of names on book jackets. It also means going beyond compensatory history by using statistics, surveys, and interviews to search for motivations, attitudes, behaviors, and patterns that have affected the development of anthropology. We must thus uncover those who are hidden behind the structure of the discipline and the university.

We will search for those who tried to make themselves visible and succeeded, those who tried and failed, and those who intentionally made themselves invisible because of their belief that by working quietly and de-emphasizing their presence, being nondistinctive in a sea of male colleagues, they would be allowed to remain part of the group. These women were determined that they be judged on the basis of their talents and merit alone, to be seen, in some cases, as "one of the boys." They tried to make sex and gender irrelevant in their professional lives. In this they failed, because in science and academe, gender is a primary field within which power is articulated. A search for power, prestige, and respect is a common theme in the many lives glimpsed in this book. Underhill, who knew what it was like to be without power, searched for an understanding of

Tohono O'Odham power through singing; Stevenson with her colleague Alice Fletcher tried to break the barriers of all-male scientific associations in their struggle for intellectual respectability. In this quest they were partially successful. But women nevertheless succeeded in enriching anthropology even if they were never treated equitably.

In this book, we try to learn from these attempts, from both successes and failures, from past struggles, strategies, defeats, and triumphs to put our own in perspective and to make it a little easier for ourselves, our students, and their students. We have as our goal to discover how women integrated themselves, remained marginal, or lived in two worlds, without negating or invalidating either of these worlds. It was a difficult quest.

Many of these essays have not been easy to write. As we discovered the difficulties that accompanied these women's careers as anthropologists, especially in their attempts to simply belong to and work in a discipline that compelled in which there was no room and little encouragement, we were at times depressed and felt we could no longer write about the painful subjects. I have been told that I am "too sensitive"; others were told they were getting caught up in things that could not be changed; still others were asked, "Why bother? The past is dead, you cannot change it." But the past is alive: norms, values, and attitudes, both implicit and explicit, are tenacious. Although there are changing definitions of professional and unprofessional behavior, perceptions of women's and men's abilities and basic natures are deeply held and unquestioned (Aisenberg and Harrington 1988). The chilly climate continues (Wylie 1991).

This is not to say that the world has not changed over time. Different generations of women have reacted differently to changed situations, and a careful periodization is needed as a framework. The 1870s and 1880s were a difficult time for budding women scientists. This was followed by a period of incipient feminization before World War II. The beginnings of the feminization of academe coincided with the women's movement (1890s to 1920s), and the subsequent backlash against women as the disciplines professionalized has been well documented by Rossiter (1982) and Rosenberg (1982). The periods coincided with the establishment of departments and the proliferation of professional organizations. The effects of these two periods as well as the two wars, the Great Depression, the Indian Reorganization Act, the G.I. Bill, and the second women's movement must all be remembered as background to avoid a too facile historicism. Concomitantly, we must remember the different nature of the country during each period. Thus, Stevenson must be seen in the context of the economic expansion and population explosion of the late nineteenth century and Underhill's work for the Bureau of Indian Affairs (BIA) in the context of World War II (Hinsley 1986b).

The most discouraging aspect of working on this volume was the knowledge that we were dealing with successes. Those who did not make it through school, who left the profession after completing their education, who worked for a few years and then seemed to disappear are still hidden. The women in this book are strong, determined, independent, and stubborn. These are the scholars who never gave up, ones who made it against all odds.[23] They endured lifetimes of low wages and lack of recognition beyond graduate school; they survived with dignity years of underemployment and obscurity. Still they persevered and made extensive contributions. Not one of them is mediocre. Although mediocre men made it into the discipline (especially in periods of university expansion and surplus wealth) women did not. They were quickly weeded out. For women, it has always been the Great Depression. Even the best were left aside if they did not work harder and live longer than men.

These women are our role models and fictive mentors. They are the atypical "firsts" and those who experienced the typical patterns of the second and third generation. Interspersed are those who will strike a chord as a remembered individual and those who will be completely unknown. As a group they are part of our collective past. If they had not tried, had not both failed and succeeded, it is probable that most of us would not be here today. We certainly would not know what we now know of ourselves, of our profession, and of our knowledge of other peoples and their lives. This book is then a celebration of their mentorship, just as *Daughters of the Desert* (Babcock and Parezo 1988) was a celebration of their accomplishments.

NOTES

1. Darnell (1972:84) has criticized the history of anthropology for this approach: "Until quite recently, the history of particular social sciences has been written from within, with an aim of providing a historical context of problems and ideas for students being socialized into a profession. . . . The result of such a perspective is too often a chronology of founding fathers suspended in an unmotivated social and historical vacuum."

2. Like other sciences, anthropological histories focus on only part of our endeavors. For example, "attention has usually been given in historical accounts of ethnology to ideational/intellectual/theoretical aspects, at the expense of sufficient examination both of ethnologists' writings addressed to audiences beyond the discipline and to their activities in academic, professional, and non-scholarly institutions" (Frantz 1985:83).

3. Women who have managed to secure permanent positions are actually the harshest critics of women. These women perpetuate the system with their own students: "Frankly, I favored my male students to my female ones. . . . I just like men better, I think, in general. We are sharing more of men's interests" (Ellis 1985). These women have adopted the attitude that since they made it through the system, anyone who has not made it in the manner they did does not have the ability to compete. "To recognize

that discrimination is a major factor in the system would be, for these women, to invalidate their own deeply felt conviction that they, at least, are meritorious and merit usually wins out" (Abramson 1975: 116).

4. Few people credit Ruth Benedict with introducing the concept of "culture shock" (Golde, ed. 1986:11) even though it is one of our central concepts. In addition, since gender and feminism are defined by the central establishment as peripheral or as very specialized subjects of interest to only a small group of individuals, works by feminists are not reviewed in major journals (Lutz 1990). This further marginalizes the research and discourse of the group. As Lutz notes, since writing is meant to be read, discussed and evaluated, the lack of citation and review marginalizes it. Women's discourse is treated by authoritative evaluators as less significant or as peripheral to the field's center.

5. Basso also recognizes the contributions of native scholars such as Helen Sekaquaptewa.

6. In British anthropology the same situation occurred for students of Malinowski.

7. Few women were charismatic in the same way as men, except possibly for Margaret Mead. Unfortunately she did not have a permanent position in a university, so she never had the same sway over students. Women's notes and findings were often appropriated. (Since this is a taboo subject in anthropology, it has probably happened to many men as well.) Missing papers of Matilda Coxe Stevenson have been found in John P. Harrington's papers in the National Anthropological Archives. He had removed her name from the copies, cut them up, and interspersed them with his own. Her work at Taos was lost by this action. Harris' (1968:367) all-too-brief mention of Cora DuBois is that a 1939/40 paper attributed to her was found in Robert Lowie's papers and that Lowie used this material without attribution in a 1960 article.

8. Hoebel does, however, go on to note that "Parsons was not a system-builder but she was far from the dry-dust accumulator that some think her to have been" (1954:723).

9. There are some notable exceptions. Bateson's (1984) memoir of her parents shows how one can study the interrelationship of culture, personal-

ity, professionalism, and gender in an enlightening narrative.

10. Of course we must use personal accounts in our historical analyses, and we should not avoid cases where two individuals, such as Stevenson and Cushing or White and Lowie, obviously disliked each other both personally and professionally. Personality did color their work. And as Curtis Hinsley (1986b) remarked at the conference, this type of information tells us much about why they felt a certain way. What must be remembered, however, is that the scale and flavor of the use of personal information differs by the gender of the author being critiqued.

11. Bunzel's career was negatively affected by gossip.

12. Men's schools were unavailable to female students in the nineteenth century, and some continued to shut women out. Moreover, women benefited from attending schools with anthropology majors. It is noteworthy that this is an important factor in later success even if the women majored in another discipline. The access for women to education also changed through time. By 1880, women constituted 32% of undergraduate students; by 1910, 40%; by 1920, 47%. Then there is a steady decline until 1950 when women made up 31%, and a steady rise to 45% in 1975 (Graham 1978:764).

13. This attitude continued even in the face of empirical evidence that married female faculty members were as productive as their male colleagues (Loeb and Ferber 1971).

14. Caldwell also noted that women were paid about half the salary of men for the same type of work.

15. Percentages of women as college professors, administrators, and instructors were 19% in 1910; 30% in 1920; 32% in 1930; 27% in 1940; 23% in 1950; and 19% in 1960 (Epstein 1970:967). She based these figures on the 1963 U.S. Bureau of Census data, vol. 1, table 202 and on 1900–1950 statistics from the U.S. Department of Labor, 1954. A jump in 1880 brought the proportion of women faculty to 32%, but the numbers of faculty were then so small and so ill defined that the proportion may be a statistical anomaly (Blitz 1974:37). The rises and falls were reflected in other professions as well. In the 1920s women constituted nearly 45% of the profes-

sional work force. This declined during the 1930s and reached a low in 1960.

16. The choice of a female faculty member was clearly not always to be desired, as witnessed in the following passage from a letter by Franz Boas to Dean E. R. Riesen of the University of Arizona. In the spring of 1931 the University of Arizona was looking for a faculty member who could teach in more than one subfield. Boas wrote,

> I have thought of the question of candidates carefully and discussed the situation with my colleagues. I confess that I cannot find a single man who would fit as well into the work proposed by you as Spier. Almost every single person whom I know is onesided; in physical anthropology, in archaeology, in ethnology, or in linguistics. The few men who might be available are all in positions which, in my opinion, they would not give up. . . . I do not know whether you can use women at all. Dr. Ruth O. Sawtell is a physical anthropologist and archaeologist. She has also studied ethnology although she has not done any field work in ethnology.

She was not offered the position. (Letter in archives, Arizona State Museum.)

17. Lander (1972:6) found that 39% of the men in anthropology have at some time served as departmental chairs, compared to 16% of the women.

18. By the end of the 1970s, women received 48% of the degrees in English, 63% in French, 40% in psychology, 29% in biology, 27% in history, 18% in political science, 13% in economics, 17% in math, 7% in physics and 4% in engineering (Anonymous 1984).

19. Included in academia is an elite and a proletariate (Wilke 1979:xii). The proletariate contains those who have been denied tenure, never obtained a tenure-track position, and gypsy scholars. To this list we can add those who are employed in marginal or peripheral institutions. As we show in this volume, working in museums, an increasingly quasi-academic institution, could become a trap and a sure way to remain in the proletariate and hence invisible to the rest of the profession.

20. Rossiter (1982:53) notes that this is not a new situation. In the 1880s and 1890s women were welcomed in two kinds of jobs: "those that were so low paying or low ranking that competent men

would not take them (and which often required great docility or painstaking attention to detail) and those that involved social service, such as working in the home or with women or children (and which were often poorly paid as well)." The most prestigious universities never considered women for regular faculty positions until well after World War II.

21. In 1969 women represented 1 in 4 of the instructors and lecturers in graduate sociology departments, but only 1 in 25 of the full professors (Rossi 1970:7). As Khasket et al. (1974:488) discovered, the status of women in microbiology is lower than that of men, and the lower status of women results, to a large degree, from inequality of opportunity throughout their careers. In history, "obtaining promotion was much harder for women than for men in the 1970s. One-third of all men who received a Ph.D. in history between 1970 and 1974 were full professors by 1980. Fewer than one-eighth of the women were. More recently 27% of the men who earned Ph.D.s between 1975 and 1978, but only 9% of the women who did so, reached associate professorial levels, with its chance of tenure" (Winkler 1981:18).

22. Service to the university in the form of time-consuming, dull, and necessary committee work is rarely valued when loyalty to the educational institution is replaced by loyalty to the discipline. "Men who have been dedicated teachers, concerned advisors to students and dutiful committee members have suffered the same professional disadvantages as the women who have performed these tasks" (Graham 1978:769).

23. I have often told my students that part of getting through graduate school is the ability to endure years of poverty and years of subordination. I have not told them of the years of subtle marginalization that will be encountered later, in the hopes that it will change.

MATILDA COXE STEVENSON:
PIONEER ETHNOLOGIST

Nancy J. Parezo

I want to do a comparatively complete and connected history of an aboriginal people whose thoughts are not our thoughts, weaving all the threads into an intelligent and satisfactory whole for the civilized students. . . . It is my wish to erect a foundation upon which students may build. I feel I can do the most for science in this way. I make no claim that my paper on Zuni will exhaust the subject. On the contrary, it but opens the subject but I think and hope it may open wide the gates for other students to pass the more rapidly over the many, many parts which I have left unexplored.

Matilda Coxe Stevenson
(NAA:MCS/JWP 5/23/00)

ANTHROPOLOGY has had the reputation of welcoming, indeed needing, women. As early as 1888, Otis T. Mason (1888:5) stated, "Who may be an anthropologist? Every man, woman and child that has sense and patience to observe, and that can honestly record the thing observed." But as in all other sciences, women anthropologists were initially tolerated during the formative period of the discipline and were accepted only in well-defined situations, encouraged to perform a set of well-bounded tasks, and then frozen out when the discipline became embedded in universities (Rossiter 1982).

As Nancy Lurie (1966:33) points out,

Doubtless the first women anthropologists encountered the general difficulties of scholarly women whose ambitions seemed presumptuous—if not actually

laughable—to many of their male contemporaries. However, not only was acceptance relatively amicable, the more perceptive men in anthropology viewed the participation of women as peculiarly enriching to the new science of anthropology, specifically in ethnology.

Valued as a helper and potential scholar who could obtain data unavailable to male researchers, a Victorian woman who insisted on a salaried career and recognition for her work quickly discovered that perceptiveness ended and ambivalence, intolerance, and obstinacy began. The career of Matilda Coxe Stevenson, the first woman to work in the Greater Southwest, demonstrates this pattern; even with the support of influential men, her road to professionalism was difficult. The intellectual community and its members' perceptiveness and intolerance affected Stevenson's career and creativity—at a cost.

Matilda Coxe Stevenson was a pioneer and explorer, scholar, activist, organizer, and wife. Her career coincided with the professionalization of anthropology. She was the only woman to break into the male scientific expeditions exploring the western frontier; no other woman geologist, botanist, or anthropologist went on these trips in a paid capacity. She loved New Mexico and Arizona despite the hardships of travel in the late nineteenth century. She became a Southwesternist, a specialist on Zuni culture, a cultural historian, an ethnologist and unilinear evolutionist, and a fighter for women's professional equality.

Stevenson was aware of her role as a woman intellectual and of her unique pioneering efforts. She also was conscious of the advantages and disadvantages that the designation "female" provided. Being a woman was valuable for her fieldwork and provided her with insights necessary to understand other peoples, but it hindered her quest for recognition within the scientific community in Washington, D.C. She waged a constant battle against being limited to the "woman's sphere" and refused to be stereotyped as docile, submissive, weak, and nonintellectual. Stevenson tried to, and indeed did, overcome these stereotypes by reacting, often aggressively, to all attempted restrictions. She worked hard and produced unquestionably accurate descriptive accounts. This same strategy has been followed by many female anthropologists such as Clara Lee Tanner (1985), who stated, "I decided the thing to do was to get to work and work hard, and lay the foundation for other women in the field."

Stevenson became a scientist and an ethnologist by being more scientific, more competitive, more impersonal, more objective, and tougher than her male contemporaries. Consequently, she suffered for her incursion into the male world of nineteenth-century science and for her vocal and unceasing demands to be treated seriously and equally. She became a legend, especially at the Smithsonian Institution, as she opened the South-west to women scholars. Her career and experiences foreshadowed many of the problems and triumphs met by later generations of women anthropologists.

EARLY LIFE

Matilda Coxe Evans (May 12, 1849–June 24, 1915) was one of five children born to Alexander Hamilton Evans of Virginia and Maria Coxe of New Jersey.[1] Evans was an attorney, writer, and journalist, as well as a minor figure in the Washington-Philadelphia intellectual community. He was an intimate friend of Joseph Henry, first Secretary of the Smithsonian Institution. As members of a privileged upper-middle-class household, Stevenson and her siblings were taught by their mother with the assistance of private governesses before attending private schools in Philadelphia (1863–1868). Matilda received her formal education at Miss Annable's Academy, a "sheltered female seminary," considered one of the finest schools of its day, where she was taught those subjects that would make her successful as the wife of a socially prominent citizen. As in all finishing schools, poise and deportment rather than intellectual curiosity were encouraged.

Returning to Washington, D.C., with her family in 1868, Matilda, contrary to expectations, studied law with her father (while serving as a law clerk in his office) and chemistry and geology with Dr. N. M. Mew of the Army Medical School. She never earned an undergraduate or advanced degree: women had few opportunities to obtain formal scientific educations during this period (Rossiter 1982). Nevertheless, she intended to become a mineralogist and work in a laboratory or undertake fieldwork. Her plans were furthered, but in a way she had not intended, when she met Colonel James Stevenson of Kentucky. They were married on April 18, 1872.

Marriage turned Matilda into an explorer. She accompanied her husband on several geological surveys in Colorado, Idaho, Wyoming, and Utah between 1872 and 1878. James Stevenson

(1840–1888), a self-taught geologist, naturalist, and anthropologist, was executive officer of Ferdinand Hayden's United States Geological Survey of the Territories.[2] Matilda helped James amass the valuable fossil and ornithological collections now housed at the Smithsonian Institution. She assisted him in his famous 1878 study of geysers in the Yellowstone region. On one trip during the mid 1870s, Matilda made her first tentative ethnographic study by visiting the Ute and Arapaho. Guided by her husband, she learned "the rudiments of ethnographic technique" (NAA:MCS/WHH 3/28/06). This technique involved asking questions of native individuals and conceptualizing cultural facts and customs as data to be treated in the same manner as other natural phenomena; the methods used in geology and natural history were extended to individuals, groups, and languages.[3] However, like all anthropologists of the period, Matilda was largely self-taught.

SOUTHWESTERN ETHNOGRAPHER

Matilda Coxe Stevenson went to the Southwest in 1879 as a member of the first collecting and research expedition of the newly formed Bureau of Ethnology under the direction of John Wesley Powell. Her official position was "volunteer coadjutor in ethnology," that is, assistant to her husband, the leader of the expedition.[4] The Stevensons, John Hillers, and Frank Hamilton Cushing arrived in Zuni on September 19 and remained for six months, occupying two rooms of the mission. Cushing wrote that the Indians brought "all sorts of their odd belongings. Day after day, assisted by his enthusiastic wife, [Colonel Stevenson] gathered in treasures, ancient and modern, of Indian art and industry" (quoted in Green 1981: 59). In addition to collecting thousands of ethnographic objects, they surveyed local archaeological sites, gathered material from caves and shrines, and amassed information on various cultural and social aspects of Pueblo life (Hardin 1983; Parezo 1987). This trip resulted in Matilda's first publication, *Zuni and the Zunians* (1881a), the first scholarly ethnography of Zuni published for a general audience. Dealing with the basic categories of Zuni life, it presaged and in many ways summarized all of Matilda's later research interests.

Throughout the 1880s, the Stevensons maintained the first husband-wife team in anthropology. Matilda was welcomed on the Smithsonian's collecting expeditions (in an unpaid capacity) because Powell and Spencer Baird, Secretary of the Smithsonian Institution, thought that she complemented her husband. As a woman, Matilda would have access to Native American women whose knowledge was crucial to anthropology but inaccessible to male researchers. Her first task was to learn about childbirth, the life of children, and women's roles in daily life. Powell and Baird felt that this information was vital if anthropology was to give a complete picture of the daily lives of noncivilized peoples.

This idea was commonly held in the Bureau of Ethnology and the Smithsonian Institution. Holmes (1916:555) reiterated it in his obituary of Stevenson:

Her researches were largely among the women of the tribe and directed toward an understanding of the domestic life and practices—a field from which men are largely excluded, for among the Zuni the women have exclusive control of the rites and observations which pertain to their sex. Her work served to round out our knowledge of tribal histories in directions hitherto imperfectly understood.

Another factor may have been that according to nineteenth-century standards of modesty, men were not supposed to discuss pregnancy, childbirth, sex, and similar topics. There was logic, therefore, in Powell's request. Riley (1984:196–97) found, not surprisingly, that frontier women's diaries mentioned Native American domestic organization, marital customs, child-raising techniques, and crafts much more often than did men's diaries.

Thus, as Mead and Bunzel (1960:205) have stated, Matilda Coxe Stevenson was the first American ethnologist to consider children and women worthy of notice. Indeed, Stevenson did produce several works that include information on children and women (1887, 1894a, 1903, 1904, 1987). But she was following Powell's suggestion and using concentration on "women's topics" as a mechanism to enable her to obtain employment and be allowed to continue ethnographic fieldwork. Her first works dealt with non–gender-specific topics, such as descriptions of archaeological pottery (1881b), the location of archaeological sites (1883), and interesting facets of Zuni life (1881a).

Stevenson's main research interests focused on religion rather than issues dealing specifically with women, children, or socialization, and she refused to be limited to those areas of culture associated with domesticity. She wrote,

I felt the need of some definite publication, a sort of foundation of some tribe, and my aim in the Zuni work was to probe to the very core of their philosophy, their religion, and sociology, and to make such a book as would be of positive value to the student of ethnology (Stevenson quoted in Hinsley 1981:222).

To bring together her interests and those of the men in authority, she concentrated on the ceremonies that women controlled and to which men had no access. Her famous monograph on Zuni children (1887) dealt principally with ceremonies that accompany childhood. Similarly, her work on Zuni games (1903) described ceremonial games. Although she received minor negative sanctions resulting from this shift in research focus, she was allowed (and later encouraged) to continue, for all contributions to knowledge were welcomed.

Fortunately, Stevenson's choice of religion as a topic did not seem unreasonable to intellectuals of the period. Civilized women were the holders of refined tastes; they held the family together, were nurturing, and were particularly susceptible to religious feelings (Riley 1984:3–9). Under-

standing religion was crucial to understanding "savage" and "barbarian" societies. In turn, this knowledge was essential to understanding evolution. Here Stevenson addressed an important intellectual problem of the period. Her research had a popular aspect as well; Stevenson's concentration on religion was an attempt to overturn the popular notion that Indians were depraved and had no religion. From her first publication she sought to show that Zuni religion was real, valid, and not the work of the devil:

Their religion is performed with decorum and solemnity. While Zuni religion is based on non-scientific principles of animism and sun worship and is not as advanced intellectually as monotheism, it is a valid system of belief and can be used to show how religion developed (1881a:29).

Stevenson did rebel against the stifling popular concept that women were unable to think scientifically. As her research topics show, she did this through subjects that could be construed as appropriate for a woman.

Stevenson quickly went beyond the sexually restricted research interests that Powell and Baird had carved out for her. She assembled information on crafts, agriculture, economics, language, medicine, housing, physical appearance (especially albinism), government, legends, myths, religion, superstitions (to use her phrase), men's and women's roles, culture history, relations with the Spaniards or Mexicans, and contemporary changes or conditions. She never depended on her status as a woman to obtain information on Zuni life from Zuni women, even though she used this as her entree. She soon worked equally with men and women. In fact, for her later work on religion, she worked closely with men. Her choice of informant depended on the individual's knowledge rather than gender. Holmes (1916:55), in accord with the prevailing stereotype, acknowledged this accomplishment, although he found it remarkable: "Having already gained the full confidence of the Zuni she succeeded in obtaining admission to a number of secret organizations and ceremonies usually forbidden to outsiders, and especially to women." Matilda Coxe Stevenson, along with Alice Fletcher and Erminnie Smith, clearly broke new ground in terms of male anthropologists' conceptions of women's scholarly abilities.

Stevenson became known for her skill in collecting ethnographic data (Tylor 1884). She always used multiple informants to check reliability, realizing quickly that "under any conditions the Indian will fool the world and laugh at us for being fooled" (NAA:MCS/HS 9/16/14). "My rule is never to regard such material of real value until it has been verified from the tongue of more than one intelligent Indian, no religious or social secret being held by any one man"(1893a: 258). Later she became even more rigorous:

Every word recorded by me is vouched for by at least three well informed men or women or both, neither one knowing that I have studied with another. When my information comes through three who agree that the matter is correct, I feel that the material may be recorded for publication with perfect safety. This is a slow way of study but it is the only sure way (NAA: MCS/JEW 6/15/14).

This methodology was standard for Bureau of Ethnology researchers, who followed Powell's general requirement for data collection (Parezo 1987). Stevenson was always careful to explain how she obtained her data and to define its quality before beginning an analysis or description. Like Powell and other anthropologists of the period, she was concerned with scientific reliability and had an aversion to falsehoods, misinformation, and hurried fieldwork. She was an excellent natural historian and field scientist.

Matilda gathered an extensive body of data. During the 1880s she and her husband made trips to Zuni almost yearly and participated in many facets of Zuni life. Like Cushing, who is noted as the first anthropologist to use participant observation, she "gained the entire confidence of the Zuni by adopting their dress, painting her face, and witnessing all their secret rites" (Stevenson 1888:137).

At the same time, the Stevensons worked less extensively in all the Rio Grande Pueblos, as well as among the Acoma, Hopi, and Navajo, partly to gain comparative material. Believing that "archaeology and ethnology must be worked together in order to secure results of real scientific value" (NAA:MCS/GHVS 6/15/14), they continued to survey archaeological sites and geological features in Arizona, New Mexico, and California. From these surveys Matilda developed a real interest in saving archaeological sites from looting, an interest she retained to the end of her life.[5]

GOVERNMENT EMPLOYEE

James Stevenson died of heart failure caused by Rocky Mountain tick fever in 1888. He had been preparing an ethnography of Zia (Sia) following their most recent trip to the Southwest. Matilda considered it vital to science to carry on their work: "My whole heart is in the work my husband left me to do" (NAA:MCS/ABR 9/21/09). Powell likewise considered the information so important that in an unprecedented move, he officially hired Matilda to put her husband's notes in order, a task that required additional independent fieldwork in 1890. Powell requested Matilda to visit Zia, Jemez, and Zuni

for the purpose of investigating the customs of the Indians of these pueblos, especially their history, mythology, medicine practices, usages with regard to the training of children, the rites and privileges pertaining to their secret societies, etc. You will pay special attention to the collection of any plants the Indians may use in their medicine and sorcery practices, obtaining their names and reputed virtues (NAA:JWP/MCS 3/15/90).

Powell, however, would not send a woman out alone; Stevenson was accompanied by an assistant, Miss May S. Clark, a Bureau stenographer who also served as photographer.

The temporary appointment became permanent in 1890 and was held until Stevenson's death in 1915. Stevenson was the first, and for a long time the only, woman to be paid as a staff government anthropologist. In fact, no other professional woman was ever permanently employed full-time by the Bureau of Ethnology (BAE). All others, including Frances Densmore, were collaborators, that is, paid by the project but not on the permanent staff, which consisted of ethnologists, assistant ethnologists, stenographers, clerks, and copyists. Many individuals, such as Washington Matthews and Cosmos Mindeleff who worked during this period, or later Franz Boas, were hired either temporarily or as collaborators. Stevenson thus had something that was quite rare in this period. Stevenson's salary, however, was always lower than those of her male contemporaries. Her salary at the time of her hire was $1,500, and it remained so throughout most of her career; in 1907, it was raised to $1,800. Her husband's salary with the Geological Survey had been $3,000 in 1888.

Stevenson was luckier than most of her male or female contemporaries in having a permanent position. It meant that she did not have to finance her own research and the publication of her monographs or continually search for funds. She was never successful in obtaining outside funding for her projects. For example, she failed to interest Mary Hemenway in funding a project to bring Hopi and Zuni artisans to the World's Columbian Exposition in Chicago in 1893 as a living exhibit. Later she approached the Fred Harvey Company for a similar project for the 1915 Panama-Pacific Exposition in San Diego without success. This placed Stevenson in a different position than Cushing, who did successfully raise funds for his project when he was furloughed from the Bureau for health reasons, and it made her dependent on the Bureau. She had to work; she was not rich and could not have continued her research without financial support. How important this secure, if at times precarious, source of employment and re-

search funds was can be seen in a situation where she almost lost them.

After publishing *The Sia* (1894a), the first major ethnography of a Rio Grande Pueblo, Stevenson recognized the now-established anthropological contention that there is always more to learn, no matter how much fieldwork has been completed, and she returned to Zuni.[6] This time she concentrated on Zuni religion, mythology, and the social organization of religious societies. During the mid to late 1890s, she lived at Zuni in the summers, returning to Washington in the winters to write up her data (1893a, 1893b, 1894b, 1898, 1903).

The manuscript on Zuni religion (1904) was conceptualized as the major work of her career. According to her yearly assignments she was to complete it by 1897, but for some unknown reason, possibly ill health, she did not. In 1899, Powell and his assistant director, William J. McGee, began sending her letters monthly asking for the manuscript; by return post she asked for an extension. Finally, on August 1, 1901, Powell lost patience and placed her on furlough due to "ill health and severe depression." Powell noted that she was often exhausted after her field sessions and that the problem, which he thought was neurasthenia, a chronic condition from which his daughter also suffered, would only go away with complete rest. "As her husband's friend," he felt the furlough was "for her own good" (NAA: JWP/MCS 1/21/02; NAA: JWP/WJM 8/14/01). Unfortunately, government employees had no paid sick leave at the time.

There was no love lost between Matilda Coxe Stevenson and Powell, although Powell and James Stevenson had been devoted friends. In a letter to Nancy Lurie, William Fenton states that "Tilly fought with Major Powell who used to fire her regularly and then she would threaten to invoke Congress on him and get herself restored to office. On one of these occasions, he got so mad he had a stroke, and that finished him" (quoted in Lurie 1966:234). Hinsley (1981:222) states that

Powell detested her. Stevenson, however, speaks very highly of Powell throughout her extensive correspondence. Stevenson, McGee, and Powell—three exceptionally strong-minded, temperamental, and opinionated individuals—were continually at odds. This time, however, Powell and McGee sent the furlough request through official channels.

The official furlough surprised Stevenson (Congressional testimony 1903), although she probably misread Powell's cues and mood. Stevenson's reaction likewise surprised McGee and Powell, for she did not react as had Cushing, who had been furloughed earlier for ill health and failure to produce a manuscript (Hinsley 1981; Mark 1980a). She fought the layoff. Since there was no official grievance procedure, she used personal and political influence to be reinstated. She wrote to McGee, who had effectively taken over daily control of the Bureau as Powell aged and who, according to Hinsley (1981:246), dictated all of Powell's correspondence and composed his annual reports. Stevenson stated her grievances and demanded to be treated as equal to other anthropologists on the staff (NAA:MCS/WJM 7/31/01). In a series of letters to McGee and Powell, she pointed out that she had worked 10- to 12-hour days in Washington and 20-hour days at Zuni and thought she could do concentrated work for longer hours than anyone else (NAA: MCS/JWP 8/15/00). She argued, in effect, that she worked harder than anyone else on the staff (i.e., any man). Powell refused to change his position. She had not fulfilled her mandate to produce a manuscript, he argued. McGee then stated that a one- to two-year furlough would be necessary to restore her to health (Congressional testimony 1903). Stevenson appealed to the administration of the Smithsonian Institution.

It is difficult to assess whether Stevenson had McGee's support. She was a very good friend of McGee's wife, Anita Newcombe McGee, an important intellectual in her own right; McGee had supported Stevenson earlier in her career and had

helped Stevenson manage her financial affairs. In fact, he held the proxy for her stock portfolio. Yet McGee implemented Powell's wishes and unquestioningly followed his intellectual and political leads. There is good evidence, however, that it was McGee who initiated the official furlough in an attempt to free funds that would enable Frank Russell, a recent Ph.D. graduate of Harvard University, to work in the Southwest. This assessment is supported by the following sequence of events constructed from BAE and Smithsonian administrative memos and correspondence. McGee wrote to Russell on January 9, 1901, stating that he was gratified that Russell would contemplate working in Washington. Russell interviewed with the BAE the next week, was hired by the Bureau on April 15, 1901, and immediately went to southern Arizona to survey ruins near Tucson and to work with the Pima near Phoenix. Almost immediately there was an extensive correspondence between Russell and McGee over the lateness of Russell's pay checks. McGee paid for some of Russell's expenses out of his own pocket until new fiscal funds could be obtained. Powell and McGee requested an increase in the Bureau appropriation, but it was not approved. On July 24, 1901, Powell wrote to the Secretary of the Smithsonian asking that Stevenson be placed on furlough commencing August 1, 1901. Stevenson began official protests on July 31, 1901. In August Russell began receiving his salary regularly and there were no more requests for emergency funds.

Not being immediately reinstated, Stevenson threatened to invoke Congress and have the appropriation to the Bureau rescinded if she was not reinstated. This was not a threat to be taken lightly. Stevenson had many important friends in Washington: Generals Sherman and Pope; Senators Teller, Logan, and Langley; Representatives Driscoll and Carlisle (Speaker of the House); Supreme Court Justice Oliver Wendell Holmes; and Presidents Cleveland and Roosevelt. Her cousin, Robley D. Evans, was a famous naval officer in the Spanish-American War; her brother Robert Evans, an admiral in the U.S. Navy, was in charge of the Pacific Fleet in the early 1900s; another brother, Richard, was a member of the House of Representatives. Within the Smithsonian she had support from Charles D. Walcott, Frederick W. Hodge, William H. Holmes, and Jessie Walter Fewkes. Secretary Samuel Langley was neutral, but he intensely disliked McGee and wanted more control over the Bureau.

While waging her political campaign, Stevenson continued to work as if she were still on the payroll and after a series of protests to the Secretary of the Smithsonian was paid from his discretionary funds for the period from August 1, 1901, to January 9, 1902. Powell, a politically astute man, knew that she could make his position as director of the Bureau of Ethnology and the U.S. Geological Survey very uncomfortable. Senator Henry Teller mediated, and after a great deal of argument, Stevenson was reinstated upon the completion of the manuscript on May 20, 1902. Frank Russell was placed "on furlough without pay for one year" the same day (NAA: JWP/SPL 5/20/02). Stevenson never received compensation for the pay she lost and was paid for the 1904 manuscript on a piecework basis, although the amount she received was closely equivalent. On June 1, 1902, she returned to Zuni.

Trying to eliminate successful women from government and laboratory staffs by using the excuse of furlough for ill health was common practice at the time (Rossiter 1982). Stevenson used strong tactics in her response because her professional position as well as her standing in the intellectual community were jeopardized—everything she had worked so hard to achieve was at stake.

There were no more official attempts to oust Stevenson from the Bureau, although Stevenson thought that McGee kept trying (Congressional testimony 1903:11). She was finally provided with an office of her own, which she had not had previously. She continued to experience minor

harrassment: McGee put her Zuni manuscript in a safe and the illustrations in the furnace room rather than prepare them for publication, and she continued to have periodic bureaucratic problems receiving pay. Her friendship with McGee ended, and her correspondence with Anita McGee ceased. Stevenson blamed McGee for her furlough. She later presented damning testimony against him during the 1903 Congressional investigation into the administration of the Bureau, and McGee lost his position. All future BAE directors left her alone. Stevenson could continue her work at her own pace with missionary zeal, and later directors could only complain that she wrote exceptionally slowly.

Stevenson believed her task as an anthropologist was to concentrate on the Puebloan Southwest and to record every phase of Indian life—in short, to produce comprehensive ethnographies before the societies were assimilated. Stevenson, like other ethnographers at the Bureau, was convinced that Native Americans would be overrun by the politically and economically dominant Anglo-American society and cease to exist as independent cultures. Cultural evolution through acculturation and assimilation was inevitable; Zuni culture was not strong enough to remain intact. In her writings she continually stressed that ethnographic data must be collected before they were irretrievably lost.

By the early 1900 she became an even more persistent advocate of the necessity of her lifelong task:

While I suffer many privations in the field and I am absolutely cut off from all intellectual companionship, I am more than willing to make any sacrifice in order to record ere it be too late, the records of these peoples (NAA: MCS/WHH 10/8/01).

I realize more fully each day, that every moment is golden for the ethnologist, for changes in the life of the Indian are becoming more rapid each year. The environment of the railroad towns is doing more to upset the autochronic institutions of the Zuni than all other influences. Now that the doors of their conventional life have been partially opened the changes are growing more and more rapid (NAA:MCS/JWP 8/30/02).

There is irony in Stevenson's insistence on salvage ethnography and her lament about the Zuni's exposure to the disreputable elements of Anglo-American society, for even as she and her husband were collecting information and objects that reflected the culture of the Zuni prior to European contact, they were trying to "civilize" the Zuni.[7] Stevenson, like the missionaries and schoolteachers of the period, tried to teach middle-class Victorian customs and concepts (such as Anglo-American concepts of time) to the Zuni. In the best known example, Stevenson tried to show We-wha how to wash clothes in a wash tub. We-wha remarked, "You do not understand that which you would teach. You do not understand as much as the missionary's wife [Mrs. Ealy]; she keeps the water in the tub and does not make a river on the floor" (Stevenson 1904:380; see also Bender 1984:210).

Stevenson clearly accepted the idea that women were the repositories of civilization and that they had a moral responsibility to elevate the Indians, that is, to enable them to become functioning members of Anglo-American society using Victorian standards (Riley 1984:14). For example, in exchange for objects collected for the Smithsonian Institution, the Stevensons gave the Zuni calico cloth, lamps, candles, soap, window glass, and milled lumber (Parezo 1986, 1987). Even though the Stevensons never forced these items on the Zuni, their presence and the amount of goods they introduced changed Zuni culture. Stevenson did come to question this practice, however. By 1904 she thought these changes toward civilization had caused the Zuni to lose more than they had gained.

So single-minded did Stevenson become in her quest, in her dedication to the science of anthropology, that she acquired a reputation for being pigheaded, humorless, insensitive, and overbearing (Lurie 1966:68–61, 234). She was by all accounts formidable. This reputation is partly due to the seriousness with which she took her task—a task she interpreted as a moral duty.

She regarded her ethnographic enterprise as a moral duty for her Native American informants as well: it was their duty to help her gather data on their lives whether they liked it or not. This attitude often placed her in disagreeable situations. Stevenson, like Cushing, encountered opposition from several Native Americans because of her insistence that they provide her with data (Pandley 1972:326–27). In fact, the *Illustrated Police News* printed a sensational story, "Cowed by a Woman. A Craven Red Devil Weakens in the Face of a Resolute White Heroine," on March 6, 1886, with a cartoon showing Matilda defending her calm husband (in the garb of an explorer) from a Hopi "attack" resulting from their insistence on trading for ethnographic items in a kiva (Babcock and Parezo 1988:11; Lurie 1966:Plate 1). Other newspapers, such as the *New York Herald,* also ran the story.

Matilda was famous and infamous, but not alone in meeting this resistance. Opposition to anthropologists and their insistence on learning secrets that were, in the native view, none of their business was not reserved for Matilda Coxe Stevenson or women in general. Fewkes (Cushing et al. 1922:273) states that similar incidents were not unusual at Oraibi. Stevenson's male colleague at Zuni, Frank Hamilton Cushing, likewise situated himself in a dramatic confrontation as a result of his insistence on sketching Zuni ceremonies. In his own account of the incident, Cushing (1882–1883) tells how he defended himself by brandishing a knife at his Zuni attackers and how, since he had shown himself to be courageous by refusing to be intimidated, the Zuni accepted him and allowed him to complete his investigations. Likewise, at Hopi, Cushing felt compelled to threaten to shoot men who opposed his trading activities in a kiva, this time without success. He had to be rescued by Mindeleff and Keam (Cushing et al. 1922; Parezo 1985).

Stevenson, however, received more bad publicity from her encounter with Native Americans than did Cushing. Leaving aside for the moment the question of personality, Cushing has never been condemned for his activities to the degree that Stevenson has been. Since there were no Anglo-American witnesses at Cushing's eipode, as there were at the one involving Stevenson, Cushing could write the account of his attack, which both he and his publicist, Sylvester Baxter, could publish. He had the opportunity to tell the events as he chose, and he chose to portray himself as a romantic, heroic frontiersman confronting and overcoming the savage Indians. Cushing was his own best publicist, a much better storyteller than Stevenson and much more adept at public relations; Stevenson never wrote about herself as the heroine of an exciting saga. Indeed, it is doubtful if she could (in all her writing she is in the background, never a prominent player); for if she had, it would have negated the strides she had made toward being recognized as an objective scientist.

Although both incidents were sensational, Stevenson's was more so because of her sex. She demonstrated courage and strength against those who would hurt or capture her and her huband. In a manner reminiscent of captivity narratives, she used neither gun nor knife but a fist and an umbrella. However, although symbolizing Stevenson's strength, the umbrella made the heroine look ridiculous and made the stereotyped savage even more of a buffoon than usual. Simultaneously, the article showed Matilda breaking the tenet for proper behavior in a middle-class, Victorian woman, who should be (according to the popular press) weak, passive, docile, pious, and submissive, show little intellectual ability, and stay at home (Riley 1984:25). Stevenson was not exemplifying these virtue but rather was aggressive in inappropriately and unexpectedly defending her husband. In a public place she crowded in front of her husband rather than remaining respectfully in the background or drawing back in

terror. The illustration thus reversed the Victorian expectation of the brave male defending the weak female. In addition, she was on a scientific expedition, exploring amid the savages, not at home raising a family. She functioned in the tough, intellectual, public male sphere of science. Thus a doubly conflicting message appeared in the article, which was resolved by having a man, trader Thomas Keam, rescue both Matilda and James Stevenson. Cushing, as a man, had no such conflict; he could rescue himself, even though he did not (by his own account).

In general, however, Stevenson seems to have had cordial relations with many Native American families and to have developed long-lasting friendships at Zuni. As Lurie (1966:55) notes:

While Stevenson never enjoyed the reverent esteem of an entire tribe, the friendships she made were intensely personal and those who called her "Washington Mother" thought of her as a real kinswoman. Furthermore, the Zuni priests did not finally open their secret ceremonies to Matilda Stevenson out of gratitude, as the Omaha leaders welcomed Alice Fletcher, but out of respect for her intellectual ability to grasp their meaning and her sense of reverential respect which exceeded that of ome of the lay Zuni.

Stevenson had several especially close relationships at Zuni—with We-wha, Naiuch, and Zuni Dick. Her friendship with We-wha was of a close relationship between two women full of warmth and affection, even though We-wha was a berdache (in Zuni, *lhamana*). We-wha, a respected tranvestite, who was able to combine a mixture of men's and women's roles and activities, was both a traditionalist and innovator and found in Stevenson one who, like herself, wanted to preserve the knowledge of traditional ways. She was "the strongest character and the most intelligent of the Zuni tribe" (Stevenson 1904:20). We-wha was an accomplished artisan, excelling in weaving and pottery. The Stevensons commissioned articles for the Smithsonian collection from her and brought her to Washington to work on linguistic and cultural studies as well as to pose as a model for exhibits.

Stevenson's friendships with Zuni men were not unusual for female anthropologists but were unusual for Anglo-American women in general in the late nineteenth century. As Riley (1984: 178) has noted, frontier women and settlers almost never developed close friendships with Native American men. In this instance, Stevenson's anthropological stance and her interest in Zuni life were crucial. She was judged to be so sincere that she was allowed to accompany the Younger Brother Bowpriest on his visits to the Great Salt Lake in the early 1880s and early 1900s, a privilege accorded to few Zuni. Stevenson never betrayed the trust of the priests by divulging the location of or looting the shrine encountered in route.

Although Stevenson clearly admired the Zuni and their religious philosophy, she was ambivalent about Native Americans in general. She overcame many popular stereotypes: she knew they were human beings and treated them as such and realized that they were not Noble Savages. Native Americans were neither industrious nor lazy: only individuals, not groups, could be so characterized. Her personal opinions and feelings were balanced and realistic compared to those of many of her contemporaries. She tried to be objective yet never overcame her Victorian upbringing or her staunch, almost unthinking support of an evolutionary paradigm. She clearly considered American Indians to be lower on the evolutionary scale than Euro-Americans; she described the Zuni as "children of nature" (1904); a "barbarous people" on "a comparatively low state of civilization" (1881a:13). Moreover, she wrote that much of their religion was "superstitious" (1887:539); "The reasoning of aboriginal people is by analogy, for at this stage of culture, science is yet unborn. So the philosopher of early times is the mythmaker" (1904:317). Like other evolutionists, she assumed that the Zuni thought differently than did civilized people. She judged Zuni practices,

customs, and beliefs in terms of Victorian moral codes; for example, when speaking of abortion she wrote, "This vice exists in Zuni" (1915a:52) and stated that some Tewa ceremonies were "shocking" (1913a).[8] Despite these prejudices, Stevenson strove for objectivity. Her feelings in her work were always secondary; she unfailingly presented Zuni religous explanations first, stating firmly that Zuni customs cannot be understood in a non-Zunian framework. All her interpretations were supported by Zuni mythology, for she argued that one must understand legends before one can understand ceremonies or secret cult societies (1894b). As a civilized scientist, Stevenson could understand why the Zuni had certain customs: "We live in a world of reality, he in a world of mysticism and symbolism" (1904:317). Different mental processes, a society's position in Tylor's evolutionary scheme, and Victorian moral codes as well as Zuni concepts formed the basis of Stevenson's explanatory model of Zuni culture.

This does not mean that Stevenson always approved of or accepted the customs she encountered. At one point she wrote that she had "never seen anything else in aboriginal life which so thoroughly aroused her indignation as did a trial for witchcraft" (1904:398). Nor does it mean that she did not try to change Zuni customs that she felt were undemocratic or barbarous. Her responese to these customs are ironic, given her quest to have the Zuni remain intact. This stance can be most clearly seen in her reactions to her encounters with witchcraft accusations: "Belief in witchcraft seems to be universal among the Indian tribes, and no great advance in civilization can be made among them until the beliefs and the accompanying practices are rooted out" (1904: 392). Witchcraft and supersition, according to Stevenson, persist among primitive peoples and the ignorant.

Stevenson wanted to understand the Zuni theological control. She also wanted the Zuni to advance out of their "ignorance." All this was to be accomplished utilizing a framework of American democracy and justice, including the idea of empirical proof of a crime, causality based on the scientific method, and the right to innocence until proven guilty, concepts not utilized by the Zuni. Stevenson tried to change the belief in witchcraft and the Zuni method of dealing with witches by attacking the Bow Priesthood. She directly questioned their authority to judge matters dealing with witchcraft allegations. In a series of incidents described in detail in *The Zuni Indians* (1904:397–406), Stevenson demonstrated her inability understand witchcraft as a means of social control. In one situation she felt that the Bow priests were condemning an individual to death unjustly for a superstition:

Near midnight the writer was notified that this man [whom Stevenson felt was unjustly accused of bewitching an individual who was ill] was to be put to death. It seemed too terrible to believe, and hastening from her camp to the village she met Nai'uchi as he was returning from the deathbed of his patient. The great theurgist and elder brother Bow priest was urged to withdraw his verdict on the ground that he might be mistaken. Since he was obdurate, he was told that the United States Government would certainly punish him. . . . [He refused.] The position of the writer was a delicate one. The man must be saved, but she must not make an enemy of a tried friend and one of the men most important to her in her studies. . . . Before night came she held a court of her own, Nai'uchi the younger brother Bow priest, and the accused being present, and the result was that the unfortunate was released. This was brought about by a declaration on the part of the writer that she had deprived the man of his power of sorcery; and he was soon at work upon his housing, fitting it for the reception of a Sha'lako god (1904:397–98).

Stevenson used similar techniques to save other accused witches, the reason for which she describes as "simply to show that it is possible, if these people are managed in the right way, to overcome their miserable superstitions" (1904: 406). Because of her successful attacks and the fact that Nai'uchi and others were arrested for

murder in 1896 after they had hung a woman accused of witchcraft, the power of the Bow Priesthood was broken. When Bunzel (1932a:536) described the situation at Zuni, she noted that the Bow Priesthood had been "reduced to three members." Likewise Smith and Roberts (1954:15) note that "the Bow priesthood has steadily declined. . . . Today there is only one remaining."

Stevenson believed that it was the Native Americans' duty to become civilized and in the process to assist her in her research on her terms. In 1879 when some people opposed her taking note on Zuni ceremonies, she sketched the ceremonies in secret. At Zia when she was met with silence (i.e., the ceremony in progress was halted) after forcing her way into a kiva, she finally left. Later she persuaded the priests to let her view and photograph the production of the altars. Apparently her method was first to attend a ceremony unannounced, to assume that her participation was permitted and tolerated, and only when this failed to try persuasion. For example,

In 1904, the writer [Stevenson], realizing that the Zuni native dyes were fast becoming a lost art, determined to secure the full complement of their colors ere it was too late. When the writer made known her desire to secure shanks of yarn of the various native colors, a number of Indians offered to do the work, but when she insisted that the dyeing be done at her camp, they protested that they could do it much better and would be less interrupted in their own homes. Innumerable ruses were offered to do the dyeing in their houses, and threats were made that it would not be done at all if it had to be accomplished away from home. A little patience and perseverance on the part of the writer brought the men and women to her camp, the clouds of discontent disappeared, and they had a merrymaking time for some days. Not only the workers were present but numbers of their relatives and intimates, and the midday meal was much enjoyed amid jokes and laughter (Stevenson 1987:299).

One of her basic arguments was followed by other Victorian anthropologists. She would tell individuals that it was their duty to record information about their lives, since they as a group would inevitably be assimilated into American society and their actions would be approved by the gods.[9] As she wrote to Holmes, "I have made this poor fellow [a Taos historian] believe that he will win the favor of his gods by allowing me to record their beliefs and so have them live always, for the gods would not wish the knowledge of their mysteries to die with his people while those of the Zuni gods will live forever because they have been recorded" (NAA:MCS/WHH 7/12/06).

In all, Stevenson worked at Zuni for more than twenty-five years—evidence of her long-standing commitment to understand the deeper meanings available to one only from in-depth knowledge of a single society. In addition to her fieldwork, she paid native informants to go to her home in Washington, D.C. (Mason 1886). During this period she collected data on many topics, including manufacture and use of native dyes, preparation of pigments, games, irrigation systems, social structure, mythology, language, philosophy, symbolism in arts, costume, and ethnobotany. She also continued to collect material culture for the Smithsonian although on a smaller scale than in the 1870s and 1880s and to help construct museum exhibits. Despite all her other interests, Stevenson still focused primarily on the minute details of the Zuni pantheon, philosophy, and ceremonies. She firmly believed, as have many other anthropologists who have worked in the Southwest, that religion was the cornerstone of all native cultures: "With these people almost every act of life assumes a religious character" (Stevenson 1904:313). In all her works she documents the importance of religion in daily life and demontrates that religious beliefs systematically form the core of Zuni philosophy, thought, and political and social organization. Religion was crucial to the Zuni's "struggle for existence." Although today Stevenson's work may appear to be disparate pieces of information, a characteristic typically ascribed to ethnographic accounts written in the period, it is her interest in religion, her belief that religion made Zuni a functioning society, that ties all her work together.

COMPARATIVE ETHNOLOGIST

In 1905 Stevenson began what she thought would be her monumental study—a comparison of the religion of all the Pueblos, to discover the underlying religious concerns and complexity of each system (see 1913a, 1913b). She envisioned this project as an extension of her work at Zuni (NAA:MCS/JWP 6/3/01). Stevenson was convinced that only after detailed fieldwork, including basic ethnographic documentation, in each Pueblo could one undertake a comparative work. The project required complicated and delicate research over a period of several years: "I must know a people well before attempting such studies, so I have stated that I come to write some of their language and to become acquainted with them" (NAA:MCS/WHH n.d./06). Until her death in 1915, Stevenson spent the greater part of each year in New Mexico, gathering facts and details.

Stevenson never completed the project, however. This was the first time in her career that she failed to produce a major monograph following an extended period of fieldwork. There are a number of reasons for this. One was her inability to work in the Rio Grande Pueblos for an extended period of time, by concentrating on one pueblo for a few years and then moving to another; instead, she worked at several at once—a few week here, a few days there. She first tried to work at Taos. When that proved futile she went to San Ildefonso, then to San Juan, Jemez, and Picuris. She tried again and again at each pueblo, year after year.

Fieldwork in the Rio Grande Pueblos was extremely difficult; few individuals would cooperate with anthropologists. Stevenson had to work in secret, for like almost all anthropologists after her, she was unwelcome in the groups as a whole although befriended by individuals. Unlike the Zuni and Hopi, societies in the Rio Grande Valley and its tributaries refused to allow outsiders access to their esoteric religious ceremonies. As a mechanism for coping with European, Mexican, and Anglo-American assimilation attempts, they had become closed societies (Dozier 1970). Stevenson's reception and her reaction can be seen in the following situation.

I spent the 22nd and 23rd at San Ildefonso observing the Eagle and Buffalo dances. The latter is the great spectacular feast of the year. I secured photographs of both ceremonies. I have never experienced such opposition to my camera—not by the elderly men who were pleased to have me make pictures but by the English-speaking "educated" Indians. I had earth thrown at me with orders not to make pictures, and when the orders were not obeyed many threats were made, one fellow taking position beside me, with a club threatening to strike, but intelligence dominated brute force, and then the men threatened to break my camera. I extended it toward him but again intelligent force dominated, and I hope that my pictures secured under such trying conditions may prove satisfactory (NAA:MCS/WHH 2/13/12).

Stevenson tried walking into kivas as she had done at Zuni and Zia, without success. When persuasion failed she tried to force the Pueblo governors to help her through political pressure via Bureau of Indian Affairs Commissioner Leupp. Although Leupp would not interfere directly, "he let the governor [of Taos] know that favors done him must be reciprocated in kind if he expects to ask additional concessions in the way of relief from taxes" (NAA:MCS/WHH 3/28/06). She used numerous devices to show the Puebloans that she represented the government and as such should be obeyed (Woodbury 1986: 4), including flying a flag at her camp. But even these aggresive techniques proved unsuccessful. Stevenson never breached the solidarity of the Rio Grande Pueblos, although her correspondence with William Holmes and Frederick Hodge shows that she thought she had and that she was always hopeful. According to John P. Harrington, a linguist and ethnographer who of-

ten visited Stevenson at her ranch and learned ethnographic techniques from her, the members of San Ildefonso considered Matilda to be a silly old woman (Lurie 1966:64). John Bodine considers her work at Taos a success, however. He notes that only Stevenson and Parsons "were able to break down the barriers of secrecy sufficiently to obtain information on the Blue Lake Ceremony" (Bodine 1988:92).

Stevenson could never admit failure in any endeavor, so it is not surprising that she refused to change her research plans and strategy. She never came to grips with, nor understood why, she was unwelcome in the Rio Grande Pueblos; she never accepted a nonindividualistic society. Instead of friendship or indifference she met rebuffs, resentment, and silence. She was not allowed to live in any of the villages, although she did occasionally stay overnight with friends in San Ildefonso. Only rarely would acquaintances in the villages risk ostracism by talking about tribal secrets. Indeed, in one case,

The man did not dare tell his wife that he was coming to me so fearful was he that his people would learn of his coming and would suspect him of imparting their secrets to me, nor did he dare remain longer than two weeks but he will return soon again, and he declares that he will continue his visits not remaining long at a time so as to avoid suspicion that would prompt his people to look for him, until he has given me a complete record of his people. He would surely meet death if he were discovered but we do not intend that he shall be discovered (NAA:MCS/CDW 2/6/09).

Stevenson tried to adopt a new field technique that was later used by other anthropologists such as Leslie White, Elsie Clews Parsons, and Ether Goldfrank, that is, working in secret outside the pueblo itself.[10] She purchased the Ton'yo Ranch adjacent to San Ildefonso as "a central place for my scientific studies" (NAA:MCS/CDW 5/8/09). She wrote, "My ranch is an ideal place to work for I can always avoid interruptions when studying or I can hide my interpreter from view"

(NAA:MCS/FWH 5/13/12). But she had little success with the new technique, for she relied too much upon participant observation. In an attempt to indirectly Taos ceremonies, Stevenson had two trusted Zuni friends attend the ceremonies and report on what they had seen. There is no evidence whether they were successful, but it is telling that the three worked steadily and productively on Zuni material, resulting in manuscripts on Zuni ethnobotany and on dress and ornamentation (Stevenson 1915a, 1987) and only a few known field notes on Taos.

Thus, Stevenson's only successful research during the period from 1906 to 1915 was a continuation of her Zuni studies. In terms of her Rio Grande research, she never had a complete data set and lacked collaboration when she did obtain information. To her this meant that her work was fragmentary and unsubstantiated. By 1910, after she had been working for four years, the Smithsonian administration began to pressure her to publish the data she had. This presented a quandary, for Stevenson always refused to publish information without supporting statements from independent sources. In addition, due to her constant switching from pueblo to pueblo, her work was unfocused. Her manuscripts were held for revision. Both Hodge and Holmes tried to warn her about what was happening but had no success. In one letter, Hodge wrote,

I believe that better, more lasting, and certainly more immediate results can be obtained by concentrating attention on a single tribe or group of affiliated tribes, such, for example, as the Tewa. To extend your work from Taos to Zuni would seem to me to lead to scattered results with nothing sufficiently intensive to afford the basis of a publication except in the indefinite future, to say nothing of the expense, which would hardly be justified, I fear, by the prospective product, if we may judge from the results of your studies thus far among the Tewa. You should concentrate on one subject, like material culture (NAA: FWH/MCS 6/2/11).

Other factors contributed to Stevenson's declining productivity and reputation. Her health was failing: her eyesight was bad, and she had what was probably angina pectoris. She once wrote, "I am stronger about the heart and do not have to dose with digitaline" (NAA:MCS/FWH 3/4/14). Her rheumatism was so severe that by 1912 she could barely write and had trouble walking. She was drinking heavily, perhaps to ease the pain. It is probable that she was becoming an alcoholic. She would request cases of scotch in her expense account (which the director would not approve). Her rationale, according to Matthew Stirling (quoted in Lurie 1966:234), was "that it was necessary in her work, since nothing else would induce the Indians to give out their more secret information." Unfortunately, as Stirling also notes (Lurie 1966:64), most people remember the disagreeable alcoholic of these later times rather than the productive, strong-willed person of earlier years.

Stevenson also overextended herself financially by trying to make the ranch pay for itself; it devoured all her savings. She became embroiled in local New Mexico politics, which resulted in numerous arguments with personnel from the Bureau of Indian Affairs (BIA) and the Santa Fe anthropological community. And most disheartening was that she was the victim of a swindle by a BIA schoolteacher, Clara D. True, and True's mother and sister and had to endure litigation that dragged on for several years.[11] Although she won all the suits, the court cases ruined her financially and emotionally.

Stevenson was convinced that the Trues had ruined her professional reputation as well. In 1909, Clara True and her sister, Miss Bryan, apparently spread rumors that Stevenson had been dismissed (NAA:MCS/CDW 5/8/09) and wrote to BIA Commissioner Leupp and William Holmes accusing Stevenson of mismanagement of government funds. Stevenson argued, "They hope in this way to get me away from my fieldwork and thereby interfere with my success" (NAA:MCS/ CDW 5/8/09). Stevenson was outraged; her cherished and hard-fought-for-reputation was more important than money. She wrote,

I have labored so hard day and night to learn what I did from the Indians and then when I saw my way clear to bring my work to an early close those women came in to interfere. You know Mr. Hodge that my life has not been mixed up with low vulgar people but it has been the very extreme from a shadow of anything vulgar. The Secretary of the Smithsonian knows the same for he was a frequent visitor at my home and knew my husband, my parents, and the people who frequented our home. He found only culture and refinement there. . . . No living creature ever heard me use a coarse word, and to be mixed up in any way with the wretched women who dared write such charges against me, and that I was expected to take any notice of such charges has almost killed me (NAA: MCS/FWH 5/28/14).

Stevenson brought a successful suit for libel against the women, an act that again depressed her bank account and halted her fieldwork. She also did not want to return to Washington after her field seasons from 1909 to 1913 because it might be construed that she had been recalled or fired because of True's accusations. Hodge allowed her to remain in the field indefinitely at her own expense so as not "to offer your enemies any ground for the unwarranted belief that their activities have been the cause of the termination of your fieldwork" (NAA: FWH/MCS 6/14/13).

So exhausting and dispiriting was this episode of her life that Stevenson's correspondence mentions almost nothing else. Gone are her long notes about interesting findings; now there are only vague hopes that she can soon return to her work. Near the end of her ordeal Stevenson wrote to Hodge (NAA: MCS/FWH 10/10/14), "I hope for a new life when I am done with those dreadful women and their vulgar attorney." But she never realized her dream, and her problems made her appear a bitter old woman to the anthropological community in Santa Fe. Less and less would she tolerate criticism: "My own ambition is to have my work live and receive favorable criticism from great men. The smaller men play no part in my life, and I have not time to reply to the absurd comments which rarely, but sometimes occur"

(NAA: MCS/CDW 2/6/09). Vindication became all-consuming.

As a result, Stevenson produced only a few short articles on the Rio Grande communities during this period, and these were little more than research reports. She never wrote her envisioned synthesis. Even with these problems, however, Matilda Coxe Stevenson completed more fieldwork in the area than had anyone previously. After her death, her protégé, John P. Harrington, "inherited" her unpublished field notes, cut many up, interspersed them with his own, and later incorporated her work into his own publications— generally without acknowledgment. (An all-too-common practice of the day; see Hinsley 1983.) It was difficult to locate Stevenson's Rio Grande materials because of Harrington's treatment, a problem that other researchers have noted as well. Bodine (1988:91), for example, noted that in 1906 Stevenson collected

the only detailed and reliable account of the annual August pilgrimage of the Taos people to Blue Lake. Her fieldnotes ultimately were obtained by J. P. Harrington. Harrington worked on Stevenson's manuscripts and particularly focused his attention on the Taos language terms incorporated in the narrative. He presumably intended to publish the Stevenson material under his own authorship since the original, now kept in the National Anthropological Archives of the Smithsonian, clearly shows that he scratched through Stevenson's name and put his own on the manuscript. Stevenson's work on Taos was not discovered until 1965, yet it will become apparent that what she collected 80 years ago is one of the most valuable sets of documents that we have on Taos Pueblo.

Stevenson's research in the Rio Grande was erased.

A FIGHT FOR RECOGNITION

Like all women scientists of her period, Matilda Coxe Stevenson continuously fought to obtain recognition for her work. At first her research was not distinguished from that of her husband. The 1879 trip and subsequent expeditions led to many unrecognized publications; Matilda helped her husband prepare the reports and catalogues of the collections that were later published in the Bureau of Ethnology annual reports (J. Stevenson 1883a, 1883b, 1884a). In a thank-you note to James Stevenson (NAA:SB/JS 3/21/82), Secretary Spencer Baird said that because all previous reports had been published only under James Stevenson's name, individuals unaware of Matilda's contribution mistakenly thought that she was not the author of *Zuni and the Zunians*. Newspaper articles listed James as the author. Actually, James disliked writing reports. As Holmes (1935:632) noted, "Although Stevenson amassed voluminous notes as the result of his observations, he was a man of action, irked by writing, and gladly turned over most of his material to his wife. He was wont to say that he was not a scientific man, little realizing that his great collection of materials would remain a valuable and in most respects unique contribution to science." James was a collector, an outdoorsman, a keen observer and administrator, and an excellent fundraiser, but he appears not to have possessed either the creative mind or the discipline needed to sit indoors writing. Creativity and synthesis he left to Matilda, areas in which she excelled.

Initially, this situation did not seem inappropriate to Matilda. In letters to friends late in her life she stated that she believed that it was the duty of every wife to assist her husband in all his endeavors and reflected that working with her adventurous husband had allowed her to leave her sheltering family. One can question whether she, unlike Alice Fletcher and Erminnie Smith, would have ventured to the Southwest on her own, much less become one of the earliest women anthropologists, if she had not first worked with her husband. However, by 1882 she resented her position of unrecognized, unimportant assistant. Much of the extreme touchiness noted increasingly after 1900 by her colleagues is a result of her frustration due to lack of professional recognition.

Not until 1885 was Matilda's contribution officially acknowledged by the government geological surveys and the Smithsonian administration (Baird 1885; Tylor 1884).[12] Stevenson received much-needed encouragement in her quest for recognition from no less a personage than Edward B. Tylor, and it can be argued that if she had not had so eminent a figure notice her publicly, she would have remained overshadowed by her well-liked and famous husband until after his death—a common situation for wives in a husband-and-wife team. In 1884, Tylor, his wife, Edward Mosley of Oxford, and G. Karl Gilbert of the U.S. Geological Survey visited the Stevensons in Zuni. The following fall in an address to the Anthropological Society of Washington, Tylor (1884:550) remarked how interesting it had been to watch the Stevensons work as an effective team at Zuni (for his remarks see p. 3 of this volume). As Lurie (1966:34) has noted, Tylor was advocating both a husband-wife team approach to research and the need for women researchers. An added benefit was his effect on the Smithsonian administration. Powell (1891), following the lead of Goode and Baird in their annual reports of 1884 and 1885 for the U.S. National Museum and the Smithsonian Institution, finally acknowledged Stevenson in the Bureau's annual report for 1886. Earlier, only James' intellectual contribution was acknowledged, although note was made that Matilda had traveled to the Southwest and helped collect artifacts. The implication was clear that collecting was not as important as analysis. James did acknowledge the help of his wife, for example, her assistance in preparing "Zuni Sand Altars," a lecture to ASW in 1885: "Mrs. Stevenson who accompanied me to Zuni attended their daily and nightly exercises, and gave much time and care to the study of their religious life. I am indebted to her for many points of information regarding their Altar worship, and the sandpaintings connected therewith. The illustrations I have here tonight are from her field sketches." This is more than the usual acknowledgment given to spouses in professional writing (Ben-Ari 1987) and demonstrates that James thought of his wife as a colleague.

Joining professional organizations is extremely important to a person's career. Membership demonstrates acceptance by the peer group of contributions to the field, validation through accepted channels, and recognition that one is deemed a serious scholar and professional. Here again, Matilda Stevenson had to fight for recognition in the male-controlled Washington intellectual community. In 1879, Powell and 25 of his friends (including James Stevenson) formed the Anthropological Society of Washington (ASW) "to encourage the study of the Natural History of Man especially with reference to America" (Lamb 1904). In 1885, Matilda (who met all the written requirements for acceptance) applied for membership, apparently as the first woman to do so. Although there had previously been no official policy excluding women, the society decided to bar all women from active or corresponding membership as a result of her request (Rossiter 1982:63, 80).[13] It may have been that men feared the feminization of their profession, which they contended would undermine their progress toward eliminating amateurism (Hinsley 1981; Kohlstedt 1978).

Stevenson, with the encouragement of Tylor and over the objections of her husband, appealed but was unsuccessful. Soon thereafter, with 10 other women she founded the Women's Anthropological Society of America (WASA) on June 8, 1885 (Holmes 1916:555; McGee 1889:16; Rossiter 1982:81–82). The purposes of the new organization were "first, to open to women new fields for systematic investigation; second, to invite their co-operation in the development of the science of anthropology" (Anonymous 1889: 240). The group invited contributions from all women who were "clear in thought, logical in mental processes, exact in expression, and earnest in the search for truth, to make contributions of ascertained and properly related facts, and thus aid in the solution of the mighty problems that make up the humanity wide science of Anthropology" (Anonymous 1885, quoted in Lurie 1966:36). WASA was one of the first scientific societies to be organized and maintained by women (Anonymous 1889:242; Croly 1898: 341; McGee 1889:22).

Stevenson was the society's first president (1885–1889), and she ensured that it rivaled other intellectual associations in Washington. The society set high standards of scholarship, and at each monthly meeting a paper of 30 minutes' duration was presented, followed by a discussion. Stevenson presented at least 7 papers, apparently the largest number by any member or invited speaker.[14] Given the lack of forums available to women, this is a remarkable output.

By February 1889, 47 papers had been presented. As Anita Newcombe McGee (1889:19) noted,

It is noticeable that the majority of the papers presented the results of personal observation on the part of their authors. They were real contributions to knowledge, generally much condensed from abundant material collected on some given subject. It results from this custom that no discussion has ever been given to the origin, antiquity, or primitive condition of man, and that no studies have been made in race classification or in philology.

This statement foreshadows the problems women would face doing physical anthropology and archaeology. Lurie (1966:36–37) found that the focus on certain subjects and neglect of others was conscious:

They appeared willing to tackle almost anything, but they emphasized the special work they could do as women. . . . Seeing themselves as capable of making special contributions to anthropology because they were women, and subscribing to views of their day that the infancy of the individual reflects the infancy of mankind, they engaged in further rhetorical questioning. In the "earliest" unfoldings of thought, language, and belief, who can collect so valuable materials as can mothers?

The subjects of the papers were general ethnography, religion, problems relating to children, customs, folklore, legends and music, housing, pottery, nutrition, and growth of children. There were also a few "nonfeminine" subjects—lighting, petroleum, and natural gas. Most papers were descriptive studies typical of the period, although an occasional theoretical or methodological paper was presented, one of which, "How to Study Children," was on a woman's subject. With the exception of papers by Stevenson, Fletcher, and Smith (who dealt with their active fieldwork with Native Americans), the papers all dealt with civilized peoples such as the Basques, Chinese, Japanese, and Russians—peoples the women had visited with their husbands. The most common topics can be classified as folklore, contemporary domestic science improvements, and reform issues.

Although Lurie (1966:37) asserts that "these women clearly accepted their role as women," I do not think it was quite that clear. Although the topics of the women's papers show a tendency toward "women's" topics, the very fact that they organized an association was a direct, if ladylike, comment on professional discrimination. These women knew they were founding a pioneer organization and would meet with resistance. According to Anita McGee (1889:16, 22),

> The purpose of this sketch will have been served if some conception has been given of this new work undertaken by women and of the progress already made upon it. We do not claim perfection in any particular, but we do believe our organization to be the minute seed from which a great forest will spring. . . . The idea was a novel one and hazardous in that only one of the participants had ever done scientific work, to wit—Mrs. Tilly E. Stevenson.

It is obvious from McGee's statements that these intellectuals were convinced that women were making contributions to anthropology because they were scientific scholars as well as mothers who were observant. It is abundantly clear that Stevenson felt this way.

Acceptance of women in professional organizations began to improve in the 1890s. In 1893, 1895, and 1896, ASW and WASA held joint meetings (Lamb 1904). Stevenson was finally invited to join the ASW on November 18, 1891.[15] After her admittance, other women were extended membership to ASW on a case-by-case basis (Moldow 1987:148). On January 3, 1899, 49 WASA members were asked to join ASW. Although there is no solid evidence for this change in ASW policy, Clifford Evans (NAA:CE/WF 6/6/58) felt, based on an analysis of ASW reports, that the association needed WASA's financial support to revitalize its flagging publication program (May 1988:6). Thus it was the women's financial rather than intellectual resources that were valued. WASA disbanded; the extensive library acquired by the women formed the nucleus of the Department of Anthropology's library at the Smithsonian Institution. Stevenson was elected to the American Association for the Advancement of Science (August 17, 1892), the Archaeological Institute of America, and the National Society of the Fine Arts and was a founding member of the Washington Academy of Sciences in 1898.

Stevenson spent a great deal of time and energy demonstrating that women were competent scientists and scholars: she served as a judge at the World's Columbian Exposition in 1893 and participated in the special congresses associated with several world's fairs. She helped plan and erect exhibits at the Louisiana Purchase Exposition, the Seattle Exposition, the World's Columbian Exposition, and the Madrid Columbian Historical Exposition. She won several awards and prizes. Much of her work was highly visible to the public and earned her numerous rewards. Her most important recognition, however, she turned down because of the libel trial in New Mexico: in 1908 Stevenson received an invitation to deliver a series of lectures at the University of Berlin— apparently the first invitation to a BAE anthropologist and to a woman. Her friend, Dr. Sophie

A. Nordhoff-Jung, a world-famous child psychologist, chided her for declining the offer. "Do you know you missed a great deal by not accepting that position in Berlin. It would have opened up a new horizon to you and I should have been so glad to have had you show those Germans what a woman can do when she has brains and is in earnest about her work" (NAA:SNJ/MCS 1/31/09). But Stevenson wanted to remain a scientific anthropologist first, a feminist second.

LAYING A FOUNDATION

Matilda Coxe Stevenson was an intelligent, self-sufficient, proud, serious, humorless, opinionated woman—a legend at the Smithsonian Institution. She refused to let people take advantage of her or regard her as a frivolous female. She generally distanced herself from others. She wanted others to judge her on the basis of her work, but anthropologists have tended to judge her on the basis of her personality in her later years, when she had become hardened and bitter due at least in part from her battles for recognition. Holmes (1916) respected her and considered her a valued friend who was "able, self-reliant and fearless, generous, helpful, and self-sacrificing"; Powell found her tiresome and quarrelsome;[16] Alfred Kidder never "cottoned much to her," according to Neil Judd (1967:57), who also found her strong-willed and dominating; Pandey (1972: 326) describes her as "an aggressive, intellectual woman who reacted strongly to anyone who did not accept her bidding." Accounts of Stevenson at the beginning of her career are neutral and favorable. While she remained her husband's helper, that is, firmly within the acceptable bounds of female behavior, she was looked upon with tolerance and favor. After his death, when she became more serious and demanded equality, she became an objectionable woman.

This sort of "ad femina" argument about the quality of an anthropologist and his or her work has always been the norm for women scholars but has been taken to extremes in Stevenson's case. For example, Jesse Green's (1981:25) assessment of Stevenson's and Cushing's work, although based on their research methods, clearly shows double standards based on sex and personality:

An aggressive and domineering person, Mrs. Stevenson pretty clearly had no sympathy for Cushing's participant approach; her own way of gathering ethnological information was more direct. In addition to buying it (at least on one occasion), she seems also (at least occasionally) to have bullied it, marching in on kiva ceremonies without invitation and threatening the Indians with the militia if they interfered with her.

Green's incomplete and inaccurate information on Stevenson is based almost solely on Smithsonian legends and Cushing's own interpretation of her: "More than one of his [Cushing's] early letters from Zuni refer to her efforts to belittle, malign, and interfere with his work" (Green 1981:24). At the same time, Green dismisses Stevenson's assessment of Cushing. Since Cushing and Stevenson disliked one another, both assessments are equally suspect.

Green's implication is that Cushing and his methods are good but Stevenson and her methods are bad. Were these individuals really different? Although Green states that Stevenson purchased her data and Cushing did not, he never gives any indication of the specific incident. Stevenson states categorically in several letters to Holmes that she will never purchase information. Cushing did not have sufficient funds to purchase information, so we do not know if he would have used this technique if he had had the opportunity. What Stevenson is probably being condemned for is the use of a paid interpreter, a commonly accepted practice in anthropology and one lauded today as nonexploitive. Green also states that Stevenson did not use participant observation methods. This is untrue. Stevenson, like Cushing, used the "good" method of participant observation. Although Stevenson did use bullying as a methodological technique, Green neglects to mention that Cushing did likewise. Stevenson is thus condemned for practices that both she and Cushing followed, as did most other anthropologists of the period. It is all too easy, and a common practice, for scholars to be harder on women than on men for the same activity. What is acceptable or tolerated in a man is not in a woman.

Although certain individuals were intimidated by Stevenson's personality and used this as the basis for dismissing her contribution to anthropology, others did use her work. No one criticized the value or quality of her fieldwork and analyses. She wanted her papers "to be of real value as references to students" (NAA:MCS/WHH 1/24/10), and they have been. Her works were used extensively by anthropologists working on the Pueblos through the 1930s. Alfred Kroeber trusted Stevenson's analyses of Zuni over Cushing's because he thought Cushing tended to overdramatize; Stevenson's analyses in contrast were impersonal, objective, and precise (Kroeber 1917 cited in Hinsley 1981:193). Her contemporaries also praised her information and presentation: Daniel Brinton (NAA:DB/MCS 6/18/95) had "a growing admiration for [her] accurate and attractive description. . . . [She had] brought forward the human element of their lives, a feature so often overlooked in the description of scientists." Frederick W. Putnam (NAA:FWP/MCS n.d.) states that her work shows that she had "secured the Pueblo's confidence and esteem and that [she had] a good knowledge of their native life, religious ceremonies, etc." Edgar L. Hewett, even though he disliked her political stance and was a supporter of Clara True, respected her firsthand knowledge of the Pueblos (Chauvenet 1983:72). Powell, who was often angry when she would not write quickly and who would object to her writing style and organizational skills, admired her thoroughness. Lurie (1966:62) states that "she collected facts, set them forth precisely and in detail, and analyzed them largely within their own context." These assessments tally with Stevenson's

own: "Perhaps I make the mistake of being too careful, and going too deeply into my subjects but to me it seems as if we owe it to future generations to proceed with great caution and avoid error. There is no science in which error is so apt to occur as in anthropology" (NAA:MCS/CDW 5/09). Further, she wrote, "I know that I am more tardy than other students in completing work for publication but I also know that when my work is published neither the Bureau nor myself can be called upon to correct errors of statement regarding the Pueblos. . . . Hurried studies among these people is time wasted" (NAA:MCS/FWH 5/13/12).

Although cited by Margaret Mead and Ruth Bunzel (1960:203–6) as a pioneer of anthropology, Matilda Coxe Stevenson has often been overlooked since World War II, overshadowed by her more flamboyant contemporary, Frank Hamilton Cushing, our new culture hero. She has become invisible. Hoebel (1954) does not mention her (indeed he mentions almost no women in his analysis). Eggan (1968) and Eggan and Pandey (1979), for example, note that Cushing's work provides an important baseline for understanding Zuni society and culture in the 1880s and 1890s. They fail to mention Stevenson's contributions. Basso (1979) has a long exposition on Cushing, but he does not mention that Stevenson was at Zuni at the same time; in his essay, Stevenson is mentioned only in passing in a photocaption.

This neglect may be due partly to Stevenson's gender (definitely due to her perceived personality); it also reflects fads in anthropological method and theory. Since World War II, Cushing's publications have been more appropriate for the types of questions being asked.[17] As texts, Cushing's works are more elegant and appear less embedded in evolutionary jargon and perspective than Stevenson's. Stevenson's work was more appropriate to the style and problems posed in the 1920s and 1930s. Today we use her work for facts, data to support or refute current ideas, or to find out what the Zuni were like in 1879. We do not use her works to obtain a "feel" for the society; Cushing's often more perceptive works are much better for this task.

Another reason for Stevenson's recent invisibility is that she never wrote theoretical essays and always stayed firmly within the dominant nineteenth-century evolutionary paradigm of Lewis Henry Morgan that was espoused by Powell and McGee for the BAE. All her writings supported Powell's general theoretical position (Hinsley 1981). She never questioned evolution or the idea that European and Anglo-American cultures were more advanced than that of the Pueblos, who were conceived of as the living representatives of earlier phases of the history of all peoples. Stevenson did not consider herself a theoretician but a scientific field researcher. Indeed, Mead and Bunzel's (1960:205) assessment of her is as "an active and industrious field worker [who] collected a large body of detailed information." She was not interested in process, although like all nineteenth-century comparative ethnologists she was interested in culture history and origins (Hinsley 1981:103). Because of this lack of concern with macrotheory, her work is of regional interest. Books on the history of anthropology have not mentioned the data gatherers but have focused on theoreticians, flamboyant personalities, and institution builders.

Matilda Coxe Stevenson endured and often overcame the conflicting messages from the field that lauded her participation yet tried to deny her professional status. In the end, she was concerned that her reputation in the field be that of a scholar who was attentive to thoroughness and ethnographic detail rather than abstract theories. She was an assembler of facts: "If I failed to tell you the facts as they are I should fail in my duty to the science I love so well and to the Institution to which my life has been so closely allied" (NAA: MCS/CDW 11/17/08). She wanted to learn the truth: "All my brains and energies are centered upon getting at the truth" (NAA:MCS/FWH 5/13/12). Her loyalties in this quest were to science, anthropology, and the Smithsonian Institution: "My great ambition is to have our Bureau become the mecca where all anthropology students will come for truth and refreshment. . . . We can have it so, if those of us who leave our science just a little better than our selfish aims will put our shoulders to the wheel" (NAA:MCS/CDW 12/1/08). And Stevenson has lived up to the goals she set herself. As one scholar notes,

For whatever failings or shortcomings she might have had, Matilda Coxe Stevenson is to be applauded for what she was able to obtain at Taos. She may not have been the equal of Elsie Clews Parsons in terms of analytical and evaluative skills, but as an ethnographer she was excellent and properly joins the ranks of those few women in the early days of American anthropology who truly contributed to the advancement of the discipline (Bodine 1988).

NOTES

I would like to thank Jerrold Levy, Nancy Lurie, Shelby Tisdale, Barbara Babcock, Nathalie Woodbury, Richard Woodbury, and Raymond H. Thompson for their insightful reading of the drafts of this paper.

1. Basic biographical information for this study comes from primary data sources in the National Anthropological Archives (NAA), obituaries, and Leonard 1914 and Marquis 1914. The most extensive sources on Stevenson are, of course, Lurie 1966 and 1971, and I have relied heavily on them. Stevenson's unpublished manuscripts are on file in separate entries and in the John P. Harrington Papers at the National Anthropological Archives, Smithsonian Institution. Additional information on Matilda Coxe Stevenson comes from the National Anthropological Archives, Smithsonian Institution: Matilda Coxe Stevenson papers (which include James Stevenson's papers); John P. Harrington papers; Bureau of American Ethnology correspondence and administrative files; 1903 congressional testimony and investigation of the Bureau; Anthropological Society of Washington records; miscellaneous information files of the Department of Anthropology, United States National Museum. Stevenson is also mentioned in the intro-

duction to annual reports of the Bureau of (American) Ethnology, annual reports of the Smithsonian Institution, and annual reports of the United States National Museum from 1884 to 1915.

2. Lurie (1966:56) describes James Stevenson as "an anthropologist by courtesy rather than training or primary inclination." James had originally gone west on the Warren Expedition in 1857–1859, served as a colonel in the Union Army during the Civil War, and then resumed geological exploration. Considered by all a generous, modest man, Stevenson was said to have had a softening influence on his wife. Stevenson mentions that she often accompanied her husband but does not always say in what year. Correspondence shows that she went on the 1872, 1875, and 1878 expeditions but not the 1874 trip (because she was in Europe with her family). She went on at least one other expedition. The Stevensons had no children.

3. Unfortunately, neither Matilda nor any other member of the Hayden expedition published the ethnographic results of the trips in Colorado and Wyoming. William Holmes and William Jackson did, however, publish the results of their archaeological trips to the San Juan region of Colorado (Holmes 1878).

4. In later years Matilda referred to herself as "Mr. Stevenson's guest" (Stevenson, 1911 manuscript p. 118, 1987).

5. In 1887–1888, Alice Fletcher and Stevenson, as representatives of the Women's Anthropological Society of America and the American Association for the Advancement of Science, lobbied Congress for passage of a bill to have Mesa Verde and the ruins on the Pajarito Plateau declared national parks (Fletcher 1888, Fletcher and Stevenson 1889). They wrote reports and drafted a bill in 1888. Illnesses in the Evans family prevented Stevenson from lobbying harder, and the bill never left committee in the Senate (NAA:MCS/GHVS 6/15/14). Mark (1980a:78) states, "Nothing much came of their efforts and Alice Fletcher realized that one of the problems was that there was no western scientific institution which could add its weight to pressure being brought to bear in Congress." The bill, however, served as the prototype of the Lacey Act of 1906. Shortly before her death, Stevenson was petitioning the New Mexico legislature to save other ruins from vandalism. Now we may see irony in these activities, for the Steven-

sons' archaeology would today be considered little more than glorified pothunting.

6. Stevenson, referring to Hermann K. Haeberlin of the American Museum of Natural History, whom she had just met while he was working on his Pueblo studies, wrote to Holmes (NAA:MCS/WHH 1/24/10): "He reminds me so much of myself after my first year at Zuni. I thought I knew it all, but returned to the pueblo to learn how little I did know."

7. Stevenson is a mass of contradictions. In one account she wrote, "In 1879 whiskey was rarely if ever used by the Zunis, but with the advance of civilization intoxicants are producing demoralizing effects on these people" (Stevenson 1904:253). Yet, according to Matthew Stirling, Stevenson late in her career

> included a case of Scotch in her expense account, which of course was turned down. She insisted that it was necessary in her work, since nothing else would induce the [Taos] Indians to give out their more secret information. It was pointed out to her that it was illegal to give whiskey to Indians. She replied that it was only illegal to sell it to them (Stirling quoted in Lurie 1966:234).

Because of Stevenson's frustration with the Rio Grande Pueblos, she had less sense of moral duty toward them than toward the Zuni. Also, Stevenson was a hard drinker and cigar smoker (Woodbury 1986:3), possibly an alcoholic by this time. The request for liquor may have been a ruse to disguise her own use of liquor. Cigar smoking was also being used as a sign of equality and emancipation by women trying to enter professional societies and attend smokers (Rossiter 1982).

8. Stevenson was upset with a Miss Arnold of Denver, "a woman who comes from a highly cultured family," who was "infatuated with a Santa Clara Indian." She found "the whole affair most disgusting" (NAA:MCS/WHH 2/12/06). Yet at the same time she states, "I claim that all persons entertaining orthodox beliefs are hampered in scientific studies especially in ethnology" (NAA:MCS/WHH 7/3/08). She could not escape her Victorian upbringing.

9. For other examples of similar arguments used by anthropologists in their attempts to secure data, especially on religious subjects, see Parezo 1983, 1985, 1987.

10. Hodge never understood Stevenson's problems in this regard. He often criticized her field methods:

If I were engaged in your present task I should expect to gain much better results and at much smaller cost, by taking a room in San Ildefonso or Santa Clara, surrounded by Pueblo life in all its phases—in other words, to be a part of the native life in a measure, rather than to attempt to bring the life of the Indian to me. This would obviate the care and annoyance of maintaining a camp and the expense of a camp helper, and would give you the obvious advantage of being one of the people among whom your studies are being conducted (NAA:FWH/MCS 6/2/11).

11. The fight with the Trues involved three suits for ownership of a camp outfit, payment for services, the use of a community ditch and land ownership. Clara True's claim on Stevenson was $1,100 (NAA:FT/ABR 6/30/00). In 1909, True brought a suit of $2,500 for services and Mrs. Randall brought one for $137 on Stevenson (NAA:ABR/MCS 11/11/08). Stevenson wrote, "I most innocently trusted Miss True to purchase the ranch for me and she kept three parcels of my land from my deed" (NAA:MCS/CDW 5/8/09). Stevenson had given the Trues $300 to buy the land (NAA:MCS/ABR 3/21/10). A jury found in Stevenson's favor and in addition awarded her $253.87 in damages from Frances D. True and Mrs. Randall, $200 in costs for lawyers' fees and court costs. Stevenson had her land restored and gained complete control over the ditch. Clara and Frances True, however, refused to honor the court order and were subsequently held in contempt of court (NAA:MCS/FWH 10/23/14). The government later brought suit against True for forgery and misappropriation of government funds.

12. Erminnie Smith and Alice Fletcher were the first women to be professionally recognized (Lurie 1966:40). Like Stevenson, Smith was interested in geology before she turned to anthropology.

13. Rossiter (1982:81) states that the reasons for this action are "because of her gender and presumed lack of field training." One can speculate that they did not consider it proper for women to attend meetings or smokers or that they thought that women were not scholars. Rossiter (1982:63) posits that Stevenson' rejection represents a backlash by the BAE and the Washington community against women. See Rossiter (1982) for other examples of the problems women had joining professional associations. The

same year, 1885, Erminnie Smith was elected an officer of AAAS. She was already a member by 1882.

14. This assertion is based on very little data, for almost none exists on the organization. Men were allowed to speak to the association although they could not become members. Otis T. Mason gave a talk on the organization of anthropology, which, according to Lurie (1966:36), the women used to help organize their society. The society published the text of Mason's talk "What Is Anthropology" in 1888 (McGee 1889). Stevenson's papers included "The Religious Life of the Zuni Child," 1886; "The Moki Indian Snake Dance" and "The Mission Indians," 1887; "The Thirteen Medicine Orders of the Zuni," 1888; "The Sandpaintings of the Navajos" and "Zuni and the Zunians," 1889; and "Foundations of the Zuni Cult," 1893, at a joint meeting with AWS. The other prolific speaker was Alice Fletcher, who had given four talks by 1889. WASA members also tended to publish in regular professional journals. For an analysis of the association, see May 1988.

15. Anita Newcombe McGee told Stevenson (NAA:ANM/MCS 11/18/91), "Hurrah! You are a member of the Anthropological Society. At the first meeting this fall there were too few members present to bring the matter up, but last night twelve were there—eight affirmative votes are required for an election, and just that number were cast. As nearly as Mr. McGee could tell the members voted as follows: Welling A, Baker A?, Mason A?, Gore N? (a guess), Pierce N?, Ward A, McGee A, Mallery A, Seeley N, T. Wilson A?, Holmes A, Flint N?. The others, Powell, Henshaw (A), and Bourke were out of the city." A was affirmative, N was negative. Powell and Bourke, a friend of Cushing, would probably have cast negative votes, since they personally disliked Stevenson.

16. In Stevenson's estate were found several original watercolors by Holmes, which he had given to her as tokens of their friendship. Holmes often tried to make Stevenson's road easier, especially when he was head of the BAE. As described earlier, Stevenson and Powell's relationship is confusing. Lurie writes (1966: 59), "It is common knowledge that she had a low tolerance of criticism of her work, even from Major Powell with whom she argued vehemently." Yet in her publications Matilda is always well within Powell's theoretical framework, and there are many letters in her correspondence at the Smithsonian Institution

where she asks for his advice. There is also the fact that Powell gave her a job in the first place. Most likely he tolerated her because of his friendship with her husband and because she does not appear to have been as demanding in the 1880s as she became in the early 1900s. Powell, in official correspondence, mentioned the value of Stevenson's work. In a letter to her (NAA:JWP/MCS 1/21/02) he states that her monograph on Zia (Sia) was an effective work and an excellent paper. Likewise,

> I have read your paper with care and also with great interest. It is a valuable contribution to anthropology and I cannot do less than congratulate you on collecting so much good material and putting it in such good shape. . . . It will be very widely read and give you reputation and you can afford to treat your subject with great care.

Even if Stevenson and Powell did not get along, she did respect his work: "I think you have a far deeper knowledge of American aboriginal life than most men" (NAA:MCS/JWP 5/23/00).

There is some evidence that Harrington found Stevenson to be a pretentious old woman. See Nusbaum 1980, p. 52, for a thoroughly unflattering story.

17. Lurie (1966:32) has noted that "early women have been relegated to no more obscurity than have many of their male contemporaries who were also remarkable pioneer spirits." However, this does not explain why Stevenson is ignored while Powell, Cushing, and Mooney are not. The fact that Stevenson did not teach and hence had no students may also be important, but neither did these other men (Hinsley 1981; Mark 1980a). Today, Cushing's flamboyance and "precocious genius" are seen as positive attributes.

ELSIE CLEWS PARSONS
IN THE SOUTHWEST

Louis A. Hieb

Her society had encroached upon her;
she studied the science of society the
better to fight back against society.
A. L. Kroeber
(1943:252)

ELSIE CLEWS PARSONS was best known during her lifetime as a sociologist, a feminist,
and a pacifist rather than as an anthropologist.
This is not to downplay her anthropological contributions, however. She was 42 when she discovered anthropology, and between 1916 and 1941
she had 95 publications concerning the Southwest, 90 of these dealing with the Puebloan
peoples of New Mexico and Arizona. In only three
years between 1916 and 1941 did she fail to have
at least one article in the *American Anthropologist*
regarding this area. It is remarkable that the most
recent anthology of publications from the *American Anthropologist* during the interwar period
makes virtually no mention of this first woman
president of the American Anthropological Association (Stocking, ed. 1976). Only during the last
few years have her contributions to all three
fields—anthropology, feminism, and sociology—
been acknowledged and analyzed in light of the
interplay of her three professional selves (Babcock
1991; Lamphere 1989; Rosenberg 1982). Indeed,

several papers from a recent American Anthropological Association meeting take the re-vision of
our view of Parsons and her scholarly endeavors a
step further. Her contributions to southwestern
studies are worthy of continued analysis.

EDUCATION AND EARLY
PROFESSIONAL APPROACH

Elsie Clews was born into "a wealthy and socially prominent family" in New York City on
November 27, 1875 (Hare 1985:18). The eldest of three children, she was the only daughter of Henry Clews, a Staffordshire potter's son
who had left England as a young man to found in
New York the banking firm bearing his
name (Boyer 1971:20; Hare 1985:23–29). Her
mother was Lucy Madison (Worthington) Clews,
a descendent of President James Madison and
granddaughter of an early governor of Kentucky,
Gabriel Slaughter. Mrs. Clews, "reputed to be
Newport's best-dressed lady of her era, declared

that each summer she set aside $10,000 for mistakes in clothing" (Cleveland Amory, quoted in Hare 1985:27).

Gladys Reichard said Elsie Clews Parsons was born "into circumstances which practically demanded that she live the life of a debutante" and her family would have preferred that she enter society. However, Parsons "early showed her determination to be free of the constraints of her social position" (Hare 1985:18), so after study with private tutors and at Miss Ruel's school in New York, she went on at age 16 to the recently accredited Barnard College. After receiving her A.B. in 1896, she stayed on for graduate study at Columbia University. Alfred L. Kroeber later recalled how "her statuesque figure floated through the seminar alcoves of the Low Library on Morningside Heights as a memorably astonishing sight" (1943:252). She received her M.A. in 1897, taught history briefly at Columbia's Horace Mann High School, and completed her Ph.D. in 1899. Her doctoral dissertation, "The Educational Legislation and Administration of the Colonies," reflected the influence of her advisor (colonial historian Herbert L. Osgood), philosopher Nicholas Murray Butler, and Franklin H. Giddings, the Columbia sociologist (Boyer 1971:20; Rosenberg 1982:153). In Giddings' sociological theory Clews found intellectual support for her own "intense devotion to individual freedom" (Boas 1942b:89), especially in his ideal of self-realization. As Rosalind Rosenberg suggests, Parsons "saw in this concept a weapon against the constraints that middle-class Victorian society imposed on female achievement" but removed it from Giddings' Spencerian evolutionary framework (1982:152).

On September 1, 1900, at Newport, Rhode Island, Elsie Clews married Herbert Parsons, a New York lawyer. Herbert was a New York City alderman who went on to become a Republican member of Congress (1905–1911), Republican National Committeeman (1916–1920), and a long-term delegate to Republican conventions. Peter Hare (1985) provides an intimate view of their courtship, open marriage, and the turbulence of an affair between Herbert and Lucy Wilson. (Wilson, an influential academic and educational reformer, was one of the first women archaeologists to work in the northern Rio Grande region.) During Herbert's tenure in Congress, the Parsons family lived in Washington and thereafter in the New York City area. Of their six children, four survived childhood: Elsie ("Lissa"), born in 1901, John Edward (1903), Herbert (1909), and Henry McIlvaine (1911).

In the early years of her marriage, Parsons continued an active academic career. From 1899 to 1902 she was Hartley House Fellow at Barnard and from 1902 to 1905 served as a lecturer in sociology. She also taught a graduate course at Columbia University on the family, in which students were required to work with underprivileged New York families (Parsons 1900). Parsons did not hold a permanent academic post after 1905 but chose to carry on independent research with a focus on "the problem of the modern family and women's place within it" (Rosenberg 1982:156). However, her first book, *The Family* (1906), grew from these lectures. Boyer (1971:20) notes, "Though a textbook, it was also a feminist tract, asserting that if women are to be fit wives and mothers they must enjoy the opportunities for development open to men." Parsons' discussion of trial marriage put *The Family* in front-page headlines (Hare 1985:14; Rosenberg 1982:161–62), but it also "brought persuasive sociological arguments to the feminist cause, explaining the modern subordinate status of women as a residue from earlier cultures which regarded menstruation, pregnancy, and childbirth with mingled awe and revulsion" (Boyer 1971:20). Parsons also observed that "ethnography had traditionally been barred to women, and because most male social scientists were themselves convinced of female inferiority, they rarely noticed the many ways in which the lives of women remained bound by patriarchal forms" (Rosenberg 1982:157).

Her concern for "the ways in which the expression of an individual's personality is affected by the conventions of society" (Hare 1985:19) appeared in book after book. In part to avoid the notoriety caused by *The Family,* in 1913 Parsons took a pen name, John Main, to argue against the oppression of women in a book entitled *Religious Chastity.* Parsons' early publications all had a marked ethnological imprint. She called *The Family* "an ethnographical and historical outline" and subtitled *Religious Chastity* "an ethnological study." A number of other popularly written books followed, all under her own name: *The Old-Fashioned Woman* (1913b), *Fear and Conventionality* (1914a), *Social Freedom* (1915), and *Social Rule* (1916h).

Social Freedom: A Study of the Conflicts between Social Classification and Personality continued Parsons' argument for the rights of the individual's personality. Much of the book concerns sexual relationships, which Parsons queried:

Since mating and parenthood are seen to be theoretically distinguishable, is not any relation of sex, we are asking, to be self-determining, arising and developing according to the natures of the lovers themselves, not to be determined by or in the interests of others, the only test of the relationship, the effect of the one personality upon the other? (1915:32)

Early reviewers felt Parsons substituted one extreme (irrational traditionalism) with another (complete individualism) and failed to define what she meant by "personality." Parsons' friend Signe Toksvig provided clarification of the key concept:

A society founded on love of personality is Elsie Parsons' first concern; and by this she does not mean a world of raw emotions or one where real differences are ignored. For empty ceremonials she would substitute genuine personal reticence, and she would acknowledge differences without being afraid of them (Toksvig quoted in Hare 1985:20).

In *The Old-Fashioned Woman* Parsons provides an insightful critique of the subordination of women in modern society and its institutions: "girls school," the "coming-out" of debutantes,

the meaning of such phrases as "I am just as glad to have a girl as a boy." She writes of the married woman (1913b:49–50):

She is forced either into idleness or into fictitious jobs by the pride of her family or by the nature of our economic organization, there being no place in it, outside of depressed industries, for a half-time worker. She is "protected" at home. She is discounted, excused, and sometimes pitied abroad. Her wedding-ring is a token of inadequacy as well as of "respectability."

She adds, "Women try hard to live down to what is expected of them."

Social Rule (1916h), Parsons' last major sociological work, is perhaps the most effective expression of her rejection of "all conventions that constrained the free expression of personality" (Hare 1985:7). Randolph Bourne, a pacifist and Parsons' friend, provides an appreciative contemporary appraisal of the book (1917:239):

Mrs. Parsons has made herself one of the few radical writers who see that central conflict between personality, which makes for life, and the interests of status, which inhibit and cramp and crush the personal life. What makes her books so fascinating is just this vision she has of the social and personal drama of the ages. There is none more compelling. As far as she is prophet, she is clear voiced for the assertion of the personal values against caste and class and social gradations. As far as she is ethnologist, she is a patient analyzer of the curious satisfactions upon which people build their codes and forms. Men and women are men and women to her whether they are guests at her most recent dinner party or her primitive friends among the Zuni Indians.

More recently Rosenberg writes (1982:169): "No other scholar had her flair for popularizing the new ideas about the cultural and psychological roots of sexual identity."

Franz Boas characterized Parsons' early work as "a strenuous revolt against convention . . . a purely intellectual criticism of fundamental forms of our modern ways of life" (1942a:481). And Hare argues that "her concerns for the ways in which the expression of an individual's personality is affected by the conventions of society" is to be found in "everything Elsie did from her first publication at the age of twenty-four in 1898 to her death in 1941" (1985:19). If this is true in general, it is not true of her writings on the Southwest after 1919 as she carefully separated propaganda from research. Indeed, her bibliography (cf. Reichard 1943) after 1917 contains only a handful of reviews and articles reminiscent of her earlier sociological period.

Nevertheless, Parsons' nonconformist temper shaped her life as it did her early books. She frequented the salon of Mrs. Mabel Dodge, where young intellectuals and radicals congregated, wrote occasionally for Max Eastman's *Masses,* and enjoyed the friendship of Walter Lippmann and other founders of the so-called New Republic group in 1914 (Boyer 1971:21; Rosenberg 1982:168–69; cf. Stocking 1976:33). She was involved in Heterodoxy, a feminist network in Greenwich Village (Schwarz 1982). She enjoyed swimming nude, would refuse "to wear a hat in New York City when all women of her social position were expected to wear hats," would "insist upon sitting with men after dinner," and would wear sandals on Park Avenue when it was not the thing to do. When scheduled to give a speech as a congressman's wife, she agreed as long as she could wear her favorite color, orange (Hare 1985:44–45). During World War I, while Herbert served in the intelligence branch of the American Expeditionary Forces in France, Elsie espoused pacifism, a position that cost her many friends (Hare 1985:107–21). In 1919 Elsie lectured at the New School for Social Research, founded in New York City by liberal and well-off New Yorkers, refugees from Europe, and various nonconforming academics. Among her first students was Ruth Benedict. Modell tells us that for Ruth Benedict "Parsons represented a woman who succeeded 'by the world's measure' without giving up her private life and, in Parsons' case, possessing the added quality of being impressively rational" (1983:114).

THE TURN TOWARD ANTHROPOLOGY

A turning point in Parsons' life came in 1915/1916. From the perspective of her contemporaries she became an anthropologist (cf. Chambers 1973:183–84; Hare 1985:135–39). Boas later wrote (1942b:89), "The contrast between their cultural behavior and our own, the influence of cultural forms upon personalities, the ways in which personalities similar to those found in our own civilization respond to the demands of their cultures, were problems that challenged her attention." Rosenberg indicates that Parsons had met Boas as early as 1907 and that in 1912 Boas helped her arrange a trip to the Yucatán (1982:166), but it is more likely (Hare 1985:136–37) that it was Pliny Goddard, A. L. Kroeber, and Robert Lowie who influenced her shift from sociology to anthropology. Early in 1916 following the publication of *Social Rule,* Goddard chided her: "Your winter activities are propaganda and your summer ones research" (quoted in Hare 1985:135). Soon the transition was complete. Leslie White writes, "Her intellectual posture shifted dramatically from the deductive sociology and weighty generalization of her earlier writings to a new concern for the smallest empirical detail of particular culture" (1973:582). From Boas' view,

she turned from the sociological study that lays primary stress upon the complexities of our culture to the wider inquiry, the question of the manner in which more primitive or alien societies have solved their problems—a necessary preliminary of the study of what is generally human and of what is historically determined. The position of women in society, the forms of the family, demanded inquiry from a wider point of view (1942a:480).

Her first published reports on Zuni show the influence of Boasian historical particularism in their meticulous recording of data, attention to folklore, and preference for empirical fact over speculative theory.

Boas, White, and others tell us what happened and when, but not why Parsons made such a radical shift from her feminist and reformist writing and activity. Rosenberg suggests, "Parsons grew discouraged over the prospects for reform in general and the woman's movement in particular"; indeed, she argues, "Whatever modest hope Parsons had for progress and reform was dashed by World War I" (1982:174, 176). She continues:

At war's end, Parsons made a final break with public life and her own brand of feminism and escaped into anthropological fieldwork . . . Her growing understanding of culture's power over the individual made her even less optimistic about individual action . . . Science, once the promise of a new era, became simply a refuge for her, in which she sought greater understanding for its own sake, not for the sake of reform (1982:176–77).

Hare tells us that Parsons "had always enjoyed adventurous trips in the wild and had an early interest in Indians. She tried unsuccessfully to persuade Herbert that they should take a trip to the Southwest on their honeymoon" (1985:123). Not until 1910 did they travel to the Southwest. In an unpublished manuscript (Parsons n.d.), she wrote of the experience: "If ever I come to work seriously in this country [the Southwest] . . . [it will be] as a student of the culture" (quoted in Hare 1985:129). This trip stimulated her reading about the area, and in the fall of 1912 Parsons went to the Southwest for a second time. Using Clara True's Pajarito Ranch near Espanola (next to Matilda Coxe Stevenson's land) as a base, she rode over 230 miles on horseback the first week to visit various Puebloan villages. Again in September and October of 1913 she visited the Southwest— notably Acoma and Laguna.

FIELD RESEARCH IN THE SOUTHWEST

Two trips to the Southwest in the summer (August) and fall (November) of 1915 began her serious ethnological research among the Pueblos. Staying in the Zuni governor's house, she met his wife, Margaret Lewis, "an extremely well-educated Cherokee once a school teacher here, who was to assist Elsie for many years to come by giving her a convenient and congenial place to stay, arranging for informants, acting as interpreter, and by writing to let her know of upcoming ceremonials" (Hare 1985 3:133).

Leaving her daughter Lissa to care for the household and the younger children, Parsons began a series of annual extended field trips to the Pueblos of Arizona and New Mexico. After Herbert's death in 1925 her travels became more frequent and extensive.

Between 1916 and 1918 Parsons produced 75 publications, including 28 on Zuni, Laguna, and Acoma. The processes of culture change, the question of Spanish influence, the role of women in society were interests that continued throughout her research in the area. She speculated that "fifty per cent of Zuni culture may be borrowed from White culture" (1918e:258n. 4). Her Zuni hosts disagreed. At one point she wrote, "'Surely, a Mexican belief,' I remarked, 'No, Zuni' [her informant replied]" (1916a:250). Nevertheless, Parsons identified a number of Zuni, Laguna, and Acoma folktales to be "probably of Spanish provenience" (1918d), without supporting evidence or argument. In "Notes on Ceremonialism at Laguna," Parsons noted that "the following data were collected during three brief visits to Laguna on my way to and from fieldwork at Zuni in the years 1917–1918" (1920c:87). Scattered references to events observed indicate that she visited Zuni for Shalako and spent two or three months at Laguna at the beginning of 1918 and again briefly in the fall of 1918. However, the quantity and variety of material published suggests she spent extended blocks of time among these western Pueblos. During this time she wrote a perceptive and well-informed critique of Kroeber's *Zuni Kin and Clan* (1918a), edited Father Dumarest's *Notes on Cochiti, New Mexico* (Parsons, ed. 1919), and began a series on mothers and children in various Puebloan villages for *MAN* (1919e, 1919f, 1921d, 1924c). An essay on "Waiyautitsa of Zuni" published in *Scientific Monthly* (1919g) was later hailed by Clyde Kluckhohn as the first publication placed squarely in the field of southwestern studies of culture and personality (1954: 685). This essay was republished in *American Indian Life* (1922a) and represents Parsons' most successful effort to popularize anthropology. Her feminist critique of modern society found expression at least once in the Southwest as well. She wrote in 1919,

At Cochiti . . . late at night my tired and sleepy Indian hostess grumbled in the soft tones no Pueblo Indian ever loses, grumbled because she had to sit up for her young husband who was spending the evening at the club, i.e., taking part in a ceremonial at the estufa. "I'll have to get him something to eat," she said, "no man here would ever cook for himself at home. They say that if they did, they would lose their sense of the trail." Rationalization of habit or desire is not confined to the peoples of western civilization (1919g:443).

Toward the end of 1918 (November 25), Parsons was instrumental in the creation of The Southwest Society. Goddard was chosen temporary chairman and Parsons temporary secretary-treasurer. As Hare has pointed out, in the years that followed, Parsons "poured many thousands of dollars into the society's treasury to support the fieldwork and publications of numerous younger anthropologists working on the Indians of the Southwest" (1985:148). Although her daughter later recalled that she "preferred men to women" (Rosenberg 1982:177), Parsons was both generous and egalitarian in her support of field research and publication. Among the southwesterners she aided financially were Ruth Benedict, Franz Boas, Ruth Bunzel, Esther Goldfrank, Berard Haile, Dorothy Keur, Morris Opler, Gladys Reichard, Ruth Underhill, Charles Wagley, and Leslie White. In addition she helped finance the field schools of the Laboratory of Anthropology in Santa Fe. Although Parsons did not establish a lasting mentoring relationship with any of the women anthropologists, she fought for their right to participate in field schools and was an important role model.

Earlier, in September of 1918, Parsons had worked with Kroeber in Zuni and here first conceived of writing *Pueblo Indian Religion* (Parsons 1939a), her most ambitious work. In late May of 1919 she and Boas made a joint trip to the Southwest for a month—he worked on Keresan language while she concentrated on genealogies. After a month in Laguna they returned to New York (Hare 1985:148–49). They were to travel together to the Southwest again in the summer of 1920 and in the fall of 1921. They never published together.

Consistent with Boasian methodology, much of the material published by Parsons derived from informants, and a lesser amount consists of descriptions of ritual or social behavior that was observed by her. She wrote in "Spanish Tales from Laguna and Zuni, New Mexico" that the first five tales were told by Wesuje of Pohuati, a colony of Laguna. She continued:

Wesuje was over eighty, and blind. He had spent his life sheepherding. These stories, and no doubt others, he used to tell to the children of Pohuati. He stopped narrating to me because a neighbor in from Laguna told him I was paying twelve dollars a story, whereas I paid him only a dollar or two for several stories. After I had stated that my rate was the same in Pohuati as in Laguna, and that his stories, besides, were "only Mexican stories," the women in his family urged him to continue; but he was obdurate. A school-girl translated (1920d:47n. 1).

A more frequent, indeed omnipresent, difficulty was Puebloan secretiveness, a challenge to Parsons especially at Taos. She wrote that on her second visit to a Laguna man living in Isleta, "He told me that his wife did not want him to talk—she is the daughter of one of the leaders in the ceremonial life of Laguna—and besides 'some smart boys,' as he called them, had advised him against talking to me, and, he might have added, frightened him" (1920b:56). She went on to say, "The only way to learn something from a Pueblo Indian, as from the secretive elsewhere, is to know something else."

This comparative technique, which she also used in collecting riddles and folktales of peoples of African descent in South Carolina and the Carribean (Chambers 1973:186), provided the basis for the systematic approach to the distribution of traits throughout the Puebloan Southwest in her later works. Indeed, the first indication of her growing recognition of variations from western to eastern Pueblos appeared this same year in "Notes on Ceremonialism at Laguna" (1920c:88 n. 1): "Hopi ceremonial organization is said to be primarily for rain, and Keresan, for curing, whereas at Zuni there are differentiated rain-making and curing groups." Starting with an account of the First Mesa *wowochim* ceremony in 1920, Parsons began including a comparative discussion (1923a: 188f) to her works, which was to continue to the end of her ethnographies of the Pueblos in 1940.

In the summer and fall of 1920, she had ventured west to the Hopi villages—especially those on First Mesa—where she was made a member of a Hopi family (1920a). This event so moved her that in *American Indian Life* (Parsons, ed. 1922) she identified herself as "Elsie Clews Parsons, Member of the Hopi Tribe." Parsons arranged for a Hopi-Tewa, Crow Wing, to keep a journal for the years 1920–1921 (Parsons, ed. 1925) and worked with a Hopi-Tewa woman, Yellow-pine, who provided information on women's roles (1921d, 1921e). Beyond this she also wrote a fine account of "Hidden Ball on First Mesa, Arizona" (1922c). Although Parsons' bibliography ultimately included over 15 publications on the Hopi and Hopi-Tewa, her fieldwork there appears to have been limited to several months in 1920–1921 and a visit in 1924.

Her greatest contribution to the study of those peoples consisted of purchasing (from Stewart Culin) and editing the manuscripts of Alexander MacGregor Stephen into "Hopi Tales" (Parsons, ed. 1929) and *The Hopi Journal of Alexander M. Stephen* (Parsons, ed. 1936). So important is this work that Fred Eggan stated at the Daughters of the Desert Conference that he considered this to be Parsons' greatest contribution to southwestern ethnography. Stephen lived at Keams Canyon and on First Mesa from 1880 until his death in 1894 and made incomparable records of Hopi and Hopi-Tewa social and ceremonial life. Parsons organized and annotated these journals and texts, drawing on her comparative knowledge and sensitivity to the richness of detail.

During 1921 and 1922 Parsons was engaged in fieldwork at Jemez, which provided the basis for *The Pueblo of Jemez* (1925). This book was the first full ethnography of a single Puebloan village ever written and included chapters on history and contemporary relations, economic life, kin and clan, personal life, secular government, ceremonial life, ritual, tales, the Pecos immigration, and comparative notes. Parsons did fieldwork again at Zuni and on occasion gathered materials on Isleta, Sandia, Taos, and elsewhere. Although her publications were always written in the east (e.g., Harrison, New York, or New York City), Parsons apparently spent most of 1921 and 1922 in the Southwest.

Her fieldwork relied heavily on informants, as has been noted; for example, she prefaced one minor article by noting, "The following notes were made during a brief visit to Isleta and at interviews with an Isleta woman at Albuquerque, in a hotel room, safe from observation" (1921a:149). For another article she wrote, "The following notes were made during a brief stay [probably in 1922] at San Felipe and during an interview of several hours at Lamy with a Santo Domingo man who succeeded in eluding his pottery selling colleagues between trains and joining me in a room off the station's patio" (1923b:485; see also her "In the Southwest" [n.d.] for a fuller account). Parsons went on to describe her approach to informants in the eastern Pueblos:

There appear to be but two methods of approach to informants: paying court for weeks, perhaps months, to the townspeople in general—"Come back again, the people will get used to you," I was advised in San Felipe; or chance interviews, preferably away from the pueblo, with persons who are more or less taken by surprise and have not time to begin to entertain the fear of consequences. In San Felipe the two best informants of the town were "progressives" and there, they said, already under suspicion. One of them was willing to work at language, and the other to put me up in his commodious house until it was learned that I had been "talking" to a girl neighbor whose father was a conservative, besides a mean man, and would betray them. Thereupon my landlord so intimidated the other man, his "cousin," that . . . I had to leave town and plan for interviews at Algodones, the Mexican settlement three or four miles away.

In November of 1923 she turned her attention to the Tewa, "past masters in the art of defeating inquiry" (1929a:7). Unlike most of her writing, one work contains considerable detail of her approach to fieldwork (1929a:7–9):

Imitating the secretiveness observed in all the Rio Grande pueblos, I settled in Alcalde, the Mexican town two or three miles north of San Juan, and, here, thanks to my helpful and understanding hosts of San Gabriel ranch, I secured informants from San Juan, Santa Clara, and San Ildefonso. My informants worked singly and in couples, niece and uncle, sister and brother, mother and daughter, one interpreting for the other. The San Juan informants were by far the best, being intelligent and scrupulous—the man the most accomplished teller of folktales I have met in any pueblo. Not merely was his memory excellent, but he was an artist, a great artist, with feeling for values, humorous and dramatic, yet using with fidelity as well as with resourcefulness the patterns of his narrative art and of his daily life. [His tales have been published in *Tewa Tales.*] Information from San Ildefonso was least satisfactory. The women were particularly timid and not well informed; the man was a threefold liar, lying from secretiveness, from his sense of burlesque, and from sheer laziness. Curiously enough, this man, whose social position is of the best, but whose veracity is of the worst according to both white and Indian standards, has probably been hitherto one of our sources of authority on the Tewa.

After three visits at Alcalde, which proved a good base also for work further afield than the Tewa, in 1926 I moved to a ranch between Santa Clara and San Ildefonso, too near either pueblo for adventure by the townspeople, always apprehensive of spies. However, I was fortunate in obtaining at this time and again in 1927 some invaluable information from San Juan and Nambe, with sidelights on Tesuque, the most conservative and tight-bound of all the Tewa pueblos. . . .

. . . Since I did not reside in any pueblo during my investigation, I will not undertake to give any general picture of town life. My short visits to all the pueblos sufficed merely to check up in a general way on maps of houses and kivas and to give me impressions I could compare with life in other pueblos in which I had lived. [The results of this fieldwork were published in *The Social Organization of the Tewa of New Mexico* in 1929.]

Meanwhile, probably in 1923, Parsons wrote two landmark essays, "Tewa Kin, Clan, and Moiety" (1924a) and "The Religion of the Pueblo Indians" (1924b) (see Spier 1943:248). Here we find the first full statements of her observations regarding variations from western to eastern Pueblos with regard to social organization and religion. Both essays use her method of arranging traits in tabular form by village or linguistic group, and both reveal a remarkable command of the relevant detail. Parsons summarized her concept (1924b:140):

There is variation from the all penetrating matrilineal clanship of the Hopi through weak clans among the Keres and Tewa to no clanship at Taos; from an equally pervasive patrilineal moiety system among the Tewa there is variation to the barest ceremonial traces of moiety classification in the west, among the Hopi and Zuni. In the west the women own the houses; in the north-east the men, a mixed system of ownership prevailing in the towns between. In the west there are efflorescent mask cult and an elaborate service of prayer-stick and prayer-feather offering, which diminish steadily to the east and north.

Not content with having made these observations, Parsons went on to ask questions, questions that continued to guide much of her later research, questions that were central to American anthropology at the time. She wrote, "Such differentiation raises a twofold problem in historic reconstruction: from what outside sources may have come these varying cultural elements, and what may have been the inter-pueblo processes of communication and imitation or of resistance to imitation?" (1924b:140). Here and elsewhere, she speculates as to the role of Mexican, Spanish, and Plains Indian influence.

In 1924 Esther Goldfrank began a study of Isleta; the following year, through her assistance, Parsons worked with Goldfrank's key informant and ultimately produced a monograph-length study, "Isleta, New Mexico" (1932a). Also in 1925 Parsons worked with a Picuris youth named Fallen Leaf, the results of which were published in 1939 as "Picuris, New Mexico" (1939b). These ethnographies were similar to her earlier work at Jemez.

Throughout many of the years during which Parsons conducted research in the Southwest, she was also collecting African-American folktales from Maine to North Carolina and throughout the Caribbean. Chambers describes her as a "scrupulous and compulsive collector of texts" whose "major theoretical interest lay in documenting diffusion of motifs or tales, usually from European sources to the New World" (1973:184). Parsons used voice recording equipment and, on occasion, took a secretary with her into the field (Chambers 1973:187). She published the texts of tales from Acoma, Laguna, and Zuni (1918d, 1920d, 1923d, 1930a, 1931b), Navajo (1923f), Jemez (1925), Tewa (1926c), Hopi (ed. 1929), and Taos (1940c).

Parsons' approach to the content of the tales is diffusionistic, attempting to show—but more often simply claiming—the European (generally Spanish) origin of each. Chambers writes, "In her attitude to folktales Elsie Parsons shared the basic materialistic assumptions of the historical-geographical school. Tales were virtually physical entities; they can travel, be spliced together, and disintegrate. Tales travel with migrating peoples; polygenesis is seldom considered" (1973:195–96). Chambers is led to assert, "She is clearly guilty of a western 'high culture' ethnocentrism and essentially denies the existence or creation of indigenous regional folklore" (1973:194). This criticism is too strong if directed to Parsons' analysis of Puebloan folktales. She wrote in *Tewa Tales*, for example (1926c:3–4),

The Pueblo novelistic type of tale, distinctive in Indian folklore, has certainly been influenced by, it may have developed from, the Hispanic or European type of "fairy tale." In most cases, the content of the Pueblo type is wholly Pueblo or Indian, but now and again, indubitable incidents from Spanish folklore are introduced, and there are many Spanish tales transposed bodily into Pueblo setting.

In seeking the historic antecedents of Pueblo culture, Parsons also examined religious practices. In "Witchcraft among the Pueblos, Indian or Spanish?" she answered tentatively that causing affliction and curing were pre-Spanish but "all these beliefs . . . were enriched by Spanish witchcraft theory, which also spread, if it did not introduce the idea that anybody might practice witchcraft" (1927:128). Later she wrote (1930b:584), "The *Koyemshi* origin tale has a distinctly Christian flavor . . . [It] is a Zuni variant of the story of Adam and Eve." Likewise, she suggested that there was a "course of development from saint to kachina" (1930b:594). And with considerable confidence she stated, "Whatever the origin of the Pueblo mask, there is no doubt that its efflorescence has been comparatively recent and that this was stimulated by the Spanish use of masks" (1933b:611)—a statement she later modified (1940b). For whatever reason, most of her later writings suggested parallels between Pueblo and Plains (1929c), Aztec (1933b), or Yuman (1937b) cultures and not a priority of one over the other. However, in a brief, late note on the humpbacked flute player she saw a possible link between Kokopelli, the locust, and the Middle American perception of "Saint Paul as the Bee god" (1938:338).

After her extended research among the Tewa, Parsons' fieldwork in the Southwest appears to have consisted of brief, strategically planned visits to Taos in January 1926 (1936a), to the Pima in December 1926 (1928a), and to San Juan in December 1927 (1930b). In 1927 she was among the Kiowa and Caddo in Oklahoma and from 1929 to 1933 in Mitla, Oaxaca, among the Zapotec. However, she returned to Taos in December 1931 to do fieldwork and made, perhaps, a final visit to Zuni in April 1932 during the year she spent with Ralph Beals among the Cahita in Sonora.

Parsons' writings in the 1930s include *The Hopi Journal of Alexander M. Stephen* (ed. 1936), the massive work she edited, and the equally massive *Pueblo Indian Religion* (1939a), which she wrote. In this period of maturity and refinement, Parsons produced an elegant summary, "The Kinship Nomenclature of the Pueblo Indians" (1932b), and placed it in the context of current discussions of kinship. In "Spring Days in Zuni, New Mexico" (1933a) she reflected upon the changes that had taken place in the 20 years since her first visit to Zuni in 1912. In contrast to the easy, anecdotal style of the Zuni essay, *Taos Pueblo* (1936a) represents the fruits of her most difficult challenge and is dedicated "To My best friend in Taos, the most scrupulous Pueblo Indian of my acquaintance, who told me nothing about the pueblo and will never tell any white person anything his people would not have him tell, which is nothing."

The secretiveness that was a challenge to Parsons had repercussions for those who agreed to be her informants. Hare writes (1985:147),

Some years after her monograph [The *Pueblo of Jemez* (1925)] was published, two Indians from the Jemez Pueblo wrote her that her book had caused people who had not given her information to be "persecuted" by people they suspected had been guilty themselves. They asked that, in the interest of fairness, she give them the names of those who had given the information. She responded that the book was not in general circulation and that she had written it only for about fifty white friends of the Indians and for the great-grandchildren of the present Jemez Indians to read when the customs had changed and might otherwise be forgotten. She suggested that they need only explain to their fellow townsmen that the "few wise white people" reading it would have no desire to interfere with their customs. Further, they should explain that there was no money made from the publication of such an historical record. Indeed, she regarded the one thousand dollars she paid to have it published as a gift to the people of Jemez from a friend.

Again, when *Taos Pueblo* was published in 1936, there were difficulties (Hare 1985:162):

This book caused much the same sort of furor among the Indians. . . . But this uproar involved her close friend Mabel Dodge Luhan and her Taos Indian husband, Tony Luhan, and consequently was much more upsetting to Elsie. She wrote Mabel that she had hesitated to publish the book, suspecting what Tony's and Mabel's reaction would be. But she had concluded that the material in the book ought to be available to students of the Southwest. She had tried to present the information in such a way that no one faction at Taos could use it against another faction and had not presented the secret information most precious to the Indians since she had never gotten them to reveal such rituals. The controversy continued, and more than a year later she felt it necessary to advise the Luhans to get people of Taos to ignore the book, as the more they talked about it, the more people would want to read it and the more likely pieces from it would be published in the newspapers. At the same time she wrote the governor and council at Taos, assuring them . . . anyone reading the book would see that I like and admire Taos people and do not wish to hurt their feelings or disturb them in any way.

Hare, however, is unaware that this furor was set off by Sophie D. Aberle, general superintendent of the United Pueblos Agency (1934–1943), who brought the book to the attention of the people in Taos Pueblo. Marc Simmons (1979:219) says this "and similar incidents reinforced

Pueblo mistrust of Anglo ways and led to a resurgence of the kind of protective secrecy once used to guard native ceremonialism and custom from Spanish interference." Parsons may have placed a higher value on her science than on Pueblo religion, but there is no evidence that she was deceptive or dishonest in her relationships with Pueblo individuals.

Aside from the early review of Kroeber's *Zuni Kin and Clan,* Parsons' few reviews were written in this final decade of her life. She was critical of Ruth Benedict—"Psychological interpretation without accompanying analysis of distribution is ever precarious" (1937a:108)—and "envious" of Ruth Underhill, whose *Singing for Power* she saw as an "aperitif" (1939e:483). And she began to rely on the fieldwork of others; George Trager (Parsons 1936a, 1940c), John Adair (Parsons 1939c, 1939d), and others working in the Southwest provided information needed to fill gaps in several of her later publications. Indeed, there is no evidence in her publications that she visited the Puebloan Southwest after her 1932 trip to Zuni. Meanwhile, Parsons was working on the publication that was the summation and high point of her research: *Pueblo Indian Religion* (1939a).

RECOGNITION OF PARSONS' CONTRIBUTIONS

The history of anthropological theory is a history of increasing disciplinary self-consciousness. During Parsons' career scholars showed little concern with the impact that questions asked had on the ethnographic descriptions produced. In Lowie's *History of Ethnological Theory* (1937), we find the first full discussion of the various schools of thought—with Parsons repeatedly recognized as a significant contributor to a number of ongoing areas of inquiry, especially kinship. Needless to say, there is a very great epistemological step from Lowie's to a work such as Dan Sperber's "Interpretive Ethnography and Theoretical Anthropology" in his *On Anthropological Knowledge* (1985).

Parsons' works are regarded as classics in the Southwest today. Just as it is hard to imagine what the development of American folklore and American anthropology would have been without her leadership and financial support, so it is difficult to imagine what we would know about the Puebloan Southwest without her monographs on Jemez, Taos, Isleta, and the Tewa and without *Pueblo Indian Religion.* Nevertheless, most of us today find Parsons' work a source of frustration. We go to her for answers to our questions only to find that her answers—for all their scientific rigor and concern for accuracy—were shaped by very different questions.

Parsons wrote little of a theoretical or methodological nature. Clearly she had a kind of conversational familiarity with the theory and method that informed the work of Boas, Kroeber, Benedict, and Lowie; nevertheless, she seldom if ever cited their more theoretically explicit works. On occasion she uses words such as *function, social organism,* and *cultural system,* but for the most part, she accepted the Boasian paradigm. The goal of Boas' anthropology, as Stocking reminds us (1976:5–6),

was essentially that of pre-evolutionary diffusionist ethnology, refashioned in the context of late 19th century science: "the genesis of the types of man." Its basic orientation was historical, but the history it sought to reconstruct (and hopefully subject to scientific law) was the history of human variability in all of its aspects. . . . Above all, Boas' anthropology was empirical. Although ultimately it sought to explain why "the tribes and nations of the world" differed, it must first trace how "the present differences developed" and before that it must accurately describe and if possible classify them.

Moreover, Stocking continues (1976:7),

The observation of behavior in the present was less important than the informant's memory of the way things were, or the details of psychic life as they "had become fixed in language, art, myth and religion." Similarly, as Dell Hymes has suggested, one can find in the analysis of cultural phenomena a common mode of attack in terms of "elements," "processes," and "patterns."

Fieldwork—especially village study rather than problem-oriented fieldwork—has almost always forced the ethnographer into a synchronic perspective. Thus, Parsons' monographs on Jemez (1925) and Taos (1936) and ultimately *Pueblo Indian Religion* contain the language of functionalism and even configurationalism. In the preface to *Pueblo Indian Religion* Parsons repeated questions typical of her research in the 1920s and early 1930s: for example, "Did cultural traits spread from group to group in various fortuitous ways or was there actual immigration by the culture carriers?" (1939a: vii). However, there is here an explicit concern with social cohesion and cultural integrity, and Parsons reflected on the recent history of anthropology (1939a: ix–x):

Once it was the fashion to collect cultural facts to string on some favored theme or fancy, by what might be called the introverted anthropological method; but today, outside of journalistic or psychoanalytic circles, it is realized that, although this method may be admirable to express personal predilections and the creative spirit, it is misleading in science, for cultural facts removed from their setting may be snare and delusion. [She noted: "I am not referring to the correlation of intertribal data or to distributional study, as I believe that 'accurate information on distributions raises problems of a basic character and helps toward their solution' " (Lowie 6: 307).] They may show how a single mind is functioning, the mind of the theorist, but not how society functions. To describe even a part of a culture is a dangerous enterprise, so interwoven is one part with another that the fabric tears when we begin to separate [the threads], leaving meaningless shreds in our hands.

She continued on a later page (1939a: xi):

This feeling of cultural integrity I have tried to recognize, convinced historian though I am. Also I have implicitly evaluated not only the instrumentalism or utilitarianism of the people which is quite generally Indian—resigned materialism Kroeber has called

it—but various habits of life and of mind which others, if they like, may call the cultural core or configuration of the Pueblos.

Nevertheless, her "primary purpose" was to "assemble and compare" (1939a: xiii). Unfortunately, the atomizing effect of the focus on elements characteristic of the trait-distribution framework meant that the relational concepts in her synchronic portraits derived from Parsons' (functionalist) understanding of the connections, not from the logical, meaningful framework of the various Puebloan peoples.

It may seem ironic that Parsons, "whose contempt for organized religion was made plain in her early publications" (Hare 1985: 45), should make Pueblo Indian religion the subject of nearly 25 years of research and writing. Parsons found Zuni religion illustrative of certain modes of thought (e.g., 1916f, 1916g, 1917g) suggestive of "science gone astray" (1939a: xi) and more generally of the impact of culture on individual personalities. However, in saying that Pueblo Indian religion was "a form of instrumentalism controlling the natural through the supernatural" (1939a: x), Parsons gave voice to a perspective widely shared in American anthropology during the interwar period. To say that an approach focused on meaning (e.g., that of Clifford Geertz or Mary Douglas or, quite differently, Claude Lévi-Strauss) rather than history or function permits a different, more sympathetic, understanding does not fault the strategies and results of Parsons' inquiry, although it does recognize the limitations present from our perspective.

Pueblo Indian Religion is a descriptive and comparative work whose constant theme is culture change, "the problem of variability" (1939a: xiv). Parsons describes the ceremonial organization, ritual, calendar, ceremonies, and worldview of the Puebloans within a comparative framework before providing a series of synchronic portraits, a "review, town by town" (1939a: 861–938). Over 300 pages are given over to descriptions of ceremonies drawn from Parsons' fieldwork and from the writings of Stephen, Matilda Coxe Stevenson, Jesse Walter Fewkes, and others. The final chapters discuss the processes of culture change—variation and borrowing and other processes of change—in a manner that reveals Parsons' omniscient command of the elements and distribution of Pueblo religions.

Parsons' colleagues recognized her contributions by electing her to the presidency of the American Folklore Society (1919–1920), the American Ethnological Association (1923–1925), and the American Anthropological Association (1940–1941). She was associate editor of the *Journal of American Folklore* from 1918 until her death. In addition, she gave financial support to these groups, particularly the American Folklore Society (Chambers 1973:197) and quietly financed many field trips by younger scholars behind the facade of The Southwest Society.

In 1940 Parsons announced publicly in the *New Republic* that she would vote for Norman Thomas for president and that she was still a pacifist. In December of the following year, just eight days before she was to officiate as president at the annual meeting of the American Anthropological Association, she died in New York City of complications following an appendectomy. At her request her remains were cremated.

Gladys Reichard recalled (1943:48) that Parsons "used to say that her idea of complete comfort was to have *at the same time* a cigarette, a cup of coffee, and an open fire. And characteristically she added quietly, 'You know it is very hard to get all three together. It is easier among Indians than among ourselves.'"

DAUGHTERS OF AFFLUENCE: WEALTH, COLLECTING, AND SOUTHWESTERN INSTITUTIONS

Susan Brown McGreevy

Adventurous thinkers, world travelers, and
generous benefactors. . . . Born to wealth and
privilege . . . it was the raw beauty of
New Mexico that captivated them.
Karen Meadows (1986:7)

Dr. Clark Wissler thought that museum work
fitted women because it was like housekeeping.
Margaret Mead (quoted in Howard 1984:87)

INTRODUCTION

The generic term *museum* refers to a wide range of
institutions: art museums, museums of science
and technology, history museums, natural history museums, and anthropology museums. The
American Association of Museums has defined a
museum as "an organized and permanent nonprofit institution, essentially educational or aesthetic in purpose, with professional staff, which
owns and utilizes tangible objects, cares for them,
and exhibits them to the public on some regular
schedule" (1973:8–9). This, however, is a modern definition based on professional standards developed over many decades.

During the late nineteenth century, the evolution of natural history/anthropology museums
was closely linked to sociopolitical agendas—
some hidden, some explicit. The emerging discipline of anthropology was rooted within major
institutions located on the eastern seaboard. As
Hinsley (1986b) has already observed, the per-

sonality of these museums was shaped by the
prominent male intellectual community of the
time. However, in basement or attic storerooms
of these institutions, collections of objects required dusting, sorting, and shelving. What
could be a more appropriate role for a woman?
Women were perceived as domestic by nature,
good housekeepers by nurture, and thus inherently suited to curatorial chores (Rossiter 1982).
Conversely, they were inherently unsuited to
function in the lofty realm of administrative and
academic decision making. Even though both
men and women served in curatorial capacities,
the museum policies, programs, budgets, and scientific research lay in the highly visible male
domain.

The collections housed in these eastern institutions were intimately related to fundamental
social and intellectual concerns of the time. In
Washington, research at the Smithsonian Institution's National Museum and the closely allied
Bureau of American Ethnology was driven by a

social evolutionary agenda. The critical political and social dilemma posed by American settlement of the West precipitated intensive study of the history and culture of the indigenous peoples whose traditional lifeways were increasingly threatened by the inexorable velocity of Manifest Destiny (Hinsley 1981).

The scientific investigation of American Indians was needed to devise appropriate strategies for replacing their traditional social systems with the accoutrements of "civilization." It was believed that the material culture of these groups could provide important clues regarding the degree of their social development. Therefore, acquisition of the "objects of others" was axiomatic to anthropological inquiry (Stocking 1985).

As Hinsley discussed at the Daughters of the Desert Conference, in Brahmin Boston, burgeoning support for southwestern research was sponsored by philanthropic enterprise rather than by the federal government. An important accident of cross-fertilization between southwestern archaeology and Bostonian philanthropy occurred when the paths of Frank Hamilton Cushing and wealthy Boston matron Mary Hemenway implausibly crossed. During the summer of 1886, Hemenway invited Cushing and his three Zuni companions to stay at her family estate on the coast north of Boston. The exotic, albeit transitory, transplant of southwestern Native Americans onto New England soil would be repeated some 40 years later when Mary Cabot Wheelwright invited Navajo medicine man Hastiin Klah to visit her summer estate in Northeast Harbor, Maine. Visits from southwestern peoples to the East Coast remained a rare phenomenon, however, and their impact on the region was limited to a small circle of receptive people. Indigenous southwestern peoples first encountered Europeans when Spanish colonization of the Southwest began in the late sixteenth century. Spaniards brought with them new crops and animals (most important, livestock, including horses and sheep) and a new repertoire of social customs

and religious beliefs. In some instances these outside influences were voluntarily integrated into the preexisting cultural patterns, although each group was discriminating, selecting only those advantageous features that were not in conflict with established values. In other cases, most notably religion, changes were arbitrarily imposed. Spanish settlement in the Southwest had a permanent impact on the material culture and socioeconomics of the region.

By the mid nineteenth century, Euro-American influences from east of the Rocky Mountains had found their way to the Southwest via the Santa Fe Trail. Although a few travelers on the trail settled in the region, the most immediate impact was found in the trade of manufactured goods. Up until this time, Native American–made objects had been necessities of everyday life. Pottery, basketry, and textiles were utilitarian by definition, although the high degree of artistic attention lavished on these prosaic objects frequently transcended their functional context. As pots, pans, and other fabricated items became more readily available, there was a gradual decline in the production of handmade household objects.

The coming of the railroad in the 1880s brought a flood—which soon became a deluge—of travelers from the East. These visitors were eager to bring home souvenirs of their experiences in the Southwest. This demand soon created a new phenomenon: a tourist/collector's market for Native American craft arts. From this point on, with encouragement from entrepreneurial agents, Native American artisans began to produce objects for this marketplace.

The romantic image of the Southwest—its compelling landscapes, its quaint and picturesque peoples—attracted not only affluent tourists, but also painters and poets, authors and anthropologists, dudes and doers. Trains brought goods and people from the East. The people brought dollars and an array of cultural baggage: ideas, assumptions, dreams, and aspirations. Among those travelers from points east were a few uncommon women whose individual and collective efforts culminated in the founding of institutions that were qualitatively different from those that had been established in their cities of origin. Inherited fortunes and philanthropic ideals were the building blocks upon which these daughters of affluence established unique southwestern museums.[1]

MAIE BARTLETT HEARD, 1868–1951

The Heard Museum, Phoenix, Arizona
Founded 1929

To establish, conduct and maintain . . .

a museum of primitive arts. . . .

To encourage research and investigation

in the science of archaeology.

(Heard Museum 1929)

The growth of Phoenix from raw desert to a fertile oasis of business and culture can be attributed mainly to eastern entrepreneurial interests. Maie and Dwight Heard propitiously arrived on the scene just as the fledgling community was poised for astonishing growth.

Maie Bartlett was born in Chicago on June 11, 1868, the eldest of four children. Like many daughters of affluence, she did not attend college, a fact she regretted. Instead she was sent to the Dearborn Seminary to be "finished" in French, art, and music, skills every incipient wife and hostess needed. Maie's father, Adolphus Clay Bartlett, was a partner in a highly successful wholesale hardware company. The Bartlett children were raised in an affluent home where the ethic of philanthropy was a second language. Collecting art was another well-established behavior in the Bartlett household. Nevertheless, the collecting habits of Maie and her sister, Florence, were to depart radically from their father's predilection for acquiring important European art.

In 1886, a distant cousin of Mrs. Bartlett, Dwight Bancroft Heard, went to Chicago to work for Hibbard, Spencer and Bartlett. Descended from a prominent lineage of Massachusetts merchants, entrepreneurial expectations had been an integral part of Dwight's early enculturation. He soon became a close friend of the Bartlett family, traveling with them in Europe and then to the Near East. His ties to the family became intimately formalized when he married the boss's eldest daughter in 1894. The next year, the family physician advised the newlyweds to seek a more salutary climate as an anodyne for Dwight's chronic respiratory problems. Although their original intent was to settle in California, a visit to Phoenix while en route changed their plans. In addition to a propitious climate, the Valley of the Sun offered exciting opportunities for Dwight's entrepreneurial aptitudes and ambitions. His health improved so rapidly that he soon became a pivotal figure in the development of Phoenix and in local, state, and national politics as well.

Dwight Heard worked diligently for Arizona's statehood and was adamant in his opposition to joint statehood with New Mexico. Arizona became a state in 1912, and Heard bought the local newspaper, *The Arizona Republic,* thereby uniting his entrepreneurial and political interests. With no previous newspaper experience, Dwight's purchase of the paper was based on his conviction that it could provide highly visible support for Theodore Roosevelt's presidential campaign. From such guileful beginnings, the paper became a highly successful and influential enterprise. Dwight's political ambitions culminated in 1924 when he ran for governor on the Republican ticket, to be defeated by only a small margin.

In addition to active participation in every aspect of her husband's multifaceted career, Maie Heard undertook impressive projects of her own. She was instrumental in the development of several important social service programs, including the establishment of The Social Service Center, the first Phoenix unit of the Young Women's Christian Association (YWCA), and the Phoenix Women's Club (Heard Museum 1951:2). These diligent efforts on behalf of others sprang not only from genuine compassion but also from a mandate for community responsibility that had been implanted at an early age. Social service was acceptable woman's work in late Victorian society (Rossiter 1982). Economic and social changes resulting from the Industrial Revolution and an ever-increasing population of immigrants from southern and eastern Europe had created a class of underprivileged and undereducated Americans. The "traditional insistence on women's innate purity and nurturance" (Smith-Rosenberg 1985: 264) delineated a role for women to play in assisting the economically and socially disadvantaged. Among the wealthy, the axiom of noblesse oblige added further impetus to social service activities.

At the same time, Maie Heard's appetite for collecting art, which also had been cultivated in the Bartlett household, became freshly aroused by the high visibility of Native American craft arts in the Phoenix area. She was not a systematic collector, nor was she particularly interested in scholarly documentation of the artifacts she acquired. Rather, her collecting endeavors were prompted by the desire to have aesthetically appealing objects as decorative accents for the Heard's home, Casa Blanca.

Heard's first acquisition was a Pima basket (Heard Museum 1979:1). The Pimas and related Tohono O'Odham made a variety of utilitarian baskets. Collectors particularly prized tightly coiled basketry trays, made of willow, with complex designs executed with splints of martynia (*Proboscidea parviflora*), also known as devil's claw. Baskets continued to be her preferred art form throughout her collecting career. However, she also acquired numerous other southwestern Native American arts: Navajo textiles; Hopi pottery, basketry, and kachina dolls; and Rio Grande Pueblo pottery. Although some of these objects were casually collected during family camping trips, most were purchased from traders or other collectors. The Heards also actively supported several archaeological projects in the area. In the

1920s, when they learned that a Hohokam ruin was being destroyed by vandals, they promptly bought the property and employed a young amateur archaeologist, Frank Midvale, to excavate it (Houlihan 1979:3). They named the site La Ciudad, and the artifacts recovered from the dig became the nucleus of the museum's archaeological collections. Gradually the collections assumed an international flavor as Heard added indigenous craft arts purchased during foreign journeys.

The collection that had begun as a shopping list for interior decorating ultimately assumed such leviathan proportions that Casa Blanca could no longer contain it, so Heard reluctantly placed many objects in storage. At the suggestion of her daughter-in-law, she began to give serious consideration to building a museum to house her collections. She was particularly excited about the opportunity to transform her collections into an educational resource for the public. She collaborated with Phoenix architect H. H. Green to design a Spanish Colonial structure, built to convey a warm, hospitable ambiance. Dwight Heard was an enthusiastic partner during all phases of planning and construction. Then, tragically, on March 14, 1929, just months before the museum was scheduled to open, he died of a heart attack. An observer noted, "The light went out for Mrs. Heard in those sad days. It was very hard for her to go back to the Museum and finish getting it ready for the opening. But she had courage and a strong sense of duty and after a time she was able to go on, this time alone" (Heard Museum 1953:4).

Maie Heard remained active in the affairs of the museum during the remainder of her life. Though Dwight Heard had had the foresight to endow the museum, his widow had sufficient independent wealth to continue to enrich the museum's collections. Ironically, the Great Depression that began the year the museum opened had a beneficial impact, for many families were obliged to sell their collections. One of the most significant acquisitions to be purchased during this time was a set of more than 100 miniature baskets that Eric Douglas, late curator of American Indian art at the Denver Art Museum, called "the finest group of Pima miniatures in the world" (quoted in Houlihan 1979:4).

The Heard Museum can be viewed as the most personal articulation of Heard's commitment to the cultural life of Phoenix, but it is not her only legacy. As a memorial to their father, she and her siblings also donated the large piece of property that became a civic center. Some of her plans for the property came to fruition before her death, most notably the renovation of the old barn as the Little Theatre and the early stages of construction of the library. (The Phoenix Art Museum was a later, and welcome, addition to the complex.)

Although failing health characterized the last years of Heard's life, her civic commitment remained indefatigable. In 1948 she was named Woman of the Year by Beta Sigma Phi, an organization that actively supports social and cultural activities in the Phoenix area. She died three years later, on March 14, 1951, in her 83rd year. Although her museum has had periods of financial adversity, the Heard Museum is flourishing. Programs, collections, exhibits, and the physical plant have experienced dynamic growth as a result of healthy support from the community and capable leadership from both administrative and academic staff. The Heard Museum has justifiably earned its reputation as an innovative institution that combines anthropology and art.

SHARLOT MADBRITH HALL, 1870 – 1943

The Sharlot Hall Museum, Prescott, Arizona
Founded 1928

I couldn't be a tame house cat woman and
spend big sunny, glorious days giving
card parties and planning dresses.
Sharlot Hall (quoted in Maxwell 1982:120)

As the only native southwesterner in this discussion of eastern transplants, the life of Sharlot Hall is an exception to the chronicle of monied independence. Hall's parents had been Kansas homesteaders who made the arduous emigration to Arizona after the calamitous drought and blizzard of 1880. Hall was 12 years old when the family settled in the Lonesome Valley area southeast of Prescott.

Hall's childhood echoed the frontier refrain: "Our lives were like those of all families on small ranches—lots of work and little schooling or other opportunities" (quoted in Maxwell 1982: 29). However, there were numerous chances for self-education. She explored the prehistoric ruins that surrounded the family homestead and developed an interest in regional archaeology that surfaced years later in the collections at her museum. Another learning experience awaited her in the territorial capital. She became fascinated with the picturesque lore associated with the governor's old log mansion. "Even then," she later recalled, "I had a dream—that someday I might live in the big log house that seemed [so] full of memory" (quoted in Maxwell 1982:35).

Hall's education received further impetus when Samuel P. Putnam, the foremost exponent of the Freethought Movement, went to lecture in Prescott. Based on the efficacy of empirical rationalism as opposed to implicit faith in divine revelation, Freethought philosophy was enthusiastically embraced by intellectual liberals throughout the country. Putnam's beliefs and personal charisma seem to have generated their own "divine revelation" within the impressionable young Hall. "It is clear from Sharlot's later writing, that whether or not a physical union had taken place, a mystical, spiritual union of tremendous import, for Sharlot, had occurred" (Maxwell 1982:51). In 1896, Putnam's sudden death, under suspicious and sordid circumstances, shocked the Freethought Movement and traumatized Hall, the faithful acolyte.

Hall's previous experiments with creative writing enabled her to externalize her anguish. Several tortured poems emerged at this time, and she penned numerous prize-winning literary articles.

Her writings came to the attention of Charles Lummis, owner and publisher of *The Land of Sunshine,* a well-respected, Los Angeles–based magazine focusing on a variety of western subjects. In spite of the magazine's popular format, Lummis was highly successful in recruiting eminent scholars, artists, and writers to contribute articles and illustrations for his publication. John G. Bourke, Frederick W. Hodge, and Dr. Washington Matthews were among those who wrote for the magazine.

Since Hall was not independently wealthy, writing for *The Land of Sunshine* provided her with needed income, as well as enhanced her literary visibility. Her poems and articles for the magazine were published in rapid succession. In 1903 Lummis invited his protégée to go to Los Angeles to become an editor for the magazine. This proved to be an enlightening and stimulating experience. Her new job provided Hall with the opportunity to associate with many of the prominent literati in the Los Angeles area, including Mary Austin and Idah Meacham Strobridge.

After a few months in Los Angeles, Hall returned home for a brief visit. During this time, she wrote a poem for *Land of Sunshine* entitled "Out West." This poem not only inspired a change of name for the Lummis magazine but also conclusively established Hall's literary reputation. Her subsequent return to Los Angeles was short-lived, for her aging mother's health was rapidly deteriorating. Hall regretfully decided that she could not permanently settle in Los Angeles.

This decision had fateful consequences for Hall's career, as she once again became immersed in the life histories of the area's colorful pioneers, who had inspired her most successful poems. Her attachment to her homeland resulted in a poem that expressed her opposition to joint statehood for Arizona and New Mexico. Her outraged sentiments were shared by a number of influential people, including Dwight Heard, who fully recognized that the poem was a "cadenced polemic, passionate with righteous indignation" (quoted in Maxwell 1982:95). Heard not only published the poem on the editorial page of Heard's newspaper but also printed it as a broadside that was distributed to members of both houses of Congress.

Hall's interest in the history and prehistory of Arizona was shared by her mentor, Charles Lummis, who had earlier founded The Southwest Society, a branch of the Archaeological Institute of America (not to be confused with Parsons' philanthropic foundation), and had established the Southwest Museum to house both prehistoric and ethnographic artifacts from California and the Southwest. Lummis believed that his museum could be the sponsor of similar institutions throughout the country, each focusing on regional collections of artifacts and documents. Hall found Lummis' idea highly provocative, and she became determined to do what she could to bring it to fruition. As Maxwell observes, "Obviously it never occurred to her that it was one thing for Lummis, being a man, to travel about the country interviewing indigenous inhabitants and quite another for a proper lady to do the same thing" (1982:97). Hall's mission to preserve the rich cultural heritage of Arizona became a political and feminist issue when the position of territorial historian was established in 1910 and a man infinitely less qualified than Hall was given the job. Although she was disappointed, she continued with her self-imposed task by collecting oral histories and regional artifacts. When the next governor astutely appointed Hall to the office, it was a landmark event; she was the first woman to hold a paid position in the territorial government. Some of the legislators were so offended by her appointment that when a constitution for the new state of Arizona was drafted, they made an abortive attempt to insert a clause that would have effectively prohibited any woman from holding public office.

In her new official capacity, Hall was able to expand her travels and research. She visited archaeological sites north of Flagstaff and east to the Hopi mesas. Subsequent journeys took her to Hubbell's trading post on the Navajo Reservation and to Mormon communities on the Little Colorado. She continued to write and to lecture, becoming widely recognized as the leading authority on Arizona history.

The achievement of independent statehood, which Hall had so eloquently supported, ironically resulted in new adversity for her when she again fell victim to politics. The position of territorial historian became that of state historian; Hall was not offered the job. Hall responded to this bitter disappointment with less resilience than she had earlier: she became despondent, ill, and reclusive. When she once again recovered after a period of several years, she began to unite her childhood dream concerning the old log Governor's Mansion with her crusade for cultural preservation. She earnestly sought funds for restoring the building. Finally, in June 1927 a reciprocal agreement was reached between Hall and the Prescott city council, awarding her a lifetime lease on the mansion and surrounding grounds. Hall agreed to have her historical collection housed in

the building now on and those to be placed on the grounds of the Governor's Mansion . . . to live in the house, and spend the remainder of her life, improving and beautifying said property. . . . Sharlot Hall was . . . the First Lady of the Governor's Mansion (Maxwell 1982:177).

In 1928 Hall went to see her old friend Charles Lummis to seek his advice about establishing a museum in the mansion. It was to be their last visit together, since Lummis died of brain cancer later that year. The following year, the effects of the Great Depression created severe hardships for already-impoverished Yavapai County and for Prescott, the county seat. Plans to raise money for the museum seemed destined to fail.

Two timely events saved the situation. With the death of her parents and her new position as mistress of the mansion, Hall no longer wanted the responsibility of maintaining the 320-acre Hall family homestead. Despite the adverse economic climate, she was able to sell it to a wealthy neighbor. Some of the money thus realized was used to support the museum. The second event was the direct result of the establishment of the Civil Works Administration (CWA) in 1933, one of several New Deal programs designed to counteract the effects of the depression. In an attempt to alleviate massive unemployment, the Works Progress Administration underwrote the costs of materials and workers for locally sponsored building projects. Hall's friend Grace Sparkes was appointed chairperson of the Yavapai County CWA and successfully obtained funding for the "construction to the west of the Governor's Mansion of a 'permanent building for the preservation of early-day Arizona relics,' to be known eventually as the Sharlot Hall Museum" (Maxwell 1982: 194). With customary eloquence, Hall acknowledged the assistance of the hundreds of relief workers who built the museum; she called the new building "The House of a Thousand Hands" (Maxwell 1982:195).

Throughout the remainder of her life, Hall continued to acquire objects for her museum. Most were historic artifacts associated with Yavapai County ranching, such as branding irons, saddles, and a variety of furniture and household utensils. Hall also arranged for several historic buildings (most notably Old Fort Misery) and a replica of a Yavapai County log house to be moved to the mansion grounds. Later, the museum also became the repository for local collections of prehistoric and historic southwestern Native American materials, including an important donation of Yavapai baskets.

Hall died of heart disease on April 9, 1943. Several years earlier, her friend Erna Fergusson had written, "For no more Sharlot Halls are being produced, and no book will ever convey the true importance of this one" (1940:184). These words seem an appropriate epitaph. Yet the story of Sharlot Hall did not end with her life. Today, her museum has grown to become a respected center of regional history. The extensively landscaped grounds now contain four buildings in addition to the Governor's Mansion. Exhibits include a sequentially organized historical survey of the area, attractively presented in appropriate historical settings, and a large display of the Native American collections. A new solar-heated research center, completed in 1979, houses an extensive library and archives, a combined community and exhibition hall, a conservation laboratory, administrative offices, and commodious, environmentally controlled storage areas. The Sharlot Hall Museum is a source of pride for Prescott and a valuable educational resource that reaches beyond the city limits.

MARY CABOT WHEELWRIGHT, 1878 – 1958

*Wheelwright Museum of the
American Indian, Santa Fe, New Mexico
Founded 1937*

And this is good old Boston,

The home of the bean and the cod,

Where the Lowells talk to the Cabots,

And the Cabots talk only to God.

Bossidy (1910)

Just as the Southwest is many miles from the affluent precincts of Boston, so too was the multicultural milieu of northern New Mexico a quantum social distance from the aristocratic society into which Mary Cabot Wheelwright was born. Most of what is known about Wheelwright's life is contained in her autobiographical memoir, "Journey Towards Understanding" (1955).[2] Unfortunately, this fascinating chronicle reveals few facts concerning the first half of her life. It is almost as if she skipped childhood, adolescence, and early womanhood to be born again at the age of 40 after the death of her mother. Information provided by family and friends has added some dimension to the portrait of her early years.

Wheelwright was born in Boston on October 2, 1878, the only child of Andrew Cunningham

Wheelwright (1827–1908) and Sarah Perkins Cabot (1835–1917). Both families were distinguished, wealthy members of the elite enclave of Boston Brahmins. Thus, Wheelwright was enculturated within an environment in which philanthropy and social service were the mandates of noblesse oblige. Like other late-nineteenth-century daughters of aristocratic background, Wheelwright did not attend school but was educated at home by governesses and tutors. She was well traveled as a result of frequent grand tours of Europe in the company of her parents.

In 1918, 40-year-old Mary Cabot Wheelwright arrived in New Mexico. Santa Fe, like Taos, had become recognized as a community that embraced renegades from the mainstream a mecca for writers, painters, and scholars. In northern New Mexico these individualists found a "New World whose terrain, climate and indigenous peoples offered a model of ecological, spiritual and artistic integration to an alienated and decadent western civilization" (Rudnick 1984: 10). Thus, while Santa Fe's physical climate proved salutary for a host of bodily ailments, the city's cultural ambience provided an anodyne for jaundiced souls.

Mary Cabot Wheelwright—the tall, angular daughter of aristocratic generations—was an improbable expatriate. Yet it appears that the constraints of Bostonian social propriety provided insufficient challenges for her lively intellect. Although she never became a full-time New Mexico resident, neither did she continue to reside in Boston. During the summer, she sailed her schooner from her home on Sutton Island, Maine, and wintered at the exclusive Cosmopolitan Club in New York City. Her continued ties with the East Coast did not, however, eclipse the compelling allure of the Southwest. Her eye welcomed the expansive panoramas and solitary spaces; her heart rejoiced in the emancipating landscape. "My particular release and joy in the East was sailing . . . and when I came to the desert, I found it gave me a similar feeling of vastness and escape, and I came to love that too" (Wheelwright 1955:7).

Wheelwright became an active member of the Santa Fe community; a participant in both the Spanish Colonial Arts Society and the New Mexico (now Southwestern) Association on Indian Affairs, an organization formed to defeat the notorious Bursam Bill legislation (1922) designed to deprive Native American peoples of their land. Nonetheless, she preferred country life and settled near Alcalde, a small Hispanic village approximately 35 miles north of Santa Fe. There, the San Gabriel dude ranch served as the base for her southwestern adventures until 1923, when she bought a historic neighboring hacienda, which she named Los Luceros after the family that had originally lived there. This gracious home was her New Mexico pied-à-terre until her death in 1958.[3]

From San Gabriel Ranch, Wheelwright began to explore the region by horseback, venturing eventually to the Navajo Reservation. According to Jack Lambert, the guide who accompanied her on those first pack trips, days in the saddle were long and hot, and camping places rough and uncomfortable (Jack Lambert 1984, personal communication). Yet Wheelwright seemed to embrace the hardships as a necessary, experiential encounter with the land. During many nights, she discovered that "the feeling of the earth when you slept on it . . . made it so much more possible to understand the connection—intimate and consoling—of the Indian to his earth" (Wheelwright 1955:7).

Although Wheelwright was not a devout adherent of institutionalized religion, she became an ardent believer in the value of spiritual enrichment and the power of mystical communion. She embarked upon an exploration of world religions and avowed that "the study of man without his religion, is like studying the ocean without its tide" (Wheelwright 1955:1). The remarkable accomplishments of the last half of Wheelwright's life were thus related to her continuing quest to understand the underlying structures of religious beliefs: myth, symbolism, and ritual. In one sense her preoccupation with Navajo ceremonialism can be viewed as a logical outgrowth of these intellectual pursuits; however, on a more practical level, fieldwork on the Navajo Reservation was an unlikely vocation for a Bostonian aristocrat more accustomed to the elegant drawing rooms of Edwardian New England. Indeed, she never gave up her personal ritual of afternoon tea—even in the most rustic circumstances.

During a horseback expedition in the early 1920s, Wheelwright visited the trading post at Nava (now Newcomb), New Mexico, owned and managed by Arthur Newcomb and his wife, Franc. The Newcombs were known for their hospitality, often inviting visitors to spend the night. However, serving as an informal "bed and breakfast" inn was not the principal function of the trading post, which was not only a center of commerce for local Navajos but also a major focal point of social intercourse for the widely dispersed population. One of the frequent visitors to the Newcombs' store was the esteemed Navajo singer Hastiin Klah.[4] By the time of Wheelwright's first visit to Nava in the early 1920s, the Newcombs and Klah had become close friends.[5] When Klah arrived at the post during Wheelwright's stay, the Newcombs introduced them— a chance encounter that transformed Wheelwright's life.

The Newcombs continued to play an important role in the collaboration that developed between Klah and Wheelwright. During one of Wheelwright's subsequent visits, the Newcombs informed her that Klah was conducting a Nightway ceremony in the desert region east of the Jemez mountains. She and her guide proceeded to the place under near-blizzard conditions, and finally "managed to reach the ceremony . . . where the dancers were to be seen through the whirling snow, while the fires blew out sideways. Out of this turmoil appeared Klah, calm and benign . . . and I got a very strong impression of power from him" (Wheelwright 1955:18). When Wheelwright asked Klah to explain the meaning of the ceremony, he asked her why she wanted to know. She responded that she was interested in religion. Klah retorted with the query, "How deep is the sea?" (Wheelwright 1955:19). Since her "chief interest had always been the ocean," she found Klah's remark to be preternaturally insightful (Wheelwright 1955:19). When Wheelwright continued to express her earnest desire to learn about the major Navajo ceremonies and related myths, Klah finally agreed to work with her because "he wanted to have some of his songs recorded [and] realized that he must have help in preserving the great knowledge he had" (Wheelwright 1955:22). And so began a journey in which two remarkable individuals from dramatically different worlds worked together to create a unique and important record of Navajo culture, a record that culminated in the foundation of an equally unique and important museum.

From the world of traditional Navajo values to friendship and collaboration with a wealthy New England spinster, Klah's journey toward understanding was as momentous an undertaking as Wheelwright's. Klah was recognized as one of the preeminent ceremonial practitioners of his time. The complex system of appropriate chants, sandpaintings, and other ritual practices associated with any given ceremony is highly esoteric and requires years of study. By the time Wheelwright met Klah, he was in his mid 50s and had mastered four complete ceremonies (Nightway, Hailway, Chiricahua Windway, Mountainway) and portions of several others.

He also had begun to weave his famous sandpainting textiles. These weavings constituted a radical departure from traditional Navajo proscriptions concerning the production of permanent sandpaintings (Parezo 1983). Klah's unorthodox behavior was due to several factors. During the 1920s, continued efforts by the federal government to assimilate Native Americans into mainstream society compounded the concerted attempts of missionaries to eradicate what

they perceived as heathen religious practices. In addition to this clear and present danger to the survival of Navajo ceremonialism, Klah's desire to assemble a record of his knowledge was due to the unexpected death of his apprentice, Beall Begay. When Begay died in 1931, Klah, who was 64 years old, realized that there would not be sufficient time to train someone else. Hence, the traditional method of perpetuating ceremonial practices from singer to apprentice was no longer available to Klah. The need to document and preserve the rich traditions of Navajo ritual beliefs and practices seemed particularly urgent.

Klah's choice of the weaving medium to record his sandpainting repertoire presents an additional cultural anomaly, since Navajo weavers are customarily women. The creation of a sandpainting textile is particularly demanding; as Reichard (1986:156) observed, "Accurate sandpaintings [textiles] contain an unlimited amount of detail which few [weavers] can master." Although it is unlikely that any female weaver would have sufficient arcane knowledge to produce a sandpainting textile, it would seem equally improbable that a singer would possess sufficient weaving skills to translate the iconography stored in his memory onto a loom. However, Klah was an accomplished weaver before he turned his skill to ceremonial interpretation. Reichard explains this apparent paradox:

If a Navajo man weaves, he is in the class of "man-woman".... Left Handed [Klah], Singer of Newcomb is the only one of this sort whom I know personally.... He weaves only sandpainting tapestries. Being an accomplished singer, he weaves the designs "out of his own head" (Reichard 1986:161).

The Navajo belief system confers special status and prestige on the "man-woman" (*nadle* in Navajo, meaning "transformed"). The *nadle* play an important role in Navajo mythology and are thought to possess special powers in the real world (Hill 1935). There are some discrepancies concerning the etiology of Klah's inclusion in the *nadle* category. However, whether he was born a hermaphrodite (Newcomb 1964:97), or emasculated as a child by the Utes to subsequently become a transvestite (Reichard 1974:141), Klah's distinguished career as singer and weaver combined both male and female activities. Wheelwright dismisses references to Klah as a transvestite as "not true" (1955:23); nor does she discuss the numerous explicit sexual episodes (including the role of the *nadle*) that are critical to the story of the Creation Myth (Wheelwright 1942). Perhaps she considered the subject too delicate for a lady to address. Nonetheless, the relationship between Klah and Wheelwright developed on the basis of mutual respect and shared interests, apparently devoid of sexual undercurrents.

Initially, Klah expressed some reluctance concerning weaving ceremonial designs. As Newcomb (1964:157) recalls, "He said that sacred symbols should not be put into a rug that would be placed on the floor and walked on every day." However, Newcomb assured him that his sandpainting textiles "would never be used on the floor, but would be hung on the wall of some museum." Although Klah's first sandpainting weavings provoked criticism and apprehension among neighboring Navajos, his prestige as a learned singer ultimately prevailed. Furthermore, he believed that the efficacy of his prayers would ameliorate the potential displeasure of powerful supernatural beings. When it became apparent that disaster had indeed been averted, Klah continued to produce sandpainting textiles and subsequently taught his nieces to weave them, too.

In addition, Klah helped Franc Newcomb and others produce watercolor reproductions of sandpaintings, thus establishing a precedent for collaboration with interested Anglos (Parezo 1983). This agenda for cultural preservation was the primary reason for Klah's decision to work with Mary Wheelwright. He perceived that the collaboration would provide further opportunity to perpetuate his vast ritual repertoire for future generations. He also recognized that Wheelwright could provide the technical resources and financial support to accomplish this goal.

For the next 15 years, Klah and Wheelwright worked closely in collecting accounts of Navajo ceremonies. During most of this time, Klah's nephew, Clyde Beyal, acted as principal interpreter. Klah introduced Wheelwright to other singers so that she could further expand her record of ceremonial information. Wheelwright paid to have the ceremonies conducted so that she could witness and record them. Payment for the transmittal of ritual knowledge was customary for apprentices and also had been a method employed by outsiders since Washington Matthews' study of Navajo ceremonialism in the late nineteenth century.[6] Nevertheless, it was hardly commonplace for a ritual practitioner to share his erudition with a non-Navajo, let alone a woman. Klah's prestige and Wheelwright's perseverance ultimately prevailed.

The years of intense collaborative research were punctuated by two trips away from the Southwest. During the summer of 1930, the Newcombs, Klah, and Beyal went to visit Wheelwright in Northeast Harbor, Maine. Wheelwright recalls that Klah made a sandpainting on the terrace of her home:

Klah wore his traditional dress of cotton trousers and lovely velveteen blouse, his silver necklace and belt, and looked wonderful against the background of the Maine woods. . . . To Klah's joy, many animals walked across his sandpainting. . . . Just before Klah left, a north wind came and destroyed it, which pleased him very much (1955:52).

In 1936, Wheelwright invited Klah and his nephew to visit her at the San Ysidro Ranch near Santa Barbara, California. It was there that Wheelwright recorded Klah's account of the Navajo Creation Myth. The Pacific Ocean had particular significance for Klah, since Navajo legend relates that Changing Woman, the most revered Navajo deity, had gone to live on an island there.

In addition to the important archive of manuscripts, recordings, and sandpainting reproductions pertaining to Navajo religion, Wheelwright also acquired Navajo baskets, jewelry, and textiles while actively supporting the survival and revival of these arts. She also worked with the New Mexico Association on Indian Affairs to develop an eastern market for American Indian arts. As with her study of Navajo ceremonialism, Wheelwright's collecting activities were part of a larger information-gathering process. She wanted to amass and organize the most complete record possible of contemporaneous Navajo life. By the early 1930s, Wheelwright became concerned with the future of her collection. "I began to realize that I had so much material that it should be in safekeeping . . . so I decided to build a repository for it" (1955:62). Fortunately, she could afford to do so. In addition to intelligence, self-reliance, and determination, Wheelwright had the independent financial resources essential for the creation of her museum.

The gift of both building and collection was initially offered to the Laboratory of Anthropology (Lab) in 1927, during the early phases of planning for the laboratory complex in Santa Fe. A controversy soon arose over Wheelwright's determination to build her museum in the shape of the traditional Navajo dwelling and ceremonial space, the octagonal-shaped *hooghan.* Because the museum was to display the sandpaintings, Klah and Wheelwright insisted that a *hooghan* was the only appropriate form to house the exhibits. The laboratory's building committee rejected the design because they believed it was incompatible with the Santa Fe style (i.e., Pueblo Revival) of John Gaw Meem's architectural plan for the laboratory complex (Wheelwright 1955:63; Lab 1931b). Further criticism of Wheelwright's plan came from influential (male) trustees, who argued that a scientific institution should not include a museum "conceived upon an emotional, rather than a scientific basis" (Lab 1931b).

Finally, after five years of troubled negotia-

tions, an irate Wheelwright withdrew her offer. She built her museum adjacent to the laboratory complex on land donated by her friend Amelia Elizabeth White. Noted Santa Fe artist-designer William Penhallow Henderson was appointed architect for the project. With Klah as consultant, the structure emerged as a larger-than-life *hooghan,* complete with interlocking cribbed-log ceiling and an east-facing door. In 1938, Henderson's unique building earned "Honorable Mention for Works of Major Importance in Architecture" from the Architectural League of New York. The citation read, "For the House of Navajo Religion, for its simple dignity and original design." Henderson's wife, distinguished poet Alice Corbin, a close friend of Wheelwright's, served as the first curator; she and Henderson lived in the museum's residential quarters until 1942.

Klah played an active role in all phases of the museum's development. He believed that this special place would provide the perfect sanctuary for his ceremonial collection, and in 1932, he left explicit instructions that his collection of ritual paraphernalia should be left to the museum in perpetuity as a research collection for succeeding generations of Navajo singers (Frisbie 1987: 252). Klah conducted a traditional House Blessing ceremony for the groundbreaking of the museum. Unfortunately, he did not live to participate in its formal opening in November 1937; he had died from pneumonia the preceding February.

The museum was first called the House of Religion (1937–1938), then the Museum of Navajo Ceremonial Art (1938–1976). The museum's original purpose was to explain Navajo religion and to serve as a research center for the study of Navajo and other world religions. Hence, the nucleus of the museum's early collections consisted of objects and archives relating to Navajo ceremonialism that had been assembled during the Wheelwright-Klah collaboration. Exhibits of sandpaintings were rotated on a seasonal basis, providing visitors with the opportunity to view a wide range of iconographic symbols and meta-physical concepts associated with Navajo ceremonialism. Interpretive texts, based on the information collected from Navajo singers, augmented the sandpainting displays. Wheelwright wanted her museum to be more than a

storehouse for museum specimens. . . . She wished to give to the Navajo and the public something transcending a mere museum, something that would catch the spirit of Navajo philosophy and give to our own people [Anglos] perhaps their clear idea of the importance of Indian myth and ritual (Lab 1931a:2).

This pioneering approach to cross-cultural understanding was in marked contrast to the display of artifacts according to typological evolutionary categories, a procedure that was still practiced at many museums throughout the country at the time.

In addition to Navajo ceremonial materials and craft arts, Wheelwright assembled important archival holdings: manuscripts from the major studies of Navajo religion (including the Washington Matthews Papers); over 500 sandpainting reproductions; a number of valuable ethnographic films; and an important archive of Navajo song texts recorded in the field by Wheelwright and others. Although Wheelwright's Navajo studies developed outside mainstream academic anthropology, the significance of her research has become increasingly recognized by Anglo scholars and Navajos alike.[7] In 1956, on the occasion of the twentieth anniversary of the museum's groundbreaking ceremony, Paul Jones, the chairman of the Navajo Tribal Council, wrote, "On behalf of the Navajo people I wish to express our thanks to Miss Wheelwright. . . . The Navajo people will be forever grateful to her for this achievement of building the things of the spirit into visible and physical form in the Museum of Navajo Ceremonial Art" (quoted in Whitehill 1962:414).

After Wheelwright's death in 1958, the museum's leadership passed to her friend and col-league Kenneth Foster. Like Wheelwright, Foster was a student of world religions. His particular interests focused on the belief systems of the Far East. Since Wheelwright had posited linguistic and symbolic connections between people of the Far East (especially Tibet) and the Navajo, she believed that Foster would be able to carry on the museum's original mission as a center for the study of comparative religion. Unfortunately, Foster was ill prepared to be a museum director, and the institution suffered from benign neglect under his tenure. When Foster died of a heart attack in 1964, the museum temporarily closed its doors while the board of trustees decided what to do next. In 1966 the board hired Bertha P. Dutton as the new director. Dutton's career as an archaeologist and museologist are discussed elsewhere in this volume by Cordell, Parezo and Hardin, and Tisdale. Dutton began her museum career as an administrative assistant/secretary to Edgar Lee Hewett. Three years later she persuaded him to create the position of curator of ethnology at the Museum of New Mexico. Dutton (1985a) wryly remembers that "in those days, you had to invent your own job in so many places." Although her work was widely recognized within Santa Fe's intellectual and cultural community, her career as curator did not admit her to the policy-making elite. Among her major accomplishments at the Museum of New Mexico was the development of a Hall of Ethnology, an interpretive exhibit of southwestern Native American cultures. However, she recalls, "That was as far as my ladder permitted, for I was only a woman" (quoted in Bernstein and McGreevy 1988:iv).

This tangential status changed radically when Dutton became director of the Museum of Navajo Ceremonial Art. Mary Wheelwright would have approved; Dutton was every bit as determined and as spirited as the museum's founder. Indeed, the two had met, and worked together, when they both served on the Board of the New Mexico Association on Indian Affairs. Since the Museum of

Navajo Ceremonial Art was not part of the state museum system, Dutton was able to exercise considerable autonomy in her new position. During her tenure the building was remodeled and exhibits of Native American art began to supplement the sandpainting displays. Furthermore, her previous museum experience enabled her to initiate modern practices, including fully cataloguing the ethnographic, archival, and library collections. Under Dutton's scholarly tutelage, the museum also regained its reputation as an important center for Navajo studies. Time proved that Klah and Wheelwright's belief that Navajo ceremonialism would disappear was mistaken. In 1976, in response to objections voiced by Navajo religious elders concerning the museum's role as a non-Navajo interpreter of Navajo religion, the museum changed its name to the Wheelwright Museum of the American Indian. At the same time, the museum gave many Navajo ceremonial materials that had been in its collections to the Ned Hatathli Cultural Center at Navajo Community College in Tsaile, Arizona, where they again reside within the four sacred mountains (Frisbie 1987:341). As the Wheelwright Museum, the new institutional mission reflected the museum's commitment to "enhance understanding between non-Indian and Indian peoples" (Wheelwright Museum 1979).

Today, the museum is a lively, dynamic institution whose purpose is "To respect and support, to record and present, the living traditions and creative expressions of American Indian peoples" (Wheelwright Museum 1992). In the Klah Gallery (the *hooghan*), changing exhibits articulate the museum's broader field of interest in documenting the ongoing vitality of American Indian creativity. However, the remarkable journey toward understanding that emerged from the collaboration between Hastiin Klah and Mary Cabot Wheelwright continues to guide the museum's mission.

AMELIA ELIZABETH WHITE, 1878 – 1972

School of American Research, Laboratory of Anthropology, and Museum of Navajo Ceremonial Art, Santa Fe, New Mexico

She was very well read and well traveled . . . a *grande dame*. She was interested in the School [of American Research] and in scholarship.
Douglas W. Schwartz (quoted in Elliott 1987:64)

Although she did not found a museum of her own, Amelia Elizabeth White's wealth and influence enabled her to play a major role in the establishment, and continued existence, of three important Santa Fe institutions: the School of American Research, Laboratory of Anthropology, and Museum of Navajo Ceremonial Art.

Amelia and her sister Martha (b. 1881) were raised in an affluent environment and socially conditioned by the tenets of altruism. Their father, Horace, was the wealthy, influential owner and editor-in-chief of the *Chicago Tribune* and the *New York Evening Post*. The White sisters first visited Santa Fe in 1923 while en route from New York City to California. They were so charmed by the Santa Fe ambience that they bought two small adobe houses at 660 Garcia Street, together with the property the houses were on—the old Armenta Spanish Land Grant, comprising many hundreds of acres. Gradually the original buildings evolved into a multistructured gracious estate that the sisters named El Delirio (The Madness) (Elliott 1987:63).

Ownership of the Armenta Grant provided an ideal philanthropic vehicle for the sisters. Beginning in 1927, plans for the construction of a private institution, The Laboratory of Anthropology, Inc., had been drafted by an elite cadre from the eastern academic establishment. Organization of the Lab was a politically motivated strategy to contravene the increasing influence of Edgar Lee Hewett, director of the School of American Archaeology (later the School of American Research) and the allied Museum of New Mexico (Stocking 1982). Although the Lab had the support of the Rockefellers, development of the project was contingent upon acquiring sufficient acreage for the envisioned complex that ultimately was to include a library, residences for visiting scholars, and a museum. The White sisters solved the problem by donating 50 acres of land on Camino Lejo, south of the city.

The Laboratory of Anthropology opened its doors in 1931 and promptly embarked on its own archaeological research agenda. Over time the Lab accumulated archaeological holdings of over 3 million artifacts and a collection of southwestern Native American art and ethnography that exceeded 50,000 display-quality objects (Ware 1986:14). In addition, the Lab was the repository for the burgeoning Indian Arts Fund collection begun by Kenneth Chapman and others in 1922 to preserve and revitalize southwestern Native American arts, which had originally attracted the attention and financial support of John D. Rockefeller, Jr. In 1928 the Indian Arts Fund was incorporated as an independent organization with its own board of trustees.

The combined effects of the Great Depression and World War II placed the Lab in precarious financial straits. In 1947, in an effort to save the Lab from complete collapse, "a merger was negotiated, and the Laboratory of Anthropology became a unit of the Museum of New Mexico" (Ware 1986:14). Under the resulting agreement, the Lab's building was given to the museum, and the collections (including the Indian Arts Fund), which continued to be housed at the Lab, came under the purview of the School of American Research. This commingling of the two organizations had important legal implications for the future of both.

The handsome Santa Fe–style (i.e., Pueblo revival) Lab building, designed by architect John Gaw Meem, contained collections storage areas, offices, research facilities, and a modest exhibit area. Other exhibits of the Lab's collections were presented downtown at the Palace of the Governors. However, the plan for a separate museum adjoining the Lab did not reach fruition for another 56 years, when finally, in July 1987, the building for the new Museum of Indian Arts and Culture was completed. Located next door to the Lab, the museum's principal function is to exhibit objects from the Lab's vast archaeological and ethnological holdings. The programs and exhibits of the Museum of Indian Arts and Culture provide public services complementary to those of the Museum of International Folk Art (discussed later) and the Wheelwright Museum, its neighboring institutions.

The "Museum Hill" complex on the Camino Lejo thus owes its existence to the generosity and foresight of the White sisters. In addition to philanthropic activities made possible by their ownership of the Armenta Land Grant, both sisters were involved with other aspects of Santa Fe life. However, Martha was more interested in raising quarter horses in Arizona and establishing the famous Rathmullan Kennels at El Delirio, an enterprise that made Irish Wolfhound breeding history during the early 1930s (Starbuck 1986:53) than in anthropology or Native American art. When Martha died in 1937, Amelia became even further committed to the development of Santa Fe's cultural and intellectual community. She was an active supporter of the Indian Arts Fund and an energetic member of the New Mexico Association on Indian Affairs. She also served on the Board of the Spanish Colonial Arts Society. White's role as a community leader brought her into frequent contact with Mary Cabot Wheelwright. Although they held each other in mutual esteem, White was one of the few persons who routinely challenged Wheelwright's adamant opinions (Lambert 1983, personal communication). Perhaps White felt secure in the knowledge that she had superior academic credentials, with a B.A. from Bryn Mawr College in Pennsylvania, one of the prestigious eastern "Seven Sister" colleges. The donation of land for Wheelwright's museum is nonetheless tangible evidence of White's respect for her friend's accomplishments.

Another abiding interest of White's from the time of her arrival in Santa Fe had been archaeology. While a member of the board of managers for the School of American Research, she developed an enduring respect for the institution's new director, archaeologist Douglas W. Schwartz, who had been appointed in 1967. Under Schwartz's leadership, the School of American Research had become a revitalized and dynamic institution, an independent research center serving "advanced scholarship" (Elliott 1987:49). As a result of her esteem for Schwartz's abilities, in 1966 White (with permission from her surviving sister, Abby) placed El Delirio in trust for the School of American Research (Elliott 1987:64). One year after White's death in 1972, the School, which had formerly been headquartered in the home of its director, Edgar Lee Hewett, moved to the elegant and spacious White estate.

Since that time, innovative programs have proliferated. An active resident scholar's program, an advanced seminar series, and a new publications department complement ongoing archaeological projects. However, the most visible component of the School's new identity resides in the Indian Arts Fund Research Center. The collection begun by Chapman and others in the 1920s grew to become one of the most important holdings of southwestern Native American art in the United States. In 1959, when the New Mexico State Legislature formally dissolved the uneasy union that had existed between the privately supported School and the state-owned Lab, a singular problem arose concerning possession of the vast collections belonging to both institutions. The trustees of both institutions ultimately decided to "vest ownership of the [Indian Arts Fund] . . . in the SAR, and subsequently it was left to the Anthro-

pology division of the Museum to determine ownership of the remainder" (Peckham et al. 1981:37). Because objects frequently had been acquired without clear title, it took three curators (Nancy Fox and Albert Ely for the museum; Betty Toulouse for the School of American Research) 10 years to inventory the collections.[8] In fact, final agreements were not reached until 1976. Once clear title to the Indian Arts Fund collection had been established, the School began to raise funds for a new building to house it. The Indian Arts Research Center opened in 1978, and another building subsequently has been added. The collections are stored on open shelves in climate-controlled vaults, accessible for research. In recognition of the unique opportunity to work with thousands of superlative artifacts, the collections have been intensively studied by Anglo-American and Native American scholars and artists. Thus, White's bequest became the catalyst for the development of a center for the study of human cultures that has gained national, and indeed international prominence.

FLORENCE DIBBLE BARTLETT, 1881 – 1954

Museum of International Folk Art,
Santa Fe, New Mexico
Founded 1953

The Art of the Craftsman is a Bond
Between the Peoples of the World.
Entrance inscription, Museum of
International Folk Art

During their lifetimes, the two daughters of Adolphus Clay Bartlett made notable and lasting contributions to the cultural life of the Southwest. As we have seen, Maie was cofounder of the Heard Museum. Her younger sister, Florence, founded an equally prominent institution, the Museum of International Folk Art in Santa Fe. Bartlett received the college education that Heard had wished for; she graduated from Smith College in 1904. After graduation, she became involved in a wide variety of social and cultural activities in Chicago.

In the early 1920s, Bartlett was among a coterie of unmarried women who founded the San Gabriel Ranch in Alcalde, New Mexico, a hospitable and stimulating respite from city life. Her initial trip to the ranch occurred only a few years after Mary Wheelwright had made her first visit there. Although Bartlett had been to the Southwest to visit her sister in Phoenix, the rural ambience of northern New Mexico presented a dramatic contrast to urban Arizona. San Gabriel Ranch was an isolated English-speaking enclave located in a remote Hispanic valley. During the day, the ranch offered a wide variety of diversions: horseback trips, wagon rides, and picturesque cowboys. The long summer evenings resounded with lively conversation and musical entertainments. However, it was the luminous presence of Hispanic and Native American cultures that provided a unique and indelible experience for San Gabriel's guests.

Bartlett was particularly enchanted with the arts and crafts produced in the nearby Hispanic villages and began to collect representative examples. Like her older sister, she had a well-trained and discerning eye. She began to collect in earnest in the late 1920s after she bought El Mirador, a large hacienda on the property of San Gabriel Ranch. Throughout the Great Depression, San Gabriel struggled for survival. Eventually, Bartlett bought the entire ranch. Soon the 20 rooms that had housed paying guests were overflowing with folk art. She gave serious consideration to establishing a museum and craft institute at the ranch, in the style of the outdoor folk museums of Scandinavia that she admired (Meadows 1986:8). The concept for a composite art school/museum also might have been influenced by the Bartlett family's close association with the Art Institute of Chicago.

However, when Bartlett realized that Alcalde was too inaccessible, she began to explore the possibility of building a museum and related craft school in Santa Fe. The Laboratory of Anthropology had surplus acres on the land that had been donated by the White sisters. Bartlett was able to acquire the land and subsequently hired John Gaw Meem, the architect who had designed the Lab, to draft plans for her school and museum complex. Although Bartlett was a wealthy woman, she did not have an infinite supply of money to spend on the project. It soon became apparent that she would have to make a difficult decision; she could not afford to build both a museum and a school. She chose the museum.

During frequent travels to far-flung and exotic places, Bartlett had acquired a large collection of folk arts. She shared with her sister an idiosyncratic addiction for collecting vernacular arts, in contrast to the acquisition of European fine arts that characterized the more conventional collecting habits of their father and brother. Perhaps the sisters' tastes reflected a declaration of independence from their childhoods, a vehicle for self-actualization. In any case, Bartlett was fascinated by the universality of the creative impulse that compelled ordinary people to fashion functional objects that were decorative as well as useful. She recognized that artifacts produced within the context of everyday life were social, as well as artistic, documents. As Glassie has observed, "It is one message of folk art that creativity is not the special right of rare individuals" (1989:88).

Since the Museum of New Mexico and the Spanish Colonial Arts Society (the Hispanic counterpart of the Indian Arts Fund) had extensive holdings of southwestern American Indian and Hispanic craft arts, Bartlett decided that her museum should concentrate on nonregional folk arts. Her personal collection, consisting of about 4,000 objects, was particularly strong in costumes and Scandinavian folk art. In 1933, as a result of her interest in the perpetuation of Swedish folk arts, she had been awarded the Vasa Order Gold Medal by King Gustav V (Museum of International Folk Art 1963:2).

Ground was broken for the Museum of International Folk Art on August 14, 1950. Although Bartlett was in Nova Scotia at the time, her thoughts were in Santa Fe. She sent a telegram that articulated her most profound convictions: "May the breaking of ground for the erection of the Museum of International Folk Art symbolize the breaking down of barriers between nations and the building up of mutual understanding among nations" (Museum of International Folk Art 1950). On October 5, 1953, Florence Dibble Bartlett officially donated the building and her collections to the state of New Mexico. Thus the Museum of International Folk Art became the third institution in the Museum Hill complex.

The legacy of Florence Dibble Bartlett received further impetus through the contributions of two gifted women whose professional expertise brought new vitality to the museum. Elizabeth Boyd White was the most overt feminist of the new professionals. Despite several marriages, she adopted the unmarked name of E. Boyd. She was a well-respected oil painter who had been instrumental in establishing the famous Rio Grande Painters group.[9] She had been educated in art history at the Pennsylvania Academy of Fine Arts and the École de la Grande Chaumier in Paris.

E. Boyd first went to Santa Fe in 1929 and returned to live there in the 1930s. She went to work for the New Mexico Federal Art Project as research artist and text author for a book entitled *A Portfolio of Spanish Colonial Design in New Mexico.* The Hispanic peoples of New Mexico have a rich tradition of weaving, tinsmithing, wood carving, and most especially, religious art. E. Boyd's interest in Spanish Colonial arts dominated the rest of her career.

During the 1940s Boyd moved to Los Angeles, where she was employed by the Los Angeles County Museum, first as librarian and then as registrar. During this time, she persuaded a friend, artist Cady Wells, to donate his significant collection of Hispanic religious art to the Museum of New Mexico. The gift was made with a major stipulation: that the Museum establish a department of Spanish Colonial arts and hire E. Boyd as curator. Boyd returned to Santa Fe in 1951. She immediately set to work to rehabilitate the moribund Spanish Colonial Arts Society,

which had been founded in the 1920s to preserve and revitalize Hispanic arts. In turn, the society helped Boyd acquire an important collection of santos for the museum (Larcombe 1983:9). She also participated in archaeological excavations of Spanish Colonial sites and was instrumental in the restoration of several important Spanish New Mexican churches. At the museum, she actively pursued her interest in Hispanic religious art, acquiring and documenting objects for the collections. In addition she helped local santeros (makers of religious sculptures and paintings) utilize the collections as a tool for refining their art. The techniques she developed for restoring santos were used at museums throughout the country. Boyd received numerous awards and ultimately became an internationally recognized authority on Spanish Colonial arts. Her scholarly research culminated in *Popular Arts of Spanish New Mexico,* published shortly before her death in 1974. Boyd's seminal research formed the foundation for all subsequent Spanish Colonial art studies, and her flamboyant individualism has become a celebrated chapter in Santa Fe's cultural history.

In 1971 the board of trustees of the Museum of International Folk Art appointed a new director, another outspoken and strong-willed woman, Yvonne Lange. Lange's background was as colorful as the folk art collections that came under her purview. A native of Trinidad, she was fluent in French and Spanish as well as English. Her life experiences had brought her into close contact with a rich variety of indigenous peoples. Before coming to the museum, she had worked at the Milwaukee Public Museum and the Smithsonian Institution. Lange was a dedicated museum professional who, at the age of 46, decided to continue her education. She was admitted into the prestigious Ph.D. folklore program at the University of Pennsylvania. In response to skepticism voiced by friends concerning the advisability of undertaking the rigors of a doctoral program at her age, Lange observed, "Knowledge is knowledge, it can't diminish you" (1987, personal communication).

Lange's dynamic leadership transformed the museum. In 1978, Alexander Girard, noted Santa Fe designer and avid folk art collector, and his wife, Susan, donated their collection of over 700,000 objects to the museum. The gift of the Girard collection and the construction of a new wing to house it was the culmination of ten years of planning, lobbying, fund-raising, and grant writing. The Girard Wing formally opened in 1982. Girard's genius found new expression in the theatrical settings he designed to display his collection. While the Girard Wing stands in visible tribute to the collection and the collector, it also bears tangible witness to Lange's generative achievement. When she retired in 1982, she was appointed director emerita.

Today, Florence Dibble Bartlett's museum is a place where objects and ideas proliferate in tandem. Permanent and changing exhibits stimulate inquiry as they recreate the social, ceremonial, and economic activities of peoples throughout the world.

MARY-RUSSELL FERRELL COLTON,
1889 – 1971

Museum of Northern Arizona,
Flagstaff, Arizona
Founded 1928

Drawn by a vast curiosity and endless enthusiasm we set out to see the mountains, the desert and the people. With packs on our backs, we climbed the San Francisco Peaks and surveyed the world about us.

Mary-Russell Ferrell Colton, 1912
(quoted in Chase 1982:2)

The history of the Museum of Northern Arizona begins with the narrative of another wife-husband team: artist Mary-Russell Ferrell Colton and zoologist/archaeologist Harold S. Colton. Although she is frequently referred to as the "wife of the founder" (see, for example, Anonymous 1971:39), unlike Winifred Gladwin, wife of archaeologist Harold S. Gladwin who founded the Gila Pueblo Museum, Mary-Russell was more than a helpmate; in fact, she played a key role in the development of several significant programs that endure today as an integral part of the museum's identity. Furthermore, her money was critical to the financial survival of the institution.

Mary-Russell Ferrell was born in Louisville, Kentucky, on March 25, 1889, and spent much of her childhood in the comfortable environs of Philadelphia suburbia. Her early aptitude for painting was nurtured and refined at the Philadelphia School of Design for Women, from which she graduated with honors in 1909. She subsequently established her own studio and was a founding member of a group of Pennsylvania women artists called "The Ten" (Chase 1982:1).

She was an avid amateur naturalist and an intrepid camper. On a backpacking trip in British Columbia, she met Harold Colton, a young zoology professor at the University of Pennsylvania. They were married on May 23, 1912. While en route to California for their honeymoon, they stopped in Flagstaff, Arizona. The small town, situated at the base of the towering San Francisco Peaks, was the portal to the Grand Canyon and to the Hopi and western Navajo reservations. The few days that the Coltons spent exploring the area changed the direction of their lives.

Mary-Russell was captivated by the artistic potential of the scenery; her husband was excited by the diversity of flora and fauna. Wanting to explore the terra incognita of Native American lands north and east of Flagstaff, they returned summer after summer. Mary-Russell began a series of paintings that established her reputation as a mature landscape artist. Harold began to survey and catalogue the rich inventory of archaeological sites in the area. The Coltons settled permanently in Flagstaff in 1926.

In 1927 Grady Gammage, president of the Arizona State Teacher's College (now Northern Arizona University), and Frank Lockwood, a member of the English faculty at the college, organized a committee of community leaders to conduct a study of the feasibility of the establishment of a regional museum of natural history (Miller 1985:125). The committee had been formed to create a viable alternative to the systematic removal of local archaeological and natural history specimens by members of scientific expeditions originating in the East. "Doctor" (a sobriquet acquired in recognition of Colton's Ph.D.) and his wife were invited to join the committee and soon became its driving force.

On May 15, 1928, the Northern Arizona Society of Science was founded. The society elected Harold Colton as president and appointed him the unpaid director of the proposed museum (Miller 1985:131). Its mission was to preserve, study, interpret, and exhibit local collections of archaeological, ethnological, and natural history materials pertaining to the Colorado Plateau. The museum opened on September 18, 1928, housed in two rooms in the Flagstaff Woman's Club building. Mary-Russell Ferrell Colton was asked to organize and head a department of arts and crafts (Miller 1985:132). When the collections outgrew the cramped quarters, the Coltons built a spacious, rambling building on their ranch property west of town. The new museum opened in 1935.

Colton's principal contributions to the museum were directly related to her artistic interests. She initiated an annual exhibition for Arizona artists that was a popular attraction from 1929 until 1936 (Heard Museum 1980:1), when it became too large for even the new museum facility. However, the quality of the museum's fine arts holdings continued to reflect Colton's finely tuned aesthetic tastes. She also was devoted to art education. She developed an innovative traveling suitcase exhibit, "Treasure Chest," that became an exemplar for outreach programs. In 1942 the Boston Museum of Fine Arts included the "Treasure Chest" in a pioneering exhibit called "The Museum in Education" (Chase 1982:3).

Colton's most enduring legacy was the creation of the annual Hopi and Navajo craft art shows. These juried sales exhibits had a profound impact on the survival and revitalization of the arts of both groups. Her familiarity with the archaeological prototypes of Hopi pottery caused her to be acutely concerned with the commercialization of the craft during the 1920s. With the exception of the beautiful Sikyatki-inspired pottery of the Nampeyo family, the distinguished tradition of finely decorated ceramic vessels had deteriorated into the production of souvenirs for the tourist market. Hopi basketry production also was in a serious decline. As Katharine Bartlett recalls, "The state of Hopi arts . . . was really at a very low ebb, everything had been reduced to a curio-type. . . . She [Colton] realized what the Hopis had done, and what they could do" (Bartlett 1987, personal communication).

During 1929, Colton visited the Hopi mesas on a regular basis, supplying materials, photographs, and actual examples of the best historic-period Hopi craft arts. She embarked upon an extensive study of Hopi vegetal dyes and encouraged the use of traditional raw materials for textile weaving, basket making, and pottery decoration. These efforts culminated in the first annual Hopi Craftsman exhibition in 1930. Many Hopis initially were skeptical about the merit of the project, but after participating craftspeople began to earn substantial money from the sales of their work, increasing numbers of artisans became involved.

Several years later, in 1938, Colton and Museum of Northern Arizona Staff Artist Virgil Hubert began to work with Hopi silversmiths to develop a distinctive jewelry style utilizing an overlay technique in combination with traditional pottery, basketry, and textile designs (King 1976:47). At about the same time, Colton began visiting the western Navajo Reservation to collect textiles, pots, and baskets for the first annual Navajo show, which opened in 1942. Colton's instrumental role in the survival and revival of Native American arts was acknowledged by the Indian Arts and Crafts Board of the United States Department of Interior in 1959 when she was awarded a certificate of appreciation, "In recognition of outstanding services in the preservation, encouragement and development of the Arts and Crafts of the American Indian. [signed] Rene F. d'Harnoncourt, Chairman" (Museum of Northern Arizona 1959). Museum staff members continue to visit Hopi villages, Navajo families, and reservation trading posts to assemble the finest available craft arts for the annual shows. Recently, a Zuni Show has been initiated by the curator of ethnology, Linda Eaton. Without a doubt, these exhibits are among the most popular of the museum's programs, attracting thousands of collectors from all parts of the country.

Shortly after the establishment of the museum, the Coltons invited Katharine Bartlett (no relation to the Chicago Bartletts) to work at the museum for the summer. "They needed someone to take care of the stuff coming out of a small [archaeological] excavation project . . . so I came down to spend the summer and I've been there ever since" (1985:3). At that time, Bartlett was about to complete her M.A. in anthropology at the University of Denver, where the departmental focus was on physical anthropology and archaeology. As Parezo and Hardin note elsewhere in this volume, Bartlett quickly became an important member of the museum's professional staff and a close and valued friend of both Coltons.

During her more than 50 years of association with the museum, Bartlett has worn many hats. Her first job was to catalogue the archaeological and ethnological collections. At about the same time, she began to help "Doctor" organize his personal library. His collection consisted of books and journals encompassing a wide variety of scientific subjects: zoology, geology, botany, archaeology, and ethnology. This core collection expanded as new donations were offered by other members of the Flagstaff scientific community.

In the 1960s the library moved to permanent quarters in the research center. Bartlett was able to hire a professional librarian to help with the task of cataloging the ever-increasing collection. The system they used was borrowed from the Laboratory of Anthropology, based on a model developed at the American Museum of Natural History in New York City, specifically designed to facilitate archaeological and ethnological research.

The library's extensive collections are used by visiting scholars from across the country. Bartlett has achieved a national reputation for her role as the Museum of Northern Arizona's librarian. She officially retired in 1978 but continues to do volunteer work at the library, where a spacious and comfortable reading room has been named in her honor. Bartlett's name has become as synonymous with the history of the Museum of Northern Arizona as is that of the Coltons. Her expertise and warm personal charm resonate throughout the institution she helped develop. About her long career, she observes with characteristic good humor, "At this point, in a museum filled with antiquities, I fit right in" (1985).

Thus, the artist and the "Doctor," with the help of their friend and assistant, created an institution that remains at the forefront of significant Arizona cultural achievements. Colton's adventurous life, artistic creativity, and enlightened concern for native peoples continue to provide enriching experiences for both local and national audiences. Today, the Museum of Northern Arizona is encompassed within a large campus with several departmental outbuildings and a research center, built in the 1950s, to house collections, archives, and the library. The main building is comprised of exhibit areas with displays pertaining to the natural history of the Colorado Plateau and interpretive exhibits that explore the lives of southwestern Native American peoples in historical and cultural context.

MILLICENT ROGERS, 1902 – 1953

*Millicent Rogers Museum, Taos, New Mexico
Founded 1953*

The discovery of Taos . . . changed
Millicent's life. It seemed to her a romantic
outpost, outside of time.

Neil Letson (1984:111)

The story of Millicent Rogers' life can be written in two distinct chapters: Before and After
Taos. Her grandfather, Henry Huttleston Rogers,
was a partner in Rockefeller's Standard Oil Company, a founder of U.S. Steel and Anaconda Copper, and owner of numerous railroads. Rogers
grew up in castles and vast estates. Her clothes
were designed by Schiaparelli and Valentina, her
jewelry fashioned by Cartier and Boucheron; her
beauty was legendary. She danced with the Prince
of Wales, dined with Clark Gable, had tea with
Ian Fleming. Yet there was a dark side to this
fable of glamour and opulence. A childhood bout
with rheumatic fever not only resulted in frail
health but also left Rogers with a presentiment of
her own mortality, which propelled the almost
pathologically frenetic pace of her life. Nor was
there a prince charming with whom she could
live happily ever after: she was married and divorced three times.

Rogers' discovery of Taos soothed her tensions and replenished her creative resources.
Figuratively, the cultural landscape of northern
New Mexico did not conform to the contours of
conventional society; literally, the endless vistas
and rugged mountains fostered new ways of
viewing reality. For Rogers, both literal and figurative landscapes were liberating. She bought a
picturesque adobe house and established a salon
for visiting luminaries, thereby threatening Mabel Dodge Luhan's hegemony as "Queen of the
Mountain" (Rudnick 1984:328). Although her
previous high society visage appears to have ac-

companied her to Taos, however, her life there
was infused with new vitality, suffused with new
vision.

Several years before Rogers established residence in Taos, her outré taste in jewelry had made
her increasingly dissatisfied with the efforts of the
famous jewelers she patronized. She began to design and eventually to fabricate her own distinctive pieces. Her work received modest acclaim
and even achieved a degree of fame with a gold
necklace she called "Figures of Growth," made for
her friend, Dame Edith Sitwell (Letson 1984:
114). In Taos, the sculptural forms found in architecture and landscape provided her a fresh
source of inspiration. The silversmithing techniques and iconographic inventory of the Navajos
and Pueblos soon became an additional catalyst
for her creativity. She rapidly matured as both designer and craftsperson.

As Rogers' interest and knowledge concerning
southwestern Native American jewelry grew, she
began to collect it. She was not interested in
recording information concerning the maker;
rather, it was the aesthetic merit of each individual object that compelled her acquisitive ardor. Ultimately, her collection consisted of some
of the most beautiful and unique American Indian jewelry available during the 1940s and early
1950s. Some were rare turn-of-the-century examples; however, she also bought contemporaneous pieces, liberally paying the craftspeople who
made them. Although jewelry remained the primary focus of her collecting activities, she did not
completely neglect other regional arts. By the
time she died, she had amassed a collection of
more than 2,000 objects that included southwestern Native American baskets and textiles as well
as Hispanic furniture and folk art.

After her death in 1953, Paul Peralta-Ramos, a
son from her second marriage, decided to build a
museum in her memory. First housed in an historic Taos home, in 1968 the museum moved to
a large, rambling adobe structure located on Taos

Mesa, four miles north of the village. Until 1977, the museum was run by Rogers' secretary of many years, Dixie Yapples, and her husband, John. During the past ten years, professional leadership and strong financial support have resulted in a spacious new gallery, expanded storage areas, and enriched collections. To visit the Millicent Rogers Museum today is to experience a rich visual feast of distinguished objects, made by native inhabitants of the Southwest, with core collections acquired by a woman with distinguished taste.

FLORENCE HAWLEY ELLIS, 1906 – 1991

The Florence Hawley Ellis Museum,
Abiquiu, New Mexico
Founded 1980

The philosophy of people is expressed in

the objects they make, but how they make

them is expressive of who they are.

Florence Hawley Ellis (1987,
personal communication)

The spectacular landscape of the Ghost Ranch country west of Santa Fe, made famous by the paintings of Georgia O'Keefe, is home to a new museum built in 1980 and named after its founder, Florence Hawley Ellis. (See Cordell's chapter for a discussion of Ellis' life and contribution to archaeology.) The establishment of this museum exemplifies the new age of professionalism with a daughter of academe in the role of museum founder.

When Ellis retired from the Anthropology Department at the University of New Mexico in 1971, she became a part-time staff member at the Ghost Ranch, a nonprofit educational institution that has operated under the aegis of the Presbyterian Church since 1955. She initiated programs in archaeology and ethnology for the ranch. During the summer months, she began to take small groups of people to survey and excavate archaeological sites in the region. They discovered the summer camps of prehistoric Gallina peoples (ancestors of today's Jemez Pueblo population) and associated artifacts. Their work attracted such great local interest that a modest exhibit was organized. From this small achievement, the idea of a museum was born. Through the support of participants in the Ghost Ranch's programs, the museum became a reality. Ellis' strong conviction that objects represent a tangible means of understanding cultures and peoples is reflected in her museum. The principal objective of the museum is to use the collections (primarily archaeological and ethnological specimens from Ellis' personal holdings) to document the life patterns of the peoples in the region: Puebloans, Navajos, Apaches, and Hispanics. Of particular interest is a large chart that illustrates the archaeological sequence of the area, beginning with the Archaic period. The connection between prehistoric Anasazi populations and present day Pueblo peoples is illustrated through a diagram of language families. With typical acerbity, Ellis observes, "That they don't speak 'Indian' is complete news to many people" (1987, personal communication).

Although the museum attracts a small number of tourists and is routinely visited by participants in the Ghost Ranch's educational programs, it is of unique value to local residents. Under Ellis' tutelage an active program has been established for schoolchildren in the area. The Florence Hawley Ellis Museum thus provides an oasis of knowledge for a very appreciative regional audience.

CONCLUSION

The apotheosis of the Bostonian establishment, the Peabody Museum at Harvard, became the repository for the southwestern artifacts collected as a result of Mary Hemenway's philanthropic largesse. In contrast, the collections acquired personally and in situ by twentieth-century daughters of affluence became the catalysts for institution building in the Southwest.

The lives and worldviews of indigenous

peoples stood in dramatic contrast to the ethos of early twentieth-century Anglo-America. Similarly, the objects made by native peoples represented a tangible symbol of new worlds discovered. Through their collecting activities, these women reified their physical and emotional separation from the social and intellectual norms of their upbringing. Yet while collecting and museum creating can be viewed within the context of self-actualization, at the same time these activities were guided by a deeply ingrained social and philanthropic conscience. Furthermore, museums were institutions that were inherently—and historically—the product of Western civilization. Thus, in one sense, the daughters of affluence were forging new frontiers; in another, they remained culture-bound to the mores and values of their forebears.

Nonetheless, from their very inception, the southwestern museums established by women had a singular ontogenesis. Rather than developing as a platform for eastern sociopolitical ideologies, each originated as an idiosyncratic response to the southwestern experience. The vast region provided literal and figurative space for fresh precedents to take root. Here the daughters of affluence found the freedom to explore the natural and cultural landscapes that surrounded them. The persuasive voice of their inherited wealth redefined the boundaries of institutional power structures. The museums they founded were intensely personal statements and, frequently, accidental inventions. The founders achieved prestige and recognition that would not have been possible in their cities of origin. Indeed, most were viewed as eccentric—at best—by friends and relatives in the East.

The era of the daughters of affluence was followed by that of professional women. Although in most instances the reins of leadership passed to men, women with advanced degrees in anthropology, history, and art history ushered in an age of scholarship that conferred new prominence on their respective institutions. Increasing professionalism resulted in more rigorous standards of practice and in vigorous growth of collections and facilities, yet each institution continues to acknowledge the totemic imprint of its founder or founders.

NOTES

1. In addition to references cited, this paper is based on the following sources:

Maie Bartlett Heard: Archives of the Heard Museum, Phoenix, Diana Pardue, librarian.

Sharlot Madbrith Hall: Archives of the Sharlot Hall Museum, Prescott, Ariz., Sue Abbey, archivist.

Mary Cabot Wheelwright: Archives of the Wheelwright Museum of the American Indian, Santa Fe, Steve Rogers, curator of collections; Archives of the Laboratory of Anthropology, Santa Fe, Laura Holt, librarian, and Willow Powers, archivist; interviews with friends and relatives of Wheelwright's conducted in 1982 and 1983 in Boston and Northeast Harbor, Maine, and in Albuquerque and Santa Fe in 1983–1988.

Amelia Elizabeth White: Archives of the School of American Research, Santa Fe, Betty Kingman, librarian emerita; and Archives of the Laboratory of Anthropology.

Florence Dibble Bartlett and E. Boyd: Archives of the Museum of International Folk Art, Santa Fe, Judith Sellers, librarian.

Mary-Russell Ferrell Colton: Archives of the Museum of Northern Arizona, Flagstaff, Katharine Bartlett, librarian emerita, Ann Walka, librarian, and Karen L. Fogg, assistant librarian.

Millicent Rogers: Archives of the Millicent Rogers Museum, Taos, N.M., Dena Lewis, registrar.

Interviews provided data for the accounts of Dutton (May 15, 1987); Lange (October 10, 1987); Katharine Bartlett (January 29, 1987); and Ellis (May 7, 1987).

2. According to Sylvia Loomis, Wheelwright's amanuensis, this autobiographical memoir was compiled over a period of time ending in 1955 (Loomis 1984, personal communication).

3. Los Luceros was entered on the New Mexico Register of Historic Places on January 9, 1970, and on the National Register on October 20, 1983.

4. In the literature Klah is referred to as Hosteen. Hastiin is the correct Navajo spelling. In Navajo his name is *Tł'aai,* left-handed. The Navajo word for ceremonial practitioner is *hataałii,* singer, in recognition of the large repertoire of chant-songs that are associated with the ceremony. Although these practitioners are frequently referred to as medicine men, singer is more faithful to Navajo usage. Navajo is often spelled Navaho: Navajo is the tribal preference.

5. Newcomb's biography of Klah (1964) was an additional result of their close relationship.

6. Two of Matthews' informants, Tall Chanter and Laughing Chanter, were Klah's Nightway teachers (Newcomb 1964:111; Wheelwright 1955:23).

7. In addition to the extensive archive on Navajo religion, Wheelwright also published numerous articles on the subject, as well as a four-volume Navajo Religion series published by the Museum of Navajo Ceremonial Art (now out of print).

8. Fox joined the staff of the Museum of New Mexico in 1954. In 1982 she was appointed senior curator of anthropology collections. She retired in 1989 as curator emerita.

9. The original group of Rio Grande Painters included Gustave Baumann, William Penhallow Henderson, Victor Higgins, John Marin, Will Shuster, and John Sloan.

Left: Mary Austin and Ernest Seton in Santa Fe. Photographer: Carol Stryker. Negative No. 14248. *Courtesy of the Museum of New Mexico.*

Below: Florence Dibble Bartlett, Director Robert B. Inverarity, and Paul Coze, representative from the French government, unpacking a gift to the museum from the French government, 1953. Photographer: E. Johnson. Negative No. 1252. *Courtesy of the Museum of International Folk Art, Museum of New Mexico, Santa Fe.*

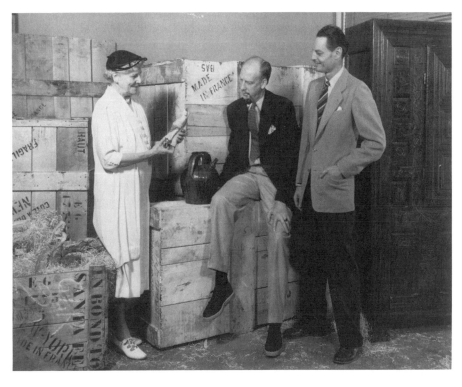

Ruth Benedict with two Blackfeet men, mid 1940s.
Negative No. 86-1323. *Courtesy of the National
Anthropological Archives, Smithsonian Institution.*

Franz Boas and Alfred Kroeber on picnic, ca. 1925.
Photographer: Esther Goldfrank. Negative No. 86-
1313. *Courtesy of the National Anthropological Archives,
Smithsonian Institution.*

Ruth Bunzel, New York City, 1985. From the video-documentary, Daughters of the Desert. *Courtesy of the Wenner-Gren Foundation for Anthropological Research.*

Harold S. Colton, Katharine Bartlett, and Mary-Russell Colton. Staff of Museum of Northern Arizona, 1936. *Back row:* L. F. Brady, John C. McGregor, Mary-Russell Colton, Harold S. Colton, Katharine Bartlett, Virgil Hubert. *Front row:* Jimmy Kewanwytewa, Lyndon Hargrave. Photographer: Watson Smith. Negative No. 12740. *Courtesy of the Museum of Northern Arizona.*

Chona making a basket, 1931. Photographer: Ruth Underhill. Negative No. UN82-328. *Courtesy of the Photo Archives, Denver Museum of Natural History. All rights reserved.*

Bertha Dutton at Las Madres site in Galisteo Basin, New Mexico, 1963. Photographer: Paul Theit. *Courtesy of Bertha Dutton and the Museum of New Mexico.*

Left: Dean Byron Cummings at Rainbow Bridge, 1953. Photographer: E. Tad Nichols. *Courtesy of the Arizona State Museum, University of Arizona, and Tad Nichols.*

Below: Florence Hawley Ellis, Gladys Phare, Emil Haury, and Clara Lee Tanner at University of Arizona field school, 1926. *Courtesy of the Arizona Historical Society/Tucson.*

Earle Pliny Goddard at Columbia University picnic, ca. 1925. Photographer: Esther Goldfrank. Negative No. 86-1315. *Courtesy of the National Anthropological Archives, Smithsonian Institution.*

Erna Fergusson, 1932. Photographer: Will Connell. Negative No. 59764. *Courtesy of the Museum of New Mexico.*

"NOT IN THE ABSOLUTE SINGULAR":
REREADING RUTH BENEDICT

Barbara A. Babcock

All our observation reinforces the testimony of our easy assent to the familiar, and we accept
without any ado the equivalence of human nature and of our own cultural standards. But many
primitives have a different experience. They have seen their religion go down before the white
man's. Their economic system, their marriage prohibitions. They have laid down the one and
taken up the other, and are quite clear and sophisticated about variant arrangements of human
life. If they do talk about human nature, they do it in plurals, not in the absolute singular, and
they will derive dominant characteristics of the white man from his commercial institutions,
or from his conventions of warfare, very much after the fashion of the anthropologist.

Ruth Benedict
(1929)

A WOMAN later described as "a tall and slender Platonic ideal of a poetess" (Barnouw
1949:242), Ruth Benedict (1887–1948) began
her study of custom by steeping herself "in
the lives of restless and highly enslaved women
of past generations" (Journal, November 1914,
AAW:132).[1] "Slowly and painfully, over many
years of frequent depression and perplexity, [she]
found a path away from the traditional set of social expectations for women to her own distinctive identity and creativity" (Bateson 1984:
118).[2] Frequently describing herself as "not having strength of mind not to need a career" (AAW:
3), Benedict was 32 years old when she discovered
anthropology and began one of the profession's
most distinguished careers. Within 15 years, she
had authored the most influential book in twentieth-century anthropology, *Patterns of Culture*
(1934b), and had been starred as a leading scientist in *American Men of Science* (Cattell 1933). Like
her friend and colleague Edward Sapir, she found
in cultural anthropology "the healthiest of all
skepticisms," and her anthropology has rightly
been described as "one great effort in behalf of the
idea of cultural relativity" (Kardiner and Preble
1961:208) and, I should add, in behalf of nonabsolutist interpretation. Given her sensitivity to
the complexity, mediatedness, and multideter-
minancies of cultures, of texts, and of the interpretation thereof, in everything she wrote "there

was always some lyrical awareness of balance and phrase which went far above and beyond the normal call of academic duty" (Barnouw 1949:242). The lyricism as well as the irony of her prose also went very much against the conventions of anthropological discourse.

I wanted so desperately to know how
other women had saved their souls alive.
Ruth Benedict (AAW: 519) [3]

From childhood, Ruth Fulton Benedict's life was characterized by a failure to fit into roles appropriate to her sex and her time. As she herself described and as her biographers Mead, Modell, and Caffrey have amply documented, hers was a traumatic, unhappy childhood. Her physician father died when she was two years old and her mother, subject to fits of weeping and paroxysms of grief, supported the family by teaching. In contrast to her younger sister, Ruth was disinclined to domestic duties in the Shattuck household, where the family moved after the death of Ruth's father. Here she escaped as often as she could with her maternal grandfather to the barn and the fields and into a world of her own imagining. If she did not want to hear her mother, at times she literally could not, for a childhood attack of measles left her partially deaf and exacerbated her sense of alienation.

Despite the difficulties of her deafness, Ruth excelled in school and found in reading and writing a legitimate escape from family relationships and duties. She received a scholarship to Vassar, where she studied English literature. By the time she graduated as a Phi Beta Kappa scholar in 1909, she had already published poetry and prize-winning critical essays such as "Literature and Democracy" and "The Racial Traits of Shakespeare's Heroes." In the fall of 1910, she joined two Vassar classmates for a year abroad, which exceeded her expectations. It was, she wrote to Florence Keys, a "realization of a dream I hoped to have that never disappointed and never seemed

empty" (RBP:RF/FK 1910). She returned to a very disappointing job as a caseworker for the Charity Organization Society in Buffalo and once again had to battle the "blue devils" of depression. In 1911, Ruth and her mother moved to Pasadena, California, to join her sister Margery and her family. Still in search of meaningful work, Ruth took a teaching job at the Westlake School for Girls.

Living in these circumstances and working with "old maids" who shared their experiences and regrets with her prompted some gloomy reflections on the role and fate of women in our society. As Margaret Caffrey points out, "She had discovered, within three years of leaving college, the limited possibilities open to women. The two most favored areas for women, teaching and social work, were female ghettos, limited in scope, salary, and status. She could not reconcile herself to a life in either area" (1989:68). And as Benedict herself wrote in her journal in October 1912, "I've just come through a year in which I have not dared to think . . . not dared to be honest, not even with myself," and went on to make the following remarks:

So much of the trouble is because I am a woman. To me it seems a very terrible thing to be a woman. There is one crown which perhaps is worth it all—a great love, a quiet home, and children. We all know that is all that is worth while, and yet we must peg away, showing off our wares on the market if we have money, or manufacturing careers for ourselves if we haven't. We have not the motive to prepare ourselves a "life-work" of teaching, of social work—we know that we would lay it down with hallelujah in the height of our success, to make a home for the right man. And all the time in the background of our consciousness rings the warning that perhaps the right man will never come. A great love is given to very few. Perhaps this make-shift time filler of a job is our life work after all. It is all so cruelly wasteful. There are so few ways in which we can compete with men—surely not in teaching or in social work. If we are not to have the chance to fulfill our one potentiality—the power of loving—why were we not born men? At least we could have had an occupation then (AAW:119–20).

In June 1914, thinking she had found her "great love," she married Stanley Benedict, a research chemist at Cornell Medical College, and settled into the life of a housewife in suburban New York City. In November of that year, after noting how happy, satisfying, and transforming her relationship with Stanley was, she outlined her plans for the winter. She hoped to study Shakespeare and Goethe, but her "pet scheme" was

to steep myself in the lives of restless and highly enslaved women of past generations and write a series of biographical papers from the standpoint of the 'new woman.' My conclusion so far as I see it now is that there is nothing 'new' about the whole thing . . . that the restlessness and groping are inherent in the nature of women (AAW:132).

The hoped-for children did not come, and Ruth was increasingly preoccupied with her "own ambitions" and her "sense of futility." "Surely," she wrote in December 1915, "the world has need of my vision as well as of charity committees; it is better to grow straight than to twist myself into a doubtfully useful footstool" (AAW:135). A year later, at Christmas of 1916, she told Stanley, "For the sake of our love . . . I must pay my way in a job of my own." He told her in return that "whatever the job, it would not hold me; nothing ever had" (AAW:138).

Benedict dealt with her unhappy marriage as she had with her childhood, by writing: "Expression is the only justification of life that I can feel without prodding. The greatest relief I know is to have put something in words" (Journal, October 1920, AAW:143). In addition to her journal, she poured her frustrations and her passions into poems, which she later published under the pseudonym Anne Singleton. Both her sense of singleness, of alienation, and her desire to escape the tyranny of custom and dreams of domesticity

in fantasy if not in fact are embodied in the last stanza of "Unicorns at Sunrise":

Throw slack the reins, and keep no memory
Of foolish dreams we dreamed of ripened corn
In barns, and red fire on the hearth. Be free
As unicorns, that are but fantasy
Unpledged to any truth, a single horn
Against reality.

(AAW:482)

Believing that "the feminist movement needs heroines," Benedict devoted much of her writing in this period of her life to "New Women of Three Centuries," her empirical biography of three different lives in three different times and places: Mary Wollstonecraft, Margaret Fuller, and Olive Schreiner. As Judith Modell has remarked,

One cannot read the drafts of "Mary Wollstonecraft" without realizing the extent to which the eighteenth-century woman's life became a model and a challenge for Ruth's life . . . that the attraction of her subject's "lavish expense of spirit" threatened her aimed-for equilibrium . . .

. . . [and that she] did not wholly anticipate the quandary she got into by sharing, even vicariously, these "enacted principles" (Modell 1983:103, 106).

The more involved she became with Wollstonecraft's "superb ego," the more her feminism became a "passionate attitude" and, as she wrote in 1916, "more and more I realize I want publication" (AAW:135). After completing a draft of the Wollstonecraft essay, Benedict sent it and a prospectus for the book, retitled "Adventures in Womanhood," to Houghton Mifflin (Benedict n.d.). "She needed the recognition represented by publisher approval to bolster her sense of worth and possibly to 'prove' her case to Stanley . . . [who] doubted her ability to stick to the project" (Modell 1983:107). When Houghton Mifflin rejected the essay in 1919, "she jammed drafts, notes, and sketches into a carton . . . [and] sent away for the course catalog from the recently established New School for Social Research" (Modell 1983:108).

> I haven't strength of mind not to
> need a career.
>
> *Ruth Benedict (AAW 1973)*[4]

In the fall of 1919, Benedict enrolled in a course very much related to her personal concerns: "Sex in Ethnology," which consisted of "surveys of a number of societies presenting a distinctive distribution of functions between the sexes, and of topical analysis of the division of labor between men and women" (New School 1919: 14). The course was taught by Elsie Clews Parsons, wealthy feminist sociologist-turned-ethnographer, who had been instrumental in founding the New School. This nonconformist woman believed that "from such rigid classification the mind as it matures seeks escape. So a maturing culture struggles against its categories" (Parsons 1915: 105). She wrote,

The more thoroughly a woman is classified the more easily is she controlled . . . The new woman means the woman not yet classified, perhaps not classifiable, the woman new not only to men, but to herself. She is bent on finding out for herself, unwilling to live longer at second hand, dissatisfied with expressing her own will to power merely through the ancient media, through children, servants, younger women and uxorious men. She wants to be not only a masterless woman, one no longer classified as daughter or wife, she wants a share in the mastery men arrogate (Parsons 1916h: 56–57).

In Parsons, Benedict found a kindred spirit and a courageous role model who "fearlessly rejected all conventions that constrained the free development of personality" (Hare 1985: 7).

Parsons had turned to ethnography after a trip to the Southwest in 1910 and had come to believe that empirical anthropology with "its techniques for studying the ways in which self-expression is checked by social forces" was a more effective way of promoting her convictions than direct propaganda (Hare 1985: 135). Of Benedict as of Parsons it could be said that "she studied the science of society the better to fight back against society" (Kroeber 1943: 252), and Parsons' preoccupation with the relationship between individual creativity and sociocultural constraints was to inform all of Benedict's anthropology. If their feminist motivations were similar, their intellectual styles and their anthropological methods were very different. Parsons was the more inductive, given to careful ethnographic description and compendia of empirical data. (See Hieb's chapter in this volume for more on Parsons' anthropological methods.) Benedict was deductive in her approach and subsequently trafficked less in description than in a "distinctive sort of redescription: the sort that startles" (Geertz 1988: 112).

During the next two years, Benedict took several more courses at New School with the brilliant and erratic Alexander Goldenweiser and was deeply influenced by this generous and enthusiastic teacher who "could smell a totalitarian under any disguise" and was "eager to build bridges over positions separated by an infinite abyss" (Hook et al. 1940: 31). "The most philosophical of anthropologists," Goldenweiser was very much concerned with psychological and psychoanalytical questions relevant to the study of culture and was responsible for "giving Benedict an early awareness of the possibility of psychological patterning at the base of culture" (Briscoe 1979: 452). After two and a half years, Parsons and Goldenweiser decided that Benedict should get a Ph.D. in anthropology, and Parsons went uptown to Columbia to recommend her to Franz Boas. "Quickly sensing the vigorously imaginative mind veiled by her painfully shy demeanor, Boas waived credit requirements," and after just three semesters, Benedict received her Ph.D. in 1923 (Stocking 1974: 71). Her dissertation, "The Concept of the Guardian Spirit in North America," was a library study that not only reflected Boas' interest in the diffusion of culture traits but also expressed Benedict's interest in the power of religious awe and in the patterns into which the vision-complex was formalized in a given culture.[5] Anticipating Lévi-Strauss' concept of *bricolage,* she concluded,

It is, so far as we can see, an ultimate fact of human nature that man builds up his culture out of disparate elements, combining and recombining them; and until we have abandoned the superstition that the result is an organism functionally interrelated, we shall be unable to see our cultural life objectively, or to control its manifestations (1923a:84–85).

Her assessment and interpretation of the diffusion studies that Boas had encouraged was expressed many years later in one of several obituary essays she wrote for her teacher:

Dissemination of traits was one of the processes that always had to be taken into account before it was possible to understand the working of the human mind in its cultural creations; it was not an end in itself nor did it by itself furnish the key to the understanding of culture. It was ancillary. The ultimate goal was to understand the process by which each human group built up its own version of life and code of behavior (1943:29).

Boas was stimulated to action "because the conditions of our culture ran counter to [his] ideals" (Boas 1938:202); his whole outlook on social life was determined by the question "How can we recognize the shackles that tradition has laid upon us? For when we recognize them, we are also able to break them" (Boas 1938:204). Between him and the quiet, questing woman who admired his energy, his principles, and his stern devotion to his discipline there developed "a mutual dependency and intellectual exchange that lasted until his death in 1942" (Modell 1975:195). As a German Jew, Boas experienced racism firsthand; as an anthropologist he believed "it is pertinent to ask whether any group has a rational basis for a claim to rights not accorded to others" (1938:203); as professor and chair of anthropology at Columbia, he was especially "hospitable" to women, remarking in 1920, "All my best students are women" (Goldfrank 1978:18). Presumably, he regarded Benedict as the best of the best,

for she stayed on at Columbia first as a teaching assistant, then as a lecturer on a series of one-year appointments after receiving her Ph.D. and became indispensable to Boas. He did not, however, give her the position of teaching his Barnard class when he gave it up in 1923. He had persuaded the Barnard administration to replace him with a full-time instructor, and since Gladys Reichard, another favorite student, was 30 years old and single, he felt she needed the job more. Benedict was sorely disappointed, and this was no doubt one of the several factors contributing to strained and distant relations between these two women over the next 25 years. (For more on Reichard, see Lamphere's chapter in this volume.) Boas did, however, conspire with Elsie Clews Parsons to provide funding for Benedict, especially after her application to the National Research Council was turned down because of her age despite Parsons' intervention. In their experience, Frank Lillie wrote, "a person who has not already become established in University work [by age 35] is not very promising material for development" (RBP: FL/ECP 5/23/24).

Whether teaching at Columbia or working on a concordance of southwestern mythology and folklore funded by Elsie Clews Parsons, Benedict lived in a New York City apartment and commuted on weekends to Bedford Hills to see Stanley and sustain a disintegrating marriage. Although she had realized in 1920 that "the more I control myself to his requirements, the greater violence I shall do my own—kill them in the end" (AAW:143), she did not separate from Stanley completely until 1930. Boas finally recognized that she needed a "real" job to support herself, and secured her appointment as an assistant professor in 1931. It was, as Sapir wrote in congratulating her, "a modest and criminally belated acknowledgement of [her] services" (RBP: ES/RB 3/16/31).

In 1922, Ruth Benedict had made the acquaintance of two individuals with whom she developed deep and mutually influential relationships.

One was linguist and anthropologist Edward Sapir, whose letter to her praising and commenting at length on her dissertation initiated a lively and voluminous correspondence in which they shared their interests in anthropology, psychology, and poetry and a friendship that lasted until his death in 1939. The other was Margaret Mead, a student in Boas' Barnard anthropology course, who became her colleague, confidante, lover, and literary executor. Mead also shared and stimulated Benedict's interests in poetry and psychology, but unlike Sapir, she took as much from if not more than she gave to the brilliant but unassuming woman who encouraged her to study anthropology and interceded with Boas to allow her to go to Samoa.

Because of her generosity of spirit and her own search for meaning as a woman, Benedict mediated between many Columbia students and "Papa Franz," edited and rewrote countless dissertations, and in later years if neither Boas or Parsons could come up with monies for research and publication, gave them "no strings attached" grants out of her own pocket. As Ruth Underhill remarked shortly before she died, "Boas and Benedict opened a door through which a light shined on me," and she was not alone in this experience. During the years (1921–1940) when Benedict was most active in the Columbia Department, 19 women and 20 men received Ph.D.'s.

Benedict preferred dealing with texts and other scholars' data, which Mead referred to as her "fondness for scrappy ethnography," for her deafness made fieldwork difficult. Nonetheless, because of the fetishism of fieldwork in anthropology[6] and because of her precarious professional position at Columbia, she pragmatically enacted this rite of passage. Her first fieldwork in 1922, under Kroeber's guidance, was with the Serrano, Southern California Shoshoneans. She never returned to these people but later published "A Brief Sketch of Serrano Culture" (1924a) and the moving "Cups of Clay" vignette in chapter 2 of *Patterns of Culture* (1934b).

In 1923, she accepted a Southwest Society fellowship to collect material for Parsons' concordance of Pueblo myths and folktales, and over a year later, she finally followed Boas, Parsons, Kroeber, and Goldfrank to the Southwest. "Still relatively whole and functioning, sharply differentiated in psychological tone from its neighbors in the same environment, Zuni culture seems to have had a great attraction for Benedict—as indeed Pueblo culture in general had for a number of alienated intellectuals" (Stocking 1974:71). The same landscape that "bit sharply into" Mary Austin's "deep self" profoundly moved Benedict. From Zuni in 1925, she wrote in exhilaration to Mead,

I've discovered in myself a great fondness for this place—it came over me with a rush—We drove in with the rain pouring down in great white separate drops and sunlit clouds and soft veils of rain shifting and forming against the far off mesa. The red terraced hillock of Zuni never looked better in any setting (AAW:291).

As she prepared to leave several weeks later, she wrote, "This is the last morning in Zuni . . . Ruth Bunzel came by Friday's mail wagon. Yesterday we went up under the sacred mesa along stunning trails where the great wall towers above you always in new magnificence . . . When I'm God I'm going to build my city there" (AAW:293).

Peoples' folk tales are their autobiography.
Ruth Benedict (1931b:291)[7]

Although hampered by her deafness and forced to work through interpreters, Benedict collected hundreds of pages of myths and tales at Zuni in 1924 and 1925 and at Cochiti in 1925, subsequently published as *Tales of the Cochiti Indians* (1931a) and *Zuni Mythology* (1935). Many years later, one of her Zuni interpreters recalled that she "spoke gently," was "polite" and "generous," and "generally worked with old men" (see Pandey 1972:333–34). Her principle informant was Nick Tumaka, whom Kroeber described as "the outstanding intellectual of the Zuni" (quoted in Parsons 1939a:64) and Benedict described in a letter to Mead: "There's something impressive in the man's fire. He might have been a really great man. And yet I think any society would have used its own terms to brand him as a witch. He's too solitary and too contemptuous" (AAW:292). Later he appeared as one of the "most striking individuals" in *Patterns of Culture* (1934b:260–61) and as Informant 7 in the introduction to *Zuni Mythology:*

He was a medicine society headman who in his young manhood was condemned by the priests as a witch and hung by the thumbs until he confessed. He turned informant against the priests and caused the elder brother bow priest to be imprisoned in a government penitentiary. He was a person of great ability, of commanding presence, and with a great personal need for achieving eminence, which he sought primarily in the medicine societies (1935:xxxix).

When Benedict left Zuni to work at Cochiti Pueblo in the summer of 1925, she planned to stay in Peña Blanca, a nearby Hispanic village, and have informants come to work with her there. Both Boas and Parsons had advised her "not to set foot . . . in Cochiti" if she wanted to work intensively with informants (AAW:299). Within days, however, she was living in the pueblo and writing to Mead, "I never do get this sense of the spiked dangerous fence that Elsie, and Dr. Boas in this case, make so much of" (AAW:299). Probably not, because the Cochitis that I know recall the same gentle, generous lady that the Zuni do, and because since the 1880s, when Bandelier was thrown out of Santo Domingo and welcomed at Cochiti, this pueblo has been more friendly to outsiders than have other Rio Grande Keres villages. Here, too, her favorite "old man" was the outstanding intellectual, widely referred to in the village as *mucho sabio*. In a letter to Mead and in the introduction to *Tales of the Cochiti Indians,* she described him as follows:

My old man is ninety and a great old character . . . He speaks excellent Spanish and I can follow a good deal when he talks it—I am angry that I have to bother with interpreters at all, but I do. He hobbles along on his cane, bent nearly double, and is still easily the most vivid personage in the landscape (AAW:300).

In another passage, she wrote,

Informant 4 was a very different individual from the others, as can be seen from the material recorded from him. He spoke Spanish fairly, and had been an adventurer all his life . . . He liked best to give "true stories" . . . His tales of the mythological heroes always emphasized their supernatural exploits in deer and rabbit hunting, and their success in turning the mockery that had been directed against them against those who had mocked them (Benedict 1931a:xiii).

Her "old man" was Santiago Quintana, the grandfather of Helen Cordero and the storyteller whom Cordero has represented in her world-famous clay figures. He was very much concerned that those who wrote about Cochiti "got the old ways right" (Cordero 1979, personal communication), and he was the valued friend and informant of several generations of anthropologists and interpreters of Cochiti life: Bandelier, Starr, Saunders, Curtis, Parsons, and finally Benedict. His son, Pablo, and daughter-in-law, Caroline, were Esther Goldfrank's hosts and helpers; his granddaughter, Helen, has changed my life by sharing her art and experience with me.

Both *Cochiti Tales* (1931a) and *Zuni Mythology* (1935) are careful, competent collections arranged in the scholarly fashion of the day into Anglo folktale categories—Hero Tales, Animal Tales, etc.—and identifying narrators only by numbers. One can presume, however, that had Benedict not been deaf and had she been able to do more fieldwork, very different texts, presentations, and interpretations would have resulted. There is much in the introductions to these collections and in her entries "Folklore" and "Myth" in the *Encyclopedia of the Social Sciences* (1931b, 1933a) that bears rereading and is quite relevant to contemporary folk narrative scholarship and the analysis of "cultural texts." In his 1937 review of *Zuni Mythology,* Stith Thompson urged all folklorists and anthropologists to read her introduction, and they should be so urged again today. Benedict's statements that "people's folk tales are . . . their autobiography and the clearest mirror of their life" (1931b:291), that myths are "a native comment on native life" (1931a:xiii), and that folklore "tends to crystallize and perpetuate the forms of culture that it has made articulate" (1931b:291) sound very like recent reflexive formulations of cockfights and other cultural texts as "stories that the _____ tell themselves about themselves." However, in these recent formulations, excepting those of James Boon, Benedict's name is noticeably absent. Yet it was she who wrote in a 1924 research proposal to study Pueblo mythology, "The advantage of mythological material over any other, for the characterization of tribal life, consists in the fact that here alone we have these things recorded wholly *as they themselves figure them to themselves* [my emphasis]" (1924b).

Given the assumptions and practices of folklore scholarship in the 1930s, which unfortunately persisted long after, her introduction to *Zuni Mythology* (1935) is particularly important in several respects: in emphasizing the value of intensive studies of the narratives of a single culture rather than a comparison of disparate elements from several cultures and a study of incident distribution; in relating narrative themes to cultural values and behavior; in debunking folklorists' myth of communal authorship and pointing out that "what is communal about the process is the social acceptance by which the trait becomes a part of the teaching handed down to the next generation" (1935:xxix); in calling attention to individual creativity "within the traditional limits" and pointing out "the possibility of the study of the native narrator, that is, the literary materials which he has at his disposal and his handling of them" (1935:xii); in describing sex differences in both the tales and the telling; and in foregrounding the aesthetic and literary qualities of such "primitive" narratives—"Mythology is a highly developed and serious art in Zuni" (1935:

xii). Here, as in "Folklore," Benedict modified Boas' culture-reflection view not only in regarding folk tales themselves as a "living, functioning" cultural trait but by emphasizing the importance of studying "local literary conventions"—"Folklore is literature and like any art it has traditional regional stylistic forms which may be studied like any other art form" (1931b:291). Perhaps most important, she eloquently evoked the power of the human imagination to make, remake, and reflect upon reality, anticipating Lévi-Strauss by several decades. In contrast to treating tales as survivals with no aesthetic or awareness thereof, she argued,

Man in all his mythologies has expressed his discomfort at a mechanistic universe and his pleasure in substituting a world that is humanly motivated and directed. He has imagined both the topography of his country and the ethical standards of his people as the outcome of human acts of the culture hero. He has recast the universe into human terms (1933a:181).

The world man actually lives in . . . always bulks very small in relation to the world he makes for himself (1933b:44).

These same values and concerns informed her editorship of the *Journal of American Folklore,* and during the 15 years (1925–1940) that Benedict edited the journal, she did much to professionalize the field of folklore and to move it beyond motif collections and distributions. In contrast to Stith Thompson, she was an early supporter of applied folklore, encouraging folk festivals and the work of the Federal Writers' Project. In the 1920s, at Elsie Clews Parsons' behest, Benedict was also involved not only with collecting and editing tales but with compiling a concordance to Southwestern Indian mythology. Two Columbia students, Gene Weltfish and Erna Gunther, assisted on this project. Benedict found this work boring and tedious and turned the project over to Gunther in 1926. What happened thereafter is unknown.

If Mead was the more powerful and intimate influence in Benedict's life and work, Sapir was the much more profound and intellectual one. Shortly after she returned from the Southwest in 1925, he wrote chastising her for not "sending verses": "I can't suffer Anne Singleton to languish into thin air. Zuni myths are important toys, of course, but your verse, even when you're not pleased with it, is a holier toy. You may quote this to Boas if you like. I have strayed from the paternal roof and no longer fear the Sire's displeasure" (AAW: 181). A year later, he sent her a verse entitled "Zuni":

> . . . Through the monotony
> Of mumbling melody, the established fall
> And rise of the slow, dreaming ritual,
> Through the dry glitter of the desert sea
> And the sharpness of the mesa keep the flowing
> Of your spirit, in many branching ways.
> (AAW: 88)

Such communications not only kept "Anne Singleton" writing poetry but heightened Benedict's awareness of the literary quality of the Zuni materials. Sapir was, however, mistaken in his 1926 admonition that her "poems [were] infinitely more important than anything, no matter how brilliant, you are fated to contribute to anthropology" (AAW: 182). As Benedict herself realized when Harcourt turned down her book of poems in 1928, "They aren't good enough to give one's life to" (AAW: 91).

In the introduction to *Zuni Mythology* (Benedict 1935), Sapir's influence is also evident in Benedict's exploration of the mechanisms of compensation and displacement operant in the translation of inhibited materials into socially acceptable terms and images, to explain striking divergences between some stories and Zuni values and behavior. From his very first letter to Benedict in 1922 concerning her dissertation, Sapir had urged her to look for psychological patterns underlying the differences in cultures and had lamented the gulf between anthropologists who studied culture as a set of institutions without reference to the individual and psychologists who analyzed the mental processes of individuals without reference to the cultural context in which they occurred.

> A culture, like an individual, is a
> more or less consistent pattern of thought
> and action.
> *Ruth Benedict (1934b:46)* [8]

The year 1927 is frequently singled out as the theoretical beginning of culture and personality studies in anthropology. Sapir's pioneer paper, "The Unconscious Patterning of Behavior in Society" (1927; reprint, Mandelbaum 1949), in which he argued that "all cultural behavior is patterned" and that "it is futile to classify human acts as such as having an inherently individual or social significance," set the frame of reference for later work in this area. He suggested,

If we can show that normal human beings, both in confessedly social behavior and often in supposedly individual behavior, are reacting in accordance with deep-seated cultural patterns, and if, further we can show that these patterns are not so much known as felt, not so much capable of conscious description as of naive practice, then we have the right to speak of the "unconscious patterning of behavior in society" (Mandelbaum 1949: 548).

Moreover, he asserted that "it is the failure to understand the necessity of grasping the native patterning which is responsible for so much unimaginative and misconceiving description of procedures that we have not been brought up with" (Mandelbaum 1949: 547). This essay also established the linguistic model for culture and personality studies that David Aberle in particular later criticized.

In September 1928, Benedict presented a paper, "Psychological Types in the Cultures of the Southwest," which not only manifested Sapir's influence but was clearly the product of 10 years of study with Parsons, Goldenweiser, Boas, and Kroeber. Because of Boas' openly expressed distaste for psychoanalysis, "it has never been sufficiently realized how consistently throughout his life Boas defined the task of ethnology as the study of 'man's mental life,' 'fundamental psychic attitudes of cultural groups,' man's 'subjective worlds' " (Benedict 1943:31). As Benedict noted in this obituary essay, as early as 1888 Boas was writing, "The data of ethnology prove that not only our knowledge but also our emotions are the result of the form of our social life and of the history of the people to whom we belong" (reprinted in Boas 1940:636). Related statements that surely influenced her approach to culture and personality and to patterns of culture are to be found in many of his writings. In his 1888 essay, he wrote, "The first aim of ethnological inquiry must be critical analysis of the characteristics of each people. This is the only way of attaining a satisfactory understanding of the cultures found in wider areas . . . to view our own civilization objectively" (Boas 1940:629). In another work first published in 1902, he added, "The actions of every individual have their roots in the society in which he lives . . . [The] style of his esoteric doctrines depends upon the general character of the culture of the tribe which has a high degree of individuality in each tribe" (Boas 1940:314–15). In 1928, he further refined the relationship of culture and personality: "Wherever there is a strong, dominant trend of mind that pervades the whole cultural life it many persist over long periods and survive changes in mode of life. This is most easily observed in one-sided cultures characterized by a single controlling idea" (Boas 1928:151). Four years later in "Configurations of Culture in North America" (1932), Benedict wrote,

Such configurations of culture, built around certain selected human traits and working toward the obliteration of others are of first-rate importance in the understanding of culture . . . Cultural configurations stand to the understanding of group behavior in the relation that personality types stand to the understanding of individual behavior . . . This force that bends occasions to its purposes and fashions them to its own idiom we can call within that society its dominant drive . . . I do not see that the development of these configurations in different societies is more mystic or difficult to understand than, for example, the development of an art style . . . These dominant drives are as characteristic for individual areas as are house forms or the regulations of inheritance (Benedict 1932:6, 23–24, 26, 27).

In assessing the influence of psychiatry on anthropology and the role played by Sapir and Benedict, Kluckhohn observed of "Psychological Types" and "Configurations of Culture" that "every page is colored by an attitude that can only be called 'psychiatric' and which must be traced eventually from the influence of psychiatry" (1944a:597). If Benedict was influenced by psychology and psychoanalysis, psychoanalysis was also influenced by her anthropology. To cite but one example, in *The Neurotic Personality of Our Time* (1937), Karen Horney "emphasized cultural conditions at the expense of the orthodox (Freudian) libidinal drives and infantile experiences" (Barnouw 1949:248) and was openly indebted to Benedict's relativism and anti-essentialism. One of the historical factors that contributed to the sudden interdisciplinary growth and influence of culture and personality studies was the arrival of refugees from Nazi Europe with Freudian and Gestalt perspectives. In the 1930s, eminent intellectuals such as Karen Horney, Erich Fromm, Franz Alexander, and Erik Erikson participated along with Benedict in Abram Kardiner's seminars, first at the New York Psychoanalytic Institute and then at Columbia as a joint effort with Ralph Linton. Benedict and Horney spent a great deal of time together during the summer of 1935, and that fall Horney taught her first course at the New School for Social Research, "Culture and Neurosis." That course and her subsequent essay (1936) of the same title were, like Benedict's "Anthropology and the Abnormal" (1934a), concerned with the extent to which neuroses were "moulded by cultural processes" and normal-abnormal categories "culturally determined."

Given Benedict's history and temperament, it should come as no surprise that she became as preoccupied as she did with understanding and writing about the deviant personality and the relativity of the definitions *normal* and *abnormal* (1934a). In a contemporaneous essay, "The Emergency of the Concept of Personality in the Study of Cultures" (1934), Sapir made the following remark, which is reflexively applicable both to himself and to Benedict:

The discovery of the world of personality is apparently dependent upon the ability of the individual to become aware of and to attach value to his resistance to authority. It could probably be shown that naturally conservative people find it difficult to take personality valuations seriously, while temperamental radicals tend to be impatient with a purely cultural analysis of human behavior (reprinted in Mandelbaum 1949:592).

In that same essay he asserted that "culture is not something given but something to be gradually and gropingly discovered" and suggested that "an excellent test of the fruitfulness of the study of culture in close conjunction with a study of personality would be provided by studies in the field of child development" (Mandelbaum 1949:595–96). Again, Sapir's proposal anticipated subsequent government-funded work that was done in the Indian Education and Research Project (1941–1947) directed by Laura Thompson and in Benedict and Mead's national character study (1947–1949) that grew out of their war work.

Culture and personality study as developed by Benedict emphasized not only child development and acculturation but the collection and analysis of life histories, for she believed as did Sapir that "there is a very real hurt done our understanding of culture when we systematically ignore the individual and his types of interrelationship with other individuals" (Mandelbaum 1949:593). In contrast to Boas, who regarded life histories as being of "limited value," Benedict argued that "life histories are important because from them one can study special cases of the kind of impact this culture has on individuals . . . Life histories are data on all kinds of problems of behavior in a tribe" (1941, in Maslow and Honigmann 1970: 321). She encouraged and enabled the publication of Underhill's *The Autobiography of a Papago Woman* (1936), the first and for many years "only substantial document on a Southwestern Indian woman" (Kluckhohn 1954:686), and wrote a foreword for it that was finally published with the 1979 edition. In the 1930s and 1940s, hundreds of life histories were collected—many of them in the Southwest—but very little was done with most of them, except to mine them for ethnographic data. In Benedict's presidential address to the American Anthropological Association the year before she died, "Anthropology and the Humanities" (1947), life histories figured prominently in her plea for science tempered with humanism:

The unique value of life histories lies in that fraction of the material which shows what repercussions the experiences of a man's life—either shared or idiosyncratic—have upon him as a human being molded in that environment. . . . But if we are to make our collected life histories count in anthropological theory and understanding, we have only one recourse: we must be willing to be able to study them according to the best tradition of the humanities. None of the social sciences, not even psychology, has adequate models for such studies. The humanities have. If we are to use life histories for more than items of topical ethnology, we shall have to be willing to do the kind of job on them which has traditionally been done by the great humanists (reprinted in Mead 1974:175).

With regard to culture and personality studies and Benedict's contribution thereto, a 1926 letter from Sapir, that other "temperamental radical," to Benedict contains a very revealing and consequential postscript:

I nearly forgot the purpose of my note, which was to tip you off to apply for a research fellowship to the Social Science Research Council . . . don't make it as technical as last year. Pueblo mythology doesn't excite people any more than Athabaskan verbs would. Take your courage in your hands, mutter loving maledictions at Boas, and come across with a live project— and you'll get what you ask for. Make it a 3 year's project on something that sounds important—say a study of the declining, or increasing, mentality of Mayflower stock . . . Follow your own intuition and your own sense of humor. To be serious—can't you devise some general subject in the American Indian field that outsiders can warm up to? Primitive dream life and its significance for general psychology theory; or Hopi culture as a response (positive or negative) to environment (AAW: 184–85).

His suggestion presumably resulted in Project 35 (later, Project 126), "The Culture and Personality of North American Indians," which began in 1931, involved research with 20 tribes, and supported countless graduate students. Dissatisfied with

'the highly formal accounts of primitive cultures which had been customarily given by ethnologists,' Benedict proposed through longer periods of residence among the respective tribes and greater attention to detail in the description of their behavior to improve upon earlier work and to study the psychological patterns as well as the overt manifestations of culture (Briscoe 1979:458).

The impact of this project was considerable— by 1935 when she wrote her four-year report, a bill had been presented in Congress through co-operation with the Bureau of Indian Affairs (BIA) to provide for ethnologists to aid in tribal administration; by 1941, the BIA had instituted an interdisciplinary study designed "to investigate the problems of personality development in relation to cultural patterning in the situational context of several Indian tribes . . . and to apply the results to the problem of Indian administration and education" (Thompson 1970:50). One of the largest programs in applied anthropology,

this seven-year project focused on southwestern tribes—the Tohono O'odham (formerly known as Papago), Navajo, Hopi, and Zuni—would have been inconceivable without Benedict's earlier work. In the "Outline for Use in the Pilot Study, Research on the Development of Indian Personality" (BIA 1942) presenting purpose, rationale, and methods, Benedict's influence is clearly evident but never officially acknowledged. The more serious appropriation and erasure was Ralph Linton's editing and publishing the book based on the fieldwork Benedict directed on the culture and personality of North American Indians. Linton, who was named chair of Columbia's Department of Anthropology in 1937, resented and competed with Benedict at every turn and in 1940 published her students' work as *Acculturation in Seven American Indian Tribes*.

Benedict also took Sapir's advice to heart, however, in writing another book on culture and personality that "outsiders can warm up to." *Patterns of Culture* (1934b), in which she described culture as "personality writ large," made anthropology "available to the man on the street" (AAW: 184–85), was translated into 14 languages, became the best-selling and most influential book in twentieth-century anthropology, and engendered considerable disciplinary debate. For all that this text, too, was subsequently misread or appropriated, it was unmistakably her own.

> Long before I knew anything at all about
> anthropology, I had learned from Shake-
> spearean criticism—and from Santayana—
> habits of mind which at length made me
> an anthropologist.
> *Ruth Benedict (1948, reprinted in Mead
> 1974:173)*[9]

Much too much has been written both pro and con about *Patterns of Culture* (1934b) in relation to culture and personality; many scholars regard the book as little more than a rendering of those ideas with regrettable generalization and over-statement into readable and accessible terms—"Psychological Types" and "Configurations of Culture" writ large. Much less has been said about the literary and philosophical pre-texts of *Patterns of Culture* or about the fact that this is the book of a poet, a philosopher, and a feminist as well as an anthropologist. Most of what has been said in this regard is negative, many anthropologists finding *Patterns of Culture*'s literary qualities or philosophical framework unfortunate or distorting or proof positive that it was not scientific. One biographer writes, "The risk in [Benedict's] aim to merge art with social science was that the scientist would tolerate art's demand for selection and distortion, and that the lay reader would not look behind art's description to the underlying reality" (Modell 1975:200). I doubt Benedict would have endorsed this either/or formulation. Her version was, as some scholars have pointed out, much more paradoxical and self-ironic (Boon 1982:44; Geertz 1988:102–28).

Herskovits was one of the very few anthropologists who saw *Patterns of Culture* as a "heartening return to the distinguished writing tradition of early anthropological literature." Even Margaret Mead (who had urged Benedict to write it all in her own style and who, with Bateson during that fateful Christmas on the Sepik,[10] was much influenced by the manuscript) felt that such an artful delineation of cultures as personalities would have only been possible for a scholar who had not really lived among the "buzzing, blooming confusion" of actual tribal situations and who had, of necessity, relied on the interpretations of native informants and other anthropologists.

Ever the positivist, Mead made a very revealing remark in a 1933 letter to Benedict from Tchambuli criticizing Radcliffe-Brown and Malinowski: "I am more and more convinced that there is no room in anthropology for philosophical concepts and deductive thinking" (AAW:334). Benedict was not convinced; for in sharp contrast to Mead's unquestioning positivism and penchant for em-piricist simplification, Benedict believed that "data were meaningless without abstraction from them of a higher order of meaning" (Briscoe 1979:461) that informed them. Twelve years earlier, one of the men Mead was criticizing had written what reads like a charter for *Patterns of Culture:*

Thus the details and technicalities of the Kula acquire their meaning in so far only as they express some central attitude of mind of the natives, and thus broaden our knowledge, widen our outlook and deepen our grasp of human nature. What interests me really in the study of the native is his outlook on things, his *Weltanschauung,* the breath of life and reality which he breathes and by which he lives. Every human culture gives its members a definite vision of the world, a definite zest of life. . . .

The study of Ethnology—so often mistaken by its very votaries for an idle hunting after curios, for a ramble among the savage and fantastic shapes of "barbarous customs and crude superstitions"—might become one of the most deeply philosophic, enlightening and elevating disciplines of scientific research (Malinowski 1921:517).

Benedict noted, "Malinowski, somewhat disappointingly, [did] not go on to the examination of these cultural wholes" (Benedict 1932:2), but Benedict did. And the same European tradition of philosophical anthropology that had influenced both Boas and Malinowski shaped *Patterns of Culture.*

Although Benedict and several of her commentators have acknowledged this heritage, Mead went out of her way to lay "the ghosts of German theoreticians" forever, denying that Dilthey and Spengler had provided an intellectual framework for Benedict's work and claiming:

The actual facts are that the theoretical part of the work . . . was worked out with reference neither to Spengler nor Dilthey. Nietzsche had been an old favorite of hers . . . As for Dilthey . . . it was Boas who insisted that she must discuss him, not out of sympathy for Dilthey's ideas but out of the special standards of scholarship which required mention of those who had used comparable ideas irrespective of whether or not one's own ideas derived from them (Mead, ed. 1973:210–11).

She wrote on at least one other occasion,

The facts . . . were quite different. Boas himself insisted that she discuss earlier German works that had a faint relationship to her thought. This was in keeping with his European scholarly insistence on establishing theoretical genealogies. So he introduced her to Dilthey, as Sapir had introduced her to Spengler. But neither writer had shaped her ideas (Mead 1974:47).

Perhaps to ensure the acceptance of her interpretation, Mead suppressed at least a page and a half about Dilthey and Spengler when she reprinted "Configurations of Culture" in her "anthological biography," *Ruth Benedict* (1974). (This was not an isolated instance, since Mead similarly denied Kardiner's influence on Benedict's work in culture and personality. More seriously, she pruned and edited Benedict's papers before turning them over to the archives at Vassar College.) Both in that essay and in *Patterns of Culture,* Benedict had remarked that "the proposition that cultures must be studied from this point of view [as patterns, configurations organized around dominant ideas] and that it is crucial in an understanding even of our own cultural history has been put forward by the German school headed by Wilhelm Dilthey" (1932:2).

For Dilthey, whom anthropologists such as Victor Turner have recently rediscovered, *weltanschauung* is not a permanent fixed structure but a dynamic living pattern that expresses itself in religious, aesthetic, and philosophic forms (see Bruner and Turner 1986). As Benedict pointed out and emulated in *Patterns of Culture,* his analysis of great philosophical configurations viewed them as "great expressions of the variety of life," exposed their "relativity," and "argue[d] vigorously against the assumption that any one of them can be final" (1934b:52). And although Benedict criticized Spengler's thesis in *Decline in the West*

(1929), she credited him for having popularizing Dilthey's insights and endorsed his notion of "destiny ideas" that "evolve within a culture and give it individuality":

These have differed profoundly one from another, and they condition their carriers so that certain beliefs and certain blindnesses are inevitable to them. Each great culture has taken a certain direction not taken by another, it has developed beliefs and institutions until they are the expression of this fundamental orientation, and the full working out of this unique and highly individualized attitude toward life is what is significant in that cultural epoch (Benedict 1932:3).

I am inclined to accept Benedict's version of the facts; I suspect there is a good deal more supporting material in her unpublished papers, and I know there is much more to be researched and said regarding Dilthey's influence, particularly his concept of understanding and his discussions of individual life and its meaning as well as the understanding of others and the objective mind (Dilthey 1961, 1976).

We may never know what Mead's motives were, but her statements and actions in conjunction with her urging Benedict to delete the "miscellaneous source materials" and the words of Boas, Lowie, and Malinowski in *Patterns of Culture* reveal an egotism and a preoccupation with originality and authority to which Benedict was constitutionally opposed.[11] Like Boas, Benedict repeatedly resisted all forms of authority, including her own. Fortunately, Mead did not have her way in this case, for the strength of *Patterns of Culture* is its intertextuality, its *bricolage. Patterns of Culture* enacts what it describes—the organization of the "rags and tatters of cultures" into a pattern through an integrating principle. It is a book made like a quilt about cultures made like quilts. Pieced quilting is, recent feminist critics and writers suggest, a trope for women's art in general and their writing in particular. The quilting analogy is valid, for the radicalness of this book, which "strikes off integration against diversity to vitalize both" (Boon 1982:107), lies in its awareness of the mediatedness of cultural interpretations and in its own nonabsolutist interpretation of "the inventions of cultures," whether by native or anthropologist or poststructuralist feminist.[12]

Just as surely as did Sapir, Benedict questioned "whether a completely impersonal anthropological description . . . is truly possible for a social discipline" and recognized that

culture, as it is ordinarily constructed by the anthropologist, is a more or less mechanical sum of the more striking or picturesque generalized patterns of behavior which he has either abstracted for himself out of the sum total of his observations or has had abstracted for him by his informants in verbal communication (in Mandelbaum 1949:593).

Few of Benedict's critics have realized that in the process of writing for "the Macy shopper," she deconstructed anthropological discourse *avant la lettre*.[13] From the kind of anthropology that Benedict practiced and wrote—and she did not make that distinction in the way that most anthropologists do—Sapir ventured to predict that

the concept of culture which will then emerge, fragmentary and confused as it will undoubtedly be, will turn out to have a tougher, more vital, importance for social thinking than the tidy tables of contents attached to this or that group which we have been in the habit of calling "cultures" (Mandelbaum 1949: 597).

With regard to this "fragmentary and confused" concept of culture, I should note that there is much more that is Nietzschean about *Patterns of Culture* than his phrases describing contrasting types as Apollonian and Dionysian. Despite Nietzsche's explicit misogyny, Benedict was, like other feminists then and now, attracted to "a gaiety and intoxication . . . that nothing else quite achieves . . . a right—poetical way of seeing" (AAW:548) and an ironic, deconstructive perspective. Contrary to Barnouw's mistaken assertion that "under her master's somewhat jaundiced

eye she turned to Nietzsche, Spengler, and Dilthey" (1949:243), Benedict was reading Pater and Nietzsche as a Vassar undergraduate. In 1926, she sent her marked copy of *Zarathustra* to Mead in Samoa with a letter from which the preceding quotations were taken. As Mead remarked in *An Anthropologist at Work*, "Nietzsche had been an old favorite of hers" (AAW:210), again acknowledging but dismissing the theoretical underpinnings of European philosophy in Benedict's work. The influence of Nietzsche, like that of Dilthey, merits further consideration.

Trained in literary criticism, Benedict read cultures and personalities as writ, as texts organized around tropes, such as the "idea of fertilization" in Pueblo culture that Hermann Haeberlin (1916) first formulated. Long before anthropologists were talking about key symbols, root metaphors, master tropes, and cultural texts and the semiotics of culture, she was teaching us to read cultures as texts and texts as cultural documents. As her student Dorothy Lee remarked,

Ruth Benedict taught us to read an ethnography as we would visit a tribe: to accord equal dignity to every datum, to read slowly and repeatedly, delving beyond the interpretative words of the writer, till we could savor the culture. She taught us meticulous attention to detail, because to her mind no detail was trivial; it was to be examined carefully as a clue to society's peculiar expression and arrangement of reality. Ruth Benedict read an ethnography repeatedly and studied the culture till she could experience reality to some extent as that group did; until their behavior and their formulations "made sense"; and the trenchant illuminative comments upon other cultures which her students like to quote, came out of this experience. When she tried to find a name for this meaning which emerged after total acquaintance with a culture, she called it "pattern" (Lee 1949:346).

Unlike many anthropologists, Benedict recognized that ethnographic description and ethnological comparison occur as writing. I can easily imagine her asking herself privately as James Boon has done publicly, "How can ethnography and literature shirk each other as long as ethnographers write? Can both be set into one critical perspective, so that our glib confidence in the boundary between two equally problematic entities may be shaken?" (Boon 1982:20). Almost 40 years ago in one of her last public addresses, "Anthropology and the Humanities," she tried to shake that glib confidence with a "heretical statement":

To my mind the very nature of the problems posed and discussed in the humanities is closer, chapter by chapter, to those in anthropology than are the investigations carried on in most of the social sciences . . .

It is important for us to be aware of what we can learn from the humanities . . . My point is that, once anthropologists include the mind of man in their subject matter, the methods of science and the methods of the humanities complement each other. Any commitment to methods which exclude either approach is self-defeating (in Mead 1974:165–66, 175–76).

Benedict never shirked literature; at the time she was writing *Patterns of Culture,* she was reading Virginia Woolf's *The Waves* (1931). Woolf's method of evoking essential spirit rather than realistically describing character appealed to her and clearly influenced her own book, "in which the complexity of human society is conveyed through the juxtaposition of distinct, particular types" (Modell 1983:192). Instead of Woolf's six characters and six different versions of a person, Benedict inscribed three cultures and three different versions of reality. In *The Waves* a central, absent character is created through the reflections of six individuals; in *Patterns,* American culture is portrayed through the images and reflections of three other cultures. Instead of writing biographies of three women as she had once planned in "Adventures in Womanhood," Benedict wrote biographies of three cultures and by implication a fourth. And, like the poet she was, Benedict constructed her argument through images—images juxtaposed in such a way that, as Clifford Geertz has pointed out, "the all-too-familiar and the wildly exotic . . . change places" (1988:106).

In contrast to Parsons' lengthy "labor of description" in *Pueblo Indian Religion* (1939a:vol. 1: xiv), Benedict took a poetic approach to inscribing the essential patterns of Pueblo experience in what was to become the most criticized section of *Patterns of Culture.* She selected and exaggerated those Pueblo culture traits that supported her conception of their Apollonian genius and overlooked those that seemed to reflect a conflicting drive, underplaying the tension and factionalism in Pueblo society. Many of the criticisms center on her minimizing Dionysian excess in the form of alcoholism and violence. In refutation of her light treatment of whipping in adolescent kiva initiation ceremonies—"The Pueblo practice of beating with stripes is likewise without intent to torture. The lash does not draw blood" (1934b: 91)—Don Datayesva's bloody autobiographical description (Simmons 1942) has been trotted out by more than one critic. From her realist's perspective, Esther Goldfrank (1945c) in particular criticized Benedict's idealistic rendering of Pueblo culture. Goldfrank's characterization is apt, for as John Bennett (1946) and others have remarked, interpretations of Pueblo culture differ markedly depending on the values of the interpreter and on whether one focuses on ideology or on praxis. Those cultural descriptions such as Benedict's and Thompson's (1945) that are elaborated on the basis of ideology, which Bennett calls "organic," see Pueblo culture and society as essentially integrated and harmonious.[14] Those such as Goldfrank's and Dorothy Eggan's (1943) that focus on praxis, which Bennett terms "repressive," emphasize the tension, conflict, and fear of Pueblo life and the extent to which the individual is suppressed and repressed.

Kluckhohn remarked to Hoebel that "Benedict did not report Pueblo society as is but Pueblo culture as conceived by the old men in particular" (Hoebel 1954:724). But does anyone, can anyone report Pueblo society as it is? Are not the old men's textualizations of their culture as valid, as important as the constructions of Pueblo life that the ethnographer writes up on the basis of his or her observations of behavior? I suspect that the truth about Pueblo culture is and ought to be somewhere in-between in the relationship between the ideal and the real, between ideology and praxis, between the Cutlass Supreme and the prayer feather on its rearview mirror—not to mention the Sacred Heart Auto League medal on the dashboard. Goldfrank is not all right, and Benedict is not all wrong. Moreover, many of those who criticize *Patterns of Culture* fail to read Benedict's own qualifications, self-criticisms, and cautionary notes.[15] For example, she wrote,

Integration may take place in the face of fundamental conflicts . . . There is always the possibility that the description of the culture is disoriented rather than the culture itself . . . It would be absurd to cut every culture down to the Procrustean bed operation that mutilates the subject and erects additional obstacles against our eventual understanding of it . . . Facile generalizations about the integration of culture are most dangerous in field-work . . . In theoretical discussions of culture, generalizations about the integration of culture will be empty in proportion as they are dogmatic and universalized. We need detailed information about contrasting limits of behavior and the motivations that are dynamic in one society and not in another. We do not need a plank of configuration written into the platform of an ethnological school. On the other hand, the contrasted goods which different cultures pursue, the different intentions which are at the basis of their institutions, are essential to the understanding both of different social orders and of individual psychology (1934b: 228–29).

On the basis of my own fieldwork, I am struck by the intuitive rightness of Benedict's characterization of Pueblo patterns and values and certainly of her interpretation of the critical differences between the Puebloans and their southwestern neighbors, which is what prompted her to write the book and its antecedent essays in the first place. At one time in my life, I divided my time between Cochiti Pueblo and the village of Cibecue on the Fort Apache Reservation, and on more than one occasion was in both places in the same day. To reduce countless images to one statement: they drink at Cochiti and it causes problems and violence, but you won't find a drunk there passed out in an irrigation ditch in the middle of the day or garbage in the front yard or a man beating a dog to death with a baseball bat. In commenting on *Patterns of Culture* and Benedict's "great theoretical and methodological contributions" based on her southwestern studies, Hoebel remarked, "It is a paradox that in spite of her highly questionable techniques of observation she was able to contribute theory and methodological devices of such great import and lasting value" (1954:724). I do not think it a paradox at all. As Boon has pointed out and as Parsons' work sometimes demonstrates, it is all too easy for ethnographers to run aground in the sands of their data, losing both their sense of irony and their sight of the larger picture.[16] Deafness, training, and temperament forced Benedict to read over the shoulder of the natives, the old men anthropologists of Pueblo society, and enabled her to go beyond or behind the minutiae of data to the integrating principles that held the "rags and tatters" together.

Neither do I think it an accident that both *The Origins of Totalitarianism* (Arendt 1951) and *Patterns of Culture* (Benedict 1934b) were written by women, for who better to describe the constraints of custom and the power of patriarchal institutions? Thanks to Mead, Modell, and Caffrey, we now know much more than we did about the feminist behind the anthropologist, but there is still much to be said about the extent to which these concerns informed Benedict's anthropology.[17] As Benedict herself remarked, "Women in the field of anthropology have contributed to its development not only as trained anthropologists, but as women" (1940c:4).

Rereading Benedict in the context of teaching a women authors course, I was struck by the feminist subtexts that I, too, had previously read over, even when on more than one occasion they break through the surface. For example, in commenting on Lowie's Shoshone material, she pointed out, "He notices the change in affect in menstrual taboos and the dropping out of the relevant customs. Childbirth and the menstruating woman have been two of the great points of departure for the tender-minded elaboration of horror and the uncanny" (1932:14). Similarly, her *Encyclopedia of the Social Sciences* (1931c) entry "Dress" discomfits conventional notions:

In more extreme instances that may be brought to bear against this theory of the origin of clothing in an instinct of modesty the very nature of the coverings themselves is the point of the argument. The codpiece which was worn in Europe about 1450 and the custom of the men of certain Papuan tribes who squeeze their members into the opening of a gourd are indicative of the exhibitionist nature of certain forms of dress. Many observers in many parts of the world have commented on the fact that the most obvious function of the genital coverings was to attract attention rather than to divert it (1931c:236).

And, most serious and most ignored of all, in the conclusion of *Patterns of Culture* she builds up to a plea for cultural relativism and tolerance by toppling images of male dominance in our own society:

The Puritan divines of New England in the eighteenth century were the last persons whom contemporary opinion in the colonies regarded as psychopathic. Few prestige groups in any culture have been allowed such complete intellectual and emotional dictatorship as they were. They were the voice of God. Yet to a modern observer it is they, not the confused and tormented women they put to death as witches, who were the psychoneurotics of Puritan New England . . . In our own generation extreme forms of ego-gratification are culturally supported in a similar business, have been again and again portrayed by novelists and dramatists, and they are familiar in every community. Like the behaviour of Puritan divines, their courses of action are often more asocial than those of the inmates of penitentiaries. In terms of the suffering and frustration that they spread around them there is probably no comparison. There is very possibly at least as great a degree of mental warping. Yet they are entrusted with positions of great influence and importance and are as a rule fa-

thers of families. Their impress both upon their own children and upon the structure of our society is indelible. They are not described in our manuals of psychiatry because they are supported by every tenet of our civilization . . . Nevertheless a future psychiatry may well ransack our novels and letters and public records for illumination upon a type of abnormality to which it would not otherwise give credence. In every society it is among this very group of the culturally encouraged and fortified that some of the most extreme types of human behavior are fostered (1934b:277–78).

Although not quite so witty, acerbic, and explicit as Virginia Woolf in *Three Guineas* (1938), written in the same decade—this was after all anthropology for the common man—Benedict just as surely drew a parallel between the development of fascism and the patriarchal family.

> Liberty is the one thing no man can have
> unless he grants it to others.
> *Ruth Benedict (1942b, in Mead 1974:146)* [18]

Although in 1934, Benedict feared that Boas had "given up science for good works" (AAW:348) and lamented the time so lost to research and writing, world events forced her to realize that anthropologists could no longer do pure science, and she followed him into the arena of public struggle against racism and intolerance. She also followed as acting head of Columbia's Department of Anthropology from 1936 to 1939. According to Mead, the dean who planned to make her the first woman chairman of a graduate department died before he could do so. After Ralph Linton was appointed chair, "he learned that Ruth had not supported his candidacy and he never forgave her" (Mead 1974:56).[19] In 1939–40, Benedict finally took a sabbatical and used it to write *Race: Science and Politics* (1940a), in which readers see writ large Boas' conviction, "It is the duty of those who are devoted to the study of social problems to become clear in regard to these questions and to see to it that through their influence the intellectual chains in which tradition holds us are gradually broken" (Boas 1938:21). She followed this with numerous articles in popular journals and the popular and controversial pamphlet coauthored with Gene Weltfish, *The Races of Mankind* (1943), of which over 750,000 copies were distributed.

In 1943, Benedict went to Washington, D.C., as head of the Basic Analysis Section, Bureau of Overseas Intelligence, Office of War Information. There, "with Mead and other anthropologists, she pioneered in the application of anthropological methods to complex societies and the study of culture 'at a distance,' working through documentary and literary materials and interviews with émigré informants in a series of 'national character' studies" (Stocking 1974:72). Benedict was particularly adept at reading cultural texts; she had, as Mead has remarked, "a disciplined and highly sophisticated approach to published materials . . . and [a] penchant for building up a picture from fragmentary data" (1974:59). Her war work produced her most elegant and eloquent book, *The Chrysanthemum and the Sword* (1946), a thematic analysis of Japanese culture based entirely on written materials and interviews with Japanese-Americans.

Several commentators have seen in this book, which "she cared more about than any other she had written" (Mead 1974:64), an integration of her different selves, the poet and the scientist: "Here at last the two halves of Benedict's own being finally merged in a book that, as Mead suggested, combined a sense of the strength and integrity of cultural pattern with the 'special poignancy of the human spirit trapped always in ways which limit its full expression' " (Stocking 1974:72). In her review, Erna Fergusson (1946b: 3) remarked that "one puts down this book feeling that our government should not delay a moment in giving Dr. Benedict another assignment to study other peoples whom we do not understand but with whom we hope to make a livable world" (AAW:428).

The government did just that. In 1947 the Of-

fice of Naval Research gave her a large grant to organize and direct a project, Research in Contemporary Cultures—the most ambitious program in anthropological research in the history of the American discipline. This and other awards and honors finally made it impossible for Columbia not to promote her to full professor shortly before her death in 1948.

Light: The more given is the more denied.
Ruth Benedict (1928)[20]

Ruth Fulton Benedict was one of the first women to attain major stature as a social scientist. When she entered anthropology in 1919, it was still an esoteric science. By 1948, when she died, an awareness of the relativity of cultural values and some grasp of the significance of the study of cultures, primitive and modern, extended far beyond anthropology. She herself played a decisive part in bringing about this transformation (Mead 1974:1).

Despite, perhaps because of this achievement, Benedict's insights were disparaged, erased, and widely appropriated, and she was subjected to discrimination, contempt, and hostility—including a failed plot to prevent her from becoming the 1946–47 president of the American Anthropological Association, which "would have discredited the delicate negotiations" for the Office of Naval Research grant (Mead 1974:69–70). I suppose I should not be shocked or surprised, for at least since the *Malleus Maleficarum* (1486), women in Western culture who showed an above-normal capacity and interest in intellectual matters were quite likely to be thought of as witches.[21] Yet, there was about Benedict a radiant integrity—Pater's "gemlike flame"—that could not be denied and a courage to carry on regardless, challenging conventional boundaries between disciplines and reorganizing our ways of making sense of the world.

Her dignity "lay in the fact that she went after important issues" (Barnouw 1949:252).[22] Like Hannah Arendt, she knew the questions were worth asking even if there were no answers, and like Mary Wollstonecraft, "she had a startling way of 'raising all the questions at once'—religious, economic, sexual, and philosophic" (AAW: 493). In one of her earliest essays (and Boas' favorite[23]), she wondered, "For what is the meaning of life except that by the discipline of thought and emotion, by living life to its fullest, we shall make of it always a more flexible instrument, accepting new relativities, divesting ourselves of traditional absolutes?" (1929:649).

Like Pater, whose conclusion to *The Renaissance* (1873) she much admired and frequently quoted, she believed that "what we have to do is to be for ever curiously testing new opinions and courting new impressions, never acquiescing in a facile orthodoxy," that "the service of philosophy, of speculative culture, towards the human spirit, is to rouse, to startle it to a life of constant and eager observation" (Pater 1873:196–97). What counted for Pater and what was distinctive about Benedict's anthropology was "the power of conceiving humanity in a new and striking way . . . selecting, transforming, recombining the images it transmits" (Pater 1885, in Pater 1914, vol. 2, p. 218).

And like Pater but unlike Mary Wollstonecraft, who disdained "to cull [her] phrases or polish [her] style," Benedict delighted in linguistic pleasure, in fine phrases, in writing anthropology like a poet. In contrast to Parsons, who gave up speaking as a woman and kept to "the straight and narrow path of kinship nomenclature and folktale collecting" (Hare 1985:139) after she turned from feminist sociology to anthropology, Benedict wrote both as a woman and as a poet. She was more blamed than praised for her sense of style. The poetess became cause to disparage the anthropologist, for "linguistic pleasure (literary language) is placed on the side of the feminine; banned, like female desire" (Jacobus 1979:14). *The Chrysanthemum and the Sword* was, one of her colleagues remarked, "almost too well written." If she spoke eloquently, she also spoke simply, lucidly. That, too, has been misinter-

preted by those who confuse density of thought with impenetrable language and fail to see that it takes courage to speak simply, particularly when one has experienced oneself as anything but simple.

In her introduction to Benedict's biography, Modell remarks that in working on Benedict's life story, she "realized how inevitably social scientists today must acknowledge her point of view" (1983:13). Unfortunately, too few do, even among those who describe themselves as interpretive anthropologists and analyze culture as text and talk of cultural tropes. The only exceptions are Boon (1982), Handler (1986), and Geertz (1988). The question is Why? What should they acknowledge of her point of view? Why do they not? Many, too many, of her words remain in darkness despite the light that she inscribed. In poems poignantly entitled "Words in Darkness" and "Moth Wing," she captured both the greatness and the fragility of her insight and the struggle that gave light:

Words in Darkness

There will come beauty in a silver rain
Out of the storm-hung heaven of my soul.
Let me remember seasons that have lain
Heavy as this with darkness and the roll
Of the on-coming thunder, and were yet
Distilled to showers crystal-cool and white
Beyond the gift of sunshine; heedless, let
The storm close cold upon me, and the bite
Of sand be on my breasts, nor question why
The silver fingers of the rain are wrought
Out of a maddened tumult and a sky
No man of all would willingly have sought.
(AAW:489)

Moth Wing

When you have cast the reckoning
Of her most wayward loveliness
And thumbed the bright frost-patterned wing
Her laughter lifted for largess
Of suffering, it will be less
Than any rag upon the wind.
Let there be end of weariness
And high endeavor, passion thinned

To songs of her great loveliness.
Weep rather for a crumpled thing
Not any jeweled words shall dress
To beauty sudden-fluttering.

(AAW:488)

NOTES

1. Throughout this essay, I have used the abbreviation AAW to refer to Benedict's unpublished and published writings edited by Margaret Mead in *An Anthropologist at Work* (New York: Avon, 1973) rather than Mead 1973, which would be misleading. A similar version of this paper was printed in *Frontiers* 12 (no. 3, 1992):39–78 with the permission of the Wenner-Gren Foundation for Anthropological Research and the University of New Mexico Press.

2. For further discussion of Benedict's ironies and her Swiftian mode of social critique, see Geertz 1988.

3. This phrase is taken from the last paragraph of Benedict's unpublished essay on Mary Wollstonecraft:

In the National Portrait Gallery hangs a picture of Mary Wollstonecraft, a picture of her as she was a few scant months before her death. I remember the child I was when I saw it first, haunted by the terror of youth before experience. I wanted so desperately to know how other women saved their souls alive. And the woman in the little frame arrested me, this woman with the auburn hair, and the sad, steady, light-brown eyes, and the gallant poise of the head. She had saved her soul alive; it looked out from her steady eyes unafraid. The price, too, that life had demanded of her was written ineradicably there. But to me, then standing before her picture, even that costly payment was a guarantee, a promise (AAW:519).

4. Mead recalls: "'I haven't strength of mind not to need a career,' Ruth Benedict used to say, with a rueful smile, during her first years in anthropology" (Mead 1973:3).

5. At this time, most of Boas' students did library dissertations and only did fieldwork after their Ph.D.'s. Kroeber and Lowie, among others, also followed this pattern. It did not, however, become grounds for criticism in their cases as it did in Benedict's.

6. See Boon 1982 and 1983 for further provocative discussion of the fetishism and conventions of fieldwork in anthropology.

7. Benedict made this statement in her *Encyclopedia of the Social Sciences* entry "Folklore" (1931b:291).

8. For further discussions of poetry, personality, and culture in Edward Sapir and Ruth Benedict, which emphasizes their differences of view, see Handler 1986. Handler overstates the case, however, in claiming that Benedict never accepted or understood Sapir's critique of reification. Like most of Benedict's commentators, he ignores her concern with the deviant, the dialectical, and the paradoxical and seems to miss her irony altogether.

9. Benedict made this statement in her 1947 AAA presidential address, "Anthropology and the Humanities," in which she argued that we can analyze cultural attitudes and behavior more cogently if we know Santayana's *Three Philosophical Poets* and Lovejoy's *Great Chain of Being* and the great works of Shakespearean criticism. Future anthropological work, too, can reach a higher level if we attract not only students of sociology but also students of the humanities.

10. Mead spent the Christmas of 1932 in the field at Ambunti, the government station on the Sepik River, with her anthropologist husband, Reo Fortune, as well as Gregory Bateson, with whom she fell in love and subsequently married. The threesome read and discussed the manuscript of *Patterns of Culture*. For a fascinating and revealing discussion of the mediations among Mead, Fortune, Bateson, Benedict, the Sepik, and Bali, and the critical role played by the manuscript of *Patterns of Culture* therein, see Boon 1985.

11. For further discussion of *Patterns of Culture* and the significance of the intertexts and concepts that Benedict retained and Mead would have weeded out, see Boon 1982:105–8.

12. See Wagner 1975 for an enlightening discussion of the invention of culture by humans in general and by anthropologists in particular.

13. This concept and construction was used in the original conference version of this essay (1986). Geertz uses the same regarding *The Chrysanthemum and the Sword* without attribution.

14. Despite her obvious indebtedness and her repeated use of the words *pattern* and *configuration*, Laura Thompson does not footnote Benedict in "Logico-Aesthetic Integration in Hopi Culture" (1945) or in

other publications and proposals associated with the Indian Education and Research Project.

15. This is notably so for Li An-Che (1937) despite the valid criticisms that he makes of her reading of Pueblo leadership.

16. For a critique of the fetishism of fieldwork, the biases of empiricism, and the conventions of the functionalist monograph, see Boon 1983. He argues,

> My point is that functionalism increasingly resisted reflexivity. As it developed as a normal science, it eliminated any sense of absurdity surrounding the investigator's position, even after the collapse of colonialism meant that the absurdities could no longer be so easily avoided . . . Functionalism became an anthropology without irony (Boon 1983:141).

Also see Clifford 1981, 1983, and 1984.

17. In a review essay, "Ruth Benedict: The Woman as Anthropologist," occasioned by *An Anthropologist at Work,* Richard Chase patronizingly remarked:

> *An Anthropologist at Work* shows that actually Mrs. Benedict was passionately committed to the Party of Woman. This book forces us to think of her as so committed and to reflect that, like any strong allegiance hers gives her work a certain bias (but also a certain clarity and intensity) which neither scientific scholarship nor the well known moral relativity of modern anthropology can conceal (1959:22).

18. This statement concludes "Primitive Freedom" (1942b), one of several popular articles Benedict published in the 1940s to encourage tolerance and relativism.

19. For more on Linton's enmity and maliciousness, see Mintz 1981:141–66.

20. This is the first line of her poem "Eucharist," published in *The Nation* (1928:296).

21. Mintz reports that in his later years at Yale, Linton publicly boasted that he had killed her: "And he produced for me, in a small leather pouch, the Tanala material he said he had used to kill Ruth Benedict" (1981:161).

22. After making this statement, Barnouw went on to remark,

> Anthropologists who classified potsherds or measured skulls could afford to criticize her methodology. Their procedures, no doubt, were impeccable in comparison to hers, but the final value of their work still remains to be discovered. Too many of Boas' students got bogged down among the intricate details of kinship-systems or basket-weaves without having much understanding of why they worked so hard. When Franz Boas published page after page of blueberry-pie recipes in Kwakiutl, the old man probably knew what he was after; but when his students did the same kind of thing, they often lacked the driving central purpose which animated Boas. They mastered techniques and methods within their special fields, but often accomplished little more than that. It requires courage to stick to the important issues, and Ruth Benedict had that courage (1949:252).

23. In a letter of January 16, 1929, to Margaret Mead in New Guinea, Benedict wrote,

> I finished my *Century* article—on time too—and even had time to show it to Papa Franz . . . I trembled when he said he wanted to see me about a point. I'd told him that I thought he'd hate the *Century* article. But no, "he thought an article like that would do more good than his book. He wished he could write in that way, but he couldn't" (AAW:311).

AMONG WOMEN: GENDER AND ETHNOGRAPHIC AUTHORITY OF THE SOUTHWEST, 1930 – 1980

Deborah Gordon

I was never ill-at-ease with [Irene Stewart] and despite our differences in life experiences we could discuss human problems, laugh together, take trips, and flourish in each other's society.

Mary Shepardson
(1986b: 29)

I am a woman and I talk to women.
Alice Marriott
(1952:47)

F ROM A feminist and postmodern perspective, there exists a notable relationship involving gender, power, and ethnographic authority among white women anthropologists in the southwestern United States and the Native American women who were their objects of study between 1930 and 1980. A type of female paternalism determined, to a large extent, how white women represented Native American women during the latter part of the twentieth century. This paternalism developed from the search for different ways of being white and female on the part of prominent female ethnographers and writers who went to the Southwest to do fieldwork. Ironically, in these anthropologists' search for difference they were constrained by authoritative social relations and, thus, literally came to know Native American women as the embodiment of their desires. The Other, which they sought in order to change themselves, was eclipsed by their own general cultural understanding of white gender relations throughout most of this century.

In its early stages, this dilemma appears most clearly in two ethnographic accounts, Gladys Reichard's *Dezba*, published in 1939, and Alice Marriott's *Maria: The Potter of San Ildefonso,* published almost ten years later in 1948. Reichard was a student of Boas and became one of the most important female anthropologists. She studied at Columbia University from 1920 to 1923, became an instructor in anthropology at Barnard College in 1923, and did most of her fieldwork among the Navajo during the 1930s. Reichard published numerous monographs on Navajo social life, particularly religious symbolism, chanting, weaving, and the practice of sandpainting (e.g., Reichard 1968). By comparison, Alice Marriott, who was the first woman to receive a B.A. in anthropology from the University of Oklahoma, was a field specialist for the Indian Arts and Crafts Board during the 1930s and 1940s. Along with collecting Native American art, she also was interested in artists' legends and histories. She worked with a number of different groups such as the Osage, Plains, Kiowa, and Pueblo Indians. *Maria* is a biography based on Marriott's work with Maria Martinez, the famous Rio Grande Pueblo potter. These specific texts, drawn from the body of each author's work, codify the dilemma of white women anthropologists who looked to Native Americans and Native American women for the reconstruction of themselves.

More recently, the emergence of feminism and Native American activism and claims for self-representation during the 1960s and 1970s have opened up different possibilities for ethnographic encounter among white women and Native Americans; these possibilities have broken from the oppressive structure of looking for a reconstructed white, female self in Native American cultures to find the gender conflicts within Anglo-American society. Irene Stewart's autobiography as told to Mary Shepardson (1980) serves as an appropriate example of this interplay of post-1960s Native American activism and Anglo-American feminism. Shepardson, who received her Ph.D. in anthropology from the University of California, Berkeley, in 1960 at the age of 54, researched cultural change and the effects of Anglo-American values on Navajo political organization. With her female colleague Blodwen Hammond she worked at Navajo Mountain from 1960 to 1962 studying social structure (Shepardson and Hammond 1970).

In the reconstruction of the history of anthropology to include women's ethnographic study in the Southwest, the more complex underside of white women's ethnographic practice needs to be examined. This underside consists of the power relations among white and Native American women, those who have conventionally studied and those who have been studied. My examination of those power relations is based on the premise that gender, the relationship of women

and men, is intersected and, thus, affected by other social relations such as race, class, ethnicity, and culture in the production of women's identity. The connections between white women's ethnographic authority and their constructions of identities for themselves and Native American women suggest that women have a stake in gender—that they are caught within the cultural constructs of gender but continually struggle with it. As such, gender is a complex and vexing problem in which women are not only victims but actors and makers of its reality.

I stress relations among women because of my desire to resist the tendency to see all power relations among women as primarily deriving from men's control of women. Although relations with men in our male-dominant society have clearly created problems and tensions among women, it has been, in large part, up to women to wrestle with and resolve these conflicts. The recent history of feminism in the United States and internationally reveals that women are struggling with the difficult challenge of sorting out illegitimate social privilege and hierarchy among women from valued distinctions such as those of cultural differences. In particular, I want to illuminate a specific set of conflicting desires for many of the white women ethnographers who studied and became involved in the lives of Native American women—the desire for both authority and equality in their relationships with Native Americans.

ETHNOGRAPHIC AUTHORITY AND POWER

In his 1983 article, "On Ethnographic Authority," James Clifford named ethnographic authority as an object of critical interest for those examining the politics of ethnographic representation. In this article, Clifford suggests that ethnographic authority is primarily an effect of the literary form of the monograph. The monograph, with its rhetorical strategies that signify objectivity and a total control and grasp of the Other, is linked historically to the rise of a particular professional persona, the participant-observer. Clifford treats the poetics of ethnographic writing as political and historical, noting that this representational practice emerged at the height of twentieth-century colonial administration. The monograph, thus, is a translation of that will to power, that Western "gaze" at the "rest." According to Clifford, with the breaking apart of the vestiges of legal colonialism during the 1950s and 1960s, the textual conventions of the monograph have been challenged in the appearance of a subgenre of anthropological writing (Marcus and Fischer 1986; Rabinow 1977). This subgenre experiments, in various ways, with the form of the monograph. As such, it breaks up the textual authority of the monograph, and for Clifford this literary subversion embodies an anticolonial political and ethical stance.

The distinction between conventional, monographic authority and experimentation, which is anti-authoritarian, is important to Clifford's article. It historicizes generic and rhetorical codes by interpreting them as complex translations of power relations. As useful as is Clifford's and other postmodernists' thinking about ethnographic authority in terms of rhetorical tropes, narrative structures, and interpretive strategies, however, the study of ethnographic authority needs to be broadened to move questions of authority and power beyond a too-narrow investigation of textual representation. The nexus of representation, participant-observation and historical circumstances, needs to be teased out in considering the politics of ethnography. To understand the politics of representing others, something similar to what Donna Haraway (1989) has called the "story-telling practices" of ethnography need to be engaged. To get at the purpose and meaning of representation, writing, and authority requires deepening our involvement with the actual stories being told in ethnographies. Haraway argues that people are constantly interpreting and telling serious tales about their world to give meaning to it, and in her recent books on the history of primate studies in the United States (1989) she proposes the concept of storytelling as a guide for hearing the multiplicity of perspectives that contest for imparting the "truth" about primates. In her concept of storytelling, people take pleasure in the actual making of the stories themselves, and that requires a technology of reading that can get closer to the actual contents of, in this case, ethnographic representation.

Linda Gordon (1988), in her recent book on the history and politics of family violence in the United States, argues that feminist analyses of a range of power relations need concepts that suggest complex struggle, not only negotiation but cooperation between those whose relationship is structured by dominance. In her study, Gordon argues against an understanding of power that is unidirectional and is about domination in the restricted sense of the repression of the ruled by rulers. She reaches for a view of power as governance, where power is cultural, deployed in specific contexts.

Gordon's argument can also be brought into a consideration of the relations between ethnographic authority and power in that she stresses that power is not just repressive but is also technical and managerial. By suggesting a historically grounded understanding of the power of modern states as it is manifested in the dynamics of social welfare, Gordon (1988:vi–vii) stresses complex "flows of initiative" of power in relations of social control. Her thinking about power dovetails with what Michel Foucault (1980) has called the "productive" character of modern politics. Although there are clearly distinctions between Gordon's and Foucault's philosophies of history, both grapple with dynamics of power that cannot be captured by Marxist political theories, which see power as domination only, or by liberal theories, which refuse to recognize inequality or oppression. What both are interested in is an understanding of power that is mobile and unstable but nonetheless not simply a continual reciprocity of moves among people. As Foucault (1980:119) argues,

If power were never anything but repressive, if it never did anything but to say no, do you really think one would be brought to obey it? What makes power good, what makes it accepted, is simply the fact that it doesn't only weigh on us as a force that says no, but that it traverses and produces things, it induces pleasure, forms knowledge, produces discourse. It needs to be considered as a productive network which runs through the whole social body, much more than as a negative instance whose function is repression.

From this perspective, ethnographic authority cannot be divorced from situations of power involving social relationships that are not simply contradictory but also circuitous. These circuits of relations deserve the demanding task of hermeneutical engagement to understand the connections between an ethnographic will to power, desire, and the knowledge produced among white women who set out to educate as well as study Native Americans.

I do not wish to consider ethnographic representations as either windows onto the world of the Other or as manifestations of ontological ambiguity, as some who have written about ethnographic representation have implied (e.g., Tyler 1986), but as woven into the social practice of storytelling. As Haraway (1989) notes, there is social practice at two levels, in the stories themselves and in the practices that make the stories possible. If we think about what makes certain interpretations possible, then we can hear ethnographic authority in between social history and the politics of ethnographic representation, not simply in the way the authorial voice, for example, is textually constituted but also in the actual making of the stories themselves.

THE DYNAMICS OF MATRONIZATION

White women anthropologists throughout the twentieth century have been part of white gover-

nance and management of Native Americans. As consultants to bureaucratic and governmental agencies, such as the Bureau of Indian Affairs, their bureaucratic role until recently was primarily as translators of cultural meanings for white administrators who needed information to supply welfare services. This management of Native American welfare included the complicated position of patronizing or, in this case, matronizing Native American women. This matronization involved genuine concern for and friendship with Native American women as well as the underlying arrogance and delusion built into translating Native American women's desires into interpretations of their needs. Although there can be no shirking from seeing this arrogance, its roots lay in more than simple bad faith. The will to power of these white women involved a desire to educate the lay public as a means of countering a general lack of empathy for and interest in Native Americans on the part of members of the white culture. Like their white male counterparts, these women saw themselves as fighting ignorance and racism through education and supporting values of tolerance, curiosity, and openness in the face of cultural differences among whites and Native Americans.

Along with wanting to educate other whites, these women also faced the difficult task of trying to understand, existentially, the damage inflicted by whites on Native Americans and their own relationship to that damage. While questions of cultural adaptation, assimilation, and diffusion run throughout the intellectual tradition of anthropology because of its strong ties to colonial administration, in the case of many individual anthropologists these interests were tinged with the desire to face squarely and respond to the violent and tragic elements of white–Native American contact. This basically liberal and ethical stance was overlaid with discontent over what it meant to be part of a group of people in whose name Native Americans had been victimized. For white women, this search for another identity was also frequently overlaid with a dissatisfaction with the male dominance of white society. For these women, this dissatisfaction meant playing out a desire, sometimes named explicitly and sometimes merely implied, to turn oneself into another kind of female by making Native American women into models of femininity. In the ethnographies I will be looking at in this chapter, comments about Native American womanhood frequently are charged with an implicit contrast with other possible ways of being female, which is not surprising given the contrastive character of anthropology. The point of this discussion of matronization is to suggest a relationship to colonialism on the part of these white women ethnographers that was neither innocent nor totally guilty but complicitous in a historically specific way.

Thus, matronization is a dynamic shot through with desires marked by race, class, and gender, and to separate out these strands is to miss the complexity of white women's position in this dynamic—one of educating themselves as well as their society. White women ethnographers both created and were caught within a historical problem of trying to change inequality but preserve difference. Ironically, in their desire to educate about cultural difference and to see themselves as, in some ways, apart from white domination, these white women saw frequently not variability or difference but the working out of gender relations of white society. Looking for a different kind of womanhood, white women anthropologists made Native American women visible to white culture as amalgamations of proper white women of the time as well as proper negotiators and resisters of white culture. These combined idealizations were based on the belief that saw white culture as fundamentally intrusive but white ethnographers as outside of this dynamic. The sense that they were outside of a perceived violent part of their culture helped white women ethnographers create a mode of relating to Native American women like mother and child. It assumed a kind of interde-

pendency in which white women tried to relinquish certain privileges and powers on the condition that Native American women love and care about them. This interdependency was not innocent but structured in part by the demand that the inevitable anger, conflict, and disagreement that Native American women might experience be suppressed so that white women could produce knowledge about them to educate the white public.

This dynamic was structured by a kind of possessiveness on the part of white women toward Native Americans, which, in cases such as that of Matilda Coxe Stevenson, was so strong that she engendered hostile relations with the Zuni. According to Nancy Parezo's biographical study in this volume, in 1879 Stevenson encountered opposition to her taking notes on Zuni ceremonies and responded by taking them secretly. By hiding her note taking, she presented herself to her Zuni informants as compliant, while at the same time she aggressively thrust herself into ceremonies where she was unwelcome. When Stevenson forced her way into a kiva, she was met with a silence that she never understood. Parezo notes that Stevenson's initial research method was to attend ceremonies unannounced and assume that her participation was accepted. If this failed, only then would she try to persuade particular Zuni to let her in. Moreover, in Parezo's words, "She would tell individuals that it was their duty to record information about their lives, since they as a group would inevitably assimilate into American society and that their actions would be approved by the gods" (p. 50). Stevenson's overriding sense of knowing what was good for the Zuni contributed to her ignorance. She literally ignored the possibility that the Zuni might not want to share everything about their culture with her. Her zealous salvaging of the Zuni for white consumption permanently damaged her ethnographic relations. By becoming a kind of "hurt mother" it also meant that Stevenson refused to read silence as culturally meaningful. She was unable to achieve the openness necessary for field-work to be more than the imposition of one's vision onto another. Although Stevenson is an extreme example, other white women anthropologists who were less insensitive personally and without Stevenson's hubris still maintained relations of authority that led to a relatively smooth practice of projection onto Native Americans. The dilemma among white women and Native American women was one of emotional ties, indeed love in some cases, among political unequals, but this struggle was not generally commented on ethnographically.

Such matronization produced certain kinds of ethnographic knowledge and, on a practical basis, permitted the kinds of stories told in Reichard's *Dezba* and Marriott's *Maria.* Irene Stewart's narrated autobiography, *A Voice in Her Tribe,* presents a somewhat different practice of authority that suggests another way of white women relating to Native American women. Reichard's and Marriott's texts were based on fieldwork conducted in the Southwest during the 1930s and late 1940s, a period of intensive academic study and political administration of Native Americans of this geographic region. Stewart's autobiography as told to Mary Shepardson, however, was published in 1980, about 25 years after their initial contact with each other, and as such is more appropriately situated within the more recent history of contact between white and Native American women. As will be shown, Stewart's text suggests a more complex dynamic than matronization. Still, it is useful to consider her account alongside Reichard's and Marriott's because hers provides a counterpoint to the central argument of this essay.

ETHNOGRAPHIC STORIES AND
THE HISTORY OF GENDER

The knowledge produced out of this dynamic of matronization suggests that the contradictions of matronization produced stories that echo the ne-gotiation of gender within U.S. society more generally. Reichard's, Marriott's, and Stewart's texts exist within three periods of gender relations in U.S. history: the late 1930s, which was the time of the Great Depression and the New Deal; the late 1940s and the postwar period; and the 1980s, after the ethnic activism and social protest of the 1960s. Linda Gordon (1988) nicely summarizes the gender relations of these time periods. Utilizing a case study of social work records on family violence in Boston, Gordon argues that gender has been interpreted differently as a result of large historical events and patterns. Like Gordon, I believe that family violence should not be seen as an aberration in relations between men and women but as an extension of "normal" conflict between the sexes in a male-dominant society. The usefulness of Gordon's account is that it reveals much about the social history of gender among those administering and those being administered within the social welfare system in the United States. Gordon's story is predominantly about certain ethnic groups—the Anglo-American, native-born whites of the middle class, the Italian and Irish immigrants who came during the great waves of immigration during the late nineteenth century and eventually came to understand themselves as Americans, and the African-Americans. Although Native Americans became a part of the welfare system during the twentieth century, their relationship to it was not the same as those of the above groups. Thus, it is possible to use Gordon's commentary on the meanings of the 1930s, 1940s, 1950s, and 1960s to illuminate the relative "whiteness" of Reichard's, Marriott's, and Stewart's texts. Gordon's descriptions of gender relations during these periods, then, provides a map of the field of referentiality within which these ethnographies exist.

As Gordon describes, during the depression years conflict between men and women was suppressed in favor of reconciliation and economic aid. Male violence was deemphasized, and the unemployed husband became a figure of social workers' sympathy. Gordon also argues that "women were consistently held responsible for the treatment of children and the general mood of the family, as men were not" (1988:22–23). Gender conflict, to the extent it was visible at all, was seen as an epiphenomenon of events outside of the family. The paradigmatic narrative here was about a husband who had been denied his manhood by economic circumstances and a wife who denied herself to help him find his male identity in other ways and to run a household in the face of this displacement of gender. The 1940s and 1950s, according to Gordon, represented a low point in public awareness of violence in the family but also the rise of psychiatric categories in interpreting its roots. She argues, "The roots of most interpersonal problems were sought in individual 'complexes,' not in cultural or structural arrangements" (1988:23).

What is essential about these decades is the kind of public denial of conflict between men and women. The denial occurred in two ways. First, there was the intensification of romantic ties between men and women after World War II, which stressed the complementarity of the sexes and the necessity of heterosexual coupling. In contrast to the period of the Great Depression during which conflict between men and women was suppressed, during the 1950s, romantic love sentimentalized conflicts, making them tautological. Second, and related to the first, was the contradiction that claimed that compulsory heterosexual romance was intensely pleasurable for women even though so many supposedly needed treatment for neuroses defined as the inability to have an orgasm or enjoy sex.

In the 1960s and 1970s, family violence was rediscovered and redefined through the social activism of the civil rights, anti-war, student, and women's movements. These movements challenged in different ways "the sanctity of family privacy, the privileged position of the male head of family, and the importance of family togetherness at all costs" (Gordon 1988:25). We are still living through the changes both addressed and brought about by these social movements, including the achievements of feminism as well as new contradictions emerging from the rise of female-headed households. I want to use Gordon's categories not so much as empirical truth but as evocative and useful mechanisms for helping to see the relative projection of cultural norms shared by diverse groups of "white" citizens, in this case white female ethnographers, onto Native Americans.

COMMUNAL MOTHERING AND WOMEN'S IDENTITY

In 1939 Gladys Reichard published *Dezba,* a biography/story of a Navajo woman who is made to represent the Navajo as a perceived totality. Reichard's preface includes a statement of her motivations for writing the book—to answer questions asked by various non-anthropologists about the Navajo. Reichard's claim to present a "picture of daily life and adaptation to objects and notions which have been introduced by whites" (1939a: v) assumed that scientific expertise on the part of anthropologists could go a long way toward changing public prejudice and violence toward Native Americans as well as developing an appreciation for a way of life different than their own. Claims of residing with native peoples was one of the practices anthropologists believed authorized their knowledge over those of lay people such as tourists and certain officials of the government (see Clifford 1983), and Reichard saw herself as writing to those whose "brief contacts" with the Navajo led them to see only a people who were "so reserved as to be stolid, so patient as to be shiftless, so mobile as to be irresponsible, so acquisitive as to be beggarly or grasping" (1939a: v). It was this overtly stereotyped image she wanted to correct.

Reichard wanted to know how Native Americans encountered and responded to white contact, which she saw as essentially intrusive. Her construction of womanhood, which she constructed and applied to both Dezba and herself, was bound up with her interest in adaption (i.e., adaptation), formulated as the transition between "old Navajo and modern white ways" (1939a:vi). The meaning of the term *adaption* in Reichard's account is interwoven with certain understandings she brought with her from white culture. These were gendered beliefs that stressed a historically specific family form emphasizing women's support in the family during a time of economic crisis. *Dezba* is a story about women influencing society through their role as communal mothers. Mothering is the bridge between the sublime and the innocent, the reconciliation of contradictions and tensions. Reichard's description of Dezba is filled with references to her quiet dignity, her gentle firmness and modesty. She is protector, defender, worrier who responds to community needs through a kind of personal involvement that demands nothing in return.

As a figure of sacrificing maternalism, Dezba is the site of adaptation; she is the figure who negotiates with whites and who constantly reminds us of the danger of involvement with whites without actively resisting their presence. Reichard's representation of Dezba's maternalism is characterized by an overall sense of loss in relation to whites. In Reichard's account, defensiveness is the only permissible action for females to take. Since women do not seek out or aspire for themselves, they do not openly confront whites who might take from Native Americans but rather yield to them to avoid trouble. Dezba possesses a kind of dignity that is not simply a sign of quiet but solid resistance to whites but also a translation of proper Anglo female behavior during this period. What assertiveness Dezba is seen to possess revolves around holding onto her children. For example, Reichard tells us that "Gray Girl was the youngest of her daughters and Dezba had long since decided to keep her a Navajo" (1939a: 60). Mothering is the signifier of resistance to whites, a positive form that works alongside the

"dull resentment in the gentle minds of Dezba and her brother" (1939a:13). Gentle Dezba, mother of her clan, negotiates white intrusion through her calm but steady refusal to be provoked by whites and by making her children the site of Navajo authenticity.

Reichard's account opens with an introduction that is a standard, general anthropological sketch of a unified Navajo culture. Its focus is the adaptation of the Navajo in relationship to other cultures, namely the Pueblo and white cultures of the geographic region. Reichard's way of coming to terms with the "mixture of the old and the new" that she sees in the Navajo is to mystify the Navajo and the landscape of the Southwest. She claims that although the Navajo may appear as modern, underneath this appearance lies a people that are either sublime, literally fixed to the "grandeur and terror" of the landscape, or else childlike and innocent, what she refers to as "children of the earth." Dezba is the locus for reconciling this contradiction between these two forces. In Reichard's account of this Navajo woman, there is a utopia of gendered identity based on women being at the center of the household with a sexual division of labor, with no apparent conflict in what is portrayed as benevolent division based on complementary functioning very reminiscent of Victorian notions of gendered complementarity (see Rosaldo 1980). Running through this mild household governed by women is the continual intruding presence of white society and Dezba's resistant role as protector of her household in her negotiation with white culture. In the household run by women, both old and new meet, and while there is an acceptance of the new found in the use of electrical appliances, overall the household represents a kind of gentile femininity understood as stasis in the face of white society, which is understood as change. White schools are a constant source of pollution and pain in Reichard's account, and white women are the principal representatives of these institutions as teachers. Ironically, Reichard separates herself from the category of white female with its sense of intrusive disciplining of Native Americans. She does not even flinch when she reports of Native American women talking in negative terms about "white girls."

The heart of Reichard's conception of gender is evident in two parts of her ethnography that show her support of a kind of male androgyny and simultaneous lack of sympathy for or interest in a female androgynous counterpart. In the story of Lassos-a-warrior, one of Dezba's relatives, his androgyny makes him a Christ-like figure who has a special responsibility and power in the community. Indeed, much of his adult life is told under the chapter entitled "Authority," and he serves as an analogue to Dezba's female authority. We are told that Lassos-a-warrior sustained an unspecified injury during his infancy that was to "deprive him of his virility" (1939a: 108). As he grew up he did not refuse the sexual division of labor with its assignments of specific tasks to men, but all could see that he was not quite a man. The outward symbol of this was his body, which was tall but slender and delicate. A more ordinary boy would have been the object of teasing, but in Lassos-a-warrior's case his companions knew of his defect and did not ostracize him for it.

According to Reichard, Lassos-a-warrior is a particular type of Navajo person, a *nadle.* Reichard quotes the meaning of *nadle* as "one who changes." This category of individuals consists of men who prefer women's activities over men's and either do women's work instead of men's or else do women's work without giving up completely men's activities. Lassos-a-warrior exhibits the latter because he learned to weave and yet remained a singer; singers were generally male religious figures whose chanting presided over such events as marriages and curing ceremonies. In Reichard's account, before Lassos-a-warrior was 30 he decided to dedicate his life to religion, giving over property to his female relatives. Like all singers, he was given the respect of The People, but Reichard claims more for him, providing him with a complementary kind of authority to the matron, Dezba:

The attainment of wealth through skill and singing was enough to merit Navajo respect and admiration, but Lassos-a-warrior, like Dezba, had more than that. He had a confident composure which nothing could disturb since he feared neither man, nature, nor even the supernatural (1939a: 112).

Reichard goes on at some length about Lasso-a-warrior's spiritual powers, which he demonstrates in the advice he gives to those who turn to him for help.

In contrast to Reichard's interest in and obvious approval of Lassos-a-warrior is her more ambivalent depiction of a tomboy. The riding of a bull by a young woman at the Navajo Tribal Fair becomes the occasion for Reichard's confusion about Navajo women who do not exhibit the quiet, controlled behavior that she finds so appealing in Dezba. In Reichard's description of a particular fair, she tells us about the gendered character of horse racing and bronc riding events. The men ride broncos and tie wild calves, generating a great deal of excitement and surprise at their skill. Riding by Navajo women is presented by Reichard through the eyes of Alnaba, one of Dezba's granddaughters, as well as through the responses of Dezba and a female friend. Alnaba, at the time of the fair, is learning to ride, and Reichard tells us that when Alnaba has mastered this skill she "would be expected to ride serenely and stately, for Navajo women were above all things dignified" (1939a:86). A surprising announcement of a young Navajo girl who will ride a wild bull takes place:

This, to Dezba as well as to Alnaba, was unheard-of. Nevertheless after some suspense, a girl who could in no way be distinguished from a boy broke through a gate riding a protesting bull. To Alnaba this girl had reached a peak in accomplishment and as she vowed to emulate her, she heard her grandmother say to the woman sitting beside her, "That girl has always acted exactly like a boy. She has never worn a dress in her life. It may be all right for her, because she goes to school and acts just like a white girl. But I would not like to have one of my girls act like that. Such sports are too rough for women" (1939a:87).

In the exchange between Dezba and her friend, this tomboyish behavior is linked to that of a "squaw dance," an event in which some young women ask men to dance in exchange for money, which they give to their families. In Reichard's description, we hear (through Alnaba's ears) Dezba and her friend's disapproval of this practice, a very common disapproval among Navajo women. Reichard's picture in this scene is confusing because she closes her description with the claim that Alnaba thought she would still like to dance. Alnaba would still like to be close to this event despite the manner in which it gets tainted by Dezba and her friend. Alnaba's excitement is not vocalized in this scene but is, nonetheless, represented; it contrasts starkly with Reichard's portrayal of Lassos-a-warrior, who is a publicly recognized androgynous male. Gender bending for men, in Reichard's account, is valued, while for women it is associated with ethnic pollution and permitted only to be a kind of secret thrill. In addition, Reichard's portrayal of whiteness as polluting can only take place as a result of her viewing whiteness as simultaneously belonging to others who are invasive and being neutral for herself. This helps account for the rather smooth, unflinching way that Reichard as a white female reports this incident.

The engendering of the Navajo, thus, revolves around a specific sex/gender system in which women are, first and foremost, communal mothers and men are either sons, absent husbands, or leaders as a result of their androgyny. This engendering of the Navajo resonates with the historical horizon of the Great Depression and New Deal, in which empathy of economic reform efforts was directed toward the unemployed man. Unemployment for men during this period was seen as a failure of manhood, and the New Deal was, in

part, an effort to boost that conception of masculinity. The milieu of the Great Depression insisted on a form of female support for men, privileging the rebuilding of men's identities and resources at the expense of female desires that went beyond the shoring up of men without jobs. In Reichard's account we see hints of the undercutting of a young woman's aspirations to participate in an activity reserved conventionally for men. Because she concludes with Alnaba's desire to ride bulls as a private fantasy, Reichard suggests that Native American women's interest in things masculine must be contained within silence. Of course, my argument that this text calls up the beliefs about men and women that Anglo-Americans were working out in response to the Great Depression does not imply that Reichard's fieldwork was useless and that her ethnography was essentially solipsistic. I am stressing the connections with her own culture to underscore some of the limits that continue to plague fieldwork among women, limits that must be faced to be changed.

ROMANCE AND GENDER OF THE 1950S: THE HETEROSEXUALIZATION OF NATIVE AMERICANS

In contrast to Reichard's biography, Alice Marriott's book focuses on the San Ildefonso potter Maria Martinez. Like Reichard, Marriott was interested in educating the white public, and she states that she was interested in "making ethnographic reports human stories" for those who "didn't yet know much about Indian women" (Marriott 1986). Marriott's biography, published in the immediate postwar period (1948), constructs a different relationship between ethnographic authority and gender by engendering Maria Martinez as a wife rather than a maternal head of the household. In Marriott's account, gender becomes heterosexualized in ways that simply are not present in *Dezba*. (By heterosexualized, I mean to suggest a significant difference between the relative looseness of the sexual and emotional ties between men and women during the depression as compared with those of the postwar period.) Reichard's biography is not about the kind of psychological/sexual intensity that is so crucial to the representation of Maria and Julian Martinez. Indeed, the fact that Maria's life story is also, in important ways, Julian's story contrasts with the relative autonomy of Dezba's tale, in which her husband is barely present. In addition, in Marriott's account, the entire political and economic development of the pueblo emanates from this couple.

Maria's identity as a potter cannot be separated from her role as her husband's psychological support, because in trying to control his drinking she involved him in making pottery. As a result of what Marriott portrays as Maria's psychological support, both Maria and Julian became successful potters, and, in turn, others in the pueblo turned to them to earn income through making pottery. Thus, Marriott's story of Maria carries a moral suggesting that the female acceptance of marriage and the responsibility for men's emotional well-being is crucial for economic growth and prosperity. This moral calls up the sex/gender system supporting the postwar suburbanization of life in the United States with its glorification of romance between men and women.

The story of Maria's personal life begins with initial resistance to and eventual acceptance of marriage. At a young age Maria attends school and becomes interested in teaching, only to be told by her sister to forget it and find a husband. After Maria tells her teacher, Miss Grimes, that she will clean the schoolhouse in exchange for social lessons, she lets her sister, Desideria, know that she may be interested in becoming a teacher. Desideria demands to know why Maria wants more lessons and why Maria wants to be a teacher, remarking, "That's all right for white people. But Indian girls don't have to be teachers. They have houses and babies to take care of" (Marriott 1948:97). Here again, as in the case of Reichard's account, deviation from gender on the part of women is marked as white and female. In the face of Desideria's disgust, Maria tries to suggest that having a house and babies takes work as well, that "you have to know how to do things, and you have to get a husband" (1948:98). She makes an implicit equivalency between marriage and teaching through the category of work, and this allows her to assert that finding a husband takes time in the same way learning to be a teacher does. Desideria, however, resists the equivalency and escalates their disagreement:

"Ana didn't know how to do things except farm," objected Desideria. "She manages her house and the baby all right."

"Well, she still had to get married first," said Maria firmly. "I don't know anybody to marry, and I'm not planning to get married."

"It doesn't have anything to do with you," snapped Desideria. "It's up to our parents to find somebody for us to marry, and to get everything ready for us."

"Maybe it is," said Maria, "but I don't know that I'll like the one they pick out for me. I might want to marry somebody else."

"If they pick him out, you've got to marry him," said Desideria, and she turned and went into the house. Maria followed her (1948:98).

In this exchange, Maria struggles to assert a different kind of female identity than one based in wifehood, but her sister denies Maria any agency in her identity. This scene is a struggle over gender in which one sister demands that the other acquiesce to her definition of femininity, and she calls on parental authority as a means of getting Maria to accept her place as a proper Native American woman. This struggle over gender evokes the 1950s preoccupation with getting women to marry. As Linda Gordon (1988) points out, during this decade tensions between men and women were explained in terms of women's neuroses. Built into this view of women's internal struggle with their femininity was the demand for therapeutic surveillance such that scores of experts offered advice about how women could overcome the psychological problems that prevented them from administering to men's needs. This scene of disagreement between women shows one woman hounding the other to give up her desire to teach. Gordon's analysis of family violence and conflict during the 1950s argues, "The 'nagging wife' of traditional patriarchal folklore was now transformed into a woman of complex mental ailments: failure to accept her own femininity and attempting to compete with her husband" (L. Gordon 1988:23). Maria, who initially wants to teach, puts those desires aside when she falls in love with Julian. The compromise worked out in the story is that Maria does become a wife but negotiates for her own choice of husband. Her parents consent to her choice of Julian, reinforcing the romantic drama of the parents' own courtship, which is told in great detail.

In the 1940s and 1950s women were instructed on how to become expert psychological supporters of men and were held responsible, as in the 1930s, for men. In this period, however, women were not temporary heads of households but silent therapists for men's problems and failures. In the lives of Maria and Julian Martinez, Marriott finds the suburbanization of gender within white U.S. society, with its tightening of the boundaries around nuclear families. Not that Maria and Julian are portrayed as living the way *Life* magazine showed family lives; the Native American practice of extended families is quite clear in this account. Rather, this practice is filtered through the dominant presence of Maria's and Julian's psychological interdependence. Marriott's text invites the reader to share in what comes close to an assigned obsession for Maria—the intense interest in what motivates Julian to behave the way he does and how to rescue him from his alcoholism. Julian is portrayed as a mystery that Maria and various men he works with

try to figure out. There is an ongoing tension throughout the story of their marriage caused by Julian's occasional drinking bouts in which he disappears for days. Maria's role is to both know and not know what he is doing, since she experiences him as drunk but never speaks directly to him about it. Rather, she and the Anglo-American and Hispanic men who employ her and Julian try to guess the reasons for why Julian drinks.

Maria's identity as an artist is bound up with her coming to terms with femininity, which is signified as wifehood, and identity, which she comes to accept through her struggle with her sister (described above) as well as the continual pieces of sage wisdom that her mother offers her. Acceptance of wifehood, in turn, leads to Maria's and Julian's effect on the political economy of San Ildefonso. They become successful businesspeople by working with white entrepreneurs who sell their pottery. Marriott represents their success in business as benefiting others; when other San Ildefonsoans challenge Maria and Julian to share their artistic and business skills so that they, too, can profit economically from an activity felt to belong to the whole pueblo, the couple includes them in the commercial pottery operation. Compared to Reichard's earlier portrayal, this ethnography is relatively less concerned with a woman as mother and more concerned with her relationship with her husband.

The central importance of Maria's psychological state makes Marriott's text more like a novel than either Reichard's biography or Stewart's autobiography. Much of the text dwells on Maria's thoughts of her husband, particularly his psychological and physical comfort. Maria tries throughout the story to keep Julian sober, and the text ends on the strange note, given its premises, of his death from alcoholism. Supposedly, Maria should have been able to free him from his disease, but what we are left with is the fact that she cannot.

WOMEN'S POLITICS AND SELF-REPRESENTATION: POST-1960S

In contrast to Reichard's portrayal of Dezba, the engendering of Stewart in her autobiography, as told to Mary Shepardson, is not figured primarily as that of a female head of the household but rather as that of a politician and legal arbitrator. Shepardson, a trained anthropologist who conducted fieldwork among the Navajo, was interested in their political and legal life. Stewart's text, published in 1980, reflects not only Shepardson's intellectual interests in the 1950s but also the increasing involvement of Native Americans in the legal and political empowerment of their tribes after the 1960s. Indeed, Shepardson's stated intellectual interests in her introduction to the text show a shift in focus away from the problem of adaptation, which was crucial for Reichard. Shepardson claims that she was able to become friends with Stewart (something that Reichard did not claim with Dezba or Marriott with Maria) because of a shared "intense interest in the building of self-government in our country's largest Indian society, a tribe which is not at the same time a 'domestic dependent nation'" (Shepardson 1980:5). Unlike Reichard, who belonged to the second generation of women anthropologists who worked in the Southwest, Shepardson falls somewhere in between Reichard's generation and the third generation of women anthropologists who attended graduate school in the 1960s. Shepardson had done fieldwork at Navajo Mountain in 1960, 1961, and 1962 and coauthored with Blodwen Hammond a functionalist and structural ethnography on Navajo social organization and kinship.

Shepardson conducted her fieldwork almost 30 years later than Reichard; more significantly, the introduction to Stewart's account was written after the 1960s and the emergence of mass social activism for Native American legal rights and cultural and political identity. It reflects the time period in which ethnic movements both took over and were given greater power in formulating public discourses and practices about their cultures. Since the 1960s, victims other than those of the working class—women, ethnic minorities, Third World peoples, lesbians, and gay men—have become much more visible culturally. These victims have had greater political power in defining their problems, and this is reflected in the relatively more mutual construction of Stewart as a Native American woman. The evidence of this mutuality is the fact that the book is an autobiography, however mediated by Shepardson, and not a biography. While this shift in genre does not guarantee either positive political identity or the achievement of practical goals, this particular autobiography suggests at least a potential recognition of the struggles for ethnic self-determination because of explicit demarcation of author, translator, and editor and Shepardson's and Stewart's roles in each. This explicitness raises the charged character of self-representation and its possibilities in ways that Reichard's and Marriott's texts do not.

In addition, Shepardson established a relationship with Native American women though a different avenue than Reichard, who learned weaving to work with Native American women. Shepardson's bond with Irene Stewart lay in their interest in Navajo self-government, reflecting a shift in meaning from studying problems of assimilation and adaptation, with their referent being whiteness. In Irene Stewart's account, the Navajo community as a whole and not the female-headed household is the place where self-government is centered. Stewart is not a head of the household but a legal arbitrator and female politician for her tribe. This shift signifies both the more general trend of the national political economy away from the nuclear family as the productive unit toward other forms of households and the changing relationship of white women to marriage and motherhood. While Reichard's text stresses mothering and Marriott's accents wifehood, Irene Stewart's account focuses on other activities. Although the family is the institution where human action occurs in Reichard's and Marriott's accounts, the nation is the space of encountering in Stewart's text. When Stewart does discuss her interaction with family members, she is working within a different construction of family than either the female household of the Great Depression or the sentimentalized husband-and-wife bond of the 1950s. In Stewart's story, her bond with Greyeyes, her husband, is one where tribal politics, elections, and community affairs dominate. As Stewart relates events from her life, the feminist preoccupations of Shepardson's culture come through. Stewart's story, in contrast to Dezba's or Maria's, is about a woman who marries a man outside her society, divorces, becomes a single mother taking many different jobs to support her family, and forms a common-law marriage with a man significantly older than herself. Unlike Reichard's biography of Dezba, Stewart's power in the community comes from her political role and community leadership in arbitration cases. Stewart's story is about the acquisition of the kind of power that goes beyond influencing people through her role as mother, and there is nothing of the kind of female responsibility for men that is present in Marriott's depiction of Maria.

In addition, the image Stewart presents of herself reflects certain contemporary feminist and ethnic ideals that stress androgyny and cultural syncretism; both approaches attempt to combine differing beliefs. Shepardson's introduction emphasizes Stewart's being of two cultures, but implicit in her description is the blending of gender as well:

She seemed at home in both cultures. At rodeos and Tribal Fairs she usually wore a velvet blouse and long satin skirt, her hair done in the special knot bound with wool which is the characteristic "national" hair style. At church she wore "Anglo" clothes. As ware-

houseman distributing grain she donned Levis and a plaid cowboy shirt (1980:6).

Stewart participates simultaneously in the production of tradition, marked in this passage as "national," in Anglo culture, and in western male culture. The explicit cross-dressing is a manifestation of the movement across differing boundaries, reflecting a historical moment in which a self-conscious conception of gender and ethnicity are not seen as opposed but existing together. Unlike in the previous ethnographies where gender is represented as a natural product of inherited ways of being, in Shepardson's introduction gender is an invented display, forged out of the play of masculine dress on a female body. In contrast to Reichard's ethnographic account where androgyny is an exclusively male prerogative, in Shepardson's image and Stewart's autobiography a kind of female androgyny is represented.

Stewart's autobiography registers not only the more recent permeability of gender but also changes in family structure. Stewart tells us of her first marriage, which ended in divorce, and the numerous jobs she took to support her children as a single mother in a chapter entitled, "A Broken Marriage and a Family to Support." There is none of the compulsive interest in trying to resolve men's problems, nor is there any sense that Stewart was responsible for her husband's irresponsibility. She describes him as a "wanderlust," a man who claimed to be job hunting but never brought home money, and she tells us how irritating it was to be married to him. Stewart's second marriage to Greyeyes appears as a relationship based on companionship and shared interests and activities, especially politics.

Her discussion of Greyeyes reflects a historical content of gender in which a different set of contradictions exists compared to the 1930s and immediate postwar period discussed previously. Stewart gives Greyeyes a certain kind of authority based on her recounting the various stories he tells her about the political history of the tribe as well as his skill and wisdom in settling an arbitration case involving marital conflict. She recounts Greyeyes' origin story of how the Navajo came under white control and how this shifted Navajo governance and created the need for an administrative apparatus. Greyeyes, who is significantly older than Stewart, is represented as a wise sage. Stewart, on the other hand, is the practicing politician, the one who was elected to this most complicated position in local government, the chapter secretary. Stewart is clearly the political actor in her family, although she implies in her discussion of how she got into politics that it was Greyeyes' interest in a local chapter dispute that enabled her to be nominated for a local position in government. Greyeyes is not patriarchal, absent, or romantically unstable, but he is given authority based on his being an elderly man. Nonetheless, because authority as a practicing politician dominates this account, it is difficult to hear Stewart's discussion of Greyeyes as some kind of subservience to her husband.

Indeed, unlike in Marriott's biography, Stewart's marital status is of relatively little importance. In her discussion of her adult life, her major passion is politics, the actual hands-on work of settling conflicts and managing the local community she represents. Her career as a politician also includes a recognition that women can work together as women to make political change happen. At one point, she mentions that Annie Wauneka, the only female Tribal Council member, supports her in her campaign for Tribal Council officer. When Stewart tells Wauneka that she thinks she will lose in the election, Wauneka responds optimistically, saying,

"Oh come on, don't talk like that; do your best and make up your mind to win. I want you to win over the two men and be with me in the council meetings. We'll join up and really work; there is plenty to do. We will go places together, so work hard. It is not hard at all when you really put all you've got into it. You've had more education than I've had."

I told Annie how I had been publicly accused of being a politician. She said, "That is all right. You are doing just that right now—talking, talking about people and community problems. Election time is a good time to show it up" (1980:57).

Wauneka supports Stewart by telling her that having another woman on the council matters to her. She encourages Stewart to think of herself as a winner and turns others' criticisms into an affirmation. The enthusiasm with which Wauneka supports Stewart suggests connections among women that include the desire to help each other achieve as individuals as well as collectively. Subjectively and collectively they exist and reinforce each other mutually. This exchange is about women's independence relative to men and their political solidarity, in contrast with the controlling character of the relationship between Maria and her sister, in which one women tries to get the other to back down from following a path leading to a world beyond marriage. The exchange between Stewart and Wauneka suggests the different historical possibility forged in the context of the women's and ethnic movements, that is, the building of resources and power for Native American women.

In addition, there is in Stewart's account a buried protest of the sexism existing in her community. She reports that when she was local chapter secretary, there were complaints over the holding of dances where some considered the behavior of youths bad. When these difficulties arose, Stewart tells us, "One man said that they should not have allowed women to hold office in the Tribal Council and chapters" (1980:61). She then goes on to tell a Navajo legend about a woman queen who had authority over women and girls but whose moral looseness led to dissent among the men and women. The women claimed their independence from the men, and the men went to make a new home for themselves. Life became hard for both the men and women, but, according to the legend, the queen and her daughter refused to do anything to bring the men and women together. Eventually, a wise owl told the woman queen to stop, and the queen admitted she was wrong. From that moment on, the men took over as rulers. Stewart never refers to this legend as sexist, but she indicates its importance: "My people have this story in mind when they criticize a woman leader. They say there will be confusion within the tribe whenever a Navajo woman takes office" (1980:57).

CONCLUSION

Clearly, Stewart's autobiography cannot be pressed into my overarching argument that white women found in Native American women's lives the preoccupation of white culture, since Stewart is not writing as a white woman. It is difficult to know from the text in what ways Shepardson shaped its contents. There is an argument to be made for the possibility that a more intersubjective relationship between ethnographer and native occurred here than in the previous accounts. I am not arguing that Reichard and Marriott somehow got the Navajo or the San Ildefonso peoples wrong or were more immersed in their historical situation than was Shepardson. What I am arguing is that the increasing political power of the Navajo to represent themselves and wrest ethnographic authority from strictly white hands has created the possibility of a new order of ethnic distinction that changes the ways white and Native American women may relate. The relationship between Stewart and Shepardson, as represented in *A Voice in Her Own Tribe*, suggests an intersubjectivity based less in a white women "helping" (either Native American women to educate the white public or themselves and their peoples) and more in a different tension. This tension involves wanting collaboration in the face of increasing claims for self-representation; the tension is based on the historically specific cross-purposes of an Anglo-American woman's desire for equality and a Native American woman's taking authority. From

this relationship develops the kind of story about gender being told in Stewart's account, one that is not simply reflective of Anglo-American women's agendas but might also be meaningful for Native American women.

As the preceding texts indicate, there have been two basic and interconnected relations between gender and ethnographic authority in Anglo-American women's ethnography of Native American women of the Southwest. These interconnected themes are designated as a practice I call matronization. Matronization was pedagogical in that it involved white women educating the public as well as attempting to educate themselves into another kind of Anglo-American female identity through a simultaneous helping and exalting of Native American women. The irony was that the white women did not escape their pre-understanding of gender formed in the cultural context of various historical events such as the Great Depression and the post–World War II period with its construction of the feminine mystique. Like paternalism, which refers conventionally to men's protection of either women or other men, matronization is complex because of its base in conflicting desires. In the assumption of protection lies a belief in the other as weak or less resourceful than the self. This posture, based in a sympathy that is dangerously myopic, has led to Anglo-American women's projection of modes of being female (these are not distinctive to Anglo-American culture but certainly of it) onto Native American women. These projections need to be defamiliarized to dislodge the knowledge produced out of stories about Native Americans that make them, too easily, characters in the gendered scripts of white culture.

Of course, Anglo-American women ethnographers, like ethnographers in general, never escape their experiences or history. This is, thus, not a condemnation of the intersubjective character of fieldwork, a call for a new objectivity that could "hear the Other" in a nonmediated way. The assumption, however, that Anglo-American culture commands and intrudes and Native American cultures only defend themselves and need a basic support in doing this disallows the kind of experience and way of being that fieldwork promises—an openness that permits a conflict of interpretations. This practice of matronization has shifted in recent history as Native Americans have claimed self-representation and self-determination for themselves in ways that have forced Anglo-American anthropologists to face them with different attitudes and beliefs. This story about white women and Native American women is not over, as Stewart's autobiography makes evident. Now that older inequalities have been altered fundamentally, we see other possible ways of caring among women, ways that do not assume that the essential act of nurturing among adult women is protection, ways that allow and foster reciprocities but, at the same time, do not lead to indifference.

WOMEN RESEARCHERS AND THE YAQUIS
IN ARIZONA AND SONORA

Kathleen Mullen Sands

The Yaquis were very interested in
their history and language. They
said to us, "I want to teach you."
Rosamond Spicer 1985

T HE Yaqui (or Yoemé) People of northwest
Mexico and Arizona are survivors. Living in
the harsh environment of the Sonoran desert—
originally in scattered *rancherías;* later, with the
acceptance of Spanish missionaries and European
agricultural methods, in pueblos; and as a result
of many having been forced off their land along
the Rio Yaqui, in Arizona in urban villages—
they have struggled fiercely and successfully to
maintain tribal identity. They have gained a reputation as exceptionally hard workers and are admired for their rich ceremonial life, which merges
indigenous and Christian beliefs and rituals. They
state proudly that the Yaqui way is "hard." Their
struggle with poverty is ceaseless, their kinship
and ritual obligations demanding, their ceremonial responsibilities draining, their history at
times catastrophic. Yet they have endured because, like so many other indigenous American
peoples, they are exceptionally tenacious and
adaptable.

Only sparse accounts of Yaqui life before the
coming of the Spanish to northern Mexico have
been handed down, but fairly comprehensive records of their cultural and social history have been
kept since that time. Thorough studies by anthropologists and cultural historians in recent decades have provided a full and often lively portrait
of Yaqui lifeways from the Conquest to the present. In part, the attention paid by scholars to the
Yaquis may stem from the fact that they have
been easily accessible in their urban villages in
Arizona. Also, the Yaqui capacity for integrating
new beliefs, rituals, and social structures into
their traditional culture while maintaining a distinct cultural identity (even when their social fabric was torn by warfare and deportation) along
with their ability to revitalize their culture in a
new environment have been compelling areas of
investigation for anthropologists. The corpus of
publication on Yaqui culture attests that the Yaquis are a people of great fascination to scholars of
culture.

The research and writing about Yaquis contributed by women, while it has not dominated
the body of Yaqui anthropological scholarship,

has made a significant contribution to contemporary knowledge about ceremonial practices, traditional lore, and the daily lives of Yaquis both in Mexico and Arizona. The study of Yaqui culture by women dates from the early 1920s, with the concentration of publication spanning the 1950s to the present. Research and analysis by these women have provided both significant works and a unique viewpoint on Yaqui culture.

THE BEGINNING OF YAQUI STUDIES: PHEBE M. BOGAN

The first anthropological study on Yaquis to be published in the United States was a master's thesis written by Phebe M. Bogan in 1922. It appeared in the papers of the Arizona Archaeology and Historical Society in Tucson, Arizona, in 1925. Based on fieldwork at Pascua Village (then on the outskirts of Tucson, but now very near the center of the city), *Yaqui Indian Dances of Tucson, Arizona* is the first of numerous studies based on fieldwork in Pascua. Although the title suggests that the report focuses on dance, the study actually describes the ceremonies of the village with emphasis on the complex Lenten rituals that culminate in La Gloria, the celebration of the resurrection of Christ. The Yaqui ceremonial calendar is most active from Ash Wednesday through Easter morning each year. During that time ceremonial societies reenact the passion, crucifixion, and resurrection of Christ in rituals that integrate traditional Roman Catholic beliefs and practices with indigenous ceremonial elements. The ceremonies require the involvement of nearly all members of the village either as active participants or in supporting roles. They culminate on Holy Saturday (La Gloria) with an enactment of the resurrection of Christ, the reconsecration of the villagers who have acted the roles of his persecutors, and a joyous fiesta.

Bogan begins her study with a brief introduction to the history and culture of the Yaquis, praising their cultural tenacity in the face of displacement from their Sonoran homeland. Comparing the Yaquis to the Pueblo cultures of the American Southwest, she presents a rather romantic and sentimental portrait, characterizing them as brave, liberty loving, and picturesque. From a contemporary perspective, her Victorian language and oversimplification (for instance, she simply says the origins of the dances she describes are "lost in tradition") are annoying, but her descriptions of the ceremonies are careful and detailed, and she provides a discussion of social and religious structures within the village, including analysis of gender roles, that later studies verify.

As one of the first women to obtain an advanced degree in the study of southwestern Native American cultures and as an early writer on Yaqui traditional life, Bogan not only had an impact on local scholars but was the first to attempt to write about the Yaquis for a popular audience. In 1926, a pamphlet based on her scholarly study was published by the Tucson Chamber of Commerce for distribution among the growing crowd of local and tourist spectators at the Yaqui ceremonies during Holy Week. With publication of this guide, Bogan disappeared from Yaqui studies and from anthropology altogether, but her pattern of fieldwork at Pascua and publication for both scholarly and popular audiences was repeated at a more complex and thorough level by another scholar of Yaqui culture, Muriel Painter.

A TRUSTED OBSERVER: MURIEL THAYER PAINTER

Painter, too, focused her work on the ceremonial life of Pascua Village, particularly the Lenten rituals. Like Bogan, she published short guides to the Easter ceremonies (1950, 1960, 1971) as well as an anthropological study (1986). However, Painter's work is much more painstaking, and her *With Good Heart* (1986) is the most comprehensive study of the Easter ceremonies that has yet been published. Bogan's tentative initiation of anthropological study of Yaqui ceremony flowered in Painter's work, partly because Painter had the benefit of a community of cultural anthropologists with whom to work, and in large measure because Painter devoted most of her adult life to fieldwork and writing about Yaqui ceremonial life.

Like many of the more famous women anthropologists, Muriel Thayer Painter, known to her friends as "Budge," was a graduate of an eastern women's college (Wellesley, in the class of 1916) and spent some time as a social caseworker in major eastern cities before going west (Babcock and Parezo 1988). Her first contacts with Yaqui culture probably came through attending the Easter ceremonies at Pascua; from the 1920s on, they attracted larger and larger followings among non-Yaquis. Or her contacts perhaps resulted from the home she had built in Tucson, which was constructed by Yaqui workmen (Slivac 1986:15). Adobe brick making and construction were major areas of Yaqui employment before World War II. Regardless, her interest was piqued.

By the late 1930s, Painter had become a dedicated observer of Yaqui culture. She was perhaps not sure initially what her unobtrusive observation would lead to and felt "reluctant to thrust herself on the Yaquis" (Painter 1986:xv), but she was serious enough about her study of ceremonies to make detailed field notes and narrative accounts of each ceremony she witnessed. Being familiar with Yaqui culture and well acquainted with Pascuans she provided anthropologist Bronislaw Malinowski his entree to the Easter ceremonies and the village in 1939 (Slivac 1986:15). His enthusiasm inspired her research. Each year between 1939 and 1954 she attended the Lenten ceremonies at Pascua and was invited to many private household ceremonies in the village as well; thus she observed, made copious notes on, and kept a diary about the full range of Yaqui ceremonial life. Through these repeated observations she came to know the subtleties and variations of the ceremonies as no other outsider has. She continued to refine her observations by continuing attendance at ceremonies until very near her death. As Edward H. Spicer wrote in his introduction to Painter's book (1986:xvi),

The total record of her notes, giving full accounts for the first fifteen years and then the major variation for another twenty, constitutes an exceptional, perhaps a unique, ethnographic account of stability and change during some thirty-five years in the forms of a single native American ceremonial.

Drawn by the rich complexity of the integration of indigenous and Christian elements in Yaqui ritual, she talked with over 80 villagers (1986: xv), collected and interpreted data on every aspect of ceremonial life—from *pascola* and deer dancers to *matachine* dancers, from altar cloths to *chapayeka* masks, from flower symbolism to Christian symbolism—and managed to bring order and clarity to this enormous archive of notes.

Though Painter, like Bogan, never held an academic position, she continued to study anthropology, sometimes attending summer field schools under Clyde Kluckhohn and Katherine Spencer (Halpern), or taking courses at the University of Arizona, or working as a research associate at the Arizona State Museum, but primarily through her own field research. In 1947, for instance, she conducted 600 hours of fieldwork; in 1948, 1,000 hours; in 1949, 1,328 hours (Slivac 1986:15). It is likely, in fact, that in her years of study of Yaqui culture, she amassed more hours of participant observation than any professional anthropologist.

As she did her fieldwork, she was also learning Yaqui terms for ritual paraphernalia and activities and informally interviewing villagers on every aspect of ceremonial life (Painter 1986:xv). Combined with her observations, these comments by Yaquis served as the basis for her culminating work, *With Good Heart,* which describes in elaborate detail (in great part using the words of Yaquis) the activities, origins, dynamics, and meanings of Yaqui ritual. In this book Painter is an observer and intermediary, centering her description on the "persisting stable core of Arizona Yaqui religious life" (1986:xxiv, xxx). Only through decades of observation and study on a very focused area of work could this discernment of the core elements of religious thought and behavior evolve and be verified. Painter's methodology—years of typed observation notes and quotations—which provides the depth and longitudinal character of her study also leaves it a bit raw. Painter works so carefully to keep her own personality out of her writing that the reader is left to supply the connecting links, to integrate the data. Her rigorous objectivity convinces but leaves an opus to be sampled rather than read, valuable for its information rather than its mode of presentation. It is, however, one of the very few works about American Indian religious thought and practice that has not raised controversy; in fact, the Yaquis have acknowledged it as an accurate portrayal of their ceremonial life.

With Good Heart has one further limitation; because it is so focused on religious ceremony, it really should be read in the context of more comprehensive ethnographic studies of Yaqui life. It is a work that was begun at about the same time as some of the ethnographies of Yaqui culture (E. Spicer 1940, 1953, 1954; Beals 1943, 1945) and perhaps fortunately was not published until the ethnographic framework to support it had been very well established.

Painter was well ahead of her time, not in her methods of observation and interviewing techniques, but in her involvement of Yaquis not simply as informants but also as partners in research and analysis. In 1941, Painter arranged to record a sermon that is presented at the end of the Easter ceremonies. Eight years later with the maestro who delivered the sermon, Don Ignacio Alvarez, and another Yaqui man who became her principal interpreter, Refugio Savala (and some technical help from an anthropologist skilled in Yaqui linguistics), she began to transcribe and translate the sermon; in 1955 it was published as a multiauthored monograph (Painter et al. 1955). During the work on the sermon, she also encouraged Savala to begin writing his autobiography, on which he worked for several years and published after Painter's death (Savala 1980), and also encouraged him in his literary work. Her dedication to scholarship on the Yaquis is apparent, but

she seems not to have attempted to gain personal recognition, perhaps because she was free of institutional pressures. At any rate, she worked slowly and cautiously, willing to credit her collaborators for their work and to share her knowledge freely. Her high standing with the Yaquis was apparent in their consultations with her on proper ways of conducting ceremonial activities, or correct adornments, or even dance patterns that they knew she had carefully recorded in the past. Thus she preserved for the community a history of ritual performance, and her notes became an archive. Always cautious and respectful in her relationship to the Yaquis, she also insisted upon protecting informants by assigning a numerical code to quotations she used in *With Good Heart.* Yaqui respect for her work and methods was clearly demonstrated when they performed a traditional religious ceremony for her death in 1975 and a death anniversary ceremony in 1976, a rare honor for a non-Yaqui.

Painter has not only served as a major force in preservation and interpretation of the Yaqui Easter ritual but has also been an intermediary between the Yaqui people and non-Yaquis with an interest in Yaqui ceremonies. Her booklets, *A Yaqui Easter* (1950, 1960, 1971) and *Faith, Flowers, and Fiestas* (with Sayles 1962), have informed tourists and local viewers, and her bylined articles (1943–1945) on the ceremonies reached a wide local audience. She also served as the Tucson Chamber of Commerce Yaqui Easter Committee Chairperson from 1942 to 1950 (Babcock and Parezo 1988), creating a liaison between the Yaquis and the city. Her scholarly and civic endeavors seemed to rise out of a consuming interest in the persistence of ethnic traditions and a desire to widen the appreciation for cultural expression through ceremony and ritual. Like Bogan, she had a dual role as scholar and popularizer of Yaqui culture, but she deepened and widened the pattern, refined the techniques of investigation and interpretation, enjoyed the benefits of consultation with a community of scholars, produced a significant scholarly work, and, because of her collaborative work with Refugio Savala, generated an autobiography written by a Yaqui.

PHOTOGRAPHY AND ETHNOGRAPHY: ROSAMOND BROWN SPICER

At the same time Painter was beginning her investigations of Yaqui ceremonial life, a young woman named Rosamond Brown Spicer, known to friends and colleagues as "Roz," was heading west in a robin's-egg-blue Model A Ford on her honeymoon to begin a year of research at Pascua Village with her husband, Edward H. Spicer, known as "Ned" (R. Spicer 1986). This year of fieldwork turned into a lifetime of dedication to studying and writing about the Yaquis for both of them. Both graduate students at the University of Chicago, Rosamond was setting out to collect data for her master's thesis, while Edward was researching material for his doctoral dissertation. They set up housekeeping in the village and went to work, sharing the day-to-day events of their neighbors from July 1936 to July 1937. At first, it was slow going, but within two months, they were both conducting interviews in Spanish (which most villagers spoke) for basic ethnographic information and were starting Yaqui language lessons (ASM:ES 1936). In the course of that year Roz Spicer observed ceremonial activities, took hundreds of photographs, kept thorough field notes, and even entered into the religious events of the village as a *cantora* (liturgical singer), a position of high status among Yaqui women.

Like Painter, Spicer's interest was in religious traditions. During the six weeks of Lent she was especially busy, relying on her husband to observe activities while she caught just enough sleep to keep going, a time she refers to as a marathon of note taking (R. Spicer 1986). She also helped Ned as he collected the ethnographic data that would result in *Pascua: A Village in Arizona* (1940). When they returned to Chicago at the end of the year, Roz wrote "The Easter Fiesta of the Yaqui

Indians of Pascua, Arizona" and received her M.A. in 1938. After several months of work with African-American youths in New Orleans and three months with the University of Chicago summer archaeological field school, the Spicer team headed back to Arizona, where Roz worked as a volunteer doing research and photography at the Arizona State Museum and Ned became an instructor in the University of Arizona's Department of Anthropology.

Like many scholarly couples, the Spicers were faced, in this period of antinepotism rules and sexist traditions, with some choices about the character of their partnership. The fact that Roz Spicer became a volunteer for the Arizona State Museum while her husband began in a salaried academic position suggests that some of the choices were out of their hands. Roz freely states, however, that choosing a family meant taking a secondary scholarly role. This choice she does not regret, since their personal relationship was truly a full partnership, but the decision meant she would never have the public recognition for her work that an academic position would have allowed (R. Spicer 1986).

Outside the academy, the partnership continued as Roz worked with Ned in collecting life histories of Yaquis at Pascua from August 1940 to December 1941 under a grant from the Social Science Research Council. Again, Roz interviewed and photographed individuals in the village. She recalls that photographing events and people in the village was permitted except when outsiders were present; later, during their research in the Yaqui village of Potam, Mexico, in 1941 and 1942, she continued to photograph, but in this case official permission was required from church officials, householders, or ceremonial leaders. In both locations, she recalls that she established rapport before bringing out her camera or seeking permission. In the course of her work in these villages from 1936 to 1979, she took over 2,000 photographs, which she is currently cataloguing for the Arizona State Museum (R. Spicer

1986). It is by far the most complete longitudinal collection of photographs on Yaqui life, for it spans a period of nearly 50 years. This archive of photographs offers a longitudinal study of Yaqui culture quite similar to, though broader in scope and different in genre, Painter's written study of ceremonial life. The photographs have appeared in all of Edward H. Spicer's books and several other books, including Painter's and Savala's, and have been exhibited at the Heard Museum and Pueblo Grande Museum in Phoenix and the Amerind Foundation in southeastern Arizona (R. Spicer 1986).

It is very clear from the handwritten field notes in the Edward H. Spicer archive at the Arizona State Museum that Roz Spicer was a full partner in the collection of data both in Pascua, which resulted in *Pascua: A Yaqui Village in Arizona* (1940) and *People of Pascua* (1988), and in Potam, which resulted in *Potam: A Yaqui Village in Sonora* (1954). Over the years of their marriage, she traveled with her husband to various field sites and professional meetings, raised three children, participated in civic groups, drew maps and printed photographs for books and articles on the Yaquis, helped found and guide the Old Fort Lowell Neighborhood Association for preservation of an important historic area in Tucson, attended art classes, taught dance classes, and from 1960 to 1963 was assistant editor of *American Anthropologist* when Ned was editor. Since her husband's death in 1983, Roz has taken up his and her own unfinished work, coediting the manuscript Ned had written from their early research in Pascua but had at the time felt was too sensitive to publish since it contained life histories; attending anthropological conferences as a speaker on Yaqui culture and her and her husband's work; and writing her own recollections of their life and work together (R. Spicer 1986).

Rosamond Spicer attends Yaqui ceremonies at Pascua Village often and is received with affection and respect. Though very modest about her professional contributions to her husband's and other scholars' research and publications, she is surely the most thoroughly informed and active non-tribal Yaqui expert living today.

LIFE HISTORIES: JANE HOLDEN KELLEY

Another of the women anthropologists with a long commitment to the study of Yaqui culture is Jane Holden Kelley, who, like Roz Spicer, has lived among Yaquis in Mexico and Arizona for periods of time, first as part of a team with her father, William Curry Holden, and later conducting research on her own. In 1971, along with her father, she brought to publication *The Tall Candle* (Moises et al. 1971), the autobiography of a Yaqui man. Retitled *A Yaqui Life,* this first autobiography written by a Yaqui records the life of a man clearly on the margins of Yaqui culture and in many ways unrepresentative of Yaqui ideals and behavior patterns. However, it provides the first intensive and full-length life history of a Yaqui individual, and it is a particularly important work because the narrator's life coincides with "a vital era of Yaqui history" (Moises et al. 1977:ix).

It is clear from the introduction to the narrative that although William Holden elicited the autobiography, the structuring and editing of the published text was Kelley's. During 1967 and 1968 she interviewed Moises to clarify details and genealogy and to flesh out events in his life; then, in close collaboration with him, she integrated the interview material into the original text he had written (Moises et al. 1977:lii–liv). Though Kelley clearly states that the intention of the narrative is not ethnographic, she also points out that although Moises "did not act out his life at the center of the Yaqui stage, he nonetheless was a knowledgeable observer of many and varied scenes" of Yaqui life and history. And she further notes that "in spite of living in non-Yaqui environments much of his life, he maintained a deep commitment to the Yaqui way" (Moises et al. 1977:lvi). Kelley's active participation in the preparation of this text for publication, particularly her analysis of the production of the text over a period of 17 years (1954–1971) as a personal chronicle that provides insight into Yaqui cultural history, establishes a stance toward the personal document as a valid means of exploring the ethnography of a culture.

Kelley pursued this position with a more clearly articulated direction in her later work *Yaqui Women* (1978). Since this is the only in-depth study of Yaqui women published to date and was authored by a very successful female scholar and teacher (chairwoman of the Department of Archaeology at the University of Calgary, Alberta), it seems appropriate in the context of this study of women anthropologists to describe the contents and methods of this work in greater detail than others included here. *Yaqui Women* raises some interesting issues about the effectiveness of women anthropologists working with women to communicate a viewpoint underrepresented in most anthropological writing.

In this book, subtitled *Contemporary Life Histories,* Kelley traces tenacity and adaptability in the lives of four women and their extended families to demonstrate the validity of the individual life history as a means of penetrating the generalities of comprehensive ethnography and vitalizing historical account with the immediacy of personal event and response to the broader cultural experience. Her study focuses on the dynamics of stability in the face of chaos. The common factor of parents who were raised in the traditional Yaqui ways before the upheavals of the 1900s provides the link between these distantly related women. Each woman is abruptly and drastically affected by the chaos of the Yaqui diaspora. Considering their similar backgrounds and beginnings, their lives are remarkably individual and varied. The four women share a sense of upheaval, hardship, and emotional stress at the loss of loved ones, but each copes uniquely. Chepa Moreno, living in Mexico, gradually but resolutely isolates herself from family and friends, illustrating a negative response to the terrors of her youth and hardness

of her maturity. Dominga Ramírez, also a Sonoran, steadily moves to the pivotal position in the family she holds together, gaining respect and admiration from many generations of Yaquis for her generosity and strength. Antonia Valenzuela, an early Arizona resident, is less directly affected by the dispersal, but because she is basically *tristeza* (sad), her role in her family has been largely passive and subservient. Dominga Tava, the other Arizona Yaqui woman, is as outgoing as Valenzuela is reclusive, having developed a broad network of community and ceremonial ties as well as family bonds, effectively demonstrating the revitalization of the Yaqui way in contemporary times. Through each woman, major historical events and cultural trends are viewed and analyzed, but primarily the women are personalized, made immediate and real—humorous sometimes, but more often intensely difficult and sometimes tragic.

Because Kelley posits the validity of personal history as a means to full comprehension of segments of (and even whole) societies, she deliberately uses the histories of these four women to demonstrate her premise: individuals as complex entities existing through time can be used as the unit of analysis to depict the historical experience of the Yaqui people. Time and change and how the four women survive and adapt to the events they experience are the focal point of the book. This method leads to concentration on range of experience rather than on typical figures and on a viewpoint that had not previously been fully explored in the context of Yaqui study, a woman's perspective. While the narrative concentrates on mature women, the portraits are not autobiographies but life history composites based on interviews with the four subjects and information about them gathered from four generations of women, usually within the same family unit. The author has attempted to minimize the problems generated by the subjective nature of life history by interviewing as many members of each family as feasible, taking variants of each life history for cross-checking, using documents where possible, and comparing individual stories with broader historical reports. Although her care minimizes false representation, she is aware that it cannot fully overcome the problems of her informants' processes of selective memory or of the events of a life subjectively perceived and presented by them. Integrating stories about the women from other informants of several generations, however, and choosing distantly related central figures does in many respects keep personal distortion minimal, since there is an area of overlap in each family history.

The structuring element of Kelley's presentation is the household. In both peaceful and chaotic times, it is the center of stress and stability, conflict and affirmation—the survival structure in Yaqui society. There is a high tolerance for stress in Yaqui family life, according to Kelley's text, perhaps because the family is rarely stable in even the best of times: separation of spouses is common, traumatic death frequent, infant and child mortality high, poverty a given, alcoholism and violence not uncommon. Out of the stress of the events of cultural history and family history comes Kelley's belief that while the family matrix is nearly indestructible, the emotional bonds that hold it together are weak. In the stories of the four women, Kelley describes few deep ties. She posits that perhaps too many forced separations have created a reluctance to rely on or even trust family members. Even beyond the effect of social upheaval, she sees Yaquis as simply unwilling to form or incapable of forming deep or enduring emotional attachments, and this viewpoint creates a consistent attitude throughout the women's narratives. While each is detailed, a rich fabric of event and response, each lacks in expression of intense emotion. In only one instance in all the apparently intimate attachments of these women to spouses or consorts does one suggest that she was enamored. Survival, Kelley says, seems to have left little energy for emotion.

This conclusion raises some interesting questions about the investigator/subject relationship and calls into question either Kelley's interpretation of her informants' lives or the often-stated notion that women are best suited to explore the female aspects of a society. The mode of presentation further emphasizes detachment through the almost exclusive use of the third person, partly necessitated by the composite approach, but nonetheless unfortunate since it tends to flatten the tone and divest the narrative of the spark and vividness characteristic of Yaqui speech. In the one instance where one of the women is directly quoted, the sense of immediacy and personality stands out brightly against the otherwise rather colorless narrative. Kelley's presentation frequently falls closer to case study than biography. Her life histories are an outsider's view, thoroughly researched and sensitively drawn but clearly documentary in intention. Her insistence on the Yaqui lack of deep bonding is finally not convincing, since she never addresses the possibility that her inference may simply be a misreading of Yaqui reluctance to discuss emotion, perhaps from modesty, or perhaps because they take the presence of emotion in intimate relationships for granted.

Kelley's argument for Yaqui emotional detachment may reflect an anthropological career primarily focused on archaeology with its emphasis on scientific objectivity. Had she come to this work from the personality and culture school of anthropology, she might have probed the emotional capacities of her subjects more fully and written about these women from a less detached perspective.

Despite its disturbing elements, Kelley's book is of great value. Nearly a third of it is an introduction that scrupulously details the aims and methodology of the work. She lays the historical groundwork for the individual lives and records her relationship with each household fully and with immediacy. Thus, in a rather tangential way, she creates a detailed contemporary life history of her time among the Yaquis as well as her relationship to each subject—a first in any study of Yaqui culture. She is, in fact, among the first anthropologists to take the risk of placing herself as a personality in an ethnographic work to analyze the effect of the fieldworker on the material gathered. She states clearly that she is seen by her informants as a *patrona,* a woman due respect, and she is protected and even indulged by them on occasion. Ultimately, her *patrona* role creates a sense of reliability in the narratives; it becomes clear in the introduction that her informants view her as a woman worthy of a sincere attempt at truth. The force of Jane Holden Kelley's character is at least as striking as the personalities of the four Yaqui women, and her effect on the communities she entered is obviously of some value not only in the production of the written life histories but for analysis of the relationships in a female fieldwork situation.

NOTABLE RESEARCHERS OF YAQUI ORAL TRADITION AND LANGUAGE

Spicer, Painter, and Kelley are the dominant women who have worked as cultural anthropologists among Yaqui peoples, and their work has provided both breadth and depth to the study of Yaqui life. But there is one area of Yaqui culture that none of them has addressed directly: Yaqui language and traditional literary expression.

The first publication on Yaqui oral tradition, *Yaqui Myths and Legends* (1959) by Ruth Warner Giddings, is the result of research for a master's thesis. Giddings worked with narrators from both Mexico and Arizona; one of her storytellers, Ambrosio Castro, is among the most renowned literary figures of modern Yaqui society. Because he has narrated only in Yaqui and Spanish, his work is not generally known in the United States.

Giddings points out in the introduction to her book that no thorough collection had been made of Yaqui oral tradition until her research in 1942. Though Edward H. Spicer (1940), Alfonso Fabila (1940), Ralph Beals (1943, 1945), Jean John-

son (1962), and William Curry Holden (Holden et al. 1936) had all collected a few stories in the course of their more comprehensive works on Yaqui culture, no attempt had previously been made to collect or analyze a large body of tales. Working with five storytellers, Giddings recorded and translated over 60 stories, both sacred and secular, many of which had never been recorded or translated before. Her presentation of the collection is also important since her introductory chapters provide a context for the comprehension of how the stories fit into the cultural life of the Yaqui people. Although this analysis is brief, it does offer a starting point for the interpretation of Yaqui oral tradition. Of even more importance is Giddings' analysis of the storytelling process in Yaqui culture and of the basic characteristics of Yaqui narrative technique and style. For instance, she points out that "although many stories show considerable foreign influence, they are usually given a Yaqui background familiar to the narrator," and later notes that "characters in early Yaqui stories are not elaborately drawn, but represent the common Yaqui personality" (Giddings 1978:16–17). She also discusses changes in story elements from pre-Conquest to modern times, pointing out, for instance, that "heroes of early tales were often obedient, wise, powerful, and great leaders or hunters. In Jesuit-period myths and tales, they become pious or sinful . . . More recent stories feature pranksters, merchants, warriors, or cowboys" (Giddings 1978:17). The primary emphasis of Giddings' analysis is literary—discussion of elements of characterization, genres, delivery style, use of setting, range of content, plot structure, degrees of belief, and function—but in discussing this aspect of Yaqui culture, she provides insights into such important elements of culture as values, kinship obligations, behavioral models, and beliefs about the spirit world.

In the area of linguistic research, Lynn Scoggins Crumrine, working with native Yaqui speakers, produced the first major study of Yaqui language, *The Phonology of Arizona Yaqui,* in 1961.

Using a three-step method—Yaqui, literal, and free translation—based on descriptions of stick figures, she developed a text that has become a standard reference on Yaqui language and has helped to establish the written form of the language for Yaquis.

Yaqui collaborators have undeniably played an important role in the interpretation of materials collected by the women who have worked to present Yaqui language and culture to students of anthropology. So it is no surprise that in 1977 Mini Valenzuela Kaczkurkin, an Arizona Yaqui woman, published a collection of Yaqui stories, *Yoeme: Lore of the Arizona Yaqui People*. Collected from five residents of Pascua Village, two men and three women, to preserve their oral traditions for future generations of Yaquis, the book includes over 80 stories ranging from mythical and traditional lore to contemporary beliefs, curing practices, and ghost stories. The variety of material Kaczkurkin presents in *Yoeme* attests to the vitality and diversity of Yaqui oral tradition in Arizona, and her introduction to each section provides an analysis of function and style. For instance, she instructs the reader that the stories are not "told purely for entertainment but as a way of teaching a moral about those things important in Yaqui life—respect for nature and living things, respect for elders, and oneself, what is good and bad and how the evil one is usually punished" (197:43). As a Yaqui scholar, Kaczkurkin addresses her work to a Yaqui audience, not to the academic world, a significant break in the history of anthropological scholarship on Yaqui culture. In her introduction she says, "I would like to help pass on some of this lore as I heard it from my Granny . . . and others. I hope these few written *cuentos* [stories] will start a renewal of the evenings of 'Did you hear the one about?' " (1977:v). Although her work is aimed primarily at her own people, her collection and presentation of stories dating from the pre-Conquest period into the present is an important contribution to the scholarly knowledge of Yaqui literary traditions.

Finally, the most recent work by women on Yaqui literary tradition is my own. In 1975, as a graduate student in literature and anthropology, I fell heir to the manuscript for the Savala autobiography that Painter had encouraged Refugio Savala to begin in 1948. He had completed it by the 1960s, but she had archived it because she felt his English was not up to publication standards. I found his language lively and distinctive and his observations and experiences of Yaqui life engaging and perceptive, so I decided the text had potential if it could be given an adequate interpretive framework. Over a period of two years, I worked with the manuscript in consultation with Edward H. Spicer, editing and structuring it, while also researching Yaqui culture, southwestern history, and other elements of the autobiography that were obscure or unclear in order to write a separate but parallel interpretation of the autobiography to be included in the published work. Near the end of my work on the manuscript, Savala, who had dropped out of sight for several years, contacted Dr. Spicer, and I was able to verify information and collaborate on changes in the text, which resulted in publication of *Autobiography of a Yaqui Poet* in 1980.

As an outgrowth of that work, I became interested in Yaqui oral tradition and set out, using the collections by Giddings and Kaczkurkin, as well as other sources and oral versions, to trace the changes and enduring vitality of an important Yaqui narrative, "The Singing Tree," in a 1983 article titled "Dynamics of a Yaqui Myth." My work again intersected with two major contributors to Yaqui scholarship when Roz Spicer asked me to work with her in editing an early unpublished book-length text on Pascua Village by her late husband (*People of Pascua* [1988]), which examines Pascua Yaquis' relationships with the other cultures in the Tucson community and contains 15 life histories from three generations. Editing this manuscript gave me the opportunity to write an afterword to the text that placed this study of cultural survival, which had been researched and drafted in the late 1930s and early 1940s, into the canon of the Spicers' writing on ethnicity. The two years Roz Spicer and I worked on editing *People of Pascua* was a particularly harmonious experience in which Spicer shared many of her memories of fieldwork and her remarkable wealth of knowledge on Yaqui culture. Thus, contemporary scholarship on Yaqui culture intersects and draws upon not only the early work of women anthropologists but also the knowledge and expertise of living women who remain active in researching and writing about Yaquis.

Each of the women who have labored to expand our knowledge of Yaqui culture has brought to her work individual interests, talents, and temperament. Some have worked quietly alone, apart from the research support of the academy; some have influenced, worked in collaboration with, or even mentored less experienced scholars. All have worked in the field in the villages of Arizona and Sonora to learn the complex and subtle ways of the Yaquis. The pioneering work of women anthropologists with Yaqui people is an enduring resource for contemporary scholars of Yaqui culture, providing the groundwork on which both men and women anthropologists may continue their investigations of these persistent people of the American Southwest.

GLADYS REICHARD AMONG THE NAVAJO

Louise Lamphere

Chance seems to have favored my introduction into the field. Why was the tribe Navaho rather than Fiji? Quite simply because there was money for a Navaho fieldtrip at the time I was ready to undertake one. Why did I find an auspicious introduction to the people upon whom I was inflicting myself? I can see several reasons for the result: one is the character (personality?) of the Navaho people and their culture, . . . and the other, the character of the white people who introduced me to them . . . That which distinguished each of these individuals from others in the same category was a willingness to view Navaho differences as legitimate and proper without assuming the customs or habits to be inferior to ours.

Gladys Reichard
(n.d.: 29)

BETWEEN 1930 and 1960, Gladys Reichard was the most important female anthropologist who studied with the Navajo, the nation's largest Native American population.[1] Almost 20 years younger than Elsie Clews Parsons and 5 years younger than Ruth Benedict, Reichard was part of the extraordinary number of women who received Ph.D.'s from Columbia during the 1920s and 1930s. Reichard, through Franz Boas' influence, obtained a position at Barnard College, where she taught for her entire career. During the 1930s she experimented with new forms of ethnographic and quasi-fictional writing, leaving several rich, descriptive accounts of Navajo weaving, family life, and ritual. As she focused more on the study of Navajo language and religion during the 1940s and 1950s, her monograph on Navajo prayer, her Navajo grammar, and particu-

larly her massive volumes on Navajo religion should have made her a major figure in Navajo studies.[2] But her work was always overshadowed by that of Clyde Kluckhohn, a full professor at Harvard University whose book *The Navaho* (co-authored with Dorothea Leighton) was, for years, the culture's major ethnographic study. Kluckhohn's research with Leland Wyman on Navajo religion and the extensive publications of Navajo myths by Franciscan missionary Father Berard Haile had more influence on other anthropologists and students of Navajo culture than did the work of Reichard.[3]

From the standpoint of the 1990s, it is possible to see in Reichard's prolific work the precursors of several methodological and theoretical trends that blossomed in anthropology in the 1960s and 1970s. Her study of Navajo prayer (Reichard

1944) seems very similar to the kind of structuralism Claude Lévi-Strauss (1963, 1964) brought to the study of Native American myth, an approach utilized by Sam Gill (1981) in his more recent analysis of Navajo prayer texts. Her work on Navajo classification of their ceremonials prefigures ethnoscience, a methodology for studying native systems of classification, which flourished in the 1960s. And her work on Navajo symbolism had a significant impact on Gary Witherspoon, whose training by David Schneider and Clifford Geertz at the University of Chicago led him to take a symbolic or interpretivist approach to Navajo categories of thought and Navajo religion. Witherspoon dedicated his book *Language and Art in the Navajo Universe* (1977) to Reichard and contributed to an issue of the *International Journal of American Linguistics* (1980) that included papers written in her honor. In Witherspoon's view (1980:1),

Gladys Reichard was an extraordinary ethnologist and an exceptional linguist. Her work has provided me with a model to emulate and an endeavor to continue. She took a holistic view of Navajo life, learning as much as she could about its many dimensions and aspects.

Still, the question remains, why did the quality of Reichard's work remain undervalued during her lifetime and until 15 years after her death?

The answer is not a simple one. The analysis in this chapter stresses the role of gender as it operated at a number of different levels throughout Reichard's lifetime. Gender is implicated in the kinds of roles Reichard played vis-à-vis her intellectual mentors and the Navajo family with whom she lived during the 1930s. It structured the professional network of anthropologists (including Reichard) that undergirded Navajo studies in the 1940s and 1950s. And it was relevant to the institutional position in which Reichard found herself as a female teacher in a woman's undergraduate college with a small department, in contrast to men in larger male-dominated graduate departments at universities (and in field

schools) where the profession of anthropology developed and expanded between 1920 and 1950.

Reichard, I believe, did not see herself as a feminist, and she would undoubtedly have played down the role of gender in shaping her life. Many of her students and anthropological colleagues emphasized her personality in contributing to her intellectual, and even social, isolation within the profession. Frederica de Laguna, one of her students who later became head of the Department of Anthropology at Bryn Mawr, in a tribute written after Reichard's death described her as "a lonely spirit." "Her attachments were warm and true, but they were not easily made" (de Laguna 1955:11). Her letters also indicate a close relationship to her mentors, Parsons and Boas, yet a distance from other women in the New York community, especially from Ruth Benedict and Margaret Mead. There were gender differences in how Reichard's personality was viewed. Women colleagues and students tended to be more positive, while male anthropologists often found her difficult, and the correspondence between her and Kluckhohn over the fine points of Navajo religion was full of harsh words. Perhaps because she was a woman, her personality could become more of an issue in the acceptance of her intellectual work, more so than for her contemporary male colleagues.[4]

There was a dialectical relation between Reichard's position as a woman (in the larger U.S. society, in anthropology, and in her fieldwork with the Navajo) and the kinds of strategies she used to order her relationships with anthropologists and Navajos. These strategies, in turn, gave shape to her research and writing. During the first 20 years of her career, Reichard as a single woman adopted a daughter role with both of her intellectual patrons, Franz Boas and Elsie Clews Parsons, and with her Navajo sponsors, Red Point and his wife, Maria Antonio, who taught her to weave and introduced her to the Navajo language and religion. Both sets of metaphorical "parents" were her mentors and teachers.

In the early period of her professional life,

gender shaped Reichard's career in enormously positive, yet limiting ways. In the course of her fieldwork, the daughter role opened up new possibilities for ethnographic description. Living within a Navajo extended family and learning to weave from its female members allowed Reichard access to the nuances of interaction between women in a matrilineal, matrilocal society. She, in turn, wrote about these experiences in three different ways (in *Spider Woman, Navajo Shepherd and Weaver,* and *Dezba*), creating texts that were innovative for their time because they focused on women and used interactive and dialogical textual strategies.

In contrast, Reichard's intellectual commitment to Boasian description steered her away from theory and developing a sense of problem and method that characterized the "cutting edge" nature of Kluckhohn's career. She had difficulty growing out of the role of an intellectual daughter but also was marginalized by the major male anthropologists who studied Navajo religion. Thus, during the last 15 years of her life (after the deaths of Boas, Parsons, Red Point, and Maria Antonio), Reichard's peripheral and contentious position within the network of those studying Navajo language and religion (both men and women) shaped her intellectual work and the acceptance of her ideas among colleagues. Her institutional position at a women's college without an anthropology department and graduate students further limited her impact on the profession as a whole. In this period the limitations of her gender role (in an American professional institutional context rather than a Navajo one) came to predominate.

These major contradictions also appear in the content of Reichard's research. On the one hand her eclectic empiricism allowed her to grasp Navajo categories on their own terms to a greater extent than Kluckhohn and Wyman were able to do, given their tendency to impose Western categories on Navajo thought. On the other hand, a lack of theory gave her work no framework. For example, *Navaho Religion* (1950) seems to be a mass of details, something like an encyclopedia, a compendium of facts that one could consult, but not a book that was easily read. Yet it contains within it great attention to Navajo categories themselves and to the role of color, direction, and gender symbolism in structuring Navajo ritual. Witherspoon (1977:1) has noted that while many have been dismayed by the "amount of unconjoined information," more recently others have perceived that in Reichard's work "there is a vision that there is a center, a core, where all things connect and according to which all facts make sense and all details derive their place and meaning." Although I would not go as far as to argue that Reichard's attention to Navajo categories and their relationship was a product of her gender (i.e., that she had a different way of looking at Navajo language and religion because she was a woman), I do believe that her insights went unappreciated until the 1970s because of her marginal professional and institutional position, which was, in turn, affected by her gender.

WOMEN AT COLUMBIA UNIVERSITY

Franz Boas molded the Columbia Department of Anthropology and the discipline itself between 1900 and 1930. He argued against the broad evolutionary schemes that characterized anthropology in the late nineteenth century and advocated the careful collection of data from a wide variety of cultures. For Boas, the diffusion of culture elements was more important than the classification of a people along a continuum that ranged from savage to civilized.

A champion of cultural relativism, later in his life Boas felt that scientific laws of human nature were difficult, if not impossible, to formulate. He argued that Native American cultures were fast disappearing with the advent of reservations, missionization, and acculturation. As a result, Boas and many of his students engaged in "salvage ethnography": the collection of myths, tales, details of kinship and social organization, items of material culture, details of phonology and grammar, and accounts of ritual practices and belief systems before cultures "died out" (Boas 1966; Stocking 1968).

By the 1920s, Boas was turning to new interests, particularly the relationship between the individual and culture, and several of his students (now mainly women), notably Ruth Benedict and Margaret Mead, began to conduct research on this topic. They continued to work extensively in the Southwest. Twenty women earned their Ph.D.'s at Columbia University between 1920 and 1940; as Boas wrote to Berthold Laufer in 1920, "I have had a curious experience in graduate work during the last few years. All my best students are women" (cited in Babcock and Parezo 1988:88). Each of these women occupied a different niche in the constellation of roles that made up Columbia's Department of Anthropology. Reichard's privileged place within Boas' circle of students and colleagues is made clear when her position is contrasted with those of Elsie Clews Parsons, Ruth Benedict, and Margaret Mead, three of the best-known female students who received Ph.D.'s from Columbia between 1920 and 1940.[5] Parsons, the oldest, was the first woman Boas interested in anthropology. From an wealthy, upper-class background and married to a Republican congressman, Parsons became a patron as well as a student of anthropology (see Hieb's chapter in this volume). She had close friendships with Alfred Kroeber, Pliny Goddard, and Robert Lowie, some of Boas' prominent male students who received Ph.D.'s before 1920. Parsons made her first trips to the Southwest between 1910 and 1913, later working at Zuni, Hopi, Cochiti, Taos, and other pueblos. Beginning in 1920 she began to fund the secretarial position in the Department of Anthropology at Columbia. She founded the Southwest Society, which, through her money, funded the research of Ruth Benedict, Ruth Bunzel, Gladys Reichard, Leslie White, and others. Her role toward many women at Columbia University, particularly Reichard, was that of mentor and patron.

Benedict, Mead, and Reichard were much younger and in some respects were all "daughters" to Boas, who by the 1920s was referred to by all as "Papa Franz." Of these three, Reichard was the most loyal and dutiful, sticking closely to Boas' approach to anthropology and living with his family. Mead and Benedict moved away from Boasian anthropology and took Boas' work into new phases, focusing on patterns and configurations that related the individual to culture. During the 1930s they participated in developing the new subfield of culture and personality (see Babcock's chapter in this volume).

In this early stage of anthropology as a profession, Boas was instrumental in finding jobs, obtaining fellowships, and acquiring research funds for all of his students. Although often marginalized within Columbia University and in the profession (partly because of his socialist political views and attacks on academic racism), Boas did find ways to support those who studied with him (Stocking 1968). He was particularly protective of his women students, taking a kindly paternalist stance towards them. Thus, Reichard received the first permanent job held by any of the women in the Columbia circle, an instructorship at Barnard College. This was a position Boas obtained for her since she, unlike Benedict, was not married and had no male to support her. In 1927, after Benedict's marriage began to fall apart, Boas attempted to obtain a position for her within Columbia's Department of Anthropology, but he was rebuffed by the administration. With a change of administrators in 1931 and a more sympathetic climate regarding the presence of women on the Columbia faculty, Boas was finally was able to secure her appointment as an assistant professor, a year after she separated from her husband, Stanley Benedict. Margaret Mead began her employment at the American Museum of Natural History in 1927 as Assistant Curator and was promoted to Associate Curator in 1942, becoming Curator only in 1964. Mead did not begin teaching at Columbia until 1934 and then only in the extension program, but she was a forceful presence in the Columbia circle of anthropologists. She later turned down a permanent position in the Columbia anthropology department, offered to her by Charles Wagley, because of the freedom of movement her museum position offered (Bunzel 1983).

In the 1920s Reichard had the most secure academic position of Boas' women students, although her place at Barnard, an undergraduate college for women, rather than at Columbia, made her more marginal than Mead and Benedict. By the 1930s, through their courses at Columbia, Mead and Benedict had a greater impact on future generations of anthropologists, even though they too faced discrimination and marginalization in the department and the discipline as a whole. Reichard's closest relationships, as the next two sections of this chapter stress, were not with her contemporaries, but with her mentors Franz Boas, Elsie Clews Parsons, and Earle Pliny Goddard, curator at the American Museum of Natural History and another Boasian. While at the beginning of her career, Reichard seemed well-placed in a secure position with important mentors; by the end of her life, she was more isolated, both intellectually and institutionally, with the result that many of her contributions, particularly to the study of women's roles and to Navajo religion and thought, have been overlooked.[6]

BECOMING AN ANTHROPOLOGIST

Gladys Reichard was born on July 17, 1893, at Bangor, Pennsylvania, where her father, Noah W. Reichard, was a respected physician. Her family was of Pennsylvania Dutch (German) heritage, and she grew up in a Quaker household. She graduated from the local high school at the age of 16, then taught for two years in a country school. "You didn't have to learn to teach in those days," Reichard said in a 1944 interview. "I was certainly awfully dumb but just the same I was in full charge at a nearby country school that had 29 pupils and 28 classes—all in one room! My father believed you should know what you wanted to study before starting at College" (McElroy 1944).[7] Between 1911 and 1915 she returned to her hometown of Bangor and taught in the public schools. In 1915, when she was 22, she enrolled in Swarthmore College. She received her A.B. in 1919, graduating as a Phi Beta Kappan. She majored in classics, intending to become a doctor, but, during her senior year, after hearing several lectures from the anthropologist who taught at Swarthmore (Dr. Spencer Trotter), she converted. She received a Lucretia Mott Fellowship for graduate study and entered Columbia University in the fall of 1919 to study with Franz Boas.[8]

Reichard received an M.A. in 1920 and assisted Boas in his classes at Barnard College during the 1920–1921 academic year. A research fellowship in 1922–1923 at the University of California at Berkeley enabled her to conduct her first fieldwork among the Wiyot and to write a Wiyot grammar as her dissertation. Boas' student Alfred Kroeber, who had become chair of the Anthropology Department, was impressed with Reichard's success in locating a Wiyot informant and obtaining several good texts. However, as he wrote in 1924 to Edward Sapir, a linguist and former Boas student, he found her overinfluenced by her mentor:

Try kidding Reichard next time. I rather liked and much admired her. Her work capacity is enormous. The chief fault I found was the super-impregnation with Boas, so that she neither gave nor received anything in her year with us. What she had, was el puro Boas; and she wanted nothing else. She did her Wiyot the way he would approve; and no doubt her Christmas paper sprang from the same motive. She is hard and efficient and charmless—the opposite of Haeberlin; but equally saturated with the old man; and Haeberlin's successor, almost, in his devotion. She's neither quarrelsome nor dogmatic, but argument with her is useless because she had Boas lock her mind and keep the key (Golla 1984:410, letter 355).

Clearly, Reichard's close association with Boas (assuming the role of an intellectual daughter) was already affecting her relations with the older generation of Boas' male students who had broken away, to some degree, from their former professor.

Reichard returned to New York in 1923 and became an instructor in anthropology at Barnard. Boas had written to her in Berkeley in January 1923, telling her that the appointment, which he was arranging, was in the final stages of approval. "You can perhaps imagine my delight at the news you sent which reached me Sunday," Reichard replied. "I hope nothing will happen because of the Trustees to dampen my ardor"(FB: GR/FB, 2/8/ 23). There is indication in Benedict's letters that she felt slighted by Boas' decision to obtain the job for Reichard. Judith Modell (1983:167) characterized Reichard and Benedict's relationship as one of "a reluctant professional respect while competitiveness characterized their personal relationship." Reichard received her Ph.D. from Columbia University in 1925, when she was 32 years old.

Reichard was almost a member of the Boas family, living at the Boas house during the winter and engaging in fieldwork during the summer. Remaining a daughter and continuing to live with aging parents or, in this case, a professor and mentor, was one of the acceptable strategies young academic women adopted as they entered the professions.[9] Reichard's correspondence with Boas dates from 1919, when she first wrote him to ask if she could study anthropology at Columbia. Her letters to Boas during the 1920s are full of chatty news to both "Mamma and Papa Franz," especially during her year in Berkeley and her year in Germany, when Boas helped her make personal and professional contacts. Some of these letters consisted of "shop" talk and clearly point out Reichard's training as a linguist in the Boasian mold. Both her letters from Berkeley and those from Idaho when she was working on the Coeur d'Alene language are full of texts, queries about each language, and tentative presenta-

tions of her data to Boas. Some of the correspondence from Germany concerns problems with getting the Navajo genealogies reproduced and published.

Later letters, especially those written to Elsie Clews Parsons, her maternal patron, are often full of news of Boas' health and moods, especially in his waning years. In 1925 she wrote to Father Berard Haile and catalogued the troubles of the Boas family that year (including the illness of Boas' daughter, the death of his son, his wife's operation, and his lame arm) as well as Reichard's own father's death. "You can easily understand how we have been thrown out of our usual schedule leaving very little time or spirit for extra work such as the Navajo. Nevertheless I occasionally eke out—steal would be more accurate—a few hours to work on it" (BHP:GR/FBH 3/12/25).

In 1929, after Mrs. Boas' death, Reichard wrote to Parsons,

It was most kind of you to send the message you did. The day your letter came Papa Franz was still too stunned to have anything from the outside register. But I showed it to his children who were constantly with him so they could use it if the opportunity seemed at hand . . . [Yesterday] He read it and then with that sweet look which comes into his eyes he said, "Isn't that just like Elsie" (ECP:GR/ECP 12/ 21/29).

In 1931 and 1932 Boas was both depressed and ill, "withering away and with no spirit at all." Reichard reported hauling Boas and his books back and forth from department to home in her car and discussed the progress of his recovery from an embolism in her letters to Parsons (ECP: GR/ECP 2/24/31; ECP:GR/ECP 1/25/32). As a devoted resident in the household, Reichard took the role of someone who communicated his emotional and physical situation to other close friends. This role of emotional mediator is often assumed by women in family networks, and Reichard's ability to take on such a position indicates her closeness and quasi-familial position in the

Boas family. She often personally attended to her aging mentor's wishes, particularly those that pertained to his work.

EARLY RESEARCH AMONG THE NAVAJO

Sometime in 1923, when she was 30, Reichard began a close relationship with Pliny Earle Goddard, Curator of Ethnology at the American Museum of Natural History. She accompanied Goddard on a field trip to the Navajo Reservation during 1923, and she returned with him again in 1924 and 1925. It is part of anthropological folklore that Reichard had an affair with Goddard, a much older, married man with a family. Certainly, she was close to him, enjoyed her fieldwork with him, and continued his work, particularly in editing the manuscript of the Shooting Chant, after his death. Her relationship with Goddard created tensions with both Boas and Goddard's wife, while Parsons remained a confidante and friend when it came to Reichard's relation with Goddard.

These first summers of research, as well as subsequent field trips, were funded by Parsons through her Southwest Society. Parsons' role of mentor and confidante emerges in their correspondence and shows that Parsons took a hand in directing the research as well as financing it. In a letter of August 16, 1923, Parsons stated, "Glad to hear that you can go on the Navaho field trip. More than twice the amount of work will be done, as I have a notion you will stimulate your colleague to work harder than were he alone" (ECP:ECP/GR n.d.). Parsons suggested that $500 is "cutting it rather close, . . . so I am enclosing a check for $200 as an emergency fund. I am wondering where you are jumping off and where you expect to be, as far as you can tell in advance." Parsons suggested that Reichard visit the Pueblos and also describe the Navajo Fire Dance. She encouraged Reichard by stating that "an intensive clan and chieftaincy study would be valuable"(GR:ECP/GR 8/16/23).[10] The next day

Reichard wrote thanking Parsons for the check, stating that they would not work on language but would focus on social and political organization, with some attention to ceremonies.

This letter and the ones that followed during the next few summers set the pattern for Reichard's correspondence with Parsons. She reported on the data she had collected and accounted for her expenses but also shared her opinions of those whom she met and her growing feelings for the Southwest and the Navajo. The letters are often open and chatty and give a clear sense of Reichard's emotional attachment to her work, her informants, and the setting for her research. In September 1923, she wrote of the first few days on the reservation:

We arrived at Aztec last Mond. & Mr. [Earl] Morris took us in hand at once. He knows the country [thoroughly] & had negotiated for a Ford for us at Farmington. On Tues. we went for it and had to wait until 3:30 while it was fixed. We have named her Elsie Elizabeth, but like naming a baby, her name is appropriate in almost no respect. She is more temperamental than a movie star & keeps Peggy busy cranking her (altho she has a self-starter), but when she does start she goes like the wind (ECP:GR/ECP 9/4/23).[11]

Reichard attended an Enemyway ceremony, also called *'ana'ji* or *nda,* a three-day chant given for patients who have become ill due to dangerous contact with non-Navajos ("enemies"). She was not impressed with (and misunderstood) the Squaw Dance, or round dance, which took place on the second night; her comments reveal how much she was disturbed by the impact of Anglo-American culture on the Navajo:

This was followed by a squaw dance—very monotonous & a mixture of old Navaho step and white man position—in fact it was pathetic and a bit disgusting. For the men were required to pay the girls before they could stop dancing & as soon as one was released the old folk on the side lines goaded her out to get another man. The girls did not look a bit happy to say the least (ECP:GR/ECP 9/4/23).

My own observation of the round dances held at *'ana'ji* ceremonies during the 1960s and 1970s indicates that the "white-man" position, perhaps a 1920s innovation, is no longer used.[12] The payment of the girls is probably more traditional than Reichard asserts, and the reluctance of the young women is more feigned than real. From my point of view this passage indicates that Reichard was willing to impose her own views on Navajo behavior, but in her published writing, her own position is not disguised as "scientific fact" but rather usually presented as her own opinion.

Reichard and Goddard traveled as a couple and used traditional field techniques. They covered several communities each summer, hired an interpreter, and worked with informants, collecting genealogies, data on Navajo clans, kin terms, Navajo names, and folklore. Her report to Parsons of their second summer's trip reveals this approach: "We spent about three weeks at Shiprock, one at Lukachukai, both places being very fertile in material and easy to work because of good interpreters" (ECP:GR/ECP 9/24/24). Reichard felt they had less success in Chinle because of an informant who insisted he had nine wives (and thus gave an "unreliable" genealogy) and an indifferent interpreter. However, at Ganado, "We had an ideal interpreter and were again able to see the *Nda* ceremony, one which was much more elaborate and complete than the one we saw last year" (ECP:GR/ECP 9/24/24). Reichard and Goddard also traveled to Gallup, with a short side trip to Zuni, before going to California to talk with Kroeber and renew acquaintances with Reichard's Wiyot and Goddard's Hoopa informants.

As a result of these three field trips, Reichard published *Social Life of the Navajo Indians* (1928). The monograph seems very much shaped by Parsons, since Reichard acknowledges using the genealogical method through Parsons' influence. She includes material on the *natc'it* (or presumed tribal assembly), which was as close to a study of "chieftaincy" as one could get. Based on her ob-

servations during both 1923 and 1924, she included a long description and pictures of the *nda* or *'ana'ji,* (which she calls the War Ceremony, but which is now translated Enemyway). There are also bits and pieces of observations in a chapter on folklore and belief, including witchcraft and divination. The monograph's most distinctive feature is the inclusion of the lengthy genealogies Reichard mentioned in her letters to Parsons. They were collected from a number of different sectors of the reservation and included 3,500 individuals (about 10% of the Navajo at the time).

Father Berard Haile had been quite helpful to Reichard and Goddard during 1923 and 1924 (as Reichard acknowledged in her chapter on the tribal assembly). He undoubtedly provided them with interpreters and even informants during their stays in Lukachukai. Reichard's early letters to Haile from 1925 and 1928 are chatty and relaxed, even though Reichard defends her criticism of Christian missionaries in a manuscript she sent to Haile. Later their relationship became more strained. The critical tone of his review of *Social Life of the Navajo Indians* for the *American Anthropologist* (Haile 1932) is similar to that of other reviews of Reichard's later work by male anthropologists. For example, Haile chastises Reichard for using the genealogical method in such a restricted number of communities and suggests that she could have constructed much more meaningful tables about clan lineages and marriage preferences from her "massive data."[13] He finds a number of errors in Reichard's data on religion and ceremonies and alludes to his own work in preparation. The *natc'it,* he argues, is the "gesture dance," not a "tribal assembly." He concludes on a kinder note that "the several chapters which treat social aspects of Navajo life are well presented, and much new material has been gathered, which is appreciated by all students of the American Indian" (Haile 1932:715).

Reichard could be equally argumentative and critical in her own reviews, which indicates that controversies over small details were often the battleground for validating one's own work as against that of others. As is particularly true in a new and developing profession, theoretical arguments are sometimes very heated. There was clearly a "battle for territory" among the major ethnographers of the Navajo between 1930 and 1960, although disagreements on how to interpret Navajo social organization continued even in the 1970s and 1980s.[14]

During the years following her first three summers on the Navajo Reservation, Reichard's research took her away from Navajo studies. She spent 1926–1927 in Hamburg, Germany, on a Guggenheim Fellowship, where she studied Melanesian design. (Boas may have arranged this fellowship to take her away from Goddard; Goddard, however, was able to visit Reichard in Rome during the International Congress of Americanists in 1926.) Reichard finished the work on the *Social Life* monograph while in Germany, having the elaborate genealogies drawn and reproduced there. She won the A. Cressy Morrison prize of the New York Academy of Sciences in 1932 for her monograph *Melanesian Design* (Reichard 1932), an innovative technological design study based on museum collections. In 1928 she went to Idaho to gather data for an analysis of the Coeur d'Alene grammar for the *Handbook of American Indian Languages* (Reichard 1938b). Boas was again able to help his protégée obtain a grant of $800 for the fieldwork through his position on the Linguistics Committee of the American Council of Learned Societies.

Pliny Goddard died suddenly in 1928, and Reichard became his literary executor. Goddard died at the Newtown, Connecticut, house that Reichard owned, and their relationship came to the attention of Dean Gildersleeve of Barnard College. Reichard may have been threatened with dismissal and had difficulties with promotions and benefits later because of this incident.

A letter from Parsons in 1928 apparently ac-knowledged Reichard's close relationship to Goddard and provided Reichard with funds to purchase the Navajo books in Goddard's library. In October Reichard answered Parsons:

Your note received Wednesday moved me more deeply than I can say. As if you hadn't done enough for us already! Just the evening before I had told Myra what might be valuable & had given up hope of having any of Dr. G.'s books, because the ones I wanted are expensive. So you can imagine—you can anyway or you would not have [thought] of the most understanding thing you could do—what your note meant to me. Perhaps when you are in the wilds with no books I can do some reference work for you or send you the books (ECP:GR/ECP 10/12/28).

Reichard's position as literary executor at first went smoothly but then ended in conflict with Mrs. Goddard, possibly as a result of Reichard's close relationship with Pliny Goddard. There are several letters to Haile attempting to arrange for him to purchase Goddard's collection of the *American Anthropologist* and the *Journal of American Folklore,* as well as a number of Bureau of American Ethnology reports and reprints. After Haile paid, Mrs. Goddard "got the idea she was being cheated or something—nobody ever knows what ideas she *will* get" and returned the check to Reichard (BHP:GR/FBH 1/19/29). Later Reichard mailed the check to Haile stating, "Do not think that *you* caused the trouble about the books. It is a circumstance too complicated to discuss and the less said about it the better anyhow" (BHP:GR/FBH 2/8/29). Finally in June of 1929, Reichard wrote to Haile that Goddard's son David had told her that the books were in the family attic and if Haile was still interested in them he could write the family directly and offer $50 for them. These letters suggest that some aspects of Reichard's relationship with Goddard (perhaps its intimate nature) rankled Mrs. Goddard and led her to interfere with Reichard's role in disposing of Goddard's library.[15]

REICHARD'S NAVAJO ETHNOGRAPHY IN THE 1930S

In 1930 Reichard returned to the Navajo Reservation, beginning a decade in which she produced her richest ethnographic material. Reichard wrote three important books in this period, each experimenting with a different type of description. Dissatisfied with the typical Boasian approach to field research, she decided to live with a Navajo family, adopting the role of daughter and student, someone who came to learn the Navajo language and how to weave. In her unpublished manuscript *Another Look at the Navajo,* Reichard gives an account of her new interests:

I had started the study of Navaho social structure by accident, the genealogical method being used by my sponsor [Parsons]. After working three summers at the job, it seemed that I had come to know a good deal about Navaho clans, linked clans, marriage and related abstractions, but little about the Navaho themselves. (Personality was not largely used at the time). I concluded that a study of structure is indispensable for any kind of social study, but that it is by no means enough for the understanding of behavior, attitude, and motivation . . . I was interested in crafts and decided that learning to weave would be a way of developing the trust of the women, as well as of learning to weave and to speak the language. By this attempt I would put myself under the family aegis; my work would at first deal primarily with women, and I could observe the daily round as a participant, rather than as a mere onlooker (Reichard n.d.: handwritten insert, p. 1).

At that point in time, it was unusual to live with a family and become intimately connected with women's activities while doing fieldwork. Living in a more detached setting was the norm: Malinowski had pitched his tent adjacent to a village of Trobriand Islanders in Melanesia, Mead had lived in a missionary's home while studying adolescent girls in Samoa, and Benedict and Bunzel had rented a house at the end of the village of Zuni, so that Benedict could work with older male informants and Bunzel with women potters (Caffrey 1989; Malinowski 1961; Mead 1928). Reichard's choice of living in a dwelling within a Navajo extended family residence group not only gave her an opportunity to learn to weave but also brought her closer to the daily interactions among women. Perhaps because it was unusual and certainly because Reichard was a woman alone, she at first found it difficult to get an Anglo-American to help her locate a family.

In 1930, when Reichard wrote to Haile asking about a singer and his family with whom she could live, she commented to Parsons on his reply:

I thought he had my point of view. He answers at length & with great detail saying he doesn't think I know enough even to wash behind the ears! Holds up Mrs Armer as a model of how to do work among the Navajo! Even mentions a nice house with curtains, easy armchair, etc. I guess except for linguistic help I can count him out (ECP:GR/ECP 2/24/37).[16]

Haile seemed to think that a young Anglo-American woman was incapable of living with a family in rather "primitive" conditions.

Even so, in the summer of 1930, Reichard spent a week in Lukachukai working with Haile's interpreter (Albert "Chic" Sandoval), but given Haile's sense that she needed a place with "window curtains," Reichard went on to Ganado with Ann Morris, the wife of archaeologist Earl Morris, to ask trader Roman Hubbell's assistance in finding a family to live with. She was much more successful this time.

We arrived—Ann left at once—on Fri. night & on Mon. at 9 a.m. I was established in my hogan. Roman knew just the family, Miguelito's, & we went up & asked them to build me a shade. But they had a storage house, [brand] new & unbuggy—but somehow I never think of bugs now! which is built just like a hogan only it is dug out & has no smokehole. It is much better protection from wind & rain (if any) than a shade could be. There is lots of wind & papers do fly around. I have all my things in this house which is only 6 mi. from Hubbell's (ECP:GR/ECP 7/6/30).

Red Point, or Miguelito, was a well-known Navajo singer (or curer) who lived near Ganado, a mile from the Hubbell Trading Post.[17] Miguelito, his wife, and his daughters had worked for Fred Harvey's Indian Department in Albuquerque, demonstrating weaving for tourists. The family traveled to San Francisco and San Diego for exhibitions in 1915, remaining in California for the greater part of two years. After returning to the reservation, Miguelito apprenticed himself to a number of singers and learned several important Navajo ceremonies over the years. In 1923 Miguelito participated in the dedication of the El Navajo Hotel in Gallup (Parezo 1983). Mary Colter, who designed the interior, used sandpainting motifs based on reproductions by Miguelito and other Navajo singers and collected by Sam Day, a trader from St. Michaels. As a Navajo who had a great deal of experience working with traders and other Anglo-Americans, Miguelito nonetheless continued a traditional way of life until his death (Reichard 1939b).

In 1930, when Reichard went to live with them, the family consisted of Red Point, Maria Antonio (his wife), and their two married daughters (Marie and Altnaba).[18] A third daughter, known as Yikadezba's Mother, lived with her husband, Ben Wilson, and their baby several miles away, although the three young Wilson girls resided with their aunts and grandmother in Red Point's residence group.

Living with a Navajo family (though in a separate dwelling) allowed Reichard to see Navajo social life from the inside. The fact that she was a woman helped her to obtain a sense of the internal core of Navajo kinship—a mother and her children. In a matrilineal society, with a tendency to matrilocal residence, the closest relations within an extended family are between a woman and her daughters. Men, both Navajo males and outsider

Anglo-Americans, are peripheral to this core; they are not part of the food preparation, child care, and weaving activities that take place daily inside the hogan. Also, since in the 1930s, Navajo men still practiced mother-in-law avoidance, a custom that pushed men further to the periphery of the Navajo matrilocal extended family. A Navajo man was not allowed to look at his mother-in-law, communication with her was always mediated by his wife, and he always left his own hogan when his wife's mother arrived for a visit. Reichard's position as a woman placed her in close contact with the women of the family, rather than on the periphery where male anthropologists and other male outsiders often found themselves when visiting or living with Navajo families.

Reichard's letters to Parsons that summer recount her experiences learning to weave and her difficulties with the Navajo language:

There are times when the language has me stopped. At such times I go to Hubbell's, stay overnight, get mail, food, etc. & start in fresh & early the next morning. Hubbells have breakfast at 6:30! I love the language but have to learn it blindly . . . [A]fter all Nav. is a hell of a language what with length, pitch, accent, verbs with a dozen principal parts, —the verbs are my Jonah—& all the rest. The FF [Franciscan Fathers'] vocabulary is very helpful but the grammar is *nil*. So I collect necessary phrases & learn them, even *use* them, & weeks after it dawns on me what they mean analytically. Well, perhaps that is the way to learn a language properly (ECP:GR/ECP 7/6/30).

Reichard also wrote of her love of the Southwest, deepened by this experience with a Navajo family:

But I want you to know that there is a kind of unexplainable balm about the S.W.—you doubtless know it already; I found it last summer and needed it even more this. There is a peace which comes to us at evening when the air is cool and the sun sets, the mountains become purple rose & blue—we are high in cedar & pinon country, a most comfortable setting— &

night settles down with the sheep in the corral & the stars & the moon & the air! Most people would hate the quiet—it *is* quiet—but I love it. It is the sort of thing some writers (a few) have gotten across, but somehow needs experiencing (ECP:GR/ECP 7/6/30).

Reichard published her experiences during that summer as well as during 1931 and 1932 in three very different books. The first, *Spider Woman* (1934a), is a personal memoir. *Spider Woman* reads like well-digested field notes, a sort of personal account of the trials of learning to weave, interspersed with descriptions of family activities—the summer sheep dip, a trip to the Gallup Ceremonials, a tornado, a sing, and even, sadly, the death of Maria Antonio during Reichard's third summer with the family.[19]

Recent discussions of ethnographic writing, particularly by James Clifford, George Marcus, Renato Rosaldo, and others, have focused on the textual strategies anthropologists have used to give authority to their accounts of other ways of life. Reichard's texts contrast in important ways with classic ethnographic writing, typified by Malinowski's *Argonauts of the Western Pacific* (1961), Evans-Pritchard's *The Nuer* (1940), and Mead's *Coming of Age in Samoa* (1928). In these books, observations and dialogue gathered in particular places and at particular times are assembled into a text containing a unified voice, that of the ethnographer representing beliefs, practices, and behaviors of a whole culture.

The position of the ethnographer is a panoptic one, above the scene of the action. The wholes represented tend to be "synchronic, products of short term research activity" sketched in the "ethnographic present" (Clifford 1988:31—32). The Trobrianders, the Nuer, or the Samoans become an absolute subject and the research process is separated from the texts it generates.

Spider Woman is much more dialogic, a goal currently espoused by many contemporary ethnographers. It contains more of the research process, the interaction between ethnographer and subject, and it records conversations as well as descriptions. Though Reichard does the recording and much of the interpreting, the voices of members of Red Point's family are heard. For example, one afternoon Reichard paid several Navajo boys for helping her pull her car out of the mud on the way home from a trip to the well to dye wool. Red Point strongly objected that Reichard paid them, since the boys had come to the rescue of a car that was carrying Navajo passengers and normally Navajos are expected to help each other without monetary payment. She describes the next morning's scene in her shelter as follows:

Red-Point was so excited last evening about the Navajo boys taking pay for helping us that he did not think of anything else. Today, as Marie is stringing the new blanket over the temporary frame and as I unwind the yarn from the skein, preparatory to winding the ball, he comes in. He is in his usual mild temper, but cannot refrain from mild remonstrance. "Too bad you paid that money. You wouldn't have had to do it if I had been here." He has come to see my first blanket. As I spread it out I tell him that at Ganado they all laughed at it. Whereupon he leaps to my defense with "Tell *them* to make one" (Reichard 1934a:60).

Although Reichard described Red Point's emotions in her words, much of the conversation is presented in his words, and Reichard herself has a place, a set of behaviors, and reactions within the dialogue. In a later chapter, she reports her own ambivalence about not taking a very sick Marie Antonio to the hospital, instead finding a singer to perform a Navajo ceremony over her. Red Point tells her, "You see we can't possibly take her to the hospital. Little-Singer died there yesterday afternoon" (Reichard 1934a:250). She then recounts her reaction:

I am shocked. I understand perfectly why my grandmother cannot go there. A place where one dies is contaminated, and if anyone goes there, he puts himself in the way of the worst. I know, too, as do they all, although they do not say it, that Little-Singer is the fourth person to die at the hospital within a week. After considering the implications I suggest, "But could the doctor come here to see her?" (Reichard 1934a:250).

The family agrees, but the doctor is not to be found, and Reichard eventually helps the family find an appropriate singer. Her attempt in this passage, both through dialogue and her own internal thought processes, is to present the Navajo view of events as well as her own. The passage is contextual, interactional, and dialogical. It is much different from a flat ethnographic statement that Navajos fear hospitals because they are places in which people die.

Throughout the book, Reichard's descriptions of the Southwest, her nights under the stars, and the sunsets are quite evocative. Designed for a popular audience, but using surprisingly modern textual strategies, the book portrays the "feel" of Navajo life as well as an Anglo-American woman experiencing that life, a combination rarely found in ethnographies of the period.

A second book, *Navajo Shepherd and Weaver* (1936), is a technical monograph on Navajo weaving. Reichard focuses on a step-by-step account of learning how to card wool, spin it, prepare a loom, and weave a rug. By the end of her first summer of fieldwork she had completed two regular-sized rugs and one very small one. At the conclusion of the third summer, she had become a proficient weaver.

In her written text, Reichard often adopted a distant descriptive prose in the "ethnographic present." For example, in describing techniques of weaving, Reichard writes about an abstract "weaver": "Although the weaver has arranged the tension rope of the loom, she has done so only casually, her purpose being merely to attach the moveable part of the loom to the loomframe" (1936:69). But then in the next paragraph she describes an actual incident with Marie and Maria Antonio as actors. "When Marie and her mother strung my first rug, one of the cross-pieces of the warpframe must have moved after the length was measured and before it was fastened. Consequently, it was at least an inch and a half longer

at the right than at the left" (1936:69). In other places, Reichard's own views come through, clearly framed in the text: for example, "I have roundly criticized the [store-bought] dyes which the Navajo must use and I think with justification" (1936:34).

These textual strategies convey the interaction between an Anglo-American outsider and her Navajo teachers. They are possible only because Reichard was a woman and thus in a position to learn a woman's craft from female instructors. Charles Amsden, a noted authority on Navajo weaving, was appreciative of this fact in his favorable review of her book, when he contrasted her approach with that of her six male precedessors who wrote as "bystanders" and observers of this "feminine craft":

Dr. Reichard, a woman, first of all learned to weave, then wrote about it as a weaver. We have long known how Navaho weaving looks; now, thanks to her, we know how it feels. She writes of the labor, the errors and frustrations and minor triumphs that lie behind the finished product on which her male predecessors fixed their admiring eyes" (Amsden 1938:725).[20]

Her third innovative book, *Dezba: Woman of the Desert* (1939a), is a novelistic account of Navajo life based on Reichard's experiences during her summers with Miguelito's family. The book centers on Dezba, the female head of an extended family. It gives a rich sense of women's roles in Navajo society and, though a novel, is used by some anthropologists as a woman's life history in undergraduate classes (since there are few such documents on Navajo females). Reichard's purpose in writing the book (1939a:v and passim) was to "answer questions asked by laymen, teachers, writers, artists and tourists whom I have met during many years of sojourn with the Navajo Indians." She portrays the problems Navajos have faced in "the seventy-year attempt to adjust themselves to the ways of an alien civilization." She felt that there was no clear-cut solution to the problems her characters faced in deciding whether or not to send their children to school, in using Western medicine or rejecting it, and in dealing with government regulations or resisting them. Dezba was a conservative Navajo woman who was ambivalent about the impact of schooling on her different children, but Reichard presented other characters who were more enthusiastic about assimilation.

Although the characters were fictitious, it seems that Dezba and her two daughters were patterned after Maria Antonio, Marie, and Altnaba. It is also possible that Lassos-a-Warrior, Dezba's brother, a *nadlay* and singer, was modeled after Hastiin Klah (*tł'ah*) or Left Handed, the singer from Newcomb, New Mexico, who worked closely with Reichard, Franc Newcomb, and Mary Wheelwright in the late 1930s.

Reichard uses several textual strategies designed to convey Navajo thoughts and feelings as well as Navajo religious beliefs. For example, she attributes aspects of the Navajo ceremonial system, normally described in the abstract, to the inner belief system of her central character. In addition, she describes her character's life situation in a way that makes it clear that for the Navajo there is an intimate connection between religious belief and bodily well-being. Thus, at the beginning of one chapter, she writes about Dezba as follows:

Dezba was brought up to believe in the relationship between man and nature sustained by ceremonial order, that order attained by song. She had never known any other religion and there was no confusion in her faith. In her youth she had been strong, healthy and full of energy. When she was about thirty-five she began to lose her ambition. She had frequent severe headaches. She had little appetite and became very thin (Reichard 1939a:93).

The chapter goes on to describe the family's active efforts to cure Dezba through the appropriate diagnosis and ceremonial.

From the point of view of the 1990s, when first-person narratives of Native Americans or novels written by Native American writers seem more "authentic" in giving voice to American Indian women, Reichard's novel may seem disappointing. Her implicit position is like that offered in many studies of acculturation and assimilation written since the 1930s. The focus is on how American Indians *adapted* to change, either individually or as a group, rather than on the economic and political factors in the larger society that forced them to change in a particular way (Lamphere 1976:6).

Deborah Gordon, in her chapter in this volume, has characterized Reichard's approach as "matronization," that is, "genuine concern for and friendship with Native American women" while at the same time attempting to "educate the lay public as a means of countering a general lack of empathy for and interest in Navajo Americans on the part of members of the white culture" (p. 157). Yet Reichard and others, Gordon argues, saw themselves outside the dynamic of power relations between Whites and Indians and made Native American women into proper models of femininity, imposing on Navajo family structure, in Reichard's case, the Anglo-American pattern where women became central to the home during the Great Depression, with its high levels of male unemployment and family abandonment.

This judgment misses Reichard's attempt to describe the internal dynamics of extended family life in a matrilineal society and her range of male and female characters. The descriptions of Dezba's participation in a sheep dip, the preparation of a Navajo dish made from ground fresh corn, and the Navajo girl's puberty ceremony are all based on careful participant observation. Though the language is often flowery, overdrawn, and not particularly close to what a description of an event in the Navajo language might be, *Dezba* takes a woman's point of view. It seems to me to be a more authentic account of Indian life than that found in such popular novels as *The Man Who Killed Deer* by Frank Waters (1942) and Tony Hillerman's mystery stories (1989a, 1989b, 1990).

By the end of three summers, Reichard had become fluent in Navajo (an extraordinary task), thanks to her teachers Red Point, Maria Antonio, Marie, and Altnaba. In the summer of 1934 she was able to get funding from the Bureau of Indian Affairs (BIA) for a Hogan School to be held at Miguelito's residence group site. The school's primary purpose was to teach literacy in Navajo to adults. For Reichard it offered the opportunity to provide an educational structure more compatible with Navajo culture, which could address some of the difficulties of the adjustment to the dominant society that she wrote about three years later in *Dezba*. Here was a school, attended by 18 students, in a home setting, where Navajos could communicate in their own language, discuss how to put technical medical English words into Navajo (such as *tuberculosis, trachoma, antiseptic*), and write about their own history and differences they saw between Navajo and Anglo-American cultures (Reichard 1934b). This experiment was possible because John Collier's administration of the BIA, beginning in 1933, was sympathetic to educational innovations that were more closely in tune with American Indian cultures, a radical change in U.S. policy.

Building on the importance of oral tradition in Navajo life, Reichard asked Red Point to be the primary teacher, providing traditional Navajo knowledge that was to be learned through writing the Navajo language. Reichard worked with the students, teaching them the symbols to use for each sound, helping them to write down vocabulary, and correcting essays. If one examines the account of the Hogan School in *Dezba,* it is clear that Reichard not only taught Navajos to read and write in their own language but also made it possible for them to devise ways in which the Anglo-American view (for example, on health and disease) could be integrated with Navajo healing and religious practices (Reichard 1939a: 130–40). Her one-summer experiment with the Hogan School was an early version of Navajo bilingual, bicultural education of the kind that only began to flourish in the 1970s with the founding

of several community-controlled schools that specialized in Navajo literacy (for example, Rough Rock, Pine Hill, Rock Point, Borrego Pass).

Miguelito died in October 1937, and his daughter, Altnaba, died the next spring. Reichard was clearly upset by both deaths. She wrote to Roman Hubbell in response to his letter telling her of the singer's death:

I am sorta numb still from the shock of your letter which arrived yesterday. Before everything I want you to know how much I appreciate your sitting down and writing me the first thing, and in such detail, too. It marks the end of an epoch with me, really I shall have to start all over psychologically and I am doubtful so far as to how I shall do it . . . But if that is true with me, how much more so with you and all those who came to depend on Miguelito for the things he had to offer. It is too unbelievable and sudden to be able to get a perspective . . . I don't seem to have any fancy words in which to say it, but it is simply that the experience with Mig's family was an event in my life and if you had not sent me to him, I should have missed all that richness (HP:GR/RH 10/14/36).

TURNING TO NAVAJO RELIGION AND WORKING WITH OTHER ANGLO-AMERICAN WOMEN

During the 1930s, Reichard's interests turned more and more to the study of Navajo religion. Living with a Navajo singer, who was a specialist in the Shooting Chant as well as several other Navajo curing ceremonies, gave Reichard the opportunity to see parts of this ceremony at the invitation of her mentor and teacher, Red Point:

Having indicated my interest in religion, I was invited to participate in an elaborate nine-day performance of Male Shooting Chant Holy at White Sands where the family lived. I had become well-informed of ritualistic procedure by an intensive study of the existing literature and was able to converse with the chanter about ceremonial lore. He had no inkling that I knew anything about anything of this kind. One time after a Navajo had voiced objections to my

presence with pencil and paper in the ceremonial hogan, the chanter came to my dwelling to excuse his
own compromise suggestion that I try to remember
instead of writing, and concluded somewhat defi-
antly, 'I'll sing over you some day!' So I did not even
have to request the part of my program I had always
planned, namely to be the 'one-sung-over' or patient
as it is sometimes called (Reichard n.d.: 5).

Between 1932 and 1937 she had seen Red Point
perform the Shooting Chant three times and also
had been a patient in the ceremony herself. Reichard has also continued the work she had begun
with Goddard by translating the text of the Male
Shooting Chant (one of the two major versions of
the ceremony) as told to Father Berard Haile by
Blue Eyes, a Navajo singer from Lukachukai, in
1924.

Early in the 1930s Reichard began to collaborate with Franc Newcomb, the wife of a trader
who operated a trading post 60 miles north of
Gallup, and Mary Wheelwright, a wealthy Bostonian. Neither of these women was a professionally trained anthropologist, but with Reichard
they became the three women who contributed
most to the anthropological study of Navajo religion and mythology. They constituted a female
network, as opposed to the male network that
consisted of Clyde Kluckhohn, Leland Wyman,
Harry Hoijer (a linguist), and Father Berard
Haile.

Reichard was particularly impressed with the
watercolor copies that Franc Newcomb had been
making of sandpaintings used by singers in the
area near her husband's trading post. In the summer of 1930, Reichard met Newcomb, and they
began a voluminous correspondence. Reichard
wrote to Parsons, "I stopped to see Mrs. Arthur
Newcomb, Miss Wheelwright's liegeman and I
venture to say hers is the most scientific collection
of sand-paintings. She has been working on them
for 12 years and is a greater hound for accuracy
than for beauty (sales value I mean)" (ECP:GR/
ECP 7/6/30).

The three women were separated by differences

of class and education, but Reichard, with her un-
pretentious, down-to-earth personality, undoubtedly was more comfortable with Newcomb than
with the upper-class Boston brahmin, Wheelwright. By February 1932, Newcomb was collecting sandpaintings of *Na'at'oee ba'aad* (Female
Shooting Chant) for Reichard, who soon suggested that they collaborate. "I think that it is
very generous of you to say that the sketches are
mine—what would you think of collaborating on
a [Na'at'oee] write up. My failing is that I am a
chronic collector" (GR:FN/GR 5/7/32). Several
months later, Newcomb replied to an apparent
offer of putting together a book on the Male
Shooting Chant,

I certainly feel like saying, "Oh, Boy!! May I, to a college instructor?" There is nothing I would like better
than to assemble a group of [Na'at'oee] paintings for
publication. This winter has almost taken the starch
out of me, but I have come to life after receiving your
letter (GR:FN/GR 1/18/33).

Reichard's impressions of Mary Wheelwright
were less favorable. In a letter to Parsons in the
summer she describes an encounter with Wheelwright that occurred when she was visiting Newcomb:

Mary Cabot doesn't think directly and sat on me so
hard I was squashed flatter than a pancake. I know I
used the wrong psychology on her, but it did make
me hot under the collar when she insinuated I was superficial (as are all who study the Navs but her!) I saw
Mrs. N[ewcomb] in Gallup and she said she was sorry
for me. Mary C. thinks in circles—like Navs! and she
explained her psychology. I don't need sympathy; I
have been squelched by such as her before, but I'm
done with her. I [thought] I was doing her a favor.
She has the idea that nobody is doing the Nav. right
but her (ECP:GR/ECP 2/13/31).

Newcomb, for her part, was equally ambivalent
about Wheelwright and often felt that she was
being exploited by the wealthy Boston patroness.
In January 1937, Reichard worked with Hastiin Klah, the singer who collaborated with New-

comb and Wheelwright. Reichard collected and translated his version of the Shooting Chant (Male Shootingway) and the myth of the Hail Chant. Klah died March 3, 1937, and his medicine bundles, copies of sandpaintings, and other paraphernalia were placed in the museum built for him by Wheelwright (Newcomb 1964). As with the death of Miguelito, Reichard was deeply affected by Klah's death. In writing to Roman Hubbell she says,

I read today in the *New York Sun* that Klah died at Rehoboth . . . When you say I live a self-centered selfish life, could it be that I have tried to build up a defense against having a load like the Navajo on my back? I might say too that I haven't succeeded in this defense. At any rate I am very sad about this affair of Klah . . . And he certainly was remarkable as a person, as a chanter and as a friend (HP:GR/RH 3/3/37).

By 1937 the product of Reichard and Newcomb's collaboration was published as *Sandpaintings of the Navajo Shooting Chant,* which included color and line drawing reprints of 44 sandpaintings, a condensed translation of the myth, and a symbolic analysis of the sandpaintings. The first book to look specifically at what is often the most fascinating aspect of Navajo ceremonies, it was also the first to look at the variations in sandpaintings during the course of a ceremony. In 1939, Reichard published *Navajo Medicine Man: Sandpaintings and Legends of Miguelito* (1939b). The volume included color reproductions of the sandpaintings Miguelito had painted for John Frederick Huckel, son-in-law of Fred Harvey, whose chain of hotels and restaurants hosted tourists throughout the Southwest. The sandpaintings came from the Bead Chant and the Male Shooting Chant, and Reichard was able to use the Blue Eyes version of the Shooting Chant myth as well as a version collected from Miguelito to interpret the paintings. Reichard interspersed descriptions of each sandpainting with portions of the myth, showing which deities are depicted in each painting. The book is a sequel to the New-

comb and Reichard 1937 publication, but with a fuller treatment of the relationship between paintings and myth.

With the death of her Navajo teachers Maria Antonio, Red Point, and Hastiin Klah in the mid 1930s and with the deaths of Parsons in 1941 and Boas in 1942, Reichard's relationships with her anthropological colleagues and others studying Navajo religion became more important in her correspondence. This mirrored her shift away from the study of women in a family context toward the broader analysis of the Navajo language, belief, and religious practice. Between 1944 and 1950, Reichard published two important books on Navajo religion.

In her short monograph *Prayer: The Compulsive Word* (dedicated to Franz Boas and published in 1944), Reichard outlined some of her analysis of Navajo religion and then analyzed the function, content, and structure of prayers. She also included the text in Navajo and English of a prayer from the Male Shooting Chant (which was transcribed by Adolph Bitanny, the most promising of the students she trained in the 1934 Hogan School). In many places the text rambles, and Reichard often gets sidetracked on questions such as whether the Navajo chanter sees the prayer as a unit and whether Navajo prayer is poetry or prose. On the other hand, her analysis of prayer structure as including an invocation, petition, and benediction is clearly an important insight that was later elaborated in Sam Gill's more exhaustive study of prayer (Gill 1981). She is able to show how a number of prayers have basically one or two structures and that repetitions and elaborations can be reduced to a small number of patterns. The monograph is full of important insights and "nuggets of information" dropped in the middle of paragraphs. For example, Reichard says that "thought is the same, or has the same potentiality, as word" (Reichard 1950:46–47), a relationship later elaborated by Gary Witherspoon (1977). Her discussion of the important Navajo concepts embedded in the phrase *sa'ah naaghaii bik'eh hozho* (in-old-age-walking-the-trail-of-beauty, according-to-old-age-may-it-be-perfect, or according-to-the-ideal-may-restoration-be-achieved) is illuminating, partly because she sticks closely to Navajo meaning and context rather than importing too many of our own conceptions into the translation.

Reichard's magnum opus, *Navaho Religion,* appeared in 1950, and *Navaho Grammar* (1951) was published in the following year. The work on religion was originally contained in two volumes, the first a discussion of Navajo dogma, symbolism, and ritual. The second volume contained three concordances, i.e, elaborate dictionaries of Navajo supernaturals, ritualistic ideas, and rites. Concordances were a tradition of the time and were used by Haile (1947) in his book on Shootingway. They were one way of handling a "mass of material that does not organize very well" (Aberle 1986).

Most would agree that *Navaho Religion* is not a book that can be read cover to cover; it is more like an encyclopedia to be consulted. Like Reichard's other writings, it is a compilation of facts much within the Boasian paradigm and very similar to Parsons' work, *Pueblo Indian Religion* (1939a). However, unlike that of Parsons who gives detailed accounts of many ceremonies drawn from her own field notes and those of other anthropologists, Reichard's work is less synthetic. Specific ceremonies and chants are not discussed as a whole but are treated under particular topics, such as the use of sex or direction in chants. It is difficult to find the overall structure of Navajo ceremonies and their origin stories. Oswald Werner, an anthropologist who has studied Navajo systems of classification (ethnoscience), provided a telling analogy (Werner, 1986, personal communication). It is as if Reichard had taken apart a motorcycle and carefully laid all the parts on the ground. Everything is there, but how it all fits together is not apparent. For those totally immersed in Navajo ritual and symbolism, there is

much to be found in the book. For someone new to the topic, it is difficult to "find the thread."

DEALING WITH THE MALE NETWORK

Reichard's work on religion brought her into disagreement with Haile, Hoijer, Kluckhohn, and Wyman on a number of points. The male network of specialists was particularly combative when dealing with disagreements. These cropped up between Reichard and Wyman, Kluckhohn, and Haile over several translations of Navajo chant names and whether to spell Navajo with a "j" or an "h."[21] Since Newcomb and Wheelwright collected sandpaintings and myth texts and were not analysts of either the religion or the language, Reichard's more technical work on these topics was primarily evaluated by the white male scholars. It is in relationship to this network and to the profession as a whole that Reichard seems like "a woman alone."

To cite the best example of the kinds of controversies that arose between Reichard and male scholars, there is a long and complex argument between Wyman and Kluckhohn, on the one hand, and Reichard, on the other, over the classification of Navajo ceremonies. Haile (1938) had a third classificatory scheme as well.[22] Basically, Wyman and Kluckhohn (1938) divided ceremonials into four main categories: Blessingway ceremonies, Holyway ceremonies (chants conducted with a rattle, which include sandpaintings and prayerstick offerings), Lifeway ceremonies, and Enemyway ceremonies. Reichard proposed a major division between those chants that emphasized good (or the transformation from neutral to sanctified) and those that emphasized evil (or the exorcism of evil). There is little difference in the placement of chants within these three classifications; in a letter Wyman wrote to Reichard, however, he vehemently objected to the classification of some of the Windways on the evil side (GR: LW/GR 3/24/46). The main contribution of Reichard's classification is that it pinpoints the major differences in function of Navajo ceremonies—the attainment of *hozho* (pleasant conditions or harmony) versus the exorcism of *hoch'o* (ugly or dangerous conditions)—two themes that run through various subrituals, prayers, and parts of larger ceremonies that, in turn, emphasize one or the other theme (see Lamphere 1969). In this sense Reichard came closer than Wyman and Kluckhohn to organizing her classification around important Navajo concepts.

Reichard's correspondence with Kluckhohn and Wyman at times was full of charges and countercharges. In a letter of November 12, 1943, Kluckhohn began by saying, "I assure you I am not 'annoyed with you' as a person. I have always genuinely and deeply, liked you as a person and I continue to." He continued in the next paragraph,

But when it comes to Navaho studies I have slowly and regretfully come to the conclusion that your views and mine as to what constitutes evidence, your views and [mine] as to the basic canons of scientific logic were so far apart that agreement was not to be hoped for. With occasional and usually utterly minor qualifications, it has been my experiences that Wyman, Hill, Father Berard and I saw pretty much eye to eye on Navaho questions—when we had talked the matter out and discussed our separate evidence with one another. This has not been the case with you so consistently—largely I am persuaded, because our basic premises seem so different (GR:CK/GR 11/12/43).

Following this opening, the letter mostly set forth Kluckhohn's objections to the term *Chant of Waning Endurance,* his arguments against the term *War Ceremony,* and his preference for spelling Navajo with an "h." He also chided Reichard for criticizing him on the basis of his lectures at Columbia University in 1939 rather than on his most recent work.

On November 17, 1943, Reichard drafted a response that she did not send. In it she defended her translation of *ha'neeneehee* and her use of the term *War Ceremony.* [23] She was particularly upset that Kluckhohn did not view her as a careful ethnographer and scientist:

Since I am condemned without a trial I shall send you only the three chapters which concern you most vitally. If you wish me to, I will cut out anything I may have said. My purpose in asking you to do so was just this as I said. There is no use in your reading any of the rest since you already know all about it. I find myself holding very curious opinions when I read your letter.[24]

In closing, Reichard commented, "I am naturally very sorry that you feel as you do; I don't know anything to do about it. I thought I presented evidence for my attitudes but since you, not having read it, do not think so, I have no basis for discussion." She signed the letter, "Yours, nice person, lousy scientist!, Gladys" (GR:GR/CK 11/17/43).

Lee Wyman attempted to mediate in a letter written to Reichard on December 3, 1943:

I would say, sit tight, try to reserve judgement until Clyde or myself has had a good talk with you in person, and in the meantime continue to be your old friendly self. You see I think you are more disturbed than circumstances warrant and that you really have not heard all of Clyde's side of the story.

Later in the letter, Wyman suggests that Reichard

accept Clyde's letter as an attempt to let you know where he stands, and also an attempt to clear the air so future misunderstanding would not crop up, and *above all* an attempt to stay on the same friendly terms as always. If you cannot swallow that and my efforts as a peace-maker are in vain, please do hold fire til one of us (or both) has had a chance to talk with you. How about it??

Whether Wyman's effort at peacemaking worked is unknown. In a letter with a missing section, possibly addressed to Wyman, Reichard again defended herself. She had heard that Kluck-hohn had told Ralph Linton, then editor of the *American Anthropologist,* that Haile was the expert on Navajo language and that "Gladys' work—especially on language—was all wet" (GR:GR/[LW] n.d.). Reichard felt Kluckhohn "double-crossed" her and that she really did not trust him. Wyman maintained that Kluckhohn might have said something like this but only in reference to one word—the translation of *ha'neeneehee.* Perhaps Wyman's intervention worked, since later correspondence between Kluckhohn and Reichard seems civil.[25]

This correspondence points up not only the heated nature of Reichard's differences with Kluckhohn, but also the way in which she was excluded from their "inner circle." Even very early on in her career, Reichard felt isolated. At one point she confessed to Parsons, "I just want to tell you how much I appreciate your keeping on believing in my job and the way I am doing it. I say this because you and Papa Franz are about the only ones who do" (ECP:GR/ECP 7/9/32).

ASSESSING REICHARD'S LIFE: PROFESSIONAL AND INSTITUTIONAL ISOLATION

Despite her very innovative work on women in the 1930s, it is difficult to argue that Reichard's intellectual and personal stance was feminist, particularly in contrast to those of Parsons and Benedict. Eleanor Leacock (1986), a feminist who was a student and research assistant to Reichard at Barnard College, remembered, "She never talked to us as women and never talked about women in the cultures she studied. My marginal notes were that [when she did talk about male and female roles] she was echoing what I would call the active/passive dichotomy which has been with us forever, and which I was already wondering about [whether it was valid or not]."[26]

If Reichard had feminist sympathies they came out primarily in her correspondence with Parsons,

the woman in the Columbia circle whose feminism was the most public. In the summer of 1929 Reichard wrote to Parsons concerning the differential treatment of three "girls" in the Laboratory of Anthropology's archaeological field school: "The main contention of them all [the men]," she wrote to Parsons,

is that girls are all right, entertaining, etc. but no good in science because you can't do anything with them. Kroeber ends all remarks with "Boas will place her." It never seems to occur to any of them that if he can, others might be able to, were they sufficiently interested (ECP:GR/ECP 8/25/29).

Later she wrote to Parsons, "Incidentally Ruth Benedict has made Asst. Prof at Columbia which is a grand scoop for feminism! If there is another woman in Columbia proper I don't know who it is"(ECP:GR/ECP 3/17/31). On the other hand, Reichard reported she felt no discrimination at the International Congress of Americanists meetings in Hamburg in 1930:

I was the only woman at the Congress Council Meeting. That fact was the only thrilling thing about it, for it was long drawn out and mostly in Spanish . . . Even tho there were few women at the Congress with a scientific interest I could not notice any discrimination. But I guess that is nonsense anyway. Birket-Smith spoke very highly of de Laguna and wants to take her with him in two years. Thilesius even now treats me as a colleague instead of as an infant in swaddling clothes as was the case when I was in Hamburg before (ECP:GR/ECP 9/30/30).

Reichard's style seems much less sophisticated than that of upper-class Parsons or even that of Benedict and Mead, whose Greenwich Village connections and interests in the arts and poetry reflected the urban intellectual milieu in which they lived. Reichard gives the impression in her letters of an enthusiastic but unpolished individual. She says things like, "I had a gorgeous summer" (ECP:GR/ECP 10/5/31) or "I'm full of prunes about the Southwest" when speaking of her experiences in 1936 (ECP:GR/ECP 10/2/36). Of the 1929 Pecos Conference she said, "We had a most awfully good time" and her initial appraisal of John Collier was that "he certainly is swell" (ECP:GR/ECP 8/25/29). She often alludes to feeling uncomfortable with upper-class women, and she disapproved of "society" and preferred straightforward interaction. It appears that she enjoyed Navajo life to a greater extent than the intellectual atmosphere of Barnard and Columbia. David Aberle (1986), who was a young researcher among the Navajo when he knew Reichard in the 1940s and 1950s, remarked, "There was a kind of naivete to Gladys' approach, and a simplicity of interpersonal style that was, I think, sort of put down both by women and men in the Columbia department." Conversely, Nathalie Woodbury (1987, personal communication), a student of Reichard's who later became an archaeologist, felt that Reichard did not play "intellectual games" in her conversations or try to "score points" with intellectual displays when with colleagues. She was very straightforward in her approach with no "guile or fancy footwork."

The Navajo appreciated Reichard's open, generous personality. She was called *'Asdzaan naadlohii* (Laughing or Smiling Woman). Margaret Jose, a Navajo nurse, met Reichard while she was working at a hospital near Fort Defiance. She spent a year in New York taking postgraduate nursing classes at Barnard and working with social service students on the Lower East Side. She attended some of Reichard's classes at Barnard and helped her translate for Navajo patients whom Reichard brought to the hospital in Fort Defiance. She described Reichard as "kind": "She was always good natured, friendly, and full of fun. I never saw her sad or anything like that . . . good natured all the time." Jose called Reichard *'Asdzaan bahozhoni* or Happy Woman (interview 1986).

Reichard's struggle for the acceptance of her views at times was a lonely one. Her isolation be-

comes clearer if we compare her intellectual commitments and her institutional situation with that of Clyde Kluckhohn. Although Reichard was a Boasian, Kluckhohn was much more interdisciplinary, reflecting his interest in the classics, a year of study in Vienna where he became acquainted with psychoanalysis, and his Rhodes Scholarship to Oxford where he read anthropology with R. R. Marrett. Kluckhohn's ideas changed and grew with American anthropology, both reflecting and shaping the interests in culture and personality and functionalism that emerged first in the 1930s and resurfaced in the Post–World War II period. One could argue that Kluckhohn's ideas "modernized," while Reichard remained a staunch Boasian long after others had turned to newer approaches and branched out beyond American Indian studies.

David Aberle (1986) has commented that Kluckhohn had a keen eye for the "à la mode" in anthropology, shifting to whatever he felt was the "cutting edge": "He understood the strategy of putting yourself in a position where you will have a lot of graduate students, which means being at a first-rate university and then going for grants that allow you to take students in the field." Reichard, whether she understood the strategy or not, could not do much about it.

Alice Kehoe, who studied with Reichard as an undergraduate and went on to Harvard to take courses with Kluckhohn, stresses that Kluckhohn and Reichard were two strong, but contrasting, personalities:

Reichard and Kluckhohn thus contrasted at every point: hidebound . . . in Boasian approach . . . vs. a fierce determination to be, and *to be seen* on the cutting edge of theory; constantly within Navajo experience for the comparative framework vs. using Navajo to explore theoretical points but not really emotionally engaged with the Navajo; working alone by choice vs. heading projects employing several graduate students; occupying a self-carved little niche vs. driven by a need to feel powerful . . . To sum up, the differences between Reichard and Kluckhohn were much more differences between personality (including ambition) and theoretical position than difference stemming primarily from gender role assignment (Kehoe 1987, personal communication).

Woodbury (1987, personal communication) basically concurs with this position:

I think Gladys would have functioned about the same way wherever she was. She had a certain personality and it had a certain effect on her professional relationships. She did her work at a time when change was just underfoot; unlike Kluckhohn she didn't reach down and grab it to enhance her position or satisfy herself with trying new ideas and ways. She was conservative and yet maybe she was ahead of her time.

In contrast to Kehoe and Woodbury, who emphasize personality, a feminist analysis of Reichard's career cannot ignore the role of gender in both shaping some of Reichard's most important contributions to anthropology and limiting her impact on the discipline. Her own gender-based strategy of living with a Navajo family (adopting the role of daughter and student) allowed Reichard to learn to weave and to view Navajo life at much closer range than others were able to do with more traditional forms of fieldwork. Her most innovative books *Spider Woman* and *Dezba* came out of this experience and provide us with rich data on Navajo women's lives through a more dialogic text than even the more well-known ethnographies of Margaret Mead.

There are three important factors that limited Reichard's impact on anthropology. First, the gender-based strategy of apprenticing herself to Franz Boas as a kind of intellectual daughter was, in the end, a liability. Those women, like Benedict and Mead, who broke away from Boas' commitment to ethnographic particularism were able to innovate theoretically and methodologically in ways that eluded Reichard. Even so, Reichard's attempt to analyze Navajo categories, symbols, and the structure of Navajo prayer in their own terms, rather than imposing more Westernized constructs (whether based on Freudian theory or scientific classification systems), prefigured structuralism and ethnoscience. That her efforts went unrecognized during her lifetime may be due partly to her insistence that there were no generalizations or overall framework (such as Kluckhohn's notion of "pattern") into which Navajo thought could be fit (a very Boasian position). By holding such a position and rejecting theory after the discipline as a whole had moved beyond Boas' position, Reichard perhaps colluded in keeping her views from gaining wide acceptance.

Second, her peripheral position within the network of scholars of Navajo religion limited her influence. That she had difficulty getting her ideas accepted by Kluckhohn, Wyman, and Haile meant that she could be dismissed in the way that Newcomb and Wheelwright were, as collectors of sandpaintings and myth texts but not serious analysts.

Third, Reichard was in an institutional situation where she had little impact on graduate students, with the exception of Eleanor Leacock, Nathalie Woodbury, Kate Peck Kent (who became a specialist in southwestern prehistoric textiles), and Katharine Bartlett (curator and librarian for the Museum of Northern Arizona).[27] In a two-person department where she had to teach a wide variety of courses, Reichard rarely had the opportunity to train graduate students, except for those who became her teaching assistants or helped with her research. Among the women who conducted research in the Southwest as described in *Daughters of the Desert* (Babcock and Parezo 1988), Reichard, unlike many, did have a Ph.D. and a full-time teaching job for her entire career. She is similar to a cluster of women archaeologists, museum specialists, and ethnographers who were in peripheral institutions: women's colleges, state universities without graduate departments, and less well known museums. Major male figures in southwestern studies such as Fred Eggan at the University of Chicago, Emil Haury and Edward Spicer at the University of Arizona, and Lee Wyman at Boston University were all members (and sometimes chairs) of departments with graduate programs. To cite the best example, Kluckhohn's position at Harvard where there was a nationally recognized anthropology graduate program meant that many well-known anthropologists of the next generation were trained by him.

Even using Reichard's personality as an explanation for her position within anthropology has a gender component. Biographers and commentators rarely argue that male contributions to a discipline hinge on their personalities, while, for women, personal style (such as their "difficultness") becomes a significant factor in their lack of renown or eminence (see the introduction to this volume and Hubbard 1990).

In all these contexts—her early apprenticeship to Boas, her fieldwork with a Navajo family in the 1930s, her marginalization within the network of those anthropologists who studied Navajo religion, and her peripheral institutional position— gender played a role, sometimes positively, but more often by limiting the impact of her work. It is gratifying, therefore, that Reichard's research has received more attention over the last 15 years.

Those who have used Reichard's early ethnographies, *Dezba* and *Spider Woman,* in their teaching have recognized her sensitive portrayal of Navajo women's lives. In the 1990s, when "objectivity" has been severely criticized within anthropology, and when characterizations of cultures that build on native concepts rather than externally imposed categories have become the accepted goal of much of cultural anthropology, Reichard's work seems very appropriate and relevant. As Ruth Bunzel said of Reichard in her 1955 tribute, "Above all in the field she never forgot that she was a human being working with subjects who were also human beings and with whom she shared a common humanity."

NOTES

1. This paper was first presented at the Daughters of the Desert Conference sponsored by the Wenner-Gren Foundation, March 15–23, 1986, at a conference center in Oracle/Globe, Arizona. I would like to thank Barbara Babcock and Nancy Parezo for their help on the first draft. I would also like to thank Elizabeth Jameson, Jane Slaughter, Rayna Rapp, and Sue Armitage for their helpful comments, which guided this revision. A version of this paper was printed in *Frontiers* vol. 12, no. 1 (1991) with the permission of the Wenner-Gren Foundation for Anthropological Research and this volume's editor.

2. Reichard's ethnographic monographs include *Spider Woman: A Story of Navajo Weavers and Chanters* (1934a), *Navajo Shepherd and Weaver* (1936), and *Dezba: Woman of the Desert* (1939a). Her other major publications on the Navajo include *Social Life of the Navajo Indians,* Columbia University Contributions to Anthropology, Vol. 7 (1928), *Navaho Religion: A Study of Symbolism* (1950), and *Navaho Grammar* (1951).

3. Kluckhohn and Leighton, *The Navaho* (1946); Kluckhohn and Wyman, *An Introduction to Navaho Chant Practice with an Account of the Behaviors Observed in Four Chants* (1940); Wyman and Kluckhohn, *Navaho Classification of their Song Ceremonials* (1938); Haile, *Prayerstick Cutting in a Five-night Navajo Ceremonial of the Male Branch of Shootingway* (1947).

4. I would like to thank Susan Armitage for this insight. This point also was discussed at the Daughters of the Desert Conference.

5. Other important women anthropologists who were part of the Columbia circle and worked in the Southwest were Esther Goldfrank, Ruth Bunzel, and Ruth Underhill. Goldfrank, who began as Boas' secretary, became a self-taught ethnographer in the mold of Elsie Clews Parsons but left anthropology during her first marriage to Walter Goldfrank. When she returned in 1937, she remained peripheral to the Mead/Benedict coalition and was somewhat envious of those women in more central positions. Her marriage to Karl Wittfogel allied her with another powerful male intellectual (apart from Boas), and much of her remaining career utilized his perspectives and sup-

ported his work. Bunzel also started as a secretary to Boas, but she went on to receive a Ph.D. on the basis of her work at Zuni. She, too, remained peripheral to the department, supported continuously on "temporary" research projects and lecturer appointments, but nevertheless was part of the Mead/Benedict coalition, especially in terms of her participation in the Linton-Kardiner seminars and her later work on culture and personality. Underhill, an older student who went to Columbia University in 1930, was perhaps the closest of these women to Reichard because of a summer's work on the Navajo reservation with a Tohono O'Odham informant and her later teaching at Barnard College. However, she left the Columbia milieu for a career in government service, a new possibility in the years of the Collier Administration of the Bureau of Indian Affairs (BIA) (see Halpern's and Tisdale's chapters in this volume).

6. Reichard's personal and intellectual life seems more that of a woman alone, harking back to Alice Fletcher's characterization of her role in anthropology in the 1880s (Mark 1988).

7. A typescript of McElroy's interview is in the Reichard collection at the Museum of Northern Arizona. Reichard evidently made some corrections in pencil, but it is difficult to tell how accurate the interview is.

8. Details of Reichard's life are taken from de Laguna 1955; Goldfrank 1956; Mark 1988; and Smith 1956.

9. I am grateful to Virginia Scharff for this point. This pattern goes back to the seventeenth and eighteenth centuries, when intellectual women studied at home and were often tutored by their fathers. In the nineteenth and twentieth centuries, professional women often formed households with other women (often called "Boston marriages") or lived in some other type of quasi-family. As an example of a woman who remained in the daughter role, Scharff mentioned June Etta Downey, psychologist and professor at the University of Wyoming who continued to live with her aging parents until they died. Virginia Scharff and Katherine Jensen, in "The Professors' Club and the Complexities of Women's Culture," a paper presented at the Conference on Women's Culture in the Great Plains, Lincoln, Nebraska, March 19, 1987, talk of these matters. Reichard, living in New York, and at some distance from her parents in Bangor, Pennsylvania, was able to become a quasi-daughter in her mentor's household.

10. The Fire Dance or Mountain Top Way is a nine-night ceremony to cure the effects of dangerous contact with mountain animals (deer, bear, mountain lion, etc.) The last night features a number of performances that take place around a large fire, including usually feather dancers and *nasjiini* who swallow long, sword-like objects.

11. Earl Morris was a prominent archaeologist who is best known for his research on Betatakin and Keet Seel, two pueblo ruins located on the Navajo National Monument. Ann Morris actively conducted research alongside her husband.

12. The couple in a picture in Reichard's book are dancing in a "white-man" position, though in the last 20 years, I have seen the dance done only in a traditional circle with each couple dancing side-by-side.

13. The Franciscan Fathers had collected large numbers of genealogies dating from the early twentieth century. If Haile was implicitly comparing his data with that of Reichard, one can imagine that he found her study less comprehensive.

14. There is still fierce defense of theoretical territory among Navajo specialists, as indicated by various disputes among ethnographers—both male and female—of my own generation. William Lyon (1989) has also assessed Reichard's relationship with other specialists and has concluded that the major factors in her rivalries were personalities, professional jealousies, and male chauvinism.

15. Goddard's daughter had a much more cordial relationship with Reichard, according to Nathalie Woodbury (1987, personal communication), and Goddard's son David seemed to be sympathetic in resolving the controversy over the sale of books to Haile.

16. Laura Armer was a professional artist and author of children's books who lived on the Navajo Reservation periodically between 1924 and 1932. She copied sandpaintings, working with a Navajo singer, taking artistic license with some of her reproductions (see Babcock and Parezo 1988). Reichard felt that Armer's paintings ran to "artiness and quantity rather than to accuracy and Indian flavor" (ECP:GR/ECP 7/6/30).

17. Miguelito was called *lichii deez'ahi* in Navajo, or "red-bluff-that-rises-up," hence Reichard's English translation of "Red Point."

18. Marie was married to Tom Curley and had two sons, Ben and Dan. Altnaba was married to Curley's son, Tom's half brother; she had one daughter, Ninaba.

19. Reichard's summers with Miguelito's family echo some of my own fieldwork experiences some 35 years later. Reichard took her own car, which soon became an important vehicle for transporting family members, and once the rainy season started, the car invariably became stuck on the muddy roads. She often took time out from her weaving to visit the Hubbells much as I retreated to my apartment in Gallup for a bath, a movie, and a respite from fieldwork. In contrast to my own fieldwork, where I always tried to live in the same hogan or house as other family members and share in the cooking, dishwashing, and housework, Reichard lived in a separate dwelling and seemed not to eat with other family members except on special occasions. I too learned to weave, but only worked on one rug, while Reichard completed several and really mastered the craft.

20. Reichard's opinion of Amsden's own book is less favorable. In a letter to Parsons containing criticism to be kept "in the bosom of the family," she found "Charlie's book" a great disappointment: "He reprints the old stuff including the old errors and illustrations. He didn't even gave a new drawing of the loom! All this seems to me inexcusable" (ECP:GR/ECP n.d.).

21. Both Hoijer and Kluckhohn agreed that Reichard should have used the term *Navaho* rather than *Navajo,* since by the 1930s most scholars were using the "h" rather than the Spanish "j." Reichard finally gave in on this point and by the publication of *Navaho Religion* was using the "h" form. Ironically, the Navajo Nation elected to have the official spelling use a "j," so Reichard's view was the one that prevailed historically.

22. I have reanalyzed Wyman's and Kluckhohn's scheme in Lamphere and Vogt (1973).

23. Kluckhohn complained that Reichard used "War Ceremony" as a translation for *'ana'ji,* which he translated as "Enemyway." For her part, Reichard found fault with the use in English of *-way* at the end

of each chant name, e.g., Blessingway, Shootingway, Hailway, when the enclitic *-ji* appears at the end of *hozhooji'* (Blessingway). She notes further that some chants are also called by a name plus the word *hataal* (singer chant). In the end the Kluckhohn and Haile preferences won out over Reichard's translations both for *ha'neelnehee* and *'ana'ji.*

24. Reichard may be referring to *A New Look at the Navajo,* a book she was still writing when she died, which presented an alternative to Kluckhohn and Leighton's book, *The Navaho.*

25. See, for example, Kluckhohn's replies to Reichard's review of Kluckhohn's *Navajo Witchcraft* (1944b); also see her comments on Kluckhohn and Leighton's *The Navaho* (1946) (GR:CK/GR 5/9/47; GR:CK/GR 2/24/no year).

26. This is not surprising, given the facts that she was teaching during the 1930s, 1940s, and 1950s, a period of feminist quiescence, and preferred to discuss "people" rather than men or women as separate categories (Woodbury 1987, personal communication). Leacock (1986) also noted Reichard's teaching style:

> She sort of struck me as disorganized, but then I realized again, looking at my notes that she was very much organized. She was very much involved in the process of working with data and really becoming immersed in data. That was her approach to teaching. Teaching is not just a matter of giving facts; you need facts to teach with. One of the emphases was on learning how to find facts and that's a selective process that involves a theory behind it.

27. See other chapters in this volume and Babcock and Parezo 1988 for biographical information on Kent, Woodbury, and Bartlett. Kent, a graduate student at Columbia, was Reichard's assistant in the Barnard undergraduate department, a position later held by Marian Smith, who became a Iroquoian archaeologist. Woodbury took courses with Reichard as an undergraduate major and was appointed lecturer at Barnard between 1952 and 1955. Leacock was an undergraduate student of Reichard's while at Barnard and helped prepare the drawings for Reichard's *Prayer: The Compulsive Word.* De Laguna took a course from Reichard in 1927, and Kehoe studied with Reichard in the early 1950s before attending Harvard, where she took courses from Kluckhohn.

Esther Goldfrank with Pueblo man. Negative No. 86-1306. *Courtesy of the National Anthropological Archives, Smithsonian Institution.*

Katherine Spencer Halpern, Malcolm Collier, and Jane Jennings (wife of Jessie Jennings who was park ranger) at Montezuma's Castle National Monument, 1937. *Courtesy of Katherine Spencer Halpern.*

Dorothy Keur and three archaeological colleagues at Big Bead Mesa excavations, 1940. Photographer: John Keur. *Courtesy of Hunter College.*

Edgar Lee Hewett in San Diego, 1932.
Photographer: Jack Adams. Negative No. 7373.
Courtesy of the Museum of New Mexico.

Clyde Kluckhohn. Photographer: John Brock.
Negative No. N24655. *Courtesy of the Peabody Museum
of Archaeology and Ethnology, Harvard University.*

Dorothea Leighton with Jennifer Fox, filmed in Santa Fe during videodocumentary session for Daughters of the Desert project, 1985. *Courtesy of the Wenner-Gren Foundation for Anthropological Research.*

Kate Peck Kent and Ramona Sakiestewa with Pueblo artist working on embroidered dance kilt at School of American Research, 1985. *Courtesy of the School of American Research.*

Right: Hastiin Klah, Navajo singer, ca. 1935.
Photographer: T. Harmon Parkhurst.
Negative No. 4330.
Courtesy of the Museum of New Mexico.

Below: Marjorie Lambert conducting visitor
tour in chapel room, Palace of the Governors,
Museum of New Mexico, ca. 1950.
Photographer: Charles Herbert.
Negative No. 1616.
Courtesy of the Museum of New Mexico.

Alice Marriott, 1939. *Courtesy of Alice Marriott.*

Maria Martinez rolling coils for pottery
walls, San Ildefonso Pueblo, ca. 1950.
Photographer: Tyler Dingee.
Negative No. 120174.
Courtesy of the Museum of New Mexico.

Muriel Painter at New Pascua during Easter
Ceremony, 1968. Photographer: Rosamond Spicer.
Courtesy of Rosamond Spicer.

Ann and Earl Morris in the field, ca. 1934. *Courtesy of
Elizabeth Morris.*

WOMEN IN APPLIED ANTHROPOLOGY IN THE SOUTHWEST: THE EARLY YEARS

Katherine Spencer Halpern

APPLIED ANTHROPOLOGY in the Southwest developed historically in a pattern similar to that found elsewhere in the world. The practical uses of anthropology had first been recognized in relation to dependent peoples and minorities. In Britain and other European countries, this meant primarily their colonial peoples, and in the United States and Latin America, the American Indians. In the last quarter of the nineteenth century, John W. Powell, director of the Smithsonian's Bureau of American Ethnology, saw the importance of government-sponsored research on American Indian cultures as a contribution to the new science of anthropology but also as a basis for government policy in its dealings with the native population. Powell's associate, William J. McGee, called this practical use "applied ethnology" (see McGee 1904:x; Hinsley 1976:45, 53, 58, 66), and Daniel Brinton was apparently the first to use the now-current term "applied anthropology" in his 1896 address to the American Association for the Advancement of Science.

In Powell's program as it developed, however, the scientific task of fact gathering took precedence over policy applications. For the most part, the early fieldworkers assumed that they were recording customs that would be lost, and they saw American Indian assimilation as inevitable. Some, like Frank H. Cushing and Edgar Lee Hewett in the Southwest, sought to understand the viewpoint of native peoples before trying to educate them to new ways, and they cautioned against using haste and force.[1] There was, however, no really systematic attempt to bring the new anthropological knowledge of American Indian life to bear on the practical problems of administration, and an assimilationist policy dominated government conduct of Indian affairs until well into the next century. When individual anthropologists became involved in action for Indian welfare, they too adopted an assimilationist stance. This was notably the case in the support of land allotments by Alice Fletcher, the pioneer woman ethnographer of Plains culture (Lurie 1966:43–54).

During this time, the institutional base of anthropology was primarily governmental, centered in Washington, D.C. By the turn of the century it was beginning to move to the universities, but not until the 1930s did academic departments begin to take an active interest in the practical implications of anthropology for contemporary life. In 1928 Boas published his *Anthropology and Modern Life*. Drastic changes in American Indian life had stimulated new academic studies of the process of acculturation. Problems of industrial organization in contemporary U.S. society became a focus of research under W. Lloyd Warner and his colleagues, first at Harvard University and later at the University of Chicago, and the Great

Depression and New Deal provided impetus to applied work in other social sciences as well. Ominous political developments in Europe increased the concern of Boas and his students about problems of race and prejudice (Benedict 1940a; Benedict and Weltfish 1943). During and after World War II many U.S. anthropologists were drawn into emergency applications of their discipline by the demand for their special knowledge, both at home and in such new areas as the Pacific Trust Territories. Formation of the Society for Applied Anthropology with its own journal in 1941 marked the professional recognition of this new field. Among the planning group that organized the society were two women, Margaret Mead and Laura Thompson, both of whom played important roles in later developments.

Against this background we will trace the history of applied anthropology as it developed during the three decades of the 1930s through the 1950s in the Southwest, paying special attention to the roles that women played in this development. In the Southwest the problems dealt with were primarily in American Indian affairs, and the focus of applied work changed over time: beginning with Indian administration, economic, and technological development; then shifting to education and community dynamics; and finally focusing on problems in medical and legal affairs. Administration holds a special place in this sequence because the administrative process itself, in the form of planned intervention, became the medium for applied work in all of these problem areas.

THE 1930S

The first formal recognition of applied anthropology occurred early in the New Deal under the auspices of the Bureau of Indian Affairs (BIA) and the U.S. Department of Agriculture. John Collier, appointed commissioner of Indian Affairs in 1933, had been active in private efforts to support American Indian rights in the Southwest. In response to increasing criticism, Congress passed the 1934 Indian Reorganization Act that in large measure reversed the current assimilationist policies, and Collier undertook a program of political, economic, and educational development that attempted to "restore to the Indian management of his own affairs" (Mekeel 1944:209). Collier's efforts to use anthropologists in this program reflected his recognition of the need to understand how human factors were interfering in Indian administration. At about the same time, the Department of Agriculture had begun to use anthropologists and other social scientists in the rural life programs of its Bureau of Agricultural Economics and Soil Conservation Service (see Redfield and Warner 1940).

Beginning to Use Anthropology in American Indian Administration

In 1933 and 1934 Collier had been in contact with anthropologists at universities and at the Smithsonian Institution to learn how they thought their discipline could be used in his new administration. His approach apparently received cordial response (see Kelly 1980:6–9). He began by making a number of temporary appointments of anthropologists to undertake special projects. Among them were two women appointed to conduct training programs for BIA teachers: Ruth Underhill, who went on to an extended association with the BIA, and Gladys Reichard, who held a brief experimental school to teach Navajo to employees on the reservation (Kelly 1980:9).

By the end of 1935, Collier had organized an Applied Anthropology Unit as an advisory group within the BIA with Scudder Mekeel as its director. Lawrence Kelly (1980) lists six participants (some used as consultants and not employed fulltime), most of whom were young anthropologists who had been working on American Indian cultures.[2] During its brief life the Applied Anthropology Unit was apparently not able to fulfill the high expectations of its inauguration. When Mekeel left the BIA in 1937, it was disbanded, primarily because of congressional opposition and curtailed appropriations. In 1944 Mekeel described some of the difficulties, as he saw them, that had limited the unit's work, chief among which were resistance and lack of understanding on the part of regular BIA personnel (Mekeel 1944:212–13; Collier 1944:424; see also Kelly 1980). He saw the need for an in-service training program to promote understanding and reduce friction between the administration and social scientists. The Education Division of the BIA was the only unit that tried out such in-service training, and it was this division that continued to be hospitable to later applied efforts.

During this period, and despite the difficulties of the Applied Anthropology Unit, two women were appointed to staff positions in what would now be termed applied anthropology, although this aspect of their contribution seems not to have been fully recognized at the time. They were Ruth Underhill, a special consultant in American Indian education, and Sophie D. Aberle, superintendent of the United Pueblos Agency from 1935 to 1944.

As a graduate student from Columbia University under Boas, Underhill began her Tohono O'Odham (Papago) fieldwork in 1930 and worked for the BIA in various capacities from 1934 to 1949. In the summers from 1934 to 1936 she gave courses for BIA teachers in Santa Fe and at the Sherman Institute in California, and from 1938 to 1944 she acted as an education supervisor for the BIA. Her preface to the 1979 edition of *Papago Woman* tells how she spent 13 years traveling among the various Arizona, New Mexico, and California reservations and studying southwestern Indian cultures, giving lectures to the Anglo teachers, and writing a series of pamphlets picturing the various peoples, which she hoped would reach both Native American and non–Native American children. Later she expanded a number of these pamphlets into books for more general popular use. Through her long professional life, and in addition to her significant contributions to Tohono O'Odham and Mohave ethnography, she continued to be a respected and effective interpreter of American Indian culture.

Dr. Sophie Aberle came from a different academic background—a Ph.D. in genetics and an M.D., followed by a period as an instructor at the Yale University School of Medicine. She gives 1927 as the beginning of her studies of the Pueblos, and in 1935 she became superintendent of the newly consolidated United Pueblos Agency (1948:25, 56). Although her activities in this position have not been described in the applied anthropology literature, her later scholarly account of contemporary Pueblo political organization in relation to the history of Pueblo land holdings and economy merits an important place in the story of the New Deal American Indian policy and reveals some of the reasons behind the continuing Pueblo success in maintaining political and cultural identity while adapting to modern conditions.[3]

Economic and Technological Development

Collier also entered into an interagency agreement with the Department of Agriculture to organize Technical Cooperation Units of the newly established Soil Conservation Service (SCS) that would employ anthropologists in their field operations. The southwestern regional office of the SCS had been especially concerned about soil erosion in its area and had developed a Human Dependency Section to provide information about the social and economic conditions of ethnic populations to aid in its conservation efforts. In the Rio Grande Valley of New Mexico, anthropologists were used in an ambitious program that focused on the cultural factors influencing land use in these Hispanic and Pueblo communities (Kelly 1980; see also Harper et al. 1943 and the Tewa Basin Study, vol. 2, reprinted in Weigle 1975). In Navajo country a stock reduction program to control erosion had met strong native resistance from its beginning. In 1936–1937 the Navajo Technical Cooperation Unit (of the BIA and SCS) employed two anthropologists, Solon Kimball and John Provinse, as field investigators and advisors in its human dependency surveys for the second stage of Navajo stock reduction (Provinse and Kimball 1942), in the course of which they discovered the key role of the Navajo corporate group of linked families that they termed the "land-use community." Although the government ultimately attained its technological objectives of reducing overgrazing and erosion, it was not similarly successful in the human impact of the program, which left a heritage of continuing Navajo hostility (Spicer 1952:185–200; Aberle 1966:73). It is only fair to note that the recommendations formulated by the anthropologists between 1936 and 1942 for changes in the government's relations with the Navajos had not been implemented (Kimball 1950).[4]

It appears that no women were used in leading positions in this Navajo project, but several were on the field staffs of the Technical Cooperation Units of the BIA and SCS for the western Navajo, Walapai, Havasupai, Gila River Pima, Tohono O'Odham, and Mescalero Apache. Underhill worked with the Tohono O'Odham and Frederica de Laguna with the Pima for brief periods (Kelly 1980:17). In 1939 Emma Reh, a nutritionist, investigated Navajo consumption habits for the SCS, and her field report presents a qualitative description of household economics that is anthropological in tone (republished in 1983).[5]

THE 1940S

During World War II anthropologists were called upon for help with new problems: acquiring information on overseas peoples, languages, and cultures; dealing with emergency conditions at home, such as the problems of war workers, consumers, and the interned Japanese; postwar population dislocations and technological and community development overseas. These demands brought anthropology to a newly aware public, and the profession responded with both enthusiasm and caution. In 1942 the newly organized Society for Applied Anthropology began to publish its own journal. Distinguished southwestern an-

thropologist Elsie Clews Parsons had just become the first woman president of the American Anthropological Association, and she devoted her presidential address ("Anthropology and Prediction," published posthumously in 1942) to the pitfalls, as well as the constructive possibilities, of this burgeoning interest in applications. At its centenary celebration in 1942, the American Ethnological Society held a symposium on acculturation and administration; according to Marian Smith, its president, this was appropriate "in a year when active participation by American anthropologists in administrative affairs [had] seen such remarkable increase" (1943:181). In this symposium, Clyde Kluckhohn's paper, "Covert Culture and Administrative Problems" (1943), discussed the implications of anthropological knowledge for administration, drawing examples from the BIA's Navajo administration.

The late 1930s and 1940s saw a steady expansion of anthropological training, and increasing numbers of women as well as men were entering the field. Opportunities opened up for women as men were drawn into military service. The extended wartime horizons meant that the Southwest no longer played as central a role as it had earlier, but it continued to be the site of several important programs. Four American Indian cultures in the Southwest were the primary focus of a large-scale project on American Indian education and administration, in which women played a major organizing role. The Southwest was also the site of a pilot project for community analysis in one of the newly established Japanese relocation centers, and toward the end of the decade Cornell University instituted field programs for training and for community research. Each of these projects had roots in Collier's initial efforts a decade earlier to bring applied anthropology into American Indian administration.

Indian Education and Administration

The Education Division of the BIA had already had some success in using Underhill's anthropological skills, and in 1941 Collier sponsored a more ambitious interdisciplinary action research project on Indian personality, education, and administration, in cooperation with the University of Chicago's Committee on Human Development. Laura Thompson, who had previously worked on problems of colonial administration in the Pacific (1940, 1941), directed the overall project. Five American Indian societies were selected for study: the Hopi, Navajo, Tohono O'Odham, and Zuni in the Southwest, and the Plains Sioux. The majority of the researchers leading these field studies were women: Thompson and Alice Joseph (a psychiatrist) for the Hopi; Rosamond Spicer, Joseph, and Jane Chesky for the Tohono O'Odham; Clyde Kluckhohn and Dorothea Leighton (a psychiatrist with anthropological training) for the Navajo; Leighton and John Adair for the Zuni; and Gordon Macgregor for the Sioux. The project made cultural background studies of these peoples and examined cohorts of school children with a battery of intellectual and personality tests, physical exams, and the collection of life histories. Local BIA personnel were drawn into the field studies where possible in accordance with the action-research objective of improving Indian administration. In Thompson's words (1950:xvi),

The aim of the research was to study the Indians both as individual personalities and as tribal societies in order to discover by scientific inquiry how the effectiveness of Indian Service long-range policy and program might be increased from the standpoint of improving Indian welfare and developing responsible local autonomy.

Four of the studies were published in the 1940s (Thompson and Joseph 1944; Macgregor 1946; Leighton and Kluckhohn 1947; Joseph et al. 1947), a summary volume from the University of Chicago Committee on Human Development on the psychological results in 1955 (Havighurst and Neugarten), and the fifth study on Zuni in 1966 (Leighton and Adair).[6] Hopes for the success of this project were high. Within anthropology there had been growing interest in interdisciplinary collaboration in the cross-cultural study of child rearing, as part of the new field of culture and personality, and the systematic accumulation of this large body of psychological data on children of five cultures was in itself a notable achievement with scientific value beyond the applied aim of the project. Director Thompson carried the burden of interpreting the significance of the project for BIA policy and administration (see Thompson 1950, 1950–51, 1951). However, at the end of the war the BIA underwent a policy reversal that returned it to assimilationist measures in response to political and public pressures, and the opportunity was lost for any extensive application of the project's findings (see Collier's foreword in Thompson 1950–51; Kelly 1954; Macgregor 1955).

The Japanese Relocation Centers and Administration

The War Relocation Authority (WRA) that administered Japanese internment camps from 1942 to 1946 turned to anthropologists and sociologists for help in understanding and managing the crises that arose in these artificially constituted and culturally separate communities. Some of the anthropologists had been employed earlier by the BIA or had been close to its operations in their own field research (e.g., John Provinse, Alexander Leighton, Edward Spicer, Morris Opler, Marvin Opler, Charles Wisdom). Provinse and John Embree, a Japanese specialist, were employed as anthropologists in WRA headquarters in Washington. Two of the ten relocation centers, the Colorado River (Poston) and Gila River centers, were in Arizona on American Indian land, and Poston was administered by the Indian Service. Although the WRA did not deal with native cultures of the Southwest, its use of applied anthropology was in the tradition originated by the BIA. Alexander Leighton, a psychiatrist with anthropological training, started a research unit at Poston, seeing this as an opportunity to study problems of relocation and community building that could be expected to arise in the postwar world (Embree 1944:278–79 n. 3; Leighton 1945; Spicer 1946). The WRA administration was fearful of community unrest, and after crises in two centers (a strike and a riot), it established a Community Analysis Section in each center to perform ongoing analysis of cultural patterns, social roles, and attitudes as they developed and to act as intermediaries between the community and administration. Most of the community analysts were men, but three women anthropologists were employed in the Arizona centers—Rosalie Wax at Gila River (and later at Tule Lake); on the Poston staff, Elizabeth Colson (Leighton 1945:373, 375), who had also been involved in Navajo work under Kluckhohn; and Tamie Tsuchiyama, from the University of California at Berkeley, who had worked on Dorothy Thomas's Japanese study (Elizabeth Colson 1987, personal communication; Thomas and Nishimoto 1946).

Community Studies: Economic and Technological Development

In the 1940s anthropologists and sociologists alike continued to work in the Hispanic villages in New Mexico. Charles Loomis, a rural sociologist who had been active in the organization of the Society for Applied Anthropology, was a leader in these studies, and he was joined by his wife in a report on rural Hispanic-Americans employed in the war industry (Loomis and Loomis 1942; see also Leonard and Loomis 1941 and Loomis and Grisham 1943). In a United Nations Educational, Scientific, and Cultural Organization (UNESCO) manual on technical change for village workers, Dorothy D. Lee authored a section on Hispanic-American villages based on both published and unpublished field studies made before the early 1950s (see Mead ed. 1953: 168–93).[7]

In northwestern New Mexico, Tom Sasaki, under the auspices of Cornell University's Field Station, undertook a study of technological change

in Fruitland, a newly settled Navajo agricultural community (published 1950). The BIA had developed irrigated land for Navajo settlement in the 1930s, but the program had met with unanticipated resistance. Navajo kinship and landholding customs adapted to seminomadic sheepherding were disrupted by the new settled life, and opportunities for off-reservation wage work drew the men away from their farms. In a related field study, Laila Shukry Hamamsy, a Cornell doctoral student who later returned to development work in her native Egypt, showed how these changes had introduced strains in the traditional matrilineal kinship system, adversely affecting the roles of women and contributing to the failure of these families to adapt to the requirements of farming (Hamamsy 1957).

THE 1950S

Applied activities continued to grow steadily during the 1950s in the fields already opened. Many of the projects undertaken by U.S. anthropologists in technological and economic development were situated overseas—in South America, the Pacific, Africa, and India. However, a Navajo community project merits attention as an example of a new approach that was coming to be known as "community development." The Southwest also saw important activity in two new fields, medicine and law. There had been forerunners in both. The 1944 publication *The Navajo Door* by the psychiatrist team of Alexander and Dorothea Leighton had been a pioneer step in interpreting how cultural beliefs and values could be expected to influence the acceptance of modern medicine, but it was not until 1953 that William Caudill's review of applied anthropology in medicine marked the first recognition of a field that soon showed unprecedented growth. In legal affairs the establishment of the federal Indian Claims Commission in 1946 had opened the door to the expert testimony of anthropologists in efforts to make some restitution for injustices in land compensation. Much of the work on claims was accomplished in the 1950s, but the broader legal applications of anthropology did not come until the 1960s and 1970s.

Community Development

A new philosophy of development work was taking shape in such diverse settings as village India, the Vicos Project in Peru, and the "action anthropology" of the University of Chicago's Fox Indian project. Community development as a concept sought through various means to aid a community in setting its own goals for change and in accomplishing them through an experience of cooperative action, as contrasted with technological change directed by outside administrators (see Van Willigen 1976). This conception of community development as a model for action had a strong influence on the overseas programs of the Peace Corps and the domestic War on Poverty in the 1960s.

From 1953 to 1960, D'Arcy McNickle, a member of the Flathead tribe who had worked in Collier's Indian Bureau and felt the urgent need for developing American Indian leadership, conducted a Navajo community project at Crownpoint, New Mexico, initially under the auspices of American Indian Development (an arm of the National Congress of American Indians) and later supported directly by private foundations. He engaged Viola Pfrommer, a health educator with overseas experience, as field representative. The program began with health issues but soon expanded into broader action—promoting construction of a building for community use and encouraging local organization. Their objective was "to learn how and to what extent a community could be helped in making its own decisions regarding development" (McNickle and Pfrommer n.d.; see also Tjerandson 1980:27–44). Their joint report is an impressive record of community cooperation and accomplishment, but as a private venture, without the continuing support that would have stemmed from being part of the larger Navajo political and administrative structure, its impact was apparently limited.

Medical Anthropology

The specialty now known as "medical anthropology" has encompassed both the study of health phenomena in academic anthropology (such as paleopathology, the comparative study of beliefs about health and illness, and curing rituals) and the applied use of anthropological knowledge and methods in the improvement of health care (such as collaboration with medical personnel in developing health policy, planning, and treatment). The work of the Leightons among the Navajo in the 1940s had contributed to academic anthropological knowledge (1942) but had also been directed to aiding health professionals to better understand their Navajo patients (1944). In 1942 Dr. Alice Joseph, who had earlier participated in the Indian Education Project, had published an article in the first volume of the journal *Applied Anthropology* discussing the relationship between physicians and their American Indian patients that showed some of the barriers to mutual understanding. In a public health journal Flora Bailey had suggested ways of helping Navajo women accept hospitalization for childbirth (Bailey 1948). Sister Mary Lucia van der Eerden had published her dissertation on traditional Hispanic-American maternity care based in Taos (1948).[8] These first examples of applied medical anthropology in the Southwest were by women who came from other professions but had been exposed to anthropological training and fieldwork. They wrote as individuals, not as part of an institutional program where they could implement their ideas.

In 1955 government responsibility for American Indian health care was transferred from the Bureau of Indian Affairs to the U.S. Public Health Service. As part of its program to meet these new service responsibilities, the Public Health Service contracted with Cornell Medical College and the School of Public Health of the University of California at Berkeley to develop projects for service, research, and training that were the first in the Southwest to bring anthropologists and medical personnel together in an institutional, multifaceted health program. John Adair headed the anthropological staff of Cornell University's Many Farms project, which worked with the physicians in devising training for Navajo health workers as aides and interpreters, in instituting a record system adapted to Navajo kinship customs that focused on the family unit, in clarifying Navajo health beliefs for medical personnel, and in collecting epidemiological data on Navajo health conditions (Adair 1960, 1963; Adair and Deuschle 1957, 1970; McDermott et al. 1960). Two women participated in the project: Cara Richards, an anthropologist whose report on cooperation between medical personnel and anthropologists shows how research can clarify misunderstandings between patients and doctors (Richards 1960); and Bernice Loughlin, a public health nurse who became an essential part of the health team in many aspects of the program (Loughlin 1962; McDermott et al. 1960; Omran and Loughlin 1972).[9]

In the University of California project the anthropologist worked with health education personnel to conduct research and develop a health education program adaptive to community needs. Margaret Clark was the first anthropologist on this team; then, from 1959 to 1964 Jerrold Levy conducted studies of community health behavior in the western Navajo Reservation and began his long-term program in Navajo medical anthropology, which has included work on linguistic barriers to health care through an interpreter training program (1964) and research on such Navajo social and medical pathologies as suicide, alcohol problems, and seizures (Levy 1965a and 1965b; Levy and Kunitz 1971, 1974; Levy et al. 1987). The new approaches developed in the Many Farms program and in Levy's work have had a lasting impact on the young physicians employed in the Public Health Service as well as on

subsequent anthropologists, including in the next decades a substantial number of women, who have continued to build an impressive and expanding body of work in southwestern medical anthropology.

Testimony for American Indian Land Claims

The employment of anthropologists to compile ethnohistorical evidence bearing on American Indian land claims may be considered applied anthropology insofar as it contributed to legal decisions and actions of practical consequence to American Indian welfare. The Indian Claims Commission Act of 1946 gave a major impetus to this work. Gordon Macgregor estimated that 20 or more anthropologists were employed by the Justice Department and an equal number by the tribal governments themselves in land claims cases (Macgregor 1955). With its large American Indian population the Southwest was an important arena for this work. Florence Hawley Ellis became one of the most active contributors in her investigations of land use and occupancy for many of the Pueblos—Zia, Santa Ana, Acoma, Laguna, Jemez, Nambe, Taos, and Hopi—and also for the Navajos. (Her original reports are listed in Frisbie 1975; they were later published in the American Indian Ethnohistory Series by Garland Publishing Company [Ellis 1974a–f].) In addition, she investigated water rights for a number of northern Rio Grande Pueblos, including Nambe, Pojoaque, Tesuque, and San Ildefonso (1967). Her earlier work had combined interests in archaeology and cultural anthropology in studies of Pueblo ethnohistory and acculturation (1937, 1948), and she had made an early nutritional study in Zia (1943); but the claims investigations involved her more deeply in providing historical documentation that was important to these American Indian peoples.

Commentaries on the claims work have emphasized two of its consequences: first, the impetus it gave to the newly developing field of ethnohistory; and second, its demonstration to the

American Indians themselves of the possibilities of acting in their own behalf by employing lawyers, anthropologists, and other specialists and by cooperating in political action with other cultural groups rather than pitting one American Indian society against another (Dobyns 1970; Lurie 1978; Manners 1974).

WOMEN'S ROLES IN APPLIED ANTHROPOLOGY

This account of women's early participation in applied anthropology in the Southwest leaves many significant questions unanswered: What backgrounds had they come from? What had been their training? Was it exclusively or predominantly in anthropology? Were they young and inexperienced or had they already become established in their fields? What had drawn them into applied work?

These women came from diverse backgrounds and do not fit a common mold. Thirteen were trained as anthropologists, but eight others came from service professions and had acquired their anthropological experience for the most part in field work. Four of the anthropologists seem to have made a major commitment to applied anthropology in the Southwest—Underhill's work in Indian education, Thompson's project in Indian education and administration, Spicer's work in Indian education and later a series of community projects, and Ellis' work on Indian land claims. For the other anthropologists (Colson, Chesky, Clark, Hamamsy, de Laguna, Reichard, Richards, Tsuchiyama, and Wax), their applied work in the Southwest came at or near the beginning of their professional careers, and a few went on to a primary commitment in applied work elsewhere while the rest combined anthropology with an academic career.[10]

The eight women from service professions came primarily from medicine and public health. Three of them made major commitments in the Southwest—psychiatrists Leighton and Joseph in medical anthropology and in the American Indian education project and research physician Aberle in Indian administration. For another three we know only of their limited participation in applied projects—Reh, a nutritionist; Loughlin, a public health nurse; and Pfrommer, a health educator. Van der Eerden was not able to continue her work because of illness, but Bailey, a school teacher, has made other substantial contributions to Navajo women's studies.

We have no clear picture of what drew these women into applied work. Those with backgrounds in medicine and public health had presumably decided on a service profession before they were attracted to anthropology. A number of the anthropologists had tried out some kind of social work or teaching on their way to the more satisfying careers that they found in anthropology (Benedict, Dutton, Reichard, Underhill), but these early trials may have been influenced by the traditional conception of social work and teaching as women's professions. Surely many women, like Benedict, Parsons, and Underhill, were keenly aware of the liberating influence of anthropology on the stereotypes of their own culture and saw it as an avenue to the understanding and ultimate correction of social injustices.

This brings us to the consideration of the social climate and institutional structure within which these women worked in the 1930s. Anthropology was still a new discipline just gaining full academic recognition. The shadow of the Great Depression had severely limited employment opportunities; this was especially true in a new and struggling field. Academic jobs for male anthropologists were scarce, and Collier's attempts to use them in American Indian administration had offered a welcome opportunity to young graduates. Except in women's colleges and in schools training for the so-called women's professions (education, social work, nursing, home economics), women had not yet been generally accepted in academic life. In the 1930s even such leading figures as Benedict, Bunzel, Goldfrank, Parsons, and Underhill had not found permanent academic appointments. By the early 1940s the wartime demand for applied anthropology was opening up employment opportunities for many among the next generation of women graduate students, although the locus for much of this demand had moved out of the Southwest.

Under what auspices and with what sources of support was applied work in the Southwest being conducted? And to what extent did these auspices provide the security and continuity of an established institutional structure? Federal agencies were the major sponsors, with universities second in importance, and American Indian organizations third. The BIA and later the WRA supported applied programs in conservation, administration, and education; the Department of Agriculture in conservation and community studies; the Public Health Service in medicine; and the Justice Department in American Indian land claims. In a number of cases these government agencies were joined by universities, sometimes with government or private foundation grants—for example, the University of Chicago for the research on American Indian education and Cornell University and the University of California for medical programs. Cornell University also maintained its own southwestern field station. The Crownpoint project for community development had originally been sponsored by an American Indian organization, but its continuing funds came primarily from private foundations. Tribal governments funded research on their own land claims.

What kind of security could these new applied jobs offer? Certainly none comparable to academic tenure. Programs under government auspices seem to have offered some continuity, as in the BIA and the Public Health Service, but for the most part they were expected to be short-term. It was understood that the WRA and the American Indian land claims would be temporary. Even for BIA programs, congressional funding was uncertain, and withdrawal of congres-

sional support had effectively terminated two important projects—the original Applied Anthropology Unit and the project on American Indian education and administration. Continuity of university support was similarly uncertain, since that also depended on government or private foundation grants.

Thus, most of the women in early applied anthropology worked under conditions of short-term and uncertain support. Perhaps they were more ready than their male colleagues to settle for these uncertainties. A few found ways to develop a satisfying role within an established agency, for example, Underhill's in BIA education and Aberle's in American Indian administration. Some men had also accepted this solution: John Provinse, for example, after an early faculty appointment at the University of Arizona and work in the Navajo SCS turned to full-time government administration that used his anthropological expertise. Some women anthropologists could presumably rely on support from their husbands' more stable academic employment. The most usual solution seemed to be a combination of academic and applied work over the course of a career. For many—Underhill, Reichard, de Laguna, Spicer, Colson, Clark, Wax, Hamamsy, and Richards—applied work in the Southwest came early in their professional careers. Ellis made her contribution to American Indian land claims later, after she had established an academic position in archaeology and ethnohistory. The latter pattern was typical of others who worked in American Indian claims and is probably common for many senior scholars who can make short-term applied commitments related to their own specialties.

This survey of women in applied anthropology in the Southwest has been limited to the first three decades of that field. Since 1960 the number of women in anthropology has greatly increased (over half the Ph.D. degrees granted in 1986 were to women—see American Anthropological Association, *Anthropology Newsletter,* April

1987). At the same time applied anthropology has seen an extraordinary expansion and diversification. A 1975 study of academic opportunities had predicted that after 1982 two-thirds of all anthropology Ph.D.'s would have to find employment outside academia, primarily in administration rather than in research (D'Andrade et al. 1975:772). Much of this employment has turned out to be in applied anthropology.[11] Government support continued in the 1960s and early 1970s, stimulated by the War on Poverty and the civil rights struggles, especially as they concerned American Indian welfare and rights, but by the end of the 1970s government funds were being sharply curtailed. Applied anthropologists faced a new situation in which they have sought, sometimes with remarkable success, new auspices and funding sources in the private sector, in state and local government, and in grass-roots organizations.

Despite these changes, our survey of early applied anthropology points to some issues that are still pertinent. First is the importance of stability and continuity in the organizational structures within which anthropologists work. Too many applied projects continue to be short-term, without sufficient time to prove themselves. Funded as demonstration projects, they may not have effective ties with the community organizations that could continue their work. A program that has been developed within an established organization has more prospect of being viable. The Crownpoint community development project shows how the valuable lessons of a demonstration can be dissipated if it does not have these firm links within the community structure.

Interdisciplinary collaboration is a second issue of continuing concern. In applied anthropology this collaboration must occur between disciplines that are separated by differences in training and objectives—on the anthropologist's side, training for research, and on the practitioner's side, training for professional action or clinical work. Many professional fields encompass within themselves

both research and practice (medicine, psychiatry, nursing, education, law), but anthropologists have had to learn, with varying success, how to bridge the gap between their academic research methods and clinical or practice methods in the fields in which they seek to work. The resulting strains for both sides are a continuing challenge. One solution from the practitioner's side has been to undertake formal training in anthropology. This has been especially fruitful in medical anthropology. The Leightons are an early example; increasingly, psychiatrists, nurses, and public health personnel have sought such training. The reverse, an anthropologist who seeks additional training in a practice profession, seems to be less common but could be as fruitful. Another solution has been for the anthropologist to become sufficiently immersed in the practice field to understand the practitioner's viewpoint from within. In the best cases, with cooperation on both sides, this becomes a successful joint effort at mutual communication and understanding, as illustrated in much of southwestern medical anthropology.

Finally, an issue still pertinent in applied anthropology concerns the maintenance of ties between it and academic anthropology. At a theoretical level, applied anthropology, despite its title, should be more than merely an application of anthropological knowledge to practical situations; it should be a source of new theoretical knowledge about the processes of social and cultural change and of administrative action (planned intervention) in social situations (see Bastide 1974 and Spicer 1976). At a personal level, too, it is important for an applied anthropologist to maintain a base in academia. Much of the satisfaction in any anthropological career lies in its intellectual and scholarly substance as well as in its contribution to practical affairs, and the richness of this contribution is in danger if separation from this scholarly base becomes too great. My own experience in schools of social work over a span of 14 years has made me especially aware of the importance of maintaining this academic tie. Since the 1950s more and more anthropologists have made applied commitments that have taken them inside professional practice fields, on faculties of professional schools, or into the action role of an administrator, where they may feel keenly the need to keep their ties to academic anthropology. With the recent growth of applied anthropology, the profession as a whole seems to be giving more recognition to the benefits that can result from maintaining this close association.

NOTES

1. See the discussion of Cushing's 1897 address to the Board of Indian Commissioners in Hinsley 1979: 28–29 and Green 1981:427–28. Hewett has been called a forerunner of modern applied anthropology (Foster 1969:199–200) for his article "Ethnic Factors in Education," where he says that the aim of American Indian education should be to make better Indians, rather than to Americanize them (1905).

2. Kelly (1980) lists Mekeel, Morris Opler, David Rodnick, Charles Wisdom, Gordon Macgregor, and Julian Steward. Van Willigen (1980:item 70) lists in addition Claude Schaeffer, Abraham Halpern, and Margaret Welpley Fisher (an official of the BIA Tribal Organization Committee).

3. See also Aberle's physical anthropology papers (Aberle 1931, 1932, 1934; Aberle et al. 1940) and her later work on American Indian policy (Brophy and Aberle 1966).

4. Kimball (1979) gives a comprehensive review of the course and significance of this landmark experience in applied anthropology.

5. Reh also participated in a southwestern food and nutrition study under the auspices of the University of Chicago (Fred Eggan 1988, personal communication). Reynolds (who used the SCS records in the Rio Grande Historical Collections, New Mexico State University Library, Las Cruces) names women who worked for the BIA and SCS Technical Cooperation Units in the Southwest during this period: Ruth D. Kolling, Katherine D. Edmunds, Louise C. Wiberg, Ruth Underhill, and Lucy Wilcox Adams (Terry

Reynolds 1986, personal communication). Of these, Underhill is the only one known as an anthropologist. Lucy Adams was an educator who lived for years on the Navajo Reservation and is the mother of anthropologist William Adams.

6. According to Kelly (1980:20), another study had been planned for Zia by Florence Hawley Ellis but was not published because of community opposition.

7. A later publication by Nancie L. Gonzalez brings together a broader range of social and historical data on New Mexico Hispanic-Americans from published and unpublished sources extending into the 1960s (Gonzalez 1967).

8. Unfortunately, van der Eerden, a member of the Medical Mission Sisters in the Southwest, became ill and was not able to implement her anthropological work (Regina Flannery Hertzfeld 1988, personal communication), but her publication remains an early landmark in applied medical anthropology.

9. The Russell Sage Foundation, whose postwar program supported use of the social sciences in the professions, also contributed to this project. Their field representative was Esther Lucile Brown, a nurse who in the 1920s had been one of the first women to receive a combined anthropology-sociology Ph.D. from Yale.

10. A number of other women in southwestern anthropology should be mentioned, whose interest in the uses of anthropology were carried out in other areas. Elsie Clews Parsons' early sociological publications were a zealous championing of women's issues. In wartime Ruth Benedict turned her special talents to anthropological efforts toward international understanding in her work on Japan, Southeast Asia, and Europe. Navajo specialist Malcolm Carr Collier later turned her attention to conducting a pioneer project on anthropology in secondary education for the American Anthropological Association (Collier and Dethlefsen 1968).

11. The following examples, from my personal knowledge, indicate something of the scope of women's applied activities in the Southwest during the 1960s and 1970s, although this is by no means an exhaustive listing:

In Development Anthropology and Government Administration: Mary Shepardson's work on the Navajo governmental system (1963) and court procedures (1965) was undertaken for its intrinsic research interest but also with the expectation that it could be useful to the Navajo in their own political development. Joan Ablon studied the results of the new federal policy to encourage American Indians to relocate in urban areas for employment (1964, 1965). Anthropologists began to participate in social impact assessments of development projects—for example, in the Navajo San Juan area, a coal and water resource study (Shepardson 1975) and the large-scale San Juan Regional Uranium Study (U.S. Department of the Interior 1980; Margaret Knight was project leader for this extensive study, which also had staff anthropologists Susan Bliss and Helen George, a Navajo). In the upper Rio Grande Valley, Sue-Ellen Jacob's evaluation of the adverse effects of a proposed dam on Indian, Hispanic-American, and Anglo farmers for the Bureau of Reclamation resulted in the cancellation of the project (Jacobs 1977). In connection with the Navajo-Hopi land dispute, anthropologists who participated in studies of the effects of Navajo relocation included three women: Elizabeth Colson, Jennie Joe (a Navajo), and Joyce Griffin.

In Education: Anne Smith, who was active in state American Indian affairs in New Mexico, wrote about their educational as well as their social and economic needs (1966, 1968a, 1968b). Cognitive anthropology made an interesting contribution to the planning of a school building that would meet the aesthetic and practical require-ments of its Navajo community (Clement 1976). An important development in educational anthropology has been the proliferation of bilingual programs in the schools, in which native linguists as well as others have participated—for example, Leanne Hinton and Lucille Watahomigie for the Yuman-speaking tribes (see their 1984 publication for other participating linguists), La Verne Jeanne for the Hopi, Ofelia Zepeda for the Tohono O'odham, and Amy Zaharlick for some of the Tewa Pueblos.

In Medical Anthropology: American Indian health continued as a focus in the Southwest. Navajo medical projects included the work of Frances Ferguson on an alcohol treatment program (1968, 1970); my own work on children's handicapping conditions, the role of interpreters as health aides, and Navajo accidents (1965, 1971, 1973); and more recently Jennie Joe's work on children's disabilities (1980, 1982). A number of women students from training programs under Levy at the University of Arizona and Ozzie Werner at Northwestern University have gone on to their own work on Navajo and Pueblo health (Tracy Andrews, LeMyra deBruyn, Ann Wright). Women also participated in an epidemiological research and training project that used a Tohono O'odham population register developed at the University of Arizona for studies of migration, upward mobility, and accidents (Julie Uhlmann, Beverly Hackenberg, and Mary Gallagher; see Hackenberg 1972).

WOMEN ARCHAEOLOGISTS IN THE SOUTHWEST

Linda S. Cordell

For women to become archaeologists in a
historically male-dominated profession, in
and of itself signifies that they are special;
they have survived and achieved success in a
profession where numerous obstacles have
been erected to full participation by women.
Jonathan Reyman
(1992:72)

This work is the most fun a person can
possibly have and still get paid for it.
Cynthia Irwin-Williams
(quoted in Williams 1981:23).

I just like the sort of challenge that prehistory
seems to give, the mystery of it . . . and finding
out about people, why they think the way they
do, and what makes human history. . . . Digging
is the part that's fun, being outdoors and digging. I don't think there is anything I love more.
Marjorie Lambert
(1985)

WOMEN have contributed substantially to
the archaeology of the Southwest as researchers, as teachers, and occasionally as planners
and administrators. Examining the role of women
in archaeology in general provides a context for a
more detailed examination of some of the women
who have chosen the Southwest as their field of
study. Moreover, the experiences of the women archaeologists in the Southwest provide a useful
contrast with the careers of women ethnologists
and with their male archaeological colleagues.[1]

WOMEN IN ARCHAEOLOGY

When archaeologists write histories of their discipline, they almost invariably write of a series of

major discoveries linked by improvements in ana-lytical methods and field techniques (e.g., Bernal 1980; Daniel 1976; Willey and Sabloff 1980). Only within the past 15 years have a few scholars explored relationships among the cultural values of the archaeological investigator and the prob-lems selected for investigation, the approaches used, and interpretations then offered of the past (e.g., Leone 1973; Schuyler 1976; Trigger 1980). It has been less than 10 years since the appearance of studies that may be viewed as examples of a reflective sociology of archaeology (Gero 1985; Gero et al. 1983) and only a few years since ar-chaeologists themselves have become concerned with issues in the archaeological study of gender (e.g., Conkey 1982; Conkey and Spector 1984; Gero 1988; Gero and Conkey 1991; Wildesen 1980; Wylie 1992). In part, the absence of time-depth on studies of gender may reflect the lack of an appropriate forum. In 1989, the Twenty-Second Annual Chacmool Conference took as its topic "The Archaeology of Gender" and was the largest gathering in the history of that confer-ence. The conference publication edited by Walde and Willows (1991) has 69 papers and runs to 615 pages. As Gero (1985:344) observes,

Archaeologists might have responded earlier, and like the socio-cultural anthropologists, participated more actively in the climate of interest in gender had it not been for the profession's traditional structure of concerns and practices which offer very low or even negative prestige for engaging in such discourse. His-torically conservative, the archaeological enterprise is also dominated by white, middle-class males. . . . This community was slow to embrace a feminist perspective.

In twentieth-century U.S. popular myth, women are viewed as being highly observant, in-tuitive, patient, good listeners, and good at learn-ing languages. These are all qualities that are deemed valuable to ethnographers. Archaeolo-gists, on the contrary, are supposed to be me-chanical, technically oriented, physically strong,

and commanding. In Hollywood's terms the ex-cavation crew is seen as a cast of thousands. These field crews are "deployed" by a leader who is in charge in nearly a military sense. The excavation leader is also supposed to be able to fix all manner of vehicles, rig generators, and prevent native la-borers or guides from stealing. In 1949, A. V. Kidder, the acknowledged dean of southwestern archaeology, wrote of this view,

In popular belief, and unfortunately to some extent in fact, there are two sorts of archaeologists, the hairy-chested and the hairy-chinned. . . . [The hairy-chested type is portrayed] as a strong-jawed young man in a tropical helmet, pistol on hip, hacking his way through the jungle in search of lost cities and buried treasure . . . [The hairy-chinned type] is benevolently absent-minded. His only weapon is a magnifying glass, with which he scrutinizes inscriptions in for-gotten languages. Usually his triumphant decipher-ment coincides, in the last chapter, with . . . [his] daughter's rescue from savages by the handsome young assistant (1949:xi).

Not only is this the popular view, but it is often the view of archaeologists themselves. As Woodall and Perricone discuss, the self-image of the archaeologist as cowboy, "marked by other facets of *machismo,* including hard-drinking and womanizing . . . emphasized by beards, jeans, and work boots (at the SAA conventions, for ex-ample) and a penchant for cowboy accouterments when possible" (1981:506–7) has had a detri-mental effect on their active support of the pres-ervation movement, which is viewed as being un-masculine. Gero (1985:344) provides further insight:

We can expect archaeologists to conform in their pro-fessional roles to the same ideological constructs they adopt to explain the past. We are alerted to certain strong parallels between the male who populates the archaeological record—public, visible, physically ac-tive, exploratory, dominant, and rugged, the stereo-typic hunter who likes his data raw. . . . Correspond-ing, then, to the stereotyped male, we expect to find the female archaeologist secluded in the base-camp laboratory or museum, sorting and preparing archaeological materials, private, protected, passively receptive, ordering and systematizing, but without recognized contribution to the productive process. The-woman-at-home archaeologist must fulfill her stereotype feminine role by specializing in the analysis of archaeological materials, typologizing, seriating, studying wear or paste or iconographic motifs. She will have to do the archaeological housework.

The myth portrays the male archaeologist as the active fieldworker who is also comfortable with high-tech analyses. The female archaeologist of the myth is engaged in simple sorting of materials, basic laboratory analysis, and library research. The degree to which the myth is reflected in practice is an empirical question worthy of continuing investigation. Gero (1985) has analyzed Mesoamerican archaeology and found that male archaeologists are overrepresented in field research and high-technology nonfield archaeometric studies (e.g., obsidian sourcing and induced hydration analyses). Female Mesoamerican archaeologists are overrepresented in nonfield library or laboratory studies.

Another way to examine the fit between the myths and reality is to examine National Science Foundation (NSF) funding, because NSF provides support for more archaeological field projects than laboratory projects. Within the NSF Anthropology Program, applications by male archaeologists are more successful overall than are applications by women in archaeology. This situation is not the case in either biological anthropology or sociocultural anthropology (Conkey 1978; Gero 1985; Yellen 1983). The NSF situation has been reviewed more recently by Stark (1991, 1992) and Yellen (1991).

There are substantial differences between the practice of archaeology and of ethnology. The differences are reflected in professional recruitment and training, and I suggest that to some extent the divergence in experiences works to discourage women from pursuing archaeology. Although the "Raiders of the Lost Ark" image of field archaeology employing a cast of thousands is blatantly unrealistic, archaeology is not a solitary occupation. Field crews generally consist of a few individuals, but crews of one or more dozen are certainly not uncommon. Field crews are also hierarchically organized. At the lowest rung are those with minimal field experience. Above these are arranged individuals with increasing amounts of field experience and specialized expertise. There is a familiar dilemma known to all archaeology students, male and female: experience in archaeology is obtained by working on excavation projects; however, to secure employment (sometimes even a place) on an archaeological project, one must have experience. In practice, initial experience can be gained by serving as an unpaid volunteer on a project, by working as a kitchen aid or in some other menial capacity and spending free time washing pot sherds or helping in any way possible, or by paying to attend an archaeological field school for which one also generally gets college credit (Gifford and Morris 1985). Until fairly recently (perhaps the late 1960s and early 1970s), mixed-gender digs were unusual. Consequently, whereas men could volunteer or be paid as menial workers on a dig, women generally could not. I suspect that the problem of the mixed dig was not solely one of propriety, although it may have been phrased as such. Rather, there is reason to suggest that excavation leaders are reluctant to assign supervisory responsibilities to women.

The ability of a woman to direct men in the field is a topic for further discussion. For example, in presenting Jean M. Pinkley with the Department of Interior Meritorious Service Award, Secretary of the Interior Udall's written citation stated, "Usually it is difficult for men to take direction from women, but Jean succeeded because when on the job she insisted in carrying her full share of the load" (cited in Thomas 1969).

Similarly, Irwin-Williams (1990:25) relates that when Marjorie Ferguson Lambert was given responsibility for a project that had been initiated under the direction of male colleagues, these colleagues claimed that the "native laborers would probably refuse to work for a woman." Nevertheless, she completed the project successfully. In archaeology, field experience is considered an essential aspect of training. A long-term apprenticeship in the field and diverse field experiences are not only highly valued but required for professional acceptance. Despite the fact that today many field opportunities for women are available, Irwin-Williams noted that "an estimated half as many opportunities are available to female students as to males" (Irwin-Williams 1990:31).

The *Anthropology Newsletter* for April 1987 informs us that "the average 1985–1986 anthropology Ph.D. . . . is 35 years old, married, white, female and childless. She holds a nonacademic job with a yearly salary of $24,000. Her name . . . is Judith." Judith is not an archaeologist. The same survey reports that rates of doctorate production among the subfields of anthropology have remained stable for the past 15 years with 49% awarded in sociocultural anthropology, 2% in linguistics, 11% in biological/physical, 27% in archaeology, and 11% recorded as "other." Yet, whereas female Ph.D.'s began outnumbering male Ph.D.'s in 1984 and continue to increase their lead, "fewer women and more men are taking Ph.D.'s in archaeology" (*Anthropology Newsletter* 28(4):12).

It is difficult to determine how many working archaeologists there really are in the United States and Canada. The Society for American Archaeology has about 3,500 members, but this number includes an unknown number of amateurs and excludes a surprising number of professionals who do not pay their dues. Nevertheless, if 3,500 is a reasonable estimate, the total number of women listed as archaeologists in the 1984–1985 *Guide to Departments in Anthropology* is 323, slightly less

than 10%. In my survey of the 1986–1987 guide, I found that 135 women archaeologists hold full-time faculty positions in the United States and Canada. In addition, 21 women work full-time in museums. Within the category of "Research Institutions," the guide includes large state- or grant-supported programs such as the Desert Research Institute and private environmental consulting firms such as Woodward Clyde Consultants. At any rate, 14 women archaeologists are employed in the research institutions listed. Finally, 89 federal archaeologists are women, but many more of these women have bachelor's or master's degrees; only 7 have the Ph.D. In general, there are not very many women who work full-time in archaeology in any setting.

Further, recognition of women within the professional archaeological community has been slow. In a paper reviewing the early contributions of women archaeologists to the field, Cynthia Irwin-Williams notes that "neither Daniels . . . in his massive history of archaeology nor Willey and Sabloff . . . in their treatment of New World archaeology, mentions a single contribution by a woman archaeologist before World War I" (Irwin-Williams 1990:6). The Society for American Archaeology was begun in 1934 by participants in Section H of the American Association for the Advancement of Science. The first annual meeting of the society was held in Pittsburgh in 1935, at which time the constitution was signed and 42 members were presented for election as fellows in the society. Of the 30 individuals who signed the society constitution in 1935, 5 were women. The entire first-year membership in the society was 328 affiliates (Griffin 1985). I do not know how many of these were women. Of the 42 names submitted for election as fellows, however, only 4 were those of women: Katharine Bartlett, Frederica de Laguna, Anna Gayton, and Florence M. Hawley (Griffin 1985).

Presidents of the Society for American Archaeology were exclusively male until 1958, when H. Marie Wormington became the first woman to hold that office. Cynthia Irwin-Williams was the second woman elected to the presidency of the society, serving from 1977 to 1979. Dena Dincauze served as president from 1986 to 1989. Prudence Rice was elected president-elect in 1989 and was the fourth female to hold presidential office in the more than 50 years of the existence of the society. In addition to the presidency of the society, which until quite recently has been considered primarily a professional honor, the most influential position within the society has been that of editor of *American Antiquity,* the scholarly journal of the society. In 1981, after nearly 50 years of publication, Dena Dincauze became the first female editor of the journal. Patty Jo Watson, whose term ended in 1987, is only the second female to edit *American Antiquity.* At least in recent years, women have routinely served on the Executive Committee of the Society for American Archaeology.

Initially, I had suspected that there would be more contemporary female archaeologists working in the Southwest or with major southwestern interests than female archaeologists working in other geographic areas. My reasoning was that, being part of the United States, the Southwest might provide fewer logistical problems than more remote areas and also be less prejudiced than Latin American or European societies against women doing essentially manual labor. Also, since females by necessity generally obtain their initial field experience in field school settings, I thought that the presence in the Southwest of the two oldest university field schools, at the University of Arizona and the University of New Mexico (Gifford and Morris 1985), might have influenced more women to continue work in the area. These expectations were not met. The 1986–1987 *Guide to Departments in Anthropology* lists the numbers of female archaeologists in full-time positions and their primary areas of research interests as follows:

TABLE I. Research area and institutional position of women archaeologists

	Teaching	Museum
General North America	25	I
Basin & West Coast	2	—
Southwest	9	2
Eastern U.S./Plains	16	5
Pacific	2	—
Mesoamerica	20	3
South America	I I	2
Asia	6	—
Arctic/Subarctic	2	—
Near East	8	—
Europe	17	2
Africa	5	—
Urban archaeology	2	I
Miscellaneous	7	I

Source: Geographic area of study and institutional positions of women holding full-time appointments as archaeologists in the U.S. and Canada as reported in the 1986–1987 *Guide to Departments in Anthropology.*[2]

Clearly, there are not more female southwestern archaeologists than female archaeologists working in comparable geographic areas. Importantly, as Irwin-Williams states (1990:32),

The most daunting difficulties, however, are encountered in finding professional employment, particularly in mainstream academic positions. . . . Most of the largest, most prestigious universities, including all of the older Eastern institutions (Harvard, Yale, Columbia, etc.), most of the largest newer West Coast schools (Stanford, University of California at Los Angeles) and most of the largest state university departments (e.g. Universities of Arizona, Colorado) had no women at all as faculty members in archaeology.

As of 1992, the University of Arizona had improved its situation with the addition of two women to the archaeology faculty. Work in federal archaeology is the only employment situation in which female archaeologists with primary interests in the Southwest are overrepresented compared to other geographic areas. This is completely understandable given the large amount of federal land in the Southwest; there are more federal archaeologists of either sex in the Southwest than elsewhere.

In sum, then, our popular myth would lead to expectations of few females pursuing careers in archaeology and achieving excellence in that field. In general, the numbers suggest that the myth is borne out in practice. Contrary to my expectations, there are not an unusual number of contemporary female archaeologists with primary research interest in the Southwest. I nevertheless maintain that those who have devoted their research careers to the Southwest have made substantial contributions to our knowledge of the prehistory of the area and often to improvements in archaeological methods of analysis. Many have also written general syntheses intelligible to nonprofessionals and to students. Some of their writings, then, have influenced greater numbers of readers than have those of male southwestern archaeologists. Thus, I suspect that more undergraduate students have read books by H. M. Wormington and Bertha Dutton than by their male colleagues.

WOMEN ARCHAEOLOGISTS IN THE SOUTHWEST

It is not possible to fully evaluate the career development and contributions of all female southwestern archaeologists. To do so would entail four times the number of pages that have been suggested for contributors. I do examine the research of a few of the best-known women, as well as women whose work represents a specific role or status within southwestern archaeology. In leaving out women such as Nathalie Woodbury, Kate Peck Kent, Clara Lee Tanner, Dorothy Keur, Florence Lister, Elizabeth Ann Morris, Helen Blumenschein, Ernestine Green, Elaine Bluhm, Vorsilla Bohrer, Emma Lou Davis, Sylvia Gaines, Dolores Gunnerson, Isabel Kelly, Linda Cordell, Dorothy Washburn, and Anne Woosley, I in no

way imply that their contributions have been unimportant. Similarly, space prohibits inclusion of younger scholars such as Patricia Crown, Patricia Gilman, Susan Kent, Frances Levine, Frances Joan Mathien, Jill Neitzel, Margaret Nelson, Janet Orcutt, Shirley Powell, Katherine Speilmann, and Patricia Spoerl. My hope is that the women who have been included will provide some insight into their career paths that may be generalized to others.

One of the more difficult patterns to evaluate is the careers of females who participated in southwestern research with their archaeologist husbands. Much of the difficulty stems from the fact that the couples themselves represent divergent models; yet it is as half of a couple rather than as an individual that the woman's name is known. Apparently in the case of the Gladwins and the Fultons, the women's role was minimal. As institution builders (Harold S. Gladwin of Gila Pueblo, and William S. Fulton of the Amerind Foundation in Dragoon, Arizona), these men had the support of their wives. There is little indication, however, that their wives participated in their work. I should mention here that although Mary-Russell Ferrell Colton might be addressed in this section, her own work with Hopi art and ethnography established her scholarship quite outside that of Harold S. Colton, her husband. Her contributions are documented in McGreevy's chapter in this volume.

A very different picture emerges in the research of Burton and Harriet Cosgrove, who were instrumental in initiating and encouraging systematic research on the Mimbres culture. Following Burton Cosgrove's retirement from business in 1924, he and his wife joined the staff of Harvard's Peabody Museum. Under the auspices of the Peabody Museum, they surveyed the Mimbres Valley, excavated Swarts Ruin and the dry caves of southern New Mexico and southwest Texas, and together began work with J. O. Brew at Awatovi. Following Burton's death at Keams Canyon in 1936, Harriet continued on at Awatovi and later at the

Peabody Museum until 1944. While it is true that Harriet Cosgrove prepared most of the drawings and contributed the analyses of pottery in "archaeological housewife" fashion, she also participated fully in the actual fieldwork (Kidder 1957).

Ann Axtell Morris, prior to her debilitating depression and illness, not only participated in Earl Morris' research but developed a unique contribution based on her skills as an artist and writer. Ann Morris at first copied the painted frieze from a prehistoric kiva bench at Mummy Cave. Later, she recorded the pictograph murals of Canyon de Chelly in paintings that were hung at the American Museum of Natural History (see Morris 1930). Her art and writing were combined in a technical work, which she coauthored with her husband and Jean Charlot, on Yucatecan Maya temple murals (Morris et al. 1931). Her popular writing included a piece on accompanying her husband on Mayan archaeological expeditions (Morris 1931) and the very successful *Digging in the Southwest* (1933). Her writing, as the Listers note, "must have prompted many a coed into anthropology" (Lister and Lister 1968: 142). Morris' contribution to popularizing anthropology is discussed on more detail in Tisdale's chapter in this volume.

The other women addressed here, whether married or not, are known for contributions to southwestern archaeology made in their own right. Some of them also achieved substantial success and recognition for their work in museums, a topic that is examined elsewhere in this volume. Here, only archaeological fieldwork and laboratory studies will be discussed, in the work of Anna Osler Shepard, Jean McWhirt Pinkley, Bertha Pauline Dutton, Florence Hawley Ellis, Marjorie Ferguson Lambert, Hannah Marie Wormington, Jane Holden Kelley, and Cynthia Irwin-Williams. These sketches should be considered introductory. Considerable detail has been sacrificed in order to be brief; each deserves more extended coverage.

Anna Osler Shepard (1903–1971)

Anna Osler Shepard was born in Merchantville, New Jersey. Her father, Henry Warren Shepard, an industrial chemist, served as her early mentor and later as her collaborator and assistant. Shepard did her undergraduate work at the Teacher's College of Southern California (now California State College at San Diego) and at the University of Nebraska, where she received her B.A. in anthropology, with a minor in philosophy, in 1928. As an undergraduate she attended the School of American Research Field School in archaeology, then at Gran Quivira, New Mexico, and she was appointed a fellow of the School in 1924. Although she began graduate work in anthropology at the University of New Mexico, she withdrew from the program because Edgar Lee Hewett would not approve her thesis topic. Her first professional position was as curator of ethnography at the San Diego Museum of Man from 1926 through 1929 (Morris 1974). Shepard's career choice was greatly influenced by Wesley Bradfield, with whom she studied at college in San Diego. While a curatorial assistant at the San Diego Museum of Man, she worked with Bradfield on the analysis of the ceramics from the Cameron Creek Village. When Bradfield became ill, she supervised the field and laboratory work on the materials from that site and assisted in the preparation of the report that was published after Bradfield's death in 1929 (Thompson 1991). From 1931 to 1936, following course work in optical crystallography at Claremont College, Shepard worked on ceramics at the Laboratory of Anthropology at the Museum of New Mexico. Her unsalaried position was funded by the Carnegie Institution and had been arranged by A. V. Kidder. This marked the beginning of Shepard's long and fruitful association with Kidder as well as the inception of the work that was her most lasting contribution to southwestern archaeology. Shepard became the authority on the technology of ceramic production, although during her lifetime, much of her work was not accorded the high regard it deserved.

Between 1937 and 1965, Shepard took classes at New York University, the Massachusetts Institute of Technology, the University of Kansas, and the University of Colorado in a variety of fields that were important to her work: chemistry, physics, mathematics, geology, mineralogy, microchemical spectroscopy, and Spanish. In 1936, while A. V. Kidder was chairman of the Division of Historical Research, Shepard began her formal affiliation with the Carnegie Institution of Washington. In 1937, under the auspices of the Carnegie Institution, she moved to Boulder, Colorado, and established her laboratory for the study of ceramic technology. Shepard's Ceramic Technology Project was directed toward making "extensive and systematic investigations which may be expected to yield data of general historical interest, rather than to provide facilities for analyses to be used for miscellaneous and unrelated identifications" (Shepard 1938:23–24). Shepard's association with the Carnegie Institution lasted until it was reorganized in 1957. From 1957 until her retirement in 1970, she was employed by the U.S. Geological Survey in Denver. While at the Carnegie Institution and the Geological Survey, she continued her work on the technology of ceramic manufacture, especially petrographic analysis, which she had first undertaken with the ceramics Kidder had excavated at Pecos (Kidder and Shepard 1936).

Shepard's publication record is outstanding. Her best-known work, *Ceramics for the Archaeologist* (1957), is, at this writing, in its twelfth printing. A pioneer in the use of optical petrography in the study of ceramic technology, "she made technological analyses of prehistoric pottery from the Southwest and Mesoamerica, carried out studies of modern Indian potters in both areas, set forth the principles of symmetry in design analysis, and reconstructed the technology to produce the unique Plumbate ware of Guatemala" (Thompson 1991:1). Today her work is frequently cited (e.g., Greib and Callahan 1987). Yet, in many ways, Shepard is a somewhat shadowy figure; her work was systematically ignored for years, and she was bothered and disappointed by the treatment her work originally received (Morris 1974:448). These observations require explication.

Shepard began her studies of ceramic technology at a time when ceramic classification was very much central to the cultural historical interests of southwestern prehistory. She was doing mainstream research. Her approach, however, was highly technical and sophisticated, and importantly, her results contradicted the theoretical norm of the time. Unlike Florence Hawley's ceramic handbook, which included observations and tests that could be conducted by archaeologists in the field, Shepard's petrographic approach required a laboratory with special equipment and training in the techniques used. It was, therefore, less accessible and less well understood in general. Further, Shepard was highly critical of the kind of ceramic classification being conducted by her contemporary southwesternists (Shepard 1939; Haury 1985). A key factor, however, is that Shepard's studies indicated that the view of economically self-sufficient Pueblo villages, where each household produced its own pottery, was untrue during some portions of the prehistoric period. The observation that until very late in the occupation of Pecos, for example, most of the painted pottery was imported from elsewhere (Kidder and Shepard 1936) was not only counter to the current opinion of Pueblo economies but anathema to those who pursued historical reconstruction by ethnographic analogies to modern Pueblos. Everyone's work was called into question, and the results and implications of Shepard's research were largely ignored. Finally, I believe that because she never taught and had not trained large numbers of students in her methods, she had no following of advocates for her approach. It has only been within the last 10 years, as archaeologists have come to appreciate the diversity in economic and possible political situations that characterized prehistoric Pueblo societies, that Anna Shepard's work has been reexamined, praised, and cited (see Cordell 1984; Plog 1980). Indeed, a recent conference was devoted solely to analyzing her contributions at which I was asked to assess the impact of her work in detail (Cordell 1991a, 1991b; see Bishop and Lange 1991).

Jean McWhirt Pinkley (1910–1969)

Jean McWhirt was born in Miami, Arizona, in 1910. The daughter of an army physician, she moved frequently during her childhood. She attended the University of Arizona, where she studied with Emil Haury, Clara Lee Tanner, and Byron Cummings, receiving her B.A. in anthropology in 1933 and her M.A. in anthropology in 1936. Upon receipt of her M.A., Jean elected to join the National Park Service, a career choice that shaped her professional development in ways that differ considerably from those of the other women archaeologists discussed here. Her first assignment was to Mesa Verde, where she worked from 1932 (as a museum assistant) to 1966, having achieved the position of chief of the Interpretive Division. In 1942, she married Addison Pinkley, who was killed in 1943 while serving in the navy on the U.S. submarine *Squalus*. In 1966, Pinkley was reassigned to Pecos National Monument, where she worked as head of a five-year excavation and stabilization program until her death in 1969. Pinkley was honored with the Department of Interior's Meritorious Service Award in October of 1967 (Thomas 1969).

Pinkley's contributions within the Park Service were outstanding. She developed the interpretive program for Mesa Verde National Park, which was a model for its time. In addition, she was instrumental in planning the Wetherill Mesa Project at Mesa Verde, a multiyear research project that involved archaeologists, climatologists, environmentalists, and other specialists. After her transfer to Pecos, her research led to the discovery of the original Pecos church (ca. A.D. 1600), the very existence of which had been unknown or questionable until her work. In recognition of her performance in the Park Service, Pinkley was honored by an invitation to a White House luncheon with Mrs. Lyndon B. Johnson in 1966 (Thomas 1969). In contrast to the research of the other women discussed here, Pinkley's work, through her interpretive program, probably has had the greatest influence on how American families and tourists understand the ancient cliff dwellers of the Mesa Verde and, by extension, the Anasazi in general. On the other hand, she had no professional or preprofessional students and only two minor publications (Lancaster et al. 1950; Pinkley 1965). In selecting a career in the Park Service when she did, Pinkley chose a situation in which not only was advancement for women unusual but traditional archaeological research and professional publication were undervalued.

Bertha Pauline Dutton (1903–)

Bertha Pauline Dutton was born in Iowa and reared there and in Nebraska and Kansas. She attended the University of Nebraska as a part-time student while she worked. Her studies included world geography and history. In 1930, Dutton was badly injured by an automobile driven by a drunken driver. During her convalescence, she learned about archaeology and the University of New Mexico from friends. With finances obtained from the settlement of damage claims from the automobile driver, Dutton was able to buy a Model A Ford and drive to Albuquerque. She registered at the University of New Mexico where she obtained her B.A. in anthropology in 1935 and her M.A. in anthropology in 1937. Dutton worked as Anthropology Department secretary for Edgar Lee Hewett. She studied with Hewett, Mamie R. Tanquist, Marjorie Ferguson Lambert, Paul A. Walter, Jr., Lansing Bloom, and Florence Hawley Ellis. She earned her Ph.D. in anthropology from Columbia University in 1952.

Dutton was employed by the Museum of New Mexico beginning in 1936 and served in several capacities, as curator of ethnology, curator of exhibits, and head of the Division of Research, until 1965. She then served as the director of the Museum of Navajo Ceremonial Art until 1975. She was honored with a Certificate of Appreciation from the Indian Arts and Crafts Board of the U.S. Department of Interior in 1967, with the New Mexico Press Women's Award in 1971, and with an honorary Doctor of Law degree from New Mexico State University in 1973.

Dutton's ethnological and museological publications are voluminous. Her archaeological research included major grants, fieldwork, and publications relating to Mexico and the Yucatán, which are beyond the scope of this discussion. Her most outstanding and well-known contributions to southwestern archaeology, I believe, have been the publication of *Sun Father's Way* (1963a), her work with the Girl Scouts, and her series of popular, well-written guides and handbooks. In 1944, Dutton conducted limited excavations at Abo, near Gran Quivira. Short reports of that work have recently been published (Dutton 1981, 1985a, 1985b). Dutton obtained research grants to conduct a survey and excavation in the Galisteo Basin during the early 1960s. Only brief reports of that work (e.g., Dutton 1966) have been published, although most of the analysis and writing are complete (Dutton 1988, personal communication). Given her extensive knowledge of the Galisteo Basin, the full reports should constitute a major contribution to late Anasazi prehistory.

Our knowledge of the prehistoric and protohistoric tradition of Pueblo kiva mural painting is scant, being limited to only a very few surviving examples; although a few other sites have yielded figures or small paintings, only Awatovi, Kawaika-a, Kuaua, and Pottery Mound have preserved examples of murals. Published description is a crucial aspect of the record of these rare materials. In *Sun Father's Way,* Dutton provides an outstanding document of the Kuaua murals. The work contains a section on the cultural and historical context of the archaeological site and the murals as well as a section describing the murals with well integrated interpretive discussion from the Pueblo ethnographic literature and American Indian informants.

During the years from 1947 through 1957, Dutton provided a summer educational program for the Girl Scouts, the Archaeological Mobile Camps for Senior Girls. These trips included visits to national parks and monuments, museums, and archaeological sites. Not only was the experience enriching for the girls who participated, but in some cases it encouraged them to go further in school than they had planned and in a few instances to study anthropology. With a keen appreciation of the kinds of questions visitors to the Southwest have, Dutton wrote and published a series of guides (pocket handbooks) on the American Indians of the Southwest (e.g., Dutton 1948, 1983). These handbooks and a series of museum catalogs (e.g., Dutton 1957, 1963b) are among the most lucid discussions of southwest American Indians and their crafts that are available for general readers.

Florence Hawley Ellis (1906–1991)

Florence May Hawley was born in Cananea, Sonora, Mexico, where her father was chief chemist for a copper mine. She was educated at home and then at public schools in Miami, Arizona. She studied at the University of Arizona, receiving her A.B. in 1927 with a major in English and a minor in archaeology. As a child, she had participated in recreational weekend digs with her family; Dean Byron Cummings was a family friend. She received her M.A. in anthropology from the University of Arizona where her fellow students included Emil Haury and Clara Lee Fraps (Tanner), all of whom were told that they might be employed by the Anthropology Department if they stayed on to complete their M.A.'s.

In addition to teaching, Florence took courses in dendrochronology from A. E. Douglass and worked with the University of New Mexico field program in Chaco Canyon (in the summers of 1929, 1930, and 1931).

Three elements important in contributing to Ellis' success in archaeology derived from this early portion of her career. First, working in collaboration with her chemist father, she accomplished the first chemical analyses of black pigments used as paint on prehistoric southwestern pottery (Hawley 1929). Since there is spatial and temporal variation in the chemical composition of these pigments in the Southwest, the distinctions have subsequently become basic to southwestern ceramic analysis. Second, Ellis participated in the initiation of dendrochronology, a technique that revolutionized southwestern archaeology by providing a reliable method for assigning year dates to archaeological sites. Third, her fieldwork at the site of Chetro Ketl in Chaco Canyon was in a geographic locale that became central in interpretations of prehistoric Pueblo development.

By 1933, the Great Depression had caused severe financial difficulties at the University of Arizona, and the young faculty were asked to take a year's leave of absence. Ellis spent the year at the University of Chicago completing her Ph.D. in anthropology (awarded in 1934). At Chicago, she studied with Fay-Cooper Cole, Robert Redfield, and A. R. Radcliffe-Brown. Fred Eggan was among her classmates. Ellis' doctoral thesis (published in 1934) provides a detailed analysis of the stratigraphy, dendrochronology, ceramics, and architecture of Chaco Canyon, based largely on her work at Chetro Ketl. The work contains one of the first archaeological applications of a statistical technique (chi-square) and describes various changes in the history of the occupation of Chaco Canyon—and its ultimate abandonment—in relation to ecological factors. The work remains an important reference today.

Due to a miscommunication between Ellis and Byron Cummings about her job at the University of Arizona, she wrote to Edgar Lee Hewett applying for an open position at New Mexico. Hewett, based on his own knowledge of her abilities and on the recommendation of Clyde Kluckhohn, offered her a contract, and in the fall of 1934 she began a teaching career in the Department of Anthropology at the University of New Mexico that lasted until her retirement in 1971. From 1937 until 1941, she spent half of each academic year at the University of Chicago, where she taught dendrochronology. She married archaeologist Donovan Senter in 1936, and their daughter Andrea was born in 1939. The marriage ended in divorce in 1947. In 1950, she married historian Bruce T. Ellis, who became curator of collections at the Museum of New Mexico in Santa Fe. This marriage lasted until Bruce Ellis' death in November 1985.

Florence Ellis had a long and productive career; she continued to be active in field research until her death in 1991. In reviewing her many contributions to southwestern archaeology, several observations seem appropriate. First, from its inception, southwestern archaeology has depended on ceramic analysis and classification as clues to chronology and culture history. In her work on ceramics, which included descriptive classification (Hawley 1936), chemical analyses of pigments, and observations about technology (Hawley 1929), she was very much part of the mainstream of archaeological research. Also, as indicated, dendrochronology serves as the baseline for southwestern chronologies, and again, Ellis' work constituted a technical expertise that was, and is still, very much in demand. Third, she developed and sustained an interest in Pueblo social organization (Hawley 1937; Ellis 1964) that was unusual among her archaeological contemporaries, and I believe, can be traced to her experiences at Chicago. In part, her approach to social organization was to examine its diversity, along with linguistic variety, as a clue to the history of various Pueblo groups (Hawley 1937). In this, her method was very Boasian. She had always been interested in detailed information; she was not impressed by works that generalized or emphasized only one set or category of data. The "answers" to questions of prehistory were to be teased from fragments of evidence from all possible sources. In her words,

At best, reconstruction of prehistory is dangerous in that consideration of every item of culture make-up is necessary for valid conclusions, and yet our only data on ancient social organization and its history must come from modern peoples. Obviously, however, the student must consider every known factor and should weigh the reconstruction with regard to each item which has not been considered or which appears to contradict the hypothesis (Hawley 1937:506).

The emphasis on detail, in my view, is reflected in different aspects of Ellis' work. Her scholarly publications, although very well written, do not read easily. They are meticulous and descriptive. The kinds of reports she wrote tend to be tightly focused. She did not indulge in grand syntheses. Ellis produced a great number of publications, yet perhaps the descriptive standards she set for herself, in addition to a relentless schedule of fieldwork and teaching, were, in part, responsible for those project reports that remain unpublished. As others have noted (Frisbie 1975:7), her emphasis on descriptive detail made her a most demanding classroom teacher.

Most of the faculty at the University of New Mexico who conducted field research in the Southwest were involved in the American Indian land claims litigation. Ellis contributed greatly in her work for Zia, Santa Ana, Jemez, Acoma, Laguna, Nambe, and Taos pueblos and most recently to ongoing water rights disputes involving Santo Domingo. She viewed participation in these activities as an anthropological obligation. In carrying out this duty, of course, she had obtained access to data that no other archaeologists working with Pueblo peoples had obtained. The results were an enhanced understanding of Pueblo prehistory and, I hope, better working relationships between American Indians and archaeologists.

As a teacher, Ellis strongly encouraged her archaeology students to get to know Puebloans; her students were expected to develop firsthand knowledge of the Pueblo villages. Finally, and I believe most importantly, in leading the University of New Mexico Field School for many years, Ellis was a model for female students who aspired to become archaeologists and may have been discouraged by male faculty who denied them archaeological field experiences. The University of New Mexico Field Schools have been mixed since 1910 when Barbara Freire-Marreco Aitken joined Hewett at Rito de los Frijoles, whether or not the director was a female. But it was in Ellis' ability to coordinate the complex undertaking, and to be the professional in charge, that she encouraged a generation of female students to go on in archaeology.

Marjorie Ferguson Lambert (1910–)

Marjorie Elizabeth Ferguson was born in Colorado Springs, Colorado. Her mother was an active member of the Daughters of the Colorado Pioneers. Her father, who was in the mercantile business, had immigrated from Scotland and was active in the local chapter of the Caledonian Society. Marjorie received her B.A. from Colorado College, where she majored in sociology and anthropology and worked part-time at the Colorado College museum. Although on graduation she was awarded a fellowship to continue her education in social studies in New York, she instead accepted Edgar Lee Hewett's invitation to pursue graduate work and teach at the University of New Mexico. She earned her master's degree in anthropology, with a minor in history, in 1931. Her thesis examined acculturation at Sandia Pueblo.

Marjorie taught at the University of New Mexico and conducted field research from there until 1937, when, at Hewett's invitation, she joined the staff of the Museum of New Mexico in Santa Fe as chief preparator in archaeology; in 1938, she became curator of archaeology. She also served as curator for historical and anthropological collections, research, and exhibits, and she was in charge of the Palace of the Governors (1955–1964). Following her retirement in 1969, Lambert was asked to join the managing board of the School of American Research, where she continues to serve and participate in a variety of the School's activities.

Her professional career and her personal life were enhanced by a good marriage. After a brief and unsuccessful marriage to George Tichy, she married E. V. "Jack" Lambert in 1950. Jack Lambert, who had taken Elsie Clews Parsons and Mary Wheelwright on their first ethnological field trips in New Mexico, encouraged her professional development and shared many of her interests (Fox 1976).

In her long and productive career, Marjorie Lambert has made contributions to the fields of history, pre-Columbian art, and museum work, in addition to archaeology. Yet, as she herself has said, "If I had my choice of taking just one of the things I did, it would probably be the fieldwork" (Lambert 1985). Indeed, I think she is best known among southwestern archaeologists for being a meticulous and successful fieldworker. She excavated at Chaco Canyon in 1932 with the University of New Mexico field program. She also worked at Battleship Rock field camp in the Jemez Mountains, at Tecolote Ruin near Las Vegas, New Mexico, at San Gabriel del Yunque near San Juan Pueblo, and at a series of important Archaic cave sites in Hidalgo County, New Mexico. Although each of these projects contributed importantly to New Mexico prehistory, I think Lambert is best known for her work at Paa-ko, which exemplifies the particular kind of research for which she is known.

Paa-ko is a large, multiplaza, late prehistoric/early historic pueblo nestled in the foothills of the Sandia Mountains not far from Albuquerque. Excavation of the site was undertaken jointly by the Museum of New Mexico and the School of American Research along with the University of New Mexico. The fieldwork was conducted between 1935 and 1937. At least part of the rationale for the work involved the potential to develop the site as a tourist center on the opposite side of Albuquerque from Kuaua. Although this goal was not realized, the site has both a prehistoric and a historic component, as does Kuaua. The published site report (Lambert 1954) presents both the historical (archival) research and detailed reporting of the archaeological work itself. Lambert's ability to tap both documentary and archaeological resources also lead her to the initial work at San Gabriel de Yunque, which proved to be the first Spanish capital in New Mexico and was later excavated under the direction of Florence Ellis (1989). Although there is nothing astounding or unusual about Paa-ko, the report achieves a level of excellence in descriptive reporting, synthesis of detail, and clarity that remains a model today. The research is cultural-historical in nature, and the interpretations are limited to comparisons with other sites or areas that may have been sources of Rio Grande populations (e.g., Mesa Verde). This kind of treatment exemplifies the archaeological research of its time, and the work at Paa-ko is among the best examples of this research era in the Southwest.

Hannah Marie Wormington (1914–)

Hannah Marie Wormington was born in Denver in 1914 and educated at the University of Denver, where she received her B.A. in 1935. While in college, she took a course from E. B. Renaud, which inspired her to continue in archaeology. Following her graduation she traveled to France, accompanied by her mother, to pursue research on the French Paleolithic. On her return, she was hired as a staff archaeologist at the Denver Museum of Natural History. In 1937, she assumed the position of curator of archaeology at the Denver Museum, holding that position until

1968. While at the museum, she received two fellowships that allowed her to undertake graduate work at Radcliffe College and Harvard University. She received her Ph.D. in anthropology, with a specialty in archaeology, in 1954 from Radcliffe College. In 1940, she married George D. Volk, and their marriage lasted until his death in 1980 (Irwin-Williams 1990:28).

Wormington's research has involved work in Paleolithic sites in the French Dordogne, Fremont sites in Utah, and Paleo-Indian and Archaic sites in Colorado and elsewhere in the western United States and Alberta, Canada. She has also represented the United States at international exchanges in the Soviet Union and China. Wormington has been tremendously active in the Society for American Archaeology, serving as vice president in 1950–51 and again in 1955–56. She was the first female elected to serve as president of the society (1968–69). In 1983, she received the Society for American Archaeology's prestigious Distinguished Service Award. Finally, in addition to her research, museum, and professional duties, Wormington has taught on a part-time or visiting basis at the University of Denver, the University of Colorado, Arizona State University, Colorado College, the University of Minnesota, and the University of Wyoming. Since 1968, she has been a research associate in Paleo-Indian studies at the University of Colorado Museum and an adjunct professor at Colorado College. In 1970–71, she was awarded a Guggenheim Fellowship and in 1977, an honorary Doctor of Humane Letters by Colorado State University.

Wormington is perhaps best known for her monographs that synthesize large and complex bodies of data. Her outstanding *Ancient Man in North America,* first published in 1939, is currently in its fourth completely revised edition (Wormington 1957). Another of her syntheses, *Prehistoric Indians of the Southwest* (1947), was the dominant text on that subject for many years and remains a classic. Wormington has collaborated in the field with a number of male archaeologists over the years—she has particularly enjoyed working with Robert Lister, William Mulloy, Joe Ben Wheat, and Mott Davis (Irwin-Williams 1990:47)—and she has encouraged women professionals as mentor and role model.

Jane Holden Kelley (1928–   )

Jane Holden was born in Lubbock, Texas, where her father, with a Ph.D. in history, taught both history and anthropology at Texas Technological College. Despite the fact that her mother came from what Kelley describes as an "incredibly sheltered Edwardian environment" (Kelley 1989:3), she had taken anthropology courses at the University of Texas, become interested in the Southwest, designed an adobe pueblo-style house, read Navajo chants, and studied the famous volumes on Native Americans written by Henry Schoolcraft in the 1850s. Dr. Holden introduced his daughter to archaeology when she was just four, and as a child, she accompanied him on summer digs in New Mexico with students from Texas Tech. Following her mother's death, when she was only eight, Kelley attended a Catholic convent boarding school, later lived on her grandmother's farm in Littlefield, Texas, and returned to Lubbock for high school.

Given her background, one might assume that Kelley's career path would have been straightforward. Indeed, she did study anthropology in college, received her M.A. and completed a two-year program at the Instituto de Antropología in Mexico City, and obtained her Ph.D. in anthropology from Harvard University. She has held teaching positions at Texas Tech, the University of Nebraska, and the University of Calgary, where she served as head of the Department of Archaeology and is now a professor. Nevertheless, she describes her career as follows:

My own case is the story of a decade-long balancing act and fragmentation. . . . I am genuinely ambivalent about whether or not it's been worth it, although at this point in my career, it seems to have paid off. There have been significant sacrifices on both sides of the fence. . . . I was 29 when I married [archaeologist David Kelley] in 1958, 30 when our first child was born, 31 when I took Special Exams, 32 when our second child was born, 36 when the twins were born and 37 when I belatedly received my Ph.D., several years behind those of my contemporaries that completed their programs. If we were to have children, which we wanted, it had to be during those years. I didn't want an either/or situation, I wanted both (Kelley 1984:16; see Kelley 1989).

Kelley has viewed her career as expedient, rather than directed, in that she has undertaken projects because they fit with her family's situation and needs. For example, she states that she undertook life history research among the Yaqui (Kelley 1978) because much of the initial interviewing could be done at home, and she could later take her family to Arizona and Sonora (Kelley 1984:18). On balance, though, Kelley has produced a coherent and important body of archaeological research in the Southwest, and she continues to add to this as well as to make contributions to the clarification of theoretical issues (Kelley and Hanen 1988).

Kelley's work has focused on the Sierra Blanca region of southeastern New Mexico (Holden 1952, 1955; Kelley 1966, 1979, 1984), an area on the boundary of the Pueblo and Plains culture areas. With the country described as marginal for Puebloan horticultural adaptation, the cultural remains have been viewed as a mixture of Anasazi and Mogollon or as just somewhat aberrant. As John Speth (1984) has noted, compared to other parts of the Southwest, this area of New Mexico is still poorly known archaeologically. Unfortunately, as well, many of the known sites have been heavily vandalized. Kelley's Ph.D. dissertation (1966), recently published by the University of Michigan (1984), described and organized into chronological phases the various sites of the Sierra

Blanca region excavated by the Texas Tech Field Schools or known only through surface survey. Kelley had been an active participant in the work and was the appropriate person to complete the analysis and writing. As she indicates, the work was done at a time when descriptive reports, cultural-historical reconstructions, and regional comparisons were the standard for archaeological investigations. These were the key features of the dissertation. The fact is, however, that the 1966 thesis was close to an underground academic bestseller because no one could hope to make sense out of the archaeology of the Sierra Blanca or neighboring regions without reading it. In essence, Kelley's cultural-historical reconstruction stood the test of time, and the detailed description she provided became indispensable for subsequent research.

Beginning in 1972, Kelley (1979) undertook a restudy of the original collections from the Sierra Blanca region; more recently, in 1984, she commenced an extensive field program in that area. Both the restudy and the new fieldwork reflect the changed perspectives archaeologists have toward their data and thus address new theoretical issues. In the late 1960s and 1970s, archaeologists became increasingly conservation-minded about their major data sources, i.e., archaeological sites. It became important to develop methods for conducting new analysis and asking new questions of previously collected material. The Sierra Blanca restudy was undertaken with these considerations in mind. It focused on a new theoretical issue, assessing regional interaction patterns that could be addressed using newly available techniques and the existing body of previously collected data. The restudy focused on modes of lithic and ceramic production and distribution in the region as reflected in the artifact collections, with some effort devoted to more detailed study of the faunal and human skeletal remains as well. The restudy was successful and is exemplary in providing new insights into the region, creating a baseline for more refined hypotheses, and demonstrating the value of tailoring research for the characteristics of specific collections.

The new fieldwork, which was recently completed, is directed toward elucidating human subsistence–environmental interactions in the region and emphasizes the roles of population dispersion and aggregation in these processes. The project takes account of the interaction of demography, settlement strategy, and environment, a contemporary theoretical concern in archaeology, as well as chronological issues more specific to the Southwest. I am convinced the project will make a major contribution to southwestern archaeology.

I would make a final observation about Kelley's research orientation and strategy. Perhaps because her teaching position in Canada is distant from the Southwest, Kelley has made an extra effort to keep informed of the developments in her area. She maintains a wide correspondence network, keeps up with an enormous amount of literature, and regularly attends U.S. national and southwestern regional meetings. The high quality of her work reflects this effort.

Cynthia Irwin-Williams (1936–1990)

Cynthia Irwin was born in Denver, Colorado. Following her mother's divorce, she and her brother were brought up by their mother and businessman–avocational historian grandfather. After her father's death while the children were still small, Eleanor (Kay) Irwin reared and supported the children alone. Irwin-Williams' interest in archaeology began in childhood, when her family spent summer vacations with a Hopi family in Arizona and engaged in hunting for arrowheads. Mrs. Irwin and her children later joined the Colorado Archaeological Society, a responsible amateur group. While she was in high school, Irwin-Williams began an archaeology club, recruiting H. Marie Wormington, Herbert Dick, and Ruth Underhill to serve as advisors.

Both Irwin-Williams and her brother, the late Henry Irwin, did volunteer work at the Denver Museum of Natural History, and both went on to professional archaeological careers. Irwin-Williams attended Radcliffe with a scholarship, earning both her B.A. (1957) and M.A. (1958) in anthropology. She earned her Ph.D. from Harvard in 1963. At Harvard, she was encouraged by Peabody Museum Director J. O. Brew. In 1962, she married nuclear chemist David Williams, spent a year on a postdoctoral fellowship at the American Museum of Natural History, and then began teaching at Eastern New Mexico University in Portales. The position in Portales represented a major compromise. David Williams took a position at Sandia Laboratories in Albuquerque, where the couple established their home. For 17 years, until their divorce in 1980, Irwin-Williams commuted nearly 500 miles, from Albuquerque to Portales, every week of the school year. Irwin-Williams served as assistant, associate, and full professor at Eastern New Mexico University. In 1977, she was honored with the position of distinguished professor of anthropology. In 1982, Irwin-Williams left Eastern New Mexico for the position of executive director of the Social Sciences Center at the Desert Research Institute in Reno, Nevada. She remained there until her untimely and unexpected death in 1990.

Irwin-Williams always played an active role in the Society for American Archaeology. In 1977, she became the second woman to be elected president of the society, and she served as chair of the society's committee on federal archaeology and in other capacities. She also served on a variety of committees for the National Science Foundation and the National Endowment for the Humanities.

Irwin-Williams has an outstanding record as principle investigator in sponsored research projects. Her research has been supported by the American Museum of Natural History, the American Philosophical Society, the National Endowments for the Arts and the Humanities, the National Science Foundation, the National Geographic Society, Sigma Xi, and the Wenner-Gren Foundation for Anthropological Research, among others. Interested in the questions of major transitions, such as from mobile hunting and gathering to sedentary agriculturalist, or from simple to complex social organization, Irwin-Williams' research encompasses major contributions to Paleo-Indian, Archaic, and Pueblo archaeology as well as archaeological method and theory.

In part because of the nature of archaeology and in part reflecting her natural inclinations, Irwin-Williams' research has a hard science orientation. She excelled in multidisciplinary approaches, geomorphology, paleoclimatological reconstructions, and synthesizing large bodies of data. She brought these assets to her Paleo-Indian work (e.g., Irwin-Williams et al. 1973; Irwin-Williams and Haynes 1970) and to her research on the southwestern Archaic and Anasazi origins (e.g., Irwin-Williams 1967, 1973, 1979). Another of her abilities was to provide lastingly useful conceptual tools. For example, Irwin-Williams argued that archaeologists must conceptualize differently those aspects of the archaeological record that inform us about basic strategies of adaptation versus those aspects of the record that inform us about the origins and histories of particular cultural traditions. Data synthesis also must then proceed on two distinct levels, one emphasizing paths of adaptation that might be expected to correlate with climatic and demographic changes and one focusing on particular tool forms and settlement behaviors that might be clues to the origins of particular groups of people. In defining Picosa (the elemental southwestern culture) and the Oshara tradition (Anasazi origins), Irwin-Williams provided the framework for describing the Archaic cultures of the Southwest. This work is conceptually precise and based on analysis of older collections as well as her own work in central New Mexico. The utility of the framework is well attested to by the

fact that it has basically withstood the test of time since its introduction in the late 1960s. During the last few years of her life, Irwin-Williams returned to her research area on the Arroyo Cuervo and some of her original questions regarding Archaic adaptations. The new work systematically integrates the ways in which the archaeological record is formed, discovered, and interpreted (Irwin-Williams 1986), a major interest in current archaeology.

Despite her love for the archaeology of Paleo-Indian and Archaic time periods, among Irwin-Williams' major contributions is her work at Salmon Ruin and her conceptualization of the Chaco Phenomenon. The two most recent major research efforts on the prehistoric Chacoan manifestations have been those of the National Park Service (R. Lister and F. Lister 1981) and Irwin-Williams' at Salmon Ruin (Irwin-Williams 1980a, 1980b). The ruins of Chaco Canyon have been a focus of archaeological investigation for nearly 100 years. Both recent projects brought modern techniques of survey, analysis, and excavation to aid in understanding Chaco and its ancient Pueblo inhabitants. Until Irwin-Williams' work at Salmon Ruin, the sites at Chaco Canyon were viewed as uniquely spectacular but representing no more than a particularly advanced branch of the Anasazi. Earl Morris' (1915) work at Aztec Ruin on the San Juan River had revealed a large structure with an early Chacoan-style component and a later Mesa Verde–style occupation. The two Anasazi branches were seen as basically equivalent and sequential. Salmon Ruin, like Aztec, has both Chacoan and Mesa Verde components and as at Aztec, the occupations are sequential. But Irwin-Williams viewed the two Anasazi manifestations as fundamentally different, and it is the difference in organization that is reflected in her having coined and used the term *Chaco Phenomenon.*

In essence, Irwin-Williams describes the Chacoan system as culturally and socially complex. She distinguishes among dispersed, nucleated, and aggregated Anasazi communities. Nucleated communities, such as the Chacoan sites including Aztec and Salmon, reflect hierarchical organization and productive specialization. They are therefore different in kind from aggregated communities, which are essentially egalitarian. The Mesa Verde occupation at Salmon and Aztec, as well as the organization of the modern Pueblo villages, reflects aggregation rather than nucleation. Irwin-Williams' view of the Chaco Phenomenon, and the Chaco system, was clearly very different from earlier conceptions. It is supported by work in Chaco Canyon itself and by the discovery of the Chaco road system and the recent documentation of the more than 70 Chacoan outliers. Basically, it is Irwin-Williams' view that prevails among southwestern archaeologists today, despite disagreement about how the Chacoan system developed and why it ultimately failed.

Prior to her untimely death Irwin-Williams had continued her fieldwork on the Archaic during the summers and her research and writing during the academic year at the Desert Research Institute. Her life had undergone several changes, and her work had been moving in new directions. She had become deeply involved in providing counseling for drug and alcohol abusers, and she had taken a number of courses in counseling. Her research had also taken on a more applied and humanistic orientation. At the time of her death she was documenting a variety of prehistoric water-control features, experimenting with prehistoric agricultural technology, and developing ways in which this low-cost, efficient technology could be used in modern Third World countries.

DISCUSSION

The female archaeologists discussed here manifest life and career patterns that differ as a group from those of female ethnologists, on the one hand, and from male southwestern archaeologists on the other. In contrast to many of the women who have contributed to ethnology, the women archaeologists on the whole have devoted many more years of their lives to fieldwork. This situation probably reflects basic differences between ethnology and archaeology. As I indicated early on, archaeology as a science is learned largely through experience and apprenticeships. Careers cannot be built on one or two field projects, no matter how well these may be carried out. The necessity for long stints in the field has seemed to select for certain kinds of women. The women archaeologists are predominantly western women who were brought up in the western United States and received much of their education in the West. They seem to be women who grew up in small towns or on ranches and in pioneer tradition were not treated very differently from their male siblings. Certainly, they seem to have been encouraged to participate in competitive activities; they were not told they should not or could not engage in particular pursuits, including archaeology.

Many of the female archaeologists were first introduced to archaeology by their parents and sometimes in the context of avocational digging. As Hinsley (1986a:218) has pointed out, archaeology as a science reflects a degree of "porousness" in demarcating professional versus amateur or avocational practice. Hinsley suggests that this characteristic is particularly salient in archaeology in the United States, where science as a whole is democratic and open. Whether or not the latter observation holds (I have doubts, due to the persistent vision of nineteenth-century English picnics, during which the major activity appears to be half of the British Isles tearing up barrows), it is true that digging for arrowheads has long been considered a healthy family activity in western states where there is plenty of land and a great many obvious archaeological sites. In any case, the avocational aspects of archaeology do seem to have been important to the recruitment of women into the field, in part because of the familial nature of the activity.

Recruitment, sponsorship, and mentoring seem also extremely important to the female archaeologists discussed. Virtually all of them mention one or a very few key individuals who encouraged them to go on. The relationship between Wormington and Irwin-Williams stands out, as do the relationships between William C. Holden and his daughter, Jane H. Kelley, between Anna Shepard and A. V. Kidder and Anna Shepard and her father, and between Florence Ellis and her father. Remarkable, however, are the number of women who were encouraged in the field or given employment by Edgar L. Hewett. Hewett, whether or not he is acknowledged and whether or not he treated women fairly, nevertheless provided more opportunities and more jobs for the women of southwestern archaeology than anyone else. Hewett was certainly no great scholar, and he antagonized the eastern academic establishment, but he provided entree into a difficult field for several very talented and dedicated women. Perhaps as more material on Hewett becomes available and subject to historical analysis, new insights into his motivations will be apparent; until then, I concur with Charles Lange's observation (1986, personal communication) that Hewett provided opportunities for women in part because he was fair and in part because he could pay them less than he would have to have paid their male counterparts.

In contrast to male southwestern archaeologists, the women have had less remunerative and less prestigious academic positions. It seems to me that they have had to work much harder, or to have produced a greater body of material for professional recognition, than their male colleagues have had to do. Although most male southwestern archaeologists do conduct many field projects in the course of their careers, they seem to establish themselves earlier on the basis of one or two projects. For example, Emil Haury attained deserved but quick recognition for his work at Ventana Cave, whereas H. Marie Wormington was only recognized by her colleagues after many years of achievement.

Finally, one must consider the ultimate regard with which the work of women southwestern archaeologists is held by their male peers. As indicated in the beginning of this essay in citing Irwin-Williams, women do not hold positions at the most prestigious institutions, nor do they hold senior positions at all the major southwestern academic departments. Although they have contributed scholarship in the mainstream of their discipline for decades, their work is often not recognized. In an article summarizing, reflecting upon, and celebrating the contributions to southwestern archaeology over the past 50 years, Haury (1985) mentions only the work of Anna Shepard, and that rather casually. Perhaps, as sophisticated as it was, Shepard's petrographic studies carried out in the laboratory are in accord with the popular myth, shared by archaeological professionals, of the role of the woman-at-home archaeologist in a male-dominated field. Her work may be regarded as proper archaeological housework.

NOTES

1. Florence Ellis, Cynthia Irwin-Williams, and Jane Kelley were invaluable and patient resources while I was preparing the conference version of this chapter. Jane Kelley has been a continuing source of insight and inspiration throughout. Chuck Lange was a thoughtful informant providing useful information. Louise Lamphere, Barbara Babcock, and Nancy Parezo made helpful, useful suggestions. A version of this chapter, entitled "Sisters of Sun and Spade, Women Archaeologists in the Southwest" was also presented at the Chacmool Conference and as "The Archaeology of Gender" published in Walde and Willows (1991).

2. These figures are now somewhat out-of-date due to the delay between the conference and publication. They are also supported by Kramer and Stark (1988) and the Society for American Archaeology (1991); therefore, I do not think the situation has changed.

THE CONTRIBUTIONS OF
ESTHER S. GOLDFRANK

Charles H. Lange

As far as I know I was the only woman to go in
the field with Boas. I was in the field in 1920, 21
and 22. Not for many weeks at a time, but, in
the summertime. It was a marvelous experience.

Esther Goldfrank
1985b

I T WAS with great satisfaction that I agreed to write this chapter, an opportunity to honor the widely recognized anthropologist Esther S. Goldfrank. This would be a chance to express in publication the thoughts I had often made known in private conversations and campus lectures over the past several decades. When I returned from service in World War II to the Department of Anthropology at the University of New Mexico to continue graduate studies leading to my doctorate, I soon needed a dissertation topic. After several false starts, my committee and I settled on an evaluation of economic factors in the culture changes at Cochiti Pueblo, New Mexico. In the immediate aftermath of World War II, it was clear that there had been significant changes and also that such changes were continuing to have an important impact on various aspects of Cochiti culture. To provide the necessary time depth and perspective, I was fortunate in being able to turn to the studies of Adolph F. Bandelier, Frederick

Starr, and Father Noel Dumarest for the late nineteenth century and the studies by the staff of Edward S. Curtis as well as those by Franz Boas, Esther S. Goldfrank, and Ruth Benedict for the early twentieth century. In a short time I had succeeded in familiarizing myself with much of this literature, augmented by such additional items as Leslie A. White's study of Keresan medicine societies and his ethnographies of the pueblos of Acoma, San Felipe, Santo Domingo, and Santa Ana as well as the numerous and diverse ethnographic and ethnological contributions of Elsie Clews Parsons. It quickly became apparent that Goldfrank's 1927 monograph was the most complete and generally helpful source in terms of my specific interests.

My own field investigations, coming another generational interval later, focused on the most recent, or postwar, phase of Cochiti culture change. Coincidentally, and fortunately for me, Cochiti Pueblo was located a few hours' drive from the University of New Mexico campus, making frequent field trips of a long day's duration practical. As an added bonus, the people of this pueblo had a reputation for being comparatively friendly and approachable. Subsequent field experiences convinced me further of the correctness of this initial impression. In retrospect, it is very difficult to pinpoint the precise moments or circumstances at which various thoughts came to me as fieldwork progressed; at some point, however, I was struck by the fact that several of my informants were the same individuals or were of the same families that had been most helpful to Goldfrank. They were openly extending a sincere welcome to me, despite their awareness (in all probability) of potential complications stemming from involvements with me. Their cordiality toward me and, in turn, toward my family never wavered even after the three of us took up residence in Cochiti Pueblo for several summers in the late 1940s.

My dissertation was completed and my degree awarded in 1951. I then began additional fieldwork at Cochiti to fill in whatever gaps I could; the augmented and revised dissertation was, of course, aimed at eventual publication. While this work was in progress, I attended the 1953 meeting of the American Anthropological Association in Tucson, Arizona. At one point in the meeting, while I was standing with a group in the hall between sessions, Professor W. W. "Nibs" Hill, my dissertation chairman, rushed up and pulled me aside, explaining, "There is someone here you should meet!" This "someone" proved to be none other than Esther Goldfrank.

Our meeting may be best characterized as a professional "love at first sight," at least for me. To be honest, I had intentionally avoided any contact with Goldfrank up to that time, except for carefully studying her monograph; I had primarily wanted to be on my own. I had also harbored a haunting fear that out of jealousy or a protective feeling in regard to "her" people, she might somehow hamper or compromise my efforts.

Upon meeting her, and after a very few minutes of conversation, I realized how completely groundless and erroneous my fear had been. Her enthusiasm over numerous ethnographic details and the sharing of field experiences, several of which involved the same individuals spanning an interval of 25 or 30 years, quickly put me very much at ease. From a strictly personal viewpoint, Goldfrank's openness and her willingness to share her people with me would have been sufficient basis for including her among the key figures of this volume on women anthropologists. Nevertheless, there are far more important grounds for honoring her and her work.

EDUCATION AND EMPLOYMENT UNDER BOAS

Esther Schiff[1] began life in New York City in 1896; she graduated from Barnard College in 1918 with a major in economics. As has been true of numerous anthropologists over the years, her one and only exposure to anthropology as an undergraduate was an introductory course taken during her final semester. Again, as in the case of several other anthropologists, this experience had far-reaching effects on subsequent events in her life. In this particular course Esther received a grade of B from her instructor, Professor Franz Boas. More importantly, however, this was the beginning of a long and rewarding association for them both.

Failing to make any real progress in the world of economics, Esther responded promptly and affirmatively to a note from Boas in the late fall of 1919 asking if she would be interested in becoming his secretary "at $25 a week and a month's vacation annually" (Goldfrank 1978:2). At that time, the end of the year 1919, the Department of Anthropology at Columbia University was housed in three rooms on the seventh floor of the Journalism Building. Boas occupied one as his office; his secretary, Esther Schiff, was in a second room; the third stood empty following the unexplained cancellation of A. A. Goldenweiser's instructorship. As of December 1919, Boas was "The Department," and Esther Schiff was "The Staff" (Goldfrank 1978:4).

As daily affairs (i.e., correspondence and other matters) occurred, it was soon apparent that this tiny department had a most valuable "angel," Dr. Elsie Clews Parsons (Goldfrank 1978:4). Not only did Parsons liberally finance field research and publication, it was she who provided the secretary's position occupied by Esther. Lacking formal training in anthropology beyond the introductory course she had taken at Barnard, Esther nonetheless derived tremendous insights and advantages from her position as secretary for the department and, more specifically, as secretary for Professor Boas. Given his prestigious position in early American anthropology, his network of contacts with European scholars and academicians, his active pursuit of diverse research interests, and his broad publication involvements, Boas was truly a major figure in the anthropological world of that time. Handling the correspondence between Boas and this far-flung and varied group of associates afforded an ideal opportunity for Esther to become familiar with these names and individuals as well as with the special interests they were pursuing. No formal university course at that time, or since, could have provided a comparable opportunity to acquire such a degree of sophistication in diverse facets of the field.

Esther's secretarial duties also provided a ringside seat to controversies in the field of anthropology such as that which arose following publication of a letter by Boas, "Scientists as Spies," in *The Nation.* This appeared in print a week before the annual meeting of the American Anthropological Association (AAA) at the Peabody Museum of Harvard University in 1919. During a AAA Council meeting held in conjunction with the convention, Dr. Neil M. Judd presented a resolution intended to disassociate the AAA from the letter by Boas that had appeared in *The Nation.* The resolution was adopted by the council, after considerable discussion, by a vote of 20 to 9.

The names of the council members taking part in this vote reads like an early "Who's Who in Anthropology." As a sequel to this action, Boas was dropped from membership in the AAA Council; he then submitted his resignation as an anthropologist on the National Research Council. Further, the Bureau of American Ethnology in Washington withdrew his honorary appointment, which he had held since 1902. A few years later, however, Boas was once again a member of both the AAA Council and the National Research Council. While obviously not of direct concern to Esther, as secretary to Boas, the activities revolving around these matters clearly contributed to her conditioning as an anthropologist. She comments now that her knowledge of these events was limited to the typing of letters for Boas; he scrupulously refrained from any additional discussion of these matters with her (Goldfrank 1978:15).

After that unpleasantness, the year 1920 brought a small but significant development in Esther's life when Boas invited her to join the Tuesday "lunchers"—a group of anthropologists who met weekly at a hotel conveniently located for staff members of both the university and the American Museum of Natural History. Regulars from the museum included Pliny Goddard, Robert Lowie, Nels Nelson, and Leslie Spier; other anthropologists joined as they came to the city and were able, such as Elsie Clews Parsons, Erna Gunther, Gladys Reichard, Alfred Kroeber, and Edward Sapir. Luncheon talk was largely focused on fieldwork, past and planned, and publication problems. Departmental affairs were rarely discussed, and such matters as the actions taken at the recent AAA meetings, never! (Goldfrank 1978:17).

FIELD EXPERIENCES

The summer of 1920 found Esther embarking on her first field experience; she joined Boas during June and July at Laguna Pueblo, New Mexico, where he was making a study of the Keres language. She writes of the experience,

In the Spring of 1920, I had already made plans to join three of my New York friends on my first trip West. We expected to leave sometime in July. Late in April I learned that Dr. Boas was returning to Laguna in June to continue his study of the Keresan language. I then started coaxing, and those who know me well will testify that I don't give up easily. "Why," I asked him, "since I am also going West, shouldn't I leave before my friends, stop off at Laguna and be some sort of help to you?" Once he had mastered his surprise at my ingenuousness, he replied "What in the world would I do with you in the field?" Actually, there wasn't much I could do for him—but time in the field, however short, could do a lot for me. Eventually Dr. Boas weakened. He would talk it over with Dr. Parsons who, with Grant LaFarge, also expected to spend some time in Laguna in June (Goldfrank 1978:40–41).

Esther was partially supported in this venture by Dr. Parsons, who, at that time, was increasingly inclined to do such things behind the facade of her own Southwest Society. Parsons had agreed, on the recommendation of Boas, to provide funds for Esther despite the fact that the latter was still an untrained and inexperienced investigator. Esther was to study cooking recipes because there was nothing esoteric about them. At Laguna, she notes, "they accepted me as the 'friend of a friend' " (Goldfrank 1985b). Because of Parsons' previous work, Esther was "spared the worry of securing informants . . . and I was assigned a simple and, from my standpoint, a very dull topic" (Goldfrank 1978:58). Parsons and LaFarge visited them briefly at Laguna before going on to do research at San Ildefonso Pueblo. All anthropologists were compelled to rely on the same small group of progressives in each village who were tolerant of Anglo-Americans and the U.S. government. These individuals were usually kin or friends, members of a clan or a political faction. Esther worked closely with women, especially Jennie Johnson, whom Parsons described as "an extremely restless informant" who was "com-

municative" but also "preferred housework to systematic presentation and discussion of kinship terms" (see Goldfrank 1978:45). Goldfrank writes,

For me, it was an exciting first session. The recording of cooking recipes and methods was continually punctuated by crying and whooping children and uninvited callers, no doubt eager to check on what was happening. When they learned what we were doing, they proved eager to show their knowledge of the culinary arts. The end result: "general confusion" (Goldfrank 1978:46).

At the close of their Laguna field season, Boas and Esther moved to San Ildefonso, where Parsons and LaFarge were still working. Within a very few days, Boas and Esther, with her appendix "kicking up," left the field to go to Albuquerque; from there, Esther went on to Los Angeles where her appendix was removed. In all it was "an exceptional setting for a first field trip and, surely, an exceptional company for an 'accidental' anthropologist" (Goldfrank 1978:58).

In 1921, after attending Boas' graduate classes and becoming part of his "family" (Goldfrank 1978:59), Esther returned with Boas to Laguna for a short time. This year Esther worked on hunting patterns (see Goldfrank 1954b) and feasts (see Goldfrank 1923). Then they went on to Cochiti; factionalism was rife throughout the pueblo when they arrived. Boas lived with John Dixon, a progressive leader, and Esther found a room at the schoolhouse. Esther studied political factionalism and social organization, and her informants were all progressives. In their work, Boas and Goldfrank were aided by *Notes on Cochiti, New Mexico,* by Father Dumarest, which had been edited and published in 1919 by Parsons. Goldfrank remembers,

My first morning after breakfast, I again wandered about the village—no informant seems to have been available for me and Dr. Boas was already working with John Dixon. In the plaza, drawing water from the pump, I saw a young woman, comely by any standard, who returned my greeting and a welcoming smile. A most encouraging gesture, I thought. I knew that women, and particularly young women, were not well informed regarding "secret" matters (men's business), but at this time I hoped to find someone willing to give me kinship terms that I could tie in with Dr. Parsons' genealogical work on Laguna (not published until 1923). And women the world over were—and are—notorious for their small talk . . .

My presence in the plaza was no surprise to the woman at the pump . . . To encourage an exchange, I asked her if she lived near the plaza . . . She did live near the plaza, she said, and asked me if I would like to visit her . . . I gladly accepted her invitation (Goldfrank 1978:79–80).

Isabel Diaz, a progressive, took Esther home. Also known as Caroline Quintana, she spoke English well and was "usually outspoken" (Goldfrank 1978:80); she helped Esther with her work on kinship, marriage, and property ownership. "Once it became known that I was a regular visitor in Isabel's house, several of her female relatives put in an appearance, and while working in a pueblo is far from a bull session, there were often as many as three Indian ladies arguing over just what who called whom" (Goldfrank 1978:81). Pedro Ramirez (Ben Quintana), Isabel's husband, "who now and again came back to the house during the day seemed eager to escape the female company" (Goldfrank 1978:82).

In the spring of 1922 Boas and Esther returned to a homecoming. Boas again stayed with Dixon, and Esther returned to the school. But after a few days she went to live with Caroline Quintana, with whom she had become good friends. Later Esther was invited to undergo an adoption ceremony into Caroline's clan, complete with head washing and feasting. "I was more than happy at this indication of their affection for me and quickly consented" (Goldfrank 1978:86–87). Caroline served as "ceremonial mother" and Esther's new name was Abalone Shell.

Supported only in part on her initial field trip, Esther received full funding from Parsons for her subsequent field trips to the Southwest—in 1921 and 1922 at Laguna and Cochiti and in 1924 at

Isleta Pueblo—although her findings were at times counter to certain ideas and conclusions then held by Parsons as a result of her experiences and studies elsewhere in the Southwest. Parsons often determined where individuals would work, with her financial support based on her quest for data to support her theories or fill gaps in the knowledge base.

In the preface to her 1927 monograph, *The Social and Ceremonial Organization of Cochiti,* Esther stated, "The material for this paper was gathered in the fall of 1921 and the spring of 1922." She added that on both visits she "accompanied Professor Franz Boas, who was making a special study of the Keres language." In between these two periods of fieldwork, in December of 1921, Esther gave her first paper at an annual meeting of the AAA in a joint session with the American Folklore Society; it was titled, "The Deer Hunt in the Southwest." It was one of 28 papers presented in all the sessions that year.

PERSONAL AND PROFESSIONAL LIFE

Completing her Cochiti fieldwork in the early summer of 1922, Esther went with Professor Boas and "Mama Franz" to Berkeley, where "Papa Franz" lectured in the University of California summer session. Not long after her return to New York City, "instead of going for a Ph.D., which [she] had intended to do" (Goldfrank 1978:92), Esther married Walter Goldfrank, the wedding taking place in early December of that year. Goldfrank, a widower, was 12 years her senior and entered into the marriage with three sons, aged 6, 9, and 12 years. In May of 1924, the Goldfranks became the parents of a daughter, Susan, and they soon moved to White Plains, New York. Goldfrank writes, "The demands of my changed situation brought my anthropological studies to a complete stop . . . But my new life was so full and fulfilling that I had no regrets at interrupting my incipient anthropological career" (Goldfrank 1978:93). She did, however, begin to write up her notes that eventually led to

The Social and Ceremonial Organization at Cochiti
(1927). In this she received no encouragement
nor sharing of data from Boas, who only wanted
to work with self-motivating individuals. He
erected no barriers to her continuing, however:

He clearly put no road blocks in the path of a woman
student because she was a woman, but he believed
marriage and a family came first in a woman's life;
and however promising a woman student might
be, he never encouraged her to limit or forsake familial duties in order to further her academic career
(1978:93).

It appears, in retrospect, that Goldfrank's three
sons and one daughter gave her a kind of special
relationship with Parsons, who also had three sons
and a daughter. Having an early involvement
with feminist movements and philosophies, and
with the example of Parsons to emulate, Goldfrank responded favorably to the suggestion by
Parsons that she "leave behind a good nurse"
(quoted in Goldfrank 1978:26) and return to the
Southwest, this time to Isleta Pueblo:

Dr. Parsons' suggestion fell on fertile soil. Despite a
full and satisfying domestic life, my early feminist involvements (among other things, I had paraded up
Fifth Avenue with a sizable Barnard contingent as
part of a campaign of Votes for Women) encouraged
me to think that, like Dr. Parsons, I might also mix
marriage and anthropology. I had a "good nurse" for
my infant daughter, a sympathetic husband, and a
maiden aunt (by affinity) who was ready and happy to
take over the reins of our household during my short
absence (Goldfrank 1978:27).

Goldfrank departed for Isleta early in November
1924. Because of her domestic responsibilities, it
was to have been only a brief visit—but the termination came even sooner than she had anticipated when she realized that to make significant
progress a considerably longer stay than she had
originally planned on would be necessary because
of the reticence of the Pueblo storytellers. The
people of Isleta were not as welcoming as those at
Cochiti. Her respondent family was not respon-

sive to or interested in her search for stories.
When she finally found someone to convey tales,
it had to be done in secret at the Alvarado Hotel
in Albuquerque, New Mexico. A follow-up field
trip was made by Parsons herself when she recognized that Esther could not leave her family again
for some time, and the same informant worked
again in Albuquerque, not Isleta (Goldfrank
1978:96–97).

For a brief period, there was thought of a joint
publication by Parsons and Goldfrank on Isleta,
made more intriguing perhaps by the fact that
although the two women were 20 years apart
in age, they had depended largely on the same
informant. In the end, the joint publication
idea was abandoned, for the fundamental reason
that their two approaches, even with the same
principal informant, were strikingly different.
Goldfrank (1978:33–34) relates the subsequent
events:

But this was not to be the end of the matter, although after the publication of my monograph on
Cochiti in 1927 I pretty much dropped out of anthropology. To be sure, I still read the journals, but I
took no courses, did no writing, and cannot remember meeting with anthropologists, not even with Dr.
Boas, until I returned to New York almost a decade
later. And it was 1940, shortly after I married Karl
August Wittfogel, before Dr. Parsons, at dinner in
her New York City apartment (besides us, only Duncan Strong and her daughter were present) referred
again to our Isleta experience. Said she, "Esther, you
were certainly a good sport to turn over your Isleta
notes to me." I answered that at the time I was sure I
would not soon be able to go back into the field—in
fact, it was 1939 before I did—and that I was then
convinced, and am indeed still convinced, that it is
deplorable to sit on untouched notes for decades (as
many anthropologists do when these notes can be
useful to others). Dr. Parsons smiled "her slow direct
smile," as Kroeber described it in 1943, and said nothing further.

I cannot help thinking she was trying to say, without putting it into words, that she recognized certain
deficiencies in her treatment of my data; she had nei-

ther cited them specifically in her Isleta monograph nor dealt in any substantial way with the theoretical points I had raised, not even with those developed in my "Isleta Variants."

Dr. Parsons died December 19, 1941. Gladys Reichard, her literary executor, phoned me shortly afterward to say that she [Parsons] had dedicated a still unpublished volume of paintings by an Isletan Indian to me. Said Reichard, "I have never known Elsie to dedicate anything to anyone before." Actually the dedication was to me and Julian H. Steward and it read, "To whom I owe the opening of Isleta." Years later Steward assured me that he had never worked in Isleta; in fact, the only contribution he might have made was in forwarding to Dr. Parsons the letter the artist addressed to the BAE . . . But whatever Steward's role may have been, I did indeed open up Isleta for Dr. Parsons.

In a later essay (1985a), Goldfrank again discusses their Isleta collaboration and the differences in their recorded data.

During this period, in Esther's words, "Walter Goldfrank died from a coronary thrombosis on a train en route to Philadelphia on a beautiful day in mid-September 1935" (Goldfrank 1978: 98). Several months later, in January of 1936, Esther Goldfrank returned to anthropology and Columbia University. "Papa" and "Mama Franz" Boas were still present in the departmental scene, but Boas was very close to relinquishing the chairmanship and retiring. He did so the next year. Professors W. Duncan Strong and George Herzog had joined the department, and two secretaries were sharing the increased demands of Goldfrank's former position. She writes,

My welcome at Columbia was extremely heartening personally, but extremely guarded when I raised the question of my scientific reinvolvement. For Dr. Boas, I was still a beloved daughter, but, as in the past, he left decision-making to me. What I would do was my affair. He neither encouraged nor discouraged my return to anthropology (Goldfrank 1978:99).

Others in the department were not encouraging about Goldfrank's prospects of finding a place in anthropology at Columbia University. Bene-

dict, however, suggested contacting Dr. Caroline Zachry, who was conducting a study of adolescents as a psychoanalyst for the Commission on Secondary School Curriculum, sponsored by the General Education Board of the Rockefeller Foundation. Goldfrank's anthropological experience, coupled with the years of raising her own family, made her a likely prospect although hardly a strong candidate. Somewhat to Goldfrank's surprise, she was accepted and soon found herself in association with a group of teachers, psychiatrically trained social workers, psychologists, anthropologists, and other specialists; all were concerned with topics and problems concerning the adolescent. In her work, Goldfrank became involved in studies of students at the Society for Ethical Culture's Fieldston School of which she was a graduate and where her daughter was then enrolled.

With the completion of the final report, this four-year (1932–1936) study came to a close, and a trip to Europe followed. Goldfrank then put forth a brief effort to write pieces that would be of interest, she hoped, to editors of the *Atlantic Monthly,* the *New Yorker,* or similar journals. Reacting quite philosophically to her several rejections, Goldfrank (1978:109–10) comments,

And while my Cochiti monograph, written in the mid-20s, has stood the test of time well (although when Fred Eggan told me long years ago he considered it the best of the short pueblo studies, I felt he was giving me more than my due) there is little to be said for it from a literary standpoint. However, working on the Fieldston report with Jenny [Jeannette Mirsky] the previous spring had not only sharpened my understanding of the school's background and relation to the Society for Ethical Culture, her proficiency as an author taught me a good deal about the art of writing. Ellery Sedwick's letter confirms this conclusion. But even after our exchange I never again submitted anything to a literary magazine. However much my writing may have improved, I have been content to send my contributions to professional journals where acceptance depends more on substance than on style.

In the fall of 1937, Goldfrank began to attend classes at Columbia University more regularly. Boas had resigned but was still using an office in the department. Ralph Linton was brought in from the outside as the new chairperson rather than the insider favored by Boas and others, Ruth Benedict. Students soon became known as "his" and "hers," reflecting and perpetuating the division within the department. The schism continued more or less unabated until Linton left in 1946 to become Sterling Professor of Anthropology at Yale. Goldfrank (1978:110–11) reflects,

> I was spared the students' worries. I did not want a degree. I was forty years old (the average age of the students was about twenty-five). I had been in the field four times. I had published and I felt confident that if I had anything worth saying I would find a platform from which to say it. And I didn't want to teach. My overriding concern was to flesh out my early field and family experiences, and since I was not working for a degree, I could be selective. Indeed, to many of the students I must have seemed little more than an aging dilettante . . . My major interest lay in theory and ethnology and, with respect to the latter, particularly in problems of social organization (which followed naturally from my work in the 20s) and of personality and culture (which through Benedict's *Patterns of Culture* had greatly stimulated research in the field by anthropologists and psychologists, and especially psychoanalysts).

In line with these interests, Goldfrank had attended sessions conducted jointly by Linton and Abram Kardiner on personality and culture. In one of these, which Goldfrank regrettably did not attend, Bunzel and Benedict reported on Zuni. Later, in his book, *The Individual and His Society,* Kardiner (1939) gave a résumé of their material, with no deviation from their interpretation of Zuni personality. Goldfrank was relieved to be told later, however, that Dr. Lawrence Kubie, a well-known psychoanalyst, had maintained at the session that the Zuni dreams collected by Bunzel were not compatible with the Apollonian image that Bunzel and Benedict were projecting. Kubie believed, as did Goldfrank, that these dreams revealed "highly aggressive personality traits that did not fit Benedict's Apollonian construct of pueblo society" (Goldfrank 1978:112).

As time passed, two distinct camps developed in the interpretation of Pueblo cultures. One consisted of Benedict, Bunzel, Laura Thompson, and numerous followers; the second involved Goldfrank, Dorothy Eggan, and, again, numerous followers. In 1946, John Bennett, an admitted outsider, discussed this dichotomy in a paper, "The Interpretation of Pueblo Culture: A Question of Values." Bennett carefully avoided taking sides in this split, characterizing the first group as having an "organic emphasis" and the second as having a "repressive emphasis" and suggesting that the issue involved a question of means and ends (Bennett 1946:372). While the first group emphasized the "ends," he argued that "to Goldfrank it is precisely the means that count and that is her bias." He continued, "She probably grants the organic, homogenous, logico-aesthetic world view, and concerns herself almost entirely with the means of achieving this. These, to her, are the important factors; these are what the social scientist should study objectively" (Bennett 1946:373). In the spring of 1939, Benedict began organizing four small field teams to work among the Blackfoot: one in the United States (the Southern Piegan studied by Wissler some 20 years earlier) and three in Canada (the Northern Blackfoot, Northern Piegan, and the Blood). Benedict asked Goldfrank to join the group; except for Lucien Hanks and his wife, Jane Richardson, the others were all graduate students in anthropology at Columbia—individuals with no field experience. Despite their differences in interpreting Puebloan culture, Benedict encouraged Goldfrank's participation and even went so far as to indicate that Goldfrank might coordinate and correlate the findings of the various researchers.

Following the summer's field investigations, Goldfrank returned to New York and spent the autumn and early winter working up her field notes. She also resumed her attendance at the sessions on personality and culture, augmented by informal talks with Linton and others. Her obvious interest, as well as her summer of fieldwork with the Canadian Blackfoot, or Blood, changed her status from that of being seated among the students attending the sessions to receiving an invitation to join Linton and Kardiner in the front row—along with special visitors and those reporting on field studies. Goldfrank comments (1978:155),

For me 1939 was a watershed year. Since my return to New York four years earlier I had been, from the standpoint of anthropology, an inquiring consumer. Now, after my summer with the Blood, I again became an eager producer. But, as could be expected, the two roles soon interlocked, as indeed they had done in the 1920s. Again I was attending classes and organizing field notes for publication.

In January 1940, on the same day that Benedict wrote to her about the possibility of returning to the Blood Reservation the following summer, Goldfrank met Karl August Wittfogel, a widely recognized scholar of Chinese society and specialist in irrigation cultures. Finding many common interests, Goldfrank and Wittfogel married on March 8, 1940.

Over the following decade, Goldfrank continued to work with her Blood material, publishing several papers using the name Goldfrank rather than Wittfogel, a practice she has followed to the present time. Three papers (Goldfrank 1951a, 1951b, 1952) brought her studies of the Blood to a close. She writes (1978:150),

It is good to know that others have been carrying on research among the Blood and related peoples. One of them, whose achievements are well known, wrote me not long ago that he had just reread my *Changing Configurations* [1945d] and found it both "informative and lively." On this comforting note I end my saga of the Blood.

In addition to her papers on the Blood, Goldfrank remained busy during the 1940s writing a number of papers on subjects ranging from the Teton Dakota to the Navajo, Hopi, and other Pueblo peoples, including Zuni and Santa Ana. One paper, invited by Erminie Voegelin for the volume honoring the recently deceased Elsie Clews Parsons, was a joint effort by Wittfogel and Goldfrank in the *Journal of American Folklore*. The paper, "Some Aspects of Pueblo Mythology and Society," rested significantly on Wittfogel's data on irrigation and appeared with him as the senior author (Wittfogel and Goldfrank 1943). From 1943 on, Goldfrank's affiliation was with the Chinese History Project at Columbia University, although her interests in North American ethnology persisted.

Goldfrank, in addition to her research, was active in professional societies. In the fall of 1945, she was nominated secretary-treasurer of the American Ethnological Society (AES) and was elected in January of 1946, serving until 1947. In 1948, she was elected president of the AES and brought the association into a closer relationship with AAA. Subsequently, she served as editor of the AES Monograph Series, a position she held until 1956.

In the summer of 1946, World War II had ended and "the Southwest beckoned" (1978:198). Goldfrank and her husband began to travel. For him it was the first visit; for her, it was the first after an absence of almost two decades. Their research centered on irrigation and related subjects. With an initial stop in Albuquerque, they visited the United Pueblos Agency and the University of New Mexico's Department of Anthropology. From there, they went to Isleta Pueblo and then retraced their steps a bit, going on to Santa Fe. After visiting the Laboratory of Anthropology, Museum of New Mexico, and National Park Service, the travelers went out to Cochiti Pueblo, where Goldfrank tried in vain to find her closest friend of 1922. Goldfrank and her husband, greatly disappointed, made their way back to Santa Fe. Talking with a shopkeeper who knew several Cochiti people, they made arrangements with a young Cochiti woman to go to the Pueblo with them for the upcoming July 14th Feast Day festivities. This attempt was successful, contact was made with the Quintanas, and a happy reunion followed.

Without going into greater detail concerning that pleasant occasion, it may be of interest to inject a few comments by way of an update. In preparing for the paper on this subject for the Daughters of the Desert Conference, I though it would be rather interesting to go to Cochiti myself, specifically to find Goldfrank's close friend and, hopefully, to obtain some pertinent reminiscences. Caroline Quintana, also a friend of ours for many years, was to celebrate her 95th birthday that May (1986). She is now a great-great-grandmother, several times over. With some prompting, hardly surprising in view of her age and the gap of almost 30 years since her last real contact with Goldfrank, the woman happily recalled Esther, who had lived with her and her family while Professor Boas had stayed with John Dixon. Her recollections focused on the fact that she did remember Esther and that "she was a very nice lady." She also remembered that Esther was several years younger than she and was pleased to have word of her. At one period of time they had exchanged letters, but that was "a long time ago."

Following the 1946 visit, Goldfrank and Wittfogel did not return to Cochiti until 1959; on that occasion, however, the recognition was instant and cordial (Goldfrank 1978:202). From there, the travelers went on to Taos and San Ildefonso. Before returning to the East, they also worked in a visit to Zuni Pueblo and a somewhat superficial look at the Navajo Reservation. In all of these visits, a major interest was the subject of irrigation and related environmental and ecological factors.

From 1947 until the early 1960s, Wittfogel divided his time between Columbia University (the Chinese History Project) and the University of Washington in Seattle (Institute of Pacific Relations). In the fall of 1952, while in Philadelphia for the AAA meetings, Goldfrank visited the American Philosophical Society's library to examine the Isleta paintings in the Elsie Clews Parsons Collection. In time, she agreed to serve as editor for the book on the paintings, which appeared in 1962 as Bulletin 181 of the Bureau of American Ethnology. This was followed in 1967 by *The Artist of "Isleta Paintings" in Pueblo Society,* which appeared as volume 5 in the Smithsonian Contributions to Anthropology.

In some respects these volumes on Isleta essentially concluded Goldfrank's contributions to Southwestern studies. Fortunately, however, additional papers have continued to appear from her hand: an introduction to a study by Marjorie Lismer on the Blood Indians (1974), the autobiographical *Notes on an Undirected Life* (1978), frequently cited in this chapter, and two more recent publications—one paper dealing with her association with Margaret Mead (1983) and the other giving an account of the collaboration between herself and Elsie Clews Parsons in the course of the fieldwork concerning Isleta Pueblo (1985a).

VALUABLE CONTRIBUTIONS

At the outset of this chapter, I indicated my personal debt as a young anthropologist to Goldfrank's sympathetic and enthusiastic assistance and encouragement. Likewise, numerous other fortunate scholars have had similar experiences, such as her colleagues on the Blackfoot field party and David French when he offered his manuscript to her as editor for a monograph in the AES Series. Subsequently, in his published *Factionalism in Isleta Pueblo,* French commented, "Gratitude is also due Esther Goldfrank for her careful editing of the paper" (French 1948:v). The same constructive criticism has been generously offered to innumerable others who have sought her advice and counsel regarding field and publication problems. In this regard, one can only regret that Goldfrank has not seen fit over the years to accept even a temporary, or visiting, teaching position despite a number of such opportunities that have been offered her. Students across the country have certainly been the losers for this reluctance on her part.

The fact that Goldfrank has not become involved in teaching on various campuses makes her long-standing pursuit of anthropological problems in the field and library and her dedication to publish her findings and interpretations without being pressured by such policies as "up-or-out" all the more significant. In this all-important regard, she has effectively served as a singular role model for her colleagues.

In a very real sense, one of Goldfrank's most valuable contributions has been the writing and publication of her autobiographical *Notes*. Her personal involvement in the early anthropology of this country, as viewed from the "center" at Columbia University and in the company of Professor Franz Boas, takes on added value and importance from the candid, documented, and detailed account she has provided. Her personal reactions to events and contemporaries, be they objective or biased, are presented for what they are worth—or as her subtitle indicates, "As One Anthropologist Tells It." For this account, alone, anthropology owes her much.

Compliments on her anthropological contributions have appeared steadily through the years. Writing in 1947, Clark Wissler commented on her analysis of the Blood, a tribe he had studied in the field some 20 years earlier: "The author is realistic in recognizing that though every Indian hopes to become rich, but few attain that level." Elsewhere in the same paper he added, "While the writer is ever ready to interpret her data, she gives most of her space to well chosen statistics and case histories. Thus, the reader can reject her assumptions of cause and effect and make his own interpretations" (Wissler 1947:308–9). A few years later, Kluckhohn, in his survey, "Southwestern Studies of Culture and Personality," wrote,

In a notable paper Goldfrank (1945[b]) comments on discrepancies in accounts of the same tribe by different field workers and criticizes various writers for un-

due emphasis upon infancy and upon the psychoanalytic point of view generally. In this and later papers she tries to restore the balance by calling proper attention to the problems of later life, especially those posed by economic and other situational factors (1954:690).

Following publication of the BAE Bulletin on the Isleta paintings, Edward P. Dozier, a Tewa anthropologist, made these remarks, among others that were generally favorable, in his review of this unique volume that Goldfrank had edited after the death of Parsons:

Credit for the publication of the paintings in the present volume is due to the efforts of Esther S. Goldfrank. Mrs. Goldfrank had color slides made of the original paintings and showed them at professional meetings and to selected audiences, attempting to find support (1963:937).

Subsequently, with the appearance of the sequel, *The Artist of "Isleta Paintings" in Pueblo Society*, Alfonso Ortiz (1968:839), another Tewa anthropologist, wrote a review that included this comment: "Goldfrank is to be congratulated for her dedication and for her labors, first in editing *Isleta Paintings*, then in attempting to piece together, from scattered and often contradictory fragments, the life, the times, and the motivation of the artist." Those familiar with the literature on the Southwestern Pueblo Indians need no reminder that the last two extracts are from reviews written by Puebloans, both well regarded in their chosen field of anthropology.

As I hope is clear from this abbreviated biography of Goldfrank and even more apparent from reading her *Notes*, she was very much an anthropological "child" of Boas. The direct-line inheritance can be readily seen in her writing. As in the case of many a strong-willed offspring, however, Goldfrank arrived at her own principles of thought, analysis, and conclusion. Although the Boasian legacy remained strong, she gave her material her own distinctive flavor.

Throughout Goldfrank's career, there is an obvious self-assurance in doing what she wanted to do. Her research and publication seemingly sufficed. She followed the lead of others (Boas, Parsons, Linton, and Kardiner), but never blindly. When her data pointed to another direction, she did not hesitate to strike out on her own. She was content to study and write; she chose not to teach and turned down several invitations to join faculties. She did not feel the need to complete a doctorate, though she momentarily considered the possibility in her earlier years. Although she maintained her independence, it is clear that she valued Boas and his ideas and writing in her earlier career, as she did the work of Wittfogel in her later years.

One gets a strong impression that Goldfrank's decisions, for the most part, were her own. One suspects that, while she might not admit it, she is quite content with her life, her achievements, and the prestige accorded her by her professional colleagues. Goldfrank (1985b) recently said, "I just did what I wanted: I wrote when I wanted, I went for my research where I wanted, and I took exception where I wanted."

Her books (included at the end of this volume) constitute a substantial and useful base from which one might profitably benefit in the pursuit of any one of a number of anthropological subjects or problems. While the base provided by Boas served as a reliable anchor, it was not necessary to maintain it rigidly without modification or expansion. Goldfrank herself recognized these points; she was inclined to be tolerant of those who saw a need to make adjustments or modifications, if necessary, in this base.

In this regard, Leslie Spier's reflections on the logical legacy of Franz Boas are relevant. What Spier says about Boas is equally applicable to "daughter"/student Esther S. Goldfrank and her anthropology:

Boas left no body of dogma as a legacy. What he established, as a foundation to modern anthropology, was a series of guiding principles for action. These are expressed in concrete contributions, with little phrasing of theoretical points in extended form. Hence our survey of central elements here must stay close to the specific as he mentioned it (1959:146).

In concluding, Spier wrote,

In many ways the most fundamental of Boas' contributions was the rigor of scientific method: careful analysis, caution, and convincing demonstration . . . Fashions change in anthropology; it is always pleasant to graze in new pastures; it is far simpler to narrow to a specialty than to harass oneself with concern for the whole. Often enough we become absorbed in some minor segment, yet scientific rigor should obligate us, like Boas, to give consideration to interrelations with other aspects of culture and bodily form . . . Much of Boas' legacy is now central in the corpus of beliefs of present-day anthropology, but some elements lie neglected awaiting the day when they will be the subject of renewed appreciation.

Having never formally taught, Goldfrank has not left the great number of students that Boas did to carry on. However, she has left a significant legacy with her steadfast independence of thought in approaching problems in the field and in the library, with her enviable record in publication, and with her pervasive interest in, and encouragement of, younger colleagues. Anthropology is most certainly in her debt.

NOTES

1. Acknowledgment must be made for the tremendous assistance derived from Goldfrank's autobiographical study, *Notes on an Undirected Life: As One Anthropologist Tells It* (1978). Without her candid and valuable account, this chapter would be much more limited in perception and content.

WOMEN IN SOUTHWESTERN
LINGUISTIC STUDIES

Leanne Hinton

> I have recorded in a hospital, when the
> singer was able to sit up long enough to
> sing, and in the issue room of an agency,
> with its meat block and boxes, in the ware-
> house of a bridge company, and in the little
> store of a Northwest Coast Indian with whaling
> equipment of various sorts on the wall.
>
> *Frances Densmore*
> *(1941:532–33).*

T HE Greater Southwest has compelled and
spoken to linguists just as it has called to
archaeologists and ethnologists. At least seven
distinct language families, including Uto-Aztecan, Yuman, Athabascan, Zuni, Kiowa-Tanoan,
Keresan, and Seri, are recognized within the
Greater Southwest (Hale and Harris 1979:170).
The American Indian languages of the region are
presently the most widely spoken native languages on the continent. Due to their relative isolation and the slower pace of urbanization and development in the region, even in the face of often
violent attempts at acculturation and European
attempts to eradicate native language use, Native
American languages and cultures have remained

more vital in the Southwest than elsewhere. Anthropological linguists have worked in the region
since the 1880s. Scholars have noted that the
Uto-Aztecan language family exhibits the greatest internal diversity and the greatest time depth
of all the language families in the Greater Southwest (Hale and Harris 1979:173). The Uto-
Aztecan speakers inhabit a large portion of the
Southwest, and the language family includes

Hopi, a majority of the Piman languages (Papago,
Upper and Lower Pima and Nebome, Northern Tepehuan, and Southern Tepehuan), the extant Taracahi-
tan languages (Yaqui-Mayo or Cahitan, Tarahumara
and Guarijio), and Huichol. To this area also belong
the extinct Opata, traditionally aligned with Taraca-

hitan, and a number of other extinct languages . . . identified with Uto-Aztecan (Jova, Suma, Jumano, Concho, Zacatec, Lagunero, and Guachichil (Hale and Harris 1979:170).

Other language families of the Southwest include Hokan (specifically, the Yuman languages), Kiowa-Tanoan (Tiwa, Tewa, Towa), Keresan, and Athabascan (Apachean and Navajo). Interspersed are language isolates such as Zuni.

The great number of distinctive language speakers living in close proximity, their prehistoric and historic intermingling, and the continued vitality and diversity of southwestern languages have made the Greater Southwest particularly attractive for linguistic study. From the time that the first word lists were collected by military and scientific personnel on the instructions of John Wesley Powell and Spencer Baird of the Smithsonian Institution, many professional and amateur linguists have studied southwestern languages for both practical and theoretical purposes, creating grammars and translation aids. Practical motivations for linguistic study have included the need to understand and interact with other peoples and, later on, for the Native Americans themselves to write or revive their languages. On a theoretical level has been the desire to understand how languages are constituted, how languages work, how language affects culture and culture affects language, and how the use of language can help us understand the prehistoric past as well as the present.

In addition to being a topic of independent research, linguistics enters into all aspects of ethnographic work. One must understand and communicate with a people to learn about the affective aspects of a culture, which include music, story, and song—areas in which the American Indian communities of the Greater Southwest have proved to be remarkably rich. Because of the close-knit relationship between music and language, not to mention the tie between ceremonial and other aspects of culture, much musical work has had implications for both linguistics and eth-

nomusicology. In fact, we might say all linguistic work has ethnological implications. Most of the ethnologists who are mentioned in this book have added to our linguistic knowledge; only a few, however, have produced work primarily linguistic in intent or have made extraordinary efforts to understand communication in the Greater Southwest. Their efforts deserve note.

I will take a slightly different approach from that taken by other volume authors. I will look briefly at how southwestern linguistics has been accomplished in the past and the place of women in this history, identifying some key individuals and indicating some of the areas in which men and women have worked. In adition to providing a historical record, this survey will set the stage for the more in-depth analysis of one linguistic pseudo-lineage, the women who have worked with Yuman speakers in both the Greater Southwest and California since 1945 and largely after 1960.

PIONEERS IN THE COLLECTION OF LINGUISTIC DATA FROM SOUTHWESTERN LANGUAGES

Linguistic studies in the Southwest mirror the development of linguistics in anthropology in much the same way as Clyde Kluckhohn has noted that anthropology is a "mirror for man" and as Keith Basso (1979:14) has noted that for ethnology "the history of research in the Southwest has been—and still is—a mirror of American anthropology." And this mirroring effect is also true of the gender divisions in the field. Women throughout the history of anthropology in the Southwest have accounted for about one-third of the individuals who have worked on language. This is approximately the same percentage that we see for sociocultural anthropologists. There is some variation by culture: for Navajo about 45% of linguists are women; for Tanoan and Uto-Aztecan approximately 35%; for Keresan only 25%; and for Yuman over 60%. There is also variation by time and research topic.

It quickly became evident to the first anthropologists in the United States that linguistic fieldwork, like ethnographic fieldwork, was sorely needed. The driving force behind the early collection of linguistic data was the desire to bring the bewildering array of distinct languages spoken by the peoples met by explorers, the military, government officials, traders, and settlers under some sort of conceptual control and ultimately colonial control. The overwhelming concern that Native American groups were undergoing such rapid change that their rich languages and cultural traditions were disappearing also compelled scholars to begin the process of cross-cultural communicative understanding. This process required more than simply identifying words and their equivalents in English and Spanish. Thus, the fieldwork was eminently feasible as more than simply a salvage operation. Marianne Mithun (1990:310) contends,

Good linguistic work in such settings has seldom been limited to the elicitations of grammatical paradigms or sentences. The rich but often fragile cultural settings of North American Indian languages have prompted a tradition of collecting texts of all kinds: religious or political oratory; legends; historical accounts; reminiscences; children's stories; descriptions of ceremonies such as naming, marriage, burial, selection and installation of leaders, etc.; various aspects of daily life, such as hunting, fishing, cooking, medicine, basketmaking, games, songs, etc., and now, with the availability of tape recorders, conversations as well. Such documentation has been valuable in itself, in many cases providing the only descriptions in the speakers' own words of earlier events and customs that are fading from memory.

Beginning with Otis T. Mason's work on synonymy around 1873, John Wesley Powell eventually involved his entire staff at the Bureau of American Ethnology (BAE) in the 1880s in developing a linguistic classification of North American indigenous groups (Hinsley 1981: 156). He intended to obtain a basic ethnographic description and word list for every group on the

continent. His concern was with discovering the historic relationships of people as evidenced in their languages, relating contemporary and prehistoric groups, and attempting to bring a bewildering array of information under control in a natural science paradigm. Curtis Hinsley (1981: 151) notes that as director of the BAE and the U.S. Geological Survey, Powell "vigorously pursue[d] the search for historical connection and the mapping of aboriginal America as aids to informed policy. This more than any other single purpose was the focus of BAE activities until the publication of the Powell linguistic map and classification of 1891"—a tour de force of taxonomic anthropology. Hinsley (1981:158) points out:

The linguistic map and classification of 1891, which fulfilled a vision shared by [Thomas] Jefferson, [Albert] Gallatin, and [George] Gibbs, proved to be the single most lasting and influential contribution of the early Bureau to American anthropology. From the beginning, linguistics was the heart of Powell's "New Ethnology," his clearest window into the mind of primitive man . . . Gibbs . . . envisioned a continental map and took important steps in that direction of collecting hundreds of vocabularies.

This flurry of activity in classifying the North American languages resulted in several early publications including the *Dictionary of Indian Tribes, Dictionary of Tribal Synonymy, Tribal Synonymy of the American Indians,* and *Cyclopedia of the American Indians* (see Hinsley 1981:157).

Several exploratory expeditions to the Southwest between the early 1880s and the turn of the century concentrated on the collection of ethnographic materials and archaeological remains for museums and private collectors (see the chapter by Parezo and Hardin in this volume). Anthropologists such as Colonel James and Matilda Coxe Stevenson, Frank Hamilton Cushing, and Jessie Walter Fewkes were sent into the field for this purpose. While collecting material objects or information on kinship relationships they also noted native terms, along with creation myths, songs, and folktales.

As early as the 1880s Matilda Coxe Stevenson was recording Zuni mythology, ceremonies, and everyday activities in the native language as well as through a native interpreter/translator. She used native terminology throughout her 1904 BAE publication *The Zuni Indians* both for material objects and for describing ceremonies and esoteric fraternities, a practice also visible in her other works. Though she dealt with linguistic data, her work cannot be considered linguistic in orientation because she made no attempt to understand the structure or semantics of the language. Nevertheless, a pioneer in the true sense of the word, Stevenson was one of the first individuals to compile a Zuni word list and to be concerned with problems of accurate translation and the use of words and concepts to understand the Zuni worldview. (She was also the first to do the same for the Havasupai, as a result of a visit by a Havasupai to Zuni country.) This unpublished work was compiled in 1885 while she accompanied her husband on a U.S. Geological Survey/BAE expedition in Arizona. The manuscripts and word lists today reside in the Smithsonian Institution.

Scholars also undertook other linguistic efforts before World War I. One of the earliest attempts at recording stories, myths, and folktales was that of Jessie Walter Fewkes and his colleague Benjamin Ives Gilman on the Hemenway Expedition. They used wax cylinders for the first time at Zuni in 1890 and again at Hopi in 1891, thereby leaving us a rich data source that has been used by many linguists and ethnomusicologists.

Since the study of song necessarily includes the study of song texts, ethnomusicologists have also contributed to the study of southwestern languages. The most famous ethnomusicologist to focus on the Southwest during that period was Frances Densmore. Born into a musical family, she learned to play the piano and studied harmony at an early age, a common practice for Victorian girls. Unlike most adolescents, however, Densmore also heard American Indian music at a Sioux encampment near her home in Minnesota (Frisbie 1988:51). With the encouragement of her mother and, later, Alice Fletcher, she completed her classical training and then turned to an in-depth study of Native American music. Charlotte Frisbie (1988:52) writes,

The year 1901 brought Densmore's first publication, her first visit to the Chippewa of Ontario, and her first transcription of a Sioux song. Accompanied by her sister, Margaret, she embarked on her first field trip in 1905, transcribing, by ear, songs of the Chippewa of Grand Portage and witnessing singing and dancing at the White Lodge Reservation, Minnesota. In May 1907, using a borrowed phonograph, she recorded Indian songs for the first time at White Earth. When she submitted the results to William H. Holmes, then chief of the Bureau of American Ethnology (BAE) of the Smithsonian Institution, he responded with enthusiasm and allotted her $150 for recording Indian songs (Densmore 1942). After purchasing a small Edison phonograph, Densmore returned to the Chippewa agency at Onigum. Later that year, with more funds she worked at White Earth. In 1908 the BAE provided her with a Columbia graphophone, a machine designed to meet demands of home recording. Later Densmore experimented with other recording devices as these were developed, however, this machine, with its galvanized iron horn, remained her favorite through 1940.

Densmore thus had musical training but no linguistic or anthropological training. Nevertheless, her contribution has been extensive; cross-cultural and literal, as a corpus of work it was eventually designed to be comparative in nature. She worked in the mode of salvage ethnography, hoping others would later analyze the over-1,000 hours of recordings she made. She collected raw data with basic musical transcriptions from most Native American culture areas. Her later work concentrated on the lyrics or the linguistic aspects of songs among a large number of southwestern indigenous groups including the Tohono O'Odham, Yuman, Yaqui, Cocopa, Acoma, Isleta, Cochiti, and Zuni (Babcock and Parezo 1988: 91). The most prolific writer on American Indian music, she wrote more than 125 articles and books that contain information on the Southwest. A modern scholar notes, "*Music of Santo Domingo* is one of Densmore's finest works and she supplies more cultural and ethnological information than is usually the case" (Roberts 1972: 247). Although some present-day ethnomusicologists criticize Densmore's work for its lack of theoretical considerations and her use of the Western twelve-tone scale and reject her statistical approach, she is recognized

as a pioneer whose attempts at comprehensive collecting spanned numerous developments in the recording industry, and whose preservationist goals, interest in the relationship between music and the rest of life, and prolific documentation of written, visual, and aural forms established a solid baseline for studies of stability and change in American Indian music (Frisbie 1988:56).

Another early ethnomusicologist/linguist was Natalie Curtis Burlin. She began her career as a musician, training in Europe. On a trip to the Southwest in 1900, she became

suddenly so deeply interested in the customs and lore and especially the music of the Indians of the region that she gave up her planned concert career. With the phonograph and later simply with pencil and paper she visited the villages and camps of the Zuni, Hopi, and other tribes and recorded their songs, poetry, and tales (McHenry 1980:58).

Like Densmore, Natalie Curtis Burlin was interested not in theoretical or interpretive studies but rather in presenting transcribed melodies in a popular format. Burlin died unexpectedly in Paris on October 23, 1921, at the age of 46, after being struck by a car. Because of her untimely death, her contributions to ethnomusicology and folklore are not as widely recognized as Densmore's. Nevertheless, her most famous work, *The Indians' Book* (Curtis 1907), as noted by Paul Burlin in a foreword to the second edition in 1923, was "widely received both here and abroad. It had instant recognition not only for the amazing accu-

racy of the musical transcriptions, but for the revelation of the Indians' aesthetic genius." And, importantly, she used her ethnomusicological, cultural, and linguistic information to help prove to a disbelieving U.S. government that southwestern Native Americans had a complex religion with deeply held beliefs and complex rituals. Through her activism and that of other reformers, laws prohibiting the practice of Native American religions were rescinded. This was the beginning of a long and fruitful relationship between linguists and Native Americans to undertake projects of benefit to the peoples themselves.

THE SECOND GENERATION: LINGUISTIC CLASSIFICATION

The work of the pioneering women previously described marks the beginning of a rich corpus of linguistic information compiled by several anthropologists who have worked to create a better understanding of the linguistic and musical diversity of the Southwest. The second generation of anthropological linguists worked on more specific problems of classification, especially in the area of kinship terminology, such as Alfred Kroeber did in his analysis of Zuni. One such individual was Barbara Freire-Marreco Aitken. After graduating from Oxford, England, Aitken went to the Southwest on a Somerville Research Scholarship. In the summer of 1910, while at the University of New Mexico's Frijoles Canyon field school in New Mexico, she was introduced to Santa Clara Pueblo by Edgar Lee Hewett. She spent the next three years collecting linguistic data at Santa Clara, at Hano (a Hopi-Tewa village in Arizona), and, briefly, among the Yavapai in Arizona. In Santa Clara, in particular, she was respected for her linguistic knowledge. In his introduction to "A Trance Experience" by Aitken (1956), anthropologist Edward P. Dozier, a native of Santa Clara, made the following comments concerning her descriptions of two accounts of differing medical practices used by the Tewa:

Although the account was related to Mrs. Aitken in English, it is remarkably close to the native idiom. Mrs. Aitken lived for extensive periods between 1910 and 1913 with the Tewa of Arizona on First Mesa and with the Tewa of New Mexico in Santa Clara Pueblo. Old residents in these two villages remember her with warm affection and speak with awe about the remarkable knowledge of the Tewa language and native customs.

Her linguistic and ethnographic data have been used by such varied individuals as John P. Harrington, Elsie Clews Parsons, Fred Eggan, Leslie White, Robin Fox, and others interested in accurate and detailed description and analysis.

Building on the work of the earlier anthropological linguists, a new system of analysis replaced the Powellian system by 1918. Mithun (1990:310) writes, "Linguistic typology and American Indian languages have long enjoyed a special relationship . . . The work of Boas, Sapir, Bloomfield, and others assured the role of North American languages in the development of linguistic theory in this century, a role that continues." A major focus of students who belonged to the Boasian-Sapir schools was on determining the cultural origins of groups such as the Navajo (Sapir 1936) and Uto-Aztecan speakers (Whorf 1935). Work in the Southwest, crucial to these studies, was built from a corpus of data that described the grammar, syntax, and words of various languages. Music was also subject to analysis: Helen H. Roberts, known also for her work with Clark Wissler and her study of Apache baskets, produced the first classification of Native American music (1936). She also produced an analysis of the music of the eastern Pueblos (Harrington and Roberts 1928; Roberts 1923). A fitting tribute to Roberts and her work has been written by Charlotte Frisbie (1986), a noted ethnomusicologist herself.

Other anthropological linguists were more culturally specific, working on classifying and understanding the language within an individual cultural framework and producing a number of grammars and grammatical sketches. For example, both Ruth Benedict and Ruth Bunzel worked extensively with Zuni linguistics. Bunzel published a grammar of Zuni that is still a definitive work, and several works on Zuni ethnopoetics (see Hardin's chapter in this volume). Benedict concentrated on developing a dictionary based on mythological and religious information (see Babcock's chapter in this volume). She also worked extensively on Cochiti. A biographer notes, "Together with Edward Sapir, she considered questions about the relationship between and among personality, art, language, and culture" (Briscoe 1979:446). Much theoretical work between the two world wars demonstrated how language, thought, and culture were combined. Southwestern languages were crucial to this work, as can be seen in Edward Sapir's *Time Perspective in Aboriginal American Culture.*

A great deal of the methodological underpinning of descriptive linguistics was worked out in the Southwest during this period. Much work was done under the auspices of the American Council of Learned Societies (ACLS) Committee on Research on American Native Languages, especially on Uto-Aztecan and Athabascan languages (Stocking 1976:27). Following the Boasian lead, this research was combined with culture history to fill in gaps in our knowledge. Folklore studies emphasizing divergence from a common source or convergence from diverse sources were in their heyday. In the interwar years, the focus on unwritten languages was coupled with an insistence on learning, analyzing, and understanding each language in terms of its own internal categories. Thus, each ethnographer produced a descriptive grammar.

Abraham Halpern, for example, was sent by Alfred Kroeber to construct the first Quechan grammar. As part of a Works Progress Administration (WPA) project, he worked with Sapir and completed his grammar before World War II. (Interestingly, very few women worked on WPA linguistic projects.) This early work on Quechan was unusual, however, for the Yuman languages were generally considered uninteresting when compared to Puebloan languages. Moreover, Hokan, the linguistic stock that includes Yuman languages, has always been problematic. When classification was a central concern, Hokan was often left to last because its nature was difficult to grasp.

The study of Athabascan languages continued at the same time. Following the pioneering investigations by Washington Matthews in the 1880s and the Franciscan Fathers in the early 1900s, Father Berard Haile, Edward Sapir, Harry Hoijer, Morris Opler, and Gladys Reichard applied vigorous scientific methods for an intensive look at Navajo and Apache languages in the 1920s and 1930s (Lyon 1989:137). Reichard, who had also conducted linguistic fieldwork with the Wiyot and Coeur d'Alene, dedicated 30 years to recording Navajo language and grammar, religion, social organization, and aesthetics (Babcock and Parezo 1988:47). Pliny Goddard is credited with having first interested Reichard in the Navajo and in linguistics (Goldfrank 1956:53), but Reichard had already completed her dissertation in linguistics under Boas before she and Goddard went to the Southwest (see Lamphere's chapter in this volume). In addition, she was the chair of the linguistics department as well as the anthropology department at Barnard College. Reichard wrote that to "investigate some of the inner meanings of Navaho religion" she felt that it was necessary to know the language, so she lived with a Navajo family for approximately three years between 1930 and 1934 (Reichard 1951:v). As a result, Reichard was one of the few anthropologists to speak Navajo fluently. After completing her linguistic training she decided to repay her intellectual and social debt to the Navajo by helping them develop a written orthography. She then taught adult Navajo interpreters to write in the Navajo Hogan School, which she organized for the BIA in 1934. The importance of this project was mentioned by D'Arcy McNickle (1979) in

his essay, "Anthropology and the Indian Reorganization Act." Unfortunately, while he mentions the roles of Father Haile, John P. Harrington, and Oliver LaFarge in the project, he fails to mention either Reichard's crucial role in developing an acceptable alphabet and grammar or her educational activities.

Reichard's linguistic work was not without its detractors, as was her ethnography; *Navaho Grammar* (1951) became controversial because she never accepted the system for Navajo transcription devised by Sapir and Hoijer. Nevertheless, she wrote (1951:iv–v) that she was

deeply obligated to the late Edward Sapir who gave unsparingly of his time when I was first studying Navaho. The fact that I have come to different conclusions from his has no relation to his kindness and generosity. Harry Hoijer, and others of Sapir's students at the University of Chicago, also helped greatly with their notes and discussions.

The issues over phonemicization, orthography, the vowel system, and semantic classification still plague Navajo linguistics. In the end, all these works greatly informed Young and Morgan's classic dictionary (1943).

THE BROADENING OF LINGUISTIC STUDIES

Only a handful of scholars were involved in linguistics when World War II began. Among these were students steeped in a Boasian approach. By 1946, because of the war effort, there was an explosion of linguistic work by men. However, as in other social sciences, few women earned their doctorates in anthropology during the 1950s. But an explosion of women entered the field beginning in the 1960s. While linguists continued their traditional research, women expanded into other useful activities, such as bilingual education, the formation of tribal orthographies, and the teaching of English as a second language, as will be shown in a case study below. Linguistics began to be divorced from anthropology, a process demonstrated by the development of separate departments of linguistics. And it is here that women and Native American scholars entered the arena. In recent decades several American Indian communities have become interested in the various issues of bilingual education and writing. This interest has given linguists the opportunity to work with many of these communities, developing writing systems and school curricula and training native-speaking educational personnel in relevant techniques of linguistic analysis.

Studies of grammatical structuring, semantics, oral literature, ethnomusicology, and worldview have dominated southwestern linguistics since the 1960s. Many new ethnographies contain important linguistic data (see Basso 1973). Ethnomusicology and ethnopoetics have been especially rich fields. For example, Basso (1973:245) observes,

Naomi Ware (1970) discusses survival and change in Pima Indian music, and Gertrude Kurath (1969) provides what is easily the most thorough and exhaustive analysis yet to appear of Tewa chants and ceremonial dances . . . It was intriguing to discover how economically some of Kurath's choreographic data could be generalized and restated in the form of order rules similar to those employed by transformational linguistics.

Kurath has done much to improve our understanding of music and dance as communication, especially in ritual contexts. Dance is conceptualized as a nonverbal code that needs a sophisticated metalanguage that can be conveyed in a kinetic notational system for cross-cultural understanding. Kurath, trained in formal dance, was the first scholar to bring such a structure to the study of southwestern dance and music. And, interestingly, she provided this framework through collaborative efforts with native speakers, musicians, and dancers, foreshadowing current linguistic collaborations. These collaborative efforts have been very important, as Kenneth Hale (1972:87) noted several years ago:

The future of American Indian linguistics (i.e. the extent to which it will advance significantly) will de-

pend critically on how successful an effort there is to engage American Indians in the active study of their own languages—not as informants as in the past, but as linguists, lexicographers, creative writers, and the like.

Ethnoscience and ethnolinguistic research have also been prominent, as evidenced by the work of Jane and Kenneth Hill (1970) and George and Felicia Trager (Trager 1971; Trager and Trager 1970). William Leap, Jack Frisch, Dennis Tedlock, Barbara Tedlock, Keith Basso, Gary Witherspoon, Norma Perchonok, and Oswald Werner (Perchonok and Werner 1969) likewise have been interested in cultural classification and lexical domains. The study of southwestern linguistics has broadened to include the total range of linguistic knowledge and anything that enables speakers to understand and create novel sentences belonging to that language. Many women have helped in this effort to broaden the field.

RECENT DEVELOPMENTS IN LINGUISTIC STUDIES

Since the development of transformational grammar and its descendants in the late 1950s, linguistic studies have become partially divided into descriptive and theoretical linguistics. Descriptive linguistics is the study and description of individual languages, and theoretical linguistics is the study of the nature of language in general. People who study American Indian languages tend to conduct descriptive studies, but their descriptions provide the fodder for linguistic theory. There have also been a large number of southwestern linguists who have refused to limit themselves to one or the other but have done both with great success. In the post-transformational struggle to control linguistics, this constructive combination has not always been easy.

Linguistics since 1960 has had a relatively large proportion of women. During this period, many women entered the field of southwestern linguistics, whereas before 1960, relatively few women were doing research in that field who were

TABLE 2. Number of women entering the field of southwestern linguistics, by time period

Date of First Publication	Number of Women
Pre-1960	
1901–10	1
1911–20	2
1921–30	3
1931–40	5
1941–50	3
1951–60	6
Total before 1960	20
Post-1960	
1961–70	15
1971–80	8
1981–82[1]	2
Total after 1960	25

1. This research period was halted at 1982, not 1990.

TABLE 3. Number of scholars studying southwestern language families

	Scholars	Women	Women as % of Scholars
Athabascan	45	18	40%
Keresan	4	1	25%
Tanoan	7	3	43%
Uto-Aztecan	53	17	32%
Yuman	13	8	62%

not primarily ethnographers, folklorists, or ethnomusicologists (see Table 2). Parezo and Babcock (1988) list 20 women who claimed linguistics as one of their specialties and whose first publication was dated between 1906 and 1961. Starting in 1963, we find a great influx of women, adding up to 25 in the 19 years between 1963 and 1982 (as opposed to the previous 18 in a span of 55 years). The decade of 1961–1970 stands out as the most dramatic time: 15 of the 25 female linguists started work in that decade (8 in 1969 and 1970 alone). There appears to be a decline thereafter; this is probably due not to a decline in women's representation in the field, but to a general trend away from American Indian linguistic studies, based on the changing foci of interest within linguistics.

It is interesting to note that among the women who started their work after 1960, the majority have focused on linguistics as their major specialty rather than simply as a minor or ancillary subspecialty. This is due in part to the history of the field of linguistics itself: few departments existed separately from anthropology departments until after World War II. This separation derived partly from the interest that developed during the war in exotic languages, especially Asian languages, which became very important to the United States for the first time. But it must not be forgotten that one southwestern American Indian language played a crucial role in World War II, since Navajo was used effectively as a code language by the United States Marine Corps in the South Pacific.

One of the best ways of looking at the present representation by women in the field is to look at the membership directory of the Society for the Study of Indigenous Languages of the Americas (SSILA). Out of 85 scholars who list themselves as specializing in languages of (or bordering on) the Southwest, 32 are women—a little under 40%. The proportion of male to female scholars, however, varies a good deal by language family. The language families of the Southwest are shown in Table 3. (The figures include scholars who specialize in languages within the family that are outside the Southwest).

WOMEN SCHOLARS OF THE YUMAN
LANGUAGES: A CASE STUDY

For most language families, the proportion of women scholars hovers at or below 40%. But Yuman languages stand out as having an unusually large representation of female scholars. Because of this predominance, the importance of the role of women in southwestern linguistics since the

TABLE 4. First publication date of scholars working on yuman languages

Year	Publications by Women	Publications by Men
1876	—	1
1885	—	1
1900	—	1
1908	—	1
1910	—	1
1911	—	1
1924	—	1
1928	—	1
1931	—	1
1942	—	1
1949	—	2
1951	—	1
1957	—	2
1958	—	1
1963	—	1
1964	1	—
1965	—	1
1966	1	1
1967	1	1
1968	2	2
1970	—	1
1971	—	1
1972	3	1
1973	1	3
1974	1	—
1975	3	—
1976	1	—
1977	3	—
1978	2	1
1979	2	—
1980	—	—

almost 90 years later; the 17 linguists who first published between 1876 and 1963 were men. But since 1964, 21 women have published on Yuman languages, compared to 12 men working in the same time period. This table, of course, does not take unpublished works into account. There were, for example, many word lists of Yuman languages collected under the auspices of the BAE in the nineteenth century. One of these, the first Havasupai word list ever collected, was done in 1885 by Matilda Coxe Stevenson, as mentioned earlier.

Again utilizing data complied by Bright (1982), women generally have tended to publish more on Yuman linguistics than have men. The 21 women and 29 men represented in the sample have published 103 and 104 works respectively—a mean of 5 per female author and 3 per male author. This productivity differential is due, in part, to historical periodicity; male linguists publishing in 1960 were very productive overall but did not specialize in Yuman linguistics. The reason for this is simple; Yuman peoples and linguistics were considered peripheral to southwestern problems and linguistics in general, due to their isolation. Topics or groups seen to be peripheral tend to have later starting dates for their concentration. The result was an intellectual vacuum for Yuman studies that women quickly filled.

The beginning of Yuman linguistic specialization, therefore, significantly coincided with the major entry of women into the field. As a result, we see a different pattern by controlling for time of publication; the 12 male authors who started work since 1960 have published less on Yuman languages than have the female authors. Several factors account for this difference. One is that more women than men have chosen Yuman languages as their major areas of specialization, and more men than women have made only brief incursions into the Yuman area while their major foci have been in other areas. Thus, the work of men has tended to be comparative—Yuman is

1960s can be illustrated through an analysis of the careers of scholars of the Yuman languages. And this case study will illustrate another point: the late entry of women into linguistic field studies. Table 4 provides the first publication date by scholars who have published on Yuman linguistics (as noted in Bright 1982). Although publications on Yuman languages began as early as 1876, no women appear as authors until 1964, like or not like other linguistic groups; that of women has been more analytic within a single language or comparative within the language family. This finding is, of course, related to the introduction of "the new ethnography" during the period and the realization that one can spend a lifetime in one culture and on one language before mining all that there is to be found and understood. On the whole, therefore, the publication statistics point out not that women are more productive than men, but rather that women have had narrower and more concentrated fields of specialization than have men.

Like the famous cohort of female ethnographers at Columbia University in the 1920s and 1930s, most of the Yuman language specialists have come from the University of California or Indiana University, the institutions that have trained the majority of linguists working on American Indian languages in the decades since 1960. Of the people who have written Ph.D. dissertations on Yuman languages, five were trained by Carl Voegelin at Indiana University, three by Mary Haas at the University of California at Berkeley, five by Margaret Langdon at the University of California at San Diego, two by Pamela Munro and one by William Bright at the University of California at Los Angeles, and one by myself at the University of California at Berkeley. Only one Ph.D. was from elsewhere: the University of Texas at Austin. This concentration in a few selected graduate schools has led to an almost familial relationship among Yuman linguists. This concept is reinforced if we think of the growth of a discipline as a whole and specialty areas within it as occurring in family trees. The strong branches are filled by mentors who provide the points of access to graduate students, legitimacy to emerging scholars, and visibility to senior scholars. The more the number of graduate student limbs, the stronger the mentoring scholar's branch. (This pattern was mentioned in the Introduction and reinforced in Lamphere's chapter on Reichard in this volume.)

One point which is notable about the Yuman family tree is the tendency of women to be trained by women. The sample is, of course, quite small, but three male dissertation advisors/mentors directed a total of two women and four men, while four female dissertation advisors/mentors directed a total of eight women and four men. Or, approaching this from the standpoint of the student, of the ten women who have written dissertations on Yuman languages, eight were trained by women. This is a somewhat stronger tendency than for the male students, where four out of eight were trained by women. This points out an important principle in the development of scholarship among women: as women become prominent in a field, they tend to attract and encourage the entry of other women. Unfortunately, male students tend not to work under female mentors, often feeling that women do not have the power necessary to propel them on their careers. In this, linguistics is similar to the other sciences. Thus, it is apparent that gender is a crucial factor in the transmission of knowledge. One reason for the dominance of women in Yuman linguistic studies has been the presence of a few strong female teachers/mentors who have attracted female students to the field.

The First Generation: Mary Haas

Mary Haas, one of the leading linguists of her era, was clearly the founder of female Yuman scholarship, even though she never published on Yuman languages herself. Haas considered herself the intellectual daughter of Edward Sapir. She received her Ph.D. from Yale University, under his tutelage, in 1935—during an era when very few women were receiving advanced degrees. Haas was then held back in her career by the Great Depression, as were almost all anthropologists, especially women. For approximately ten years after her graduation, there were no linguistics positions available in any university, nor for the first five years were there applied or governmental jobs such as those that a few archaeologists or cultural anthropologists were lucky enough to obtain. Instead, like Bunzel, Haas earned her living working on research grants and was as a result tremendously productive (Eggan 1986). She devoted herself to fieldwork in the Southeast, working on Natchez, Creek, Koasati, and other languages. This work was funded by Boas' Committee on Native American Languages. Though enduring a financially bleak period, Haas did establish her reputation and was able to attend the 1936 Linguistic Institute in Ann Arbor, Michigan, a landmark institute that enabled her, along with Zellig Harris, George Trager, C. F. Hockett, Kenneth Pike, Morris Swadesh, Norman McQuown, Carl Voegelin, and Harry Hoijer, to train in applied linguistics (Cowan 1979). (Note the lack of other female participants.) While using American Indian languages, the institute concentrated on methodology.

During World War II, Haas was appointed as the first fellow in the Intensive Language Program of the ACLS. The war brought a sudden imperative need for research and improvement in language instruction for the Asian languages, to assist the troops in the Pacific theater. At that time there was not a single trained individual in the United States who could teach any oriental language, except for the written Chinese and Japanese languages. The War Department quickly recognized the imperative of a conversational approach to the teaching not only of Japanese and Chinese but also Thai and Vietnamese. They turned to anthropologically trained linguists who had worked with unwritten American Indian languages. Haas went first to Washington, D.C., and then to the University of Michigan, where she worked with native Thai speakers to develop methodologies, protocols, teaching materials, and instructional techniques. She then conducted a successful pilot project at Ann Arbor, teaching Thai conversation to army intelligence and communication personnel. Mortimer Graves, executive secretary of the ACLS,

provided fees for the Thai students who participated and who were known as informants (following the then current anthropological practice; we all lived to regret that term). When [Haas] was well along with the analysis, [Graves] asked her to run a class in which the students would work directly with Mary, observing her analytic techniques, learning what Thai they could in the process but also learning how to analyze a language. Meanwhile, she converted what knowledge she had gained into teaching materials to be used in class. This was the genesis of the "linguistic method" of language teaching, later known as the "Army method" (Cowan 1979:160).

A. L. Kroeber at the University of California at Berkeley called for the development of a similar teaching program in Asian languages on the West Coast. Soon Haas was sent to Berkeley along with another linguist, Murray Emeneau, to help develop the Army Specialized Training Program. Haas trained native speakers of several Asian languages to serve as conversation instructors in conversation, while she concentrated on lectures about grammar, semantics, and phonology. The program was successful.

After the war, when the Department of Oriental Languages at Berkeley initiated courses on Thai and Vietnamese, both Haas and Emeneau joined the department. Here they continued their instruction and research. Soon thereafter, Emeneau was instrumental in obtaining funding for a study of California Indian languages, which was designed to follow Kroeber's and his students' earlier work on grammar. The Survey for the Study of California and Other Indian Languages was formed with Mary Haas as director. Six months later, the Department of Linguistics was founded, lending permanence to the Survey. Haas served as chair of the department for many years, the first woman to become chair of a linguistics department in the country.

When the Survey was first established, scholars from all over the country were brought in to work with native speakers both on their reservations and on campus. Because much progress was made, Haas soon grew to feel that the Survey provided an excellent pedagogical and methodological training ground, and she shifted the emphasis of the program to graduate training. She sent students out of the classroom to obtain actual field experience throughout California and Arizona. Although many worked on grammar, they studied all aspects of language. (This approach has since been used by Oswald Werner for his Navajo linguistic field school.) Under her direction, close to 50 dissertations were written on California and southwestern American Indian languages. Three of these dealt with Yuman languages: Margaret Langdon on Diegueño, James Crawford on Cocopa, and Mauricio Mixco on Kiliwa.

When Haas retired in the late 1970s, she had a worldwide reputation as one of the leading scholars in linguistics. Even though she never conducted research in the Southwest, she trained a cadre of scholars who today specialize in southwestern languages. These individuals in turn have trained students to work in the Greater Southwest. And it was Haas' student Margaret Langdon who went on to become the leading scholar in Yuman linguistics. Thus, if Haas is the trunk of our family tree for linguistics, Langdon is the main branch.

The Second Generation: Margaret Langdon

Margaret Storm was born in Belgium in 1926 and lived there through the chaos of World War II. Immigrating to the United States in 1947, she went to Berkeley, California, in the 1950s, where she found a secretarial position at the University of California. Soon, desiring more intellectually stimulating work, she decided to return to school. Influenced by the work of Edward Sapir, she decided to major in linguistics. Haas admitted her into the linguistics department in 1958; in rapid succession she earned her B.A., M.A., and Ph.D. Haas assigned her to work on Diegueño, a Yuman language of southern California. (Assignment by

a mentor of the initial language to be studied by a new scholar is quite common in linguistics.) Storm began fieldwork in 1963 with Ted Cuoro (her main linguistic consultant) through the assistance of another female anthropologist, Florence Shipeck, an archaeologist and applied ethnologist who had trained at the University of Arizona and taught at the University of Wisconsin and had conducted a number of ethnohistoric studies on Yuman peoples. On Storm's second field trip to southern California, she met Richard Langdon; they were married in July 1964.

While working on her dissertation, Margaret Langdon was offered a position in the newly formed Department of Linguistics at the University of California at San Diego (UCSD). She started teaching there in the fall of 1965 and finished her dissertation in 1966. Throughout her career Langdon has dedicated her research primarily to Yuman languages. She has been the major influence in Yuman studies through her own research, her direction of five dissertations on Yuman subjects, her establishment of an archive of Yuman languages (which has served the needs of many scholars), and her development of a yearly conference on Hokan languages, in which the Yuman element has always been dominant.

The First Hokan Conference took place under Langdon's direction at UCSD in 1970. As a yearly endeavor it was extremely successful. Because of its growing size, Langdon felt the need to establish a smaller and more focused institute that would concentrate specifically on Yuman issues. Thus, in 1975 she organized and sponsored the First Yuman Languages Workshop, also at UCSD. Since then the workshops have been held annually at different universities and organized by a variety of scholars. The emphasis of the workshops has varied depending on critical problems in the field; sometimes billed as Yuman, sometimes Hokan or Hokan and Penutian, the workshops on occasion have been even more broadly based to include every large grouping of American Indian languages in order to contextualize Hokan and Yuman problems. The strength of Yuman studies has always been clear at these workshops regardless of the yearly emphasis: papers on Yuman studies always far outnumber papers on any other language group. This centrality is in very large part due to Langdon's charismatic teaching, empirical and theoretical advances, and strong encouragement of scholarship in the field.

Langdon has also had a strong influence as a result of a more recent project, the Comparative Yuman Dictionary. In this multifaceted and multiyear project, Langdon is the coordinator of the other investigators, who have gathered published and unpublished materials on all Yuman languages. The final dictionary will be the most comprehensive comparative lexical project ever completed on an American Indian language family.

Beyond these organizational and networking projects, which have been so important in encouraging others in their pursuit of Yuman linguistic studies, Langdon has been the most prolific author on Yuman languages. Her research has had three main thrusts: (1) comparative work in Yuman and between Yuman and other languages (e.g., Hinton and Langdon 1979; Langdon 1974, 1975a, 1975b, 1976a, 1976b, 1977a, 1977b, 1977c, 1977d, 1979; Langdon and Munro 1979); (2) major descriptive studies of Diegueño (e.g., Hinton and Langdon 1979; Langdon 1970, 1976c) and Quechan and Cocopa (Langdon 1977b, 1978; Langdon and Munro 1980); and (3) Diegueño language preservation and language renewal (Couro and Langdon n.d.). She is as highly respected by the Diegueño community as by the academic linguistic and ethnological community. She envisions her work and her participation in Diegueño life as applied, relevant to community needs, and collaborative. Her linguistic work is designed to be of and for the people as much as of and for her linguistic colleagues. And she has passed on this perspective. Of Langdon's five stu-

dents who wrote dissertations on Yuman languages, two (Pamela Munro and Leanne Hinton) have themselves gone on to direct other graduate students on Yuman languages and insist that they work intimately and collaboratively with native peoples.

The Second Generation: Pamela Munro

Born in Niagara Falls, New York, in 1947, Pamela Munro attended Stanford University before pursuing graduate work in linguistics at the University of California at San Diego. Luckily she was assigned to Margaret Langdon as a graduate research assistant upon her arrival. Their close association sparked the development of her interest in Yuman languages and gave her the firsthand training needed by all scientists to succeed. She was also exposed to Uto-Aztecan languages when she took a field methods course in Luiseño. Interested in language contact and convergence, she went to the field in 1971 to study Chemehuevi (a Uto-Aztecan language) and Mojave (a Yuman language). These two groups live along the Colorado River in Arizona and have begun to intermarry as well as trade. During this research she found herself increasingly drawn to interesting problems in Mojave syntax, which became the topic of her dissertation.

Rather than focusing exclusively on Mojave and other Yuman languages, Munro has always been interested in the many different language families found both within and outside the Southwest. Besides her major specializations in Yuman and Uto-Aztecan, since 1977 she has been working with Muskogean speakers. Despite these wide-ranging interests, her publication record on Yuman languages ranks second only to Langdon's. Her major focus in Yuman studies has been topics in Yuman and Mojave morphology and syntax (for example, see Munro 1973, 1976a, 1976b, 1976c, 1980a, 1980b, 1981c, 1982; Munro and Haiman 1983). A great deal of her work has been comparative in nature as well (Munro 1973b, 1981a, 1981b). And like Langdon, she has been sensitive to the impact of her work on the Mojave community and has developed a practical writing system and a dictionary for community use.

Munro is a gifted teacher and has done much to encourage the entry of other linguists into the Yuman arena. In 1974 she became an assistant professor at the University of California at Los Angeles (UCLA), where she is now a full professor. Two dissertations on Yuman languages have been written under her direction (by Lynn Gordon and Heather Hardy), while another on morphology utilized a great deal of Yuman data (by Tracy Thomas Flinders).

The Second Generation: Leanne Hinton

I began my work with Yuman languages in 1964 while an undergraduate student, at first working within the field of ethnomusicology. I met Margaret Langdon in 1966 and collaborated with her on various projects dealing with Diegueño. After many years of indecision as to whether I wanted to work in linguistics or ethnomusicology, in 1971 I finally entered graduate school at UCSD as Langdon's student and received my Ph.D. in 1977. From 1976 to 1978 I taught at the University of Texas at Dallas and then moved to the University of California at Berkeley to replace Mary Haas, who had recently retired. I am presently an associate professor there.

Unlike other Yuman scholars, I have focused on the languages of the Upland Yumans, which had not been studied since Kroeber's Laboratory of Anthropology field school with the Yavapai in the 1930s. My dissertation deals with the linguistic perspective of Havasupai songs. The combination of music and language has remained one of my central interests, and I have published various papers on language and music in Yuman (e.g., Hinton 1974, 1976, 1980, 1982, 1984a) as well as sociolinguistic approaches to language change (Hinton 1979, 1980). Like other linguists I have worked in areas that combine language and other

aspects of culture, especially textual analyses (Hinton 1977a, 1978; Hinton and Watahomigie 1984). Like Langdon and Munro, I have been deeply involved in developing written versions of Yuman languages (Hinton 1977b) and bilingual education, serving as codirector of the Havasupai bilingual education program for several years. We have developed a writing system and many materials for the program, including many unpublished children's books, a dictionary, a curriculum guide for teaching the Havasupai language, and a guide to reading and writing the Havasupai language (Hinton 1984b, 1984c). I have also organized and presented many training seminars for bilingual education staff on the Havasupai and Hualapai reservations and have taught several summer linguistics workshops in Arizona for bilingual education staff members of Yuman tribes.

The Third Generation: Bendixon, Norwood, Gordon, Hardy, Joel, and Kendall

I selected Langdon, Munro, and myself as examples of the second generation for special mention because we happened to play an important role in the family tree of the Yuman scholars. This is due in part to the fact that we have all been situated at campuses of the University of California system, where we have had ample access to both students and other established Yuman scholars. Women who received their Ph.D.'s later in the 1970s have not had this advantage. Because of fewer available positions in the core area, they have by necessity scattered through the country to positions at far-away institutions. Unfortunately, like other students in the late 1970s and early 1980s, the high unemployment rates in anthropology and linguistics forced many of these linguists into other careers. The situation was similar to that encountered by Haas in the Great Depression. The women in the first category who received Ph.D.'s at the University of California schools in linguistics with specialization in Yuman languages include Langdon's students Birgitte Bendixon and Susan Norwood, Munro's students Lynn Gordon and Heather Hardy, and William Bright's student Judy Joel (1964). Outside the University of California system, only one woman has written a dissertation on a Yuman language: Martha Kendall.

All of this third generation are at the beginnings of their careers, and their research topics show the continued breadth and depth of interest in Yuman linguistics of their mentors. Birgitte Bendixon is one of the few phonologists to look closely at Yuman languages; she has published one paper on Cocopa rhythmic structure (1979) and completed her dissertation in 1980 on phonological and temporal properties in Cocopa. Susan Norwood has written several manuscripts on Quechan and Diegueño and completed her dissertation on progressives in Yuman and Romance languages in 1981. She then spent several years working and studying indigenous languages in Nicaragua and is now back in San Diego teaching and resuming her Yuman studies. Lynn Gordon's Yuman specialization is Maricopa, a language that has gone unstudied since Leslie Spier's classic work. Gordon's dissertation (1980a) was on Maricopa morphology and syntax; she has also written many other works on aspects of Maricopa (e.g., Gordon 1979, 1980b, 1981, 1982, 1983a, 1983b). She is presently on the faculty at Washington State University.

Heather Hardy has also worked on understudied areas of Yuman, beginning with her 1979 dissertation on Yavapai syntax (1979c). Hardy teaches in the English Department at North Texas State University in Denton, Texas. Despite her present geographic isolation from Yavapai territory and from the intellectual centers of Yuman studies, she has contributed numerous articles on Yavapai (e.g., Hardy 1979a, 1979b, 1980, 1981, 1982) and comparative Pai (1979a).

Judy Joel was the first woman to write on Yuman languages since Matilda Coxe Stevenson: her 1964 paper on classification and taxonomy was actually earlier than Langdon's first publication.

She was awarded a Ph.D. from UCLA in 1966 for her dissertation on Paipai phonology and morphology. Joel has continued her interest in Paipai, which is peripheral to the Southwest, and comparative Yuman. She has developed a close collaboration with Langdon, whom she considers to be her mentor in southwestern Yuman linguistics, and has taught special classes at UCSD several times. Her home institution is Indiana University Southeast, where she is now a professor.

Martha B. Kendall, the only woman to get a Ph.D. as a Yuman specialist outside the University of California system, wrote her dissertation on Yavapai in 1972. She is presently on the faculty at Indiana University, where she was a student under Carl Voegelin. Carrying on the Voegelin tradition, she has been a highly productive scholar and colleague. She has been editor of abstracts for the *International Journal of American Linguistics,* which is the major publication outlet for American Indian linguistic research, as well as editor of *Anthropological Linguistics,* a journal published by Indiana University. She has written numerous articles on Yavapai and other Yuman languages (e.g., Kendall 1975, 1976, 1977). Like others, she has also turned her hand to practical applications of linguistics in the Yavapai community.

Lucille Watahomigie

Although most of these influential women received Ph.D.'s in linguistics, one woman without an advanced degree in linguistics must be included in this chapter because of her impact. Lucille Watahomigie, a native speaker of Hualapai and director of the Hualapai bilingual education program, has been an exceedingly important force in Yuman linguistics in recent years. She received a master's degree in education at the University of Arizona and immediately established the Hualapai Bilingual/Bicultural Education Program in 1976. This has been one of the most successful bilingual education programs in North America, and it now serves as a model program for native peoples. Watahomigie is visited regularly by the staff members of other tribal programs. In addition, she gives dozens of presentations every year all over the country, demonstrating the Hualapai program and its curriculum and materials.

When Watahomigie first established the program, she and her new staff attended a Summer Institute of Linguistics training program but found its approaches unsuited to their particular needs. Watahomigie then made a trip to San Diego, where she met with Langdon and me. This proved to be the beginning of a long working partnership, which later came to include many other linguists as well. I was then developing a practical writing system with the Havasupai, and I consulted frequently with Watahomigie. My work with the Havasupai bilingual program was greatly aided by ideas that Watahomigie developed for the Hualapai program. Watahomigie later initiated the notion of summer linguistic training workshops for bilingual educators in Yuman languages, and we, with the help of linguists William Leap and John Rouillard, developed a proposal to the U.S. Department of Education to fund the workshop. This was the beginning of what is now a yearly workshop (presently funded by Title VII and usually housed at Arizona State University) to train southwestern Native Americans in linguistic methodology.

As an outgrowth of her work in the bilingual education program, Watahomigie has also collaborated on several works of linguistic importance (e.g., Powskey et al. 1980; Hinton and Watahomigie 1984; Watahomigie 1967). Of special importance to southwestern linguistics is the *Hualapai Reference Grammar* (Watahomigie et al. 1982), a thorough, detailed grammar. It is the first Yuman grammar written by individuals with linguistic training who also have the full benefit of native speaker intuitions. Like most of the women whose work has been described here, Watahomigie is still early in her career, and we can

happily expect much more from her in the future. She is currently collaborating with Professor Akira Yamamoto on a large dictionary of the Hualapai language.

Watahomigie's work reminds us that Native American groups, Athabascan and Uto-Aztecan speakers as well as Yumans, have developed a keen interest in their languages. They are concerned with what is being published about them and how this is presented. Native collaborators have gained a great deal of power in this area. The Havasupai tribal council, for example, now exerts the right to approve all publications that concern them; included in their considerations is how useful the research is to them as a community. Hualapais and Havasupais as a result are increasingly collecting their own data and turning to linguists more than cultural anthropologists to help train them to undertake their own studies. The collective authorship that has resulted has greatly improved southwestern linguistics.

CONCLUSIONS

Yuman linguistic studies are presently in a time of great flowering. Most of the dominant figures in the field are still actively producing. The majority of these are women who began their work after 1960. Some strong women, especially Haas and Langdon, have largely shaped the course of Yuman studies. The history of Yuman studies since 1960 has been characterized by a closely knit, expanding network of scholars who maintain very close contact with each other. The network consists of both men and women, but it is the women who emerge as the primary cohesive force in the field and in the field's extended family. This pseudo-family has influenced the theoretical and practical development of the study of Yuman languages and in turn all of southwestern linguistics.

Pseudo-lineages have also been important to women in anthropology, of course. Columbia

University and New York City, as the home of several anthropological institutions, in the 1920s and 1930s saw a large group of prominent women—Elsie Clews Parsons, Ruth Benedict, and Margaret Mead followed first by Ruth Bunzel, Gladys Reichard, Erna Gunther, and Esther Goldfrank and later by Gene Weltfish and Eleanor Leacock. Cohorts were also evident at the universities of Arizona, New Mexico, Chicago, and even Denver. While these situations are important, more closely akin to the linguistic pseudo-familial network may be the students who worked in the Navajo area under Clyde Kluckhohn: few students earned degrees under his tutelage at Radcliffe College and Harvard University, but many women from other universities claimed to have been strongly influenced by him, so his influence stretched out to other places in much the same way as Langdon's workshops have done. Based on a mutual interest in a research area and topic, Kluckhohn influenced anthropologists from Florence Hawley Ellis to Katherine Spencer Halpern to Mary Shepardson to Louise Lamphere. And the students of these women are carrying on the legacy. This type of lineage in anthropology deserves further attention.

The strong intellectual kinship lineage has meant that individuals were included or excluded based on training and membership rather than gender. Thus, in linguistics there is a tendency for individuals to be taken seriously based on with whom they studied. There is thus an element of a "good old boys" and a "good old girls" network in southwestern linguistics. This has allowed some elements of personality bias to creep in that are absent in periods when pseudolineages are not evident. This networking is most evident in periods when there are strong, dominant personalities in the areas. In southwestern linguistics, Sapir, Whorf, Hoijer, Voegelin, Kroeber, and Haas are a few such dominant personalities. These charismatic leaders have had an effect on which languages individuals study and the topics and theoritical frameworks that are focused on. For

men and women who have developed in the pseudo-kinship modes, the language group of the professor/mentor has become the first choice for study. This mechanism has meant that language families have been studied differentially through time.

The family metaphor for the growth of linguistic studies by women can also be seen in the role that families actually played in the development of Yuman linguistic studies. Langdon was a very dedicated family individual. She did not want to travel far from her family to some exotic place while her child was growing up. Thus, she and several of her students opted for Yuman linguistics because fieldwork could be undertaken close to home. In addition, mastering the structural nuances of a language takes a long period of time, years of repeated visits to native collaborators. This requirement for field studies was also evident for those who worked in museums, as Parezo and Hardin's chapter in this volume documents. It was more crucial in linguistics and ethnomusicology than in the study of material culture and art, for to be taken seriously as a linguist one has to be a field linguist and demonstrate the ability to handle and manipulate formal description as well as to learn other languages.

While I have concentrated primarily on Yuman languages, where women have played a notable role, it should not be forgotten that in other language families in the Southwest, female scholarship has likewise blossomed since the 1960s. Southwestern linguists such as Elizabeth Brandt, Jane Hill, Eloise Jelenik, Sally Midgette, and Susan Steele are prominent scholars at several southwestern institutions. Each is training other women students to work in Uto-Aztecan and Athabascan languages. Also similar to the trends in Yuman, other language families exhibit the concurrent development of the application of linguistics for the benefit of the American Indian speech communities and an increase in the number of scholars who are of Native American descent. Notable American Indian women who specialize in southwestern languages include Ofelia Zepeda (Tohono O'Odham), Laverne Jeane (Hopi), and Navajo scholars Alice Neundorf, Ellavina Perkins, Irene Silentman, and Mary Ann Willie. We expect that these women will in turn develop into strong branches in their linguistic family trees.

I have not, of course, done justice to the large number of female scholars in the Southwest who have worked on language families other than Yuman. Some of the scholars mentioned above and elsewhere in this volume, such as Matilda Coxe Stevenson, Barbara Freire-Marreco Aitken, Frances Densmore, Natalie Curtis Burlin, Ruth Benedict, Ruth Bunzel, and Gladys Reichard (to name only a few), have done very important linguistic work. All, however, worked independently (with the exception of Benedict and Bunzel at Zuni) and did not develop a cadre of students to carry on their work and perspectives. What I hope has become clear by concentrating on scholarship in a single language family is how great a change has occurred in the degree of participation by women in scholarship since the 1960s. It will be interesting to see if this is a permanent change.

Left: Edward Sapir at New Haven, Connecticut, 1936 or 1937. *Courtesy of Sapir family.*

Below: John Wesley Powell at desk at Bureau of American Ethnology, ca. 1895. Staff photographer. Negative No. Port. 64-A-13-A. *Courtesy of the National Anthropological Archives, Smithsonian Institution.*

Left: Gladys Reichard at the Museum of Northern Arizona, early 1950s. Staff photographer. Negative No. 12887. *Courtesy of the Museum of Northern Arizona.*

Below: Anna Shepard examining pottery at the Pecos exhibit, Museum of New Mexico, mid 1930s. *Courtesy of the Carnegie Institution, Washington, D.C.*

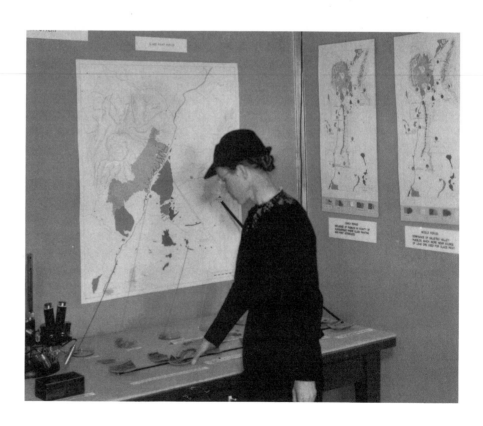

Mary Shepardson and Blodwen Hammond leaving for the Navajo Rservation, 1960. *Courtesy of Mary Shepardson.*

Matilda Coxe Stevenson with Pueblo woman, mid 1890s. Negative No. 55286. *Courtesy of the National Anthropological Archives, Smithsonian Institution.*

Ruth Underhill at Jemez Springs, New Mexico, 1936. Photographer: Frederica de Laguna. Negative No. Un84-042. *Courtesy of the Photo Archives, Denver Museum of Natural History. All rights reserved.*

Laura Thompson, Rosamond Spicer, and Dorothea Leighton at the reception for the opening of the Daughters of the Desert exhibit, 1986. Photographer: Janice Dewey. *Courtesy of the Southwest Institute for Research on Women.*

Left: H. Marie Wormington on archaeological excavation, 1938. *Courtesy of Marie Wormington.*

Below: Mary Cabot Wheelwright and Jack Lambert near Soap Creek, Arizona, 1927. *Courtesy of the Wheelwright Museum of the American Indian.*

Amelia White with one of the Russian wolfhounds,
Santa Fe. *Courtesy of the School of American Research.*

Nathalie Woodbury at NAASA Seminar, 1960. Staff
photographer. Negative No. 13784. *Courtesy of the
Museum of Northern Arizona.*

ZUNI POTTERS AND THE PUEBLO POTTER: THE CONTRIBUTIONS OF RUTH BUNZEL

Margaret Ann Hardin

All ethnological information comes to us through the medium of another mind,
and, with data so complex and subtle as those of human civilization, no matter
how clear and honest that mind is, it can absorb only what is congenial to it,
and must give it out again through such means of expression as it may command.

Ruth L. Bunzel
(1932b:547)

THE *Pueblo Potter: A Study of Creative Imagination in Primitive Art* (1929) was Ruth L. Bunzel's first monograph. A major resource for scholars interested in the traditional artist, it has been particularly influential among North Americanists, both cultural anthropologists and archaeologists, for whom it has provided major examples of how artists work within traditional styles. Available since 1972 in a widely distributed paperback edition, it is also read by non-anthropologists interested in Native American art and culture and by Native Americans, including the Zuni. Because of its influence, *The Pueblo Potter* is an important book deserving careful scrutiny.

The Pueblo Potter has been of great importance to me in my own work. It provided many of the strategies with which I began my research on pottery painting in a Tarascan village and, subsequently, the comparative basis used by others to discuss my own contributions (Watson 1979:

282–83). When I began teaching the anthropology of art at the University of Maine in the 1970s, I assigned Bunzel's book as a major reading, for in it she touched upon many of the problem areas that interested me. I reread *The Pueblo Potter* on a regular basis in much the same spirit an anthropological linguist rereads Edward Sapir's *Language* (1921). In dealing with the basic problem of how artists perform within the traditionally defined limits of established styles, Bunzel touched upon most of the issues that I considered to be pertinent and important.

The Pueblo Potter assumed a different significance for me when I began to work with Zuni pottery in the collections of the Smithsonian Institution during the late 1970s. Most of Bunzel's fieldwork was conducted at the Pueblo of Zuni where she lived during the 1920s with the family of a major potter, Catalina Zuni. While the Zuni pottery painting of the 1920s described by Bunzel differed in content and, especially, in variability from that of the period of the Smithsonian collections of the late nineteenth century, Bunzel had illustrated *The Pueblo Potter* with Smithsonian vessels and had used these earlier collections as the basis for her discussion of stylistic change. *The Pueblo Potter* became, for me, a crucial historical document as I sought to understand what had happened to Zuni pottery in the last century.

I went to Zuni first to study the current state of pottery-making and then to serve as the guest curator of a tribally organized exhibit of traditional Zuni ceramics (Hardin 1983). I found that it was not unusual for Zunis to be familiar with *The Pueblo Potter.* The volume was available in community libraries and was a standard resource in the high school art room. During the course of exhibit planning, Zuni committee members asked me what I thought about *The Pueblo Potter.* As I sought to understand what was being said and requested, and chose my answer, I began to reconsider how potters are presented in the book and whether this presentation reflected the intellectual standards or conventions of the day as taught at Columbia University or reflected Ruth Bunzel's interactions with and ideals of the Zuni potters and the Zuni community. To establish this, *The Pueblo Potter* must be seen in the context of Bunzel's entire contribution to anthropology and in terms of contemporary Zuni views about pottery and Bunzel.

BUNZEL'S FIRST FIELD RESEARCH

When Ruth Bunzel began the field research that served as the foundation for *The Pueblo Potter,* she had barely started her training as an anthropologist. When I visited her in August of 1976, she told me that she had originally intended to visit Ruth Benedict in the field while Franz Boas was in Europe during the summer of 1924. At that time Bunzel was employed as Boas' secretary in the Department of Anthropology at Columbia University, having taken over that position in 1922 from Esther Goldfrank. Her salary, like that of Goldfrank's, was paid by Elsie Clews Parsons.

Having graduated from college in 1918, Bunzel was searching for a career. With little to do that summer, she stated,

I thought that if I could see an anthropologist at work at the most crucial and mysterious part of his study, and perhaps try a bit on my own, I would know whether or not I wanted to be and could be an anthropologist. So I thought that I would take my vacation time and a few dollars I had saved for a trip to Europe and instead meet Ruth Benedict at Zuni. My plan was not too ambitious—I was a good stenographer and I would take down folk tales and interviews in shorthand, and do all our typing. Ruth Benedict seemed pleased with the suggestion so I took it to Boas (Bunzel quoted in Mead 1959b: 33).

On Boas' advice, however, she changed her plans:

Boas heard me out, snorted in his inimitable fashion and said, "Why do you want to waste your time typing?" (He always thought typing a "waste of time," though Heaven knows he wasted enough of his own precious time on similar donkey work to know that the gremlins didn't do it after funds were spent on informants.) (Bunzel quoted in Mead 1959b: 33–34).

She remembers that Boas said,

"What are you going to do?" And I said, "I don't know." And he said, "Don't waste your time. Do a project of your own." But I said, "Professor Boas, I'm not an anthropologist. I can't do that." He said, "You're interested in art. They make pottery there. Go do a project on the relationship of the artist to her work." So I had a problem to work on (Bunzel 1985).

Boas continued, "'I have always wanted someone to work on the relation of the artist to his work.' (Boas always had a long list of problems that he hoped someone would work on, things that he had started and hadn't had time to go on with, or things that had just occurred to him.)" (Bunzel quoted in Mead 1959b: 34).

Reflecting Boas' interest in the individual, Bunzel's assigned task was to study how Zuni potters operated within their traditions. Because she already knew something about artists in her own society from her undergraduate education (although she had had no formal training in art history), she decided to agree with Boas' plan. Pottery was, of course, a major art form in Pueblo society, and pottery-making was a prerogative of the female role. Whether Bunzel would have chosen this project for herself is, in light of her later comments, a reasonable question:

Furthermore, out of all the ways in which one can work in a foreign culture, each anthropologist has one which is preferred (though, of course, not to the exclusion of other methods) and which for him seems most natural and most promising. He will use this method whenever the situation permits, and it is right that he should do so because a person picks up more cues in a field which is familiar and natural to him. I, for instance, am only a moderately good observer. I have had to train myself to look at things, to observe them precisely and attentively. Even so, I miss many subtleties that would be picked up by someone for whom visual experience is the primary method of orienting himself in life. On the other hand, I am naturally very alert to those nuances in verbal communication that can reveal more than the informant intended to say (Bunzel 1952:xiv).

Bunzel, however, had an assignment and "had about four or five weeks to become an anthropologist and plan a project" (Bunzel 1985).

I was really alone in a big sea and I had to swim. I assumed that the Zuni artists were not going to be any more articulate about what they were trying to do than the poets and painters I had met in Greenwich Village, and that direct questioning would get me nowhere (Bunzel quoted in Mead 1959b:34).

With a shove from Boas, which meant instructions to read H. K. Haeberlin's *The Idea of Fertilization in the Culture of The Pueblo Indians* (1916) and a book on Northwest Coast basketry technology (Haeberlin et al. 1925) and to go and look at some pots, Bunzel developed innovative methods, perspectives, and techniques. As she remembered her dilemma,

I had to figure out what to do with art. So I spent the next couple of weeks down at the American Museum of Natural History photographing all the Zuni pottery, all the Pueblo pottery, too. I had all these photo-graphs to take along with me to show the people and get them started (Bunzel 1985).

Bunzel had some ideas. She noted, "I had to approach the problem indirectly. I decided on three lines of approach—criticism, instruction, and problem solving. . . . Three weeks later I was on the train to Zuni" (Bunzel quoted in Mead 1959b:34).

In addition to the direct influence of Boas, the desire to please her employer, and the decision whether she should pursue an anthropological career, Bunzel had another reason for choosing pottery production as her first project: pottery was made by women. According to Bunzel,

Zuni is a woman's society and women have a great deal of power and influence, [although] women don't have access to all the ceremonials and of course the early anthropologists of the Southwest all dealt with ceremonials—the men's part of culture. I felt there was a great lack of knowledge about people's lives—particularly about women. . . . So being a woman, that was the obvious place to start (Bunzel 1985).

Benedict and Bunzel each began her work under the most difficult of circumstances, the behavior of anthropologists having been the immediate cause of a recent political upheaval (see Bunzel 1952:xiv–xvi; Pandey 1972).

When Ruth Benedict and I first arrived at Zuni the village was in one of its periodic states of upheaval in which anthropologists figured. The "progressive" faction, favorable to Americans and friendly to anthropologists, had been ousted after unsuccessful attempts by anthropologists [Frederick Hodge] to photograph the midwinter ceremonies, and its members were so discredited that any contact with them would have been disastrous. We were consequently faced with the necessity of finding informants among the conservative and traditionally hostile group that was now in power (Bunzel 1952).

They had intended to stay with Margaret Lewis, with whom Elsie Clews Parsons had lived (Parezo 1992). Lewis, however, was a member of the disgraced progressives. Luckily they were befriended by Flora Zuni (Pandey 1978), an employee at the government school who spoke English and was a member of the household of one of the leaders of the ultraconservative faction. Her mother, Catalina, was also a competent and active potter. Of the experience Bunzel wrote to Boas,

Well, two days—or is it two years—ago we set up house keeping a la Zuni. Mrs. Lewis is no longer here so we have been thrown on our own resources. It was not a great surprise because Hodge had warned me of the possibility. It seems that Mrs. Lewis has gotten herself badly involved in the religious rumpus, and as a result did not get a school appointment for next year. Nevertheless, our hearts went down into our toes when we got here and actually found her gone, and our letters lying undelivered in the post office. We went to Flora as a next resort and were received like princes and rented from her a house on the edge of the village where we are more than comfortable (FB: RB/FB 8/6/24).

Because of the political situation at the pueblo, Bunzel conducted her fieldwork within the confines of Catalina Zuni's family and its immediate social network (Bunzel 1972: xiv–xvi, 63). Flora served as an interpreter, Bunzel (1952: xv) noted, "but only with members of her own family. . . . For the first week it seemed doubtful that we would be able to remain, but through a mixture of caution and luck we survived." The family provided the necessary fictive kinship attachments and roles needed for a single woman living in a society where marriage and children were expected. Bunzel lived for five summer seasons and a couple of winters with Flora Zuni (1924–1929) and was formally adopted into her family and made a member of the Badger clan in 1926. She was given the name *Maiatitsa,* which means "Blue Bird," in honor of her blue smock (Fawcett and McLuhan 1988: 30). The two women developed a lasting friendship. Flora Zuni has stated that

[Bunzel] was just like a sister to me. We lived together for a while in the old house and then moved to this new house. I washed her hair and my children

used to bring her drinking water from the day school. She was very hardworking like me. She used to grind cornmeal for our [religious] doings, go to the fields with men to work there, and helped my nieces with their homework. Once she got after one of the teachers for giving them too much homework and after that they treated our children nicely. . . . Bunzel was a good woman. She liked people and was always good to children. She used to go to [the Zuni] night dances in the winter. Once I got after her because she spoiled one of my nicest dresses. She borrowed it for a dance and then sat on the dirt floor wearing my dress. I remember her getting upset only once when she was followed by some boys who said dirty things to her. She talked back in Zuni and scolded them. They got scared and ran away. Boys were nice and obedient in those days (Zuni quoted in Pandey 1972: 333).

Anthropological fieldwork confined to the context of a single family shaped the way in which Bunzel conducted her field research. She continued to use this method when working with other cultures and in other situations: "My preferred method of work is to become attached to a single family, living as intimately as possible within the orbit of their lives, identifying as fully as possible with them and learning to see the culture through their eyes" (Bunzel 1952: xiv–xv).

For Bunzel the results of this arrangement were highly productive. She worked closely with Flora Zuni's mother, Catalina ("Lina"), a 65-year-old woman who spoke no English and was "an excellent potter and a real artist" (FB: RB/FB 8/6/24). Catalina had "been practicing her art for at least forty years. . . . She was an able informant on all matters of religious belief and practice, knew many esoteric ceremonies and imparted freely whatever she knew" (Bunzel 1972: 69). In addition, Bunzel obtained "from various members of Flora's large family short texts on everyday activities—planting, harvesting, housebuilding, baking, cooking—and short simple descriptions of ceremonies" (FB: RB/FB 7/25/26). She even was able to obtain an autobiographical text of major events in Catalina's life (Bunzel 1933: 74–96).

Bunzel tried to fit as closely as possible into the orbit of the Zuni family's life and to "see the culture through their eyes" (Bunzel 1952:xv).

Bunzel studied Zuni pottery-making by learning to make pottery: "I felt that instruction was very important in how they visualized, how they thought about what they were doing. So I said I wanted to learn how to do it and got people to teach me. I was never very good at it" (Bunzel 1985). She also watched potters and recorded what they said about their work and asked potters, especially Catalina, to comment on photographs of pots and about the designs she had them draw on paper. Bunzel was soon recognized at Zuni as a novice potter, and "at one point she could walk about with a pot on her head, and climb a ladder balancing a pot with her hand" (Fawcett and McLuhan 1988:31). While Bunzel characterized her later work on Zuni kachinas (1932c) and ritual poetry (1932d) as "using a conceptual scheme native to the culture as the structural framework of research" (Bunzel 1952: xv), in this context she does not mention her work on pottery.

The Pueblo Potter was only the beginning of Bunzel's contribution to Zuni ethnography (see Parezo 1992). In all, she spent several field seasons at Zuni, going more deeply into Zuni life and values. Her most substantial contributions were in the area of Zuni religion and its associated myth and ritual poetry (Bunzel 1932a, 1932b, 1932c, 1932d). In addition, she did extensive work on Zuni language and in culture and personality studies (Bunzel 1935, 1953). Her work on Zuni economics, summarized in "The Economic Organization of Primitive Peoples," contains beautifully drawn characterizations and explanations of associated Zuni values (Bunzel 1938a). She also published ethnographic texts (Bunzel 1933) gathered during her third Zuni field season.

When I went as a new student of Zuni ceramics to ask her questions, Ruth Bunzel graciously answered them. She quickly added that she had gone on to do other things, in particular, to study economics and culture change. It is ironic that of all of Bunzel's careful work, it is her first work, *The Pueblo Potter,* which has had the most influence on anthropology and related fields. Putting aside regionally specific comparisons such as those of Parezo (1983:126), Stanislawski (1978:215–16), and Hill (1977:56), which utilize Bunzel's conclusions on learning patterns, let us briefly examine the broader influence of *The Pueblo Potter.*

THE PUEBLO POTTER

Bunzel's monograph provides a major case study for the allied fields of anthropology and sociology of art. For example, *Art in Primitive Societies* (Anderson 1979), a standard introductory text, lists Bunzel's study as a suggested reading after three of seven chapters. In the same text, Anderson draws upon Bunzel's scholarship to provide examples of the unconscious nature of aesthetic socialization (Anderson 1979:116–18), values in maintaining style boundaries (1979:124–25), and cultural restraints on innovations (1979: 162–64). In an earlier statement, Robert Redfield (1971) cites Bunzel to illustrate the unconscious and culturally specific nature of aesthetic judgments. John Anson Warner in his paper on the individual in American Indian art (n.d.: 1–2) characterizes Bunzel's contribution in the following manner:

Ruth L. Bunzel illuminates the relationship of an artist to his or her society in her classic volume *The Pueblo Potter: A Study of Creative Imagination in Primitive Art,* where she remarks on individual creativity in Pueblo pottery. Despite the manifest examples of individuality apparent in the work of Puebloan potters, Bunzel recognized that its expression took place within the narrow confines of what Puebloan society allowed.

Warner quotes Bunzel's initial definition of the problem (Bunzel 1972:1), which emphasizes the social limits of artistic activity and compares art styles to human languages. He then states that "this view of individuality and art is widely accepted in sociological circles" (Warner n.d.: 3).

Ethnoarchaeologists (Arnold 1983) and archaeologists (Muller 1979) have also found Bunzel's linguistic analogy attractive. Muller (1979: 172) uses Bunzel to stress the unconscious operation of style in support of his own particular linguistic analogy:

As a study of the relationships of artists to their work and to each other, *The Pueblo Potter* (1929) still stands out. Bunzel paid particular attention to the way a potter viewed her work and the work of her contemporaries and found good evidence that the conscious ideas of these potters were by no means identical to the actual structures of the style. Although it is discouraging to not be able to get to actual structures of such a style simply by asking the artist, the differences between the so-called 'real' and 'ideal' should come as no surprise to anthropologists. There are not innumerable examples of the difference between what people think they are doing and what they actually do. Bunzel showed that an aesthetician can no more expect a formal organized statement of a style from an artist than a linguist can expect a finished and explicit grammar from a native speaker of a language (Muller 1979:159).

The Pueblo Potter provided a key ethnographic analogy for archaeologists seeking to reconstruct social organization from the distribution and associations of portions of pottery decoration in archaeological context. In their classic form, these arguments assumed that knowledge of a preference for pottery design was passed from mother to daughter in a reliably unconscious and mechanical fashion (Hill 1970:57–74; Longacre 1970:27–32). *The Pueblo Potter* was cited to support this line of reasoning (Hill 1970:57; Longacre 1970:28).

ZUNI POTTERS IN *THE PUEBLO POTTER*

Zuni potters provided Bunzel's most elaborately drawn example of "the manner in which individuals operate within the limits of established style" (Bunzel 1972:1). Zuni pottery also played a key role in Bunzel's arguments as the most extreme example of artists bound by the limits of their tradition. She considered Zuni, together with Acoma, to best represent indigenous conditions (1972:5) because pottery production in those pueblos was still primarily for household use. However, she found it advisable to pursue her interest in artistic creativity in other pueblos. In the introduction to *The Pueblo Potter,* Bunzel clearly stated the role she assigned the Zuni example in her argument: "Most of the fieldwork for the present study has been done at Zuni, although the stagnation and inferiority of the art there has made it advisable to include surveys of villages where commercial success has stimulated new and interesting developments" (1972:5).

Bunzel intended to study the relationship between style and artistic creativity. She defined decorative style as the "mode of plastic expression characteristic of any group at any given time" (Bunzel 1972:1). She thought of style in terms of limits and expected that most artists in traditional societies would remain within these limits (1972:86). Having defined the traditional case, Bunzel equated it with the Zuni potter of the 1920s. Her purpose at Zuni was to discover the unconscious processes through which the potter's work was kept within the boundaries set by tradition. She argued that the processes were sensual, intuitive, and largely dependent upon the visual image. While Bunzel recognized that style also changed gradually (1972:1), she reserved her praise for the more abrupt departures from tradition that occurred at Hopi and San Ildefonso (1972:88–89). She considered the processes that resulted in these new kinds of pottery to be of a different order, involving the ability to experience mentally what had not been experienced sensually (1972:90)—in other words, to be artistically creative.

Bunzel began her discussion by outlining the underlying principles of Zuni pottery design (1972:13–29). She provided a brief analysis of Zuni design layout, characterized in terms of patterns of explicit (involving boundary lines) spatial division and associated patterns of design repetition. Bunzel's discussion of the number of design repeats focused on potters' stated preferences and on the discrepancies between these stated ideals and actual practice.

Bunzel's discussion of Zuni designs and how potters use them relied heavily upon a corpus of partial vessel decorations drawn on paper by a single Zuni potter. These partial vessel decorations provided Bunzel's evidence that "the Zuni artist recognizes that her designs can be analyzed into smaller units" (1972:23). The corpus was also reproduced in an appendix to illustrate Bunzel's contention that the Zuni analytical process was limited in nature:

I reproduce the collection precisely as it was made, since it represents better than any comments the extent and limitations of native analysis. These are not design elements in any sense that would satisfy a sophisticated analyst of design. They are patterns adapted to use on special parts of vessels. Native analysis goes no further. These are psychological elements, although they might be reduced to a very much smaller number of structural elements (1972:23).

The 1924 corpus, supplemented by further ethnographic observation and photographs of nineteenth-century vessels, was the basis of Bunzel's enumeration of Zuni pottery designs. In her discussion she unhesitatingly accepted these "psychological units" as given, as focused on identifying representational designs. She first distinguished two painting styles, sacred and secular. The sacred style, which she argued is completely distinct, used a few representational designs. By contrast, the secular style employed a larger number of designs. Here Bunzel's chief concern was to determine the extent to which designs were representational, which she did by choosing those few designs she termed "representatives," thus characterizing the large remainder as "geometrical patterns."

Bunzel concluded her summary of design principles with a consideration of the overall charac-

teristics of Zuni design. Based on potters' comments as well as the vessels themselves, these characteristics included the proportion of design to ground, the relative use of colors and textures, the preference for particular symmetry patterns at the level of motif, and spatial subdivision (1972: 28–29).

Having established the principles of Zuni pottery design, Bunzel turned her attention to the potter at work. Potters stated that the designs they painted were first visualized in detail (Bunzel 1972:50–51). The design was carefully planned in the potter's mind and, in fact, measured out on the vessel before the painting was begun. Zuni potters condemned those who copied designs. They claimed that their own designs were unlike those of other potters and that they did not repeat their own designs in their own work. Bunzel emphasized what she saw as a discrepancy between potters' theory and practice:

Even at Zuni where the inventive faculty is at the lowest ebb and where choice of design is narrowly circumscribed by prevailing taste, in spite of all this, each pot is approached as a new creation, the decoration of which is evolved only after much thought and inner communings. However much theory and practice may be at variance, there can be no doubt concerning the theory. And strangely enough it is at Zuni where the ideal is stated with greatest conviction, that it is most frequently violated (1972:52).

Bunzel found the Zuni pottery designs of her day to be repetitious in both decorative content and treatment. She emphasized potters' lack of awareness of the rules they followed. Potters' ability to sustain contradictions between theory and practice was then attributed to the visual and, thus, unanalytical nature of their thought processes. Turning again to the corpus of isolated designs, she argued that potters' inconsistent and limited application of design names provided further evidence of the unanalytical nature of the Zuni approach to the pottery painter's task (1972:53– 55). For Bunzel, the instruction of novice potters and the criticism of local and exotic vessels provided further information about the lack of creative processes at Zuni. In both cases, she emphasized the preoccupation with technical excellence in painting as evidence of the largely unanalytical nature of the design processes.

Bunzel argued that the large majority of Zuni pottery designs were not symbolic in nature. In doing this she rejected potters' claims that every design had a name and a story (1972:69). She also disagreed with earlier researchers who assumed to varying degrees that the designs used by Zuni potters were meaningful (Cushing 1886; J. Stevenson 1883a, 1883b, 1884b; M. Stevenson 1904).

Bunzel's distinction between sacred and secular pottery painting styles was crucial to her treatment of Zuni design symbolism. She identified what she felt were two separate categories of pottery, which overlapped in neither decoration nor context of use. The sacred style used a limited number of isolated representational designs. Statements recorded by Bunzel make it clear that Zunis considered these designs to be representational: "These are all creatures who frequent springs. If we paint them on our bowls, our bowls will always be full of water like the springs" (Catalina Zuni quoted in Bunzel 1972:69). Vessels termed secular by Bunzel were covered with complex painted decorations. She argued that the designs painted on these vessels were not symbolic in nature, but she recognized three exceptions. Bunzel dismissed obviously representational birds and deer as recent additions to the secular style. She concluded that the image of the "road" with its nearly ever-present line break symbolized the life of the potter. In addition, she somewhat grudgingly advanced the stylized feathers painted on the outside of most Zuni bowls to the status of symbol. Bunzel based her argument for the lack of symbolism in Zuni design on a particularly strict and narrow definition of symbol, which she shared with her mentor Franz Boas (Boas 1955). In Bunzel's words, "We are justified in using the word symbol where the association between de-

signs and the object or idea suggested is fixed and recognized. Zuni designs with their shifting meanings are neither tribal nor individual symbols" (1972:69).

Bunzel's conclusions about symbolism were based on the corpus of 94 designs drawn on paper. She had Catalina Zuni, the potter who drew the designs, identify them in 1924 when they were drawn, and she had them identified again in the summer of 1925 (we do not know if she used Zuni again as the 1925 respondent). Bunzel found the two sets of design identifications to be inconsistent (1972:69–70), but since they did not point toward symbolism as she defined it, she considered the evidence conclusive:

These designs were drawn for me by an old Zuni woman, an excellent potter who has been practicing her art for at least forty years. . . . She was an able informant on all matters of religious belief and practice, knew many esoteric ceremonies and imparted freely whatever she knew. If, therefore, there is any esoteric symbolism in Zuni pottery designs, as has been claimed by Cushing and others, this information could be secured from this woman (1972:69).

Bunzel's treatment of design symbolism was intricately related to assumptions about the direction of change in the Zuni painting style. From examining museum collections of late nineteenth-century Zuni pottery, Bunzel recognized that the style had once exhibited a greater range of variability (1972:16–20, 62–63), and she suggested that the loss of variability was of two kinds: fewer designs were used, and the freedom with which these designs were arranged decreased. Bunzel related this to the limited number of Zunis active as potters in the 1920s (1972: 62–63). Thus, demographic pressures affected design range and variability. In addition, she linked the increasingly fixed character of Zuni design to its increasingly symbolic character. Her argument was aided by the fact that the two secular Zuni designs that she considered to be symbols (paths and feathers) had fixed usages. She rejected an alternative theory that Zuni designs had once been symbolic but had been secularized; that is, that while specific meanings had been lost, knowledge of their significance persisted. Bunzel concluded that "Zuni design is not less but more symbolic than it was seventy-five years ago" (1972:70).

RECONSIDERATION OF BUNZEL'S CONCLUSIONS ON ZUNI POTTERY DECORATIONS

In summary, Ruth Bunzel found Zuni pottery decorations to be the most limited and routine of the Pueblo traditions on which her study focused. Given her assessment of Zuni design, she found it strange that Zuni artists approached pottery painting with intense concern for the originality of their designs. Bunzel used what she saw as a contradiction between practice and theory to argue that the painting process was a visual, intuitive, and largely unanalytical one. She continued to argue from a series of perceived contradictions between potters' statements and practices. For example, she noted discrepancies between general statements of design principles and specifics of particular designs. While potters claimed that the designs they painted were meaningful, Bunzel found that she was not justified in calling most Zuni designs "symbols" within her (and Boas') restricted definition.

The corpus of Zuni designs drawn on paper presented Bunzel with special problems. She was forced to recognize that unlike the potters of Acoma, Hopi, and San Ildefonso, Zuni potters consciously built up designs from recognized elements (Bunzel 1972:87). For this reason, she devoted considerable attention to the corpus, arguing that design names did not constitute a consistent, complete, and, therefore, analytic terminology. The related possibility that the Zuni designs in the corpus were (or had been) symbolic in nature presented an analogous problem; that is, the possibility made it more difficult for Bunzel

to argue that the potter was largely unconscious of what she was painting.

Much of Bunzel's argument against the symbolic nature of Zuni design was based on her assessment of the potter's identification of the designs drawn on paper. Reexamination of her responses suggests alternative explanations for the potter's apparent inconsistencies in naming designs. The corpus consists of 94 designs; however, 2 are obvious representations and 10 are only named once. Of the 82 remaining designs, 25 are consistently named. Of the 57 inconsistent responses, 18 focus on attributes at different levels of naming. The remaining 39 appear to be contradictory; that is, different labels are applied to the same element or to the entire design on successive occasions. The weight of the evidence (Bunzel 1972:25, 18, 39) lies slightly with consistency of meaning.

Bunzel's arguments of inconsistency are usually difficult to assess because they cannot be reconstructed; half of the material used in her comparisons (i.e., what Bunzel saw in the field) is unavailable to us today. Thus, the designs painted on paper present a unique opportunity to reexamine the potter's behavior. We are reminded that there are many ways to explain seeming contradictions. Is it appropriate in the Zuni case to apply strict Boasian standards for symbolic status, which require that the association between design and referent be unchanging and universally recognized within the culture (Boas 1955)? Here it seems appropriate to offer a Zuni comment, "Do you people really think that way?"

Other reasons also suggest that Bunzel's treatment of the Zuni potter should be reconsidered. Contemporary research conducted in the Zuni community does not unequivocally support Bunzel's conclusions, as would be expected in any community. That is, what Zunis say about their traditional pottery suggests alternative interpretations. Potters' practice of their art today differs from Bunzel's findings in key ways. Further, Zunis who have read *The Pueblo Potter* are not comfortable with the view of the potter and her pottery presented by Bunzel. While it is difficult to control for changes over time, one person commented that he preferred Cushing to Bunzel. Of Cushing he said, "He got a little bit more of the right idea" (personal communication).

A closer review of two of Bunzel's areas of interest—thought processes in pottery painting and design meaning—from a contemporary perspective sheds further light on the issues. This information is derived from the interviews conducted for *Gifts of Mother Earth* (Hardin 1983).

Thought Processes in Pottery Painting

Contemporary Zuni potters are quite analytical about design when the occasion calls for it; that is, they dissect vessel decorations and find new uses for the parts. For example, a portion of a design from the body of a water jar might be adapted to a bowl exterior. A design from a bowl interior might be "turned inside out" to fit on a globular canteen. On other occasions, potters insist that they stick to their own designs, handed down in their family. Then, as now, legitimating the right to use a design is an important issue for Zuni potters, as it is with other Zuni artists. Statements about creating one's own designs must always be considered in the broader context of Zuni society, in which knowledge is privileged and rights to knowledge are compartmentalized.

Compartmentalization of knowledge at Zuni has other implications for Zuni pottery-making. Potters talk about "having to make" a vessel. This means that a vessel is ordered for a specific religious context. The potter is thought to benefit generally but receives no compensation. In these cases, vessels are thought of as tokens of existing types. The cultural mechanism for making a vessel anew is quite specific. The potter receives instructions from the person who "needs it." This may be a detailed discussion of the vessel's size and form, together with an explanation of the necessary details of its use. In some cases, the motifs required and even their location on the vessel

must be specified. In addition to detailed verbal instructions, the potter may receive information in the form of broken pieces of the vessel she is replacing. The individual needing the replacement rejects the pot if its attributes are not those required. Usually another potter is then asked to make the vessel. What has been outlined here is a mechanism by which a potter can make a vessel, perhaps with meaningful designs, without knowing the meanings of those designs.

Design Meanings

Let us reexamine Bunzel's argument about design symbolism in the light of contemporary Zuni belief about their traditional ceramics. Her argument began with a strict dichotomy between sacred and secular painting styles. Zunis today contend that the distinction between sacred and secular styles (as opposed to specific vessels) is an inaccurate and artificial one. They point out that vessels more frequently associated with domestic use (for example, water jars) also find use in religious contexts. That is, the appearance of a vessel does not unambiguously indicate its function. They go on to say that Zunis do not segment their lives into religious and non-religious components; rather, traditional beliefs permeate every aspect of Zuni life.

Broader examination of the literature and of documented museum collections supports Zuni statements. In fact, vessels associated with religious contexts of use are quite varied. The category contains vessels painted in Bunzel's secular style and in her sacred style, as well as in other Zuni painting styles. Zuni practice before and after Bunzel's observations calls into question her distinction between sacred and secular.

Bunzel asserted that the meanings she collected were not the remains of a coherent symbolic system. If anything, she felt such a system might be developing. Today Zunis wonder about the actual meanings of designs. When looking at unfamiliar designs, they try (with varying degrees of success) to pick out familiar motifs and to assign representational meanings to them. The dominant belief at Zuni today is that designs on traditional vessels were intended to be meaningful, just as rock art is meaningful. According to contemporary Zuni theory, traditional vessels together with their decorations draw their meanings from their contexts of use. It is difficult to logically separate context and meaning. Thus, an unrecognized vessel may draw a comment "Who had it?" meaning what religious group had it, or "Has it been lost?" Such vessels are those which are made anew for religious use. They are said to be lost when their type is no longer in active use. The meanings of vessels and designs are thought to be lost through the same process. For example, a twentieth-century engineering project obliterated a spring and is said to have resulted in the loss of the vessels used to gather water on pilgrimages to the spring. In keeping with this line of reasoning, one vessel form no longer actively used but still remembered was included in the pottery exhibit "Gifts of Mother Earth" by Zuni committee members "so that it would not be lost." Thus, Zunis today hold a theory of contextual meaning and use it to explain how specific vessels together with their meanings may become lost. This Zuni theory of design meaning provides an interpretation of recent Zuni ceramic history that contradicts Bunzel's prediction that Zuni designs would acquire more fixed meaning rather than lose them.

CONCLUSIONS

This chapter's assessment of Bunzel's treatment of artists in *The Pueblo Potter,* in light of the Zuni evidence that was central to her argument, reveals that in one way the book was a rigorously circumscribed study of the potter's practice of her art. *The Pueblo Potter* paid little attention to the role of ceramics in Zuni life. Bunzel's conclusions that the artistic process was largely an unconscious one and that Zuni designs were not symbolic in nature followed from the definition of the problem with which she, under Boas' guidance, began her study.

By focusing on some of the problems generated by Bunzel's approach, and the approach of other Boasians, I have not meant to show that Bunzel's work is without value. Indeed, the opposite is the case. It has been possible to reexamine her analysis only because Bunzel published potters' responses as they were given (both in the design corpus and in the body of her text); she collected an extraordinary array of information during several difficult field seasons. The success of *The Pueblo Potter* must be attributed to her ability to assemble this information in support of her argument. Bunzel likewise viewed her efforts as the beginning of a new approach to anthropological study:

I was too ignorant at the time to know that I was pioneering; that I was on the frontier of a whole new field of anthropology; that this was the first tentative approach to the study of the individual in culture; the first attempt at a systematic study of behavior. I didn't know that I was employing "participant observation" and "projective techniques" because I had never heard of these things (Bunzel quoted in Mead 1959b:34).

She would have been pleased to know that the Zuni still use and discuss her work.

IN THE REALM OF THE MUSES

Nancy J. Parezo and Margaret A. Hardin

> Dr. Clark Wissler thought that museum work
> fitted women because it was like housekeeping.
> *Margaret Mead*
> *(quoted in J. Howard 1984)*

> Men are in the top jobs and
> women are doing the work.
> *Bertha Dutton*
> *(1985a)*

ON AUGUST 1, 1879, James Stevenson, his wife (Matilda Coxe Stevenson), photographer John Hillers, and Frank Hamilton Cushing traveled to the Southwest on the first expedition sponsored by the Bureau of Ethnology of the Smithsonian Institution. Their goals were to report on archaeological remains, continue earlier geological surveys, study architecture and domestic arrangements, and collect ethnographic specimens from the many Native American groups in New Mexico and Arizona for the U.S. National Museum (Hardin 1983; Parezo 1985, 1987). They collected over 40,000 objects from the western Pueblos, Rio Grande Pueblos, Navajos, and Jicarilla Apaches. Shipped to the Smithsonian Institution for use in exhibits at the numerous world's fairs, as well as in the museum, were pottery, domestic objects, weapons, clothing, basketry, toys, and musical instruments. When processed and analyzed, these objects served as the basis of several scholarly catalogues and articles authored by James Stevenson (1883a, 1883b, 1884a, 1884b) and were used by many other scholars as data for evolutionary theories, as evidence for cultural histories and for the continuity of Puebloan peoples from the prehistoric past into the present, and as symbols of cultures.

The gathering, display, and use of objects by anthropologists in the late nineteenth and early twentieth centuries was conceptualized as a way to salvage disappearing cultures and a means for anthropologists to define and describe cultural traditions. Material culture constituted rich anthropological data. But for the items made by other cultures to be used by anthropologists, objects had to be catalogued, classified, described, housed, and cared for in central locations, that is, in a museum. To perform these time-consuming, tedious, and invisible tasks required more than the work of a single individual; for example, Matilda Coxe Stevenson had to help her husband in order for the catalogues to be published as quickly as they were. She wrote many of the object descriptions that appeared in her husband's publications and prepared pots for exhibition. But in her handmaidenly role, she received no visible credit for these activities.

This pattern—anthropological collecting associated with museum-based research and exhibition, an interest in material culture as a focus of scholarly projects by both men and women, the publication of results by a senior scholar with the unacknowledged assistance of others (generally, but not always, women)—was quickly established and became the hallmark of anthropological research in the Southwest. By the beginning of World War I, anthropologists had collected hundreds of thousands of pieces of ethnographic and archaeological art and material culture from groups throughout the Greater Southwest. These men and women published hundreds of scholarly analyses, descriptive monographs, exhibit catalogues, and popular accounts of the objects made and used by Native Americans (Parezo et al. 1991). In fact, the majority of anthropologists who went to the Southwest published at least one article or book on material culture or included material culture in their general treatises. To work with art and material culture was especially common for women anthropologists. By 1985, over 1,190 women had collected, studied, and published works on Native American ethnographic arts and crafts. (This is 74% of the over 1,600 women identified for this project.) Although many of these women penned a single contribution, others produced a significant corpus of knowledge: Ruth Bunzel, Dorothy Dunn, Kate Peck Kent, Mary Lois Kissel, Franc Newcomb, Elsie Clews Parsons, Gladys Reichard, Helen Roberts, Matilda Coxe Stevenson, Clara Lee Tanner, Ruth Underhill, Gene Weltfish, and Mary Wheelwright are but some of the most well known. Prolific writers who are not as readily recognized include Laura Armer, Ina Sizer Cassidy, Maria Chabot, Elizabeth DeHuff, Hester Jones, Ruth Kirk, Frances Sanita, Opal Singer, Margaret Smith, and Betty Woods. And it goes without saying that all the archaeologists identified by Cordell in her chapter in this volume worked with material culture. Concentration on material culture and art became a specialty of women anthropologists.

It is not surprising, given the number of women who have published in this area, that many were employed in museums. In fact, the museum was one of the major homes for women working in southwestern anthropology; as Edgar Lee Hewett told Marjorie Lambert, "I approve of lady curators because they are such good housekeepers" (Lambert 1985). Despite this convergence of women and museum anthropology in the Southwest, the women who worked in museums, beginning in the 1930s, are now often obscure and fuzzy historical figures even though they have made numerous contributions. This adumbration is due to the nature of museum work and the structure of museums, which came to be dominated by a hierarchy of authority polarized by gender at the time women entered the institution in significant numbers. Moreover, conceptions of women's work confined women to the support positions in museums, with the exception of the founders analyzed in McGreevy's chapter in this volume. The realm of the muses enabled women to have meaningful work in anthropology, but it was, simultaneously, a trap that marginalized women by identifying them with undervalued, albeit necessary, labor—i.e., housework, primary and secondary education—and with traditional stereotypes of women as behind-the-scenes assistants.[1]

ANTHROPOLOGY AND MUSEUMS

In the late nineteenth and early twentieth centuries, anthropology was embedded in museums; the collection and study of ethnographic and archaeological artifacts played an important role in the professionalization of the discipline (Parezo 1987). Objects were considered "an essential part of the provision of basic documentation of human cultures at specific points in time and space, quite comparable to the recording, in written form, of data on the nonmaterial aspects of these cultures" (Sturtevant 1977:1). Collecting and studying material culture was viewed as an activity essential to understanding non-European peoples because it could be used as evidence for theories of evolution, diffusion, innovation, cultural change, and cultural continuity. In addition, it enabled anthropologists to create taxonomies of cultural types, an essential evolutionist activity that initially brought the unknown world under scientific control; later these taxonomies could be extended to serve as the conceptual bases for such anthropological cornerstones as culture areas and trait distributions. The collection and study of material culture epitomized salvage ethnography, which held that if native peoples were destined to assimilate or die out in the face of "superior" cultures, it was the duty of anthropologists to save as much as possible of their tangible and intangible culture for future generations (Parezo 1987).

Museums, as institutions designed to house and preserve collections of all kinds, especially those that expanded human knowledge and understanding, were the logical bases from which to begin a discipline that was conceptualized as natural history. In the West as well as the East it was common for anthropology departments to develop out of, or in conjunction with, university or large natural history museums (i.e., the University of New Mexico, the University of Arizona, Yale University, the University of California at Berkeley, the University of Pennsylvania, the University of Michigan, the University of Washington, and Harvard University). Even the University of Chicago and the Field Museum, Columbia University and the American Museum of Natural History, and the University of Wisconsin and the Milwaukee Public Museum were conceptualized as intellectual units. (They have since split.) Museums and universities continued to be complementary institutions (Sturtevant 1969: 623–24) between 1910 and 1930 even though there were more anthropological jobs in museums than in university departments; much of the teaching in universities was done by anthropologists who had joint appointments. A good deal of the anthropological research of the period was

likewise carried out in what Stocking has called "non or quasi-academic contexts." He continued, "Aside from the money appropriated for government anthropology, research was supported largely by individual philanthropy, channeled through the museums; universities provided little if any money for anthropological research" (Stocking 1976:9). In fact, the opportunity for research and access to funds made museums seem like ideal institutional settings for anthropologists. A common career pattern for both men and women was to begin their careers in museums, usually during their graduate years and as their first jobs, and then shift to other institutions—research centers, universities, and government agencies. As examples, Franz Boas, Florence Hawley Ellis, Alfred Kroeber, Robert Lowie, Paul Martin, and Leslie White followed this pattern. (Lowie would have spent more of his career in a museum if he had not been fired by the American Museum of Natural History during World War I because of his German heritage.) Others began in museums, shifted to universities and applied work, and returned to the museum setting (i.e., Nancy Lurie) or held joint appointments (i.e., Emil Haury, James Griffin, and Gordon Willey). Several noted anthropologists, such as Margaret Mead, Clark Wissler, and Herbert Spinden, worked in museums for their entire professional careers.

And working in museums, with the entailing special challenges and opportunities, has influenced anthropology as a whole:

Archaeology and ethnology in the museum context surely reinforced the historical orientation of anthropological theory, just as the object-orientation of museum collections sustained a particular attitude toward ethnographic data. More importantly, the whole culture-area approach, although in a sense the natural outgrowth of the Bureau of Ethnology program for mapping the continent, was very heavily conditioned by the problems of museum exhibition. Beyond this, the museum context, in which all the subdisciplines save linguistics were visually represented, obviously helped to reinforce the embracive tendency of the discipline, as well as its ties to the natural rather than the social sciences. The impact of the museum orientation continued to be felt throughout the 1920s, which were still a period of museum growth—although by the time the depression forced a sharp cutback in museum activities, their importance was already being undercut by other institutional developments (Stocking 1976:10).

As this transition progressed, museums came to be conceptualized as the place where men and women, with a few notable exceptions, were employed because they could not "make it" in the university. This perception and preconception crystallized in the 1930s during a time when the discipline, museums, and universities were becoming increasingly stratified. The reasons for this transition were varied, resulting partly from changes in the nature of the discipline, the questions asked about other peoples, the methodologies and techniques utilized to gain new knowledge, and the nature and locale of scientific research in general. This trend was evident in all the natural sciences—biology, botany, zoology, evolutionary systematics, and geology. When science gave high priority to describing and classifying disparate observations, progress in these disciplines depended heavily on collections. Thus, in the late nineteenth and early twentieth centuries, disciplines with a taxonomic paradigm, which included anthropology, tended to be centered in museums.

When experimentation and laboratory analysis took precedence after World War I, there was less apparent need for collections. The natural sciences, following the lead of the physical sciences, became centered in universities, which could support laboratories with government assistance. These teaching institutions had pools of inexpensive labor—students—to perform semi-skilled or skilled but tedious jobs. Museums came to be seen as the storehouses and repositories for evidence, be it physical objects or tape recordings and field notes, rather than the locale where new

knowledge was generated. And there was some validity to this perception; as the collections grew and grew, more and more time was required for preservation and maintenance of the evidence (i.e., the patrimony or heirlooms of past intellectual endeavors), activities that became associated with housekeeping. Less and less time was available for original research. This gradual transition occurred during a period when collecting expeditions became more expensive and hence rarer and as isolated donations of objects with less secure documentation increased. As a result, museum scientists began to be seen as individuals who initiated fewer major intellectual breakthroughs than did university scientists. By the beginning of World War II, museums had come to be regarded as places that held the results of past research rather than places for generating new knowledge.

Anthropology museums were not as marginalized as were those of other disciplines, such as biology, because the major university departments remained connected to museums and archaeology continued to be a classifying discipline. Collections were (and remain) as indispensable for archaeological research as they were in 1890, even though documentation requirements, the diversity of specimens collected, and the idea of what constitutes an object that carries data (i.e., whole pots versus potsherds) have changed. Thus, the marginalization scenario was not as evident, nor has it been as critical, in archaeology as it has been in ethnology and physical anthropology. Archaeology's period of systematization occurred later than ethnology's. Whereas ethnologists before World War I were concerned with bringing order to the potentially confusing array of peoples encountered for the first time, archaeologists did not have the conceptual or methodological tools to bring order to their data base until 1920 (e.g., Willey and Sabloff's Early Classification-Historical Period of 1914–1940). Archaeologists during this period were concerned with the development of cultural sequences, developing typologies and regional syntheses (Willey and Sabloff 1980). Museum collections were essential for this activity. Therefore, archaeology remained embedded in museums, especially the large natural history and university museums, until the 1960s.

In cultural anthropology, changes in the nature of the research endeavor meant that objects were not required for the analysis of social organization, customs, or beliefs, although they were rich in information. Cultural anthropologists could talk to people, unlike archaeologists who had to utilize the objects people left behind. In addition, fewer ethnologists were given the extensive training needed to analyze material objects by the mid 1930s. As a result, ethnologists came to ignore material culture or felt it had only descriptive or curiosity value, that it was of little use for theoretical arguments (Wissler 1914; Fenton 1974; Ford 1978; Sturtevant 1969, 1977; Thompson and Parezo 1989). This perception was ironically reinforced by Franz Boas' rejection of museums (Freed and Freed 1983; Jacknis 1985) for political reasons. Boas' fight to control the discipline and his theoretical debate with evolutionists and diffusionists, who were often employed by museums and whose theories were based on material objects, were closely associated. This trend was reinforced by the structural-functionalists, who relegated material culture to the appendices of their books, and by the growing interest among other scholars in behaviorist research in modern communities and the search for solutions to practical problems. Much of the change of the museum anthropologist's status in the field has been, therefore, related to the role of material culture, art, and technology studies in ethnology (Thompson and Parezo 1989). As ethnology grew increasingly close to the other social sciences, the ties to museums and natural history were weakened (Stocking 1976:11).

Although museums were no longer *the* center of research they had been in the nineteenth century, collections research remained crucial to the definition of a museum in the 1920s, 1930s, and 1940s. All individuals who worked in a museum conducted formal or informal research on the objects housed in their institutions, for collections research is crucial to the definition of a modern museum. Collections managers needed to properly identify an object to correctly fill out a catalogue card; a conservator needed to analyze the materials used to produce an object to treat it without inflicting additional damage; a curator needed to understand the use of an object to impart knowledge to the public or pen a scholarly paper. By and large, these research activities, extensive and detailed as they were, produced cultural and object-specific descriptions rather than theoretical generalizations about the nature of society and culture. And it was theoretical innovations that were sought and rewarded in anthropology.[2]

The marginalization of museum anthropology was also due to the changing demographics of the discipline. Universities in the United States, especially research universities, grew phenomenally during the mid to late twentieth century. As a result, academic departments grew in size to a much larger extent than did museums, even though the number of museums expanded as well. While the number of museum anthropologists remained approximately the same in the early 1960s as it had been in the 1930s, the number of non-museum anthropologists increased dramatically (Collier and Fenton 1965:111). Thus, a smaller proportion of anthropologists worked in museums by the start of World War II, and this proportion declined even further during the explosion of university professorships in the late 1950s and 1960s. By and large, only archaeological curatorships grew numerically during the past 40 years, reflecting in part the development of cultural resource management programs, the continuation of archaeological research expeditions, and the curtailment of systematic ethnological collecting. Many ethnology/cultural anthropology positions were eliminated from museums during this same period.

These shifts in anthropology's occupational structure and theoretical orientations occurred simultaneously with a shift in funding for research (from patronage in museums to government and foundation sponsorship) and a change in museums themselves (from institutions designed primarily for research to ones intended to serve the general public through exhibits and interpretive programs). Institutions like the Smithsonian Institution and the American Museum of Natural History had initially been conceptualized by founders, directors, and staff members as institutions whose primary purposes were to generate new knowledge and house specimens for investigators. Secondarily, they were to have been institutions that would disseminate general knowledge (Powell 1887:612). With increasing public concern about the need for mass education in a democracy, museums, especially non-university museums, began to emphasize public programs. This shift created a tension in museums—should their mission be directed toward collecting and preservation for scholarly research or toward public education and interpretation through exhibits? Today, of course, museums as institutions have become the primary center for the dissemination of scientific information to the public. It is in museums that most people encounter anthropology and its central concepts for the first time. While curatorial staff members still conduct research, they also emphasize the reinterpretation of known scientific facts and theories for an educated but uninformed public. This is a teaching function; and teaching, as Tisdale demonstrates in her chapter in this volume, is associated with women. And in our society, education is, unfortunately, not considered as prestigious an activity as is research.

The museum world that developed in the 1930s was in some sense growing away from the university by developing different goals and priorities. Museums were simultaneously places where knowledge was objectified; treasure houses that stored the booty and heirlooms of our past and the glorification of our wealth; research laboratories designed to increase understanding and produce new knowledge; temples and sacred spaces that inspired awe and contemplation; informal schools convened to disseminate information; display arenas that often rivaled Disneyland; and community centers that drew people together for leisure and civic activities. Museums were complex institutions whose goals were to preserve, study, and interpret objects that illustrated natural and cultural phenomena to increase knowledge and thereby educate, entertain, and enlighten. Museums were educational institutions that presented information, concepts, relationships, myths, and worldviews of folk culture through the medium of tangible objects as presented in exhibits, educational programs, and books in a nontechnical (i.e., jargon-free), voluntary, and, as was hoped, understandable form. They were, in short, exciting places to work because of the complex and varied duties; one had to be flexible. They provided staff with a worthwhile and culturally valued avocation and occupation.

Museum staff members provided objects with explanations and meanings and translated these to visitors who were conceptualized as the general public with a tenth-grade education. They tried to help people cope with their world and document their past while stimulating curiosity so that visitors would wish to learn more about a subject on their own. Unlike schools, museums educated through visual symbols and metaphors rather than by the spoken and written word. The central goal or message of the anthropology museum in this educational forum was to help people understand other ways of life, to train them to distend judgment about customs and beliefs that were difficult to comprehend so that they would not pass judgment until the other culture's way of life was understood in its own context. Curators tried to instill respect for other peoples and their ways of life by eliminating stereotypes.

Museums sought to accomplish this by transmitting information about the inhabitants of an area in contradistinction to ourselves. For the Southwest this was done through evolutionary models of primitive vs. civilized, nonliterate vs. literate, us vs. them, and in a pluralistic model, ethnicity. Today this paradigm is being interpreted as the appropriation of the aboriginal past or the packaging of natives by a capitalist, postcolonial society, often for a crassly commercial purpose. (In fact, museums, especially art museums, have been marginalized from scholarly communities because of their appropriation by commercial concerns.) Museums have been involved in selling the Southwest and its native peoples. In the 1920s and 1930s, however, these activities were seen as saving and preserving others for our future. In the process, objects and people were placed on pedestals as they were taken from one culture and reintegrated into our own. The heirlooms that were saved were simultaneously given new value, depersonalized, and authenticated. Because of these translation, valuating, and authenticating roles, the curator in a southwestern museum was an important and highly respected individual in the Southwest. And her or his role was especially important in those periods when the sale of native art was exceptionally big business. Museums mediated between the world of the collector/dealer and the world of the native maker; in many ways they distorted reality by continuing folk culture preconceptions of Native Americans.

Museums were (and still are) exceptionally expensive institutions; a museum existed for the good of a community and often became a community center in orientation and outlook. It could less and less frequently remain an ivory tower. All museums served society in that they provided for the pulling together of relevant items and for their identification and annotation as a first step towards understanding. Staff in museums collected, accepted from others, and cared for those objects society deemed should be saved

"forever"; that is, in trust for the use of future generations. Curators and directors had a huge investment in these objects, and they evaluated and imputed significance to them. Thus, museums, while saving and caring for society's heirlooms, also defined and valuated that which was worth preserving. Museums saved and housed these objects for current use, not only to hoard them for the future. Museums were active places as well as quiet havens. Research at all levels of this endeavor was crucial. This made museums a scholarly resource, simultaneously archives for the preservation of the evidence of conclusions and centers of active research toward new conclusions. This work was creative, varied, and exciting; and it was in part what drew both men and women to museums. Like a faculty position in the academy, curatorship in the museum provided the opportunity for learning in a highly responsible and opportunistic way. As Marjorie Lambert said, "I think that working in the museum has been an exciting career, primarily because it provides opportunities for fieldwork" (Lambert 1985).

The museum's dualism produced a tension. Museums as institutions exhibited a number of conflicting functions that completed for scarce resources and were often burdensome. The goals of different staff positions were contradictory as well: conservators and collections managers or curatorial assistants tried to minimize use of the collections to preserve them for as long as possible. Meanwhile, exhibit coordinators, curators, and researchers utilized objects as much as they could even though use meant that a given object might not last as long as forever.

In the nineteenth century, women were seen as culture bearers, the individuals who would civilize the wilderness and preserve culture through community service and social work. As McGreevy documents in her chapter in this volume, women often preserved culture through volunteer activities and philanthropy. Given the conceptions of women's natural abilities and the duties for which they were fitted, working with objects, especially caring for art or craft items, came to be considered proper duties for women, like teaching. Women were associated with crafts rather than fine art; native peoples were thought to make crafts, not art; native women were assumed to make utilitarian objects rather than ceremonial objects; the objects made by women were considered decorative and therefore without intellectual content. It made sense for women, therefore, to care for them. This pervasive taxonomy of women's work and cultural realms has influenced the production of knowledge for decades. It is no surprise, therefore, that many women who became anthropologists in the 1920s, 1930s, and 1940s found homes in museums and studied objects. Women were welcomed in museums because of their abilities; women sought out jobs in museums partly as an alternative to university teaching positions that were unavailable and partly because of their commitment to public education. It is also not surprising that most of these women were archaeologists and that museum jobs became available as museums came increasingly to be seen as peripheral to the discipline's core institution—the university department. Once inside the museum, women found open to them those aspects of museum work that emphasized their nurturing and handmaidenly role in society. Women today outnumber men in the museum field. As in psychology, the professionalization of the field coincided with the feminization of the field. Museum work has become a female-dominated occupation, but this does not mean that women control the institutions. Women are instead concentrated at the bottom of the prestige scale.

As a result of this complex transition in the disciplines, universities, and museums, male research scientists (except during periods of temporary recession) declined museum job offers. Simultaneously, women began working in museums, especially in the areas associated with the institution's housekeeping and educational areas. Given the sex-typing of museum jobs, to be de-

scribed in the next section, women tended to hold positions in which they cared for or preserved the objects/heirlooms, while men held positions that used the objects. This dichotomy between preservation and use produced institutional problems.

HANDMAIDENS IN THE BASEMENT: THE MUSEUM HIERARCHY

Museums are hierarchical organizations that exhibit characteristics of universities and corporations; this structure developed in the early twentieth century during initial attempts to professionalize. Museums differ from university departments, however. Academic departments are a community of peers, embedded in an age-graded rank system. These peers temporarily elect one of their rank to serve as chair or coordinator. Although the head or departmental chair can often yield a great deal of power, there is essential equality among faculty members at each step in the progression from junior to senior rank. In the past, some departments had only one professor; all others were assistant or associate professors. As has been noted throughout this volume and elsewhere (Rossiter 1982), women were more slowly hired into tenure track positions and had lower retention rates and slower advancement in rank. But within the system they could, with luck and exceptional tenacity, make it to the top of the rank system; thus, Florence Hawley Ellis and Clara Lee Tanner as permanent faculty members could become full professors before they retired. Below this rank are temporary faculty—peers who do not have permanent positions and a few support staff members. There is little mobility from the staff to the faculty positions.

A research curator in a major museum needs to have the same educational credentials and research experience as a university professor. (In the 1930s both curators and professors at all but elite institutions needed only M.A. degrees.) The curator is part of the same professional structure and works toward the same goals of increasing knowledge about other peoples with the hopes of receiving the same rewards and prestige. However, while museums offer intellectual freedom for scholars, museum work requires a team: no single individual can conceptualize, research, design, implement, and erect an exhibit. This means that the museum structure is more discrete than that of an academic department, consisting of a series of specialized positions that are not interchangeable. Because of the necessary team approach, there is less individual freedom for professionals than in an academic department, where at a certain level all professors are equal and interchangeable. Although each professor is a specialist in a certain area of knowledge, each performs the same function—teaching, conducting research, and providing service to the university and profession. This produces an equivalency. This system of peer equality is absent in museums. The museum world is dominated by a partial hierarchy of authority.

Museums have an essentially two-tier system conceptualized as a stratified team of specialists (an elite)—scientific curators and administrators—and support staff and technicians (the proletariate) under the direction of a benevolent dictator or general who organizes a vision for the institution and makes sure the team carries it through. Power and authority accrue to the top position; the team approach means that the director receives credit for all successful projects and takes the blame for all unsuccessful projects that come to the attention of the public. Support technicians perform essential yet invisible functions that the public rarely sees or understands; these are essentially the handmaidenly positions that tend to be filled by women with the exception of exhibit personnel (who use power tools—a male activity). Directors, head curators, research curators, and researchers generally tend to be men; educators, collections staff, and office staff tend to be women. There is very little, if any, mobility from support positions to the more prestigious

and visible research/curatorial and administrative positions; as in universities, to move requires an advanced degree. The ranked age-grade system for curatorial staff is absent in all but the largest museums. Museums exhibit power relations structured by differentiation between the elite and the proletariate. This system was in position by the 1930s, even though it began much earlier.

The elite curatorial positions are highly respected by the general public and the profession, at least in theory. Curators care for our valued things. They, like faculty, are allowed the freedom to conduct research and produce new knowledge; they and the directors hold the positions toward which a scholar aspires. Each has a territory and a recognized specialty. As Mead (1965:17–18) wrote,

Each curator is responsible for one area of the world or else for one aspect of anthropology; the objects in his office speak for his special interest. A curator's office is a workshop. Here he spreads out new specimens to catalogue or old ones to study. Here he makes selections or exhibits, comparing his field notes and his field photographs with objects collected on a recent field trip or perhaps a half-century ago. Here he also answers all kinds of questions over the telephone. . . . Here he also talks with people who bring in specimens they would like to have identified. And here in the Museum the anthropologist hopes and plans for his next field trip.

Curators spend a great deal of time authenticating and contextualizing objects. This authority accrues to the museums and the high-level positions within it. Simultaneously, however, it requires housekeeping, because caring for the collections requires keeping them safe from harm and clean. Curators and their assistants spend a great deal of time, as one noted,

trying to keep the dust off, and trying to keep them from being rubbed or crowded or whatever else might hurt them. . . . One of the big problems in the whole area of museum storage is to get the pieces put away in such a manner that they can be used for study or can be seen, so that we can tell how many pieces we have and know just what types of materials we do have at any one time. It isn't a matter of piling them tightly in a box and closing the lid and locking it. All these things must be distributed in some way in the storage area so that they can be of value to visiting scholars or to people in the Museum who are working with them (Gifford quoted in Mead 1965: 772–73).

This is time-consuming and tedious work. In many ways, curatorship is scientific housekeeping, according to Harry Shapiro (quoted in Mead 1965:73); its essential features are dusting, shelving, sorting, protecting, knowing where things are. It is situated in the basement or the attic, away from the public, primarily for the safety of the objects. It is, therefore, hidden; it is the private side of the museum. As Gifford states, one does it to assist other people who use the collections; rarely does one do it for one's own research. It takes so much time to curate a collection that one rarely has time to use it oneself. So one looks forward to going to the field. The notion of a curator having more time for professional activities than does a faculty member is an illusion. A curator does what a professor does as well as performing more community service.

While collecting and assembling a potentially confusing array of objects, museum curators and their assistants conserve and preserve heirlooms so that they can be used by future scholars. The goal is to prolong the life of objects as far into the future as possible. This is a fiduciary responsibility and involves caretaking—the invisible museum function. If museum curators who write books, conceptualize and prepare exhibits, and give lectures are visible to the pubic, the helpers—called curatorial assistants, registrars, or collections managers—are invisible. Taking care of a collection is never-ending and exceptionally time-consuming work. One never catches up. It is neither glamorous nor engendering of rewards as is writing a book, conducting fieldwork in ex-

otic places, or producing a major exhibit. Yet it is absolutely crucial to the continuous functioning of the institution. And it calls upon the "feminine" skills of observation, patience, and dexterity.

This pattern of women being concentrated at the bottom of the prestige scale and in positions that have the largest concentration of volunteers thus has a long history, although there has been some improvement since the 1960s. One scholar notes the sex-typed pattern of employment in natural history museums as well:

Sex-segregated employment was also underway in the expanding world of natural history museums in the late nineteenth century. Although there are instances of women assistants on museum staffs as early as the late 1860s, more were added in the next few decades to help museums cope with the explosive growth in collections brought back from the increasing numbers of expeditions to far-off places. The whole scale of natural history was changing. A naturalist, for example, who might formerly have devoted his career to the classification of the flora and fauna of a given region would now be overwhelmed by the vast quantities of specimens that were piling up. Entire museums were necessary to house them, and staffs of bright (but poorly paid) assistants would be needed to catalog and classify them and to publish taxonomic descriptions. Although women were accepted in this new kind of work, and by 1873 twelve were listed as working at Harvard's Museum of Comparative Zoology, they received far less publicity than did the women astronomers (Rossiter 1982:87).

In addition, the second tier of temporary second-class peers was found between the elite and the proletariate:

Likewise, in the anthropological museums of this period, women began in the 1880s to hold marginal positions, from which they often made sizable contributions to science. Women anthropologists in these years were often loosely affiliated, almost "free-lance," field workers who were only rarely paid a salary but who were allowed to publish in the museum's proceedings and to have some official museum identification, which aided them, in the field. Among the most notable of these women were Alice C. Fletcher, Erminnie A. P. Smith, and Zelia Nuttall, who were affiliated with the Peabody Museum of Archaeology and Ethnology at Harvard, the University Museum of the University of Pennsylvania and the museum at the University of California at Berkeley. A few other, wealthier, women also took up the matronly role of financial patron and power-behind-the-director at late-nineteenth-century anthropology museums. Two of these powerful women were Sara Yorke Stevenson at the University Museum of the University of Pennsylvania in the 1890s and her protégée, Phoebe Apperson Hearst, who started her own museum at the University of California in 1901 (Rossiter 1982:59).

A case in point of the entrenched nature of this dichotomy is the U.S. Museum of Natural History (Smithsonian Institution) in Washington, where from the 1840s until 1963 almost all women held secretarial/clerk-typist or janitorial positions (Dodson 1986:35). There were no women curators; there were numerous female volunteers. All women scientists held unpaid positions as honorary Smithsonian fellows, associates, and collaborators. Several female anthropologists, such as Betty Meggars and Nathalie Woodbury, were married to Smithsonian curators and research scientists; because of nepotism rules they were ineligible for paid positions. After World War II, a few women did work in educational outreach programs and as administrative support staff members, but the first female curator in anthropology was not hired until the early 1980s!

This dichotomized situation at the Smithsonian stemmed directly from the need to professionalize in the face of increasing criteria for university employment and from the influence of the legendary Matilda Coxe Stevenson. Stevenson, with her infamous personality and her constant disagreements with Powell (see Parezo's chapter in this volume), served as an excuse for a more general pattern that occurred between 1880 and the 1920s, which has been identified by Rossiter (1982:xvii):

Increasingly in the 1880s and thereafter, educated women joined scientific organizations and sought work in museums and observatories, thus seeming to most men to be encroaching upon what had formerly been exclusively masculine territory. Such incursions brought on a crisis of impending feminization, and a series of skirmishes in the 1880s and 1890s in science. Although still allowed to enter most areas of science, they could hold only subordinate, close to invisible, and specifically designated positions and memberships. In this context at least part of the so-called "professionalization" of science in the 1880s and 1890s begins to look more like a deliberate reaction, conscious or not, by men against the increasing feminization of American culture, including science, at the end of the century. Ejecting women in the name of "higher standards" was one way to reassert strongly the male dominance over the burgeoning feminine presence. Thus, even though women could claim by 1920 that they had "opened the doors" of science, it was quite clear that they would be limited to positions just inside the entry way.

Museums exhibited this same pattern in their hierarchical structure, and at the same time they became the place where mentors could put women they did not want to lose from the profession yet did not want to let into the more prestigious academic department.

Exhibits, a product of the museum, reinforced and reflected this sexual hierarchy. Exhibits were not only about objects; they were also about the people who made and used them. Exhibits created and substantiated societal myths and reinforced preconceptions about basic cultural categories in the United States, including the subordinate status of women and their place in the home, because they were public discourse. They did this by portraying women from other cultures in a manner that reflected middle-class, Anglo-American ideals and realities. Ever since the 1893 World's Columbian Exposition, when William H. Holmes developed life group exhibits to show objects in a life group setting, life-sized exhibits have depicted American Indians "wearing real clothing engaging in typical activities using actual objects [that] appeared to possess a quality of human interest that attracted the attention of people of all ages and both sexes" (Ewers 1955:4).

Meant to be realistic, action oriented, and noncontroversial—an improvement over the rows upon rows of decontextualized stone tools and pottery bowls—life groups were a type of habitat group designed to put the visitor in the midst of nature and make culture a part of nature. They brought nature to the city dweller. Almost all life groups used anthropologists as models (occasionally a Native American was brought to the museum to model) and depicted an idealized nuclear family of a man, a woman, and one or two children. They showed no extended families and no old people. And, of course, it was extremely rare for a woman to be standing by herself or for two women to be shown together working or interacting. (The only exceptions were the stiff mannequins that wore costumes.) Figure positions and diorama layouts reflected status ideals as well as cultural roles. Men tended to be positioned standing and women kneeling. This made the man the center of interest because the viewer's focus is drawn to a standing figure, which always predominates a landscape. While men faced the visitor, eye to eye, women generally faced the rear wall. When women figures faced forward, their eyes were lowered; there was no direct eye contact with the visitor. Thus, women were seen to have a shy, modest demeanor.

Women in exhibits were usually passive; when active, they were hardworking housewives. They ground corn or made useful utensils to hold food—almost always sitting on the floor to perform such tasks, while a man stood around, unintentionally reinforcing the preconception that men did not do household tasks. More commonly, women received food, raw materials, luxury items, or clothing from a man. Rarely were women the givers and men the receivers. Women were portrayed as helpers rather than as independent active participants in the culture (Parezo

1988b). Rarely did women work or act in the public domain. Native American women in exhibits thus reflected the Victorian and Edwardian ideal of the woman who remained in the home while her husband went out to work and brought home resources. When the woman did work, she cooked, sewed, and made a good home for her family. The exhibits portrayed an idealized cultural foil for modern European and American civilization, reinforcing preconceptions of what was right and natural for gender relations. And museums kept portraying this timeless model even when the rest of anthropology was rejecting unilinear evolutionary theories. No wonder the message that was being portrayed—that all women are hardworking but passive housewives who receive the gifts of men—was reinforced in the occupational structure of the museum. According to the model, women belonged in the basement as the museum's hardworking but quiet housewives.

SOUTHWESTERN WOMEN
ANTHROPOLOGISTS IN THE MUSEUM

Museums developed in the East, and the earliest museologists were men; women, when they held positions in the late nineteenth and early twentieth centuries, were, with the exception of a few individuals such as Matilda Coxe Stevenson and Frances Densmore, collectors and collaborators, clerks and typists—a situation common to all sciences (Rossiter 1982). Women entered museums in the 1920s, when museums were expanding across the country, primarily as collection assistants and support staff, i.e., in technical rather than elite scientific positions. As the Great Depression intensified and university professorships became almost nonexistent for everyone, women who wanted to work in anthropology, especially archaeology, were drawn to and hired by museums. This was partly because they were willing to accept less pay, to work in western rather than eastern museums and in small rather than large institutions. "Anthropology and museums have the reputation of being poorly paid and we knew that when we went into it" (Lambert 1985). Since then, with few exceptions, museum anthropologists have been paid about two-thirds of what their university counterparts have earned.[3] Lambert (1985) noted that she never earned more than $10,000; moreover, she said,

Every now and then the paper would publish salaries of top people in the museum and you'd find out someone whose job you were partly doing was getting more money. . . . I know two men I worked with were getting $100 to $150 a month more than I was and I was doing exactly the same work at the same title. And you know what the excuse was? "Well, we're the head of our families, you're not." . . . They thought they were giving us a break by having us in the profession. They didn't come right out and say it, but I'm sure that's what it was. And their attitude was, if she wants to have everything, why doesn't she go and find a man with money and marry him? I think that attitude still persists.

Discrimination in pay was not uncommon. Bertha Dutton (1985a) felt, "Because I am a woman I have never received more than $12,000 a year for all that I've done." And it should be mentioned that Dutton overcame all the odds and was one of the first women museum directors in this country (see McGreevy's chapter in this volume). By contrast, her male counterparts earned on the average at least 50% more. This double system also surfaced in slower advancement rates, as it had in the university: Dutton commented, "All the way through if I hadn't been a woman, I'd be in a higher place" (1985a). Even Margaret Mead noted the discrepancy: "Being a woman, I was not paid as well or advanced as fast as the men in the Department, but I did have a lot of freedom to do as I liked" (Mead 1965:117).

Women in the 1930s and 1940s did gain academic freedom and freedom from the home and were rewarded with a job and security. (Although there was no tenure system in museums, few people in curatorial positions were ever fired.)

This was, and still is, very important to museum professionals. But once a group of professionals enters an institution en masse and accepts less pay, the pay scale for the entire institution begins to fall. Since American society places value on occupations based on how well they pay, a lowering pay scale adds to the profession's marginalization. And, unfortunately, the freedom was often wishful thinking. As Lambert (1985) remembered,

When I went into the museum, we were told we would spend half the time doing curatorial work, and half the time on our own research. It never did work out that way. The duties you had just took too much time. I sometimes thought that if I was in a department I would get time to do fieldwork. I think maybe I missed it because they do have summers free to do fieldwork.

All museums lacked resources to perform their tasks well; and it can generally be said that curators tried to do their jobs well. Women, because they were often in support positions or at the bottom of the curatorial hierarchy, received less support than their male counterparts for the same amount and type of work. They often were presented with the expectation that they could miraculously produce results with no financial or technical assistance. The experience of Margaret Mead at the American Museum of Natural History illustrates this problem common to women who worked in all museums:

When I arrived home [from a field trip] and came to the Museum, it was explained that there was no real office free for me. I would have to take a kind of cataloguing room up in the sixth floor tower, where old Mr. Sabine sat putting numbers on specimens of new collections. I was next to youngest of the departmental members (Dr. Shapiro was the youngest) and I was a girl. Dr. Wissler used to say that museum work fitted women because it was rather like housekeeping. And in fact, most of the "housekeeping" then was done by Miss Bella Weitzner, who came to the Museum straight from high school and later was appointed to the scientific staff. When she retired, she was Associate Curator of Ethnology (Mead 1965 : 116).

Research curatorships were professionally useful only if there was an assistant to help look after the collections. Unfortunately, the situation for most women was the same as that encountered by Bertha Dutton at the Museum of New Mexico:

You get enough money to go into the field and study people and learn about their culture or you go into the field to do archaeology and recover materials. And then you have just three months to do it. Then you come back to your job and everything has accumulated there and you have to dig in harder than ever to get back to the string that you were following when you left for the field. You have to do your laboratory work or your writing work at home or during holidays or weekends. And there is no money or help for that (1985a).

In the museum, curatorships with curatorial assistance were the quality jobs; they afforded the greatest freedom and, with luck, ample opportunities for fieldwork. These were the only positions recognized by academic anthropologists as the equivalent to university professorships. Women curators did obtain as much research time as they could, which generally was not enough. H. Marie Wormington (1985) noted, "I got very little time for research, but somehow managed to get my papers written. Digging is the part that's fun." There was general agreement among those interviewed that male curators received more research time than did female curators. In Wormington's case, even though she stated that "the most blatant forms of sexism had died down by the time I got there" (1985), getting research opportunities required hiding her gender as well as a great deal of persistence.

In 1985, Wormington described her professional problems. She began working for the Denver Museum of Natural History on a temporary basis in 1935. In 1937, the new director, Mr. A. M. Bailey, "discovered there was a woman and an archaeologist on the staff. He wrote to the di-

rector of the board of trustees suggesting that I be removed. He felt there was no place for either in the museum and the combination was lethal." The board, however, retained Wormington on a full-time basis and "that began 33 years of problems with the director." Among other things, he would not give her in-house financial or clerical support for her fieldwork activities, kept her salary at half the rate of other curators on the staff, and required her to work weekends and perform hostess duty. When Wormington wrote articles for scientific journals he told her to use her initials, H. M., not her name, Hannah Marie, for he "felt that nobody would read a book written by a woman." Finally in 1968, when Wormington was on sabbatical as a visiting professor at Arizona State University, the director managed to remove her by simply eliminating the position. "Bailey was able to fire me after granting me a year's leave of absence to teach at ASU. He just wrote me a letter saying he was closing the department. The following year he opened up a new department of anthropology."

A few women did obtain and keep these respected positions with the help of supportive male directors, as Cordell notes in her chapter. Marjorie Lambert worked her entire career for the University of New Mexico and the Museum of New Mexico, essentially for Edgar L. Hewett, "a wonderful teacher and a good friend" (Lambert 1985). Hewett was a power broker in New Mexican archaeology and western higher education. An institution builder, he controlled anthropology at the Museum of New Mexico, the School of American Research, the University of New Mexico, and later the San Diego Museum of Man and the University of Southern California (Chauvenet 1983). Lambert was appointed supervisor of the University of New Mexico's field school in 1934:

In the spring of 1937 Hewett told me he was going to trade Paul Reiter—the Curator of Archaeology at the Museum of New Mexico—to the University because he wanted me to come up to Santa Fe and work for him at the Museum of New Mexico. So I became the Curator of Archaeology. I went in first at a pre-parator's salary. I held the post until 1959 when I became the Curator of Anthropological Exhibits and General Anthropology (Lambert 1985).

Lambert remained with the institution until her retirement in 1969 (thereby exhibiting the institutional loyalty so striking of women who worked in museums), although the road was not always easy. "It was extremely hard for women to break down the pride in men," she noted in 1985. Many of Lambert's male archaeological colleagues resented having a woman around, and Lambert (1985) felt ambivalent about Hewett's double standards with regard to pay and duties:

I was hurt because Dr. Hewett was so good to me, and he thought the world of me—and he was sort of a father figure to all of us. It was like having your own father doing a dirty trick to you. When I got the Pa'ako job, for example, there had been a man ahead of me who hadn't done very good work for three months. I found out he was getting almost $200 a month more than me. I found that out at a time when I was taking $25 a month out of my own salary to have the shovels and picks sharpened. I paid for the photographs, too, out of my own salary. That's the only thing I hold against Hewett. Otherwise, he was a wonderful person.

Even for these "equivalent" positions under "supportive" directors, some curators were more equal than others.

Women fulfilling the motherly role were quite common in corporations and in academe. Kanter (1977) found that women were expected to carry out mundane tasks in support of male colleagues. Women curators mentioned that they had receptionist duties not required of their male counterparts. For example, at the Museum of New Mexico the curators went out to lunch every day to socialize and discuss business. The female secretary who sat at the front desk and served as security guard while welcoming visitors also needed a daily lunch break. Lambert remembered, "If there was not enough in the budget to keep the museum open during lunch, the women curators

would have to tend the desk while the men went out to lunch—two- or three-hour lunches at that" (1985). None of the men were asked to take over this duty. In addition, women curators, like support staff, were asked to work longer hours and "were made to do things that the men didn't want to do. That sort of discrimination has gone on throughout my career. But I think women are better at standing up for their rights now than when I started. We wouldn't have dared then—jobs were so scarce" (Lambert 1985).

Another reason that many women anthropologists worked in museums, in addition to a lack of alternatives, was that many museums required a B.A. or M.A. degree to obtain an entry-level position, and they were happy to have individuals who had obtained their education in the West, not only at elite eastern schools. (Ph.D.'s were later required for research curatorial positions in larger institutions.) Marjorie Lambert, for example, obtained a M.A., as did Katharine Bartlett and Kate Peck Kent. Women with anthropology M.A.'s were much more likely to work in museums than in anthropology departments in the Southwest; Clara Lee Tanner was the rare exception, and it is significant that she obtained a teaching position at her alma mater. Ironically, there was even the feeling that Ph.D.'s were unnecessary for women curators. Several were discouraged from finishing their studies. Lambert (1985), for example, wanted to continue her education:

I wanted to go to Harvard, Columbia, or Chicago. I wanted to do that more than anything, and Hewett wouldn't let me. He didn't think it was a good idea. He wanted me to go to USC and that wasn't a good school. Then I talked to Dr. Mera about it, and he said that if I was going to spend my life in a museum, he didn't see that a Ph.D. was important.

In the 1930s, museums even came to be seen as the place where one could enter the profession with no advanced degree. Journals such as the *AAUW Journal* and the *Independent Woman* (published by the National Federation of Business and Professional Women) urged women to turn a hobby, a unique interest, or a skill into a job. Dorothy Thomas's "Exploring the Museum Field" in 1933 described the work of several women at the American Museum of Natural History, including Margaret Mead, and encouraged women to think that by starting as volunteers they could rise to interesting positions. Unfortunately, any job that can be obtained through volunteerism has the taint of amateurism.

Thus, museum work offered women a foot in the door, a way into the profession on a permanent basis, but at a price. The reasoning went that because women had fewer credentials and were really only volunteers, directors were justified in giving them lower salaries and positions such as assistantships. Occasionally, the foothold did enable a few women (e.g., Bertha Dutton and Marie Wormington) to hold jobs while they slowly worked toward their Ph.D.'s. During the 1930s, the alternatives to a job while one was going to school were a scholarship (very rare for women), the task of putting pot sherds together in the university museum basement (very common for both men and women), or government projects (often closed to women). The museum was the ideal place to learn the trade. Clara Lee Tanner (1985) mentioned spending hours in the basement of the Arizona State Museum. This educational apprenticeship, based on the need for quantities of cheap labor for time-consuming and tedious but necessary tasks, was considered especially appropriate for women. It was reinforced by the sexual division of labor in the field schools, where women were more likely to be assigned duties in the laboratory, washing sherds, reconstructing pots, or numbering lithics (all of which were registration or cataloguing skills needed to prepare objects that had been discovered, so that the senior male anthropologist could identify and analyze them) rather than surveying or digging. Lambert exemplified this: "Hewett appointed me instructor in the department at UNM. They opened up the

big excavations at Bandelier and Kuaua. Gordon Vivian was in charge of the excavations at Kuaua. I was appointed in charge of lab materials" (Lambert 1985). The field laboratory was the equivalent to the museum collections storage area. The assignment of women to the tent out of the sun was the standard practice at the University of Arizona and the University of New Mexico field schools for many years, the practice lasting longer in Arizona than in New Mexico (Ellis 1985, personal communication).

Thus, while they were graduate students, Clara Lee Tanner and Florence Hawley Ellis were given lab work that trained them for museum work while Emil Haury helped Byron Cummings excavate. Later, because he had excavation experience, Haury was asked by Cummings to accompany him to Cuiculco in Mexico. The two women were not. The same was true for Anna Shepard at the University of New Mexico—she worked in the laboratory but did little excavation. Hewett did let some women excavate, which is one reason why so many women went to the University of New Mexico field school rather than the University of Arizona field schools.

This gender-specific division of labor in school solved, if one may, the conceptual dilemma in archaeology identified by Cordell—the "expedition mentality." The classical idea of archaeology involved going on a quest-like expedition to face hardships in faraway places. An expedition meant enduring difficulties such as finding water, digging latrines, and surviving in a manly manner. Placing the women in the tent-laboratory kept them safe and sheltered. They could assist yet not get in the way. This created a spatial, social, and conceptual polarity between the excavation area and the camp-lab, which was reflected later in the museum building. Those men who did allow the small but insistent group of women on excavations reinforced the dichotomy because they felt that women had special skills—such as illustrating artifacts and record keeping. These skills could best be performed in a sheltered area.

We are not implying that women did not enjoy laboratory work. Many did. We do want to note that women had fewer alternatives than male students and that their alternatives trained them for support positions in museums. The alternative was to market traditionally female skills—secretarial, as Bertha Dutton did, or writing for a popular audience, the path chosen by Gertrude Hill and the women documented in Tisdale's chapter. A combination of the two types of skills were what was needed for that first museum position.

Sometimes women had mobility between institutions and across the country, but most women stayed in the Southwest and in museums because of an abiding love for the institution and the place, moving laterally within the institution. Women could secure positions in western museums much more easily than in eastern museums because these institutions were smaller in size and had a greater emphasis on exhibition and public education. This attitude is evident in the following letter from Frederic Douglas to Jesse Nusbaum:

Most of my ideas revolve about the central thought that it's better to belong to a small live museum than a big dead one. The odor of stagnation was pretty evident. Instead of revising their public exhibitions, most of which need it badly, most of the eastern folks just sit and putter or write books they can't afford to publish. What those birds need are some bright young things with an idea for making good looking displays. They're all so hopped on research that they have lost the art of reaching the public effectively through displays (DAM:FD/JN 9/20/34).

All of Douglas's assistants were women, for he felt they were especially gifted in these areas and had great energy and ideas. Kate Peck Kent, for example, worked in museums for most of her early career before teaching at the University of Denver. Kent enjoyed museum research: "Many women go into museums. It is a pleasant experience" (Kent 1985b). Trained by Douglas at the

Denver Art Museum, she assisted him for years, both before and after completing her master's degree. Unfortunately, there was never enough money to make her position permanent, as Tisdale discusses in her chapter in this volume. When Douglas retired, a male curator from an eastern institution rather than his more highly qualified and experienced assistant, Kate Peck Kent, took over his post.

Katharine Bartlett's professional life illustrates women's careers in western museums. Bartlett joined the staff of the newly formed Museum of Northern Arizona in 1930 after graduating with an M.A. in archaeology and physical anthropology from the University of Denver. Harold S. Colton asked her to come to the museum after hearing her research presentation at an American Association for the Advancement of Science meeting in Tucson. Her first job was classified as temporary summer employment. She catalogued artifacts from a small excavation under the direction of Lyndon Hargrave and John McGregor, because "they needed someone to take care of the material from the excavation" (Bartlett 1985). Pleased with her performance, diligence, and attention to detail, Colton asked her to remain: "I came to spend a summer and I've been here ever since" (Bartlett 1985). This was a very common pattern for women museum anthropologists. They were initially noticed for their independent and sophisticated scientific research abilities, then hired and retained for traditional female helping skills. Nevertheless, Bartlett and others remained extremely loyal to their institutions and directors and often stayed with one museum for their entire career. This loyalty has been recognized: speaking of Bartlett, Dorothy House concluded, "She is a unifying spirit. She has through time helped the institution maintain its identity. It's terribly valuable to have that continuity here. She is still a resource after 59 years" (quoted in Bartimus 1989).

But there were opportunities and there were traps. Bartlett became the general assistant to the

Coltons, and she lived with them for many years, becoming much like an impoverished cousin: "I got to be a member of the family, almost" (Bartlett 1985). Working on whatever needed doing during the day, she wrote articles at night: "Most of the research I did I worked on in the evenings. After dinner we just sat around the fireplace and I worked on whatever kind of research I had going on" (Bartlett 1985). Bartlett produced an exceptionally wide-ranging list of publications, over 70 articles and appendices in respected reports and journals, on everything from lithic technology to Spanish–Native American relations. But most of these were short descriptions and analyses; there is not the all-important monograph or book. She never had the opportunity.

Bartlett was indispensable to the Museum of Northern Arizona, for she was needed to manage the daily operations. "In those days when I was an anthropologist, the staff was so small we all did everything" (Bartlett quoted in Bartimus 1989). But, as usual, some individuals did more of everything than did others. The museum would not have been successful if Bartlett had not done all the registration, cataloguing, budget preparation and accounting, correspondence, and editing. She also assisted with the annual Hopi and Navajo Craftsmen shows, managed the houses and the research associate program, "wrote lots of site cards," and performed "unending other tasks." She never led an archaeological project, nor was she able to return to the large-scale analyses that had been the impetus for Colton's hiring her. Male archaeologists (usually graduate students from the University of Arizona) were brought in for these research tasks. Bartlett thus worked on small projects by necessity, as she herself recognized:

I have dabbled in everything under heaven: a little research here, a little research on something else. I have written things on history, Indians, Indian History, Indian arts and crafts, museums. . . . I kept thinking I should concentrate on one thing, but I never managed. . . . I think the only continuous thing that I

have really had an interest in was the museum as a whole (quoted in Bartimus 1989).

Bartlett actually pursued a very pragmatic and successful plan of research and publication that has been followed by other museum anthropologists—small projects based on accessible museum collections and limited research goals that could be attained by working intermittently. Collections research lent itself to this strategy. "The kind of fieldwork I did was in museums," Kent (1985b) remembered. This also suited her time schedule, for Kent balanced a family with her work. She firmly stated,

It never occurred to me that I wouldn't get married at some point nor did it ever occur to me that there was something difficult about deciding whether to get married or to have a career. There never seemed to me to be the choice. . . . I received a great deal of support from my husband. The only problem was how to juggle a family and outside interests and jobs. You have to work twice as hard and I don't think that unless you are physically very strong you can do it. The only person who ever really figured it out was Margaret Mead (Kent 1985b).

Bartlett, Kent, and others were assisted in this research strategy through museums such as the Museum of Northern Arizona that had their publication outlets, e.g., *MNA Museum Notes, Plateau, MNA Bulletins,* and *MNA Research Reports. Museum Notes* was designed for members of the museum; in the 1930s it contained annual reports, lists of acquisitions, research progress reports, and short articles (two to six pages) describing the results of staff endeavors. At first these articles were highly detailed, written for other anthropologists, geologists, and naturalists. As a corpus, they form a significant body of regional information that is still widely cited. *Museum Notes* was not theoretical, however, and was equivalent to the "Reports and Comments" section in the *American Anthropologist* or *American Antiquity.* With time, as the funding structure of the institution changed and came to depend on outside funding by the public rather than on the Colton family fortune, *Plateau* became more popular; it was eventually transformed into a glossy picture magazine in the late 1970s. *Museum Notes* (whose name was changed to *Plateau*) thus became an extended exhibit designed for the educated general public.

A similar transformation occurred in the journals of the Southwest Museum (*The Masterkey*), the Museum of New Mexico (*El Palacio*), and the American Museum of Natural History (*Natural History*). Museum curators and staff members were expected to contribute to these publications, often on a monthly or bimonthly basis. Dutton, for example, published over 150 articles; all but 3 were in *El Palacio, New Mexico Magazine, Museum News, Southwest Monuments Monthly Reports, Southwestern Lore,* or *Indian Life.* Dutton did manage to publish a number of professional monographs through the museum series at the same time, but she had no articles in *American Anthropologist* or *American Antiquity.* She was allowed little time and received no encouragement to publish in these professional outlets. And in fact, writing for and eventually becoming responsible for membership journals became a burden for Dutton, Bartlett, and Lambert, especially during World War II. Dutton, however, reconciled this by seeing the task as an educational duty that demanded and engendered a special kind of writing, one that would help eradicate illiteracy: "I've always tried to introduce new words and explain them, and to educate people" (Dutton 1985a).

Museum publication outlets, especially research reports, actually gave an advantage to museum anthropologists, both men and women, that was not available to academically based anthropologists. However, the magazines involved a different style of writing than is found in research monographs, articles, and reports. In some cases the magazines were much more journalistic; in all cases they were more descriptive—informative but not exceptionally analytical. They were seen as low-level interpretation. There were constant deadlines, so often the work showed signs of having been done more quickly than the author would have liked. Also, since they were not refereed, they brought less professional status to the author, although more public recognition. And as Cordell notes in her paper, directing large excavation projects and writing a monograph as the senior or sole author was what brought the greatest rewards in anthropology, not penning numerous articles on a series of small discrete projects. Women published hundreds of articles in these regional and in-house publication outlets and made a tremendous contribution to our knowledge base in the process.

Women often moved from job to job within an institution rather than change institutions; it was harder to move from a western to an eastern institution because of preconceptions about the West's "backwardness." (Unfortunately, western anthropology museums began to develop on the cusp of the great museum period in the East.) Eventually, for example, Katharine Bartlett became the librarian and archivist for the Museum of Northern Arizona. "I think that I really enjoyed the library almost more than any of the other things that I've ever done. It was very interesting and really wonderful to be able to help people find what they needed for their research projects. I really enjoyed that" (Bartlett 1985). Bartlett was in many ways the glue that held the museum together—the essential helper sometimes acknowledged and frankly beloved by all anthropologists who have ever gone through the halls of the Museum of Northern Arizona. She was the trained specialist and generalist that every museum must have. And this role suited her inclinations and personality. As she herself analyzed her role: "I was a jack-of-all-trades. I am not a leader, but a follower. Diversification is my motto. I've done just about everything you can think of in a museum" (1985). One can still go to Bartlett to find something, just as everyone went to Bella Weitzner at the American Museum of Natural History. Both always knew exactly where the elusive object, book, or piece of paper was hidden. Bartlett and Weitzner were the history of their institutions. Neither ever attained a curatorship or formal recognition in their own institution of their true worth.

Bartlett has obtained some recognition in the field. Nevertheless, although she is known to most Southwesternists, other anthropologists who became collections managers, exhibit designers, educators, and registrars remain invisible. For example, Florence Connolly, Leona Cope, Barbara Cortright, Carol Cox, Emily Davis, Mabel Mason DeBra, Margaret Estep, Helen Forsberg, Mona Hanks, Gertrude Hill, and Hilda Hobbs all had advanced degrees in anthropology and conducted independent research. Each published a few articles at the beginning of their careers and then spent the rest of their lives caring for the collections, building exhibits, and assisting research curators and visiting scholars. We know next to nothing about them; many probably left the field.

These women and others have eluded all our efforts to collect information about them. We only have occasional glimpses. For example, Kathleen Scheifele worked at the Heard Museum after graduating from the University of Arizona, having specialized in archaeology and museology. She received excellent recommendations from Emil Haury and Ted Sayles, with whom she had worked in the laboratory at the Point of Pines field school (DAM: TC/FD 7/25/52). Her position at the Heard Museum was Curatorial Assistant, but she was essentially a secretary. She never became a curator, and one can only surmise that she married or left the field for some other reason.

Slightly more well known but still elusive was Aileen O'Bryan Nusbaum. Nusbaum was the wife of archaeologist Jesse L. Nusbaum, and they lived and worked both in Santa Fe and at Mesa Verde (1921–1931). In Santa Fe, Jesse was first an archaeologist and later the director of the Laboratory of Anthropology. Aileen accompanied her husband on his expeditions and collected legends and origin myths from different southwest-

ern groups (Nusbaum 1926, 1956). In addition, she wrote children's stories and pageants that utilized Native American themes. These were illustrated with her own drawings (Nusbaum had studied art and drama at the Sorbonne.) While at Mesa Verde, Nusbaum upgraded the small museum established by Jessie Walter Fewkes in 1918 and built exhibits that can still be seen today (D. Smith 1988; J. Smith 1981). She continued to utilize her expertise at the Laboratory of Anthropology until she and her husband divorced.

There is some evidence that women anthropologists and museum specialists became librarians and archivists when it became evident that there was no upward and little lateral mobility, job security, or even the possibility of a living wage in museums. Economic necessity forced many women to return to "female" jobs. Alice Stallings, Curatorial Assistant at the Laboratory of Anthropology, changed professions when her archaeologist husband returned to Harvard University to complete his doctorate:

We have all taken two cuts this year, so that when Sid's salary stops the last of August, mine alone doesn't stack up well. Therefore I am looking for another job, anything, anywhere, that will up the level again. I'd dearly love it to be something to do with anthropology but after all, we are not the only ones counting pennies, so I shall not be choosy (DAM: AS/FD 6/26/39)

She eventually found a job in a library. Another scholar, Gertrude Hill, graduated from the University of Arizona and published extensively on southwestern Native American art, especially Piman basketry and Navajo jewelry (Hill 1937a, 1937b, 1938a, 1938b, 1942a, 1942b, 1947). She held a series of low-paying, temporary jobs in southwestern museums and finally went to the University of Denver's library school in 1944, completing her apprenticeship in the Denver Art Museum library (DAM: FD/LM 9/26/44). Unable to obtain employment in Colorado, she returned to Santa Fe and became the librarian at the Museum of New Mexico. Although the position paid less than other librarianships back East that she had been offered, she chose the Museum of New Mexico because she could continue working in her primary area, the American Southwest, and even find time to publish a bibliography (Hill 1954). However, she never returned to material culture research, although she did manage to produce articles dealing with literature and archival research (Hill 1957, 1958, 1961). Frances Reynolds at the Denver Art Museum and Ruth D. Simpson of the Southwest Museum and the Heard Museum also followed this course.

The transition from student archaeologist to museum professional to librarian was also common for women who married, left the field temporarily to have families, and then tried to return. Adelaide Chamberlaine Law provides a brief case. Law obtained a B.A. from the University of Arizona, training in archaeology and museum methods under Dean Byron Cummings, and an M.A. in archaeology from the University of New Mexico under Hewett in the early 1930s. In addition, she continued her advanced course work at the Cincinnati Art Academy. She quickly obtained employment at the Southwest Museum as a research assistant and curator of exhibits. She held these posts for five years. She was noted by colleagues for her nonaggressive personality, her talent, and her versatility (DAM:HJ/FD 1/21/41). While at the Southwest Museum she designed and built all the habitat groups, "gathered and arranged the materials for the director's lectures," ran the docent program, gave lectures to women's clubs, and produced traveling exhibits for schools. Her independent research project was a compilation of Keres vocabulary, focusing on Cochiti. Her friend and colleague Hester Jones observed, "Her chief informant is a most intelligent young woman from Cochiti capable of giving her grammatical forms and definitions" (DAM:HJ/FD 1/21/41). Either unable to publish or not interested in publishing, Law produced a series of "anonymous" exhibits and gave public

lectures. She was easily forgotten when she left the Southwest Museum to start a family. After a divorce, she again sought employment. After two years of searching in the early 1940s, she returned to school and became a librarian, finding employment at the Monk Library in Arizona (DAM:HJ/FD 1/21/41, 3/3/41, 9/8/46; DAM: FD/HJ 3/6/41).

The ultimate support position, barring that of wives of anthropologists who volunteered their time, labor, and intellect, was probably held by Bertha Dutton, whose career is described by Cordell and Tisdale in this volume. Dutton's extensive skills helped her to become an anthropologist. She noted, "Secretaries were rare things out here in this country so many years ago. And this was my job. So I went to Peru as Hewett's secretary—even though I had completed my degree and was a graduate student. I did find time to make a study of Inca architecture" (1985a). Following this expedition, Hewett hired her as his personal assistant in his capacity as director of the Museum of New Mexico. She remembered,

Then I went to work for the museum up here, when Dr. Hewett brought me up here to be his assistant and that was a very fine opportunity to live this way of life. I was given $100 a month. In those days I needed 30 cents every day to survive. $100 a month was the same salary without a master's degree or a doctorate that I had left in Lincoln years before I came out here (Dutton 1985a).

Dutton remained in the position of director's assistant for many years, simultaneously serving as Curator of Ethnology. For this latter position, Dutton had to carve out her own niche and convince Hewett that she could be a curator in addition to performing her regular duties. Dutton thus "kept rein on Dr. Hewett's galloping projects. . . . Bertha designed the furniture, the modular cases, and exhibits. Thousands of specimens were catalogued, photographed and storage space prepared for them" (Bohrer 1979:10–11). In 1946–1947 Dutton received a sabbatical with half-pay to attend Columbia University and obtain a doctorate (awarded in 1952). And "on December 31, 1946, Bertha's own tie of apprenticeship was cut by Edgar L. Hewett's death" (Bohrer 1979:11). With the death of her mentor, Dutton ceased being the director's permanent assistant and was given an independent curatorship by the new director, Sylvanus Morley. Thus, at the age of 44, after completing all course work for a Ph.D. (a requirement not required of any of the other curators) and publishing at least 6 monographs and 125 articles, Dutton was given the position she so richly deserved. Dutton had simply been too valuable as a helper to be given independent status.

CONCLUSION: THE REWARD STRUCTURE OF ANTHROPOLOGY

In the nineteenth century, women were looking for ways to expand their educational horizons. Without access to higher education, they looked for new means of informal learning. One scholar notes, "Attending public lectures and visiting museums both quickly became accepted as properly "womanly" behavior in American cities and towns" (Rossiter 1982:3). This, the tradition of volunteerism, and the subtle power of women's purses opened the museum world to women.

Women entered museums as assistants, volunteers, and affiliated field workers. As the nature of museum work changed, more assistants and fewer scientists were needed—reinforcing the pyramidal and hierarchical structure of the institution. Jobs were downgraded conceptually even as they become more demanding. Pay was lowered. (The term *proletariatinization* has been applied to the phenomenon [Brienthal and Konz 1976:318].) This, in turn, allowed the jobs to be feminized—that is, women could become curators. What we see in museums is unfortunately the dominant pattern for scientific institutions: "Most female assistants remained at the same level for decades, and thus had no alternative but to make a whole

career out of a job that should have been just a stepping stone to more challenging and prestigious roles" (Rossiter 1982:56).

Women anthropologists entered anthropological museums in paid positions when material culture articles in major journals were declining (Sturtevant 1969) and the demand for museums to serve as centers of public education and entertainment through exhibitions and public programs was increasing. These public duties began to take up more and more time for curators. Though highly rewarding individually, anthropology has rarely considered exhibitions as prestige activities, certainly not ones on a par with publications. Exhibits were ephemeral (90% of all exhibits have never had accompanying catalogues), were rarely based on original research, contained synthetic, simplified knowledge, and constituted received wisdom. Exhibits did not, and generally still do not, carry authorship credit; the curator received little visible recognition for the intellectual content of the work. Assistants, exhibit designers, and preparators received none. The museum staff constituted an anonymous team. Curators with exhibition and education duties had little time to publish the scholarly works that did bring disciplinary recognition. Without large numbers of students who would consider themselves disciples, the curator's contribution remained unacknowledged. It is little wonder that we had so much difficulty discovering women museum anthropologists. The museum was an institution that effectively portrayed "the invisibility of the servant female in western society" (Warren 1988:18).

Museums have also been marginalized because they appeared to be behind the times. This is partly due to the nature of exhibit work, which is very expensive and by its nature always out-of-date. In exhibits, museum anthropologists display established truths rather than the newest or debated truths. These simplified and noncontroversial truths are continuous introductions designed for nonspecialists. Curators spend much of their time working for and instructing nonanthropologists, an activity that, as Tisdale shows in her chapter, has rarely been rewarded by the academic side of the profession. This activity has been augmented through educational programs—an activity even more devalued by the profession, as Lambert (1985) said: "There was no docent program [at the Museum of New Mexico] and part of the time you had to spend taking school groups around. The men on the staff wouldn't do it. They left it to the women. . . . But I felt again that it was part of my job to teach and to go out and give lectures at clubs."

Using museum collections was also, unfortunately, a double-edged sword. While the objects under review were readily available for researchers, there was a higher valuation placed on "original" fieldwork, that is, going to exotic places by oneself or as a member of an expedition and finding something new to Anglo-Americans and Europeans. By definition, museum collections were not new; they were the result of someone else's research endeavors, second-hand data that "belonged" to the original researcher even if that individual did not, nor ever intended to, use them. This valuation implied that research using museum data was the equivalent of library research. By definition, library research was second-class research in a profession that valued travel, hardship, exoticness, and originality.

Anthropological curators understood this and knew that the academy-bound members of the profession would not value the labor required to write an effective and informative exhibit label (consisting of no more than three sentences to convey a complicated idea or process) to the extent that they valued the effort to write a site report, an ethnography, a regional synthesis, or a theoretical article. Curators also realized that it was harder in many ways to write an exhibit label than a book. Wormington (1985) noted, "It's more work. If you're writing in technical jargon, you can just zip the thing out. But if you want to make it intelligible to the layman, you rewrite

and you rewrite, and there's a lot more work than doing a strictly technical publication." And of course, it was just this ability to synthesize and simplify in the sense of making difficult concepts understandable that women working in museums were justifiably proud of: "I think my greatest contribution has been in making things available to the layman as well as to the professional, and . . . in my ability to synthesize—to pull things together—and to publish them" (Wormington 1985). Thus, the women who worked in museums felt that this undervalued activity was their strength even if, like Lambert, they preferred to excavate or write scholarly articles. Some even felt that educating in a nontraditional manner was their greatest contribution to the field.

Given the situation for women in museums—the constant attention to curatorial and support detail and the hierarchical structure—the expectations of publishing were normally low and limited in scope. Because of the low opportunities for publishing major monographs, the lack of students, and the requirement for work in a popular genre, all much more expected of women than men, women curators have been hidden in our textbooks and histories. And women have known this and accepted it while they have attempted to overcome it.

Most people in the United States have discovered anthropology in museums. (Today this introduction is joined by specials from the Public Broadcasting System.) Since the 1930s, museums have seen themselves increasingly as educational institutions, the places that dejargonize the discipline so that it can be understood by a non–technically proficient but intelligent public. And women led in this effort. In fact, they embraced it wholeheartedly, considering the enterprise vital to the success of the discipline and the betterment of the country: "I think it is very important for a public who is interested in archaeology to have it available. It can offer a great deal—an understanding of what the human race is all about. I feel that prehistory is like history. You can't understand the present without knowing something about the past" (Wormington 1985).

Women curators were dedicated and provided a great service to anthropology. "We loved our work and were in it for the love of the work. I still think that is more important, but you do have to live" (Lambert 1985). Claiming that anthropology was the basis for a way of life and museums were institutions from which to apply anthropology to life was a common sentiment: "If you are an anthropologist, you have to apply anthropology. It is a wonderful field. I'm not leaving any children, but I've helped educate hundreds of children, and I've done all I could for my fellow man" (Dutton 1985a).

These idealistic women were pragmatic as well: "It was my training that gave me the vision, and I was just a woman who did what was to be done at the moment," noted Bertha Dutton (1985a). One of the goals of women anthropologists in the 1930s and 1940s was to be accepted on an equal footing with their male colleagues. Museums provided one avenue for gaining admittance to the field, but it became an often-vicious circle by 1940. Much of the necessary work that women did in museums could be and was conceptualized as worthwhile community work and housekeeping that had cultural value and social prestige but little prestige in the profession. However, it was better than unemployment or being a secretary, to paraphrase Bertha Dutton. Unfortunately, to keep from being trapped, women had to work not just twice as hard as men, but three times as hard—just to prove themselves. Men did not notice the difference: "They thought they were giving us a break by having us in the profession" (Lambert 1975). Women worked in marginal, subordinate positions in what was termed "women's work" because of economic considerations. One scholar notes, "Women were willing to do the often tedious and difficult tasks required for far lower salaries than would satisfy competent men. The women had so few other opportunities that they grabbed these low-ranking jobs and often did superbly well with little support" (Rossiter 1982:60).

In spite of the odds against them and the marginalization, women realized that they had played an important role by working in museums. In many ways, Marjorie Lambert (1985) summed up the feelings of all the women who worked in museums: "I don't see how you could regret a career in anthropology, no matter where it leads you."

NOTES

1. We would like to thank Richard and Nathalie Woodbury, Raymond H. Thompson, Shelby Tisdale, Linda Cordell, and J. J. Brody for their suggestions on this manuscript. This paper was not presented at the 1986 Daughters of the Desert Conference, although the issues in it were extensively discussed there. A version of this paper was presented by Parezo at the Chacmool Conference, The Archaeology of Gender, in the session "The Status of Women in Archaeology" in Calgary, Alberta, Canada, November 11, 1989.

2. It is interesting to note that museums became so marginalized in the minds of historians of anthropology that Goldschmidt's *The Uses of Anthropology* (ed. 1979) has no mention of museums. Nor does Mandelbaum, Lasker, and Albert's *Resources for the Teaching of Anthropology* (1963).

3. Surveys by various museum organizations, individual museums, and the American Association of Museums have demonstrated that this situation has not changed over the years. At the University of Arizona, for example, museum professionals with equivalent degrees, years of service, and publication records are paid almost one-fourth less than individuals housed in the Anthropology Department.

THE WOMEN WHO OPENED DOORS:
INTERVIEWING SOUTHWESTERN ANTHROPOLOGISTS

Jennifer Fox

Anthropology, a new science, welcomed the stranger. As a science which accepted
the psychic unity of mankind, anthropology was kinder to women . . . This professional
tradition of liberality has not been complete or unblemished . . . Women have been
made more welcome than in other professions, but not unequivocally.

Margaret Mead
(1960:5)

M ARGARET MEAD'S comments speak to the ambiguity of women's experience in American anthropology during its early years. On the one hand, women in the first few decades of this century were given access to graduate education in various academic disciplines, including anthropology—a right that women of the preceding decades had fought hard to win.[1] On the other hand, earning a degree in anthropology did not give women equal access to the career opportunities and professional recognition enjoyed by their male counterparts.[2] Cast in the role of "stranger" and concerned with their own place in the discipline of anthropology as well as in society more generally, a number of early women anthropologists set a precedent for examining the conventional gender roles and relations of the peoples they studied. Many of their inquiries along these lines, like those of subsequent anthropologists, were obliquely reflexive; by focusing on issues of gender in other societies, they aimed for what Elsie Clews Parsons termed an "ethnological inkling of themselves" (1913:v). That is, they used their understanding of gender in other societies to shed light on their own in a critical way.

One goal of the Daughters of the Desert Oral History Project was to remove deflectors and hold a lens more directly to the conventional gender roles and relations of our own society as they have affected women working in the field of anthropology itself. It is fortunate that a number of the women pioneers in American anthropology are still alive and willing to share impressions of their experiences along these lines. Between July 1985 and March 1986, I interviewed 18 of these senior women anthropologists for Barbara Babcock and Nancy Parezo. Each of the women who were interviewed had conducted ethnographic or archaeological research on Native Americans of the Southwest.[3] The interviews were done with an open-ended format based on a schedule of 30 basic queries. The questions were designed to elicit comments about each subject's education; the influence of others on her intellectual and professional development; her experiences in the professional arena; her fieldwork in, and relationship to, the Southwest; her personal orientation to her work; her influence on others; and the contributions she has made. As mentioned in the preface, much of the questioning was specifically oriented toward having these women assess how gender may or may not have influenced their professional experiences.

A caveat or two is needed before proceeding with the analysis: the content of the interviews was necessarily restricted by the focus of the questioning, the short amount of time I was able to spend with each subject (from 3 to 12 hours), and the individual's willingness to discuss sensitive issues with a young relative stranger. In constructing ourselves through discourse, we all engage in a certain amount of editing—emphasizing some issues and suppressing others depending on our purposes and our public. We are not always conscious of this. The interviews, therefore, should be viewed as subjective documents (Watson 1976), but documents from which a picture of 18 distinguished, productive, and resolute women emerges.

OPENING DOORS

While reviewing the hours of interview tapes, a comment made by psychiatrist-ethnographer Dorothea Leighton helped to make much of the richly diverse material fall into place. On a late autumn afternoon in Santa Fe, as we discussed her life and career, Leighton commented that she could remember no overt differences between the treatment of women and men during her graduate school training in the 1930s. She then added with a chuckle, "One thing, though—I wondered if I should open a door if I got to it first, or allow a man to do it. Sometimes you'd be scolded

hard if you opened it yourself because they were still gentlemen to some extent. I don't think the women cared, but it was a nuisance not to know what to do" (Leighton 1985). Leighton's literal wondering which doors to open plays into a figurative sense of opening doors. When women of her generation opened new doors of opportunity by stepping outside of established gender roles and pursuing careers in nontraditional areas, they faced uncertainties about the consequences of their actions. These women had to deal creatively with new situations that relatively few women before them had encountered and also had to accommodate their lives to their chosen unconventionality.

From the interviews, a number of patterns emerged regarding how these individuals shaped, responded to, and made sense of their experience in the context of systems that did not always favor women. These patterns have echoed through the history of women's involvement in anthropology, as evidenced by other chapters in this volume.[4] Cross-cutting these patterns is the issue of perceived discrimination: the degree to which certain gender distinctions have been internalized by the individuals involved and have been experienced as "natural" rather than discriminatory. From my perspective—that of a 29-year-old doctoral student in many ways the intellectual granddaughter of these women—it was against the backdrop of this issue that attitudinal differences between our generations emerged. And it is precisely through these differences that I have come to appreciate how the doors opened by my foremothers have helped raise the level of expectations about gender equality that many of us hold today.

STRIKING A BALANCE

Because the family is traditionally the realm most closely associated with women in our society, marriage and family life are obvious areas of experience potentially affected by women's career choices, and vice versa. Seven women who married and raised children all treated as natural the idea that they should bear the primary responsibility for child rearing.[5] Yet each developed her own strategy for coordinating marriage, child rearing, and career concerns.

Two of the women, Rosamond Spicer and Dorothea Leighton, combined child rearing, domestic responsibilities, and professional teamwork with their husbands. Rosamond ("Roz") began her formal training in anthropology as an undergraduate at Northwestern University, then continued her graduate work at the University of Chicago in 1934. As she put it, she and her husband-to-be, Edward Spicer, walked into the department at the same time, soon fell in love, and married in 1936 (Spicer 1985). Newly wedded and endowed with a departmental research grant, the Spicers undertook their first ethnographic fieldwork, with the Yaqui (Yoemé) Indians of Arizona, as a team in the fullest sense—a busyman's honeymoon. From the Yaqui material Roz wrote her M.A. thesis and Ned his Ph.D. dissertation. By the time the first of their three children was born in 1940, Roz had decided not to make the tremendous sacrifice that would be required of her children for her to pursue a Ph.D. and advance her own career. Instead, she managed the household, raised the children, carried out numerous civic and artistic projects, and lovingly assisted Ned in all aspects of his work "so that he could have the career."

Dorothea Leighton met her husband-to-be, Alexander Leighton, while they were medical students at Johns Hopkins University. In 1939, following two years of marriage and a psychiatric residency, the Leightons took "a leave-of-absence from medicine in order to see what other people were like" (Leighton 1985). With the aid of a Social Science Research Council fellowship they spent the fall semester auditing anthropology courses at Columbia University and attending the important Kardiner-Linton seminars. In the winter, at the suggestion of Clyde Kluckhohn, they set off for New Mexico to live among the Navajo.

The Leightons subsequently involved themselves in a series of research projects combining their interest in medicine with anthropological insights. When their two children were born, Leighton continued her own research projects and assisted her husband in his research and teaching but spent less time on project matters and more time attending to their home and children. Only after their divorce in 1965 did Leighton pursue a teaching career of her own.

While Spicer and Leighton have each made contributions to anthropology in her own right, both openly expressed intellectual and professional subordination to their husbands. In speaking of Ned, whom she described as "truly gifted," Roz related, "I thought it important for him to develop and do as much as he could. He needed to be freed from a great many other things so he could do that" (Spicer 1985). Dorothea, with characteristic modesty, credits Alec with having had "all the bright ideas in our career" (Leighton 1985). Yet as these women narrated their lives, it was clear how greatly each had contributed to her husband's work through her professional assistance and through the responsibility she had taken as homemaker and primary care-giver to their children.

Kate Peck Kent and Clara Lee Tanner, specialists in southwestern Native American craft arts, described themselves as having had two full careers by combining research, teaching, and familial responsibilities. Kent had become interested in material culture as a museum assistant during her senior year at the University of Denver. Upon graduating in 1935 she decided to pursue this interest as a graduate student in anthropology at Columbia University. Dissatisfied after two years of study, she married and returned to Colorado to work as Assistant Curator of Indian Art at the Denver Art Museum. In 1947, while her husband was overseas for the war, Kent completed course work for an M.A. in anthropology at the University of Arizona using a special scholarship obtained through the sponsorship of Harold S. Colton (Bartlett 1985). By 1951 she had written her

M.A. thesis, had her first two children to care for, and began a 26-year teaching career in anthropology at the University of Denver. To devote what she felt was adequate attention to her family, Kent taught only part-time until 1966 but always remained active in her research on southwestern prehistoric textiles, as Tisdale notes in her chapter in this volume. Like others, Kent (1985b) said she had "worked twice as hard as you would if you were having just a career or just a family . . . But that is the way my generation did it because you didn't think about househusbands or somebody sharing half the load the way they do now."

Tanner's career was well underway by the time she decided to marry in 1936. One of the first three students to receive a bachelor's degree from the newly formed Department of Archaeology at the University of Arizona in 1927, Clara Lee completed her M.A. the following year. She was immediately hired by Byron Cummings as an instructor in the department, eventually attained a professorship, and continued teaching there until her retirement in 1978. Tanner always maintained a lively interest in southwestern American Indian craft-arts—a topic on which she has written voluminously—and delivered numerous public lectures, in addition to her heavy course load of four courses per semester. The birth of her daughter in 1940 gave Tanner "two full-time jobs," and she "didn't fudge on either one" (Tanner 1985).

The paths that Kent and Tanner followed in balancing their families with their careers converge at a number of points. Neither saw family and career as an either/or issue; both felt the need to make career adjustments once they had children. Both spoke of their husbands as being highly supportive of their career decisions, if traditional in their role expectations. Kent (1985b), for example, related that her husband, Arthur "always helped tremendously around the house and with the kids. In that way I was lucky, but it never occurred to me to question that I was in charge of the house and family. That just seemed

to me to be part of my role." Finally, both Kent and Tanner minimized the difficulty of balancing research and family by focusing on topics specific to the region in which they worked and lived, topics that could for the most part be carried out through the study of museum collections.

Florence Hawley Ellis was another of the first three individuals to receive a B.A. and an M.A. in archaeology at the University of Arizona. In 1933 she went on to earn a doctorate from the fledgling University of Chicago Anthropology Department, based on her previous archaeological research at Chaco Canyon in New Mexico. The following year she was hired as an assistant professor at the University of New Mexico, where she taught until retiring in 1971. In her first years at the university, an unsuccessful marriage left her with an infant daughter, Andrea, whom she had to support financially and raise alone. In assessing the situation, Ellis stated matter-of-factly that she had fortunately been "raised simply to be independent." She continued, "And I suppose it is well that I was, because I would have had a heck of a time in all those years that I had to manage for myself" (Ellis 1985). With "no husband on deck," Ellis maintained a full-time teaching career, kept up an active research schedule, and saw to her home and child with "the time [she] could steal from something greater." When possible, she incorporated Andrea into her professional activities, taking her along on visits to the pueblos and on archaeological excavations, where she had "a kiva for a play-pen."

Six of the women interviewed were married but had no children.[6] Again, each of these women expressed the naturalness of the idea that she should pursue her own career after marriage and the great freedom she felt to do so. All those who discussed their marriages related that their husband's supportiveness and their lack of children contributed to the sense of professional freedom they shared.[7]

Of the women in this group, only Nathalie Woodbury did not continuously earn her own income. She had gone to Barnard College in 1935 intending to major in anthropology. Under the guidance of Gladys Reichard, who *"was* the department then," she completed her degree and headed across the street for graduate work at Columbia University (Woodbury 1985). In 1942, after completing all the requirements for a doctorate short of writing her dissertation, she left Columbia University for several years of research and teaching in New York and New Mexico. In the summer of 1946 she met archaeology student Richard Woodbury while directing the lab at the University of Arizona's Point of Pines field school. In 1948 they married, and the following year Richard received his Ph.D. in archaeology from Harvard University. The Woodburys subsequently made a series of moves based on his career opportunities because "Dick has been the prime marketable product—you have to be practical," as Nat related in her usual forthright manner. By and large the two lived on his salary while Nat "took opportunities as they came along," including several years of teaching anthropology and serving in higher administration at Barnard College, editing the American Anthropological Association newsletters and bulletins, and serving on the administrative boards of various anthropological organizations. In her words (1985),

Being married to an anthropologist meant that I was not pulled away from my field. I've always managed to have a satisfactory professional association wherever I've been that could give me an identity, and I just proceeded to do my thing—some of which has coincided with Dick's, and some of which has not.

Woodbury characterized her situation as "like being on a mini-MacArthur [Fellowship]" because she had had the freedom to do what she wanted without the constraints of university employment. "Looking back on it from my advanced years," she reflected, "what I really like is problem-solving, and action, and editing, and administering things—and that's what I do" (1985).

Marriage also did not interfere with the career

of Katherine ("Kay") Spencer Halpern, in part because she did not marry until her mid 50s. In discussing how marriage fit into her career plans, she stated:

I certainly never made any intentional decisions for or against getting married . . . As anthropology graduate students at the University of Chicago we weren't making decisions between a career and marriage. We were all going to have careers of some sort, and some of us were married and some of us weren't (Halpern 1985).

Kay had entered the graduate program in anthropology at the University of Chicago in 1936 after a B.A. at Vassar and a year of graduate work in social welfare. The following summer she and two of her classmates split a fellowship to attend the University of New Mexico's field school at Chaco Canyon, which according to Halpern was "just an excuse" for them to get to the Southwest. There she introduced herself both to Clyde Kluckhohn, who became a valued friend and important figure in her anthropological development, and to the Navajo, whom she has both studied and assisted through applied work intermittently over the course of her career—an activity to which she all too modestly refers in her chapter on applied anthropology in this volume. Throughout her long and intricate career Halpern has combined her love of anthropological research with her concern for social welfare and mental health. "At each stage of my career there was both the straight academic interest and always an interest in applications." By the time she received her Ph.D. in 1952, she had begun to move away from traditional anthropological employment toward teaching and research in social work. In the mid 1960s she shifted back to anthropology through her renewed applied work with the Navajos and in her marriage to linguistic anthropologist Abraham Halpern. In 1970 she accepted a professorship in anthropology at American University.

In general, marriage emerged as a nonissue to each of these women. All seemed to welcome it as a complement to their professional lives and as something that at times helped them to further their career goals. None saw marriage in itself as a bar to professional pursuits, though more stated that she had tailored her plans to suit her husband's career than that her husband had altered his plans to suit his wife's career. Only with the entry of children into the picture did any feel that it was necessary to alter substantially her professional involvements.

CREATING ALTERNATIVES

In 1916, feminist social psychologist Jesse Taft wrote in her doctoral dissertation,

Everywhere we find the unmarried woman turning to other women, building with them a real home, finding in them the sympathy and understanding, the bond of similar standards and values, as well as the same aesthetic and intellectual interests, that are often difficult of realization in a husband, especially here in America where business crowds out culture (Taft 1916:10–11).

If marriage did not fit into the lives of the remaining five women with whom I spoke, close companionship with another woman sometimes provided an alternative.[8] Three of these women— Bertha Dutton, Katharine Bartlett, and Alice Marriott—spoke at some length about friendships they developed with other women who have shared both their homes and their interests.

Bertha Dutton, an energetic octogenarian who spent "half a century setting trails around the Southwest," first went to the region from Nebraska in 1932 (Dutton 1985a). Unable to "stand the humdrum nature of being a business clerk," Dutton was drawn to the University of New Mexico's Department of Anthropology with its promise of hands-on learning through participation in field schools—a promise she said "sounded good to this country girl." Simultaneously studying and working as departmental secretary under Edgar L. Hewett, Dutton completed her undergraduate degree in 1935, then set to work on her

master's degree. The following year Hewett hired her as assistant in his capacity as director of the Museum of New Mexico in Santa Fe. She remained with the museum in a series of positions until her retirement in 1965, stopping long enough to earn a doctorate at Columbia University in 1952. In 1966, at age 63, Dutton took on the directorship of the Museum of Navajo Ceremonial Art (Wheelwright Museum) in Santa Fe and remained there until a second retirement in 1975.

Dutton's friendship with Caroline Bower Olin began in the early 1970s when the latter went to work as a curator for the Museum of Navajo Ceremonial Art and to continue her research on the artistry of Navajo sandpaintings. The two women "just hit it off immediately" and became fast friends. At first Olin rented a room in Dutton's ranchito, but Dutton said (1985a), "now she lives here as a permanent associate. We're both as stubborn and as independent as can be . . . She's a classical archaeologist and I'm a Southwestern archaeologist. She's interested in art and I'm interested in art; she's interested in music and I'm interested in music, so it works out beautifully." Dutton's attitude that "people should help each other out" is reflected in her friendship with Olin. For more than a decade the two have provided each other with steady companionship, traveled extensively together, and collaborated on a number of research and writing projects.

Katharine Bartlett discovered anthropology as an undergraduate at the University of Denver, where "one or two courses really sold me," she recalled with quiet enthusiasm (1985). After completing her bachelor's degree in 1929, Bartlett remained at Denver for graduate training. A trip to the 1930 American Association for the Advancement of Science meetings in Tucson proved to be a key event in her life. There she met Harold and Mary-Russell Colton, founders of the Museum of Northern Arizona in Flagstaff (as McGreevy recounts in her chapter in this volume), and stayed with them on her way back to

Denver. Shortly after the trip she received a letter from Colton inviting her to work in Flagstaff for the summer to handle artifacts from a small excavation project the museum was sponsoring. Bartlett, just finishing her thesis and in need of a job, accepted the offer. The summer job stretched into the fall and eventually developed into a permanent position. She said (1985), "I came down to spend the summer and I've been here ever since." In her long affiliation with the museum, Bartlett had done whatever needed to be done— "Diversification is my motto," she said in 1985—which included administration and curation of the collections, assisting with the museum's annual Hopi and Navajo art shows, editing and contributing numerous articles to the museum's publications, and establishing and directing the museum's library.

For about the first 25 years of her association with the museum, Bartlett lived with the Coltons "and got to be a member of the family, almost." Through Mary-Russell she met Jean Foster, a "very talented" individual who "preferred to be self-employed." The two developed a friendship, eventually moved in together, and then built a house which Foster designed and helped construct. Foster shared Bartlett's enthusiasm for archaeology, and in 1957 the two collaborated on a project in which they documented prehistoric sites in Glen Canyon that were soon to be destroyed by a dam project. Their camaraderie lasted until Foster's death several years ago. "I enjoyed being with her," Bartlett reminisced (1985); "I miss her a lot."

Alice Marriott, who described herself as "more of an anthropologist than anything," spent over 40 years as a free-lance researcher and writer (Marriott 1986). While working as a librarian in Oklahoma after earning a bachelor's degree in 1930, Marriott was exposed to books on the American Indians of the region, which piqued her curiosity about anthropology. She decided to pursue the subject, and in 1935 completed a second B.A. from the University of Oklahoma in the newly formed Anthropology Department. A great deal of independent fieldwork and a position with the U.S. Department of the Interior's Indian Arts and Crafts Board from 1938 to 1942 brought Marriott into contact with many native peoples of the Plains and the Southwest. Her interest in the lives of these peoples is reflected in the many novels, short stories, and popular books she wrote, as is analyzed by Gordon in her chapter in this volume.

In 1960 Marriott established Southwest Research Associates with her friend and fellow anthropologist Carol Rachlin. They had met when Rachlin had gone to Oklahoma to conduct research on Plains Indians textiles. As Marriott recalled (1986), "My mother looked [Carol] over, and looked me over, and she said, 'You're not going to send that child back to the Shawnee by herself.' And I said, 'No Ma'am,' handed her the keys to the spare bedroom, and she moved in." After that the two collaborated on much of their research and writing. Living and working together was a boon to both of them, they agreed. Marriott especially appreciated the companionship of Rachlin, who is completely deaf, when her own eyesight failed. "She's the eyes and I'm the ears," Alice joked (1986); "together we get around."

TIES THAT NURTURED

The women who entered anthropology in the first few decades of this century generally did so lacking the power to move through the ranks of the profession on a par with their male counterparts, as noted in Parezo's introductory chapter in this volume. In the context of academic systems generated and sustained by male authority, a few forward-thinking men emerged as figures who actively assisted female students in their pursuit of anthropology. As I interviewed one woman after another, I was struck by the recurrent mention of several such individuals and the paternal imagery used to describe them.

"Papa Franz" Boas, a German Jew whose personal experience instilled in him a special sensitivity to discrimination, was particularly "hospitable to women," and "thought they had grey matter in their heads" (Bunzel 1985). Boas used his enlightened attitude and his position as chair of the Department of Anthropology at Columbia University to train and send numerous women anthropologists into the field. Among them were two of his secretaries, Esther Goldfrank and Ruth Bunzel.

Esther Goldfrank, the first to address Boas as "Papa Franz," went to work as his secretary in October 1919 with a degree in economics from Barnard College and little conception of anthropology. Though she said she was "never a very good typist . . . Boas didn't seem to mind," and she found the work far more engaging than her previous job on Wall Street (Goldfrank 1985b). When Boas made plans to travel to the Southwest for ethnographic fieldwork the following summer, Goldfrank announced to him, "You've got to take me." As Lange notes in his chapter in this volume, Boas took her request to heart and secured enough extra money from Elsie Clews Parsons, who was funding his research and paying Goldfrank's salary, to take her along for a few weeks of fieldwork at Laguna Pueblo. "When I got back," she recalled (1985b), "I just settled down to become a secretary again." But Boas invited her to accompany him the following two summers for additional fieldwork at Laguna and Cochiti pueblos. In 1922, during her third summer of fieldwork, Goldfrank decided to resign from her post as secretary and to begin graduate work in anthropology at Columbia University. Her plans were soon changed by marriage and children, but in 1936 she returned to Columbia for further training, fieldwork, and research in anthropology, again nurtured by Boas.

Ruth Bunzel, another Barnard College graduate, went to work as Boas' secretary on the heels of Esther Goldfrank in 1922. In the spring of 1924, Bunzel informed Boas that she was planning to spend her vacation accompanying Ruth Benedict and taking dictation for her on the latter's summer field research at Zuni Pueblo. "Don't waste your time!" Boas exhorted her: "Do a project of your own." Bunzel then "had four or five weeks to become an anthropologist and plan a project" (Bunzel 1985). The project she chose dealt with the relationship of the Zuni potter to her work—a study on which she based her doctoral dissertation and her well-known *The Pueblo Potter* (1972), as Hardin documents in her chapter in this volume. In reflecting on Boas' holistic vision, Bunzel stated that "he thought women could do things and could get into places men couldn't" and were thus necessary to help paint a balanced picture of any culture. "But," she added, "he never felt women had to do only women's things" (1985).

Edgar L. Hewett, a magnate of New Mexico archaeology for several decades, was remembered by his students Bertha Dutton and Marjorie Lambert as a "father figure to all of us" (Lambert 1985). Lambert first learned of Hewett and his activities in southwestern archaeology when he went to lecture at Colorado College, where she was pursuing an undergraduate degree. When she finished in 1931, a fellowship offer attracted her to the University of New Mexico, and she began to study with Hewett. In 1934 Hewett appointed Lambert field supervisor of the University of New Mexico field school; in 1937 he moved her to the Museum of New Mexico in Santa Fe, where she remained as a curator until her retirement in 1969. Lambert (1985) stated that at a time when male archaeologists were sometimes resentful of having a woman around, she was grateful to Hewett for the opportunities he provided: "He was a wonderful teacher and a good friend."

Tanner (1985) described her mentor, Byron Cummings, as "a remarkable man" who "had a breadth of vision I think is so important in a teacher." His vision demonstrably included a place for women in archaeology, and Tanner and

Ellis are two of the women he helped to establish themselves in the discipline. In a similar vein, Fay-Cooper Cole, chair of anthropology at the University of Chicago, welcomed women as students in his department and treated them with fairness and respect. Both Rosamond Spicer (1985) and Katherine Halpern (1985) spoke of "Papa Cole" as a kind and generous individual who was always cognizant of the interests of his students, regardless of whether they were men or women.

Likewise, three of the women who conducted ethnographic research among the Navajo—Katherine Halpern, Dorothea Leighton, and Mary Shepardson—spoke warmly of Clyde Kluckhohn as an individual who gave them tremendous moral support and assisted them in achieving their professional goals. Although none was formally his student, their mutual interest in the Navajo brought these women into lasting associations with him. "He had a very special interest that women should be able to be in anthropology and do anthropology," Halpern (1985) said, "and respect for women who worked in anthropology." Both Halpern and Shepardson noted that without Kluckhohn's encouragement during their graduate training, they probably would not have continued in the discipline.

The concept of women's networks, popular among academic feminists today as a strategy for accomplishing goals, was something the women I interviewed did not feel had been available to them when they were pursuing an education and establishing themselves as professionals. Shepardson's (1986) assessment that "no women helped me because there were none around" accurately summarized the experience of most. A few isolated women—notably Elsie Clews Parsons, Ruth Benedict, and Gladys Reichard—were mentioned as individuals who offered support and guidance but had little power to help their female students secure a place in the professional realm.

Others, however, did mention close teamwork with a female colleague as a means by which they achieved intellectual and personal satisfaction in a professional setting that sometimes left them feeling isolated or marginalized. In addition to teams mentioned in the previous section, several more merit consideration.

Mary Shepardson entered anthropology in mid-life after a career as a social worker and after a marriage. Her vacation visits to Chinle on the Navajo Reservation with her husband had aroused her curiosity about the people she saw there; she decided to pursue course work in anthropology to learn more about them. She returned to her alma mater, Stanford University, where she was "reluctantly admitted" because of her age. There she met "Blodwen Hammond, a fellow middle-aged M.A. student in the department" (Shepardson 1986b). The two became friends and through the course of their training provided one another with moral support and amicable competition for grades. When Shepardson earned her master's degree in 1956, she was barred from continuing for a Ph.D. "You have two strikes against you," she was told: "Your age and your sex" (Shepardson 1986b). In addition, her motivation for wanting a Ph.D. was questioned since she had a husband to support her. Discouraged but not deterred, Shepardson gained admittance to the University of California at Berkeley through the intervention of Clyde Kluckhohn. Here she completed her Ph.D. in 1960. Her friend Hammond, who received similar treatment at Stanford University, did not go on. Not wanting Hammond to languish, Shepardson made her a research associate in 1960 when she received a postdoctoral fellowship to continue her work among the Navajo. "I knew how frustrated she was, and I asked her to come along," Shepardson remembered (1986b). She incorporated Hammond into every phase of her research on Navajo kinship, politics, and community, from fieldwork to publication. "In the end we got that not only could we stand to live together under difficult situations, we could write things together . . . Really you do twice as much work if you're working with somebody. It's really great—it's wonderful" (Shepardson 1986b).

Dorothy ("Dodie") Keur's long association with Hunter College had begun in the early 1920s, when she chose that school for her undergraduate training. She had taken the one course offered in anthropology at the time, and when she had graduated in 1925 her professor had asked if she would like to stay on as his assistant. Keur (1985) laughed as she remembered her promise to return half of her meager monthly salary to the professor so that he could buy American Indian artifacts for the collection over which she presided as his assistant. After three years Keur was promoted to instructor of anthropology, at which point she began taking graduate courses at Columbia University to "keep a little ahead of the students" she was teaching (Keur 1985).

Keur completed her Ph.D. in 1940 with a dissertation on Navajo archaeology. During her entire graduate career she had maintained her teaching position at Hunter College and had eventually attained a full professorship. She remained with the college until her retirement in 1966. Keur placed much of her emphasis at Hunter College on developing the anthropology department. Her partner in the endeavor was Elsie Viault Steedman, another Hunter College alumna who had begun graduate work under Boas at Columbia University but had never completed her doctorate. "You don't hear of her," Keur stated (1985), "because she put her whole emphasis on building anthropology at Hunter College, very unselfishly really." Among their joint accomplishments were the creation of a highly acclaimed physical anthropology lab, the organization of a memorable lecture series funded by the Wenner-Gren Foundation, and the gradual addition of new faculty and courses to the department. Keur recalled (1985) that she and Steedman "didn't always agree, of course, but had an excellent working rapport." Keur felt grateful for having had the opportunity to work closely with Steedman toward their common goals and considered

their contributions to the department at Hunter among her most satisfying achievements (Keur 1985).

In the mid 1950s, Florence Hawley Ellis, as a result of her regional archaeological background and close association with the Puebloans, was asked to assist in a land claims litigation involving Zia, Santa Ana, and Jemez pueblos. Ellis felt a responsibility to honor the request: "I think if you have learned a good deal from the Indians then you ought to be able and willing to give back to [them] whatever they can use of your understanding of things" (Ellis 1985). One land claims case led to another, and eventually Ellis had more to do than she could manage alone. Her daughter, Andrea Ellis-Dodge, then joined Ellis in her work. Looking back on the experience, Ellis (1985) felt that "the relationship between us . . . had always been close . . . We've always enjoyed very much the same things." Working together, especially among the pueblos where Ellis-Dodge had spent much of her childhood, had come very naturally to the mother-daughter team. The work had occupied much of their time and had been a gratifying part of their relationship.

NO PLACE FOR WOMEN

Halpern recalled that when she began to consider the various professions she might enter, she was "scared off from medicine—from trying to be a women working in medicine at the very beginning of my career" (Halpern 1985). She turned instead to anthropology "because in anthropology there were a number of women from a very early date and I think I sensed that they were welcome." This sense, however, was tempered by the admonitions given her when she began graduate school at the University of Chicago, as recounted in the introduction to this volume. There was "no place for women in anthropology," she was told; nobody was assured of finding work in the discipline at the time. The Great Depression took its toll, especially on women. Ruth Bunzel's experience was similarly equivocal: "I came in at a time when things were opening up for women. There was no difficulty in fieldwork . . . but women had a tough time in getting appointments in anthropology. There were no jobs and they didn't go to women when they did turn up" (Bunzel 1985). This equivocal sense of welcome manifested itself in various ways. A number of experiences were telling reminders of the barriers women have faced—and those they have broken down—in their pursuit of professional fulfillment.

In 1928 Laura Thompson entered Harvard University for graduate work in anthropology with a B.A. from Mills College. As a woman, she was not allowed to enroll directly at Harvard University but was registered instead through its women's undergraduate branch, Radcliffe College. Thompson remembers her year at Harvard as one of tremendous alienation. Because she was a woman, many professors barred her from attending their courses, and she had to be given tutorials on the side. In one course that she was allowed to attend, the professor "went out of his way to make off-color remarks about women" (Thompson 1985). After a year of this treatment, Thompson transferred to the University of California at Berkeley, where "there was the freedom of the West," and completed her Ph.D. in 1933. She went on to distinguish herself with pioneering work in applied anthropology. "I could have been discouraged by my year at Harvard," she noted (1985), but her belief that women are "indispensable to anthropology" and her love of the discipline had kept her in touch with her goals.

H. Marie Wormington, an expert on Paleo-Indian archaeology, took her undergraduate degree from the University of Denver and began graduate work at Harvard University in 1937. Fortunately, the more blatant forms of sexism "had died down by the time I got there" (Wormington 1985). Wormington juggled graduate school, marriage, and a full-time position as Curator

of Archaeology at the Denver Museum of Natural History, finally completing her doctorate in 1954. Although Wormington's gender did not create significant problems for her at Harvard University, this was not the case at the museum. She had been working for the museum on a commission basis in 1935 when an unexpected change in directors occurred. When A. M. Bailey, the new director, "discovered there was a woman and an archaeologist on the staff, he wrote to the director of the board of trustees suggesting that I be removed" (Wormington 1985). He felt that there was no place for either in the museum and that "the combination was lethal." Because his tenure had not officially begun, the board quickly hired Wormington on a full-time basis, "and that began 33 years of problems" (Wormington 1985). Among other things, Bailey would not give Wormington in-house financial support for her archaeological fieldwork, he kept her salary at half the rate of that of male curators on the staff, and he would allow her to publish her books with the museum press only under her initials because he "felt that nobody would read a book written by a woman." In 1968, when Wormington was on leave for a year as a visiting scholar at Arizona State University, the director managed to remove her simply by eliminating the position. Wormington's many professional contributions—for which she received the Society for American Archaeology's Distinguished Service Award in 1983—stand as a tribute to her talents and perseverance in light of the difficulties she faced at the museum.

"Because I am a woman, I have never received more than $12,000 a year for all that I've done," Dutton forcefully stated (1985a). The problem of unequal pay for equal work was the most frequently mentioned evidence of gender discrimination experienced by those interviewed. As these women had begun their careers, the excuse that women did not need equal pay because they were not family heads had been a frequently invoked and seldom challenged justification for gender-based discrepancies in pay. "I think that I was exploited all those years, and I don't think that your generation lets itself be exploited that way," Kent (1985b) said thoughtfully: "I did an awful lot of work for not much money. And it wasn't until, I think, probably the early '60s that the women on campus at the University of Denver began to make noises about equal pay for equal rank."

Lack of job security is another pattern, which, though not explicitly mentioned by many of these women, is evidenced by an examination of their curriculum vitae. Bunzel, for instance, spent her entire career as a lecturer, research associate, and adjunct professor at Columbia University. Kent was never on a tenure track. Thompson, Shepardson, Halpern, Leighton, Woodbury, and Goldfrank each spent many years working on a project-by-project basis. In reflecting on the instability she had experienced, Bunzel (1985) said, "There was a time when I wanted to have a stable position, but it wasn't in the cards . . . I had no illusions. I knew as a woman it would be difficult."

Tanner and Ellis, both of whom were fortunate enough to have secured tenure track positions early in their careers, mentioned that their promotion records did not compare favorably with their male colleagues. Ellis (1985) found this especially frustrating in light of her "far bigger list of publications" than the men in the department and the heavier teaching load she had been required to carry. Dutton (1985a), too, sensed that "all the way through if I hadn't been a woman, I'd be in a higher place." Lambert's experience at the Museum of New Mexico also fit the pattern of more work for less pay and fewer opportunities for advancement than had been available to the men on the staff. She pointed out that the women had worked longer hours and had been "made to do things that the men didn't want to do . . . That sort of discrimination has gone on throughout my career." "But," she added, "I think women are

better at standing up for their rights now than when I started. We wouldn't have dared then—jobs were so scarce" (Lambert 1985).

On the issue of professional recognition, half of the women expressed the belief that women overall do not stand on an equal footing with men. "I think in anything a woman has to be twice as good and work twice as hard as a man to be recognized," Spicer (1985) remarked. Ellis (1985) agreed "that in general, if a woman produces something she gets about half the credit that she might if a man had produced the same thing."

Mary Shepardson (1986), who had experienced a double dose of discrimination because of gender and age, was the most vocal about the sorts of problems that women have faced. Her voice was full of emotion as she assessed the general situation in light of her own experiences at Stanford:

I think it's a historical thing that they could get away with stuff like this . . . [and] that they felt they were perfectly justified in doing this—this telling you about all the strikes against you . . . "for your benefit" so that you aren't misled, to know that it was foolish even to want to go ahead, that there was no place—when what they should have done, if this was the situation, they should have gone ahead and broken it down.

In general, however, these women downplayed negative experiences of the sort just mentioned. Most preferred to see these incidents as relatively isolated events in otherwise productive and fulfilling lives. "I'm afraid I didn't have any struggles that make dramatic reporting," folklorist Frances Gillmor (1985) remembered as we sat talking in her Tucson home. "I've never felt [gender discrimination] anywhere, at any time, about anything."

Gillmor first went to Tucson in 1927 "to get away from the Chicago winters." She enrolled in the English program at the University of Arizona and the next year completed the bachelor's degree she had previously begun at the University of

Chicago. While working on her master's project—a biography of Louisa Wade Wetherill—Gillmor spent ample time visiting the Wetherill family on the Navajo Reservation. Her contacts with the Navajo inspired her 1930 novel, *Windsinger.* Upon completing her master's degree in 1931, Gillmor was hired to teach in the English Department at the University of Arizona. She divided her time between teaching in Tucson and conducting research and working toward her doctorate at the Universidad Nacional Autonoma in Mexico City. She continued to teach at the University of Arizona until her retirement as a full professor in 1973. In reflecting on each stage of her career, Gillmor (1985) emphasized the ease with which she achieved her goals and the lack of discrimination she felt along the way: "That's been a pleasant aspect of all my teaching, and everything else."

MARGINS OF OPPORTUNITY

The lack of bitterness exhibited by these women and the hesitancy with which many of them spoke about gender discrimination in their lives at times led me to wonder if they have somewhat suppressed their memories of being treated unfairly and the accompanying feelings of frustration. Gender discrimination, as Ellis (1985) said, "is, of course, discouraging when you stop to think of it, so you just don't dare stop to think of it. All you do is just see what you can do to get around the situation at the moment and go ahead with your work." When these women did state that discrimination had affected them, I sensed that they viewed it as something they had been powerless to fight in the context of their own lives. However, each seemed to feel a challenge—and a responsibility—to help change the general situation through positive action. Their strategy, as a rule, was not to draw attention to discrimination, but instead to demonstrate what women have to offer the profession through their own contributions. In Tanner's words (1985), "I decided the thing to do was to get to work and work hard, and lay the foundation for other women in the field." And this is precisely what she and the others set about doing.

Often lacking the opportunity—and sometimes the desire—to work within the academic mainstream, many of the women had carved out their own professional niches on the margins. Museum work and popular writing were two avenues open to these women, as other essays in this volume explore in depth. Without exception, each individual who has engaged in one or both of these activities emphasized how satisfying she has found such work and how it has provided a forum to reach the general public with anthropological insights. Wormington (1985), for example, felt that her "greatest contribution has been in making things available to the layman as well as to the professional." Although Tanner (1985) had been told by her colleagues that writing for the general public "wouldn't get her anywhere academically" ("And it didn't," she added), she had persevered, to her great personal satisfaction. When Marriott (1986) was asked why she chose not to write for an academic audience, she answered emphatically, "What's the use of taking in our own laundry, for heaven's sake?"

Operating on the margins of the discipline had given some of the women the freedom to be quite creative in their work. Several explicitly mentioned that being innovative or pioneering in new areas was a gratifying aspect of their careers: Thompson spoke with pride about her role in the development of applied anthropology; Leighton said how pleased she was to be recognized as a pioneer in medical anthropology. Dutton (1985a), when she spoke of her idea to create a Hall of Ethnology at the Museum of New Mexico, remarked that "you have to invent your job in so many places." Edgar L. Hewett had consented to her proposal, and Dutton "had the pleasure to design a whole museum." Similarly, Ellis discussed her conscious experimentation with new archaeological techniques. For instance, as

Cordell discusses in her chapter in this volume, Ellis was one of the first to use statistics in archaeological research; she developed a new method for excavating prehistoric ash piles; and she was a pioneer in the use of tree-ring dating. Regarding the latter, she "decided that this would be a good thing to be in because if you could have a specialty you were more likely to be wanted, which was a point especially for a woman" (Ellis 1985).

Working at women's colleges or in areas combining anthropology with fields traditionally open to women had made several women feel very much at home in their professional environments. Keur, for example, had enjoyed a remarkably stable career with little sense of discrimination. She attributed part of this to the fact that Hunter College had been exclusively a women's college when she had begun to teach there. "There were always more women than men, and the women were always the top people in administration" (Keur 1985). Gillmor (1985), whose experiences were similar to Keur's, said that the University of Arizona English Department had had other women faculty members and that some women have long had an accepted place in that field. Halpern (1985) spoke of a similar sense of place in her professional pursuits. "I think part of it was that for most of my career I wasn't in an academic setting," she suggested. "I was also in a field, mental health and social work, where there were many, many women. Both psychiatry and social work have used women as much as anthropology has, or more."

Given the scarcity of stable positions available to women, it is no surprise that several emphasized the serendipitous and episodic nature of their careers. Goldfrank (1985b), for example, described herself as having had an "undirected life" (and "happily so") in which she had merely taken opportunities as they had come along. It was "more luck than brains," she quipped. Leighton (1985), too, spoke of her luck in having been given unexpected opportunities. "I was very in-terested in the work I was doing, and I guess probably part of that was due to the fact that it changed so often. There's a kind of thread going through it, but the circumstances and the reasons and everything else changed a lot from one level to another." Woodbury (1985) characterized herself as being "infinitely adaptable" and told me that everywhere she has gone, she has found opportunities that have allowed her to put her anthropological training to good use: "I've always enjoyed having jobs in which you took anthropology and used it in nontraditional ways."

With World War II came the creation of new professional opportunities for women anthropologists. This occurred for two reasons. First, many anthropologists, female and male, were hired to work as analysts on war-related matters; among the female anthropologists were Halpern, Spicer, Bunzel, and Leighton. Second, because many male anthropologists were involved in the war effort, women were able to move into a few of the openings the men left. The large, multidisciplinary Indian Education Research Project coordinated by Laura Thompson provides a ready example. Thompson (1985) said that "because of the war, the bulk of the work was done by women." Spicer and Leighton are among the many women who worked on the project, which aimed systematically to assess the government's administration policies toward American Indians, particularly in the Southwest.

FINDING A PLACE

The Greater Southwest, with its rich archaeological record and "ethnology on the hoof" (Woodbury 1985), gave each of the women interviewed for this project an opportunity to prove herself professionally through fieldwork. It also gave many of them the satisfaction of forming lasting bonds with the region and its native peoples. A number of reasons as to why these women found a place in the harsh terrain of the Southwest emerged in the course of the interviews.

First there is the seduction of the environment itself, an environment whose limitless expanses, sharp contrasts, and clean aesthetic fostered a sense of freedom and well-being in those who went there. For Tanner (1985), who grew up and remained in the region, "the Southwest itself has something you can't put your fingers on—it just is—and it is beautiful, and it is vast." The Southwest is also a place that at the time foregrounded how arbitrary the conditions of survival were in professional settings that were sometimes hostile to women. It is a place, Thompson (1985) suggested, that "shows you survival in the raw." And the Southwest is a place where the cultural past and present coexist and merge with the landscape to create an all-embracing sense of continuity and otherness that allowed these women to establish new identities for themselves.[9] "I think the big draw was the color," Keur (1985) remembered, "the fact that here you felt American Native cultures still lived . . . Here were these great, marvelous ruins, and here were Navajos living their own kind of life. You stepped into their culture. That was the great appeal—here you were in an entirely different cultural milieu."

The cultures that these women stepped into frequently became a part of their being: "The Indians have molded me," Dutton (1985a) stated, "and I want them to know it." Lambert (1985) felt that she has "learned so much from the Indians" and has enjoyed her contacts with them: "I wouldn't change those contacts for anything, and I think I'm a better person having had them." Thompson's association with the Hopi led her to conclude that "we're handicapped in our dualistic view of life. We could learn a lot from the Hopi view."

Several women spoke of their adoption into pueblo families. At Cochiti Pueblo, Goldfrank (1985b) had been taken in as the "daughter" of Caroline Quintana. Goldfrank related how Quintana had "washed my hair and [taken] me out into the sun," and had given her a Keresan name meaning "Abalone Shell." Bunzel had been adopted at Zuni Pueblo and had been given the Zuni name for "Bluebird." Dutton (1985a) had been given her place in the Marmon family at Laguna Pueblo. "When my mother died," she reminisced, "Susie Marmon said, 'Let me be your mother,' and adopted me." Ellis (1985) had developed lifelong friendships at Zia Pueblo, and when her daughter had been born, Andrea had been adopted and "given her proper clan."

Shepardson's reception by the Navajo was a refreshing change from her treatment at Stanford. After her first field experience, Shepardson received a letter from the head of the Navajo tribal records saying that although previously she had thought that anthropologists "just came to look at us like bugs. . . . I think you are a friend of ours" (quoted by Shepardson 1986b).

If "the special qualities of women are not recognized in the academic world" (Bunzel 1985), they sometimes give women an edge in fieldwork. Marriott said of her entry into anthropology,

I began reading everything I could get in ethnology, and I began to get kind of bothered about it because all these things were written by men about men. And even with one year's experience I could see that . . . there were two parallel cultures together, and nobody had paid any attention to the women . . . So, I began concentrating on women: women's [lives], women's ways, women's tricks if they have them.

Marriott's ability to "relate to women" and her friendship with Maria Martinez had led to her sensitively written portrait, *Maria: the Potter of San Ildefonso* (1948).

Bunzel (1985) said that her entrée to Zuni culture had been through the women: "I felt there was a great lack of knowledge about people's lives, particularly about women. So being a women, that was the obvious place to start." Goldfrank (1985b), too, spoke of her acceptance into the women's circles at Cochiti Pueblo: "Usually my audience and helpers were a group of women . . . By and large it was a women's party."

Those who had studied several of the pueblos

felt that their acceptance, in part, had been due to the fact that women are accorded a great deal of respect in matrilineal societies. Ellis (1985) suggested, "When the Pueblo Indians think of you as a woman, I don't think they think of you as a lower creature the way our men tend to do." Bunzel (1985) similarly stated that "Zuni is a women's society. The women have a great deal of power and influence, so it's a good place for women to work."

The types of information that some of these women had pursued among the native peoples of the Southwest also had facilitated their acceptance. A large component of Thompson's Indian Education Research project had involved administering psychological tests to Zuni, Hopi, Navajo, and Tohono O'Odham children. "Women were especially suited to this kind of fieldwork," Thompson maintained (1985). "Women are accepted in the field as being naturally interested in children."

Those who had taken their own children into the field believed that they had had a special advantage in their work as well. Spicer said that the Tohono O'Odham had appreciated her bringing her infant son into the field: "I certainly think that having my child with me was helpful there. They recognized that I was a normal kind of person and they appreciated the fact that I would bring a child out here to be with me. They simply trusted me more." Ellis, too, felt that taking her daughter with her had facilitated her acceptance by the Puebloans. "There's no question," she asserted, "that if you take a child into a Pueblo with you, you are ahead of the game."

ACROSS GENERATIONS

In the course of these interviews, I sometimes sensed uneasiness with the explicitly stated feminist orientation of the project. Looking back on our interactions, I now wonder if the term *feminism* suggested to them a denigration or devaluation of the feminine. I detected in each an easy

acceptance of her femininity and a desire to maintain a certain amount of difference between the sexes. "I'm not uncomfortable being a woman at all," Halpern stated (1985). "I've rather enjoyed it." All, I think, preferred to see themselves as anthropologists who happened to be women rather than as women anthropologists. Yet the fact that they were both, and were able to accomplish as much as they did when they did, generated in me a note of respect and admiration for each of them. The women of my generation have benefited by, and built on, the gains made by these earlier women. Today, as we open new doors to more equal opportunities, we should not forget the doors opened for us by our foremothers.

NOTES

1. This research was made possible through the generous support of the Wenner-Gren Foundation for Anthropological Research. My thanks go to Lita Osmundsen, Barbara Babcock, and Nancy Parezo for enabling my participation in this project and for their immeasurable guidance in carrying it out.

2. See Rosenberg (1982) and Rossiter (1982) for insightful and in-depth treatment of these educational and career trends for women in academe generally, with some attention to anthropology in particular.

3. The interviews were recorded variously on audio- and videotape as described in the preface. The originals are housed in the archives of the Wenner-Gren Foundation for Anthropological Research in New York City.

4. See also Modell 1983 for an eloquent and thorough treatment of Ruth Benedict's quest for patterns in her own life and work.

5. The women in this group are Florence Hawley Ellis (2 marriages, 1 child from the first), Esther Goldfrank (2 marriages, 1 child and stepchildren from the first), Kate Peck Kent (3 children), Dorothea Leighton (2 children and 1 foster child), Mary Shepardson (1 stepchild), Rosamond Spicer (3 children), and Clara Lee Tanner (1 child).

6. This group consists of Katherine Spencer Hal-

pern, Dorothy Keur, Marjorie Lambert (2 marriages), Laura Thompson (3 marriages), Nathalie Woodbury, and Hannah Marie Wormington.

7. Laura Thompson did not discuss her marriages. Marjorie Lambert characterized only her second husband as supportive of her career.

8. The unmarried women interviewed are Katharine Bartlett, Ruth Bunzel, Bertha Dutton, Frances Gillmor, and Alice Marriott.

9. This point was made by Barbara Babcock in her opening remarks for the Daughters of the Desert public conference, published in part as the introduction to the illustrated catalogue (Babcock and Parezo 1988:1–5).

WOMEN ON THE PERIPHERY
OF THE IVORY TOWER

$

Shelby J. Tisdale

Anthropology is considered an intellectual
quest; it's a science. What's important are
the ideas and the transmission of those
ideas to the next generation.
Joan Mark
(1986)

Dedication to anthropology is like dedication
to one's religion, it is a way of life.
Florence Hawley Ellis
(1985)

P OPULARIZING is one of the most undervalued and underrewarded forms of anthropological discourse. Generally considered atheoretical, descriptive, and unscientific, attempts to
educate the public by demystifying, dejargoniz-
ing, humanizing, and in many instances romanticizing anthropology are often viewed with mistrust by the profession. As a result, the discipline
has stigmatized and peripheralized those individuals who have attempted to introduce anthropology to the general public. Although some men
have been involved in the popularization of the
discipline, it has primarily been women who have
met the challenge to bring scientific inquiry and
anthropological concepts into the realm of public
understanding. Although this was unrecognized
and unrewarded in the past, recent discourse
among anthropologists suggests that support
from the general public may be necessary to carry
the discipline into the future (see issues of the *Anthropology Newsletter* beginning in May 1991). Anthropological discoveries and concepts have become popular themes for Hollywood productions
(such as the Indiana Jones movies), television programs, and numerous articles in popular magazines and local newspapers. This increased media
exposure suggests that there exists a public that
has a genuine interest in anthropology. In addition, the anthropologists who are generally mentioned and remembered by the public are those
who have had the unique ability to communicate
their discoveries to a public audience; this includes such famed anthropologists as Margaret
Mead, Ruth Benedict, Ashley Montague, the
Leakeys, and Donald Johanson.[1]

Chartered to understand the cultural diversity
of the world, anthropology as an academic discipline has been directed by world economic and
political decisions. Because anthropology is embedded in this political-economic milieu, it has

kept its knowledge primarily locked within an Ivory Tower. The Ivory Tower is herein defined as a cohort made up of tenured professors in prestigious universities such as Harvard, Columbia, Chicago, Yale, Michigan, Pennsylvania, and the University of California at Berkeley, who set the standards by which the rest of the discipline is judged. At the time that a large number of the women in this volume were entering the profession, the anthropologists already well established in the Ivory Tower were men who were well published, were widely cited by other anthropologists in publications and classrooms, and had a select group of graduate students who carried on their theoretical and methodological approaches and concepts. Although not everyone in academe was a privileged member of the Ivory Tower, all used and continue to use its criteria and standards to judge the work of their colleagues. This concept differs somewhat from the more general definition of the Ivory Tower as including all universities and colleges with scholars who are generally removed from the practical affairs of the rest of society. One of the goals of anthropologists in this Ivory Tower has been to socially reproduce themselves by transmitting their knowledge to a select group of individuals in formalized classroom settings. This is ironic; for example, Nathalie Woodbury (1985) has remarked, "I'm always surprised at how receptive people are to anthropology and its concepts, how curious they are about it, how much they want to know, and yet, how little the profession as a whole and many of its followers give." As indicated by the opening quotation from Mark (1986), only the knowledge of the profession's privileged members is transmitted to the next generation and will influence its theoretical direction; all other information is generally considered peripheral and less important.

To advance as a science, anthropology had to maintain an element of mystery through the development of a particular jargon that one had to have special training to understand. There was also the need to sustain scientific objectivity over subjectivity because it was felt that if the discipline became too generalized it would not be able to maintain its tenuous position in academe. Ruth Benedict noted,

This scientific framework in which anthropology has worked and developed has not prevented it from falling into error or from exploring blind alleys. Anthropology, like any science, must constantly rephrase its questions in the light of new discriminations in its own field and of new knowledge available to it in the work of other sciences. It must constantly try to profit by methods and concepts which have been developed in the physical and biological sciences, in psychology and in psychiatry (quoted in Mead 1974:165).

Unlike the hard sciences, anthropology was and continues to be based on human discovery and understanding, which is dynamic and constantly changing. Like the hard sciences, anthropology applies scientific methods and models to fieldwork and analyses. These are difficult to replicate from one society to another, whereas the replication of experiments is essential to scientific inquiry.

Numerous women anthropologists were unable to gain entree into graduate departments, yet they were dedicated to the principles of the anthropological approach. As Fox notes in her chapter in this volume, they saw anthropology as a way of life, a philosophy that would make the world a better place. They concentrated their efforts on teaching undergraduates and popularizing anthropology through their writing and public lectures. Popularizing and educating are important aspects of the career histories of many women anthropologists. While anthropology was struggling for recognition as a separate discipline and a legitimate science, women were making major contributions. Chapters throughout this volume note the various research contributions as well as the theoretical and methodological achievements that a number of women have made. Another aspect remains to be discussed, however: the women who were on the periphery of the Ivory Tower.

Through their undergraduate teaching, public lecturing, and popular writing, women played an important role in influencing young people and the public to take an interest in anthropology. This is one area where women in particular have been extremely active. They were motivated by the general concern of the discipline at the time—that Native American cultures were vanishing and that the information for each group needed to be recorded in full descriptive detail. They helped formulate the public's attitude toward native peoples by demonstrating the wealth and richness of Native American cultures of the Southwest. Although they are discussed in great detail elsewhere in this volume, I would like to point out that women such as Marjorie Lambert, Bertha Dutton, and H. Marie Wormington played a major role in popularizing anthropology and the Southwest by concentrating their efforts on teaching a general audience through public lectures and museum exhibitions about the Southwest's prehistory, history, and contemporary cultures; in articles in museum catalogues, newsletters, and popular magazines; and in books (see Cordell's chapter for details on their careers as archaeologists and Parezo and Hardin's chapter for a discussion of women anthropologists who worked in museums). Dorothy Keur, Kate Peck Kent, and Clara Lee Tanner, who are examined in this chapter, worked in colleges and universities where they could teach about the cultural diversity of the native peoples of the Southwest in lower-division courses; at the same time they also gave numerous public lectures. Other women wrote novels, popular anthropology books, or travelogues about the Southwest or worked as activists for Native American rights: of these Frances Gillmor, Mary Austin, Erna Fergusson, Ann Axtell Morris, and Ruth Murray Underhill are discussed here.

Unfortunately, we know little about many of the women who have devoted their lives to disseminating anthropological knowledge. The staggering number of popularizers who have gone unrecognized by academe includes writers such as Laura Armer, Margery Bedinger, Ina Sizer Cassidy, Amy Passmore Hurt, Wilma Kaemlein, Dorothy Pillsbury, Toney Richardson, Frances Sanita, and Opal E. Singer, to name but a few. Hundreds of women amassed information on the arts and crafts of the Southwest, for example, Martha Beckwith, Willena D. Cartwright, Jane Chesney, Mary Cynthia Dickerson, Marjorie Givens, Margaret Schevill Link, and Grace Taft, of whom we know little or nothing. Others are to us little more than authors of brief articles in *New Mexico Magazine, Plateau, Arizona Highways, El Palacio,* or *Desert Magazine.* The list could go on and on.[2]

Popularizing the discipline and educating college and university undergraduate students and the general public have been important parts of the career histories of many women anthropologists. Popularizing and educating were ways in which women were able to overcome their marginality. In this they succeeded brilliantly. Indeed, popular work made some professional and activist anthropologists better known to the general public, especially in the Southwest, than to scholars in the elite institutions located elsewhere.

It is time to celebrate the contributions of these women who dedicated their lives to popularizing anthropology and the Southwest as lecturers, educators, writers, and activists at the expense of being peripheralized by the Ivory Tower. The following biographical vignettes are of women who were educators and popularizers of the discipline. These two categories are not mutually exclusive; there is overlap in individual interests and the audiences on which these women focused during the courses of their diverse careers. Some of these women were trained at Ivory Tower institutions such as Columbia University, a few received their education at universities in the Southwest, and others were not anthropologists at all; nevertheless, they deserve credit for bringing anthropology and the understanding of cultural diversity into the public domain. Although the focus of this volume is on women anthropologists who worked in the Southwest, women outside of anthropology and academe also had an indirect effect on the discipline through various methods such as writing descriptive novels, lecturing to the general public, teaching outside of academe, educating the intellectual tourist, and advocating Native American rights, all of which were embedded in emotion and love for the Southwest as a place and the native peoples that were part of its landscape. These women's contributions demonstrate that careers and contributions need to be broadly defined. While many of these women will have been discussed in other chapters of this volume, some will be introduced for the first time. It is my intention to emphasize the "voice" of these women; therefore, quotes from interviews are utilized to emphasize or clarify particular points.

WOMEN WHO POPULARIZED ANTHROPOLOGY THROUGH FORMAL EDUCATION

Women in the United States are generally thought to be natural teachers, especially of children and young adults. During the last two decades of the nineteenth century, several independent women's colleges such as Smith, Wellesley, Bryn Mawr, and Baltimore College for Women were founded. Barnard College was established as Columbia University's coordinate institution for women in 1889. However, as Rossiter (1982:52) argues, while this movement made higher education available to women,

little thought had been given to the careers that such graduates might take up. Because of the prevailing notion of "separate spheres" for the two sexes, it was assumed that most women were seeking personal fulfillment and were planning to become better wives and mothers. Advocates of their study of science saw it as offering a rigorous and satisfying intellectual experience to women who led essentially "aimless lives."

After the turn of the century there was an increase in the number of women entering higher education; nevertheless, they were limited to teaching in women's colleges or teaching undergraduates at larger colleges and universities. While most of the women in the following vignettes were unable to gain entree to the Ivory Tower, each one influenced young anthropology students in her own way and blazed the trail for the rest of us to follow. Ruth Benedict, Gladys Reichard, and Florence Hawley Ellis were exceptions to the rule of women being relegated to teaching positions in less prestigious institutions. In terms of their overall careers, Benedict, Reichard, and Ellis made it into the Ivory Tower, where they placed tremendous emphasis on teaching both undergraduates and graduates; yet they also dedicated time to popularizing the discipline outside of the classroom through public lectures and popular writing and by inviting amateurs as well as students to participate in research projects, as Ellis did on her archaeological excavations. They felt that this was crucial to the dissemination of anthropological knowledge. Although their professional careers are discussed in more detail elsewhere in this volume, we cannot neglect the role they played in making anthropology a popular subject.

Ruth Benedict

Ruth Benedict taught at Columbia University, had graduate students, and was remembered not only by her students but by the discipline as a whole for making major contributions to anthropology; nevertheless, it had taken her a long time to be recognized and rewarded. One area that has still been undervalued is Benedict's involvement in several causes and events throughout her career, especially during World War II. Modell (1988:4–5) maintains that

her work as an anthropologist was pedagogical: she taught her audience the virtues of "seeing how other people arrange their lives," the necessity of tolerating individual differences if a society is to survive, the power of culture over nature. Human beings, she wrote, can change the terms of their existence and, with insight brought by anthropology, can make these changes wisely.

Victor Barnouw, one of Benedict's graduate students at Columbia, is cited (Hatch 1973:75) as having said, "Like most of Ruth Benedict's students, I looked up to her with a mixture of veneration and bewilderment." Although her hearing impairment made her appear aloof and shy, she was remarkably generous with her time and money to both her friends and students (Hatch 1973:75). During her tenure at Columbia she "had a decisive influence on the careers of Margaret Mead, Ruth Underhill, and Ruth Bunzel" (Babcock and Parezo 1988:27).

As a writer, Benedict is best known for two classic works: *Patterns of Culture* (1959a [1934]), one of the most widely read books in anthropology, and *The Chrysanthemum and the Sword* (1946). During the 1930s and 1940s Benedict directed her writings toward an educated popular audience in a series of articles for the *New Republic, Atlantic Monthly,* and *UNESCO,* as well as numerous reviews of work by her colleagues for the *Herald Tribune.* At the same time she was trying to reach a second audience primarily made up of the nonanthropological scientific community and policy makers. Although not as well known, Benedict's *Race: Science and Politics* (1940a) was "designed to shock readers out of complacency and deflect the world from its precipitous course into disaster" (Modell 1983:249). Caffrey (1989:292) points out that

the book was not on the "cutting edge" of knowledge, not an original creative contribution to scholarship, but instead reiterated ideas that had become clichés in anthropology by 1939, although they remained fresh and startling to the largely uninformed general public she was trying to reach.

Benedict complained of Boas' intensified interest in race and militant anti-Nazi activities in 1934;

however, as Mead (1959a:348) notes, Benedict was eventually

seized by the urgency of the problems facing the world and the obligation as an anthropologist to take part. She never acted as a simple citizen—perhaps here vestiges of her belief in causes lingered—but always as an anthropologist within a certain area of competence. In this way the years of active work on the question of race and on the wider questions of democracy began.

Mead (1959a:53) points out that by the time the United States entered into World War II, both Boas and Benedict had become "actively involved in a series of battles over academic freedom that brought them into conflict not only with Stalinists but also with anti-Stalinists who periodically accused them of having Communist sympathies." While on sabbatical in California (1939–1940), Benedict wrote *Race: Science and Politics,* on which Mead (1959a:350) claims she "worked with devotion and without delight as if in payment of a moral debt which anthropologists owed a world threatened by Nazism." *Races of Mankind,* a pamphlet she wrote with Gene Weltfish in 1943, was a simplified version of *Race.* It was Benedict's attempt to reduce inequality and racism. Unfortunately, *Races of Mankind* was denounced in Congress as subversive "because of a tactical error committed in the writing in stating badly that some Northern Negroes had scored higher in intelligence tests than had some Southern whites" (Mead 1959a:353). This was not acceptable within the framework of the wartime security structure.

Throughout this period Benedict devoted herself to a great deal of lecturing and writing on race, war, and democracy. Her discussions of these matters as an anthropologist "became known far outside the small circle of her profession" (Mead 1974:54). At the same time her works drew both criticism and praise from a professional and a lay audience. Modell (1983:287) describes this contrast in reviews of Benedict's writings:

Reviewers and essayists, anthropologists and nonanthropologists, commented on the evident pedagogical purpose in all her writings. The fact that Ruth directed her anthropology to current events and crises drew both negative and positive response; few failed to mention that she wrote, and practiced, an anthropology formed by contemporary problems and addressed to common readers.

Reviewers of *Patterns of Culture, Race,* and *The Chrysanthemum and the Sword* debated the virtues of popularizing—at least semi-popularizing—anthropology. The issue united otherwise differently motivated reviewers, who questioned the effect of literary techniques on scientific inquiry. Discussion revolved around the relationship of science and aesthetics, in research and in presentation. Ruth herself had been clear: She wrote to educate her readers in a science and used artistic devices to make the lessons not just palatable but meaningful in day-to-day experience.

Reviewers of her books ended up discussing the definition of science and, specifically, the degree to which anthropology *was* a science. Again Ruth was clearer than many of her critics. Hers was a "humanistic science," she said, a science pursued and publicized for the purpose of improving human lives.

Although she was praised for her humanitarian work, it was not considered scientific and did not advance her career in academe. According to Modell (1983:287), she was often "dismissed for making judgements, misunderstood as bias and subjectivity."

Gladys Reichard

Like Benedict, Gladys Reichard chose to combine her teaching and field experiences with popular and scholarly writing. At Barnard College, an undergraduate women's college which was connected to an elite institution, Columbia University, Reichard worked primarily with undergraduates. Reichard was committed to advancing the professional careers of her female students, as Kate Peck Kent (1985b), her assistant, remembered: "She was so bright. Her mind worked so fast you couldn't keep up with it. She was fun to work for. She assumed you had a

brain." Like Kent, students such as Ruth Underhill, Marian Smith, and Eleanor Leacock, to name but a few who worked under Reichard's direction, went on to establish themselves in the discipline.

Reichard's commitment to teaching anthropology grew out of her previous experiences; like many other women of her generation she taught in an elementary school before pursuing a career in anthropology. This experience and her dedication to making anthropology understandable to a wide audience informed her teaching strategy. In her discussion of Reichard's method of teaching, Leacock (1988:303) contends,

Not only did Gladys Reichard integrate the personal and intellectual in her anthropology, anthropology itself was the major integrating force in her life. She became close personal friends with the anthropologists with whom she had studied or worked: Boas, Lowie, and especially Pliny Earle Goddard, who had introduced her to the Navajo. She was much concerned with the teaching of anthropology as well as her own research and writing, and gave great thought to it.

A popular teacher in her large introductory classes, Reichard incorporated her fieldwork and analyses into her teaching (Leacock 1988:306), and this influenced the career choices of her students. Kent (1985b) claimed, "She was good on material culture—especially weaving. I think her interests rubbed off on me, too."

Reichard had the ability to advance her knowledge and research for both a scholarly audience within academe and a popular audience. Her popular publications, based on her experiences among the Navajo, captivated the public and scholars alike. Her popular writing emphasized the beauty and feel of Navajo life. Leacock (1988:307) points out that "when she wrote a book on the Navajo for a popular audience, she made the stature and authority of Navajo women a central theme." Likewise, her popular work often preceded her scholarly work in ways that profoundly influenced the discipline. Lyon (1989:138) maintains,

Her intensive studies led first to a popular book, *Spider Woman* (1934), an autobiographical account of her life with the family of Miguelito, then a technical account of weaving, *Navajo Shepherd and Weaver* (1937). This was followed by a fictionalized biography of Miguelito's wife, *Dezba, Woman of the Desert* (1939) . . . *Dezba* should be given some credit for introducing a new genre into Navajo scholarship: the biographical study.

Lyon adds that "her writings had a certain charm and human interest; the reader came to care about, became bonded with Spider Woman, who obviously was Gladys living in a primitive hogan learning to weave, and about Dezba and her family." Today Reichard's *Spider Woman* (1934a) would be considered reflexive in terms of the postmodernist approach to anthropology, and *Dezba* (1939a) would be referred to as ethnobiography.

Florence Hawley Ellis

Florence Hawley Ellis was a dedicated and rigorous teacher as well as researcher, as Cordell and Fox have documented in their chapters in this volume. In 1934 when Ellis began her long teaching career there was only one other woman faculty member at the University of New Mexico: Mamie Tanquist, a member of the Sociology Department. This was not unusual for most anthropology departments in the 1930s. Of Ellis' tenure at the university, Bock (1989:3) contends that she and Donald Brand were "demanding teachers who insisted that archaeological and ethnological studies be integrated and reflect a deep understanding of environmental contexts." This was quite different from the isolationist approach dictated by the separation of the four subfields of the discipline. Over the past few decades, ethnoarchaeology and ethnohistory have become important approaches increasingly integrated into graduate programs at large universities such as the University of Arizona.

Throughout her career at the University of New Mexico (1934–1971), Ellis taught over 20 different courses on the archaeology, ethnology, and material culture of the Southwest at both the undergraduate and graduate levels. Theodore Frisbie (1975:7) claims that

Florence was never a static teacher. Each year her courses were taught in a manner that brought the latest theoretical approaches and her own stance into focus. Florence's mind was and is that of a thinker. Her own research, as well as that of others, constantly provided stimulation for her students, as well as herself . . . When it was exam time, students often displayed mild hysteria, because the amount of material she covered in her courses was always extensive . . . Her exams stressed thinking with the data, rather than straight regurgitation, and thus to survive, you were forced to learn to think.

In addition to her classes at New Mexico she ran several archaeological field schools in Chaco Canyon and in the northern Rio Grande area. This eventually had a far-reaching influence, national in scope.

Today Ellis is recognized for the training of numerous archaeologists. According to Babcock and Parezo (1988:125), Ellis "devoted her time to research and teaching. Through the University of New Mexico field schools and classes, Ellis introduced numerous students to Southwestern archaeology and taught them 'anthropology that wasn't just out of books.'" Continuing with her research and teaching long after her retirement, Ellis was given an honorary doctorate degree at the University of New Mexico in 1988 (Bock 1989:13).

Clara Lee Tanner

A scholar who devoted her life to teaching both undergraduates and the general public was Clara Lee Tanner. Offered a teaching position at the University of Arizona in 1928, she stayed for the next 50 years and was eventually given an honorary Ph.D. shortly before she retired. Tanner taught numerous courses covering a variety of subjects during her teaching career at the University of Arizona. She began with courses on Greek,

Roman, Egyptian, and Asiatic archaeology. As the department grew and changed its focus from archaeology to anthropology, Tanner began teaching introductory courses in all four subfields and turned her attention to native peoples of the Southwest. In 1940 she added courses on southwestern Native American art, which became some of the most popular in the university. When asked if she enjoyed teaching, Tanner (1985) emphatically responded, "Oh, I loved it. I enjoyed it thoroughly . . . It's hard work, if you do it honestly . . . But, then to be able to help someone else learn in the process, it's a very gratifying thing."

Besides her commitment to teaching, Tanner was dedicated to presenting public lectures, which she saw as her civic duty:

I became interested in writing early in the 1930s. And also in public speaking. I was not able to participate in city activities—you know, volunteer things—because of my hours. And so, I decided early in the game, that anyone who asked for a public lecture I would be glad to do it if I was free. And that has been my policy all along (Tanner 1985).

At the age of 85 she continues to give a dozen lectures a year and serves as a judge in at least two Native American art shows. Over the years she has given thousands of talks in public forums throughout the Southwest. Tanner not only disseminated information verbally but also published popular and semi-popular articles on southwestern Native American art to ensure that correct information was made available to a public audience. Her extensive list of publications includes numerous articles in *The Kiva* and *Arizona Highways*.

Although Tanner felt that theory and its requisite jargon was not coincident with the needs of popular writing, her technical writings have been widely cited. Several of her publications on Native American arts and crafts, such as *Southwest Indian Craft Arts* (1968), *Prehistoric Southwestern Craft Arts* (1976), and *Indian Baskets of the Southwest* (1983), are extremely valuable to students,

professionals, and the general public. These publications have also been invaluable to museum curators and collections managers who are charged with the identification, interpretation, and care of ethnographic and prehistoric objects. Collectors and lovers of Native American art use her books as orientations to the field and as guides for understanding technology and quality.

Tanner realized that her male colleagues at Arizona did not share her interest in writing factual, descriptive, and nonjargonized accounts of the native populations of the Southwest. Over the years, the department increasingly emphasized abstract and mid-level theory. She argued, however, "If you are going to write about facts you don't get into theory too much . . . And I felt that the facts were very important and quite necessary to an understanding of our native peoples in particular, specifically that area [of art], that being my area of interest" (Tanner 1985). This is not to say that others in the department did not use facts; rather, they combined facts with a theoretical and interpretive framework that required specialized knowledge to understand. Tanner tried to write in a way in which the information would speak for itself.

As a result of the decisions she made and the history of professional discourse, Tanner taught for 50 years before she was promoted to full professor. The lack of a Ph.D. limited her career both financially and professionally: other Arizona faculty members concurred that the "lack of a Ph.D. hurt academically" and slowed her promotion to full professor (Lytle-Webb 1988:352). Despite this slow rate of promotion Tanner was dedicated to the University of Arizona. She had other academic and professional offers, but she wanted to continue her research on southwestern Native American arts and crafts, to live in the Southwest, and to teach at Arizona. This took courage, since her decision to focus on a popular audience almost cost Tanner her career:

My popular writing was not helpful in any kind of progress. And I don't think that was gender, I think it was just simply attitude . . . I talked to two heads of my college, college deans, about this very subject. Both of them said, "I approve highly of this being done, but it isn't going to get you anywhere professionally" (Tanner 1985).

Fully aware of the effect popularizing would have on her career, Tanner decided to go in this direction anyway. Many other women, like Tanner, made this conscious decision to make their own way in the discipline even though the university community disapproved and felt that popularizing the discipline was marginal to its scientific endeavors. Tanner sacrificed rapid career advancement to maintain her principles and ideals concerning the popularization of anthropology and thereby assured that the information gained through research was brought into the public domain.

Kate Peck Kent

Kate Kent is one of the few women in this volume whom I have had the privilege of knowing personally. Although I did not take any formal anthropology classes from her, I was most definitely one of her students. I met Kent after she had retired from the University of Denver and was studying the Navajo textile collection at the School of American Research in Santa Fe. She had just published *Prehistoric Textiles of the Southwest* (1983a) and *Pueblo Indian Textiles* (1983b) and was working on *Navajo Weaving: Three Centuries of Change* (1985a). The time that I spent with her was all too brief, but during the three-and-one-half years that I was acquainted with her, she was always willing to share her vast array of anthropological knowledge with me as she did with all of her students. She felt that "if you get your training in anthropology, it does set up a particular point of view, which is really what anthropology is. It gives you a perspective that no other discipline gives you, a curiosity about other people" (Kent 1985b). Of her own contributions to anthropology Kent (1985b) said,

In terms of the profession, I think my writing on archaeological textiles is something no one else has

done or does any more. That should stand. In terms of other less measurable contributions, I think what has been most rewarding and maybe most significant is turning young people on to certain aspects of the field. And personally, that is more satisfying to me than recognition for the writing and research.

Kent was introduced to prehistoric textiles in 1937 while working for Frederic H. Douglas, Curator of Indian Art at the Denver Art Museum. Her analysis of cotton fragments from Montezuma Castle National Monument in Arizona launched her on a lifetime of research on southwestern prehistoric, historic, and contemporary textiles (Schevill 1989:3). As Fox notes in her chapter, after receiving a B.A. at the University of Denver in 1935 and working at the Denver Art Museum for one year, Kent went to Columbia University for graduate work on a resident scholarship. As a graduate assistant to Gladys Reichard, she taught Reichard's classes for one semester. Prior to completing her M.A., however, she returned to Denver and secured a position as the assistant curator of Indian art at the Denver Art Museum in 1937. When Douglas was drafted, she served as Acting Curator of Native Arts from 1942 to 1944. After his return she held a series of part-time positions and went to the University of Arizona, where she completed her M.A. in 1950. She hoped to secure a permanent position when Douglas died of cancer, but the museum's board of trustees felt that curators should be men and not women. They also felt that as a married woman with a family Kent did not need the job! Kent, nevertheless, managed to balance a career and family obligations, but the lack of a full curatorship and a Ph.D. undoubtedly prevented her from advancing in the profession as rapidly as her male colleagues (see Fox, this volume).

Kent's "fieldwork" focused on museum collections, and she was a storehouse of knowledge in her expertise on prehistoric and historic Pueblo textiles. After more than 30 years of dedicating her life to the study of textiles she would still get excited when making a new observation or interpretation, which was highly contagious to anyone within hearing range. Her old friend and noted textile specialist Joe Ben Wheat notes,

Kate used museums as resources in her teaching, whether for formal teaching, or for that which involved research into Pueblo textiles and embroidery or the exploration of early Hispanic weaving. To Kate, museum collections constituted not only a major resource for her own research, but a resource for the guidance and inspiration of her students and colleagues. In teaching the skills needed for museum work, Kate raised the level of appreciation and understanding that students had for material culture, and, most important, she fostered the spirit of inquiry which enabled them to translate the museum objects from curio to common human experience (Wheat 1989:30).

Kent not only viewed museums as places in which research could be conducted, she felt that it was important that museums be professionalized. For this reason she stressed the training of curators, collection managers, and registrars and incorporated museology into her course curricula. As a result, "she was deeply concerned with museum training and many curators around the country acquired their professional standards and enthusiasms in her classes" (Whiteford 1988: 956).

In an obituary in *American Anthropologist,* Whiteford (1988:956) sums up Kent's career in the following words:

Her enthusiasm for textile research was equaled only by her devotion to teaching and her family. She was a great teacher and was absorbed with her students from her first appointment as a part-time instructor . . . in 1950 until she retired as associate professor emerita from the University of Denver in 1976.

Unfortunately, Kent was never awarded tenure nor promoted to full professor:

I wasn't on the regular faculty. I was adjunct with year-to-year appointments. One year I ran the department—that was full-time, but I still wasn't on tenure track. The department head was on sabbatical. I was the only one there, I think. It was a very small de-

partment, and still is. I think I was exploited all those years . . . I did an awful lot of work for not much money (Kent 1985b).

Regardless of this lack of advancement there is no doubt about what Kent thought of teaching:

I loved teaching. I would still love to teach, but only a few students at a time, and what I want to teach, and what they are interested in. I liked the last few years. I taught graduate students, who were already mature and had their interests. They knew more than I did about a lot of things (Kent 1985b).

Realizing how limited careers are for women in academe without a Ph.D., Kent always encouraged her students, especially women, to continue with their education after the M.A. and to acquire a doctorate. She felt that this might give women the opportunity to gain equal footing with men.

Kent is one of the few anthropologists to be memorialized by her students and colleagues: in a special invited session at the 1988 American Anthropological Association meeting in Phoenix; in a special issue of *Museum Anthropology* dedicated to her; and in a memorial exhibit commemorating her contributions to both anthropology and museums at the Wheelwright Museum of the American Indian in Santa Fe, which opened approximately two weeks after her death.

Dorothy Louise Keur

Dorothy Keur began her career as an archaeologist "with a distinguished monograph on Big Bead Mesa [1941], a Navaho fortress archaeological site, which she analyzed in terms of ethnographic acculturation" (Irwin-Williams 1990: 20). Although Keur is known as an archaeologist and as a cultural anthropologist for her ecological research in the Windward Islands and the Netherlands with her husband, she is best known as a teacher and for "her efforts to develop undergraduate anthropology at Hunter College" (James 1988:181).

Graduating from Hunter College in 1925, Keur became interested in anthropology after taking a summer course from Edward Sapir at Columbia University and another the following year (1926) from Leslie Spier. Shortly after receiving her M.A. from Columbia in 1928, Keur went to the Southwest, where she was "thrilled with the living Native Americans and the archaeological remains" (Keur 1985). There she met Edgar Lee Hewett and made arrangements to attend his archaeological field school at Chaco Canyon, where she received her basic archaeological training.

While teaching full-time at Hunter College, Keur worked toward and completed her Ph.D. in anthropology at Columbia University (Babcock and Parezo 1988:143). She commented, "I had the privilege of studying under Benedict, Weltfish, Spier, and Sapir. I crammed in everything I could so I could give an introductory course in anthro at Hunter and keep a little ahead of the students" (Keur 1985).

Although her groundbreaking excavations of Big Bead Mesa and in the Gobernador area allowed her to document for the first time Navajo life and Navajo-Pueblo relations in the Pueblo Refugee period, Keur (1985) felt her major contribution to anthropology had been teaching at Hunter College:

When I began anthropology, everyone I knew—friends, relations, and even other academicians—thought of anthropology as the study of oddities by eccentrics. And yet, it gave me such a sense of unity with mankind, a reaching out, a feeling of touching other human beings, and a feeling of my own insignificance—one tiny being out of all those billions of human beings on the earth. I love that feeling, and was very stimulated by it, and also by the concept of the relativity of values . . . I wanted to explore other values, other peoples' lives, and also to teach that to thousands of others—not that they would ever become professional anthropologists, but that they would have a viewpoint. In a way, it is a viewpoint of life. It's a philosophy; it's humanity. I just loved it.

During her 37 years at Hunter, Keur progressed from lab assistant to full professor, as Fox notes in her chapter in this volume. She taught a "multi-plicity of courses" and established a laboratory for physical anthropology (Keur 1985). James (1988: 184) notes, "Despite many handicaps, Keur and [Elsie] Steedman developed such a fine collection of primate and human skeletal material and instruments that Sherwood Washburn called Hunter the best equipped undergraduate laboratory of physical anthropology in the United States."

Keur also served in administrative and advising capacities along with carrying a heavy teaching load. Of her contribution to the development of anthropology at Hunter, Keur (1985) said,

I had a rather large role. I really think that is my big contribution: to the development of anthropology to the general undergrad body at Hunter. It doesn't seem like a big accomplishment professionally. In those early years you almost didn't want to go around saying "I'm just a teacher of anthropology." If you weren't a great field researcher, you were really looked down upon. Certainly at Columbia I had to overcome that. I had to accept a back seat vis-à-vis professional stardom.

As the Wheelwright Museum did for Kent, Hunter College recently curated an exhibition in honor of Keur as a way to recognize and acknowledge her contributions to the development of its anthropology department (McClendon 1991).

Dorothy Dunn

Not all anthropological teaching was done in the university, nor was it necessarily done by trained anthropologists. As a teacher and artist, Dorothy Dunn bridged the gap between the understanding of "Indian" art and "Anglo" art. Through her efforts, as well as those of members of the Indian Arts Fund in Santa Fe, native peoples were able to move into the realm of art, away from being considered simply craftspeople, and thereby increase their incomes considerably. As an art teacher in The Studio at the Santa Fe Indian School, Dunn took on the role of mediator and cross-cultural educator between Native Americans and Anglos through her emphasis on understanding artistic appreciation and aesthetics. Her activities have positively affected the public and Native Americans alike.

Earlier attempts to train Native American artists had depended on the teacher's initiative, which was in "clear opposition to official Indian Bureau policies" (Brody 1971:126). Prior to 1932, art classes had been taught for personal and recreational benefit at the primary levels. Not until formal art classes were taught at the Santa Fe Indian School did the government explore the personal and professional benefits of art training for Native Americans. Among these pioneer teachers who were "especially dedicated and imaginative people" was Dorothy Dunn (Brody 1971:126). An Indian Service teacher at the BIA day school in the late 1920s, Dunn used art as an aid in teaching English and other subjects by having her students paint pictures of their own life experiences. She hoped to "use art to build respect among her charges for their own cultural traditions and as a medium for personality development" (Brody 1971:127).

Dunn left the Indian Service in 1928 to complete her formal education at the Chicago Art Institute. Working on a plan for a painting studio at the Santa Fe Indian School, she returned to the Southwest in 1932. Her goal was "to study Indian painting as art and, as an artist and research person, to assist in its creative development by Indian students through exploration with them of their own heritage of art forms and symbols" (Dunn 1960:18). Brody (1971:128) claims,

Through the Santa Fe Studio, Miss Dunn became the single most influential individual for an entire generation of Indian painters. The Studio became the model for art departments at other Indian Schools, and no significant changes in method or philosophy occurred until thirty years after she began her work. Virtually all of the important Indian painters of her generation came under her guidance or were taught by her students, and in turn they taught most Indian artists of the succeeding generation . . . The work of these artists must be considered a product of the dis-

tinctive painting style developed at the Studio from 1932 to 1937.

Although Native American artists had long been painting pottery, weaving textiles, creating silver jewelry, and working in other media, Dunn influenced a different art medium, that of easel painting within the confines of a studio. According to Gibson (1981:294), "During the 1930s The Studio enrollment averaged 130 pupils. They studied composition, drawing, design, and painting. Initially, Dunn had only one student helper, and she divided the students into eight classes of from fifteen to thirty-two. Elizabeth Willis DeHuff later taught art there." The distinctive style Dunn encouraged at the Santa Fe Studio was based on the imagination of her students; it has come to be recognized as quintessential southwestern "Indian" painting.

Even though most of her students were from the southwestern Pueblos and the Navajo and Apache reservations, Dunn also had students from the northern and southern Plains. Dunn's students became free-lance artists or art teachers or were employed as commercial artists, illustrators, or muralists (Gibson 1981:294). Dunn later devoted her time to public lectures, judging, promoting, and curating invitational exhibitions in museums across the country. Her collection of easel art has been seen and admired by thousands of people. The modern success of her students and their art could not have happened without her vision. Her legacy continues at the Institute of American Indian Art in Santa Fe, where several Native American artists continue to receive their formal training.

WOMEN WRITERS WHO POPULARIZED THE SOUTHWEST

One way in which the Southwest came alive was through the efforts of those authors who wrote popular articles and books that captivated the imagination. This style of writing was done by the professional woman anthropologist as well as the advocate and the nonacademic. Some of the better-known anthropologists having already been discussed in this volume and touched on again in the earlier sections of this paper, I would now like to turn to those women who are not as well known, yet deserve acknowledgement for their direct contributions to making the Southwest an area of both scholarly and popular interest and for their indirect contributions to the field of anthropology.

Both men and women have worked to popularize and romanticize the Southwest as a place and southwesterners as a people. Some early publications on the Southwest were written by men such as Adolph Bandelier, Oliver LaFarge, Charles Lummis, and Carl Lumholtz, who romanticized archaeological discoveries and the Native Americans they encountered. One purpose for their particular genre of writing was partly to raise general interest in their individual research projects in hopes of securing additional funding. Several women, on the other hand, wrote nonacademic, personal accounts that came straight from the heart. For some the goal was to generate popular interest in and increase awareness of the Southwest and for others the goal was to promote anthropology by focusing on a shared human experience. Because of their atheoretical approach and personalized accounts, these women were peripheralized by members of the Ivory Tower. Interestingly, this approach eventually became a popular form of ethnography among some male anthropologists such as Clifford Geertz (1988) and Paul Rabinow (1977).

Frances Gillmor

An anthropologist, folklorist, and English professor at the University of Arizona, Frances Gillmor has ventured into several arenas throughout her long and productive career. Gillmor has written columns for newspapers, novels, and biographies, as well as scholarly works. Writing was Gillmor's life. Not having given a lot of thought to career goals or direction, she said that "opportunities just came up. I was writing from my childhood on, so there was never any decision about whether I should write—I just did" (Gillmor 1985).

Awarded an academic scholarship, Gillmor attended the University of Chicago for two years from 1921 to 1923. Instead of completing her degree she went to work as a newspaper reporter in Florida. Her mother's illness took the family to Arizona in 1926, and Gillmor resumed her studies at the University of Arizona, where she received a B.A. in 1928 and an M.A. in 1931 in English. Her interest in the Southwest already kindled, she went to the Navajo Reservation to conduct thesis research, which entailed collecting biographical data on Louisa Wetherill, a well-known trader at Kayenta. This ultimately resulted in the publication of *Traders to the Navajo* in 1934, a collaboration between Gillmor and Wetherill.

Her relationship with the Wetherills provided Gillmor "an entree into Navajo life rarely afforded non-natives, particularly women, at the time. In addition to customs, she observed numerous tribal rituals such as sand-painting ceremonies while a guest on the reservation" (Kibbee 1988: 116). Her interest in these ceremonies resulted in the publication of *Windsinger* in 1930, "notable for its authentic description of Navajo customs and beliefs" (Kibbee 1988:116). This novel captures much of the flavor of Navajo life in a way that ethnographic description does not. Like LaFarge, Gillmor wanted to convey what it was like to be a Navajo, to live on the reservation, even if the daily situations were contrived. Gillmor thought the novel provided a better forum for the conveyance of emotions, values, and customs than did the dry description of traits common to the ethnographic monographs of her day.

Gillmor taught in the English Department at the University of New Mexico before returning to the University of Arizona in 1934, where she stayed throughout the remainder of her career. She was fortunate in her ability to combine teaching with her scholarly pursuits. After publishing another novel, *Fruit out of the Rock* (1940), and several short stories, she became interested in Aztec ethnohistory and culture. Gillmor remained a dedicated teacher at Arizona and pursued her career as a scholar by teaching only one semester a year at the university. According to Kibbee (1988:118), while Gillmor was on leave

she pursued her research, writing, or continuing education. She preferred not to devote her energies to both teaching and research simultaneously, fearing that students would not enjoy her full attention if research were competing for her time. She enjoyed a warm relationship with her students; and in recognition for her talents in the classroom, she was awarded the University of Arizona's Creative Teaching Award in 1970.

She continued her education at the Instituto de Filosofía y Letras in Mexico, where she studied Aztec codices. Returning to Mexico a year later to study at the Universidad Nacional Autononoma de Mexico, she "began the laborious research on her principal project, a biography of Nezahualcoyotl, poet-king of the Aztecs and ruler of Texcoco in the fifteenth century" (Kibbee 1988: 116). In 1949 Gillmor published this research as *Flute of the Smoking Mirror*. While a full professor of English at Arizona she was awarded a doctorate from the Universidad Nacional Autonoma at the age of 54.

Gillmor felt it was important to "preserve and study the oral traditions of her beloved Southwest" (Kibbee 1988:117). In 1943 she founded and directed the Folklore Archive (now the Southwest Folklore Center) at the University of Arizona (Babcock and Parezo 1988). There

Gillmor endeavored to collect a body of materials from which scholars might draw. This material included verbal arts—legends, tall tales, family stories, proverbs, and jokes—as well as examples of traditional wisdom, such as superstitions or remedies. She recognized that the Southwest possessed a rich vein of lore that, unlike that of the southern Appalachians, had yet to be tapped . . . Serving as a catalyst, Gill-

mor organized and inspired a dedicated corps of professionals, students, and laypersons to recognize and preserve the oral traditional culture of the region. Through her tireless efforts and infectious enthusiasm, she generated a climate of awareness and appreciation of regional folkways that was to become her legacy (Kibbee 1988:117).

A scholar, teacher, and popularizer, Gillmor aimed to link academe to a general audience. Unlike most women she managed to successfully move between the academic and popular spheres, combining many genres of writing.

Mary Austin

Although she was not a trained anthropologist or folklorist, Mary Austin is discussed here because of her concern for the environmental preservation of the Southwest and its native peoples and her advocation of anthropology. Compared to Alice Corbin Henderson, Mabel Dodge Luhan, and numerous other poets, writers, and artists who had already been political activists in other parts of the country before gravitating to the Southwest, Austin was extremely prolific. She wrote 27 books and over 250 articles in which she helped to romanticize the Southwest. As a trained naturalist in California, Austin identified strongly with the land. In describing Austin's writing, Fink (1983:ix) claims,

All of her writings are in a sense autobiographical. Even when she wrote of the land, she reflected the despair and ecstasy of her own experience. However, in her formal autobiography, *Earth Horizon,* she presented only those aspects of her life about which she wanted the world to know. It is in her novels and short stories, as well as in her intimate letters to those with whom she was on most intimate terms, that the rest of her story is revealed.

Babcock and Parezo (1988:205) point out that Austin's writings not only expressed her "passionate identification with the land" but also "her outrage against the mistreatment of its native inhabitants and the misuse of women's gifts."

Austin not only wrote about the Southwest but

also joined Mabel Dodge Luhan and other New Mexican intellectuals and artists in the fight against the Bursam Bill, which proposed to take away approximately 60,000 acres of Pueblo land and the accompanying water rights (Simmons 1979:215). Like several other women of this time period such as Natalie Curtis Burlin, Alice Fletcher, and Sharlotte Hall, Austin was a complex and dynamic woman:

A feminist, naturalist, mystic, and writer, she was involved with aspects of the human condition which are ageless. In an era when minority groups were despised and dispossessed, she carried their cause to the highest offices in the land. In a society in which women were treated as chattels, she spoke out for the right to self-realization with candor and eloquence. In a country where natural resources were taken for granted and the land ruthlessly exploited, she interpreted man's abiding relationship and responsibility to the earth with a depth and understanding unsurpassed by later environmentalists (Fink 1988:1).

Austin's popularizing was directed toward educating specific groups—Washington, D.C., policy makers and bureaucrats. Recognizing the threat of contemporary capitalist Anglo-American society to the Native American and Hispanic cultures of the Southwest, she utilized her political activism to help preserve their cultural heritage. Concerning Austin's activism against the assimilation policies of the federal government during the 1920s, Gibson (1981:293) claims that

Mary Austin was largely responsible for the change in public policy concerning Indian art. She insisted that the humane and intelligent policy for the federal government was to lift the rule against expressing Indianness. Her position was that the most effective way to renew the Indian was to permit him self-determination rather than to require him to follow the white man's road. And the suppressed Indian arts, so vital to tribal as well as national culture, could be saved only through education.

Babcock and Parezo (1988:205) add that she "also gave generously of her time and money to the Indian Arts Fund" in Santa Fe. The Indian Arts Fund had been formed by leaders of the Santa Fe artists' colony, which included Mary Austin along with Kenneth Chapman, Frank Applegate, and John Sloan, to encourage the preservation and continuation of southwestern Native American arts, especially Pueblo pottery. As part of her effort she penned several works on Pueblo pottery.

Popularizers were often political activists. Like Austin, several other writers in the Southwest opposed the East Coast and European establishments and argued that a new national culture could be built upon the framework of indigenous myths and symbols. In her discussion of Luhan, Henderson, and Austin, Rudnick (1987:22) argues that

in spite of their tendency to romanticize and at times racially typecast these cultures, they were among the first generation of Anglo-Americans to promote attitudes toward the Indians that were neither racist or assimilationist . . . Their decision to root their own writing in the common experiences of the folk was integral to their belief in a democratic ideal that would destroy the distinctions between so-called "high" and popular culture.

If Austin had been a trained anthropologist and had had an academic position she would have been considered an action anthropologist, which Mark (1986) points out is considered of lesser importance and peripheral to the discipline's theoretical approach. Nevertheless, she would have been in good company, as Halpern demonstrates in her chapter discussing women applied anthropologists.

Erna Fergusson

Another writer who played an active role in popularizing the Southwest, Erna Fergusson, is one of the few women discussed in this paper who had been born and raised in the region. Living almost all her life in Albuquerque, New Mexico, Fergusson was familiar with the landscape and the indigenous peoples of the region. She received her B.A. in education at the University of New Mexico in 1912 and her M.A. in history at Columbia University in 1913, then returned to Albuquerque to teach in a public school until 1916. During World War I she was the state supervisor of the Red Cross, which allowed her to "visit every village in the State and to know its people" (Simms 1976:46). This gave her an intense exposure to New Mexican life and the land. Fergusson became a reporter for *The Albuquerque Herald*. Finally bored with writing "society notes," she began writing a series of feature articles entitled "Do You Remember Old Albuquerque?" (Simms 1976:46). She had planned to write about something different each week including such subjects as historical events, associations, and buildings. Through this experience she developed the straightforward style of writing for which she became known. Remeley (1969:10) notes that although these articles were "sometimes dull and stylistically awkward," they contained "amusing descriptions of the old Albuquerque Erna had known as a child around the turn of the century."

With her knowledge of New Mexico and interest in the Native American cultures, Fergusson centered on what was termed the "dude wrangling business"—taking tourists to American Indian dances in the area. This eventually developed into the Koshare Tours that she organized with Ethel Hickey in 1921. Describing this business and educational endeavor, Fergusson stated, "We took people out to see Indian dances, starting with Isleta and San Felipe, and gradually spreading out until we were taking people to the Snake Dance in Arizona and the Shalako at Zuni" (quoted in Simms 1976:46). They used women as guides instead of the rough-and-tough cowboys that were generally employed by the resorts and hotels. These Koshare guides were supposed to be intelligent, talkative, and knowledgeable about the area, a tradition continued by the Harvey Company (Thomas 1978). The success of the Koshare Tours prompted the Fred Harvey Company to purchase the enterprise and to hire Fergusson to train the Harvey Couriers who acted as guides for the Indian Detours. Fergusson began training the first twenty Couriers on April 15, 1926.

These "Detours" provided Fergusson with the opportunity to see and lecture about the history, customs, folklore, and archaeology of the Southwest. The lectures and discussions became the foundation of her numerous publications on the region. The most popular and widely read has been *Dancing Gods* (1957, originally published in 1931), a book about American Indian ceremonials that was used to train the Couriers but also captivated the imagination of the East Coast tourist and made the Southwest alive and accessible. To this day this book "stands unsurpassed as an authentic, readable work on southwestern Indians and their ceremonials" (Keleher 1964:348). This feeling for the area was repeated in her other works, especially *Our Southwest* (1940), *Murder and Mystery in New Mexico* (1948b), and *New Mexico: A Pageant of Three Peoples* (1951). These books are "among the best written about the region, for they are blended of knowledge, love and understanding" (Powell 1964:142).

Fergusson had a vision of the Southwest as place, as people, as historical events; a personal place of pageantry and mystery. She wrote the following as a summary of what the Southwest meant to her:

A far-flung land of ample visions, and its own unconquerable defenses against too much encroachment on the part of man. Climate and weather also on a grand scale, wonderful to live with for sunshine and clean air, heavenly at its best, magnificent in its fiercest moods and so found untamable to man's duller ways. Here man has seldom succeeded for very long in modifying nature; he must conform or perish. And . . . the Southwest means to me its people, representing every stage of development from vestigial paganism and barbarism to the most modern manifestations of the arts and sciences. And despite all our shortcomings, a generally decent regard for human differences that makes for easy and civilized living (Fergusson 1948a: 202).

Fergusson began an entirely new career with the success of *Dancing Gods,* which "subsequently led to national recognition as an authority on the Southwest, from the dual aspect of author and lecturer" (Keleher 1964: 348).

Although Fergusson wrote primarily of her beloved New Mexico, she also had a great interest in Latin America. This interest in Latin America had been prompted by Hubert Herring, a faculty member of Claremont College in California, who had asked her to speak at seminars for the Committee on Cultural Affairs in Mexico, Guatemala, and South America. Her first book on Mexico, *Fiesta in Mexico* (1934), was followed by several others on Latin America. These included *Guatemala* (1937), which recorded her impressions of the indigenous peoples of that country; *Venezuela* (1939), a travel book; *Chile* (1943), hailed as the best book on the country at the time; and *Cuba* (1946a). In Remeley's analysis of Fergusson's writing he contends that

the body of her work gives a balanced view of both the pleasant and unpleasant aspects of a geographical region and a varied culture. If she ever felt herself a rebel, it does not show in her writing. The final product is an affirmative description of a heritage she felt positively about (1969: 2).

Fergusson's writing "expresses an understanding of other cultures and suggests how Anglo-Americans might interact with them for the richer preservation of the best in all" (Remeley 1969: 2). Powell (1964: 143) describes Fergusson's writing as "straightforward, clear, simple, intended to say what she means and to mean what she says."

Fergusson wrote several articles for journals as travelogues and as critical reviews of federal government policies such as the Bursam Bill in the 1920s, the treatment of the Navajo (which re-

sulted in the sheep reduction program under John Collier of the Bureau of Indian Affairs), and the exploitation and erosion of the Rio Grande Basin by native New Mexicans and Anglos overgrazing and stripping away the timber (Remeley 1969). Remeley explicitly notes (1969: 30), "She is completely in sympathy with the Indian and his threatened way of life, and she occasionally seems to practice an inverse discrimination against the Anglo intruders. She is down on Indian agents and efforts of government bureaus to educate the Indian for assimilation." Yet, while a champion of Native American causes, Fergusson did not appear concerned about her own role in romanticizing and popularizing the very people she sought to protect from exploitation by tourists and assimilation.

Lawrence Powell best describes Fergusson's style of writing as a "middle ground" between that which was required for the popular general audience, journalism, and academic scholarship: "She is a combination of scholar, reporter, and able prose writer. Her style is clear and simple, her emotions cool. Every now and then, however, they light up, and we get passages of transcendent writing" (Powell 1964: 144). Like Austin, Fergusson's concern for Native American rights brought her national recognition that would not have been possible had she chosen a strictly academic career. Remeley (1969: 37–38) sums up her career as a writer and tour guide:

Erna Fergusson helped make the Southwest and Latin America seem like real and accessible places for the general American reader. She was read widely. Features on her Koshare Tours and reviews of her books appeared in nearly every newspaper in the country. She was the twentieth century's popularizer of the Southwest and a spokesman for those little understood people, Indians and Spanish Americans.

Ann Axtell Morris

Several women ethnographers and archaeologists such as Elizabeth Crozier Campbell, Hattie

Cosgrove, Winifred Gladwin, Pearl Beaglehole, and Rosamond Spicer earned recognition while working alongside their husbands. The best known, Ann Axtell Morris, was the wife of Earl H. Morris, himself one of the most respected southwestern archaeologists of the twentieth century. Watson Smith (1985) remembered her as a "beautiful, vivid, vigorous, young woman" married to Earl, "who was quite dull, a reclusive kind of guy." Ann Morris did not limit herself to a single career; she was "talented as an archaeologist, author, and artist" (Irwin-Williams 1990:12).

By the time Ann Axtell was six years old, she knew exactly what she wanted to do when she grew up. She declared: "I want to dig for buried treasure, and explore among the Indians, and paint pictures, and wear a gun, and go to college" (see Morris 1933:12). These were not common goals for a young girl at the turn of the century, but Morris accomplished them, thereby realizing her ambitions and becoming a meticulous archaeologist and scientific chronicler. Ann Morris collaborated with her husband on several projects in the Southwest and Mesoamerica: working in Chichén Itzá she recorded the wall murals in the Temple of the Warriors, and in the Southwest she focused her attention on pictographs, the first in a series of prominent women scholars to do so. Unfortunately, her name will not be found on a library shelf as the author of works on these subjects. Irwin-Williams (1990:12–13) contends that even though

she collaborated with her husband on virtually all of his work and is reported to have written significant parts of the technical reports, her own best known credited publications are both nontechnical and designed for a general public (*Digging in Yucatan,* 1931; *Digging in the Southwest,* 1933).

Watson Smith (1985) describes *Digging in Yucatan* as a "young, ripe, happy person's story of the fun of digging in the dirt" that "appealed to the public." Morris' autobiographical and descriptive account of the life of a southwestern archaeologist in *Digging in the Southwest* began, in the 1933 edition, with the following metaphorical definition of archaeology:

Archaeology might be defined as a rescue expedition sent into the far places of the earth to recover the scattered pages of man's autobiography. Some of these life notes are scribbled in ancient inks; unfamiliar lines; some are not writing at all as we recognize the word. But a message is there just the same. Buildings of carved stone, rudely dug caves, carefully woven blankets, molded bits of pottery, all have their tale to tell, when the scattered paragraphs are arranged in order (Morris 1933:xv).

This descriptive account of working as a southwestern archaeologist continues to be read by a popular audience today, composed of young and old. It has been in print for almost 60 years. As Charles Lange (1986) noted at the Daughters of the Desert Conference, Morris' *Digging in the Southwest* "is the greatest recruiting device ever written for archaeology. Many people have been attracted here because of her work." Indeed, one may ask whose contributions are more widely read—the description and analysis of how archaeology is undertaken and constituted, or the results of those endeavors, which are sequestered away in scientific journals and out-of-print museum publications? Which has the more lasting effect in the development of anthropology?

Ruth Murray Underhill

Griffen (1988:355) describes Ruth Underhill as an "ethnographer, civil servant, and author, [who] was known for her work with Southwest Indian groups, especially the Papago, as well as her more general books and pamphlets on North American Indians." Underhill's interest in literature as an undergraduate student, her fascination with languages, and her interest in understanding people compelled her to become an anthropologist. Entering anthropology as a middle-aged graduate student, Underhill became completely immersed in the discipline. Sands (1984:4) claims that "her personal narrative gives us a glimpse into the motives and skills this very independent woman brought to the Southwest in the mid-1930s."

While working on her Ph.D. at Columbia University, Underhill visited the Tohono O'odham (previously called Papago) Reservation in Arizona four times and stayed with Clara Lee Tanner in Tucson. These trips resulted in her dissertation, entitled *Social Organization of the Papago Indians,* eventually published in 1939. As a graduate student she was an assistant in anthropology under Gladys Reichard, who had Underhill participate in "an experimental seminar, called the Hogan School, in which the Bureau of Indian Affairs (BIA) aimed to teach Navajos to write the Navajo language" (Griffen 1988:357). That same summer (1934), Underhill taught an in-service course in applied ethnology to the BIA (Griffen 1988: 357). This introduction to applied work led to Underhill's commitment to make anthropology of use to the wider society, the profession, and the people who were studied.

Underhill was hired by the Sherman Indian Institute in Riverside, California, for the summer of 1935 to present a series of lectures to BIA personnel about various tribes with which they would be working and conducting surveys and needs assessments. During the fall she continued her applied work at the Tohono O'odham Reservation headquarters in Sells, Arizona, by reviewing the proposed tribal constitution required under the New Deal, a result of the Indian Reorganization Act and the administration of the BIA under John Collier and his emphasis on tribal self-governance. The proposed constitution did not reflect Tohono O'odham social and political organization, in Underhill's judgement, and she argued against its adoption. As a result, Underhill was banned from participation in further government projects dealing with the tribe (Griffen 1988: 358). Collier felt that the anthropologists hired to conduct economic and cultural surveys of the various groups of the Southwest had to have the

"right personality and the proper perspective" to get along with and be sensitive to the untrained BIA employees. Griffen notes:

He then proceeded to remove Underhill as head of the Papago survey team because he felt BIA personnel would resent her involvement in the project and because his personal experience with professional women in administrative and executive positions had been most discouraging. Underhill did not take part in the Papago survey, and it was never published (Griffen 1988:358).

Nevertheless, during the summer of 1936 Underhill was able to complete seven pamphlets in the Indian Life and Customs Series for the BIA, one of which was eventually published as *People of the Crimson Evening* (1951a). While intended for a specialized audience of BIA and Public Health Service workers, these works have been available to the general public. In 1936 she also published *The Autobiography of a Papago Woman,* which is both a biography of Chona and autobiography of herself. Despite the merit of this work she had difficulty getting it published because of the newness of the writing style and mode of presentation. In the end it was accepted because it was brief. As Sands (1984:9) points out, in "1936 her approach was considered unreliable, even unprofessional . . . Her method was too literary in a time when science was the criteria." Convinced that cross-cultural understanding could best be served through popular forms such as narrative, she persisted in her work.

Underhill was a prolific writer of both scholarly and popular books and articles for both a professional and a public audience. Her work is "well crafted, unsentimental, remarkably direct and explicit for its time, and stylistically sophisticated" (Sands 1984:10). The books that she wrote for the Indian Service, which include *Southwest Indians: An Outline and Ceremonial Organization* (1934), *The Papago Indians of Arizona and Their Relatives, the Pima* (1941), *Navaho Weaving* (1944a), *Pueblo Crafts* (1944b), *Work-a-Day Life of the Pueblo* (1946b), and *Here Come the Navaho!* (1953a), were some of the most widely read books of the region, and most are still in print. They have also been used for introductory anthropology and regional classes for years; for example, Tanner used *Pueblo Crafts* as a text in her American Indian art classes through the 1970s. During the time that Underhill served with the Indian Service she visited almost every reservation in the country and found that Native American children had not been taught their own history; this discovery resulted in a series of books illustrated by American Indians to be used as high school books.

For 13 years Underhill was involved in American Indian education for the BIA. Upon retirement from the BIA in 1948 she became a professor at the University of Denver, where she taught in the Department of Anthropology until her retirement in 1952. During this time she wrote *The Navahos* (1956) and *Red Man's Religion* (1965) as well as several books on the Tohono O'odham. (See Halpern's contribution to this volume for more details on Underhill's career as an applied anthropologist.)

In 1984 Underhill was "honored for popularizing anthropology in a responsible manner, for her early work in applied anthropology and the study of women's roles, and for her scholarship and teaching" by the American Anthropological Association (AAA) (Griffen 1988:359). Underhill's long-term relationship with the Tohono O'odham resulted in numerous publications on their religion and social organization such as *The Autobiography of a Papago Woman* (1936), *Singing for Power: The Song Magic of the Papago Indians of Southern Arizona* (1938), *Social Organization of the Papago Indians* (1939), and *Papago Indian Religion* (1946a), along with several popular books, including *Ceremonial Patterns in the Greater Southwest* (1948), *Red Man's America: A History of Indians in the United States* (1953b), and *Red Man's Religion: Beliefs and Practices of the Indians North of Mexico* (1965). Prior to being paid homage by the AAA, she was recognized and honored by the Tohono

O'odham themselves in 1979 (Herold 1980). Although her books contain valuable ethnographic information, especially on Tohono O'odham social organization, ceremonies, and rituals, her work is rarely cited.

Unfortunately, Underhill's work was often dismissed by anthropologists in the Ivory Tower because it was so well written, something Underhill worked at very diligently. As a result, her work has been analyzed more from a literary perspective than an anthropological one (see Gordon's chapter in this volume). This has served to marginalize her contributions in the literature on the history of anthropology. Like numerous other women anthropologists, Underhill also wrote novels, poetry, and biographies because she felt they captured the essence of a culture better than an ethnographic monograph. This, in turn, further marginalized her because novels were not felt to be as authentic as descriptive ethnographies— some of the information presented in novels was considered to be made up and not based on observational fact. As such it could be dismissed, and by extension the corpus of Underhill's work became suspect. This situation was met by all popularizers.

PERIPHERALIZED BY ACADEME

With few exceptions, these women have been neither written into the histories of anthropology nor given credit for the contributions they have made to the development of the discipline. It took Benedict 25 years before being awarded a full professorship. Reichard spent her entire career at Barnard, an undergraduate women's college. Tanner was denied promotions because of her popular writing and interest in southwestern Native American arts and crafts. Kent was never awarded tenure and remained a part-time instructor even though she chaired the department at one time. Keur was half administrator, half teacher, yet she goes unrecognized for building up an anthropology department at an undergraduate college.

Morris, Underhill, and Fergusson found creative alternatives to academe. But their efforts have not been valued by anthropology except within the region itself. Why is this so? Is it because these women dared to break the mold established by the Ivory Tower while anthropology was still in its nascent stage? They followed their hearts and worked hard to take anthropology off its dusty shelves and introduce its concepts to an audience outside of academe. The reward structure in academic institutions did not approve of this approach because it was seen to be without academic controls: anyone could give a public lecture, anyone could call himself or herself an anthropologist. There were few, if any, peer reviews of their publications; consequently, much of their work was viewed as lacking quality controls.

While Gillmor is recognized as an academic, her concentration on folklore and her popular style of writing kept her on the periphery of the Ivory Tower. By contrast, Austin was not an academic, but her popular novels about the Southwest and her role as an activist to preserve the natural environment of the Southwest and its native peoples should not be overlooked. The fact that popularizers were primarily women made it easier for the Ivory Tower to peripheralize them and place them in positions with low visibility and limited possibilities for advancement. Popularizing anthropology and advocacy were considered outside of academe, and the Ivory Tower mistrusted both. Popularizing demystified the discipline and brought it under public scrutiny, and the style of writing was viewed as too personal by academe—all of which resulted in a sense of mistrust toward popularizing as well as advocacy because those practices were no longer "objective."

CONCLUSION

Mark's (1986) comment that women viewed anthropology as a "quest or way of life" instead of as a job or profession is the underlying theme for most of the women in this chapter. The common

glue that binds these particular women together is that they became anthropologists, educators, activists, and popular writers because they were curious about the prehistory, history, and contemporary lives of other peoples, especially the native peoples of the Southwest. They wanted to demystify anthropology through the elimination of jargon and to introduce the aura or feel for the region and its peoples based on human experience. Some women were able to accomplish this by teaching undergraduates in academic settings, while others reached out to a more general public audience through their work in museums or by writing popular articles, travelogues, novels, and books.

The dedication of these women who chose to popularize and demystify anthropology in some ways did a disservice to the women who remained in academe: this disadvantage derived from the characterization of women as popular writers, since popularizing the discipline was not valued. Tanner (1985) noted, "My audience has been the general public, intentionally, positively, definitely . . . I knew there was an intelligent public out there, and that is the main reason that I have continued writing in that particular field, even though I was told it wouldn't get me anywhere academically."

To be published, several women were forced (or chose) to direct their writing toward a popular audience instead of a scholarly one. This may stem from the fact that most professional journals were edited by men, who decided what was to be published and determined what was important to the discipline at the time. Lutz (1990:616) found that

women's writing enters the standard journals and other writing venues of the discipline at a rate that suggests that their voices are not excluded from the field. Writing is, however, intended to be read, discussed, and evaluated, and it is in these activities that women's work is marginalized—that is, treated by authoritative evaluators as peripheral to the field's center or less significant than men's work. Listening to women's voices in academia follows patterns established by the culture at large; previous research demonstrates that readers' or listeners' assessments of the value and importance of a statement are definitively influenced by the gender of the author of that statement.

We know from an analysis of university records and compilations of theses and dissertations on Native Americans that hundreds of women have been trained as anthropologists, folklorists, art historians, and sociologists, yet few are found in our histories. We remain ambivalent about them because many have been popularizers. This ambivalence has resulted in mistrust of women scholars by the Ivory Tower because the style of writing has often been nontechnical and the material presented has often not been based on empirical data collection; instead, it has often been impressionistic and full of anecdotes that bring the people of the Southwest to life. The writing style itself thus has frequently been personalized.

There were rich alternatives to academe. Some of the women discussed here may not be famous according to the written histories of anthropology, but their efforts have brought about public awareness of the importance of understanding cultural diversity in a pluralistic society. They have made major contributions to the study of humanity and to the discipline of anthropology as a whole, contributions that can no longer be overlooked. Women in anthropology have balanced the scales of fieldwork and theoretical paradigms to gain a fuller and deeper understanding of humankind. Anthropology has been successful as a discipline because the larger society has thought it was valuable; yet, ultimately, the larger society has known about anthropology and its purposes because of the popular and pedagogical efforts of individuals like the women presented in this chapter who have been peripheralized by the Ivory Tower.

The popularizers of the discipline are the leaders and activists; they have led the way to our present concern that an understanding of cultural diversity exist not only at a global level but at the university and college campus level as well. It is time that they be recognized and celebrated for their efforts. Administrators in academic institutions should acknowledge the expertise that exists in anthropology departments on their own campuses; by the same token, anthropology faculty members should recognize their importance in directing the future understanding of cultural diversity on their own campuses as well as on a global level. It may be time to come down out of the Ivory Tower and no longer peripheralize colleagues for their efforts to popularize anthropology.

We have no one to blame but ourselves if the public does not understand our messages. Anthropology has an important role to play in educating the global public of the importance of cultural diversity and understanding, especially at a time when international relations have become more intertwined with our daily lives. As noted in a recent *Anthropology Newsletter* (May 1991), David Givens asked AAA members to respond to the two major issues he raised: "(1) What are the top three anthropological issues that should be communicated to the public in the 1990s?, and (2) How should they be communicated and who should communicate them?" Member responses and comments were then published in a special edition of the *Anthropology Newsletter* (October 1991), which was dedicated to "Projecting Anthropology to the Public." There has been a continuing dialogue among members in subsequent issues of the *Newsletter* concerning the representation of anthropology to the public. May we take this as evidence that the Ivory Tower has recognized that we have entered an era of shared information and that by keeping valuable cultural information sequestered within its realm it is doing a disservice to humanity? Or is public demand for knowledge challenging its very foundation? Is it possible that what these women have been attempting to do all along—to bring anthropology into the public domain—is finally gaining credibility and validity in the Ivory Tower? We can only hope so.

NOTES

1. I would like to thank Nancy Parezo for giving me the opportunity to be included in this important volume on women anthropologists who chose the Southwest as their research area. The Greater Southwest being the focus of my own anthropological research, I feel a certain affinity with these women. This paper was not presented at the Daughters of the Desert Conference in 1986; however, through Dr. Parezo's generosity I have had access to the conference tapes and the individual taped interviews of the living "daughters" from 1985 to 1986. I would also like to thank Nancy Parezo, Kelley Hays, Kathy McCaston, and Marjorie Lambert for reading earlier drafts of this paper. Their comments are most appreciated.

2. It would be impossible to include the hundreds of women that I would like to include in this chapter. As I began this project I had no idea of the massiveness of such an endeavor. Fortunately, a tremendous amount of data had already been collected by Nancy Parezo and Barbara Babcock, in which at least 1,600 women had been rediscovered. All of these women certainly deserve a place in the history of anthropology and have played an important role, albeit an unrecognized one, in contributing to its foundation and popularizing the Southwest.

CONCLUSION:
THE BEGINNING OF THE QUEST

Nancy J. Parezo

It is a matter of the living and the dead
[being] caught up together, in an operation of bringing order and significance
to aspects of the present we feel we know,
and of the past we try to apprehend.
Rosemary Firth
(1985:22)

To consider one sex while ignoring the other
is like looking at an old family photograph
in which the males occupy the foreground
as distinct figures, while the females are an
undifferentiated blur in the background.
Linda Reiber and Jane Mathews
(1982:41)

IT HAS BEEN a premise of this volume that understanding the effect of gender on anthropological careers is crucial for understanding anthropology as an endeavor: "In all the activities of fieldwork, from the course of one's academic career, to entering the field, to putting on one's clothes in the morning, to writing up field notes, and drafting articles for publication, gender shapes the task. It is inescapably our task to see the shaping through the shapes" (Warren 1988: 58–59). Building on the solid foundation of feminist theory, discourse analysis, and the history of anthropology, which is part of the paradigm shift that calls for greater equity and equality in professional disciplines, we have dealt with issues of setting (fieldwork situations and the workplace) and process via the personal biography and career history of the researcher rather than specifically with the outcome of research and intellectual production. We have done this by expanding the types of allowable questions we could ask and by analyzing the hidden perspectives and careers of women who worked in one culture area, the Greater Southwest, at specific historical moments.

I have entitled this essay both a conclusion and the beginning of a quest. While we are at the end of this volume, we are at the beginning of an allegorical and actual journey. As protagonists, we have set forth to find something that is missing and needed by the society for its continued well-being. Like all quests, this involves hard work and adventure, even danger, for our activities have begun to uncover some hard truths that we would like to dismiss. In our quest we are searching for our legendary heroines and trying to understand their lives. As a first step in the process, we have begun to write a new version of the history of anthropology in this book, one that is more than compensatory by redefining the boundaries of the discipline to take into account all of anthropology's players as active agents. Just as excellence for men resides in action, so does it for women. Thus we have shown that women have not been passive but that barriers have made it appear so.

Now we must try to draw conclusions about the place of gender in anthropological careers. This will be a complicated task, for each author has selected themes that have reflected individual concerns and intellectual bents. In addition, it is very difficult to generalize from the individualistic experiences of a handful of women who were not chosen randomly to the profession as a whole and difficult to distinguish those experiences common to both men and women from those restricted to women. No single narrative can typify our understanding of women in anthropology; for women anthropologists, like men anthropologists, are not a homogeneous group. Different generations found a historically specific set of circumstances that offered different challenges, opportunities, and solutions. Wars, economic depressions, recessions and upswings, the presence or absence of a strong women's movement, changes in national politics, preconceptions of women's abilities and proper societal roles, and the size and configuration of the universities and other workplaces affected women's lives. And, of course, even within a time period women chose different routes that met individual needs and circumstances.

Although definitive conclusions are elusive, we can see indicators of how women reacted to pervasive social norms and situations and constructed their own lives. From these emerging patterns we can begin to posit a model for being a woman anthropologist and ask more sophisticated questions. Although we cannot deal with all the issues that were identified in the chapters or at the conference, we can comment on a few themes: marginality, strategies for overcoming marginality and fostering success, husband-and-

wife teams, mentoring, and the Greater Southwest as a research locale for women.

THE ROAD TO SUCCESS

As noted throughout this book, women have encountered many institutional roadblocks—from lack of employment opportunities and access to resources to harsher criticism of their work than that of men—but they have not been passive. Women have actively confronted and overcome obvious and intentional, as well as subtle and unintentional, career barriers that placed them in marginal positions compared to men seeking anthropological careers. The history of anthropology for women is replete with challenges to obtain access to institutions (including higher education), the disciplinary power structure, resources, professional organizations, programs, jobs, students, and rewards: in short, to full participation, acceptance, equality, and recognition. Marginality and career barriers have prevented more women than men from reaching their full potential, made them compromise and accept situations in ways not required of men. While all professionals face challenges and must pass rites of passage as they progress on their career paths, women encounter additional obstructions not met by men. Rosenberg (1982:xxi) has contended that the story of women in academe has been one "of frustration felt by those whose work was celebrated in graduate school but who could find no academic position in which to carry on their research." Rossiter (1982:xii), likewise, concluded that "women's experiences, hitherto so obscure, demonstrate that there were very definite limits to the supposed openness and rationality of the scientific community in the years before 1940." Aisenberg and Harrington (1988:xii) discovered a similar pattern in the 1980s; women had the "experience of professional marginality and of exclusion from the centers of professional authority—for the academic profession there is such a thing as *women's* experience." The roadblocks that handicapped women in the 1880s, 1920s, and 1930s are as pervasive today as they were 50 or 60 years ago.

Women scholars are almost by definition marginal. Marginality, to borrow the concept from sociology and political science, can be defined as the state in which an individual "lives in two different worlds simultaneously, one of which is, by prevailing standards, regarded as superior to the other" (Klein 1974:171–72). For anthropology, the worlds of men and women as public versus private spheres (the workplace and the home) in the general society form the backdrop for professional participation. In front of this are the prestigious worlds of universities and scientific communities, which are male dominated and controlled. These worlds of male scholarship are felt to be superior to and noncomplementary to women's worlds; women's "sex status is defined within the cultures of professions as inappropriate. Thus women find the institutionalized channels of recruitment and advancement, such as the protegee system, are not available to them" (Epstein 1970:968). Because of this incompatibility there were barriers to women's full acceptance in any discipline (see Astin 1969; Bernard 1964; Kanter 1977; Rosenberg 1982; Warren 1988).

Gender preconceptions affected a woman's perception of her ability to participate in the scholarly world, just as it did the perceptions of the individuals who controlled the discipline. We have seen ample evidence throughout this book that attitudes and assumptions about female nature have both assisted and hindered women in the anthropological enterprise. The extreme view of incompatible male and female worlds excluded women's participation in anthropology except as unpaid helpers of professional husbands and fathers or as dilettantes pursuing a hobby; the concept that men and women might be different but were not incompatible allowed women with creativity to participate as professionals.

As women have sought to actively pursue anthropology as a career, their lives have often been dominated by professional marginality. Women could either capitalize on gender stereotypes and use them for short-term gain, often in sex-typed employment, or women could challenge them when they proved too restrictive. But women could not ignore gender preconceptions and resulting marginality; they had to work with this as a cultural and social backdrop. As a result, women more often than men have had to balance the demands of living in two worlds; of their families and roles as wives and mothers with their roles as scholars, academics, and fully employed professionals. This, and the fact that they have had to work at institutional margins, has meant that women have had to develop their own methods and integrative strategies to fulfill career aspirations. In some ways, women have had to make choices not required by men; in other ways they have had fewer options and fewer choices.

Due to conflicting demands, women anthropologists have had to make strategic behavioral decisions on how to use opportunities in order to overcome structural and cultural constraints.[1] The resulting integrative strategies have ranged between two extremes—acceptance and confrontation. Women could confront the system, view themselves as scientists or scholars (identifying with male scholars), and act in the academic work according to the prevailing normative standards of professional, male-oriented anthropology and be seen, at least initially, as unfeminine, or they could view themselves and act according to the prevailing standards of femininity and be seen as exceptional women. There was also a range of accommodating behaviors and styles between these two extremes, and women could identify with either or integrate parts sequentially.

Acceptance as a style involved conservatively adhering to "proper" feminine behavior and accepting relatively without protest the time period's gendered division of labor as typical. Being a "good girl" (Aisenberg and Harrington 1988: 17) and acting like a lady while simultaneously using socially acceptable mechanisms within the permissible realms of female behaviors was the hallmark of this approach. As a strategy of maintaining the status quo, women searched for ways to enter the field without calling their femininity into question, while gently expanding the bounds of proper behavior. Women using this strategy worked hard, often behind the scenes (in women's areas), made few demands, let the rewards of their work accrue to others (usually their male superiors), and blended into the background. One way they did this was by calling on what Mead (1986) has identified as their "deeply feminine interests and abilities." This was most evident in research topics and specialties that were chosen in such a way that they reflected traditional female concerns and were not threatening to men.

Anglo-American women and men have had special work and interest spheres that crystallized in the late nineteenth and early twentieth centuries. These included philanthropy, "Culture," literature, domesticity and child rearing, the arts, and music for women, while math, politics, economics, business, engineering, and science were reserved for men. These spheres were reflected in the choice of anthropological research topics. We have numerous examples of women who intentionally studied folklore, literature, poetry, music, and art—more than one would have expected given random choice in subject matter. Even a brief review of the works penned by women who worked in the Greater Southwest shows a heavy emphasis on "women's issues"—culture and personality studies, child rearing, acculturation, socialization, health and nutrition, and humanistic topics. Many of these topics were pursued with either male or female native collaborators. While we cannot say definitively that the choice of research topic was due to the acceptance by the researcher of traditional gender models, either of his/her own society or of that being studied, there is a tendency for those who chose an acceptance strategy to focus on women's topics and for women who were confrontational to be more wide-ranging or focus on the mainstream topics

of the period, regardless of whether those topics were regarded as male or as female subjects. While the acceptance strategy emphasized women's "unique skills and special talents," it was limiting. Considered of minor theoretical importance, competition for preeminence in women's areas was minimal. As Rosaldo (1974:17) has remarked, anthropologists are "heirs to a sociological tradition that has seen women as essentially uninteresting or irrelevant." Women's information was needed for a holistic ethnographic picture but was simultaneously not felt to be crucial for understanding the workings of society conceptualized as "men's worlds."

The limitations of the acceptance approach can be seen in the following example. Olive E. Hite was a member of the Women's Anthropological Society in the late 1890s. She had been interested in folklore for many years, and in 1897 she decided to compile her information on the Penitentes with whom she had first worked in 1866. She gingerly approached Frank Baker, professor of anatomy at Georgetown University and editor of the *American Anthropologist,* on January 22, 1898:

I take the liberty of submitting to you, for your opinion, as to its availability, a story of "The Little People," which is generally believed in New Mexico. The letter which I give in its entirety, was written by an American several years ago [herself] and the extracts from Don Amado Chavez's communications to me are of above recent date and whilst I do not think the matter is such as you would care to publish in the *Anthropologist*—a greater honor than I could ever possibly hope for—I would esteem it more than an ordinary favor if you could suggest some semi-scientific paper that might be willing to use it . . . The scientific world is enough interested, I feel, in the possibility of learning about the idea of the Little People that it has prompted me to write the article and to take up a little of your valuable time in asking you to read it (NAA:OH/FB 1/22/98).

Note the roundabout way Hite asked for her paper to be published, the terms she used, how she used a man (Don Chavez) as an authority figure, how she referred to an imaginary author (never actually naming herself), how she did not presume to claim authority for herself since this was inappropriate for a woman especially when addressing a learned man, her attempt to make folklore scientific as a means to get her work published, the self-deprecating tone, and the idea that publishing is a favor to women bestowed by powerful men. How different is her submissive approach from that adopted by Jessie Walter Fewkes or F. W. Hodge when they requested that their works be published. In their correspondence with Baker,[2] they assumed their work was important and made demands for specific publication dates. It would have been inappropriate for Hite to make such demands. It is noteworthy that her article was never published and that she did not try again after this one unsuccessful attempt.

Such an extreme acceptance style was not used by the women covered in this book, and we must question whether anyone who followed it could have successfully undertaken a career; one would not have been taken seriously and would have had to constantly work from a position of weakness. Academic success takes self-confidence, posturing, and the ability to win an intellectual debate by forcefully stating one's views. By doing what they were told, women appeared patient, deferential, and nonpersuasive, hence weak. Consequently it was concluded that they were not committed to their work. Acceptance seems to have been more common among women who began but then left the field, such as some of those identified in the chapter on museums.

But there were others, such as Clara Lee Tanner, Franc Newcomb, and Kate Peck Kent, who adopted a nondemeaning modified acceptance or accommodation style: they emphasized the fact that they were ladies, adhered to the merit dream—"that true merit will somehow be evident and recognized by professional authorities without self-advertisement" (Aisenberg and Harrington 1988:52), and hoped that women would secure jobs and rise through the ranks because they were good anthropologists, had excellent well-trained minds and original ideas, were methodologically sound, were committed to the field, and had evidence of performance in the form of completed research projects and publications. But the academic world is no different from any other workplace where image, appearance, opportunity, and luck are important. This meant that eventually these women had to live with the knowledge that they would not have equal professional status. From this base they used their feminine status to carve out a place in the profession that, given enough time, would be recognized as important. But one had to make a 40-year commitment to be successful.

Women who adopted a modified acceptance strategy tended to concentrate on areas that minimized their potential, or actual, competition with men. This included such strategies as working on peripheral topics (art or child rearing), developing a non-theoretical but descriptive writing style, emphasizing their roles as teachers rather than researchers, and popularizing anthropology. They did not strive to change the profession or make groundbreaking, risky, or contentious theoretical contributions but defined niches for themselves in limited subject areas where they could become the recognized experts. They thus simultaneously conformed to many of the long-held ideals of femininity and quietly pursued their scholarly activities. (This does not mean that they were not argumentative with regard to their interpretations and factual data.) They tended to be well-known and respected by the public later in life. Like the acceptance strategy, this is ultimately a nonthreatening, status-quo approach. Women recognized and accepted the inequalities, problems, and barriers as things they could not change. Instead they tried to work around them—to whittle away at the edges—by working hard, ignoring the discrimination, hoping no one noticed them, demonstrating that they were not bad risks (even if other women were), holding long-term goals, and making compromises that involved minimal risks. Rossiter (1982 : 129) has seen this as a "strategy of deliberate overqualification and personal stoicism."

Accommodation meant not making too many waves, especially around powerful men. (People learned the lesson of Matilda Coxe Stevenson quickly, for she had paid dearly for her confrontational style.) One had to be careful using this approach, however, and could not call too much attention to oneself by clashing with men directly. This caution can be seen in the fact that women saw other women, but rarely men, as intellectual rivals and criticized women in ways that called into question their rivals' femininity.[3] For example, Florence Hawley Ellis (1985) disapproved of Anna Shepard as a scientist because "she was one who never felt the necessity of acting or looking particularly feminine." Ellis continued,

I think a woman has got to compete as a woman, not as a man. That's the only chance she had . . . I think the approach to be taken is the approach that I have taken, not only while I was teaching but afterwards, of being pleasantly dressed—a pleasant thing to look upon—and doing every little thing that is seen to be pleasant femaleness. And you have to show that you're not going after them [men]. You are just being a pleasant piece of the landscape.

Ellis also stressed that adaptation and accommodation were crucial for success and that one had to quietly accept this situation:

The discrimination was discouraging when you stopped to think of it. So you just don't dare stop to think at all. All you can do is just see what you can do to get around the situation at the moment and go ahead with your papers. You may go home and do a lot of weeping first and then wipe your tears and settle down to your paper and pencil.

Feminine adaptation required that one not be sensitive but focus singly on the ultimate career goal. Katherine Spencer Halpern (1985) reflected, "I think I'm not one to be very sensitive to discrimination against women. One just got ahead with the job."

The confrontational style, the extreme from the acceptance style, was used by idealistic, stubborn, liberal/radical women who continually fought against all societal stereotypes of women and worked for the feminist goal of full equality or by those who were "masculinely oriented" (Mead 1986). Stevenson and Elsie Clews Parsons are two prime examples of individuals who opposed the existing system when they insisted on being taken seriously and treated equally. Confrontation involved insisting on being employed, being paid equally, and never allowing others to show or accept discrimination in any form; as a result, this "bad girl," non-status-quo strategy gained one a reputation for being a "pain in the ass" or "scandalous." Often calling on feminist rhetoric, confrontationists actively pushed for inclusion in the male community based on the adoption of the prevailing standards of male scientific conduct. This included the elimination of a "feminine" gender role in anthropology, which was seen as constraining academic opportunities. For nonfeminists it also meant that one forcefully stated that science was genderless and that issues of family were nonexistent. Laura Thompson (1985) emphatically denied that being a woman ever affected her career or that a feminine perspective entered her work. Like other women of her period, she, along with her male colleagues, even repudiated the feminist critique. (This is similar to what happened earlier; see Lowie and Hollingworth 1916.)

Periodization also affected women's adherence to and feelings about feminism. As Fox and Gordon indicated in their chapters, women saw feminism and the role of a strong feminist voice in their lives and their works differently, depending on when and where they lived. Esther Goldfrank reacted violently when asked about feminism because of the political implications of the term. Stevenson identified more strongly with science than with feminist political activism, yet she worked for women's rights. Other women were not interested in feminism as a paradigm for their research but felt they were feminists in their lives. Still others were ambivalent. This variation results in part from the great changes in the meaning of the concept as well as the strategies women chose. Women who followed an acceptance or a modified acceptance/accommodation strategy did not feel they were feminists. Some women who used the confrontational strategy did. And even for this group there is a periodization that is evident in their writing. It is well accepted that Ruth Benedict and Parsons compartmentalized their discourse, writing poetry under pseudonyms, disguising or eliminating their feminist writings under pressure to conform to standards of scientific, objective, and apolitical academic anthropology. Thus, even for confrontational women, certain areas of writing and theoretical statements were too controversial and too dangerous to use. A strong feminist confrontational style would have led to ostracism or blacklisting as happened to Marxists (not even Communists) during the McCarthy era.

While a woman using a confrontational strategy could smoke a cigar and use all sources of power to gain admittance to scientific societies, she could not be a visionary eccentric like Frank Hamilton Cushing.[4] Eccentricity was a very dangerous oppositional strategy for women because it meant flouting the value of scientific life and could only be used by artists. And even direct confrontation that demonstrated complete identification with male academicians was not possible for an entire career. More often than not, individuals who "rocked the boat" or called the system into question did so for a limited number of years. Women had to make compromises because a confrontational style was very wearing. Even Parsons, the most effective confrontational woman, ultimately compartmentalized her reformist, politically active voice and her empirical discourse. Babcock (1986) contended at the conference, however, that Parsons remained an invisible feminist even after she had turned to anthropology, although she did modify her style to be accepted into the anthropological community.

A modified confrontational/accommodation style was used by those who had been confrontational and were tiring of the stress and by women who had begun with a modified acceptance strategy and wanted more visibility. Working within the mainstream of anthropology, individuals such as Goldfrank, Ruth Bunzel, and Benedict were bored with women's topics (studying women and children) and dealt with both male and female worlds. They used "male" analytical techniques, "female" intuition and insights for their interpretations, quantitative as well as qualitative analyses. Often using a feminist paradigm, they studied what was current in the field at the moment and attempted to make theoretical contributions that would be judged on their own merit. Great variation runs through these women's choices of research topics (as it does for men), for women's work is as affected by intellectual generation as by gender. Because of this, these women could openly debate men as well as women on almost equal terms. As a result, they had increased visibility often early in their careers. They did not have to wait for the accumulation of a lifetime of effort.

Commonly, successful women used accommodation styles—modified versions of the two extremes—at different points in their careers; many went back and forth between the accommodation/acceptance and the accommodation/confrontational styles. This was necessary because "women in any culture play many roles, simultaneously and over the course of a lifetime" (Mukhopadhyay and Higgins 1988:465). In addition, there is a good deal of difference in the anthropology produced by Stevenson and Ruth Underhill, Parsons and Dorothea Leighton, Benedict and Thompson, and Goldfrank and Sophie Aberle; this dissimilarity required the use of different strategies. Needs and responses varied through time because research questions, research situations, the world, ideas about women, and the institutional settings changed. Accommodation could be achieved because there had been women who had confronted the system and had made it possible for a larger number of women to enter anthropology and learn to function in institutions created and controlled by men.

Integrative strategies were made visible through a number of mechanisms, themes, and characteristics. Although I have not systematized or prioritized these mechanisms that enabled women to orchestrate an integrated strategy (because we do not yet have enough data), I have isolated a few that appear to be important: some for specific styles, others regardless of the style chosen. Care must be taken, however, to remember that women are not a homogeneous group leading uniform lives and that adoption of these general integrative strategies and specific mechanisms has been contingent on the history, professionalization, and institutionalization of anthropology.

MECHANISMS AND TECHNIQUES FOR OVERCOMING MARGINALITY

Successful women had to be independent, unconventional, tenacious, stubborn, and ambitious. They had to want a career and a life beyond the home; exhibit a passion for learning; desire an active life that included exotic adventures or socially meaningful experiences; not mind having to be an overachiever; and strive to do something that involved interesting work. They had to feel that no matter what happened in their lives, they could, with a positive attitude, make it. This confidence was often embedded in their view of anthropology.

To be young and energetic and bright in the twenties, recalled another Boas protegee, the anthropologist Ruth Bunzel, was to face stirring choices. "Some of us fled to the freer air of Paris," she said, "and eventually retired. Some of us joined radical movements, and sold the *Daily Worker* on street corners, and some of us went into anthropology, hoping that there we might find some answers to the ambiguities and contradictions of our age and the general enigma of human life . . . It was inconceivable that this cultural upheaval would not be reflected in so sensitive a discipline as anthropology" (Howard 1984:69).

A commitment to anthropology, a sense that it was an integrating factor in one's life was a dominant motif for Gladys Reichard, Stevenson, Thompson, Dorothy Keur, and others. One had to feel that being an anthropologist made a difference because of the sacrifices involved. For example, Thompson (1985) remarked, "I always felt one person could make a difference, and I still do." As a group women anthropologists demonstrated a desire not to accept old roles that limited women's behavior to the home; they searched, however quietly, for new avenues that would lead to the center of anthropology. But one had to be realistic to attain this goal; Goldfrank declared (1985b), "I'm a realist, not an idealist." And it was how one defined *realistic* that led to different integrative styles—in some instances this meant confrontation, in others acceptance/accommodation, and in still others confrontation/accommodation.

A characteristic of confrontational women was their restlessness and rebelliousness—many sought freedom from the drawing-room domesticity of Boston and New York. To fight the good fight often meant that one felt one was alone in the world. Confrontation is always lonely because people mistrust a fighter and do not want one for a colleague since the protagonist is "not easy to live with." Confrontational women tended to have strong personalities and not be pliable or facile. Gertrude Kurath, for example, was described by an anthropologist as "frightfully serious" and because of this was felt to be difficult to relate to.[5] Parsons had few close friends but many admirers. Confrontational women were respected, even when their enemies employed leveling mechanisms.

Even those who followed a modified acceptance style mentioned loneliness, for most worked in situations where there were few other women. This had ramifications for the building of cohorts (see below); rarely were professional women able to organize groups of like-minded women. To succeed, women had to align themselves with men, especially those in positions of power, but unfortunately, wives of male faculty members often insisted that their husbands not work with women professionals. The lack of support networks and access to gain this support was a common theme for all women. It required that women strive for self-sufficiency and redefine themselves. Goldfrank voiced this view of the individual walking a singular path towards independence, a path that included struggling against exclusion by powerful individuals. Independence was crucial for Ellis (1985) also: "The idea of not being dependent was just part of my family's philosophy . . . We were raised simply to be independent. And I suppose I was because I would have had a heck of a time in all those years that I had to manage for myself."

Importantly, one had to think one was intelligent even when others stereotyped women as frivolous and suggested that one return to the home; as Mary Austin stated, "Why on earth, or why in heaven, should anybody make a mind like mine and then not use it?" (quoted in Fink 1983). And successful women had, no matter which strategy they used, a dauntless spirit and inexhaustible energy—they were able to work with little sleep and to endure. As Tanner (1985) summarized, women had "two full-time jobs that you didn't fudge on." These women did not give up, even in the face of the numerous problems mentioned throughout this volume. In fact, their tenacity and aggressiveness sometimes clashed head-on with generally accepted ideas of proper feminine behavior, even for those pursuing an acceptance strategy.

Family and Marriage

One of the most difficult and crucial decisions for a woman was whether to combine a professional career with marriage and a family. As Kent (1985b) stated, "My only problem was how to juggle a family and outside interests and jobs. You have to work twice as hard and I don't think that unless you are physically very strong you can do it. The only person who ever really figured it out was Margaret Mead." For those who chose to marry, trying to balance a family and career were very important.

It goes without saying that a family and a career required a great deal of accommodation and compromise; as the literature has proved, children (and societal conceptions of parental obligations) are the number one reason women have had trouble progressing as rapidly as men. Indeed, many women considered striving for an advanced education with a subsequent professional career and marriage to be incompatible choices and so chose one or the other. Several women chose not to marry, for staying single meant greater mobility and freedom. (It is interesting to note that many women felt that not having children gave them more time to pursue their professional interests, yet at the same time they saw their students as their children.) Others who chose a family and followed an acceptance strategy dropped out of the profession or vicariously worked through their husbands' careers (see below). Some women who felt careers and families were incompatible worked on each sequentially. They raised families and then began their careers, a decision that meant they were much older than their cohort, or they began their careers, stopped while they had their families, and later returned as their children aged. Thus, this problem of role definition involved not only the choice of appropriate modes of professional conduct but also the timing and prioritization of activities.

If one saw families and careers as compatible and tried to continue working while raising small children, a great deal of flexibility was required. Tanner continued to work after the birth of her child, as did Ellis. And children were even seen as an advantage in the fieldwork situation: "There is no question but if you take a child into a pueblo with you, you are ahead of the game" (Ellis 1985). Rosamond Spicer found similarly that the Tohono O'Odham saw her as a "normal" human being when she had her children with her. One always had to make career adjustments once one had children, and it helped to have a very supportive husband, as did Kent. (A nonsupportive husband usually meant one had to drop out of the field, as happened to Barbara Aitken, or divorce.) Anthropological activities for women with small children tended to be limited to volunteerism or part-time endeavors. Still other women, like Kent, adjusted their place of employment; for those with small children, working in a museum was an excellent solution to fieldwork. Nevertheless, there were limits to even these advantages; it is noteworthy that women who continued to work had few children—only one or two.

Alternate Employment and Research Strategies

Often denied access to prized jobs—such as those in Research 1 Universities—women developed alternative employment strategies and redefined the nature of anthropological products to adjust to their lifestyle requirements. For example, popularizing was an ideal solution for those who followed the acceptance strategy (because one could work part-time) and for individuals who had a personal desire to take anthropology beyond the ivory tower. An individual like Dama Margaret Smith could be a free-lance writer for *Arizona Highways* or *Desert Magazine* and still raise a family in the remote corners of Arizona. (Her husband was a National Park Service ranger.) Popularizing anthropology, either from within or outside the academy, was conceptualized as women's work. Some university-based anthropologists, such as Boas, wanted a wider audience for anthropology, but their writing styles were too difficult for nonanthropologists. Rather than change, these men encouraged women students to undertake the task. Thus, professionals such as Reichard and Underhill wrote popular accounts of their fieldwork as well as scholarly theses.

Although popularizing did provide women with an outlet, it was not without its pitfalls. Popularizing was mistrusted by the inward-looking university community, for popularizers worked under a set of rules that differed from that of the male-dominated academy. Competition for success was measured in different terms, and, in fact, many men did not vie for these positions because of this. Nonacademic, full-time popularizers (e.g., Alice Corbin Henderson, Mary Austin, Mary Colter, Mabel Luhan Dodge, and Erna Fergusson), by using these different rules, could also help create the Southwest in the process (Remley 1969; Weigle 1989). Through idealized tours, the decoration and construction of hotels, brochures, and advertising, the Southwest of dreams emerged as well as the Southwest of reality. Others wrote novels that captured the flavor of the Southwest. Photographers and artists graphically portrayed the variety of Native American peoples using sharp and soft foci in their portraits and landscapes. Their work both compelled and repelled; Tanner began to take anthropology outside the academy because she felt that many popular authors provided misinformation to the public. But, as McGreevy and Tisdale remind us in their chapters, other popularizers saved as much as they invented. And part of their preservation efforts resulted in an activism (see below) that has yet to be thoroughly explored or appreciated (see Weigle and Fiore 1982).

Women preferred to be gainfully employed in anthropology, for it was very hard to maintain a professional identity without a job. Employed individuals, unfortunately and unintentionally, distrust those without jobs; they think there must be something wrong with the person who does not hold a lucrative position. Rarely do they question whether there are enough jobs for the professional population, why some positions are seen as acceptable and others not, or why only certain types of individuals are able to secure the lucrative positions. This is a form of victimization that requires a very strong will and exceptional self-confidence to overcome. Unemployed anthropologists must maintain a faith in their work, often at great emotional cost. To obtain jobs, especially during periods of extreme economic hardship, women (from their marginal positions) have had to be exceptionally conventional or extremely creative. This necessity became even more crucial as the discipline professionalized and had increasingly stringent basic requirements for admission to the work force.

As shown throughout this book, women were highly creative in their search to find a place in southwestern anthropology, regardless of the strategy they followed. Inventing one's own job, however, meant it was often outside of, or on the fringes of, the discipline's institutional base. This could be very positive: a few women worked in women's colleges, comprehensive universities, or institutions where they controlled the finances and mission of the institution. Many women also found employment in institutions felt to be appropriate for women—museums, secondary schools and junior colleges, tourism, and government service—or the applied arena. In fact, these were often women's preferred institutional homes:

I did not feel any [gender discrimination] at all, in spite of Lloyd Warner's warnings that I would receive less pay if I worked at Harvard University. I think part of it was that for most of my career I wasn't in an academic setting. I was also in a field, mental health and social work, where there were many, many women. Both psychiatry and social work have used women as much as anthropology has, or more. So I was really working through a field in which this would not be a barrier (Halpern 1985).

Women who combined an interest in theoretical research and its practical applications found less discrimination, because there were many women in social work, education, and health. Women had a small advantage in these fields because they were seen as women's worlds. And they had an added benefit. One of the hallmarks of women's anthropological endeavors is that their work be relevant, even though relevance takes different shapes in different periods (Leacock 1986) and varies by integrative strategy. Taking this perspective as a starting and end point, many

women adapted those tenets of Victorian society that were identified as women's work—bringing civilization to unknown places—to their anthropology. It comes as no surprise that a number of women came to anthropology from social work or took their anthropology into the field to help others. Halpern's chapter contains examples of women's attempts to utilize anthropology for the betterment of all people, not only other anthropologists. Indeed, Halpern (1985) herself was responsible for much work in medical anthropology: "I wanted to be in public health. It was a mission." For women, the economic chaos of the Great Depression and the political reforms of the New Deal provided opportunities to pursue research, educate government officials, and help Native Americans. Part of a worldwide phenomenon for anthropologists during the period (James 1973), women anthropologists took full advantage of it. In fact, working directly to improve the social conditions of Native Americans has recently been noted to be a hallmark of southwestern anthropology (Frantz 1985; Kelly 1985): "Probably ninety percent of all anthropologists who were professionals during the period [early 1930s–1950s] were at some time or another engaged in matters of public concern" (Goldschmidt 1979:1). For others, World War II was the high point of their careers:

I have the feeling on the basis of those anthropologists whom I know who did war-related work (Ruth Benedict, Margaret Mead, Alexander Lesser and a number of others) that it was for many of them, the very zenith—the pinnacle of their careers because they felt perhaps for the first time in their lives that what they were doing was really important. It was not only an intellectually motivated activity but an activity connected with saving lives and destroying fascism (Mintz 1986).

As Halpern concludes in her chapter, women have been at the forefront of these important efforts to make anthropology relevant to society.

This commitment to taking anthropology beyond the ivory tower often found its expression in activism. Activism was a very successful strategy for politically astute women because of our conceptual models of women as cultured and refined in contrast to wild, savage, and rough men (see Ortner 1974). It also stressed the ideals of cooperation and social concern felt to be congenial to the female temperament (Rosenberg 1982). Although this model of female and human nature has been questioned cross-culturally (MacCormack 1980), it is still valid as part of the paradigm under which women scholars and amateurs worked and could be used by those following any integrative style. Activism combined with a romantic view of the Southwest was the hallmark strategy of several women, such as Natalie Curtis Burlin, who led the fight for American Indian rights. One of our foremost folklorists and ethnomusicologists, she successfully convinced Washington politicians that Native Americans should have religious determinacy, thereby lifting the assimilationist ban against the singing and playing of Native American music. Other women supported and encouraged American Indian arts and crafts and lobbied for the preservation of prehistoric ruins and the establishment of national parks. As several authors mentioned, Ellis' commitment to the American Indian land claims work was part of her quest "to give back to them whatever they can use of your understanding of things. You stand, really between them and the white man" (Ellis 1985). Activism allowed women to be mediators between two worlds. The strategies they used to overcome marginality could be effectively used to help others who also inhabited marginal worlds.

Women tended to work in the subfield with the least resistance to women—ethnography. In ethnography a woman could work on her own (or travel with a companion of her own choosing), while in archaeology there was a hierarchical and team arrangement to fieldwork. Teams of men, as Cordell has shown, were not hospitable to women. Women, thus, could have more control over their work by becoming cultural anthropologists and be more demanding in their pursuit of recognition. By and large the archaeologists who

worked before 1960 followed a modified acceptance strategy, working hard yet quietly. It is also noteworthy that the women who pursued archaeology were westerners, not individuals who came from the East Coast on archaeological expeditions. We are still not sure how this affected the development of anthropology; but for women archaeologists, there seems to have been a need to remain in the area to take advantage of proximity. This may partly have been due to financial considerations; since women lived in the area year-round, they could excavate more cheaply. If they had lived on the East Coast, as did Alfred Kidder, for example, they would have needed a different type of resourcefulness or opportunity to obtain resources for an expedition. This was much more difficult for women than men, and it was never easy even for men to mount an expedition.

Finally, to be successful, women had to see an opportunity and seize it: "It's knowing people, knowing what the opportunities are, and keeping your ears open that makes things happen for you" Dutton (1985a) told us. Or, as Woodbury (1985) summed up her career, "I just took opportunities as they came." The opportunity could be serendipitous or the result of years of preparation, hard work, and well-thought-out plans. A trajectory toward a professional goal was important so that one did not create the impression of frivolity. Many women did not work in all areas, as mentioned above; they choose their research topics and societies with care. For example, Ellis (1985) said, "I decided that this [dendrochronology] would be a good thing to be in because if you could have a specialty you were more likely to be wanted, which was a point especially for a woman." This strategy of specialization had its drawbacks as well as its assets. Although it made women valuable because of their specialized knowledge and skills, it meant that they were not seen as mainstream in the same sense as those who undertook basic ethnographic or archaeological research. But in general, it was beneficial because special talents have been sought out regardless of attitudes concerning women (Epstein 1970:979).

Enabling Families

Getting a head start or having luck helped. Many of the women who "set the trails" in the Southwest were literally the daughters of distinguished men who enabled them either intellectually or financially. None of the women encountered during this project were the daughters of the poor; all were raised in middle- and upper-class homes where advanced education for women was accepted or considered desirable.[6] This is a common pattern for women academics; women tend to come from higher socioeconomic classes than do academic men and are more likely to have fathers who are in professional occupations (Simeone 1987:14).

Having money definitely privileged; it made women independent. Several women inherited fortunes from their fathers that they used for the betterment of anthropology. Parsons had so much money that she did not need to work. In fact, she financed the fieldwork of almost everyone who worked in the Southwest for many years. One reason why so many individuals worked in the Southwest was Parson's enabling funds and her suggestions of how these funds should be utilized.[7] Likewise, Mary Wheelwright, Katharine Bartlett, and Mary-Russell Colton could found museums and research institutions and leave their personal stamp on them. Burlin, Alice Fletcher, Elizabeth White, Mary Hemenway, and Phoebe Hearst could use inherited wealth or family influence to finance research expeditions, make collections, and underwrite field schools. Their vision and subsequent influence on anthropology has been enormous (Woodbury and Woodbury 1988).

Money also empowered pioneers to test the bounds of unconventionality. Parsons, for example, returned to her teaching position at Barnard College after the birth of her children. One scholar writes of Parsons,

Her passion for sociology, together with her husband's tolerant attitude, did much to make this unusual combination of motherhood and teaching possible. Without her family's wealth, however, and the large homes and retinue of servants it could command, her unconventional achievement might never have been realized. Though realized according to the strictest rules of New York society life, Elsie Clews Parsons succeeded better than most other women of her generation in ignoring the social conventions of her time, simply because she could afford to do so (Rosenberg 1982:154).

Even unexpected funds from an automobile accident, as Cordell and Fox relate in their chapters, served a purpose in enabling Dutton to leave the confines of a traditional supporting job in the Midwest and pursue her dream of becoming an archaeologist. The transformative power of enabling wealth and anthropology allowed her to build a new identity. Other women who lacked inherited wealth or steady employment at a decent wage were not so lucky. Many dropped out of anthropology, much to our loss.

MENTORS, PATRONS, AND SUPPORT GROUPS

Anthropology was, and still is, a "small world" where influential target people with strong personalities act as gatekeepers. These individuals either close or open doors. Those who open them serve as role models, help find the neophyte's first job, write letters of recommendation, and introduce new scholars to the established community with a *Good Housekeeping* stamp of approval." One cannot underestimate the role played in the development of southwestern anthropology by gatekeepers, especially male scholars who were, in Bunzel's (1985) words, "hospitable to women and thought they had grey matter in their heads." Luckily, several influential and eminent men in key schools demonstrated that they valued women's contributions and took them seriously, and a few had even had a female mentor themselves: "I can remember Kluckhohn spoke with such admiration for certain women whom he'd had as his mentors" (Halpern 1985). Others had a desire for fairness and justice, an intellectual skepticism about untested stereotypes about women's so-called limited potential, which they found to be based on unsupported biological models. Often these men had democratic proclivities and had experienced some form of discrimination themselves.[8] Many liked and admired women, especially those women who showed intelligence and the ambition to pursue meaningful work.

In almost every case, senior male professors opened doors. In archaeology, Cummings of the University of Arizona encouraged Tanner and Ellis; Renaud helped Bartlett, Kent, and Lambert at the University of Denver; Hewett welcomed women such as Lambert, Dutton, Aitken, and Keur to the University of New Mexico's field schools. In ethnology there was Kroeber at the University of California at Berkeley and Kluckhohn at Harvard University who gave moral support and saw women as "remarkable," even if they did not know what to do with them. And it was not only as formal teachers that mentors were important; other senior anthropologists met along the way played crucial roles as enabling individuals in critical periods. Thus, Ellis was grateful to Hewett for his finding the money to publish her dissertation so she could receive her doctorate before she began teaching.[9] Kluckhohn helped many women even when they were not officially his students; for example, Halpern (1985) said, "I had a summer's fieldwork in the Southwest and I had Kluckhohn for an advisor there. He really became the most important person for me in my anthropological development. He was more important than the Chicago professors."

Kluckhohn exhibited one of the key features of the mentor or older friend—creative flexibility. For example, Kluckhohn picked up Halpern, Carr, and Wooley at the train station and took them to the University of New Mexico field school in Chaco Canyon. Halpern (1985) described the occasion:

I had been told by someone at Chicago who had been a student of Kluckhohn's at Harvard that even though he was supposed to teach archaeology, he could probably be persuaded to have students do some ethnological fieldwork . . . He asked us what the three of us

expected to do. I told him, "I hope to do ethnology with you." He said, "But there's no ethnology at the summer field school." That was the first reception of it, but he immediately figured out ways to use us for ethnology. He arranged for us to have an interpreter, and we worked with Navajo clans in the Pueblo Alto area, around Chaco Canyon. It was a wonderful summer for the three of us. Kluckhohn was always so encouraging to any of his students and perhaps even more so to his female students. I know that not everyone feels that way. Some students crossed or annoyed him. But the ones I know for whom he was an important figure got an awful lot from him. He took care that they should get opportunities. I know other women who felt the same way . . . I feel that he was terribly important in the role of women in anthropology. I don't think that I would have thought that I could be an anthropologist if he hadn't encouraged me in the early days.

Kluckhohn thus had an interest in helping and encouraging others, opportunities for fieldwork, a number of projects that could be done and to which he let students have publication rights, and control of the resources. And he could call on friends to help students: Kluckhohn was very influential in getting Mary Shepardson into Berkeley when she was denied admission at Stanford University because of her age.[10]

Although important, these men were all too few. As has been found in other sciences (Blackburn et al. 1981), men who sponsored women students supported a disproportionate number. And they did this at some risk to their reputations; Hewett was much criticized for his support of women, and "there were anthropologists who objected to Boas' custom of bringing to lunch his secretaries, budding anthropologists who could take shorthand" (Mead 1960:5). Fortunately for women, male gatekeepers ignored the criticism.

Father Figures

As numerous studies have demonstrated, actual and fictive fathers serve as key figures in the success of women (Henning and Jardin 1977). The image of the father figure is very strong. Hewett was "a father figure to us" (Lambert

1985); Fay-Cooper Cole was "Papa Cole" to both Spicer and Halpern because he was a man who was "good at getting things for students" (Halpern 1985); Robert Redfield, although a "very distinguished and somewhat remote man," sponsored Halpern for a Social Science Research Council fellowship—"I knew he liked my work" (1985). And there was Franz Boas at Columbia University, affectionately described by his women students as "Papa Franz." As Stocking (1976:7–8) has demonstrated, this family analogy is strong in anthropology, often used instead of the concept of "school":

A more illuminating metaphor is suggested in Kroeber's comment that Boas was "a true patriarch"—a powerful and rather forbidding father figure who rewarded his offspring with nurturant support insofar as he felt that "they were genuinely identifying with him," but who was indifferent and even punishing if the occasion demanded it . . . There are obvious analogies to the psychodynamics of a large late-Victorian family: the oedipal rebellion of certain older male offspring, the rejected sons, the sibling rivalries, the generational and sexual differentiations—most notable in the softening of the patriarch toward the younger generation of daughters, who called him "Papa Franz" and accepted the sometimes ambiguous benevolence of a man who facilitated the entry of many women into the discipline, but who still tended to assume that, in the world as it was then constituted, wives and secretaries could not enjoy all the prerogatives of professionalism.

This "father of American anthropology" (La-Barre 1949:156) was the most important gatekeeper for women who came to the Southwest. His sensitivity led him to welcome women, even if he felt that his female students were unusual and he did not recruit them. In 1920 he wrote to Berthold Lauffer, "I have a curious experience in graduate work during the last few years. All my best graduate students are women" (quoted in Goldfrank 1978:8). During his tenure at Columbia University, over 20 women received Ph.D.'s in anthropology, most of them conducting fieldwork in the Southwest. Boas was extraordinarily supportive, partly spurred on by Parsons. As Bunzel (1985) remembered, "Boas was hospitable to women. He thought women could do things and could get into places men couldn't . . . But he never felt women had to do only women's things." Boas was an extraordinary mentor. Although the extraordinary mentor is not uncommon in science (Crane 1972), what is unusual in this case is the number of women and their concentration over a short time in the female cohort, Boas' support of the cohort during their crucial training period and throughout their professional careers, and his general respect for women.

The Cost of Mentoring

Mentoring has effects other than simply helping an individual get started on a career path. Mentors surround themselves with students who are expected to carry on the mentor's work and research agenda, to perpetuate him or her after retirement. As such, mentors tend to be slightly autocratic, to decide where people go—especially on first, and in the case of Boas' students, subsequent field trips. (This happened to Reichard, Benedict, and Bunzel, as Lamphere has demonstrated in her chapter.) Almost all the women from Columbia University were directed to the Southwest partly because it was seen as safe and exotic but still part of the United States—only Mead rebelled and went to the South Pacific (see below). Like all mentors with rebellious children, Boas was furious with her. Thus, many women came to the Southwest because they were directed there by influential individuals whom they respected and because men who controlled field and funding situations encouraged them to do so.

Many first- and second-generation women became fictive daughters: "The brilliant graduate student can attach herself as an intellectual daughter to an older male colleague emphasizing loyalty and dependency" (Douvan 1976:14). While the encouragement and approval of a male faculty member as teacher and colleague was crucial for advancement from the 1920s through the 1950s, male disapproval hindered if not suppressed budding careers. This made mentoring problematic. Women learned that they had to be wary of those who had decided a priori, based on existing stereotypes of women's abilities, what was best for them and what they needed. Even with the best of intentions, there was little regard or consideration for what women wanted or needed. There is a sense of betrayal in accounts of women who knew they were being paid less by their mentors for more work than were men, always had to remain in awe of and support their fictive fathers, and could never call their loyalty into question. Daughters remained daughters even if they were 40 or 50 years old. They never truly became colleagues.

One reason for this is the conscious or unconscious sense of obligation engendered in women by male mentors who reminded women that they had been admitted to the academy or museum through the back door. Several women began their careers in traditional women's jobs and fell into anthropology through the opportunity of serving a Great Man. For example, Bunzel (1985), as has already been noted throughout this volume, was Boas' secretary: "I wasn't an anthropologist; I was a secretary. I think I had about four weeks to become an anthropologist." She always thanked Boas for giving her the opportunity. Likewise, Goldfrank (1985b) tried anthropology on her summer vacation from her secretarial job, and Dutton (1985a) was able to complete her education and find employment because she served as Hewett's secretary. She had gone into anthropology because, as she said, "I couldn't stand the humdrum nature of being a business clerk," yet she was so valuable as a secretary that she continued to serve in this capacity even after she became a curator at the Museum of New Mexico. A valued assistant was more important than a colleague.

The mentor's protection and encouragement at one stage meant discouragement and hindrance later, for it kept women from entering the competitive arena for jobs. Women professionals were rarely given the choice of being protected or being independent. Independence was viewed as meaning "no job." Unfortunately, dependence sometimes meant the same thing because the mere existence of the sponsor-protégée (i.e., master-apprentice) relationship hindered female advancement (Epstein 1970). Men tended to let their male apprentices go earlier then their "daughters"; women remained helpers because of the prevailing notion that women needed to be cared for. Men questioned whether women could or would become their intellectual successors, so entrenched were the notions that a woman's other (and primary) roles—wife and mother—would force her to curtail her professional commitments and that she would be taken care of by a husband so she would not need a permanent job. Boas, for example, regarded Benedict first as a wife and secondly as a scholar; she would be "amply supported . . . someone for whose talents he must find work and a little money, someone on whom he could not make extreme demands and for whom he need not be responsible" (Mead 1959a: 343). Later, when Benedict separated from her husband and pressed for professional standing, Boas secured an assistant professorship for her. Boas worked harder promoting male students for career lines than he did female students and primarily helped women when it was obvious they were not going to be married. When Goldfrank returned to Columbia University and anthropology on the death of her husband, Boas still thought of her as a beloved daughter, but, she writes, "as in the past, he left decision-making to me. What I would do was my affair. He neither encouraged nor discouraged my return to anthropology" (Goldfrank 1978:99). He did not find her steady employment.

One of the reasons that many of the women we interviewed and those who have written biographies have not publicly stated that they had barriers to overcome has to do with the mentoring relationship and their simultaneous gratitude and frustration. It was prudent to act as if there were no problems or barriers and to not question the generosity of their mentors or the system. As Rossiter notes,

however deserving a woman might be, promotions were gifts from one's colleagues, particularly the powerful ones. If a woman expected to be promoted at such institutions merely because her work was good, she might well be disappointed because a promotion required the initiative and intervention of someone strong enough to override the resistance and criticism that would come at all levels of the appointment process, from chairmen to deans to presidents and boards of trustees. Her promotion would be a personal gift. She could take no initiative, such as to threaten to leave to accept an offer elsewhere, since she would only get one. Nor was her status transferable—to leave one job was not to go to an equal or better one elsewhere—it was, rather, to fall to the bottom, as a middle-aged lecturer, instructor, or assistant professor, or if married, perhaps to unemployment, because of antinepotism (Rossiter 1982:189–90).

This pattern was very common in anthropology. Few of the women who worked in the 1930s wanted to be branded a "troublemaker." It was better to remain silent and not upset the mentor.

Women Mentors and Friends

Mentor-teachers were not only men; women also played important roles in helping and empowering other women. The greater the women faculty/women student ratio, the greater the number of women graduates who subsequently attain professional standing (Tidball 1974:52). The role of crucial older women is prominent in the biographies of women successful in the academic world (Angrist and Almquist 1975; Douvan 1976; Mead 1972; Solomon 1985; Speizer 1981; Spender 1981). Women helped both directly and indirectly. Mary Roberts Coolidge, the first woman sociologist at the University of California at Berkeley, helped female students such as Isabel Kelly complete their educations.

She served as role model and sponsor, helping to obtain funding for Kelly's first research projects. Indirectly, through their writings, women established pseudo-matrilineages, building on each other's scholarship. This is clearly evident in Hinton's chapter on linguistics and in those that describe the women who attended Columbia. Empowerment by women also occurred informally; for example, Parsons finished Stevenson's monumental work on Pueblo religion, and Benedict and Bunzel built on each other's work at Zuni. As Bunzel (1985) said of Benedict, "She was very supportive . . . What I learned from her is so much a part of myself I can't sort it out."

Sometimes just meeting a woman at the right time provided the model and direction a woman needed to make a decision about pursuing a career. Halpern (1985) heard Mead lecture at Vassar College and discovered anthropology, and later she met Benedict in Washington:

I was a young anthropologist very interested in her work, and we would meet her in meetings and see her at parties. My impression of her was that when you talked to her about her work at any point, she was so interested in what you thought, what you had gotten out of the movies you had both seen. She was a wonderful, gracious lady. We weren't working closely with her, but saw her work and had a taste of what she was like.

And the same can happen for men. Fred Eggan (1986) remembered,

Bunzel was the greatest fieldworker we've had in the Southwest, man or woman, and Gladys Reichard and Ruth Underhill were outstanding. There [was] a whole group of important women who in my undergraduate and graduate days we all thought were really remarkable, since they were doing things that we looked forward to maybe doing and we were very much impressed by what they had done.

Friendship enabled as well. Sapir and Mead deeply influenced Benedict. Tylor gave an important endorsement to Stevenson at a time when she needed the approval of a successful male anthropologist to gain credibility. And the most important intellectual friendships were with fellow graduate students and colleagues, as David Aberle (1986) noted at the conference. Although we have not gone into this aspect deeply enough, it may be here that the ultimate influences on a career can be found.

Cohorts and Critical Mass

Since fellow graduate students and age-grades are crucial informal teachers and mentors, the presence or absence of women is important in determining the success of women. The presence of a critical mass is necessary in any group; that is, a minority group cannot be represented by a token member if the minority group as a whole is to have any influence, be taken seriously, and have their voices heard and their positions respected. One-third membership is needed for the agenda of the group to have any chance of success. Thus a minimum number of women was necessary in the profession as a whole and in individual departments for women as a group to succeed. Both in Britain and in the United States during the 1920s there were approximately equal numbers of male and female graduate students in anthropology for the first time. This critical mass at Columbia University, for example, had staggering effects for southwestern anthropology; the presence of Benedict and Boas on the faculty and the sponsorship of Parsons enabled Underhill, Bunzel, Mead, Goldfrank, Reichard, Kent, Keur, and Woodbury to become anthropologists. Goldfrank (1978: 18–19) remembered that

there can be no doubt that the war had significantly affected college attendance. Young men had been conscripted and young women had become career-minded. Jobs were plentiful but a college education gave promise of a better one—in fact, that last point as being regularly stressed during my years at Barnard—and with its many inviting areas for fieldwork and many problems still unresolved, anthropology may well have attracted more qualified women students during these years.

Boas' doctoral students between 1900 and 1916 had been men, with two exceptions: Laura E. Bennett and Martha Beckwith. Then, between 1920 and 1940, the pattern changed; both sexes were equally represented—20 men and 20 women earned their Ph.D.'s. With the advent of the women's movement, women provided support for each other. They sought practical advice, provided moral and emotional support, and imparted intellectual guidance and critique. After 1941 (until the mid 1960s) the pattern changed again; 193 men but only 111 women completed their degrees. What we see in the 1920s and 1930s we do not see again until the 1970s and 1980s.

Although there is no question that numbers make a difference, we still need to ask why in New York City and why in the 1920s were women welcomed in anthropology and so drawn to the field? Much more research needs to be done, but one hint comes from Stocking. While describing the situation in the aftermath of Boas' censure by the American Anthropological Association, Stocking contends that

fired by patriotic indignation against the pacifist-oriented and predominantly immigrant Boasians, reinforced by a reaction against cultural anthropology in the Waspish "hard" science establishment, the forces of resentment accumulated in the course of the Boasian redefinition of American anthropology exploded in brief eruption (1976: 1–2).

The issue was power: control of the new funding agencies, control of the discipline and its standards, and the self-determination of anthropology as a science. As Stocking explains, the Boasians mobilized

all their forces, adeptly politicking with the neutrals, and seizing a critical moment to force a compromise . . . were able to split the so-called "Maya-Washington crowd" and save the unity of the Association . . . The "scientific" status of anthropology, which was to a considerable extent the heritage of its association with the evolutionary tradition and its ties to the biological sciences, was sustained—not just for physical anthropology, but for all the component sub-disciplines, and most importantly, for the cultural an-thropological orientation that was to dominate the profession (1976:2).

While remaining the central figure in twentieth-century anthropology, Boas had fewer male stu-dents after this incident and more female stu-dents. It is probable that there is a connection; male students are less likely to study with a ques-tionable male figure than are women. Fewer men applied to work with Boas at Columbia; they went to Harvard, Chicago, or Berkeley instead. This created an opening for women, which they seized.

Although mentoring, role models, and cohorts helped, they were not always essential for a career. The lack of mentors, especially female mentors, had its effect and was often noted; Shepardson (1986a) remembered, "No women helped me be-cause there were none around." While today there is good evidence that female students are more likely to major in departments where there are female faculty members (Angrist and Almquist 1975), there were no women faculty members for Tanner, Marriott, Parsons, Ellis, and Thompson. And when mentors were there, they were often not in positions of power or influence. Thus, women have made it primarily without female help. As a result, most of the women met in this book could not picture themselves as role models, but this is not surprising since the category of "role model" did not appear in the literature until 1973 (Speizer 1981:693). There were firsts be-fore the critical mass—those who demonstrated that it was possible to commit oneself to work and succeed; there is no question that they are our role models.

HUSBAND-AND-WIFE TEAMS

A special type of mentoring relationship enabled several women to become anthropologists; these women went on their first expedition because they shared (or came to share) their husband's in-terests and work. Husbands would send wives to gather data inaccessible to them, and soon the women would keep their own field journals, as did Rosemary Firth (1972). In this way women gained knowledge and expertise that was as valu-able as a graduate education; there is no question that Stevenson gained some of her scientific train-ing in this way. Unfortunately, this level of com-petence, because it was not obtained in the "or-dinary" way via graduate school, could rarely be translated into a paying job. It could, however, be used to further a husband's career.

The team approach was rewarded and rein-forced by the university system, a phenomena Pa-panek (1973:858) has called the "two-person single career":

Colleges and universities, large private foundations, the U.S. government (particularly the armed forces and the foreign service), and similar institutions all develop their own version of the two-person career pattern among their employees. They all communi-cate certain expectations to the wives of their employ-ees. These expectations serve the dual function of reinforcing the husband's commitment to the insti-tution and of demanding certain types of role perfor-mance from the wife that benefit the institution in a number of ways.

In universities the career was the prerogative of the male. But the marriage partner spent enor-mous amounts of time researching, editing, typ-ing manuscripts, and co-writing grant proposals, articles, and books under the authorship of the individual with the professional credentials and position. This support was accepted as proper be-cause it was a central tenet of twentieth-century culture that wives support and work to advance their husband's careers, much as it was expected that women help men in the workplace. Some-times the female member of the team became the photographer and was recognized for her crucial effort, as was Spicer. Occasionally it was the hus-band who provided research support, as was the case for Clara Lee and John Tanner. More com-monly the woman accepted this situation and thought it was normal because the husband was the more intellectually deserving or because he was the better anthropologist. Goldfrank saw herself as intellectually subordinate to Wittfogel. Leighton felt that her husband Alexander was the one who developed the ideas and initiated their projects. Spicer (1985) said, "Ned was the brilliant and gifted one and the greatest contribution I could make was to help support him in his career and part of that included bringing up the children." Endorsement of the situation is very common (Aisenberg and Harrington 1988), especially for those following an acceptance or modified acceptance strategy.

In a two-career team, the woman's professional advancement was subordinated to her husband's. It is a well-known fact that in a two-career family it has been more common for the wife's career to be disrupted as the husband moves to new institutions. This means that as an accompanying spouse, the wife had fewer employment opportunities and often had to begin her rise again from a tenuous position. Added to this was the high level of unemployment in anthropology over the last hundred years. This situation was abetted or reinforced by anti-nepotism rules or other barriers that prevented the wife from obtaining a paying job of her own at her husband's university. This required the professional wife to be creative and also in some cases provided a desired flexibility: "Being married to an anthropologist meant that I was not pulled away from my field. I've always managed to have a satisfactory professional association wherever I've been that could give me an identity—and I just proceeded to do my thing" (Woodbury 1985).

One of the most common professional identities for married women was the research associateship, which kept them in science and was especially important for women with experience but no advanced educational credentials. But research associateships were positions with lower status—the paid/unpaid assistant—than a permanent professorship. This system kept competition

down but took a toll on many individuals and held others back because it limited opportunities and choices. Thus, the old norms of women's domestic roles rather than their ambitions for intellectual and public fulfillment meant that many women were not given the opportunity to make their own choices.

There were advantages and disadvantages to the team approach. For women who placed the priority of the family above that of holding a full-time position, a husband-wife approach was ideal because it allowed them to combine their family responsibilities and science in a way that was socially and personally acceptable. Eventually this created problems, however; Leighton did not obtain a permanent position until after her divorce. In fact, she was not taken seriously when she applied for several positions because it was assumed that she would accompany her husband, take care of the children, and would rather assist him than work independently.[11] Being a full-time co-researcher while continuing to have the primary responsibility for the home and child rearing takes its toll on a marriage. In addition, there was a general lack of recognition for the spouse's contribution; publications generally came out only under the man's name, as Papanek (1973:862) has discovered:

It is probably correct to say that openly acknowledged collaboration, in the context of a two-person career, is not very frequent. This ambivalence surrounding the wife's contribution suggests that many institutions, again particularly in the academic world, recognize the fragility of male self-esteem in American society and have adopted a number of ways of safeguarding it.

Women would be credited with the photographs, a second-class activity in the dissemination of anthropological knowledge, National Geographic Society fees notwithstanding. By and large, professional wives of high achievers became especially invisible. This was not always the case, and there were notable exceptions of well-known teams in which each scholar was an equal partner and credited as such; for example, Ernest and Pearl Beaglehole and Dorothea and Alexander Leighton wrote together. Their works benefited from their combined efforts, and there are certainly unique insights into cultural worlds separated by gender that can result from collaboration by husband-and-wife teams.

Unfortunately, all too often, the husband was the primary fieldworker, and his topics were seen as being the most important. He was free to pursue his work full-time; the wife still had control of and responsibility for the management of the household. Highly trained women professionals all too often had to subordinate their expertise, thereby reinforcing the notion that "the social place of women in Western society has traditionally been to stand behind men, out of their sight: as mothers, wives, nurses, secretaries, and servants" (Warren 1988:18). I can think of no cases in the Southwest where the woman professional was blessed with full-time secretaries and research associates (and housekeepers) by marriage; I can think of several for men. And sadly, the wife could not translate her new informally acquired education into a paying position or independent recognition until after the husband's death. It was only upon the attainment of the status of widowhood that wives actively returned to the profession and were recognized as independent scholars.

THE LURE OF THE GREATER SOUTHWEST

We have focused on women who worked with the native inhabitants of one culture area in order to limit the scope of this project; but in the process of our controlled comparison we have discovered much more. The reasons for our choice of the Greater Southwest (the southwestern United States and northwestern Mexico) and, as it turned out, for the choices of those who worked here were many. The first were historical depth, the amount of anthropological activity, and evident patterning through time. Native American peoples have had a long history of coping with

strangers who wished to learn about their cultures. Indeed, as William H. Holmes reported following the 1876 Hayden expedition, the Southwest offered "rich rewards" for anthropologists interested in ancient and living peoples. And anthropologists came here to such an extent that by the 1930s there were jokes that a Navajo household consisted of a Navajo family and an anthropologist. Goldfrank remembered (1978:38), "For some time before I joined Dr. Boas, the Southwest had been a major field of interest, and this continued to be so during my years at Columbia, and indeed for many afterward."

"The Southwest is many things to many people" (Babcock 1990:384). To Benedict, the Southwest was a place of vistas and peace and magnificence. To Goldfrank (1985b), anthropology in the Southwest was "a woman's party." To Parsons, fieldwork in the Southwest was an escape from public life and her earlier commitment to social reform (Rosenberg 1982:176). To Mary Shepardson (1986a:1), it was home:

Whenever I see the road sign, YOU ARE ENTERING THE NAVAJO INDIAN RESERVATION, I feel a lift of the heart. The sight of every sculptured canyon, every red rock mesa, the first flock of sheep herded by an Indian child, woman, or man on horseback, the distant dome of Navajo Mountain, the first overlook into Canyon de Chelly, Old Shiprock rising from the sand intensifies my delight. Months and months of living and working with Navajo Indians are distilled into the essence of joy.

The Southwest was simultaneously a place, a people, and a concept. And it especially had an allure for women as an almost ideal fieldwork locale.

The Southwest as Research Locale

As analyzed in *Daughters of the Desert* (Babcock and Parezo 1988) and alluded to in the preface, the Greater Southwest had much to offer anthropologists. As a locale it was an ideal place for fieldwork of both a theoretical and an applied nature. The Land of Enchantment contained such rich archaeological remains that one almost fell over the sites; cliff dwellings were visible from miles away. These ruins could be surveyed and excavated to answer sophisticated questions as well as provide information on the culture history of various groups. Nor had the contemporary populations died out, been displaced, or moved from their traditional homelands during America's expansion. There were numerous, highly diverse native groups whose life styles ranged from technologically simple hunters and gatherers to agriculturalists with complex organizations; for all groups there was a rich and extensive folklore. Even as late as the 1930s there were people who could remember what life had been like before the reservation period and reflect on how it had changed since the coming of Anglo-Americans. It was evident that there was continuity between contemporary inhabitants and peoples of the past and that the peoples of the area had lasting and deep bonds to the region that had not been eradicated by contact with European cultures. These regional characteristics were very important considerations for anthropologists before World War II (Parezo 1987). For example, Kluckhohn "was particularly enthusiastic about New Mexico as a living laboratory for anthropology" (Bock 1989). He saw the Southwest as the ideal place to study the role of environment on culture and society and the unique features of multicultural settings (Kluckhohn 1937).

By 1940, the Greater Southwest was the most systematically studied region in the world, and this fact was widely recognized. Scholars noted, for example,

Nowhere in North America is as much work of significance for anthropological theory being done today as in the Southwest. As the aboriginal societies of other areas become even more things of the past, the Southwest will continue to grow in importance for some time to come (Hoebel 1954:725–26).

The great store of data [on the Pueblos] has been used constantly by students of this or that particular problem in the origin and development of human culture, by assiduous workers at the task of the reconstruction of the history of the American Indian, or by others

concerned with the special puzzles of the rise and fall of the prehistoric civilization of the Southwest (E. Spicer 1948:78).

Basso (1973:221) echoed this view years later:

Anthropologists have been investigating indigenous cultures of the Southwestern United States and northern Mexico for three quarters of a century and have produced a body of literature on the subject which in terms of sheet magnitude and richness in detail probably surpasses that of any ethnographic region in the New World . . . [F]ar more impressive than the bulk of this material, however, is the extent to which it reveals the decisive role played by earlier generations of Southwestern ethnologists in stimulating the growth of American ethnological theory . . . Between 1968–1972, Southwestern ethnologists have not been lacking for things to do. To the contrary, their enthusiasm has been unflagging, their energy quite enormous, and their published output just a little shy of prodigious.

The Greater Southwest thus has been the place where theories were generated, where facts were discovered that called for theoretical revisions, where the whole of life could be studied. It has also been anthropology's training ground, especially for archaeology, as Cordell observes in her chapter; many anthropologists came here to undertake their first professional endeavors—and their second and third as well, for anthropologists have had a tendency to return to the areas in which they were trained. It is no wonder that thousands of men and women came to the Southwest. It provided an ideal research locale recognized by teachers and students alike as the place where one could become established in anthropology. But it was also much more.

The Southwest's Indescribable Romance

The Southwest had another characteristic that meant generations of anthropologists would need to return. Goldfrank (1978:42) recounted discussions at Columbia University in the 1920s and 1930s: "The Southwest was a frequent topic of conversation. Research there was seen to be intriguing, frustrating, and challenging. The strands of knowledge in the Southwest always remained tangled." Lambert (1985) expressed the same sentiments when she told us why she never wanted to leave the Southwest: "I liked the challenge that prehistory seemed to give, the mystery of it, and finding out about the people here." John Bennett (1946:361) likewise voiced the view that in the Southwest there was "a pervading sense of mystery and glamour of the country itself." Regardless of style, the Greater Southwest had the aura of the unknown, that which would always require further study.

And in the Southwest the research locale and gender became interconnected. "A good deal of ethnology and archaeology in the Southwest has been done with a kind of eager reverence for turquoise, concho belts, Snake Dances and distant vistas" (Bennett 1946:365). This gendered romance can be clearly seen in the chapters by Babcock, Gordon, and Sands, where the texts of women writers are shown to reflect setting and the interpretive moment. In addition, it draws on the notion that all anthropological writing is autobiographical as well as scientific or humanistic (Fabian 1983). Of course this varied through time, and what may at first glance appear to be a gender-specific voice may be an artifact of historical style. An interest in narrativity and rhetoric was characteristic after World War I, for example, and was strengthened by the romanticist current found in certain intellectual circles, where members were "conscious of their own group identity" (Stocking 1976:32). As part of a cultural self-criticism, romanticists turned to the Native American Southwest to validate their concepts. Likewise,

At first the students of Pueblo culture seem to have been strongly motivated by what can only be called a sort of romantic wonder. How can such things be? they seem to be asking. How could these highly organized communities grow up in what seemed such a forbidding environment? Must we continue to call people who carry out such beautiful and elaborate ceremonies savages or primitive peoples? Early stu-

dents like Matilda Coxe Stevenson, Adolf Bandelier, Edgar Lee Hewett, and Frank Hamilton Cushing went to the Rio Grande pueblos and Zuni with a strong feeling for the romantic elements in the life they were studying. It is to their writing that we must still go if we are looking at Pueblo life as a sort of escape from our own. They have brought it into our culture in terms of the strange and wonderful (E. Spicer 1948:83).

For nonromanticists, the Southwest was a research locale where facts should be soberly recorded and where the act of recording became an end in itself.

Societies that Respected Women

If the Southwest as place called, it was the Southwest as people that compelled. "Zuni is a woman's society. The women have a great deal of power and influence, so it's a good place for women to work," Bunzel told us in 1985, while Ellis (1985) said, "When the Pueblo Indians think of you as a woman, I don't think they think of you as a lower creature the way our men tend to do . . . These Pueblo women are given an equality that is then passed onto the rest of us when we come into the picture." The respect for women noticed in Puebloan cultures was a definite lure to women who realized they were not treated with equality in their own society.

Women anthropologists were drawn to matrilineal societies, where women were respected for their talents and it was felt they would have access to information and be treated better than in societies where women had low status. Few women worked in patrilineal or bilateral societies in the Southwest until after World War II. This situation changed as the debate on whether gender roles for both the fieldworker and the cultural hosts and hostesses were negotiable (Hunt 1984; Lederman 1986). When it was felt that gender affected rapport and defined the quality and type of data that could be gathered (Warren and Rasmussen 1977), the fieldworker was caught in the roles designated for men and women in the culture under study as well as those of her or his own culture, with the result that women had limited access to masculine settings and men had limited access to feminine settings. At these times, women and men studied gendered worlds. Women tended to go to matrilineal societies and men to patrilineal societies or those with strong male age groups or the like. This idea of gender as an ascribed role or one that is difficult to negotiate was commonly held in the social sciences but debated in the 1920–1930s and again in the 1970s–1980s. During these periods gender was "part of the structural grounds upon which negotiation took place" (Warren 1988:9), and women went further afield in the types of societies they studied and the situations they entered.

Whether the female anthropologist and her mentor (if it was her first trip) viewed gender as an ascribed or a negotiable role affected the choice of field site. Women who saw gender as nonnegotiable and wanted to fit into established roles for women in the society they studied tended to choose cultures in which women had a high status and were respected. They avoided cultures in which women had a low status because they would be dismissed and would have a difficult time fulfilling their task of data gathering. Those who saw gender as negotiable worked in a wider variety of cultures. Since there were so many southwestern societies that respected women, however, this was more a factor for coming to the culture area than for making a cultural choice within the area.

Cross-Cultural Friendships

The idea of ascribed or negotiated gender roles as well as the type of integrative style chosen by the individual woman had implications for relations with native peoples (and men too: see Angrosino 1986). By and large, women anthropologists were respected for the help they could give to their cultural hosts and hostesses regardless of gender style because of the mutual respect and reciprocity that developed into lifelong friendships. For example, Underhill wrote histories and stories for the people who became her friends. As a Tohono O'Odham linguist said of her, "Sometimes we don't know the whole story and we can look at her books to see what it should be. We trust Underhill" (quoted in Anonymous 1980:3). In the process of repeated fieldwork endeavors, intimacies developed across cultural boundaries because anthropologists were able to transcend their own culture and become figurative daughters, mothers, and elder sisters. This gave many women a new sense of self and purpose, for they were given new names and adopted into clans and families. Parsons had her hair washed at Hopi to make her a member of the community; Bunzel was adopted not once but twice at Zuni; at Cochiti, Caroline Quintana washed Goldfrank's hair and named her Abalone Shell; and when Dutton's mother died, Susie Marmon of Laguna adopted her. Women came to the Southwest as strangers and left as kin. They were given a proper place in the native social order, which they valued throughout their lives. As Underhill reflected, "They [the Tohono O'Odham] were so good to me. They were always kind and willing and caring and helped me whenever I needed help so that I sort of remembered it as an ideal place to go" (quoted in Anonymous 1980:3).

This does not mean that women renounced their own society; they all returned to their other lives at the end of research trips. "It is worth noting that virtually no European anthropologist has been won over personally to the subordinated culture he [or she] has studied; although countless non-Europeans, having come to the West to study its culture, have been captured by its values and assumptions" (Asad 1973:17). As in other colonial situations, "a fair skin and Caucasian physical characteristics set the anthropologist off not only as a foreigner, but also as someone of a higher status than the 'natives'" (Warren 1988:25). These characteristics permitted women fieldworkers opportunities for cross-gender behavior not open to native women. And older women anthropologists—such as Shepardson, Underhill, and later in her life, Stevenson—were culturally androgynized; their grey hair gave them access to all in the culture.[12] Thus, older, non-native women in particular were not confined to women's worlds; but even younger women could work with both men and women. All mentioned that they had no major problems conducting fieldwork and that being a women was a definite asset. In fact, if they had been male they could not have conducted their research with the success they did. Thus, women gained visibility and access within American Indian men's worlds in contradistinction to women's invisibility in Western cross-gender settings.

The Effect of Colonialism

The relationships between women anthropologists and native informants/collaborators must be situated in time as well as place, however. The regional integration of the United States as a nation and its uneven economic development is crucial to understanding how women (and men) anthropologists were treated. The effects of colonialism were felt by all anthropologists. Pueblo "secretiveness," reticence, and factionalism colored the research efforts of Stevenson, Parsons, Goldfrank, Benedict, and Bunzel just as it did those of Harrington, White, Stephens, Eggan, and Fewkes. (As Parsons [1929a:7] stated, the Puebloans were "past masters in the art of defeating inquiry.") And several female anthropologists used the colonial power structure to further their own ends, as did men. The encounters with Native Americans must, therefore, be couched in the unequal power structure of colonialism. One scholar notes,

It is this encounter that gives the West access to cultural and historical information about the societies it has progressively dominated, and thus not only generates a certain kind of universal understanding, but also re-enforces the inequalities in capacity between the European and the non-European worlds or derivatively, between the Europeanized elites and the "traditional" masses in the Third World (Asad 1973:16).

Anthropology is a discipline that has contributed to and used asymmetrical power relationships. While sympathetically recording indigenous customs and structures, anthropologists have contributed, sometimes indirectly, toward maintaining the colonial power structure; this is most clearly seen in the chapter on Stevenson.

Anthropology, of course, is not simply a reflection of colonial administration or ideology, but it should be stated that female, like male, anthropologists were members of a political system and that this influenced relationships with Native Americans with whom they worked. Lamphere (1989:523) has recently commented upon the issue and its effect on the research endeavor and product:

Given Pueblo resistance to researchers, especially those who wanted to know about religion, information was always obtained piecemeal. Anthropologists were never able to present a "seamless whole" nor could they have "pitched their tents among the natives." Like others of the period Parsons relied primarily on information from one family (the host) and from a small circle of paid informants. In most secretive pueblos like Isleta, notes were made during interviews in a hotel room or at a nearby Spanish village. This relatively clandestine research (although Parsons took care never to reveal the names of her informants) gives us (in the 1980s) the sense that anthropologists were almost prying information, often secret, out of the "natives."

Few Southwestern researchers were engaged in writing with the kind of ethnographic authority that claimed that "I was there, so you are there." Instead, a scholarly article was often a blend of different voices—the anthropologist as observer, the native as co-observer answering the anthropologist's questions "on the spot," the notes of previous anthropological observations, and a narrative of a "prototypical" ceremony by a native informant.

Gordon extended this idea further in her chapter discussing gender and ethnographic authority by demonstrating how the notion of the Southwest, the sex of informant/collaborators, and the desire for freedom (see below) combined in the work of many women anthropologists. This was often expressed as a feeling of kinship with peoples who have been marginalized. While there is no question that gender relationships in the wider society colored and framed ethnographic work as the women tried to reconstruct themselves, what is still needed is a study that looks at the uneven regional economic and political development in the United States and Mexico as the context for these relationships. As Sidney Mintz reminded us at the conference, we must embed the relationships between anthropologists and native collaborators in·a comparative framework that considers differentiated regional development in terms of national economic and political history. This study as envisioned must consider the gradual appearance of an imperialistic philosophy of a national destiny and the reasons Native Americans were displaced as well as how firmly and openly they resisted outside forces. In short, we need to better contextualize the Southwest in the history of nation-states to truly understand the actual and symbolic relationship between gender, peoples, and place.

A Place to Be Free

The Southwest as a regional entity was conceptualized as America's last frontier. To romantic individualists it was the Wild West, a place where people could be free to live as they wanted. For others it was less an escape than the last chance at cultural salvation. Men and women such as Bandelier, Cushing, Lawrence, and Dodge saw New Mexico and Arizona and the Native American societies there as the means by which Anglo-American society could be restored. Highly disillusioned with capitalism, industrialism, puritanism, and rural morality, they went to the Southwest to learn how society could be reintegrated (Hinsley 1986b). In the American Southwest, they thought, could be found the bases for a better nation, and if this could not be translated into reform, at least liberal individualists could live without the constraints of middle- and upper-class American society. Thus, the last frontier, the last vestige of pure Native American

cultures living on their own lands, made the Southwest a place for individuals who felt alienated from their own society yet wanted to return to simpler times in order to save civilization from the effects of industrialization.

Many anthropologists entered the field because they felt they were dissatisfied and unconventional. Anthropology has appealed to those who do not want to blindly follow the taken-for-granted aspects of their own society and its oppressiveness. The Southwest called to these individuals because it meant freedom and independence; it was a place where one could prove oneself. Thompson (1985) compared Berkeley to Harvard: "There was the freedom of the West." As Hieb hypothesized, the West allowed Parsons to escape the confines of New York City society—to be free of her social position—so she could follow her intense commitment to individual freedom. The West was the place where one overcame the constraints society imposed on women; it meant sexual and intellectual freedom. Working with Native Americans in the West was simultaneously an escape and an active political statement. Of course, men as well as women have rebelled against society and sought out places where they could be respected for their normalcy, their strengths, and their differences. While for some this simply meant the Southwest was a good place to live and work, for others it became a romanticized quest, as mentioned above. Escape to the Land of Enchantment was glorified and reproduced, for the Southwest meant an idealized life, preferable to the complexity of life, as well as an exotic research locale.

The lure of the Southwest was so strong that one group of women remained, forgoing mobility and increased salaries. Their acceptance in western institutions, the perception that these were humane places to work, their desire for intellectual freedom, and the love of place held people in the Southwest:

I didn't want to leave the Southwest. Paul Martin said I made a great mistake staying here. He said, "You should have left when Hewett died. You could have gotten a job at any of the leading museums in the country. We would have welcomed you." But at that time in my life I had become enamored with New Mexico. I loved the contacts with the Indians which I knew I would lose. I knew that I could lose close and immediate contact with the archaeological sites . . . so I didn't consider leaving (Lambert 1985).

I knew that if you were with UNM you were getting lower salaries than you might get if you were in the Midwest or farther east. And I got some offers but I didn't want to live in those areas. I wanted to live out here and be with my Indian friends and the archaeology that went with them. And I just figured, well, OK. That's the price, you pay for it. So what? And I think this is the kind of thing that you have to decide in the long run. You do the best you can under the circumstances (Ellis 1985).

Practical considerations also entered into the decision to remain in the Southwest. It was cheaper and easier to conduct fieldwork in the Southwest than it was to go to the Kalahari Desert, especially with children in tow. Women recognized that although they were quite successful in obtaining research support, especially fellowships, securing expeditionary funds would have been exceptionally difficult. Additionally, in the western United States, academic traditions were less entrenched than in the East. Given the lower population densities it was impossible to support sex-segregated institutions, so coeducation was the norm. The staffing problems in the West's rapidly expanding public land-grant system encouraged coeducation. Without secure endowments, western universities needed women. Since there were fewer women's colleges in the West, there was no "tradition" to break.

The lure of the West for professional women seeking employment was recognized early. In 1912, C. H. Handschin published a survey of women teachers in colleges. He found that the proportion of women teaching in state colleges was 9% nationwide but 14% west of the Mississippi; in the Northeast the percentage was less

than 6%. Handschin's reasons for this difference were (1) women were not conservative and the West was more liberal; (2) there were more co-educational institutions in the West; (3) most of the western schools were founded after women began to compete for college positions; and (4) the lack of funds in the West meant lower salaries for faculty. Women were willing to accept lower pay. Thus the West, including the Southwest, provided opportunities, dignity, freedom, and a foot in the door.

A Safe Place to Work

In addition to being a fruitful arena for anthropological research, a place with remarkably varied landscapes that compelled some and repelled others, the Greater Southwest was conceptualized as an ideal (and in many ways the only) place for women because it was "safe" while still being exotic enough for anthropological research. Safety in the field was a common dilemma for women anthropologists and their mentors (see Easterday et al. 1977; Golde 1986). One needed to study noncivilized peoples, to live among "primitive" peoples, or to excavate the remains of past civilizations in remote locales to validate credentials, yet "primitives" and "savages" may not know how to behave "properly" (i.e., in the Victorian sense) toward women. Feminist scholars have long noted the captivity literature that voiced concerns, preconceptions, and prejudices about how European or Caucasian women would be treated by Native American, Black, and Asian men if they traveled alone (Hellerstein et al. 1981; Riley 1984).[13] Women anthropologists were by definition in danger.

Living in dangerous and unknown field situations was always perceived as a special problem for the single female. For example,

In 1932 Camilla Wedgewood received a fellowship from the Australian National Research Council to carry out fieldwork in Melanesia on culture contact . . . [Her male European colleagues] in New Guinea did not welcome the idea of a single woman coming out to do fieldwork on her own. This was a period in the history of New Guinea in which the fear among whites of sexual assault to females was at its height . . . with little concrete evidence that white women were actually in danger of sexual assault. But [one male wrote that] "if any more lady anthropologists are thinking of coming out here you had better suggest that they bring a husband with them. I know of no place where a woman can work without fear of molestation from the natives" (Lutkehaus 1986:778).

Relatives also expressed concern about safety, although in different terms. Goldfrank (1978:42) remembered her first field experience: "Some of my aunts and uncles thought it dangerous for a young woman to live in an Indian village and even more dangerous to live there with a male companion, even if he was Professor Franz Boas, and almost forty years my senior. I had no such concerns." Thus the fear of rape, molestation, death, the possibility of scandal, sexual advances, the destruction of reputation, and loss of health were common concerns with which all women anthropologists had to deal. The Victorian era and its preconceptions of the helpless female as potential victim died hard and affected the choice of field site.

As a compromise, women, if they did not undertake fieldwork with their husbands, were expected to take a female companion and go somewhere "safe," that is, to a group that had been visited before by anthropologists, a requirement placed on Stevenson by Powell. Boas, for example, often talked about the health, safety, and vulnerability of women in the field and wanted them to go to the Southwest because it was safe. Mead presented a problem for him in this regard. She was his only female student who refused to conduct her dissertation research in the Southwest. Boas tried to discourage her with a "sort of litany of young men who had died or been killed while they were working outside the United States" (Mead 1972:129). Boas and Sapir argued that she was too small, young, and inexperienced to endure the hardships of the South Pacific by herself

without her husband. Mead persevered, however, by pointing out that they were acting in an arbitrary manner.

Actually, the Greater Southwest as a research locale was seen simultaneously as safe and unsafe based on one's preconceptions about the specific native groups; there were the "peaceful," settled, agricultural Puebloans who were safe and the "warlike," hunting, semisettled Apacheans who were not safe. The preconception of an "untamed" group overrode the matrilineality benefit of some of the groups. Zuni was the ideal field site; it was safe, exotic, remote, yet easily reached by a rigorous but not hazardous journey. Women were respected there, and Zuni was a functioning culture that was used to (or minimally tolerant of) anthropologists. Accessibility and safety were the reasons why so many women worked with Pueblo groups and so few women worked in the remote regions of the Sierra Madres or with peoples who were categorized as hunters and gatherers. Few women worked with the Apachean groups, with the exception of the Navajo, because it was felt they had not really been subdued. This idea was reinforced by the death of Henrietta Schmerler in 1931.

Schmerler, a student at Columbia University, went to study the Western Apache on the Fort Apache Reservation in the summer of 1931. Benedict at the time was running the Laboratory of Anthropology's Ethnology Project on the Mescalero Apache Reservation in New Mexico for which Schmerler had been an unsuccessful applicant. Schmerler decided, however, to go into the field on her own, against the advice of Benedict, who felt she was naive and unprepared and romanticized the fieldwork situation: "Schmerler insisted on going to a reputedly fierce tribe and without a well-defined project" (Modell 1983:181). She refused, for financial reasons, to live with an Apache family or employ a female companion. She erected a small tent in the woods, away from any encampments, and did not align herself with a kinship group. "Her instructions were also to make friends of the women and let the men go. Her better judgement went down before an excess of enthusiasm," Reichard wrote to Jesse Nusbaum (quoted in Woodbury 1987:3). "Miss Schmerler, who greatly admired Margaret Mead, was determined to duplicate her South Seas work in the Apache context and especially to gather material about Apache sex life. This is a subject about which Apache elders do not speak easily to virtual strangers, and they refused to cooperate" (Opler 1987:3). Based on information in the files of the Laboratory of Anthropology, Claire Farrer discovered that Schmerler became romantically involved with a White River Apache man and feared the advances of another.

After a few weeks of fieldwork, disaster struck. A young Apache asked her to attend a ceremony with him, and she accepted in a manner he misunderstood. "The youth who slew her interpreted her emphasis on sex in her research as a sign of looseness and invited her to ride behind him on his horse, something that young people of the opposite sex among the Apache do not do unless they are courting. Miss Schmerler, unaware of this, accepted" (Opler 1987:3). After they rode away from the camp, the young man made advances and was rebuffed. He became angered at the rejection; struggle, assault, and death were the result. Schmerler, whom one contemporary Columbia University student felt never should have been allowed to undertake fieldwork anywhere because she had trouble opening the doors at the university, never tried to understand proper female Apache roles and behaviors, was too impatient to learn, and had a tendency to barge into situations without thinking. Boas, when he heard the news, wrote to Benedict on August 27: "Gladys [Reichard, who was on the Navajo reservation that summer,] sent me the first full report about the sad Schmerler affair. It is dreadful. How shall we now dare to send a young girl out like this? And still. Is it not necessary and right?" (quoted in Howard 1984:128; Mead 1959:410).

Benedict replied: "I know it is one of those unprecedented things that cannot be foreseen or guarded against, and yet I think of endless points at which I might so easily have made different arrangements. I think especially of your saying as we came down 119th Street, 'Isn't it a rather untamed tribe?' " (quoted in Modell 1983:181).

The incident reawakened the debate about the safety of women in the field and the appropriateness of funding women students for fieldwork by the Laboratory of Anthropology and other institutions (Anonymous 1931). Defending the right of women to conduct fieldwork, Matthew Stirling, director of the Bureau of American Ethnology, noted that

this might have happened among any other group of people in similar circumstances . . . There is no real reason why a white woman would be in greater danger among Indians than among her own people, provided she has sufficient knowledge of Indian ways. It would seem inadvisable, however, for a young woman to live all alone in a remote region in any circumstances (quoted in Anon 1931:184–85).

Almost 40 years later I received similar sage advice from my professors before I left to undertake fieldwork.

Is the Southwest Unique?

The Greater Southwest is a wonderful place for women to work, but is it unique as an anthropologically compelling setting? The staggering number of men and women who came here and the proportion of women in relation to men is impressive and lends credence to this idea, as do the numerous characteristics that called individuals, be it the sense of place, freedom, research opportunities, or friendship with marginalized peoples. Since we did not conduct a comparative research project, we do not know whether the Greater Southwest is an exceptional culture area or whether we have a difference of scale. As Eleanor Leacock reminded us at the conference, there are very strong parallels between the statements of southwestern anthropologists and women who worked in Canada and the Arctic. The sense of escape to less male-dominated societies, the impressive landscape (bleak and foreboding in its own way), the opportunity to collaborate with fascinating natives called adventurous women. As in the Southwest there were professionals such as Regina Flannery, Margaret Lantis, and Ruth Landers and amateurs such as Mrs. Hubbard and Heliuz Washburne. "Some of the more flamboyant personalities were marginalized because they were flamboyant, not because they were women or because they were amateurs" (Leacock 1986). Thus, it may be that anthropology as a fieldwork endeavor that involved travel to exotic places where women could be treated with respect, do interesting things, and overcome society's constraints was what compelled. For we know that it is in travel that many women have found what they have been seeking: "In their various travels, women move intellectually as well as literally to places that seem hospitable to the identity they are seeking" (Aisenberg and Harrison 1988:25). But do women anthropologists go to those cultures where there is greater openness than in the United States? We need comparative studies of other culture areas to see how gender and place articulate before we can posit a definitive answer.

CONCLUSION: BEING A WOMAN ANTHROPOLOGIST ISN'T EASY, BUT IT'S BETTER THAN BEING A PHYSICIST

Thus in time, may be written a psychology of women based on truth, not opinion; on precise not on anecdotal evidence; on accurate data rather than on remnants of magic. Thus may scientific light be cast upon the questions so widely discussed at present and for several decades past, whether women may at last contribute their best intellectual effort toward human progress, or, whether it will be expedient for them to remain in the future as they have in the past, the ma-

trix from which proceed the dynamic agents of society (Leta Hollingworth 1914:99, quoted in Rosenberg 1982:103).

Anthropology, like all professions, has myths—one of these myths is that women have been welcomed in the profession because they were needed. It would be more accurate to say that they were tolerated in certain areas because they were useful and at times even respected. As a result, being a female anthropologist, while it had its rewards, was not easy because anthropology was embedded in institutions and a society where women intellectuals were seen as unusual and deviant. Women were not encouraged to aim for the top. In this, anthropology was like other sciences:

From the beginning of her professional training, the woman microbiologist feels handicapped by lack of encouragement and proper role models. She generally receives little advice regarding her professional future and rarely feels pushed to take the most challenging position. Should she be married, she feels that her mobility is severally restricted. Even though the subjective natures of these feelings may be interpreted as projections of failure, subtle inducements for women to stay at lower levels may well exist, in addition to more objective measurements, such as lower salary levels and slower professional advancement (Khasket et al. 1974:492).

But what were the other choices? To middle-class women the university represented the one institution open to them that led to respectable employment—teaching (Rossiter 1982:44)—even though being born a women meant gender disparities in hiring, salaries, promotion, employment status, and access to academic positions that continued into the 1970s and 1980s (Sanjek 1982). All women thus have had to search and fight for their place in the system, not simply as surrogate males but on their own terms through the use of integrative strategies. Sometimes this has been easy, sometimes difficult, for definitions of marginality have varied through time, correlated with economic conditions and the professionalization of the discipline and academia.

Generational concerns influenced the extent of the welcome or exclusion. Stevenson could enter anthropology because of the great fluidity of the period when "processes of economic, social and demographic differentiation in the late nineteenth century [meant] new roles and opportunities were unfolding at the same time that new persons were becoming available to fill them" (Rossiter 1982:xvi). Stevenson, and Parsons a few years later, could be confrontational in her style and make inroads because of this fluidity. Likewise, the rigidity and backlash that occurred in the 1930s limited Reichard's, Bunzel's, and Underhill's careers. There is a reason that Henrietta Burton could only find work in a home economics department and that she used a modified accommodation style even as she penned what has proven to be one of the most important economic analyses of Pueblo art. "Conservatives came forward to stress the less threatening goals of building up and striving for excellence within women's separate realms, as at the women's colleges, in the schools of home economics, and in several separate women's clubs in science" (Rossiter 1982:xviii).

Women anthropologists, however, were never quite as contained in the post-1920 period as women were in other sciences because, after all, anthropology needed women. Simply the prevalence of the idea meant that women could gain a foothold in the profession. Thus, anthropology has been more welcoming than other sciences because of its basic philosophy: "The catholicity of anthropology, with its ideological insistence on the psychic unity of man, and its tradition of disregard of race, ethnicity, age and sex as a criteria for academic posts or research capabilities" was what distinguished anthropology from other fields, according to Mead (1973:3). Women could enter and succeed in the field. Women have had a harder time in disciplines such as medicine and physics with a high degree of objectification

and depersonalization of people where the aspects of self are alienated from traditional feminine socialization patterns. In fields such as psychology, anthropology, and literary criticism where people are not so depersonalized, women have fared better (Douvan 1976:12–13). And women recognized this fact.

Never since I drifted into anthropology, have I regretted my choice. When I faced at the age of 46 the dilemma of commuting 110 miles a day or giving up the profession of anthropology, my sister-in-law Ruth Lee Thygeson said, "What will you do with the next fifty years of your life?" . . . Field work cured me of hedonism, ethnocentrism and boredom . . . Field work is the adventurous, exhilarating part of social and cultural anthropology, but I believe that it is the combination of the personal with the scholarly that holds me fascinated and is lighting up those last fifty years of my life (Shepardson 1986a:56–57).

Anthropology thus has had its special rewards. This is why we were able to find successful women and why they are hidden, absent from our textbooks. Nevertheless, entering anthropology, like other sciences, "had occurred at the price of accepting a pattern of segregated employment and underrecognition, which, try as they might, most women could not escape" (Rossiter 1982: xviii). Women discussed in this book illustrate how unusual yet how common women's success was in the sex-segregated university labor market, how hard it was to realize the full potential of that success, and the contributions that nevertheless resulted. In this, women anthropologists' experiences, situations, and responses mirrored those of women in other disciplines.

Women have always been a major force in our society, yet their histories have been relegated to second-class status or ignored, hidden by a structure that reinforces exclusion in which men serve as the norm by which women are evaluated. Countless theories have been proffered to explain or justify this "condition of women." Most have been proven false, shown to be based on erroneous premises or assumptions (Solomon 1985), but we are still fighting a battle to get people to conceive of women without stereotypes. Although we are enlightened in comparison to the days when thinking was considered too much for women's brains, we still need to ensure that the theories developed and espoused by women are taken as seriously as, judged equally with, and recognized similarly with regard to merit as those of men.

To do this we need to rethink our internalized assumptions, bring to light the unspoken agreements and the implicit contrasts that people have in the past unconsciously agreed to. We must question the structure and the dynamics that allowed people to be hidden from our view. And we need to alter how we view success in a discipline and reanalyze the toll that academic life takes on both men and women. As David Aberle reminded us at the close of the conference, "We will not understand some of the issues we have discussed fully except by finding and using equivalent data on men, and not only look at the superstars. I think of all the men of the generation before me at Columbia who disappeared from anthropology. We need to know about them, too."

Since the 1970s universities have tried to improve the recruitment, advancement, and retention of women. Despite all the efforts, insufficient progress has been made in achieving diversity with regard to gender and race in both student bodies and faculties/professional staffs (Spector 1988:3). The number of female students has increased to the point that there are now more female than male college students, but the number and proportion of female faculty members has remained small:

The proportion of women on faculties appears to actually have declined from 1920 through 1970. Even during the 1960s women failed to gain ground. Women have a smaller proportion of full-time faculty at every rank except instructor at the end of the decade than they had at its beginning. The problem is especially acute at elite institutions and at high ranks (Menges and Exum 1983:124).

Although numerical documentation of barriers is well established, documenting and understanding deep-set and unquestioned values held in academia, regardless of discipline, on the value of diversity and the ability of women and minorities to attain the "high standards" of these institutions has been evasive. To influence and improve the position of women, we need to educate those in power so that they will understand the traditions that have led to major roadblocks for women—what it means to have to overcome (or be defeated by) barriers—to isolate and define the special problems faced by women both inside and outside academia. There is a need for concrete quantitative and qualitative data. Special commissions and task forces in almost every state are now amassing these data on salary inequities and the differential treatment of women in areas of instruction, hiring, evaluation, promotion, and institutional rewards. Unfortunately, most of these are sitting gathering dust. Little is changing. Needed, therefore, are case histories that illustrate the problems as they occurred in the past hundred years and special case histories that deal with specific disciplines. Especially telling will be comparisons of the disciplines that are held to be closed to women and those that are open to women. We can then see what "openness" means.

The quest, or the political agenda, of this book has been to overcome sexism. One of the challenges of the 1990s will be to create an environment in which talent can be expressed and nurtured, in which people can work to their greatest productive and creative potential in our academic and research environments regardless of gender, race, ethnicity, class, or age. One step in accomplishing this goal is to know the past in order to understand the present and change the future. We must assess the situation under which our professional ancestors worked in order to see the roots of perceptions and misperceptions, to set the record straight, to ask the right questions, to allow people to speak without fear of consequences for their careers, to make sure that we all overcome the same clearly identified hurdles to achieve a successful career and not be stopped by differentially erected and hidden obstacles. We are still not very far along in this quest for a humane discipline and university.

One can succeed against great odds and significantly shape anthropological understandings, public conceptions, and government policies. But we must be vigilant and ensure that women are no longer displaced in official histories of anthropology. We have a legacy that must not be forgotten and must be understood if we are ever to have a discipline that is truly based on its own conceptions of the value of diversity and the dignity of people. This will be a challenge, for anthropology has followed the pattern of the other sciences: open at first because of recognized necessity, but later, when in the process of professionalizing, marginalizing women. Periodically it would open again for a brief time, then close when the power base was threatened and when tremendous sources of money were involved. The fact that the population of women anthropologists made inroads during the 1920s, stabilized briefly during the early 1930s, declined in the next two decades as resources became scarce, and declined significantly when research funds exploded is a lesson we should all remember because it can too easily happen again.

Women are indispensable to anthropology.
Laura Thompson
(1985)

NOTES

1. The concepts of marginality, structural constraints, opportunity variables, and integrative strategies find their counterpart in the political conduct of women (Carroll 1985; Shapiro 1983).

2. Correspondence for these transactions can be found in the National Anthropological Archives, files on the American Anthropological Association.

3. Reichard, however, had intellectual rivalries with men, so the point cannot be taken too far. Although there may have been heated arguments earlier with men over specific factual and interpretative points, men were not seen as rivals, especially by women who chose a modified feminine strategy.

4. None of the women anthropologists who worked in the Southwest "went native," as Cushing is often either accused of or glorified for having done (Basso 1979).

5. Gertrude Kurath taught for years at the University of Michigan in adjunct and temporary positions. Even though she was the most prolific ethnomusicologist of her era, the world's expert on dance, since her husband was a professor in linguistics she could not break through the nepotism barrier. In addition, her field was considered marginal to both anthropology and music.

6. This does not mean that all were wealthy. Several women talked about living hand-to-mouth while they secured their Ph.D's.

7. Parsons would also finance the publication of dissertations (a prerequisite for obtaining a Ph.D. in that period), give scholarships and fellowships, underwrite the publication of her and her colleagues' work, and generally keep the professional associations solvent.

8. Marginality and discrimination often makes people more creative, empathetic, and tolerant both in their writings and in their relations with others. For example, Stocking (1976:3) asserts that "Boas' cultural marginality as Jewish German, his early field experience, and his difficulties establishing himself professionally in the United States, helped to create an experiential standpoint from which a systematic critique could be developed."

9. During this period a Ph.D. candidate had to have his or her dissertation published before the degree was officially conferred. This was a real financial hardship and one of the reasons many men and women did not finish and why others took so many years to complete their degrees.

10. "Kluckhohn had respect for women who worked in anthropology. The way he talked about Mead and Benedict and acted toward them, he had a special interest that women should be able to be in anthropology and do it" (Halpern 1985).

11. This was also a problem on women's field trips. Alexander Leighton expected Dorothea to conduct full-time research but still assume all the responsibility for their children and the household. According to Dorothea this put strains on their marriage that ultimately led to divorce.

12. At the same time there was a rich literature penned by women explorers who had traveled far and wide to remote areas of the world by themselves or with a companion.

13. Negotiated gender can only be carried so far, however. Research in U.S. society (e.g., Gurney 1985) has shown that there is a level beyond which an individual is not culturally androgynized.

REFERENCES

ARCHIVAL SOURCES OF CORRESPONDENCE

ASM   Arizona State Museum, University of Arizona, Tucson.

1936   Edward H. Spicer: Personal Correspondence. Franz Boas to E. R. Riesen.

BHP   Berard Haile Papers. (AZ 132). Box 3a, Folder 5. University Library, University of Arizona, Tucson.

Gladys Reichard to Berard Haile: March 12, 1925; January 19, 1929; February 8, 1929.

DAM   Denver Art Museum, Denver.

Thomas Cain to Frederic Douglas: July 25, 1952. Heard Museum Correspondence File in the Native Arts/Anthropology Department.

Frederic Douglas to Hester Jones: March 6, 1941. Museum of New Mexico Correspondence Files.

Frederic Douglas to Leslie Murphy: September 26, 1944. Museum of New Mexico Correspondence Files.

Frederic Douglas to Jesse Nusbaum: September 20, 1934.

Hester Jones to Frederic Douglas: January 1, 1941; March 3, 1941; September 8, 1946. Museum of New Mexico Correspondence Files.

Alice Stallings to Frederic Douglas: June 26, 1939. Laboratory of Anthropology Correspondence File.

ECP   Elsie Clews Parsons Papers. American Philosophical Society, Philadelphia.

Elsie Clews Parsons to Gladys Reichard: August 16, 1923.

Gladys Reichard to Elsie Clews Parsons: September 4, 1923; September 24, 1924; October 12, 1928; August 25, 1929; December 21, 1929; July 6, 1930; September 30, 1930; February 13, 1931; February 24, 1931; March 17, 1931; October

5, 1931; January 25, 1932; July 9, 1932; August 26, 1935; October 2, 1936; February 24, 1937; January 20, no year; n.d.

FB   Franz Boas Papers. American Philosophical Society, Philadelphia.

Ruth Bunzel to Franz Boas: August 6, 1924; July 25, 1926.

Gladys Reichard to Franz Boas: February 8, 1923.

GR   Gladys Reichard Papers. (AZ1). Museum of Northern Arizona Library, Flagstaff.

Clyde Kluckhohn to Gladys Reichard: November 12, 1943; May 9, 1947; February 24, no year.

Franc Newcomb to Gladys Reichard: May 7, 1932; January 18, 1933; May 1933.

Elsie Clews Parsons to Gladys Reichard: August 16, 1923.

Gladys Reichard to Clyde Kluckhohn: November 17, 1943.

Gladys Reichard to [Leland Wyman]: n.d.

Leland Wyman to Gladys Reichard: December 3, 1943; March 24, 1946.

HP   Hubbell Papers (AZ 375). Special Collections, Main Library, University of Arizona, Tucson.

Gladys Reichard to Roman Hubbell: October 14, 1936; March 3, 1937.

NAA   National Anthropological Archives, Smithsonian Institution, Washington, D.C.

Spencer Baird to James Stevenson: March 21, 1882.

Daniel Brinton to Matilda Coxe Stevenson: June 18, 1895.

Clifford Evans to William Fenton: June 6, 1958.

Olive E. Hite to Frank Baker: January 22, 1898. AAA Files.

Frederick W. Hodge to Matilda Coxe Stevenson: June 2, 1911; June 14, 1913.

William H. Holmes to Matilda Coxe Stevenson: March 28, 1906.

Anita Newcombe McGee to Matilda Coxe
Stevenson: November 18, 1891.

W J McGee to Frank Russell: January 9,
1901.

Sophie A. Nordhoff-Jung to Matilda Coxe
Stevenson: January 31, 1909.

John Wesley Powell to SPL: May 20, 1902.

John Wesley Powell to W J McGee: August
14, 1901.

John Wesley Powell to Matilda Coxe Stevenson: March 15, 1890; August 1,
1901; January 21, 1902.

Frederick W. Putnam to Matilda Coxe Stevenson: n.d.

A. B. Reneham to Matilda Coxe Stevenson:
November 30, 1908.

Matilda Coxe Stevenson to Frederick W.
Hodge: May 13, 1912; May 28, 1914;
March 4, 1914; October 10, 1914; Octo-
ber 23, 1914.

Matilda Coxe Stevenson to William H.
Holmes: October 8, 1901; February 12,
1906; March 28, 1906; July 12, 1906;
n.d., 1906; July 3, 1908; January 24,
1910; February 13, 1912.

Matilda Coxe Stevenson to W J McGee:
July 3, 1901.

Matilda Coxe Stevenson to John Wesley
Powell: May 23, 1900; August 15, 1900;
June 3, 1901; August 30, 1902.

Matilda Coxe Stevenson to A. B. Reneham:
September 21, 1909; March 21, 1910.

Matilda Coxe Stevenson to Hermann
Schweitzer: September 16, 1914.

Matilda Coxe Stevenson to G. H. Van
Stone: June 15, 1890; June 15, 1914.

Matilda Coxe Stevenson to Charles D. Walcott: November 17, 1908; December 1,
1908; February 6, 1909; May 8, 1909;
May 1909.

Matilda Coxe Stevenson to John E. Watkins: June 15, 1914.

Frances True to A. B. Reneham: June 30,
1900.

RBP   Ruth Benedict Papers. Correspondence.
Vassar College, Poughkeepsie, N.Y.
Ruth Fulton to Florence Keys: 1910.

Frank Lillie to Elsie Clews Parsons: May 23,
1924.

Edward Sapir to Ruth Benedict: March 16,
1931.

REFERENCES

AAW [Ruth Benedict]. 1973. *An Anthropologist at
Work,* ed. Margaret Mead. New York: Avon
Books.

Aberle, David. 1961. Navaho Kinship. In *Matrilineal Kinship,* ed. David M. Schneider and Kathleen Gough, pp. 96–201. Berkeley: University Press.

————. 1966. *The Peyote Religion among the Navaho.*
Chicago: Aldine.

————. 1973. Clyde Kluckhohn's Contributions to
Navajo Studies. In *Culture and Life,* ed. Walter W. Taylor, John L. Fischer, and Evon Z.
Vogt, pp. 83–93. Carbondale: Southern Illinois University Press.

————. 1986. Discussion Comments, March 17.
Daughters of the Desert Conference. Globe,
Ariz.: Wenner-Gren Foundation for Anthro-
pological Research.

Aberle, Sophie F. 1931. Frequency of Pregnancies and
Birth Interval among Pueblo Indians. *American Journal of Physical Anthropology* 16:63–80.

————. 1932. Child Mortality among Pueblo Indians. *American Journal of Physical Anthropology*
16:339–49.

————. 1934. Maternal Mortality among the Pueblos. *American Journal of Physical Anthropology*
18:431–35.

————. 1948. *The Pueblo Indians of New Mexico: Their
Land, Economy and Civil Organization.* Memoirs of the American Anthropological Association No. 70. Menasha, Wis.: American
Anthropological Association.

Aberle, Sophie D., J. H. Watkins, and E. H. Pitney.
1940. The Vital History of San Juan Pueblo.
Human Biology 12:141–87.

Ablon, Joan. 1964. Relocated American Indians in
the San Francisco Bay Area. *Human Organization* 23:296–304.

————. 1965. American Indian Relocation: Problems of Dependency and Management in the City. *Phylon* 26:4 (Atlanta University).

Abramson, Joan. 1975. *The Invisible Woman: Discrimination in the Academic Profession.* San Francisco: Jossey-Bass.

Adair, John. 1944. *The Navajo and Pueblo Silversmiths.* Norman: University of Oklahoma Press.

————. 1960. The Indian Health Worker in the Cornell Navajo Project. *Human Organization* 19:59–63.

————. 1963. Physicians, Medicine Men, and Their Navajo Patients. In *Man's Image in Medicine and Anthropology,* ed. Iago Galdston, pp. 237–57. New York: International Universities Press.

Adair, John, and Kurt Deuschle. 1957. Some Problems of the Physicians on the Navaho Reservation. *Human Organization* 16:19–23.

————. 1970. *The People's Health: Anthropology and Medicine in a Navajo Community.* New York: Appleton-Century-Crofts.

Adair, John, et al. 1957. Patterns of Health and Disease among the Navajos. *The Annals* 311 (May): 80–94.

Ad Hoc Committee, American Anthropological Association. 1979. Report. *Anthropology Newsletter* January: 1.

Aisenberg, Nadya, and Mona Harrington. 1988. *Women of Academe: Outsiders in the Sacred Grove.* Amherst: University of Massachusetts Press.

Aitken, Barbara. 1956. A Trance Experience. *Plateau* 28(3): 67–70.

American Anthropological Association. 1986. *Guide to Departments of Anthropology.* 25th ed. Washington, D.C.: American Anthropological Association.

————. 1987. *Anthropology Newsletter* 27(4).

American Association of Museums. 1973. *Museum Accreditation: Professional Standards.* Washington, D.C.: American Association of Museums.

Amsden, Charles. 1938. Review of *Navajo Shepherd and Weaver* by Gladys Reichard. *American Anthropologist* 40(4): 724–25.

Anderson, Richard. 1979. *Art in Primitive Societies.* Englewood Cliffs, N.J.: Prentice-Hall.

Angrist, S. S., and E. M. Almquist. 1975. *Careers and Contingencies: How College Women Judge with Gender.* New York: Dunellen.

Angrosino, M. V. 1986. Son and Lover: The Anthropologist as Non-Threatening Male. In *Self, Sex and Gender in Cross-Cultural Fieldwork,* ed. T. L. Whitehead and Mary Ellen Conaway, pp. 64–83. Urbana: University of Illinois Press.

Anonymous. 1885. *The Organization and Constitution of the Women's Anthropological Society.* Washington, D.C.: Privately printed.

————. 1889. The Women's Anthropological Society of America. *Science* 13(321): 240–42.

————. 1929. Stevenson, Matilda Coxe. *National Cyclopedia of American Biography,* 20:53–54. New York: James T. White.

————. 1931. Women Students among Indians. *El Palacio* 31(12): 184–86.

————. 1938. Women in Our Economy. *Journal of the American Association of University Women* 31(3): 171.

————. 1971. Dr. Harold Sellers Colton (1881–1970), Obituary. *Plateau* 43(4): 147.

————. 1980. Papago Tribe Honors Ruth Murray Underhill. *Anthropology Newsletter* March: 3.

————. 1981. *Higher Education.* Washington, D.C.: National Center for Educational Statistics.

————. 1984. *Digest of Educational Statistics.* Washington, D.C.: National Center for Educational Statistics.

————. 1988a. *Higher Education.* Washington, D.C.: National Center for Educational Statistics.

————. 1988b. A Two-Tiered Faculty System Reflects Old Social Rules that Restrict Women's Professional Development. *Chronicle of Higher Education* Oct. 26: A56.

Arendt, Hannah. 1951. *The Origins of Totalitarianism.* New York: Harcourt Brace.

Arnold, Dean E. 1983. Design Structure and Community Organization in Quina, Peru. In *Structure and Cognition in Art,* ed. Dorothy K. Washburn, pp. 56–73. Cambridge: Cambridge University Press.

Asad, Talal. 1973. Introduction. In *Anthropology and the Colonial Encounter,* ed. Talal Asad, pp. 9–20. New York: Humanities Press.

Astin, Helen S. 1969. *The Woman Doctorate in Amer-*

ica: Origins, Careers, and Family. New York: Russell Sage Foundation.

Astin, Helen S., and Alan E. Bayer. 1973. Sex Discrimination in Academe. In *Academic Women on the Move,* ed. Alice Rossi and A. Calderwood, pp. 139–79. New York: Russell Sage Foundation.

Babcock, Barbara A. 1982. Clay Voices: Invoking, Mocking, Celebrating. In *Celebrations: Studies in Festivity and Ritual,* ed. Victor Turner, pp. 58–76. Washington, D.C.: Smithsonian Institution Press.

———. 1983. Clay Changes: Helen Cordero and the Pueblo Storyteller. *American Indian Art* 8(2): 30–39.

———. 1985. Modeled Selves: Helen Cordero's "Little People." In *The Anthropology of Experience,* ed. Edward Bruner and Victor Turner, pp. 316–48. Urbana: University of Illinois Press.

———. 1986. Discussion Comments. Daughters of the Desert Conference. Globe, Ariz.: Wenner-Gren Foundation for Anthropological Research.

———. 1990. By Way of Introduction. *Journal of the Southwest* 32(4): 383–99.

———. 1991. Introduction. In *Pueblo Mothers and Children: Essays by Elsie Clews Parsons, 1915–1924,* ed. Barbara Babcock, pp. 1–27. Santa Fe, N.M.: Ancient City Press.

Babcock, Barbara A., and Nancy J. Parezo. 1988. *Daughters of the Desert: Women Anthropologists and the Native American Southwest, 1880–1980: An Illustrated Catalogue.* Albuquerque: University of New Mexico Press.

———. 1990. Review of *Ruth Benedict* by Margaret M. Caffrey. *American Anthropologist* 92(4): 1093–94.

Bailey, Flora. 1948. Suggested Techniques for Inducing Navaho Women to Accept Hospitalization during Childbirth and for Implementing Health Education. *American Journal of Public Health* 38: 1418–23.

———. 1951. Review of *Navaho Religion: A Study of Symbolism* by Gladys Reichard. *Journal of American Folklore* 64(254): 434–36.

Baird, Spencer. 1885. *Annual Report of the Smithsonian Institution for 1884.* Washington, D.C.: GPO.

Barber, B. 1962. *Science and the Social Order.* New York: Collier Books.

Barnouw, Victor. 1949. Ruth Benedict: Apollonian and Dionysian. *University of Toronto Quarterly* 3: 241–53.

Bartimus, Ted. 1989. Walking Resource Guide since 1930, Katharine Bartlett Has Been Contributing to the Museum. *The Flagstaff Sun,* September 20, p. A6.

Bartlett, Katharine. 1985. Interview (with Jennifer Fox) for the Daughters of the Desert Oral History Project. August 24, Flagstaff, Ariz. Audio Recording. New York: Wenner-Gren Foundation for Anthropological Research.

Basso, Keith H. 1973. Southwestern Ethnology: A Critical Review. *Annual Review of Anthropology* 3: 221–52.

———. 1979. History of Ethnological Research. In *Southwest,* vol. 9 of *Handbook of North American Indians,* ed. Alfonso Ortiz, pp. 14–21. Washington, D.C.: Smithsonian Institution Press.

Bastide, Robert. 1974. *Applied Anthropology.* New York: Harper and Row.

Bateson, Mary Catherine. 1984. *With a Daughter's Eye: A Memoir of Margaret Mead and Gregory Bateson.* New York: William Morrow and Co.

Beals, Ralph L. 1943. *The Aboriginal Culture of the Cahita Indians.* Ibero-Americana No. 19. Berkeley and Los Angeles: University of California Press.

———. 1945. *The Contemporary Culture of the Cahita Indians.* Bureau of American Ethnology Bulletin No. 142. Washington, D.C.: GPO.

Ben-Ari, Eyal. 1987. On Acknowledgements in Ethnographies. *Journal of Anthropological Research* 43(1): 63–84.

Bender, Norman J., ed. 1984. *Missionaries, Outlaws, and Indians: Taylor F. Ealy at Lincoln and Zuni, 1878–1881.* Albuquerque: University of New Mexico Press.

Bendixon, Brigitte. 1979. Aspects of Rhythmical Structure of Cocopa. In *Proceedings of the 1978 Hokan Languages Workshop,* ed. James E. Redden, pp. 72–90. Occasional Papers on Linguistics No. 5. Carbondale: Southern Illinois University.

———. 1980. Phonological and Temporal Properties in Cocopa. Unpublished Ph.D. dissertation, University of California, San Diego.

Benedict, Ruth. 1923a. *The Concept of the Guardian Spirit in North America.* In Memoirs of the American Anthropological Association No. 29, pp. 1–97. Menasha, Wis.: American Anthropological Association.

———. 1923b. Critical Note of the Relation of Folklore to Custom, etc. *Journal of American Folklore* 36:104.

———. 1924a. A Brief Sketch of Serrano Culture. *American Anthropologist* 26:366–92.

———. 1924b. Research Proposal 2. Ruth Benedict Papers, Vassar College, Poughkeepsie, N.Y.

———. 1928. Eucharist. *The Nation* 1927:296.

———. 1929. The Science of Custom. *Century Magazine* 117(6): 641–49.

———. 1930a. Psychological Types in the Cultures of the Southwest. In *Proceedings of the 23rd International Congress of Americanists,* September 1928, pp. 572–81. New York: The Science Press. (Reprinted in *An Anthropologist at Work,* ed. Margaret Mead, pp. 258–61. New York: Avon Books, 1959.)

———. 1930b. Animism. *Encyclopedia of Social Sciences,* vol. 3, ed. Edwin R. A. Seligman, pp. 65–67. New York: Macmillan.

———. 1930c. Child Marriage. *Encyclopedia of the Social Sciences,* vol. 3, ed. Edwin R. A. Seligman, pp. 395–97. New York: Macmillan.

———. 1930d. Eight Stories from Acoma. *Journal of American Folklore* 43:59–87.

———. 1931a. *Tales of the Cochiti Indians.* Bulletin of the Bureau of American Ethnology No. 98. Washington, D.C.: GPO.

———. 1931b. Folklore. *Encyclopedia of the Social Sciences,* vol. 6, ed. Edwin R. A. Seligman, pp. 288–93. New York: Macmillan.

———. 1931c. Dress. *Encyclopedia of the Social Sciences,* vol. 5, ed. Edwin R. A. Seligman, pp. 235–38. New York: Macmillan.

———. 1932. Configurations of Culture in North America. *American Anthropologist* 34:1–27.

———. 1933a. Myth. *Encyclopedia of the Social Sciences,* vol. 11, ed. Edwin R. A. Seligman, pp. 178–81. New York: Macmillan.

———. 1933b. Magic. *Encyclopedia of the Social Sci-*

ences, vol. 10, ed. Edwin R. A. Seligman, pp. 39–44. New York: Macmillan

———. 1934a. Anthropology and the Abnormal. *Journal of General Psychology* 10:59–82. (Reprinted in *An Anthropologist at Work,* ed. Margaret Mead, pp. 262–83. New York: Avon Books, 1959.)

———. 1934b. *Patterns of Culture.* Boston: Houghton Mifflin.

———. 1934c. Ritual. *Encyclopedia of the Social Sciences,* vol. 13, ed. Edwin R. A. Seligman, pp. 396–98. New York: Macmillan.

———. 1935. *Zuni Mythology.* 2 vols. Columbia University Contributions to Anthropology Vol. 21. New York: Columbia University.

———. 1938. Religion. In *General Anthropology,* ed. Franz Boas, pp. 627–65. Boston: Heath.

———. 1940a. *Race: Science and Politics.* New York: Modern Age.

———. 1940b. Review of *Pueblo Indian Religion* by Elsie Clews Parsons. *Review of Religion* 4: 438–40.

———. 1940c. Women and Anthropology. In *The Education of Women in a Democracy.* New York: The Institute of Professional Relations for the Women's Centennial Congress, November 1940.

———. 1940d. Women and Anthropology. In *Report of the Commission on Education and the Woman's Centennial Congress in New York City, 1940.* (Reprinted in *Women's Work and Education* 11 (3): 11.)

———. 1942a. Anthropology and Cultural Change. *The American Scholar* 11(2): 243–48.

———. 1942b. Primitive Freedom. *Atlantic Monthly* 169:756–63. (Reprinted in *Ruth Benedict,* ed. Margaret Mead, pp. 134–46. New York: Columbia University Press, 1974.)

———. 1943. Franz Boas as an Ethnologist. In *Franz Boas, 1858–1942,* ed. Alfred Kroeber, pp. 27–34. Memoirs of the American Anthropological Association No. 61. Menasha, Wis.: American Anthropological Association.

———. 1946. *The Chrysanthemum and the Sword: Patterns of Japanese Culture.* Boston: Houghton Mifflin.

———. 1948. Anthropology and the Humanities. *American Anthropologist* 50:585–93. (Reprinted in *Ruth Benedict,* ed. Margaret Mead, pp. 165–76. New York: Columbia University Press, 1974.)

———. 1959. *Patterns of Culture.* Boston and New York: Houghton Mifflin [1934].

———. n.d. Adventures in Womanhood. Unpublished ms. on file, Ruth Benedict Papers, Vassar College, Poughkeepsie, N.Y.

Benedict, Ruth Fulton, and Gene Weltfish. 1943. *The Races of Mankind.* Public Affairs Pamphlet No. 85. New York: Public Affairs Committee.

Bennett, John W. 1946. The Interpretation of Pueblo Culture: A Question of Values. *Southwestern Journal of Anthropology* 2(4): 361–74.

Bernal, Ignacio. 1980. *A History of Mexican Archaeology: The Vanished Civilizations of Middle America.* London: Thames and Hudson, Ltd.

Bernard, Jessie. 1964. *Academic Women.* University Park: Pennsylvania State University Press.

Bernstein, Bruce D., and Susan Brown McGreevy. 1988. *Anii Anaadaalyaa'igii: Continuity and Innovation in Recent Navajo Art.* Santa Fe, N.M.: Wheelwright Museum of the American Indian.

Bidney, David. 1953. *Theoretical Anthropology.* New York: Columbia University Press.

Bishop, Ronald, and Frederick W. Lange, eds. 1991. *The Ceramic Legacy of Anna O. Shepard.* Boulder: University Press of Colorado.

Blackburn, Robert T., David W. Chapman, and Susan M. Cameron. 1981. Cloning in Academe: Mentorship and Academic Careers. *Research in Higher Education* 5: 315–27.

Blitz, Rudolph C. 1974. Women in the Professions, 1870–1970. *Monthly Labor Review* 97(5): 30–41.

Boas, Franz. 1888. The Aims of Ethnology. In *Race, Language, and Culture* by Franz Boas, pp. 626–38. New York: Macmillan (1940).

———. 1902. The Ethnological Significance of Esoteric Doctrines. In *Race, Language, and Culture* by Franz Boas, pp. 312–15. New York: Macmillan (1940).

———. 1928. *Anthropology and Modern Life.* New York: W. W. Norton.

———. 1938. An Anthropologist's Credo. *The Nation* 147(9): 201–4. (Reprinted and expanded as "I Believe." In *I Believe,* ed. Clifton Fadi-

man, pp. 19–29. New York: Simon and Schuster, 1938.)

———. 1940. *Race, Language, and Culture.* New York: Macmillan.

———. 1942a. Elsie Clews Parsons, Late President of the American Anthropological Association. *The Scientific Monthly* 54: 480–82.

———. 1942b. Elsie Clews Parsons. *Science* 95: 89–90.

———. 1955. *Primitive Art.* New York: Dover [1927].

———. 1966. *Kwakiutl Ethnography.* Chicago: University of Chicago Press.

Boas, Franz, ed. 1938. *General Anthropology.* Boston: Heath.

Bock, Philip K. 1989. Anthropology at the University of New Mexico, 1928–1988: A Trial Formulation. *Journal of Anthropological Research* 45(1): 1–14.

Bodine, John J. 1988. The Taos Blue Lake Ceremony. *American Indian Quarterly* 12(2): 91–126.

Bogan, Phebe M. 1925. *Yaqui Indian Dances of Tucson, Arizona.* Tucson, Ariz.: The Archaeological Society.

———. 1926. The Yaqui Indian Dances. *Progressive Arizona* 2(5): 21–22, 35.

Bohannan, Paul, and Mark Glazer, eds. 1973. *High Points in Anthropology.* New York: Alfred A. Knopf.

Bohrer, Vorsilla L. 1979. Bertha Pauline Dutton: A Bibliography. In *Collected Papers in Honor of Bertha Pauline Dutton,* ed. Albert H. Schroeder, pp. 1–32. Papers of the Archaeological Society of New Mexico Vol. 4. Albuquerque: Archaeological Society of New Mexico.

Boon, James A. 1982. *Other Tribes, Other Scribes: Symbolic Anthropology in the Comparative Study of Cultures, Histories, Religions, and Texts.* Cambridge: Cambridge University Press.

———. 1983. Functionalists Write Too: Frazer/Malinowski and the Semiotics of the Monograph. *Semiotica* 46(2/4): 131–49.

———. 1984. Folly, Bali, and Anthropology or Satire Across Cultures. In *Text, Play, and Story: The Construction and Reconstruction of Self and Society,* ed. Edward M. Bruner, pp. 156–77. Washington, D.C.: The American Ethnological Association.

———. 1985. Mead's Meditations: Some Semiotics

from the Sepik, by Way of Bateson, on to Bali. In *Semiotic Mediation: Sociocultural and Psychological Perspectives,* ed. Elizabeth Mertz and Richard J. Parmentier, pp. 333–57. Orlando, Fla.: Academic Press.

Bossidy, John Collins. 1910. Toast, Holy Cross Alumni Dinner. Worcester, Mass.

Bourne, Randolph. 1917. A Modern Mind [Review of *Social Rule*]. *The Dial* 62:239–40.

Bowen, Eleanor S. 1954. *Return to Laughter.* Garden City, NY: Doubleday.

Boyd, E. 1974. *Popular Arts of Spanish New Mexico.* Santa Fe: Museum of New Mexico Press.

Boyer, Paul S. 1971. Parsons, Elsie Clews. In *Notable American Women, 1607–1950,* vol. 3, ed. Edward T. James, pp. 20–22. Cambridge, Mass.: Harvard University Press.

Brew, J. O., ed. 1968. *One Hundred Years of Anthropology.* Cambridge, Mass.: Harvard University Press.

Bright, William. 1982. *Bibliography of the Languages of Native California.* Metuchen, N.J.: Scarecrow Press.

Briscoe, Virginia Wolf. 1979. Ruth Benedict, Anthropological Folklorist. *Journal of American Folklore* 92(366): 445–76.

Britenthal, Renate, and Claudia Konz. 1976. Beyond Kinder, Kuche, Kirche: Weimar Women in Politics and Work. In *Liberating Women's History: Theoretical and Critical Essays,* ed. Bernice A. Carroll. Urbana: University of Illinois Press.

Brody, J. J. 1971. *Indian Painters and White Patrons.* Albuquerque: University of New Mexico Press.

Brophy, William A., and Sophie D. Aberle, compilers. 1966. *The Indian: America's Unfinished Business.* Report of the Commission on the Rights and Responsibilities of the American Indian. Norman: University of Oklahoma Press.

Bruner, E., and Victor Turner. 1986. *The Anthropology of Experience.* Urbana: University of Illinois Press.

Bunzel, Ruth. 1932a. Introduction to Zuni Ceremonialism. In *47th Annual Report of the Bureau of American Ethnology for 1929–1930,* pp. 467–544. Washington, D.C.: GPO.

———. 1932b. Zuni Origin Myths. In *47th Annual Report of the Bureau of American Ethnology for the Years 1929–1930,* pp. 545–609. Washington, D.C.: GPO.

———. 1932c. Zuni Kachinas. In *47th Annual Report of the Bureau of the American Ethnology for the Years 1929–1930,* pp. 837–1086. Washington, D.C.: GPO.

———. 1932d. Zuni Ritual Poetry. In *47th Annual Report of the Bureau of the American Ethnology for the Years 1929–1930,* pp. 611–835. Washington, D.C.: GPO.

———. 1933. *Zuni Texts.* Publications of the American Ethnological Society No. 15. New York: G. E. Stechert.

———. 1935. Zuni. In *Handbook of American Indian Languages,* vol. 4, ed. Franz Boas, pp. 388–515. New York: Columbia University Press.

———. 1938a. The Economic Organization of Primitive Peoples. In *General Anthropology,* ed. Franz Boas, pp. 327–408. New York: D. C. Heath.

———. 1938b. Art. In *General Anthropology,* ed. Franz Boas, pp. 535–88. New York: D. C. Heath.

———. 1952. *Chichicastenango, a Guatemalan Village.* Publications of the American Ethnological Society No. 22. New York: J. J. Augustin.

———. 1953. Psychology of the Pueblo Potter. In *Primitive Heritage,* ed. Margaret Mead and Nicolas Calas, pp. 266–75. New York: Random House [1929].

———. 1955. Gladys A. Reichard—A Tribute. In a memorial booklet published by Barnard College.

———. 1960. Section Introductions. In *The Golden Age of American Anthropology,* ed. Margaret Mead and Ruth L. Bunzel. New York: George Braziller.

———. 1972. *The Pueblo Potter: A Study of Creative Imagination in Primitive Art.* New York: Dover Publications. [Original published by Columbia University Press, New York, 1929.]

———. 1983. Interview with Charles Wagley. University of Florida. Ms. on file at Wenner-Gren Foundation for Anthropological Research and Smithsonian Institution.

———. 1985. Interview (with Jennifer Fox) for Daughters of the Desert Oral History Project. July 2, New York, NY. Video Recording.

New York: Wenner-Gren Foundation for Anthropological Research.

Bureau of Indian Affairs. 1942. Outline for use in the Pilot Study, Research on the Development of Indian Personality. Washington, D.C.: National Archives.

Burton, R. E., and R. W. Kebler. 1960. The "Half-Life" of Some Scientific and Technical Literatures. *American Documentation* 11:18–22.

Caffrey, Margaret M. 1989. *Ruth Benedict: Stranger in This Land.* Austin: University of Texas Press.

Caldwell, A. Ellis. 1921. Preliminary Report of Committee W on the Status of Women in College and University Faculties. *AAUP Bulletin* 8(6): 21–32.

Carnegie Commission on Higher Education. 1973. *Opportunities for Women in Higher Education.* New York: McGraw Hill.

Carroll, Susan. 1985. *Women as Candidates in American Politics.* Bloomington: Indiana University Press.

Cattell, James McKeen, ed. 1933. *American Men in Science.* New York: Science Press.

Caudill, William. 1953. Applied Anthropology in Medicine. In *Anthropology Today,* ed. A. L. Kroeber, pp. 771–806. Chicago: University of Chicago Press.

Chamberlain, Mariam, ed. 1988. *Women in Academe: Progress and Prospects.* New York: Russell Sage Foundation.

Chambers, Keith S. 1973. The Indefatigable Elsie Clews Parsons—Folklorist. *Western Folklore* 32:180–98.

Chase, Katherine. 1982. *Mary-Russell Ferrell Colton and the Museum of Northern Arizona.* Flagstaff: Arizona Bank.

Chase, Richard. 1959. Ruth Benedict: The Woman as Anthropologist. *Columbia University Forum* 2(3): 19–22.

Chauvenet, Beatrice. 1983. *Hewett and Friends: A Biography of Santa Fe's Vibrant Era.* Santa Fe: Museum of New Mexico Press.

Clement, Dorothy C. 1976. Cognitive Anthropology and Applied Problems. In *Do Applied Anthropologists Apply Anthropology?* ed. Michael Angrosino, pp. 53–71. Southern Anthropological Society Proceedings No. 10. Athens: University of Georgia Press.

Clifford, James. 1981. On Ethnographic Surrealism. *Comparative Studies in Society and History* 23(4): 539–64.

———. 1983. On Ethnographic Authority. *Representations* 1(2): 118–46.

———. 1984. Dada Data. *Sulfur* 10:162–64.

———. 1988. *The Predicament of Culture.* Cambridge, Mass.: Harvard University Press.

Clifford, James, and George Marcus, eds. 1986. *Writing Culture: The Poetics and Politics of Ethnography.* Berkeley: University of California Press.

Codere, Helen. 1986. Field Work in Rwanda. In *Women in the Field: Anthropological Experiences,* ed. Peggy Golde, pp. 143–64. Berkeley: University of California Press.

Cole, Jonathan R. 1970. Patterns of Intellectual Influence in Scientific Research. *Sociology of Education* 43:377–403.

———. 1979. *Fair Science: Women in the Scientific Community.* New York: Free Press.

Cole, Stephen, and Jonathan R. Cole. 1968. Visibility and the Structural Bases of Observability in Science. *American Sociological Review* 33: 397–413.

———. 1973. *Social Stratification in Science.* Chicago: University of Chicago Press.

Collier, Don, and William N. Fenton. 1965. Problems of Ethnological Research in North American Museums. *MAN* 65(100): 111–12.

Collier, Jane, and Sylvia Yanagisako. 1987. *Gender and Kinship: Essays toward a Unified Analysis.* Stanford, Calif.: Stanford University Press.

Collier, John. 1944. Collier Replies to Mekeel. *American Anthropologist* 46:422–26.

Collier, Malcolm C., and E. S. Dethlefsen. 1968. Anthropology and the Pre-Collegiate Curriculum. *Human Organization* 27:11–16.

Colson, Elizabeth. 1970. Report of the Subcommittee on the State of Academic Women on the Berkeley Campus, 1970. Green Hearing, Discrimination Against Women, Hearings before the Special Subcommittee on Education of the Committee on Education and Labor, House of Representatives, 91st Cong., 2d Sess. on Section 805 of HR 16098, pp. 1143–1221. Washington, D.C.: GPO.

Colton, Mary-Russell Ferrell. 1965. *Hopi Dyes.* Museum of Northern Arizona Bulletin No. 41.

Flagstaff: Museum of Northern Arizona.

Conkey, Margaret W. 1978. Participation in the Research Process: Getting Grants. Paper presented at the 77th Annual Meeting of the American Anthropological Association, Los Angeles.

———. 1982. Archaeological Research, Gender Paradigms, and Invisible Behavior. Paper presented at the 81st Annual Meeting of the American Anthropological Association, Washington, D.C.

Conkey, Margaret W., and Janet D. Spector. 1984. Archaeology and the Study of Gender. In *Advances in Archaeological Method and Theory,* vol. 7, ed. Michael Schiffer, pp. 1–38. Orlando, Fla.: Academic Press.

Cordell, Linda S. 1984. *Prehistory of the Southwest.* Orlando, Fla.: Academic Press.

———. 1991a. Sisters of the Sun and Spade: Women Archaeologists in the Southwest. In *The Archaeology of Gender,* ed. Dale Walde and Noreen Willows, pp. 502–9. *Proceedings of the 22nd Annual Chacmool Conference.* Calgary: The Archaeological Association of the University of Calgary.

———. 1991b. Anna O. Shepard and Southwestern Archaeology: Ignoring a Cautious Heretic. In *The Ceramic Legacy of Anna O. Shepard,* ed. Ronald Bishop and Frederick Lange, pp. 132–53. Boulder: University Press of Colorado.

Couro, Ted, and Margaret Langdon. n.d. *Let's Talk "Iipay Aa": An Introduction to the Mesa Grande Diegueno Language.* Ramona, Calif.: Ballena Press.

Cowan, J. Milton. 1979. Linguistics at War. In *The Uses of Anthropology,* ed. Walter Goldschmidt, pp. 158–68. American Anthropological Association Publication No. 4. Washington, D.C.: American Anthropological Association.

Crampton, C. Gregory. 1977. *The Zunis of Cibola.* Salt Lake City: University of Utah Press.

Crane, Diana. 1972. *Invisible Colleges: Diffusion of Knowledge in Scientific Communities.* Chicago: University of Chicago Press.

Croly, Jane C. 1898. *The History of the Women's Club Movement in America.* New York: Knopf.

Crumrine, Lynne S. 1961. *The Phonology of Arizona*

Yaqui. Anthropological Papers of the University of Arizona No. 5. Tucson: University of Arizona.

Crutchfield, R. S., and D. Krech. 1962. Some Guides to the Understanding of the History of Psychology. In *Psychology in the Making,* ed. Leo Postman, pp. 3–27. New York: Knopf.

Curtis, Natalie. 1907. *The Indians' Book.* New York: Harper and Brothers.

Cushing, Frank Hamilton. 1882–1883. My Adventures in Zuni. *Century Illustrated Monthly Magazine* 25:191–207, 500–11, 26:28–47.

———. 1886. A Study of Pueblo Pottery as Illustrative of Zuni Culture Growth. In *Fourth Annual Report of the Bureau of American Ethnology,* pp. 476–521. Washington, D.C.: GPO.

Cushing, Frank Hamilton, J. Walter Fewkes, and Elsie C. Parsons. 1922. Contributions to Hopi History. *American Anthropologist* 24(3): 253–98.

D'Andrade, Roy. 1975. Minorities in Anthropology Higher Degree Programs. *Anthropology Newsletter* 16(9): 19–23.

D'Andrade, R. G., E. A. Hammel, D. L. Adkins, and C. K. McDaniel. 1975. Academic Opportunity in Anthropology, 1974–1990. *American Anthropologist* 77:753–73.

Daniel, Glyn. 1976. *A Hundred and Fifty Years of Archaeology.* Cambridge, Mass.: Harvard University Press.

Darnell, Regina. 1972. The Professionalization of American Anthropology: A Case Study in the Sociology of Knowledge. *Social Science Information* 20(2): 83–103.

Deegan, Mary Jo. 1978. Women and Sociology. *Journal of the History of Sociology* 1:11–32.

de Laguna, Frederica. 1955. Gladys Reichard: Appreciation and Appraisal. In a memorial booklet published by Barnard College.

Delamont, Sara. 1987. Three Blind Spots? A Comment on the Sociology of Science by a Puzzled Outsider. *Social Studies of Science* 17:163–70.

Delgado, Richard. 1984. *The Imperial Scholar: Reflections on a Review of Civil Rights Literature.* University of Pennsylvania Law Review No. 132. Philadelphia: University of Pennsylvania.

Denmark, F. L. 1980. Psyche: From Rocking the

Cradle to Rocking the Boat. *American Psychologist* 35 : 1057–65.

Densmore, Francis. 1941. The Study of Indian Music. In *Annual Report of the Smithsonian Institution,* pp. 527–50. Washington, D.C.: Smithsonian Institution.

Dobyns, Henry F. 1970. Therapeutic Experiences of Responsible Democracy. In *The American Indian Today,* ed. Stuart Levine and Nancy O. Lurie, pp. 171–85. Baltimore, Md.: Penguin Books.

Dodson, Shirleen L. 1986. Smithsonian Women: Seizing the Opportunities. In *Women's Changing Roles in Museums,* ed. Ellen C. Hickes, pp. 35–37. Washington, D.C.: Smithsonian Institution.

Dolby, R. G. A. 1971. Sociology of Knowledge in Natural Science. *Science Studies* 1 : 1–21.

Douglas, J. D. 1979. *Investigative Social Research: Individual and Team Field Research.* Newbury Park, Calif.: Sage.

Douvan, Elizabeth. 1976. The Role of Models in Women's Professional Development. *Psychology of Women Quarterly* 1(1): 5–20.

Dozier, Edward P. 1963. Review of Elsie Clews Parsons' *Isleta Paintings* (ed. Esther S. Goldfrank). *American Anthropologist* 65(4): 936–37.

———. 1970. *The Pueblo Indians of North America.* New York: Holt, Rinehart and Winston.

Dumarest, Father Noel. 1919. *Notes on Cochiti, New Mexico,* ed. Elsie Clews Parsons, pp. 139–236. Memoirs of the American Anthropological Association No. 6. Menasha, Wis.: American Anthropological Association.

Dunham, Ralph, Patricia Wright, and Marjorie O. Chandler. 1964. *Teaching Faculty in Universities and Four-Year Colleges.* Washington, D.C.: Office of Education.

Dunn, Dorothy. 1960. The Studio of Painting, Santa Fe Indian School. *El Palacio* 67(1): 16–27.

———. 1968. *American Indian Painting of the Southwest and Plains Areas.* Albuquerque: University of New Mexico Press.

Dutton, Bertha. 1948. *New Mexico Indians.* Santa Fe: Museum of New Mexico.

———. 1957. *Indian Artistry in Wood and Other Media: An Exhibition in the Hall of Ethnology, Museum of New Mexico.* Papers of the School of American Research and Museum of New Mexico No. 47. Santa Fe, N.M.: School of American Research.

———. 1963a. *Sun Father's Way: The Kiva Murals of Kuaua.* Albuquerque and Santa Fe: University of New Mexico Press and The School of American Research.

———. 1963b. *Navajo Weaving Today.* Santa Fe: Museum of New Mexico Press.

———. 1965. *Indians of the American Southwest.* Englewood Cliffs, N.J.: Prentice-Hall.

———. 1966. Prehistoric Migrations into the Galisteo Basin, New Mexico. *Actas y Memorias, XXXVI Congreso Internacional de Americanistas,* pp. 1287–99. Seville, Spain: Universidad de Sevilla (1964).

———. 1970. *Let's Explore Indian Villages Past and Present.* Santa Fe: Museum of New Mexico Press.

———. 1981. Excavation Tests at the Pueblo Ruins of Abo, Part 1. In *Collected Papers in Honor of Erik Kellerman Reed,* ed. Albert H. Schroeder, pp. 177–95. Papers of the Archaeological Society of New Mexico No. 6. Albuquerque: Archaeological Society Press.

———. 1983. *American Indians of the Southwest.* Revised edition. Albuquerque: University of New Mexico Press.

———. 1985a. Interview (with Jennifer Fox) for the Daughter of the Desert Oral History Project. August 1 & 2, Santa Fe, N.M. Audio and Video Recording. New York: Wenner-Gren Foundation for Anthropological Research.

———. 1985b. Excavations at the Pueblo Ruins of Abo, Part 2. In *Prehistory and History in the Southwest, Collected Papers in Honor of Alden C. Hayes,* ed. Nancy J. Fox, pp. 9–104. The Archaeological Society of New Mexico, No. 11. Santa Fe, N.M.: Ancient City Press.

Dutton, Bertha A., and Caroline B. Olin. 1978. *Myths and Legends of the Indians of the Southwest.* San Francisco: Bellerophon.

Easterday, L. D., D. Papademas, L. Schor, and C. Valentine. 1977. The Making of a Female Researcher: Role Problems in Field Work. *Urban Life* 9(3): 333–48.

Edmunson, Munro S. 1973. The Anthropology of Values. In *Culture and Life*, ed. Walter W. Tylor, John L. Fischer, and Evon Z. Vogt, pp. 157–97. Carbondale: Southern Illinois University Press.

Eells, Walter C. 1958. Highest Earned Degrees of Faculty Members in Institutions of Higher Education in the United States, 1954–55. *College and University* 34(1): 5–38.

Eggan, Dorothy. 1943. The General Problem of Hopi Adjustment. *American Anthropologist* 45: 357–73.

Eggan, Fred. 1968. One Hundred Years of Ethnology and Social Anthropology. In *One Hundred Years of Anthropology*, ed. J. O. Brew, pp. 119–52. Cambridge, Mass.: Harvard University Press.

———. 1986. Discussion Comments. Daughters of the Desert Conference. Globe, Ariz.: Wenner-Gren Foundation for Anthropological Research.

Eggan, Fred, and T. N. Pandey. 1979. Zuni History, 1850–1970. In *Southwest,* vol. 9 of *Handbook of North American Indians,* ed. Alfonso Ortiz, pp. 474–81. Washington, D.C.: Smithsonian Institution Press.

Elliott, Malinda. 1987. *The School of American Research: A History, The First Eighty Years.* Santa Fe, N.M.: School of American Research.

Ellis, Florence Hawley. 1937. Pueblo Social Organization as a Lead to Pueblo History. *American Anthropologist* 39:504–26.

———. 1943. An Inquiry into Food Economy and Body Economy in Zia Pueblo. *American Anthropologist* 45:547–56.

———. 1948. An Examination of Problems Basic to Acculturation in the Rio Grande Pueblos. *American Anthropologist* 50:612–25.

———. 1964. *A Reconstruction of the Basic Jemez Pattern of Social Organization, with Comparison to Other Tanoan Structures.* University of New Mexico Publications in Anthropology No. 11. Albuquerque: University of New Mexico.

———. 1967. Water Rights Studies of Nambe, Pojoaque, Tesuque, and San Ildefonso. Mimeograph prepared for BIA.

———. 1974a. *Archaeological Data Pertaining to the Taos Land Claim, Pueblo Indians 1.* American Indian Ethnohistory Series. New York: Garland Publishing.

———. 1974b. *Archaeological and Ethnological Data: Acoma-Laguna Land Claims, Pueblo Indians 2.* American Indian Ethnohistory Series. New York: Garland Publishing.

———. 1974c. *Anthropology of Laguna Pueblo Land Claims, Pueblo Indians 3.* American Indian Ethnohistory Series. New York: Garland Publishing.

———. 1974d. *Anthropological Evidence Supporting the Land Claims of the Pueblos of Zia, Santa Ana, and Jemez.* American Indian Ethnohistory Series. New York: Garland Publishing.

———. 1974e. *The Hopi: Their History and Use of Lands.* American Indian Ethnohistory Series. New York: Garland Publishing.

———. 1974f. *Navajo Indians 1: An Anthropological Study of the Navajo Indians.* American Indian Ethnohistory Series. New York: Garland Publishing.

———. 1974g. List of Mimeographed Mss. on Land Claims for Pueblos of Zia, Santa Ana, Jemez, Hopi, Nambe, and for the Navajos (1956–1962). In *Collected Papers in Honor of Florence Hawley Ellis,* ed. T. Frisbie, pp. 17–18. Papers of the Archaeological Society of New Mexico No. 2. Santa Fe: Archaeological Society of New Mexico.

———. 1985. Interview (with Jennifer Fox) for the Daughters of the Desert Oral History Project. August 4 & 5, Santa Fe, N.M. Audio and Video Recording. New York: Wenner-Gren Foundation for Anthropological Research.

———. 1989. *San Gabriel del Yungue as Seen by an Archaeologist: Florence Hawley Ellis.* Santa Fe: Sunstone Press and Florence Hawley Ellis Museum of Anthropology at Ghost Ranch, Abiquiu, New Mexico.

Embree, John. 1944. Community Analysis—An Example of Anthropology in Government. *American Anthropologist* 46:277–91.

Epstein, Cynthia Fuchs. 1970. Encountering the Male Establishment: Sex-Status Limits on Women's Careers in the Professions. *American Journal of Sociology* 75(6): 965–82.

Evans-Pritchard, E. E. 1940. *The Nuer.* Oxford: Oxford University Press.

Ewers, John. 1955. Problems and Procedures in Modernizing Ethnological Exhibits. *American Anthropologist* 57(1): 1–12.

Fabian, Johannes. 1963. *Time and the Other: How Anthropology Makes Its Object.* New York: Columbia University Press.

Fabilia, Alfonso. 1940. *Las Tribus Yaquis de Sonora.* Primer Congreso Indigenista Interamericano, Departamento de Asuntos Indigenistas, Mexico, D. F., ed. Farnham, Christine. 1987. *The Impact of Feminist Research in the Academy.* Bloomington: Indiana University Press.

Fawcett, David M., and Teri McLuhan. 1988. Ruth Leah Bunzel. In *Women Anthropologists: A Biographical Dictionary,* ed. Ute Gacs, Aisa Khan, Jerrie McIntyre, and Ruth Weinberg, pp. 29–36. Westport, Conn.: Greenwood Press.

Fenton, William N. 1974. The Advancement of Material Culture Studies in Modern Anthropological Research. In *The Human Mirror: Material and Spatial of Man,* ed. Miles Richardson, pp. 15–36. Baton Rouge: Louisiana State University Press.

Ferber, Marianne. 1986. Citations: Are They an Objective Measure of Scholarly Merit? *SIGNS* 11:381–89.

Ferguson, Frances. 1968. Navajo Drinking: Some Tentative Hypotheses. *Human Organization* 27:159–67.

———. 1970. A Treatment Program for Navajo Alcoholics. *Quarterly Journal of Studies on Alcohol* 31:898–919.

Fergusson, Erna. 1934. *Fiesta in Mexico.* New York: Alfred A. Knopf.

———. 1937. *Guatemala.* New York: Alfred A. Knopf.

———. 1939. *Venezuela.* New York: Alfred A. Knopf.

———. 1940. *Our Southwest.* New York: Alfred A. Knopf.

———. 1943. *Chile.* New York: Alfred A. Knopf.

———. 1946a. *Cuba.* New York: Alfred A. Knopf.

———. 1946b. Review of *The Chrysanthemum and the Sword* by Ruth Benedict. *New York Herald Tribune Weekly Book Review,* December 1, 1946, p. 3.

———. 1948a. What the Southwest Means to Me. *Arizona Quarterly* 4(3): 197–202.

———. 1948b. *Murder and Mystery in New Mexico.* Albuquerque: Merle Armitage Editions.

———. 1951. *New Mexico: A Pageant of Three Peoples.* New York: Alfred A. Knopf.

———. 1957. *Dancing Gods.* Albuquerque: University of New Mexico Press {1931}.

Fink, Augusta. 1983. *I-Mary, A Biography of Mary Austin.* Tucson: University of Arizona Press.

Firth, Raymond. 1963. Aims, Methods and Concepts in the Teaching of Social Anthropology. In *The Teaching of Anthropology,* ed. David Mandelbaum, Gabriel W. Lasker, and Ethel M. Albert, pp. 127–40. Memorandum No. 94. Washington, D.C.: American Anthropological Association.

Firth, Rosemary. 1972. From Wife to Anthropologist. In *Crossing Cultural Boundaries: The Anthropological Experience,* ed. Solon T. Kimball and James B. Watson, pp. 10–32. San Francisco: Chandler Publishing.

———. 1985. Bernard Deacon: An Intimate Memoir. *Anthropology Today* 1:21–22.

Fletcher, Alice C. 1888. On the Preservation of Archaeologic Monuments. In *Proceedings of the American Association for the Advancement of Science,* vol. 36, p. 317.

Fletcher, Alice, and Tilly [Matilda] C. Stevenson. 1889. Report on the Committee on the Preservation of Archaeological Remains on the Public Lands. In *Proceedings of the American Association for the Advancement of Science,* vol. 37, pp. 35–37.

Ford, Richard I. 1978. *Systematic Research Collections in Anthropology: An Irreplaceable National Resource.* Cambridge, Mass.: Peabody Museum for the Council for Museum Anthropology.

Foster, George M. 1969. *Applied Anthropology.* Boston: Little, Brown.

Foucault, Michel. 1978. *The History of Sexuality: Introduction.* New York: Pantheon.

———. 1980. Truth and Power. In *Power/Knowledge: Selected Interviews and Other Writings, 1972–1977,* ed. Colin Gordon, pp. 109–33. New York: Pantheon.

Fox, Nancy. 1976. Marjorie Ferguson Lambert. In *Collected Papers in the Honor of Marjorie Ferguson*

Lambert, ed. Nancy Fox, pp. 1–18. Papers of the Archaeological Society of New Mexico No. 3. Albuquerque: Archaeological Society of New Mexico.

Frantz, Charles. 1972. *The Student Anthropologist's Handbook.* Cambridge, Mass.: Schenkman.

——. 1985. Relevance: American Ethnology and the Wider Society, 1900–1940. In *Social Contexts of American Ethnology, 1840–1984,* ed. June Helm, pp. 83–100. Washington, D.C.: American Ethnological Society.

Freed, Stanley A., and Ruth S. Freed. 1983. Clark Wissler and the Development of Anthropology in the United States. *American Anthropologist* 85(4): 800–25.

Freeman, Jo. 1970. Women on the Social Science Faculties since 1892, University of Chicago. In Discrimination Against Women, Hearings before the Special Subcommittee on Education of the Committee on Education and Labor, House of Representatives. 91st Cong., 2d Sess., on Section 805 of HR 16098, pp. 994–1003. Washington, D.C.: GPO.

French, David H. 1948. *Factionalism in Isleta Pueblo.* American Ethnological Society Monograph 14. New York: J.J. Augustin.

French, Fran. 1979. The Rules Keep Changing Every Day. In *The Hidden Professorate: Credentialism, Professionalism, and the Tenure Crisis,* ed. Arthur S. Wilke. pp. 135–39. Westport, Conn.: Greenwood Press.

Fried, Morton H. 1971. Employment of Women in Anthropology. *Anthropology Newsletter* 12(2): 6–7.

——. 1972. *The Study of Anthropology.* New York: Thomas H. Crowell.

Frisbie, Charlotte J. 1987. *Navajo Medicine Bundles or Jish: Acquisition, Transmission, and Disposition in the Past and Present.* Albuquerque: University of New Mexico Press.

——. 1988. Frances Theresa Densmore. In *Women Anthropologists: A biographical Dictionary,* ed. Ute Gacs, Aisha Kahn, Jerrie McIntyre, and Ruth Weinberg, pp. 51–58. New York: Greenwood Press.

——. 1989. Helen Heffron Roberts (1888–1985): A Tribute. *Ethnomusicology* 33(1): 97–111.

Frisbie, Theodore R. 1975. A Biography of Florence Hawley Ellis. In *Collected Papers in Honor of Florence Hawley Ellis,* ed. Theodore Frisbie, pp. 1–12. Papers of the Archaeological Society of New Mexico No. 2. Santa Fe: Archaeological Society of New Mexico.

Frisbie, Theodore R., ed. 1975. *Collected Papers in Honor of Florence Hawley Ellis.* Papers of the Archaeological Society of New Mexico No. 2. Santa Fe: Archaeological Society of New Mexico.

Gacs, Ute, Aisha Khan, Jerri McIntyre, and Ruth Weinberg, eds. 1988. *Women Anthropologists: A Biographical Dictionary.* New York: Greenwood Press.

Gailey, Christine. 1985. The State of the State in Anthropology. *Dialectical Anthropology* 9(1–4): 65–91.

Geertz, Clifford. 1988. *Works and Lives: The Anthropologist as Author.* Stanford, Calif.: Stanford University Press.

Gero, Joan. 1983. Gender Bias in Archaeology: A Cross-Cultural Perspective. In *The Socio-Politics of Archaeology,* ed. Joan Gero, D. Lacy, and Michael Blakey, pp. 51–57. Department of Anthropology Research Report No. 23. Amherst: University of Massachusetts.

——. 1985. Socio-Politics and the Woman-at-Home Ideology. *American Antiquity* 50: 342–350.

——. 1988. Gender Bias in Archaeology: Here, Then, and Now. In *Feminism within the Science and Health-Care Professions: Overcoming Resistance,* ed. Sue V. Rosser, pp. 33–43. New York: Pergamon Press.

Gero, Joan, and Margaret W. Conkey, eds. 1991. *Engendering Archaeology: Women and Prehistory.* Oxford: Basil Blackwood.

Gero, Joan, David Lacy, and Michael Blakey, eds. 1983. *The Socio-Politics of Archaeology.* Anthropological Research Report No. 23. Amherst: University of Massachusetts.

Gibson, Arrell Morgan. 1981. Native American Muses. *New Mexico Historical Review* 56(3): 285–306.

Giddings, Ruth Warner. 1959. *Yaqui Myths and Legends.* Anthropological Papers of the University of Arizona No. 2. Tucson: University of Arizona Press. (Reprinted 1978.)

Gifford, Carol A., and Elizabeth A. Morris. 1985. Digging for Credit: Early Archaeological Field Schools in the American Southwest. *American Antiquity* 50:395–412.

Gill, Sam D. 1981. *Sacred Words: A Study of Navajo Religion and Prayer.* Westport, Conn.: Greenwood Press.

Gillmor, Frances. 1930. *Windsinger.* New York: Minton, Balch and Co.

————. 1934. *Traders to the Navajo: The Story of the Wetherills of Kayenta.* Boston: Houghton Mifflin.

————. 1940. *Fruit out of the Rock.* New York: Duell, Sloan and Pearce.

————. 1949. *Flute of the Smoking Mirror: A Portrait of Nezahualcoyotl, Poet-King of the Aztecs.* Albuquerque: University of New Mexico Press.

————. 1985. Interview (with Jennifer Fox) for the Daughters of the Desert Oral History Project. August 21, Tucson, Ariz. Audio Recording. New York: Wenner-Gren Foundation for Anthropological Research.

Givens, David. 1991. Special Theme Issue of AN. *Anthropology Newsletter* 32(5): 48.

Glassie, Henry H. 1989. *The Spirit of Folk Art: The Girard Collection at the Museum of International Folk Art.* New York: Harry N. Abrams.

Golde, Peggy. 1986. Odyssey of Encounter. In *Women in the Field: Anthropological Experiences,* ed. Peggy Golde, pp. 67–93. Berkeley: University of California Press.

Golde, Peggy, ed. 1986. *Women in the Field: Anthropological Experiences.* Berkeley: University of California Press.

Goldfrank, Esther. 1923. Notes on Two Pueblo Feasts. *American Anthropologist* 25(2): 188–96.

————. 1926. Isleta Variants: A Study in Flexibility. *Journal of American Folklore* 39(151): 70–78.

————. 1927. *The Social and Ceremonial Organization of Cochiti.* Memoirs of the American Anthropological Association No. 33. Washington, D.C.: American Anthropological Association.

————. 1937. Culture Takes a Holiday. Profile of Ellery Sedgewick. Unpublished ms. Washington, D.C.: National Anthropological Archives.

————. 1943a. Historic Change and Social Character: A Study of the Teton Dakota. *American Anthropologist* 45(1): 67–83.

————. 1943b. Review of Leslie A. White's *The Pueblo of Santa Ana. Journal of American Folklore* 56(221): 233–34.

————. 1943c. Administrative Programs and Changes in Blood Society in the Reserve Period. *Applied Anthropology* 2(2): 18–24.

————. 1945a. Irrigation Agriculture and Navaho Community Leadership: Case Material on Environment and Culture. *American Anthropologist* 47(2): 262–77.

————. 1945b. Review of Mischa Titiev's *Old Oraibi. American Anthropologist* 47(2): 300.

————. 1945c. Socialization, Personality, and the Structure of Pueblo Society (With Particular Reference to Hopi and Zuni). *American Anthropologist* 47(4): 516–37.

————. 1945d. *Changing Configurations in the Social Organization of a Blackfoot Tribe during the Reserve Period.* American Ethnological Society Monograph 8. New York: J. J. Augustin.

————. 1946a. Review of A. H. and D. Leighton's *The Navajo Door. American Anthropologist* 48(1): 97–98.

————. 1946b. More about Irrigation Agriculture and Navaho Community Leadership. *American Anthropologist* 48(3): 473–82.

————. 1946c. Linguistic Note to Zuni Ethnology. *Word* 2(3): 191–96.

————. 1948a. The Impact of Situation and Personality on Four Hopi Emergence Myths. *Southwestern Journal of Anthropology* 4(3): 241–62.

————. 1948b. Review of Buwei Yang Chao's *Autobiography of a Chinese Woman. American Anthropologist* 50(2): 314–15.

————. 1948c. Review of Albert O. Hara's *The Position of Women in Early China. American Anthropologist* 50(2): 316–17.

————. 1949. Presidential Report at Annual Meeting of the American Ethnological Society, December 30, 1948. *American Anthropologist* 51(2): 371–72.

————. 1951a. Observations on Sexuality among the Blood Indians of Alberta, Canada. In *Psychoanalysis and the Social Sciences,* vol. 3, ed.

Geza Roheim, pp. 71–98. New York: International Universities Press.

———. 1951b. "Old Man" and the Father Image in Blood (Blackfoot) Society. In *Psychoanalysis and Culture,* ed. George B. Wilbur and Warner Muensterberger, pp. 132–41. New York: International Universities Press.

———. 1952. The Different Patterns of Blackfoot and Pueblo Adaptation to White Authority. In *Acculturation in the Americas,* ed. Sol Tax, pp. 74–79. 29th International Congress of Americanists. Chicago: University of Chicago Press.

———. 1953. Review of Evon Z. Vogt's *Navajo Veterans—A Study of Changing Values. American Anthropologist* 55(2): 248–50.

———. 1954a. Discussant of Ruth Underhill's paper, Intercultural Relations in the Greater Southwest. *American Anthropologist* 56(3): 658–62.

———. 1954b. Notes on Deer-Hunting Practices at Laguna Pueblo, New Mexico. *Texas Journal of Science* 6(4): 407–21.

———. 1955. Native Paintings of Isleta Pueblo, New Mexico. *Transactions of the New York Academy of Sciences* Ser. 2, 18(2): 178–80.

———. 1956. Gladys Amanda Reichard, 1893–1955. *Journal of American Folklore* 62: 53–54.

———. 1958. Review of Joseph F. Rock's *The Zhi ma Funeral of the Na-khi of Southwest China. American Anthropologist* 60(1): 191–92.

———. 1960a. Review of Vera Laski's *Seeking Life. American Anthropologist* 62(3): 538.

———. 1960b. Review of Charles H. Lange's *Cochiti, A New Mexico Pueblo, Past and Present. American Anthropologist* 62(6): 1075–77.

———. 1964. Review of Leslie A. White's *The Pueblo of Sia. American Anthropologist* 66(3): 680–82.

———. 1967. *The Artist of "Isleta Paintings" in Pueblo Society.* Smithsonian Contributions to Anthropology 5. Washington, D.C.: GPO.

———. 1968. Review of Joseph P. Donelly, ed. and trans., *Wilderness Kingdom: Indian Life in the Rocky Mountains: 1840–1847: The Journals and Paintings of Nicholas Point, S.J. American Anthropologist* 70(4): 839–40.

———. 1969. Concerning "People of the Middle Place." *American Anthropologist* 71(1): 92.

———. 1974. Introduction to Marjorie Lismer's *Adoption Practices of the Blood Indians of Alberta, Canada. Plains Anthropologist* 1(2): 19–63.

———. 1978. *Notes on an Undirected Life: As One Anthropologist Tells It.* Queens College Publications in Anthropology No. 3. Flushing, N.Y.: Queens College Press.

———. 1983. Another View: Margaret and Me. *Ethnohistory* 30(1): 1–14.

———. 1985a. Two Anthropologists, The Same Informant: Some Differences in Their Recorded Data. *Journal of the Anthropological Society of Oxford* 16(1): 42–52.

———. 1985b. Interview (with Jennifer Fox). Daughters of the Desert Oral History Project. July 3, New York, N.Y. Video Recording. New York: Wenner-Gren Foundation for Anthropological Research.

Goldfrank, Esther S., ed. 1962. *Isleta Paintings.* Introduction and Commentary by Elsie Clews Parsons. Bureau of American Ethnology Bulletin 181. Washington, D.C.: GPO.

Goldschmidt, Walter. 1979. Introduction: On the Interdependence between Utility and Theory. In *The Uses of Anthropology,* ed. Walter Goldschmidt, pp. 1–13. Washington, D.C.: American Anthropological Association.

Goldschmidt, Walter, ed. 1979. *The Uses of Anthropology.* Washington, D.C.: American Anthropological Association.

Golla, Victor, ed. 1984. *The Sapir–Kroeber Correspondence: Letters between Edward Sapir and A. L. Kroeber, 1905–1925.* Report No. 6. Survey of California and Other Indian Languages. Berkeley: University of California.

Gonzalez, Nancie L. 1967. *The Spanish Americans of New Mexico: A Heritage of Pride.* Albuquerque: University of New Mexico Press.

Goode, William. 1957. Community within a Community: The Professions. *American Sociological Review* 22: 194–200.

Gordon, Deborah. 1988. Writing Culture, Writing Feminism: The Poetics and Politics of Experimental Ethnography. *Inscriptions* 3/4: 7–24.

Gordon, Linda. 1988. *Heroes of Their Own Lives: The Politics and History of Family Violence.* New York: Viking Books.

Gordon, Lynn. 1979. -k and -m in Maricopa. In *Studies of Switch-Reference,* ed. Pamela Munro, pp. 119–44. Papers in Linguistics No. 8. Los Angeles: University of California.

———. 1980a. Maricopa Morphology and Syntax. Unpublished Ph.D. dissertation, University of California, Los Angeles.

———. 1980b. Relative Clauses in Maricopa. In *Proceedings of the* 1979 *Hokan Language Workshop,* ed. James E. Redden, pp. 15–24. Occasional Papers on Linguistics No. 7. Carbondale: Southern Illinois University.

———. 1981. Evidentials in Maricopa. In *Proceedings of the 1980 Hokan Languages Workshop,* ed. James Redden, pp. 59–69. Occasional Papers on Linguistics No. 9. Carbondale: Southern Illinois University.

———. 1982. Inferential Constructions in Maricopa. In *Proceedings of the 1981 Hokan Languages Workshop,* ed. James E. Redden, pp. 15–23. Occasional Papers on Linguistics No. 10. Carbondale: Southern Illinois University.

———. 1983a. Some Maricopa Auxiliaries. In *Proceedings of the 1982 Conference on Far Western American Indian Languages,* ed. James E. Redden, pp. 1–12. Occasional Papers on Linguistics No. 11. Carbondale: Southern Illinois University.

———. 1983b. Switch Reference, Clause Order, and Interclausal Relationships in Maricopa. In *Switch Reference and Universal Grammar,* ed. John Haiman and Pamela Munro, pp. 83–103. Philadelphia: John Benjamins.

Graham, Patricia A. 1978. Expansion and Exclusion: A History of Women in American Higher Education. *SIGNS* 3:759–73.

Green, Jesse, ed. 1981. *Zuni: Selected Writings of Frank Hamilton Cushing.* Lincoln: University of Nebraska Press.

Greib, Phil R., and Martha M. Callahan. 1987. Ceramic Exchange within the Kayenta Anasazi Region: Volcanic Ash-Tempered Tusayan White Ware. *The Kiva* 52(2): 95–112.

Griffen, Joyce. 1988. Ruth Murray Underhill. In *Women Anthropologists: A Biological Dictionary,* ed. Ute Gacs, Aisha Khan, Jerrie McIntyre, and Ruth Weinberg, pp. 355–60. New York: Greenwood Press.

Griffin, James B. 1985. The Formation of the Society for American Archaeology. *American Antiquity* 50:261–71.

Gurney, J. N. 1985. "Not One of the Guys": The Female Researcher in a Male-Dominated Setting. *Qualitative Sociology* 8(1): 42–62.

Hackenberg, Robert H. 1972. Modernization Research on the Papago Indians. *Human Organization* 31 (2): 111–240.

Haeberlin, H. K. 1916. *The Idea of Fertilization in the Culture of the Pueblo Indians,* pp. 1–55. Memoirs of the American Anthropological Association No. 3. Lancaster, Penn.: American Anthropological Association.

Haeberlin, H. K., James A. Teit, and Helen H. Roberts. 1925. Coiled Basketry of British Columbia and Surrounding Areas. In *41st Annual Report of the Bureau of American Ethnology, 1919–1924.* p. 119–484. Washington, D.C.: GPO.

Hagstrom, Warren O. 1965. *The Scientific Community.* New York: Basic Books.

Haile, Father Berard. 1932. Review of *Social Life of the Navajo Indians* by Gladys A. Reichard. *American Anthropologist* 34(4): 711–15.

———. 1941. Reichard's Chant of Waning Endurance. *American Anthropologist* 43(2): 306–11.

———. 1947. *Prayerstick Cutting in a Five-Night Navajo Ceremonial of the Male Branch of Shootingway.* Chicago: University of Chicago Press.

Hale, Kenneth. 1972. A New Perspective on American Indian Linguistics. In *New Perspectives on the Pueblos,* ed. Alfonso Ortiz, pp. 87–111. Santa Fe, N.M.: School of American Research.

Hale, Kenneth, and David Harris. 1979. Historical Linguistics and Archaeology. In *Southwest,* vol. 9 of *Handbook of North American Indians,* ed. Alfonso Ortiz, pp. 170–77. Washington, D.C.: Smithsonian Institution Press.

Halpern, Katherine Spencer. 1965. Index of Navajo Children with Handicapping Conditions (Crownpoint, N.M.). Ms. prepared for Indian Health Service. Washington, D.C.: U.S. Public Health Services.

———. 1971. Navajo Health and Welfare Aides: A Filed Study. *Social Service Review* 45:37–52.

———. 1973. Navajo Accident Patients. Paper Presented at the Annual Meeting of the Society for Applied Anthropology.

———. 1985. Interview (with Jennifer Fox) for Daughters of the Desert Oral History Project. September 3, Santa Fe, N.M. Audio Recording. New York: Wenner-Gren Foundation for Anthropological Research.

Hamamsy, Laila Shukry. 1957. The Role of Women in a Changing Navaho Society. *American Anthropologist* 59:101–11.

Handler, Richard. 1986. Vigorous Male and Aspiring Female: Poetry, Personality, and Culture in Edward Sapir and Ruth Benedict. In *Malinowski, Rivers, Benedict, and Others: Essays on Culture and Personality,* vol. 4 of *History of Anthropology,* ed. George W. Stocking, pp. 127–55. Madison: University of Wisconsin Press.

Handschin, C. H. 1912. The Percentage of Women Teachers in State Colleges and Universities. *Science* 35(889): 55–57.

Haraway, Donna. 1986. Primatology Is Politics by Other Means. In *Feminist Approaches to Science,* ed. Ruth Bleier, pp. 38–67. New York: Pergamon Press.

———. 1989. *Primate Visions: A History of the Craft of Story Telling in the Sciences of Monkeys and Apes, United States, 1920–1980.* Boston: Routledge, Kegan Paul.

Hardin, Margaret Ann. 1983. *Gifts of Mother Earth: Ceramics in the Zuni Tradition.* Phoenix, Ariz.: The Heard Museum.

Hardy, Heather. 1979a. The Development of the Pai Vowel System. In *Proceedings of the 1978 Hokan Languages Workshop,* ed. James E. Redden, pp. 29–41. Occasional Papers of Linguistics No. 5. Carbondale: University of Illinois.

———. 1979b. An Integrated Account of the Morpheme in Tolkapaya. In *Proceedings of the 1978 Hokan Languages Workshop,* ed. James E. Redden, pp. 19–28. Occasional Papers on Linguistics No. 5. Carbondale: Southern Illinois University.

———. 1979c. Tolkapaya Syntax: Aspect, Modality, and Adverbial Modification in Yavapai Dialect. Unpublished Ph.D. dissertation, University of California, Los Angeles.

———. 1980. The Story of /o/ in Tolkapaya: A Problem of Homophony. *Proceedings of the 1979 Hokan Languages Workshop,* ed. James E. Redden, pp. 53–59. Occasional Papers on Linguistics No. 6. Carbondale: Southern Illinois University.

———. 1981. Behavioral Verb Constructions in Tolkapaya. Native Languages of the Americas: Prospects of the 80s. *Journal of the Linguistic Association of the Southwest* 4(2): 108–22.

———. 1982. The Use of Auxiliaries as a Cohesive Device in Tolkapaya. In *Proceedings of the 1982 Conference on Far Western American Indian Languages,* ed. James E. Redden, pp. 15–23. Occasional Papers on Linguistics No. 11. Carbondale: Southern Illinois University.

Hare, Peter H. 1985. *A Woman's Quest for Science: Portrait of Anthropologist Elsie Clews Parsons.* Buffalo, N.Y.: Prometheus Books.

Harper, Allen G., Kalervo Oberg, and A. R. Cordova. 1943. *Man and Resources in the Middle Rio Grande Valley.* Albuquerque: University of New Mexico Press.

Harrington, John P., and Helen H. Roberts. 1928. Picuris Children's Stories with Texts and Songs. In *43rd Annual Report of the Bureau of American Ethnology for 1925–1926,* pp. 289–447. Washington, D.C.: GPO.

Harris, Ann S. 1970. The Second Sex in Academe. *AAUP Bulletin* 56(3): 283–95.

Harris, Marvin. 1968. *The Rise of Anthropological Theory.* New York: Thomas Y. Crowell.

Hartman, Heidi. 1981. The Family as Locus of Gender, Class and Political Struggle: The Example of Housework. *SIGNS* 6(3): 366–94.

Hatch, Elvin. 1973. *Theories of Man and Culture.* New York: Columbia University Press.

Haury, Emil W. 1985. Reflections: Fifty Years of Southwestern Archaeology. *American Antiquity* 50:383–94.

Havighurst, Robert J., and Bernice L. Neugarten. 1955. *American Indian and White Children.* Chicago: University of Chicago Press.

Hawley, Florence (also under Ellis, Florence Hawley). 1929. Prehistoric Pottery Pigments in the Southwest. *American Anthropologist* 31: 731–54.

———. 1934. *The Significance of the Dated Prehistory of Chetro Ketl, Chaco Canyon, New Mexico.* University of New Mexico Bulletin, Monograph Series No. 1, Part 1. Albuquerque: University of New Mexico.

———. 1936. *Field Manual of Prehistoric Southwestern Pottery Types.* University of New Mexico Bulletin, Anthropological Series No. 1, Part 4. Albuquerque: University of New Mexico.

———. 1937. Pueblo Social Organization as a Clue to Pueblo History. *American Anthropologist* 39: 504–22.

Heard Museum. 1929. Articles of Incorporation.

Heiss, Ann M. 1970. *Challenges to Graduate Schools.* San Francisco: Jossey-Bass.

Hellerstein, Erna O., Leslie P. Hume, and Karen M. Offen, eds. 1981. *Victorian Women.* Stanford, Calif.: Stanford University Press.

Helm, June, ed. 1966. *Pioneers of American Anthropology.* Seattle: University of Washington Press.

———. 1985. *Social Contexts of American Ethnology, 1840–1984.* Washington, D.C.: American Anthropological Association.

Henning, Margaret, and Anne Jardin. 1977. *The Managerial Woman.* New York: Doubleday.

Herold, Joyce. 1980. Papago Tribe Honors Ruth Murray Underhill. *Anthropology Newsletter* 21(3): 3.

Hewett, Edgar L. 1905. Ethnic Factors in Education. *American Anthropologist* 7: 1–16.

Hill, Gertude. 1937a. The Art of the Navajo Silversmith. *The Kiva* 2(5): 17–20.

———. 1937b. *The Art of the Navajo Silversmith.* Ysleta, Tex.: Edwin B. Hall. (Reprinted 1939 as *Use of Turquoise among the Navajo.*)

———. 1938a. Turquoise: Its History and Significance in the Southwest. Unpublished master's thesis, University of Arizona.

———. 1938b. The Use of Turquoise among the Navajo. *The Kiva* 4(3): 11–14.

———. 1942a. Notes on Papago Pottery Manufacture at Santa Rosa. *American Anthropologist* 44(3): 531–33.

———. 1942b. On Bone Daggers. *Society for American Archaeology Notebook* 2: 38.

———. 1947. Turquoise and the Zuni Indians. *The Kiva* 12(4): 42–52.

———. 1954. *Bibliography of Pueblo Indian Dances and Ceremonies.* Santa Fe: Museum of New Mexico.

———. 1957. Folklore in Southwestern Literature with Special Reference to New Mexico. *El Palacio* 64(10): 265–71.

———. 1958. New Mexico at the 1885 World's Fair. *El Palacio* 65(6): 234–36.

———. 1961. Henry Clay Hooker: King of the Sierra Bonita. *Arizoniana: The Journal of Arizona History* 2(4): 12–15.

Hill, James N. 1970. *Broken K Pueblo: Prehistoric Social Organization in the American Southwest.* Anthropological Papers of the University of Arizona No. 18. Tucson: University of Arizona Press.

———. 1977. Individual Variability in Ceramics and Prehistoric Social Organization. In *The Individual in Prehistory: Studies of Variability in Style in Prehistoric Technologies,* ed. James N. Hill and Joel Gunn, pp. 55–108. New York: Academic Press.

Hill, Jane H., and Kenneth C. Hill. 1970. A Note on Uto-Aztecan Color Terminology. *Anthropological Linguistics* 12: 231–38.

Hill, W. W. 1935. The Status of the Hermaphrodite and Transvestite in Navajo Culture. *American Anthropologist* 37: 273–79.

Hillerman, Tony. 1989a. *Talking God.* New York: Harper & Row.

———. 1989b. *A Thief of Time.* New York: Harper & Row.

———. 1990. *Coyote Waits.* New York: Harper & Row.

Hinsley, Curtis M., Jr. 1976. Amateurs and Professionals in Washington Anthropology, 1897–1903. In *American Anthropology: The Early Years,* ed. John V. Murra, pp. 36–68. Proceedings of the American Ethnological Society for 1974. Seattle: University of Washington.

———. 1979. Anthropology as Science and Politics: The Dilemmas of the Bureau of American Ethnology, 1897–1904. In *The Uses of Anthropology,* ed. Walter Goldschmidt, pp. 15–32. American Anthropological Association

Special Publication No. 11. Washington, D.C.: American Anthropological Association.

———. 1981. *Savages and Scientists: The Smithsonian Institution and the Development of American Anthropology, 1846–1910.* Washington, D.C.: Smithsonian Institution Press.

———. 1983. Ethnographic Charisma and Scientific Routine: Cushing and Fewkes in the American Southwest, 1879–1893. In *Observers Observed: Essays on Ethnographic Fieldwork,* vol. 1 of *History of Anthropology,* ed. George Stocking, Jr., pp. 53–69. Madison: University of Wisconsin Press.

———. 1986a. Edgar Lee Hewett and the School of American Research in Santa Fe, 1906–1912. In *American Archaeology Past and Future: A Celebration of the Society for American Archaeology, 1935–1985,* ed. David J. Meltzer, Don D. Fowler, and Jeremy A. Sabloff, pp. 217–35. Washington, D.C.: Smithsonian Institution Press.

———. 1986b. Discussion Comments. Daughters of the Desert Conference. Globe, Ariz.: Wenner-Gren Foundation for Anthropological Research.

Hinton, Leanne. 1974. The Old Lady's Song: A Poetic Analysis of a Havasupai Song. *Linguistic Notes from La Jolla,* pp. 19–35.

———. 1976. Havasupai Medicine Song. *Alcheringa, Ethnopoetics* 3.

———. 1977a. The Tar Baby Story: A Diegueno Text. In Yuman Texts, ed. Margaret Langdon. *International Journal of American Linguistics, Native American Text Series* 1(3): 101–6.

———. 1977b. Literacy and Linguistics: The Havasupai Writing System. *University Museum Studies* 11: 1–16.

———. 1978. Coyote Baptizes the Chickens. In Coyote Stories, ed. William Bright. *International Journal of American Linguistics* 1(4): 117–20.

———. 1979. Irataba's Gift: A Closer Look at the s*sO Soundshift in Mojave and Northern Pai. *Journal of California and Great Basin Anthropology–Papers in Linguistics* 1: 3–37.

———. 1980. Vocables in Havasupai Songs. In *Southwestern Ritual Drama,* ed. Charlotte J.

Frisbie, pp. 275–305. Albuquerque: University of New Mexico Press.

———. 1982. Sound Symbolism. In *Hualapai Reference Grammar* by Lucille J. Watahomigie et al., pp. 404–10. American Indian Studies Center. Los Angeles: University of California.

———. 1984a. Havasupai Songs: A Linguistics Perspective. Turbingen, W. Germany: Gunter Nass.

———. 1984b. *Curriculum Guide for Havasupai Grammar.* Peach Springs, Ariz.: Havasupai Bilingual Education Program.

———. 1984c. *Havasupai Dictionary.* Peach Springs, Ariz.: Havasupai Bilingual Education Program.

Hinton, Leanne, and Margaret Langdon. 1979. Object-Subject Pronominal Prefixes in La Huerta Diegueno. In *Hokan Studies, Papers from the First Conference on Hokan Languages,* ed. Margaret Langdon, pp. 113–28. The Hague: Mouton.

Hinton, Leanne, and Lucille J. Watahomigie, eds. 1984. *Spirit Mountain: An Anthology of Yuman Story and Song.* Sun Tracks. Tucson: University of Arizona Press.

Hodgen, Margaret T. 1964. *Early Anthropology in the Sixteenth and Seventeenth Centuries.* Philadelphia: University of Pennsylvania Press.

Hoebel, E. Adamson. 1954. Major Contributions of Southwestern Studies to Anthropological Theory. *American Anthropologist* 56(4): 720–27.

Holden, Jane (see also under Kelley, Jane H.). 1952. The Bonnell Site. *Bulletin of the Texas Archaeological and Paleontological Society* 23: 78–132.

———. 1955. Preliminary Report on the Bloom Mound, Chaves County, New Mexico. *Bulletin of the Archaeological Society* 26: 166–81.

Holden, William Curry, et al. 1936. *Studies of the Yaqui Indians of Sonora, Mexico.* Texas Technological College Bulletin Series No. 2, Vol. 12, No. 1. Lubbock: Texas Technological College.

Hollingworth, Jane. 1914. *Functional Periodicity: An Experimental Study of the Mental and Motor Abilities of Women during Menstruation.* New York: Teacher's College, Columbia University.

Holmes, William H. 1878. Report on the Ancient Ruins of Southwestern Colorado, Examined during the Summers of 1875 and 1876. In *10th Annual Report of the U.S. Geological Survey of the Territories for 1876,* pp. 383–408. Washington, D.C.: GPO.

———. 1916. In Memoriam: Matilda Coxe Stevenson. *American Anthropologist* 18(4): 552–59.

———. 1935. John James Stevenson. *Dictionary of American Biography* 17:631–32.

Honigmann, John J. 1976. *The Development of Anthropological Ideas.* Homewood, Ill.: Dorsey Press.

Hook, Sidney, Ruth Benedict, and Margaret Mead. 1940. Alexander Goldenweiser: Three Tributes. *The Modern Quarterly* 11(6): 31–34.

Horney, Karen. 1936. Culture and Neurosis. *American Sociological Review* 1:221–35.

———. 1937. *The Neurotic Personality of Our Time.* New York: W. W. Norton and Company.

Hornig, Lilli S. 1980. Untenured and Tenuous: The Status of Women Faculty. *Annals of the AAPSS* 448:115–25.

———. 1984. Women in Science and Engineering: Why So Few? *Technology Review* 87(8): 29–41.

Houlihan, Patrick. 1979. Lecture to the Scottsdale Historical Society. Ms. on file, Heard Museum Archives, Phoenix.

House, Dorothy. 1980. Mary-Russell Ferrell Colton. Nomination for Arizona Women's Hall of Fame, November 25. Heard Museum Archives, Phoenix.

Howard, Jane. 1984. *Margaret Mead: A Life.* New York: Simon and Schuster.

Howe, Florence. 1984. *Myths of Coeducation: Selected Essays, 1964–1983.* Bloomington: Indiana University Press.

Howe, Florence, ed. 1977. *Seven Years Later: Women's Studies Programs in 1976.* Washington, D.C.: National Advisory Council on Women's Educational Programs.

Hubbard, Ruth. 1990. *The Politics of Women's Biology.* New Brunswick, N.J.: Rutgers University Press.

Hughes, Helen M., ed. 1973. *The Status of Women in Sociology, 1968–1972.* Washington, D.C.: American Sociological Association.

Hunt, Jennifer. 1984. The Development of Rapport

through the Negotiation of Gender in Field Work among Police. *Human Organization* 43(4): 283–96.

Hutchinson, Emilie. 1929. *Women and the Ph.D.* Greensboro: North Carolina College for Women.

Hymes, Dell J. 1962. On Studying the History of Anthropology. *Kroeber Anthropological Paper* 26:81–86.

Irwin-Williams, Cynthia. 1967. Picosa: The Elementary Southwestern Culture. *American Antiquity* 32:441–56.

———. 1973. *The Oshara Tradition: Origins of Anasazi Culture.* Eastern New Mexico University Contributions in Anthropology 5(1). Portales: Eastern New Mexico University.

———. 1979. Post-Pleistocene Archaeology, 7000–2000 B.C. In *Southwest,* vol. 9 of *Handbook of North American Indians,* ed. Alfonso A. Ortiz, pp. 31–42. Washington, D.C.: Smithsonian Institution Press.

———. 1980a. Investigations at Salmon Ruin: Methodology Overview. In *Investigations at the Salmon Site: The Structure of Chacoan Society in the Northern Southwest,* ed. Cynthia Irwin-Williams and Phillip H. Shelley, pp. 107–70. Portales: Eastern New Mexico University.

———. 1980b. San Juan Valley Archaeological Project: Synthesis, 1980. In *Investigations at the Salmon Site: The Structure of Chacoan Society in the Northern Southwest,* ed. Cynthia Irwin-Williams and Philip H. Shelley, pp. 135–211. Portales: Eastern New Mexico University.

———. 1986. The Density-Dependent Method in Archeological Site Survey. Ms. in possession of Cordell.

———. 1990. Women in the Field: The Role of Women in Archaeology before 1960. In *Women of Science: Righting the Record,* ed. G. Kass-Simon and Patricia Farnes, pp. 1–41. Bloomington: Indiana University Press.

Irwin-Williams, Cynthia, and C. Vance Haynes, Jr. 1970. Climatic Change and Early Population Dynamics in the Southwestern United States. *Quaternary Research* 1:59–71.

Irwin-Williams, Cynthia, Henry T. Irwin, George

Arorino, and C. Vance Haynes, Jr. 1973. Hell Gap: A Paleo-Indian Occupation on the High Plains. *Plains Anthropologist* 18:40–53.

Jacknis, Ira. 1985. Franz Boas and Exhibits: On the Limitations of the Museum Method of Anthropology. In *Objects and Others: Essays on Museums and Material Culture,* vol. 3 of *History of Anthropology,* ed. George W. Stocking, pp. 75–111. Madison: University of Wisconsin Press.

Jacobs, Sue-Ellen. 1977. Social Impact Assessment: Experiences in Evaluation Research. In *Applied Anthropology and Human Ethics, Part 3, El Llano Unit of San Juan Chama Project.* Occasional Papers in Anthropology. Mississippi State: Mississippi State University.

Jacobus, Mary, ed. 1979. *Women Writing and Writing about Women.* London: Croom Helm.

James, Alice. 1988. Dorothy Louise Strouse Keur. In *Women Anthropologists: A Biographical Dictionary,* ed. Ute Gacs, Aisha Kahn, Jerrie McIntyre, and Ruth Weinberg, pp. 181–86. New York: Greenwood Press.

James, Wendy. 1973. The Anthropologist as Reluctant Imperialist. In *Anthropology and the Colonial Encounter,* ed. Talal Asad, pp. 41–70. New York: Humanities Press.

Jenkins, J. Rockwood. 1951. Maie Bartlett Heard. Eulogy delivered at memorial service, April 12. Ms. on file, Heard Museum Archives, Phoenix.

Joe, Jennie R. 1980. Disabled Children in Navajo Society. Ph.D. dissertation, University of California, Berkeley.

———. 1982. Cultural Influences on Navajo Mothers with Disabled Children. *The American Indian Quarterly* 6:170–90.

Joel, Judy. 1964. Classification of the Yuman Languages. In *Studies in California Linguistics,* ed. William Bright, pp. 99–105. Publications in Linguistics No. 34. Berkeley: University of California.

———. 1966. Paipai Phonology and Morphology. Unpublished Ph.D. dissertation, University of California, Los Angeles.

Johnson, George E., and Frank F. Stafford. 1979. Pecuniary Rewards to Men and Women Faculty. In *Academic Rewards in Higher Education,* ed. Darrell R. Lewis and William G. Becker, pp. 231–43. Cambridge, Mass.: Ballinger.

Johnson, Jean B. 1962. *El Idioma Yaqui.* Mexico, D.F.: Instituto Nacional de Antropología e Historia.

Joseph, Alice. 1942. Physician and Patient: Some Aspects of Inter-personal Relations between White Physicians and Indian Patients. *Applied Anthropology* 1(4): 1–6.

Joseph, Alice, Rosamond B. Spicer, and Jane Chesky. 1947. *The Desert People: A Study of the Papago Indians.* Chicago: University of Chicago Press.

Judd, Neil M. 1967. *The Bureau of American Ethnology: A Practical History.* Norman: University of Oklahoma Press.

Kaczkurkin, Mini Valenzuela. 1977. *Yoeme: Lore of the Arizona Yaqui People.* Tucson: University of Arizona Press.

Kaduschin, C. 1968. Power, Influence, and Social Circles: A New Methodology for Studying Opinion Makers. *American Sociological Review* 33:685–99.

Kanter, R. N. 1977. *Men and Women of the Corporation.* New York: Basic Books.

Kardiner, Abram. 1939. *The Individual and His Society: The Psychodynamics of Primitive Social Organization.* New York: Columbia University Press.

Kardiner, Abram, and Edward Preble. 1961. *They Studied Man.* New York: The World Publishing Company.

Keleher, W. A. 1964. Erna Mary Fergusson, 1888–1964. *New Mexico Historical Review.* 39(4): 345–50.

Keller, Evelyn Fox. 1985. *Reflections on Gender and Science.* New Haven, Conn.: Yale University Press.

Kelley, Jane Holden. 1966. The Archeology of the Sierra Blanca Region of Southeastern New Mexico. Ph.D. dissertation, Anthropology Department, Harvard University.

———. 1978. *Yaqui Women: Contemporary Life Histories.* Lincoln: University of Nebraska Press.

———. 1979. The Sierra Blanca Restudy Project. In

Jornada Mogollon Archaeology, ed. P. H. Beckett and R. N. Wiseman, pp. 107–32. Las Cruces and Santa Fe: New Mexico State University Press and Historic Preservation Bureau, Department of Finance Administration, State of New Mexico.

———. 1984. *The Archaeology of the Sierra Blanca Region of Southeastern New Mexico.* Anthropological Papers of the Museum of Anthropology, University of Michigan, No. 74. Ann Arbor: Museum of Anthropology, University of Michigan.

———. 1989. Being and Becoming. Paper delivered at Women in Archaeology: The Second Annual Symposium on the History of Theory in American Archaeology. 54th Annual Meeting of the Society for American Archaeology, April 5–9, Atlanta.

Kelley, Jane H., and Marsha P. Hanen. 1988. *Archaeology and the Methodology of Science.* Albuquerque: University of New Mexico Press.

Kelly, Lawrence C. 1980. Anthropology and Anthropologists in the Indian New Deal. *Journal of the History of the Behavioral Sciences* 16:6–24.

———. 1985. Why Applied Anthropology Developed when It Did: A Commentary on People, Money, and Changing Times. In *Social Context of American Ethnology, 1840–1984,* ed. June Helm, pp. 122–38. Washington, D.C.: American Ethnological Society.

Kelly, William H. 1954. Applied Anthropology in the Southwest. *American Anthropologist* 56: 709–16.

Kendall, Martha B. 1975. A Preliminary Survey of Upland Yuman Dialects. *Anthropological Linguistics* 17(3): 89–101.

———. 1976. *Selected Problems in Yavapai Syntax: The Verde Valley Dialect.* New York: Garland Press.

———. 1977. The Upland Yuman Numerical System. In *Proceedings of the 1976 Hokan-Yuman Languages Workshop,* ed. James Redden, pp. 17–28. Museum Research Record No. 11. Carbondale: Southern Illinois University.

Kent, Kate Peck. 1983a. *Prehistoric Textiles of the Southwest.* School of American Research. Albuquerque: University of New Mexico Press.

———. 1983b. *Pueblo Indian Textiles: A Living Tradition.* Santa Fe, N.M.: School of American Research Press.

———. 1985a. *Navajo Weaving: Three Centuries of Change.* Santa Fe, N.M.: School of American Research Press.

———. 1985b. Interview (with Jennifer Fox) for the Daughters of the Desert Oral History Project. September 4, El Rito, N.M. Audio Recording. New York: Wenner-Gren Foundation for Anthropological Research.

Kessler, Suzanne J., and Wendy McKenna. 1978. *Gender: An Ethnomethodological Approach.* New York: John Wiley and Sons.

Keur, Dorothy Louise Strouse. 1941. *Big Bead Mesa: An Archaeological Study of Navaho Acculturation, 1745–1912.* Memoirs of the Society for American Archaeology No. 1. Menasha, Wis.: Society for American Archaeology.

———. 1985. Interview (with Jennifer Fox) for the Daughters of the Desert Oral History Project. August 6 & 7, Santa Fe, N.M. Audio and Video Recording. New York: Wenner-Gren Foundation for Anthropological Research.

Khasket, Eva Ruth, Mary Louise Robbins, Loretta Levine, and Alice S. Huang. 1974. Status of Women Microbiologists. *Science* 183(4124): 488–94.

Kibbee, Jo. 1988. Frances Gillmor. In *Women Anthropologists: A Biographical Dictionary,* ed. Ute Gacs, Aisha Kahn, Jerrie McIntyre, and Ruth Weinberg, pp. 115–119. New York: Greenwood Press.

Kidder, Alfred V. 1949. Introduction. In *Prehistoric Southwesterners from Basket-maker to Pueblo* by Charles A. Amsden, pp. xi–xiv. Los Angeles: Southwest Museum.

———. 1957. Harriet and Burton Cosgrove. *New Mexico Quarterly* 27:52–55.

Kidder, Alfred V., and Anna Shepard. 1936. *The Potter of Pecos,* vol. 2. Papers of the Phillips Academy Southwest Expedition No. 7. Andover, Mass.: Phillips Academy.

Kimball, Solon. 1950. Future Problems in Navajo Administration. *Human Organization* 9(2): 21–24.

———. 1979. Land Use Management: The Navajo Reservation. In *The Users of Anthropology,* ed.

W. Goldschmidt, pp. 61–78. American Anthropological Association, Special Publication No. 11. Washington, D.C.: American Anthropological Association.

King, Dale Stuart. 1976. *Indian Silverwork of the Southwest,* vol. 2. Tucson: Dale Stuart King.

Klein, Viola. 1974. *The Feminist Character: A History of an Ideology.* Urbana: University of Illinois Press.

Kluckhohn, Clyde. 1927. *To the Foot of the Rainbow.* New York: Century.

———. 1933. *Beyond the Rainbow.* Boston: Christopher.

———. 1937. The Field of Higher Education in the Southwest. *New Mexico Quarterly* 7:23–30.

———. 1943. Covert Culture and Administrative Problems. *American Anthropologist* 45:213–27.

———. 1941. Patterning as Exemplified in Navaho Culture. In *Language, Culture and Personality,* ed. Leslie F. Spier, pp. 109–30. Menasha, Wis.: Sapir Memorial Publication Fund.

———. 1944a. The Influence of Psychiatry on Anthropology in America during the Past One Hundred Years. In *One Hundred Years of American Psychiatry,* ed. J. K. Hall et al. New York: Columbia University Press.

———. 1944b. *Navajo Witchcraft.* Boston: Beacon Press.

———. 1949. Introduction: The Ramah Project. In *Gregorio, the Hand–trembler* by Alexander H. and Dorothea Leighton. Papers of the Peabody Museum of Archaeology and Ethnology Vol. 40 No. 1, pp. v–x. Cambridge, Mass.: Peabody Museum.

———. 1951a. Foreword: A Comparative Study of Values in Five Cultures. In *Navaho Veterans* by Evon Z. Vogt. Papers of the Peabody Museum of Archaeology and Ethnology Vol. 41 No. 1, pp. vii–xii. Cambridge, Mass.: Peabody Museum.

———. 1951b. Values and Value-Orientations in the Theory of Action. In *Towards a General Theory of Action,* ed. Talcott Parsons and Edward Shils, pp. 388–433. Cambridge, Mass.: Harvard University Press.

———. 1954. Southwestern Studies of Culture and Personality. *American Anthropologist* 56(4): 685–708.

Kluckhohn, Clyde, and Dorothea Leighton. 1946. *The Navaho.* Cambridge, Mass.: Harvard University Press.

Kluckhohn, Clyde, and Leland C. Wyman. 1940. *An Introduction to Navaho Chant Practice with an Account of the Behaviors Observed in Four Chants.* American Anthropological Association Memoir No. 53. Menasha, Wis.: American Anthropological Association.

Kohlstedt, Sally Gregory. 1978. Working in from the Periphery: Women in Nineteenth Century American Science. *SIGNS* 4(1): 81–96.

Kramer, Carol, and Miriam Stark. 1988. The Status of Women in Archaeology. *Anthropology Newsletter* 29(9): 1, 11–12.

Kroeber, A. L. 1917. *Zuni Kin and Clan.* Anthropological Papers of the American Museum of Natural History No. 18 (2). New York: American Museum of Natural History.

———. 1943. Elsie Clews Parsons. *American Anthropologist* 45:252–55.

Kuhn, Thomas. 1962. *The Structure of Scientific Revolutions.* Chicago: University of Chicago Press.

Kuper, Adam. 1985. *Anthropology and Anthropologists: The Modern British School.* London: Routledge and Kegan Paul.

Kurath, Gertude, and A. Garcia. 1969. *Music and Dance of the Tewa Pueblos.* Albuquerque: University of New Mexico Press.

Laboratory of Anthropology. 1931a. Report of the Conference between the Building Committee and Mary Cabot Wheelwright, October 15. No. 89 LAZ.0020.2A. Laboratory of Anthropology Archives, Santa Fe, N.M.

———. 1931b. Alfred V. Kidder to Board of Trustees, December 3. No. 89 LAZ.020.2A. Laboratory of Anthropology Archives, Santa Fe, N.M.

LaBarre, Weston. 1949. Toward World Civilization. *The Survey* 85:153–56.

Laird, Carobeth. 1975. *Encounter with an Angry God.* New York: Ballantine Books.

Lamb, Daniel S. 1904. The Story of the Anthropological Society of Washington. *American Anthropologist* 6(n.s.): 564–79.

Lambert, Marjorie Ferguson. 1954. *Paa-ko: Archaeological Chronicle of an Indian Village in North Central New Mexico.* School of American Research Monographs No. 19. Santa Fe, N.M.: School of American Research.

———. 1985. Interview (with Jennifer Fox) for the Daughters of the Desert Oral History Project. September 2, Santa Fe, N.M. Audio Recording. New York: Wenner-Gren Foundation for Anthropological Research.

Lamphere, Louise. 1969. Symbolic Elements of Navajo Ritual. *Southwestern Journal of Anthropology* 25(3): 279–305.

———. 1976. The Internal Colonization of the Navajo People. *Southwestern Economy and Society* 1:1–23.

———. 1978. Long Term Research among the Navajo. In *Long Term Research in Anthropology,* ed. Elizabeth Colson, Thayer Scudder, and R. V. Kemper, pp. 15–44. New York: Academic Press.

———. 1986. From Working Daughters to Working Mothers: Production and Reproduction in an Industrial Community. *American Ethnologist* 13:118–30.

———. 1989. Feminist Anthropology: The Legacy of Elsie Clews Parsons. *American Ethnologist* 16(3): 518–33.

Lamphere, Louise, and Evon Z. Vogt. 1973. Clyde Kluckhohn as Ethnographer and Student of Navaho Ceremonialism. In *Culture and Life,* ed. Walter W. Taylor, John Fischer, and Evon Z. Vogt, pp. 94–135. Carbondale: Southern Illinois Press.

Lancaster, J. A., Jean Pinkley, P. Van Cleave, and Don Watson. 1950. *Archaeological Excavations in Mesa Verde National Park, Colorado.* National Park Service Archaeological Research Series No. 2. Washington, D.C.: GPO.

Lander, Patricia A. 1972. Male and Female: New Data from the AAA Membership Survey. *Anthropology Newsletter* 13:8–10.

Langdon, Margaret. 1968. The Proto-Yuman Demonstrative System. *Folla Linguistica* 2(1/2): 61–81.

———. 1970. *A Grammar of Diegueno: The Mesa Grande Dialect.* Berkeley: University of California Press.

———. 1974. *Comparative Hokan-Coahuiltecan Studies: A Survey and Appraisal.* The Hague: Mouton.

———. 1975a. Kamia and Kumeyaay: A Linguistic Perspective. *Journal of California Anthropology* 26:64–70.

———. 1975b. Boundaries and Lenition in Yuman Languages. *International Journal of American Linguistics* 41:218–33.

———. 1976a. The Proto-Yuman Vowel System. In *Hokan Studies,* ed. Margaret Langdon and Shirley Silver, pp. 129–48. The Hague: Mouton.

———. 1976b. Metathesis in Yuman Languages. *Language* 52:866–83.

———. 1976c. The Story of Eagle's Nest—A Diegueno Text. *International Journal of American Linguistics* Native American Series 1:113–33.

———. 1977a. The Origin of Progressive Markers in Yuman. In *Proceedings of the 1977 Hokan-Yuman Languages Workshop,* ed. James E. Redden, pp. 52–57. University Museum Studies No. 11. Carbondale: Southern Illinois University.

———. 1977b. Yuma (Kwtsaan) after 40 Years. In *Proceedings of the First Yuman Languages Workshop,* ed. James E. Redden, pp. 43–51. University Museum Studies No. 11. Carbondale: Southern Illinois University.

———. 1977c. The Semantics and Syntax of Expressive "Say" Constructions in Yuman. In *Proceedings of the Third Conference of the Berkeley Linguistic Society* 2:1–11. Berkeley: University of California.

———. 1977d. Stress, Length, and Pitch in Yuman Languages. In *Studies in Stress and Accent,* ed. Larry Hyman, pp. 239–59. Occasional Papers in Linguistics No. 4. Los Angeles: University of Southern California.

———. 1978. Animal Talk in Cocopa. *International Journal of American Linguistics, Native American Text Series* 44:10–16. Bloomington: Indiana University.

———. 1979. Some Thoughts on Hokan with Particular Reference to Pomoan and Yuman. In *The Languages of Native America,* ed. Lyle Campbell and Marianne Mithun, pp. 592–642. Austin: University of Texas Press.

Langdon, Margaret, and Pamela Munro. 1979. Subject and Switch Reference in Yuman. *Folia Linguistica* 13:321–44.

———. 1980. Yuman Numerals. In *American Indian and Indoeuropean Studies: Papers in Honor of Madison S. Beeler,* ed. Kathryn Klar, Margaret Langdon, and Shirley Silver, pp. 121–35. The Hague: Mouton.

Lange, Charles H. 1959. *Cochiti: A New Mexico Pueblo, Past and Present.* University of Texas Press. (Reprinted by Arcturus Books, Southern Illinois University Press, 1968.)

———. 1986. Comments. Daughters of the Desert Conference. Globe, Ariz.: Wenner-Gren Foundation for Anthropological Research.

Langness, L., and G. Frank. 1981. *Lives: An Anthropological Approach to Biography.* Novato, Calif.: Chandler and Sharp.

Larcombe, Claudia. 1983. E. Boyd: A Biographical Sketch. In *Hispanic Arts and Ethnohistory,* ed. Marta Weigle, pp. 3–13. Santa Fe, N.M.: Ancient City Press.

Leacock, Eleanor Burke. 1977. Women in Egalitarian Societies. In *Becoming Visible: Women in European History,* ed. Renate Bridenthal and Claudia Koontz, pp. 11–35. Boston: Houghton, Mifflin.

———. 1981. *Myths of Male Dominance.* New York: Monthly Review Press.

———. 1986. Discussion Comments, March 17. Daughters of the Desert Conference. Globe, Ariz.: Wenner-Gren Foundation for Anthropological Research.

———. 1988. Gladys Amanda Reichard. In *Women Anthropologists: A Biographical Dictionary,* ed. Ute Gacs, Aisha Kahn, Jerrie McIntyre, and Ruth Weinberg, pp. 303–9. New York: Greenwood Press.

Leaf, Murray J. 1979. *Man, Mind and Science: A History of Anthropology.* New York: Columbia University Press.

Lederman, R. 1986. The Return of the Redwoman: Fieldwork in Highland New Guinea. In *Women in the Field: Anthropological Experiences,* ed. Peggy Golde, pp. 261–88. Berkeley: University of California Press.

Lee, Dorothy. 1949. Ruth Fulton Benedict (1887–1948). *Journal of American Folklore* 62(246): 345–47.

Leighton, Alexander H. 1945. *The Governing of Men.* Princeton, N.J.: Princeton University Press.

Leighton, Alexander H., and Dorothea Leighton. 1942. Some Types of Uneasiness and Fear in a Navaho Indian Community. *American Anthropologist* 44:194–210.

———. 1944. *The Navaho Door.* Cambridge, Mass.: Harvard University Press.

Leighton, Dorothea. 1985. Interview (with Jennifer Fox) for Daughters of the Desert Oral History Project. November 21 & 22, Santa Fe, N.M. Audio and Video Recording. New York: Wenner-Gren Foundation for Anthropological Research.

Leighton, Dorothea, and John Adair. 1966. *People of the Middle Place.* New Haven, Conn.: Human Relations Area Files Press.

Leighton, Dorothea, and Clyde Kluckhohn. 1947. *The Children of the People.* Cambridge, Mass.: Harvard University Press.

Leonard, John W., ed. 1914. Stevenson, Matilda Coxe. *Woman's Who's Who of America, 1914–1915,* p. 781. New York: The American Commonwealth Co.

Leonard, Olen E., and Charles P. Loomis. 1941. *Culture of a Contemporary Rural Community: El Cerrito, N.M.* U.S. Department of Agriculture, Bureau of Agricultural Economics, Rural Life Studies No. 1. Washington, D.C.: GPO.

Leone, Mark P. 1973. Archaeology as the Science of Technology: Mormon Town Plans and Fences. In *Research and Theory in Current Archaeology,* ed. Charles Redman, pp. 125–50. New York: Wiley and Sons.

Letson, Neil. 1984. A Woman of Some Importance. *Connoisseur* June:110–15.

Lévi-Strauss, Claude. 1963. *Structural Anthropology.* New York: Basic Books.

———. 1964. *The Raw and the Cooked.* New York: Harper Torch Books.

Levy, Jerrold. 1964. Interpreter Training Program. Mimeograph, U.S. Public Health Service.

———. 1965a. Navajo Suicide. *Human Organization* 24:308–18.

———. 1965b. *Indian Drinking: Navajo Practice and*

Anglo-American Theories. New York: John Wiley and Sons.

Levy, Jerrold, and Stephen J. Kunitz. 1971. Indian Reservations, Anomie, and Social Pathology. *Southwestern Journal of Anthropology* 27:97–128.

———. 1974. *Indian Drinking: Navajo Practices and Anglo-American Theories.* New York: John Wiley and Sons.

Levy, Jerrold, Raymond Neutra, and Dennis Parker. 1987. *Hand Trembling, Frenzy Witchcraft, and Moth Madness: A Study of Navajo Seizure Disorders.* Tucson: University of Arizona Press.

Li An-Che. 1937. Zuni: Some Observations and Queries. *American Anthropologist* 39:62–76.

Linton, Ralph, ed. 1940. *Acculturation in Seven American Indian Tribes.* New York: Appleton-Century.

Lister, Florence, and Robert H. Lister. 1968. *Earl Morris and Southwestern Archaeology.* Albuquerque: University of New Mexico Press.

Lister, Robert H., and Florence C. Lister. 1981. *Chaco Canyon Archaeology and Archaeologists.* Albuquerque: University of New Mexico Press.

Loeb, Jane, and Marianne Ferber. 1971. Sex as Predictive of Salary and Status on a University Faculty. *Journal of Educational Measurements* 8(Winter): 235–44.

Longacre, William A. 1970. *Archaeology as Anthropology: A Case Study.* Anthropological Papers of the University of Arizona No. 17. Tucson: University of Arizona Press.

Lonn, Ella. 1924. Academic Status of Women on University Faculties. *Journal of American Association of University Women* 17(1): 5–11.

Loomis, Charles P., and Glen Grisham. 1943. The New Mexico Experiment in Village Rehabilitation. *Applied Anthropology* 2(3): 13–37.

Loomis, Charles P., and Nellie H. Loomis. 1942. Skilled Spanish American War-Industry Workers from New Mexico. *Applied Anthropology* 2(1): 33–36.

Loughlin, Bernice W. 1962. A Study of the Needs of the Pregnant Women in a Selected Group of Navajo Women. Master's thesis, School of Public Health, University of North Carolina.

Lovano-Kerr, Jessie, and Rachel Fuchs. 1983. Retention Revisited. *Journal of Educational Equity and Leadership* 3(3): 219–30.

Lowie, Robert H. 1937. *The History of Ethnological Theory.* New York: Farrer and Rinehart.

Lowie, Robert, and Leta Hollingworth. 1916. Science and Feminism. *Scientific Monthly* 4(9): 277–84.

Lurie, Nancy O. 1966. Women in Early Anthropology. In *Pioneers of American Anthropology: The Early Uses of Biography,* ed. June Helm, pp. 29–81. Seattle: University of Washington Press.

———. 1971. Stevenson, Matilda Coxe Evans. In *Notable American Women, 1607–1950,* vol. 3, ed. Edward T. James et al., pp. 373–74. Cambridge, Mass.: Belknap Press of Harvard University.

———. 1978. The Indian Claims Commission. *Annals of the American Academy of Political and Social Science* 436 (March): 97–110.

Lutkehaus, Nancy. 1986. "She Was VERY Cambridge": Camilla Wedgewood and the History of Women in British Social Anthropology. *American Ethnologist* 13(4): 776–98.

———. 1990. Refractions of Reality: On the Use of Other Ethnographers' Fieldnotes. In *Fieldnotes: The Makings of Anthropology,* ed. Roger Sanjek, pp. 313–23. Ithaca, N.Y.: Cornell University Press.

Lutz, Catherine. 1990. The Erasure of Women's Writing in Sociocultural Anthropology. *American Ethnologist* 17(4): 611–27.

Lyon, William H. 1989. Gladys Reichard at the Frontier of Navajo Culture. *American Indian Quarterly* 13(2): 137–63.

Lytle-Webb, Jamie. 1988. Clara Lee Fraps Tanner. In *Women Anthropologists: A Biographical Dictionary,* ed. Ute Gacs, Aisha Kahn, Jerrie McIntyre, and Ruth Weinberg, pp. 350–60. New York: Greenwood Press.

MacCormack, Carol P. 1980. Nature, Culture and Gender: A Critique. In *Nature, Culture and Gender,* ed. C. P. MacCormack and Marilyn Strathern, pp. 1–24. Cambridge: Cambridge University Press.

MacCormack, Carol, and Marilyn Strathern, eds. 1980. *Nature, Culture, and Gender.* Cambridge: Cambridge University Press.

McDermott, W., K. Deuschle, J. Adair, H. Fulmer, and B. Loughlin. 1960. Introducing Modern Medicine in a Navajo Community. *Science* 131:197–205, 280–87.

McElroy, Elsie. 1944. Dr. Gladys A. Reichard—The Pollen of Dawn Has Instructed Her. Typescript. Ms. on file, Reichard Papers, Museum of Northern Arizona Archives, Flagstaff.

McGee, Anita Newcombe. 1889. *Historical Sketch of the Women's Anthropological Society of America.* Washington, D.C.: Privately printed.

McGee, William J. 1904. Report of the Director. In *23rd Annual Report of the Bureau of American Ethnology for 1901–1902,* pp. ix–xiv. Washington, D.C.: GPO.

McGrath, J. E., and I. Altman. 1966. *Small Group Research: A Synthesis and Critique of the Field.* New York: Holt, Rinehart and Winston.

Macgregor, Gordon. 1946. *Warriors without Weapons.* Chicago: University of Chicago Press.

———. 1955. Anthropology in Government: United States. In *Yearbook of Anthropology,* ed. W. L. Thomas, pp. 421–33. New York: Wenner-Gren Foundation for Anthropological Research.

McHenry, Robert, ed. 1980. *Liberty's Women.* Chicago: Merriam-Webster.

McNickle, D'Arcy. 1979. Anthropology and the Indian Reorganization Act. In *The Uses of Anthropology,* ed. Walter Goldschmidt, pp. 51–60. American Anthropological Association Publication No. 4. Washington, D.C.: American Anthropological Association.

McNickle, D'Arcy, and Viola G. Pfrommer. n.d. Dine? Txah: A Community Experience. (Report of Crownpoint, N.M., Project 1953–60). Ms. on file, Newberry Library, Chicago.

Malefijt, Annemarie de Waal. 1974. *Images of Man: A History of Anthropological Thought.* New York: Alfred A. Knopf.

Malinowski, Bronislaw. 1961. *Argonauts of the Western Pacific.* New York: Dutton [1922].

———. 1967. *A Diary in the Strict Sense of the Term.* New York: Harcourt Brace.

Malleus Maleficarum. 1928. Translated and with an introduction, bibliography, and notes by Rev. Montague Summers. New York: Blom, Inc.

Mandelbaum, David G., ed. 1949. *Selected Writings of Edward Sapir in Language, Culture, and Personality.* Berkeley: University of California Press.

Mandelbaum, David G., Gabriel W. Lakser, and Ethel M. Albert. 1963. *Resources for the Teaching of Anthropology.* Memoirs of the American Anthropological Association No. 63. Washington, D.C.: American Anthropological Association.

Manners, Robert A. 1974. Introduction to the Ethnohistorical Reports on the Land Claims Cases. (Reprinted in each volume of the Garland Series on American Indian Ethnohistory; see Ellis 1974.)

Manners, Robert A., and David Kaplan. 1968. *Theory in Anthropology: A Sourcebook.* Chicago: Aldine.

Marcus, George, and Michael Fischer. 1986. *Anthropology as Cultural Critique: An Experimental Moment in Human Sciences.* Chicago: University of Chicago Press.

Mark, Joan. 1980a. *Four Anthropologists: An American Science in Its Early Years.* New York: Science History Publications.

———. 1980b. Reichard, Gladys. In *Notable American Women,* vol. 4, ed. Barbara Sicherman and Coral Hurd Green, pp. 572–74. Cambridge, Mass.: Harvard University Press.

———. 1986. Presentation and Discussion Comments. Daughters of the Desert Conference. Globe, Ariz.: Wenner-Gren Foundation for Anthropological Research.

———. 1988. *A Stranger in Her Native Land: Alice Fletcher and the American Indians.* Lincoln: University of Nebraska Press.

Marquis, Albert Nelson, ed. 1914. Stevenson, Matilda Coxe. In *Who's Who in America: 1914–1915,* vol. 18, pp. 2239–40. Chicago: A. N. Marquis.

Marriott, Alice. 1948. *Maria: The Potter of San Ildefonso.* Norman: University of Oklahoma Press.

———. 1952. *Green Fields: Experiences among the American Indian.* New York: Dolphin.

———. 1986. Interview (with Jennifer Fox) for the Daughters of the Desert Oral History Project. March 31, Tucson, Ariz. Audio Recording. New York: Wenner-Gren Foundation for Anthropological Research.

Maslow, Abraham H., and John J. Honigmann. 1970. Synergy: Some Notes on Ruth Benedict. *American Anthropologist* 72(2): 320–33.

Mason, Otis T. 1886. The Planting and Exhuming of a Prayer. *Science* 8(179): 24–25.

———. 1888. *What is Anthropology?* Washington, D.C.: Judd and Detweiler, Women's Anthropological Society.

Maxwell, Margaret. 1982. *A Passion For Freedom: The Life of Sharlot Hall.* Tucson: University of Arizona Press.

May, Laurie D. 1988. The Women's Anthropological Society, 1885–1899: "Earnest in the Search for Truth." Master's thesis, George Washington University, Washington, D.C.

Mead, Margaret. 1928. *Coming of Age in Samoa.* New York: Morrow

———. 1959a. *An Anthropologist at Work: Writings of Ruth Benedict.* Boston: Houghton Mifflin. (Reprinted 1973.)

———. 1959b. Apprenticeship under Boas. In *The Anthropology of Franz Boas: Essays on the Centennial of His Birth,* ed. Walter Goldschmidt, pp. 29–45. Memoirs of the American Anthropological Association No. 89. Washington, D.C.: American Anthropological Association.

———. 1960. Introduction. In *The Golden Age of American Anthropology,* ed. Margaret Mead and Ruth L. Bunzel, pp. 1–12. New York: George Braziller.

———. 1965. *Anthropologists and What They Do.* New York: Franklin Watts.

———. 1972. *Blackberry Winter: My Earlier Years.* New York: William Morrow.

———. 1973. Changing Styles of Anthropological Work. *Annual Review of Anthropology* 3: 1–26.

———. 1974. *Ruth Benedict.* New York: Columbia University Press.

———. 1986. Field Work in Pacific Islands. In *Women in the Field,* ed. Peggy Golde, pp. 293–331. Berkeley: University of California Press.

Mead, Margaret, ed. 1953. *Cultural Patterns and Technical Change.* New York: United Nations Educational, Scientific, and Cultural Organization.

———. 1973. *An Anthropologist at Work: Writings of Ruth Benedict.* New York: Avon Books. [Reprint of 1959 edition.]

Mead, Margaret, and Ruth L. Bunzel, eds. 1960. *The Golden Age of American Anthropology.* New York: George Braziller.

Meadows, Karen. 1986. Sisters in Spirit: Florence Dibble Bartlett, Mary Cabot Wheelwright and Amelia Elizabeth White. *El Palacio* 92(1): 7–11.

Mekeel, Scudder. 1944. An Appraisal of the Indian Reorganization Act. *American Anthropologist* 46: 209–17.

Menges, Robert J., and William H. Exum. 1983. Barriers to the Progress of Women and Minority Faculty. *Journal of Higher Education* 54(2): 123–44.

Merton, Robert K. 1957. *Social Theory and Social Structure.* Glencoe, IL: The Free Press.

Miller, Jimmy H. 1985. *A Philadelphia Brahmin in Flagstaff: The Life of Harold Sellers Colton.* Ph.D. dissertation, departments of History and Political Science, Northern Arizona University. Ms. on file, Museum of Northern Arizona Archives.

Mintz, Sidney W. 1981. Ruth Benedict. In *Totems and Teachers: Perspectives on the History of Anthropology,* ed. Sydel Silverman, pp. 141–70. New York: Columbia University Press.

———. 1986. Discussion Comments. Daughters of the Desert Conference. Globe, Ariz.: Wenner-Gren Foundation for Anthropological Research.

Mithun, Marianne. 1990. Studies in North American Languages. *Annual review of Anthropology* 19: 309–30.

Modell, Judith Schachter. 1975. Ruth Benedict, Anthropologist: The Reconciliation of Science and Humanism. In *Toward a Science of Man: Essays in the History of Anthropology,* ed. Timothy H. H. Thoresen, pp. 183–203. The Hague: Mouton.

———. 1983. *Ruth Benedict: Patterns of a Life.* Philadelphia: University of Pennsylvania Press.

———. 1988. Ruth Fulton Benedict. In *Women Anthropologists: A Biographical Dictionary,* ed. Ute Gacs, Aisha Kahn, Jerrie McIntyre, and Ruth

Weinberg, pp. 1–7. New York: Greenwood Press.

Moises, Rosalia, Jane Holden Kelley, and William C. Holden. 1971. *The Tall Candle: The Personal Chronicle of a Yaqui Indian*. Lincoln: University of Nebraska Press.

———. 1977. *A Yaqui Life: The Personal Chronicle of a Yaqui Indian*. Lincoln: University of Nebraska Press.

Moldow, Gloria. 1987. *Women Doctors in Gilded-Age Washington: Race, Gender, and Professionalization*. Urbana: University of Illinois Press.

Moore, Eoline W. 1946. Women Faculty Members in Alabama Colleges in Wartime. *Journal of American Association of University Women* 39(3): 150–51.

Moore, Henrietta. 1988. *Feminism and Anthropology*. Cambridge, Mass.: Polity Press.

Morlock, Laura. 1973. Discipline Variation in the Status of Academic Women. In *Academic Women on the Move*, ed. Alice S. Rossi and Ann Calderwood, pp. 255–312. New York: Russell Sage Foundation.

Morris, Ann Axtell. 1930. *Rock Paintings and Petroglyphs of the American Indian*. New York: American Museum of Natural History.

———. 1931. *Digging in Yucatan*. Garden City, N.Y.: Doubleday, Doran and Company.

———. 1933. *Digging in the Southwest*. New York: Doubleday, Doran and Company. Morris, Earl H. 1915. The Excavation of a Ruin near Aztec, San Juan County, New Mexico. *American Anthropologist* 17:656–84.

Morris, Earl H., Jean Charlot, and Ann Axtell Morris. 1931. *The Temple of the Warriors at Chichen Itza, Yucatan*. 2 vols. Carnegie Institution of Washington Publication No. 406. Washington, D.C.: Carnegie Institution.

Morris, Elizabeth A. 1974. Ana O. Shepard, 1903–1973. *American Antiquity* 39:448–51.

Mukhopadhyay, Carol C., and Patricia J. Higgins. 1988. Anthropological Studies of Women's Status Revisited: 1977–1987. *Annual Review of Anthropology* 17:461–95.

Muller, Jon D. 1979. Structural Studies of Art Styles. In *The Visual Arts: Plastic and Graphic*, ed. Justine M. Cordwell, pp. 139–211. The

Hague: Mouton de Gruyter.

Mullins, N. C. 1968. The Distribution of Social and Cultural Properties in Informal Communication Networks among Biological Scientists. *American Sociological Review* 33:786–97.

Munro, Pamela. 1973. Reanalysis and Elaboration in Yuman Negatives. *Linguistics Notes from La Jolla* 5:56–62.

———. 1976a. *Mojave Syntax*. New York: Garland.

———. 1976b. Subject Copying, Auxiliarization, and Predicate Raising: The Mojave Evidence. *International Journal of American Linguistics* 42:99–112.

———. 1976c. Mojave Modals. In *Proceedings of the First Yuman Languages Workshop*, ed. James E. Redden, pp. 55–62. University Museum Studies No. 7. Carbondale: Southern Illinois University.

———. 1980a. On the Syntactic of Switch-Reference Clauses: The Special Case of Mojave Comitative. In *Studies of Switch Reference*, ed. Pamela Munro, pp. 145–59. Papers in Linguistics No. 8. Los Angeles: University of California.

———. 1980b. Types of Agreement in Mojave. *Proceedings of the 1979 Hokan Languages Workshop*, ed. James E. Redden, pp. 1–14. Occasional Papers on Linguistics No. 7. Carbondale: Southern Illinois University.

———. 1981a. Two Notes on Yuman "Say." In *Proceedings of the 1979 Hokan Languages Workshop*, ed. James E. Redden, pp. 70–77. Occasional Papers on Linguistics No. 9. Carbondale: Southern Illinois University.

———. 1981b. Mojave -k and -m: It Ain't Necessarily So. In *Proceedings of the 1980 Hokan Languages Workshop*, ed. James E. Redden, pp. 124–29. Occasional Papers on Linguistics No. 9. Carbondale: Southern Illinois University.

———. 1981c. Vowel-Initial Roots in Yuman. In *Proceedings of the 1981 Hokan Languages Workshop*, ed. James E. Redden, pp. 24–36. Occasional Papers on Linguistics No. 10. Carbondale: Southern Illinois University.

———. 1982. *Transitivity*. New York: Academic Press.

Munro, Pamela, and John Haiman, eds. 1983. *Switch Reference and Universal Grammar.* Philadelphia: John Benjamins.

Murphy, Eula Parker. 1953. Lecture to the Maie Bartlett School. Ms. on file, Heard Museum Archives, Phoenix.

Murphy, Robert. 1976. *Selected Papers from the American Anthropologist, 1946–1970.* Washington, D.C.: American Anthropological Association.

Museum of International Folk Art. 1950. Florence Dibble Bartlett File. Museum of International Folk Art Archives, Santa Fe, N.M.

———. 1963. A Tribute to Florence Dibble Bartlett by Her Friends. Trustees, October 5. Florence Dibble Bartlett File. Museum of International Folk Art Archives, Santa Fe, N.M.

Museum of Northern Arizona. 1959. Certificate of Appreciation, Mary-Russell Ferrell Colton File. Museum of Northern Arizona Archives, Flagstaff.

Nader, Laura. 1986. From Anguish to Exultation. In *Women in the Field: Anthropological Experiences,* ed. Peggy Golde, pp. 94–116. Berkeley: University of California Press.

National Center for Educational Statistics. 1981. *The Condition of Education.* Washington, D.C.: GPO.

Newcomb, Franc Johnson. 1964. *Hosteen Klah: Navaho Medicine Man and Sand Painter.* Norman: University of Oklahoma Press.

Newcomb, Franc J., and Gladys A. Reichard. 1937. *Sandpaintings of the Navajo Shooting Chant.* New York: J. J. Augustin.

New School for Social Research. 1919. *Bulletin.* New York: New School for Social Research.

Norwood, Susan. 1981. Progressives in Yuman and Romance. Unpublished Ph.D. dissertation, University of California, San Diego.

Nusbaum, Aileen O'Bryan. 1926. *Zuni Indian Tales.* New York: G. P. Putnam's Sons.

———. 1956. *The Dine: Origin Myths of the Navajo Indians.* Bureau of American Ethnology Bulletin No. 163. Washington D.C.: GPO.

Nusbaum, Rosemary. 1980. *Tierra Dulce: Reminiscences from the Jesse Nusbaum Papers.* Santa Fe, N.M.: Sunstone.

Oates, Mary J., and Susan Williamson. 1978. Women's Colleges and Women Achievers. *SIGNS* 3(4): 795–806.

Omran, A. R., and Bernice Loughlin. 1972. An Epidemiological Study of Accidents among the Navajo Indians. *Journal of the Egyptian Medical Association* 55 : 1–22.

Opler, Morris E. 1987. Response to Dr. Farrer. In Past is Present. *Anthropological Newsletter* March: 3.

Ortiz, Alfonso. 1968. Review of Esther S. Goldfrank's *The Artist of "Isleta Paintings" in Pueblo Society. American Anthropologist* 70(4): 838–39.

Ortner, Sherry B. 1974. Is Female to Male as Nature Is to Culture? In *Women, Culture and Society,* ed. Michelle Rosaldo and Louise Lamphere, pp. 67–87. Stanford, Calif.: Stanford University Press.

Painter, Muriel Thayer. 1950. *The Yaqui Easter Ceremony at Pascua.* Tucson: Chamber of Commerce.

———. 1960. *Easter at Pascua Village.* Tucson: University of Arizona Press.

———. 1971. *A Yaqui Easter.* Tucson: University of Arizona Press.

———. 1986. *With Good Heart: Yaqui Beliefs and Ceremonies in Pascua Village.* Tucson: University of Arizona Press.

Painter, Muriel Thayer, Refugio Savala, and Ignacio Alvarez. 1955. *A Yaqui Easter Sermon.* University of Arizona Social Science Bulletin No. 26. Tucson: University of Arizona.

Painter, Muriel Thayer, and Edwin B. Sayles. 1962. *Faith, Flowers, and Fiestas: The Yaqui Indian Year.* Tucson: University of Arizona Press.

Pandey, Triloki Nath. 1972. Anthropologists at Zuni. *Proceedings of the American Philosophical Society* 116(4): 321–37.

———. 1978. Flora Zuni—A Portrait. In *American Indian Intellectuals,* ed. Margo Liberty, pp. 217–25. 1976 Proceedings of the American Ethnological Society. St. Paul: West.

Papanek, Hanna. 1973. Men, Women, and Work: Reflections on the Two-Person Career. *American Journal of Sociology.* 78(4): 858–72.

Parezo, Nancy J. 1983. *Navajo Sandpainting: From Religious Act to Commercial Art.* Tucson: University of Arizona Press.

———. 1985. Cushing as Part of the Team: The Collecting Activities of the Smithsonian Institution. *American Ethnologist* 12(4): 763–74.

———. 1986. Now Is the Time to Collect. *Masterkey* 59(4): 11–19.

———. 1987. The Formation of Ethnographic Collections: The Smithsonian Institution in the American Southwest. In *Advances in Archaeological Method and Theory,* vol. 10, ed. Michael Schiffer, pp. 1–47. Orlando, Fla.: Academic Press.

———. 1988a. Matilda Coxe Stevenson. In *Women Anthropologists: A Biographical Dictionary,* ed. Ute Gacs, Aisha Kahn, Jerrie McIntyre, and Ruth Weinberg, pp. 337–43. New York: Greenwood Press.

———. 1988b. A Glass Box for Everyone: Displaying Other Cultures. Paper presented at the American Anthropological Association Meeting, November 1988, Phoenix.

———. 1992. Ruth Bunzel: The Search for the Middle Place. Introduction to *Zuni Religion* by Ruth Bunzel. Albuquerque: University of New Mexico Press.

Parezo, Nancy J., Ruth Perry, and Rebecca Allen. 1991. *Southwest Native American Arts and Material Culture: A Resource Guide.* 2 vols. New York: Garland Publications.

Parrish, John. 1962. Women in Top Level Teaching and Research. *AAUP Bulletin* 4(2): 99–107.

Parsons, Elsie Clews. 1900. Field Work in Teaching Sociology. *Educational Review* 20: 159–69.

———. 1906. *The Family.* New York: G. P. Putnam's Sons.

———. 1913a. [John Main] *Religious Chastity.* New York: G. P. Putnam's Sons.

———. 1913b. *The Old Fashioned Woman: Primitive Fancies about the Sex.* New York: G. P. Putnam's Sons.

———. 1914. *Fear and Conventionality.* New York: G. P. Putnam's Sons.

———. 1915. *Social Freedom: A Study of the Conflicts between Social Classification and Personality.* New York: G. P. Putnam's Sons.

———. 1916a. A Few Zuni Death Beliefs and Practices. *American Anthropologist* 18: 245–46.

———. 1916b. The Zuni Adoshle and Suuke. *American Anthropologist* 18: 338–47.

———. 1916c. The Zuni Lamana. *American Anthropologist* 18: 521–28.

———. 1916d. The Zuni Molawia. *Journal of American Folklore* 29: 329–99.

———. 1916e. A Zuni Detective. *MAN* 16: 99–100.

———. 1916f. Zuni Inoculative Magic. *Science* 44: 469–70.

———. 1916g. The Favorite Number of the Zuni. *Scientific Monthly* 3: 596–600.

———. 1916h. *Social Rule: A Study of the Will to Power.* New York: G. P. Putnam's Sons.

———. 1917a. Ceremonial Friendship at Zuni. *American Anthropologist* 19: 1–8.

———. 1917b. All Souls Day at Zuni, Acoma and Laguna. *Journal of American Folklore* 30: 495–96.

———. 1917c. The Antelope Clan in Keresan Custom and Myth. *MAN* 17: 190–93.

———. 1917d. *Notes on Zuni, Part I.* Memoirs of the American Anthropological Association, 4(3). Menasha, Wis.: American Anthropological Association.

———. 1917e. *Notes on Zuni, Part II.* Memoirs of the American Anthropological Association, 4(4). Menasha, Wis.: American Anthropological Association.

———. 1917f. Is the Office of Governor among the Pueblos Spanish? *American Anthropologist* 19: 454–56.

———. 1917g. Reasoning by Analogy at Zuni. *Scientific Monthly* 4: 365–68.

———. 1917h. Zuni Conception and Pregnancy Beliefs. In *Proceedings of the 19th International Congress of Americanists for 1915,* pp. 379–83. Washington, D.C.

———. 1918a. Review of *Zuni Kin and Clan* by A. L. Kroeber. *American Anthropologist* 20: 98–104.

———. 1918b. Notes on Acoma and Laguna. *American Anthropologist* 20: 162–86.

———. 1918c. War God Shrines of Laguna and Zuni. *American Anthropologist* 20: 381–404.

———. 1918d. Pueblo-Indian Folk-Tales, Probably of Spanish Provenience. *Journal of American Folklore* 31: 216–55.

———. 1918e. Nativity Myth at Laguna and Zuni. *Journal of American Folklore* 31:256–63.

———. 1919a. Increase by Magic: A Zuni Pattern. *American Anthropologist* 21:279–86.

———. 1919b. Census of the Shi'wanakwe Society of Zuni. *American Anthropologist* 21:329–35.

———. 1919c. Note on Navajo War Dance. *American Anthropologist* 21:465–67.

———. 1919d. Teshlatiwa at Zuni. *Journal of Philosophy, Psychology and Scientific Methods* 16:272–73.

———. 1919e. Mothers and Children at Laguna. *MAN* 19:34–38.

———. 1919f. Mothers and Children at Zuni. *MAN* 19:168–73.

———. 1919g. Waiyautitsa of Zuni, New Mexico. *Scientific Monthly* 9:443–57.

———. 1920a. A Hopi Ceremonial. *Century* 101:177–80.

———. 1920b. Notes on Isleta, Santa Ana, and Acoma. *American Anthropologist* 22:56–69.

———. 1920c. Notes on Ceremonialism at Laguna. *Anthropological Papers of the American Museum of Natural History* 19:85–132.

———. 1920d. Spanish Tales from Laguna and Zuni, New Mexico. *Journal of American Folklore* 33:47–72.

———. 1921a. Further Notes on Isleta. *American Anthropologist* 23:149–69.

———. 1921b. Notes on Night Chant at Tuwechedu which Came to an End on December 6, 1920. *American Anthropologist* 23:240–43.

———. 1921c. The Pueblo Indian Clan in Folk-Lore. *Journal of American Folklore* 24:209–16.

———. 1921d. Hopi Mothers and Children. *MAN* 21:98–104.

———. 1921e. Getting Married on First Mesa, Arizona. *Scientific Monthly* 13:259–65.

———. 1922a. Waiyautitsa of Zuni, New Mexico. In *American Indian Life*, ed. Elsie Clews Parsons, pp. 157–73. New York: B. W. Huebsch.

———. 1922b. Oraibi in 1920, Shomopavi in 1920. *American Anthropologist* 24(3):294–97.

———. 1922c. Hidden Ball on First Mesa, Arizona. *MAN* 22:89–91.

———. 1922d. Winter and Summer Dance Series in Zuni in 1918. *University of California Publications in American Archaeology and Ethnology* 17:171–216.

———. 1923a. The Hopi Wowochim Ceremony in 1920. *American Anthropologist* 25:156–87.

———. 1923b. Notes on San Felipe and Santo Domingo. *American Anthropologist* 25:485–94.

———. 1923c. Laguna Genealogies. *Anthropological Papers of the American Museum of Natural History* 19:133–292.

———. 1923d. The Origin Myth of Zuni. *Journal of American Folklore* 36:135–62.

———. 1923e. Zuni Names and Naming Practices. *Journal of American Folklore* 36:171–76.

———. 1923f. Navaho Folk-Tales. *Journal of American Folklore* 36:368–75.

———. 1923g. The Hopi Buffalo Dance. *MAN* 23:21–26.

———. 1923h. Fiesta of Sant' Ana, New Mexico. *Scientific Monthly* 16:177–83.

———. 1924a. Tewa Kin, Clan and Moiety. *American Anthropologist* 26:333–39.

———. 1924b. The Religion of the Pueblo Indians. *Proceedings of the 21st International Congress of Americanists*, pp. 140–48. The Hague: E. J. Brill.

———. 1924c. Tewa Mothers and Children. *MAN* 24:148–51.

———. 1924d. *The Scalp Ceremonial of Zuni.* Memoirs of the American Anthropological Association No. 31. Menasha, Wis.: American Anthropological Association.

———. 1925. *The Pueblo of Jemez.* Papers of the Southwestern Expedition No. 3. Andover: Phillips Academy.

———. 1926a. Ceremonial Tewa du Nouveau Mexique et en Arizona. *Journal de la Societe de Americanistas de Paris* 18:9–14.

———. 1926b. Der Spanische Einfluss auf die Marchen der Pueblo-Indianer. *Zeitchrift fur Ethnologie* 58:16–28.

———. 1926c. *Tewa Tales.* Memoirs of the American Folklore Society No. 19. New York: American Ethnological Society.

———. 1926d. Ceremonial Calendar at Tewa. *American Anthropologist* 28:209–29.

———. 1927. Witchcraft among the Pueblos, Indian or Spanish? *MAN* 27:106–12, 125–28.

————. 1928a. Notes on the Pima, 1926. *American Anthropologist* 30:445–64.

————. 1928b. The Laguna Migration to Isleta. *American Anthropologist* 30:602–13.

————. 1929a. *The Social Organization of the Tewa in New Mexico.* Memoirs of the American Anthropological Association No. 36. Menasha, Wis.: American Anthropological Association.

————. 1929b. Masks in the Southwest of the United States. *Mexican Folk-Ways* 5:152.

————. 1929c. Ritual Parallels in Pueblo and Plains Culture. *American Anthropologist* 31:642–54.

————. 1930a. Zuni Tales. *Journal of American Folklore* 43:1–58.

————. 1930b. Spanish Elements in the Kachina Cult of the Pueblos. *Proceedings of the 23rd International Congress of Americanists,* pp. 582–603. New York: The Science Press.

————. 1931a. Review of *Notes on Hopi Clans and Hopi Kinship* by Robert H. Lowie. *American Anthropologist* 33:232–36.

————. 1931b. Laguna Tales. *Journal of American Folklore* 44:137–42.

————. 1932a. Isleta, New Mexico. In *47th Annual Report of the Bureau of American Ethnology,* pp. 192–466. Washington, D.C.: GPO.

————. 1932b. Kinship Nomenclature of the Pueblo Indians. *American Anthropologist* 34:377–89.

————. 1933a. Spring Days in Zuni, New Mexico. *Scientific Monthly* 36:49–54.

————. 1933b. Some Aztec and Pueblo Parallels. *American Anthropologist* 36:611–31.

————. 1933c. *Hopi and Zuni Ceremonialism.* Memoirs of the American Anthropological Association No. 39. Menasha, Wis.: American Anthropological Association.

————. 1936a. *Taos Pueblo.* General Series in Anthropology No. 2. Menasha, Wis.: American Anthropological Association.

————. 1936b. Early Relations between Hopi and Keres. *American Anthropologist* 38:554–60.

————. 1936c. The House Clan Complex of the Pueblos. In *Essays in Anthropology Presented to A. L. Kroeber,* pp. 229–31. Berkeley: University of California Press.

————. 1937a. Review of *Zuni Mythology* by Ruth Benedict and *Zuni Texts* by Ruth Bunzel. *Journal of American Folklore* 50:107–9.

————. 1937b. Naming Practices in Arizona. *American Anthropologist* 39:561–62.

————. 1938. The Humpbacked Flute Player of the Southwest. *American Anthropologist* 40:337–38.

————. 1939a. *Pueblo Indian Religion.* 2 vols. Chicago: University of Chicago Press.

————. 1939b. Picuris, New Mexico. *American Anthropologist* 41:206–22.

————. 1939c. The Franciscans Return to Zuni. *American Anthropologist* 41:337–38.

————. 1939d. The Last Zuni Transvestite. *American Anthropologist* 41:338–40.

————. 1939e. Review of *Singing for Power* by Ruth M. Underhill. *American Anthropologist* 41:482–83.

————. 1940a. Relations between Ethnology and Archaeology in the Southwest. *American Antiquity* 5:214–20.

————. 1940b. A Pre-Spanish Record of Hopi Ceremonies. *American Anthropologist* 42:541–42.

————. 1940c. *Taos Tales.* Memoirs of the American Folklore Society No. 34. New York: American Ethnological Society.

————. 1941. Review of *The Hopi Child* by Wayne Dennis. *Journal of American Folklore* 54:221–23.

————. 1942. Anthropology and Prediction. *American Anthropologist* 44:337–44.

————. 1962. *Isleta Paintings.* Bulletin of the Bureau of American Ethnology No. 181. Washington, D.C.: GPO.

————. n.d. In the Southwest. Unpublished manuscript, American Philosophical Society.

Parsons, Elsie Clews, ed. 1919. *Notes on Cochiti, New Mexico* by Noel Dumarest. Memoirs of the American Anthropological Association No. 6(3). Menasha, Wis.: American Anthropological Association.

————. 1922. *American Indian Life.* New York: B. W. Huebsch.

————. 1925. *A Pueblo Indian Journal, 1920–1921.* Memoirs of the American Anthropological Association No. 32. Menasha, Wis.: American Anthropological Association.

————. 1929. Hopi Tales by Alexander MacGregor Stephen. *Journal of American Folklore* 42:1–72.

———. 1936. *The Hopi Journal of Alexander M Stephen,* 2 vols. Columbia University Contributions to Anthropology No. 23. New York: Columbia University Press.

Parsons, Elsie Clews, and R. L. Beals. 1934. The Sacred Clowns of the Pueblo and Mayo-Yaqui Indians. *American Anthropologist* 36:491–514.

Pater, Walter. 1873. *The Renaissance.* (Reprinted New York: The Modern Library.)

———. 1885. *Marius the Epicurean: His Sensations and Ideas.* 2 vols. (Reprinted London: Macmillan, 1914.)

Peckham, Stewart, Nancy Fox, and Marjorie Lambert. 1981. The Lab's Modern Era: 1947–1981. *El Palacio* 87(3): 32–42.

Perchonok, Norma, and Oswald Werner. 1969. Navajo Systems of Classification: Some Implications for Ethnoscience. *Ethnology* 8:229–32.

Pezzullo, Thomas R., and Barbara E. Brittingham. 1979. The Assessment of Salary Equity: A Methodology, Alternatives and a Dilemma. In *Salary Equity: Detecting Bias in Salaries among College and University Professors,* ed. T. Pezzullo and B. Brittingham, pp. 1–23. Lexington, Ky.: Lexington Books.

Pinkley, Jean M. 1965. The Pueblos and the Turkey: Who Domesticated Whom? In *Contributions of the Wetherill Mesa Archeological Project,* ed. Douglas Osborn, pp. 70–72. Memoirs of the Society for American Archaeology No. 19. Menasha, Wis.: Society for American Archaeology.

Plattner, Stuart, Linda Hamilton, and Marilyn Madden. 1987. The Funding of Research in Socio-Cultural Anthropology at the National Science Foundation. *American Anthropologist* 89(4): 853–66.

Plog, Stephen E. 1980. *Stylistic Variation in Prehistoric Ceramics: Design Analysis in the American Southwest.* New York: Cambridge University Press.

Pollard, Lucille A. 1977. *Women on College and University Faculties.* New York: Arno Press.

Powdermaker, Hortense. 1967. *Stranger and Friend: The Way of an Anthropologist.* New York: W. W. Norton.

Powell, John Wesley. 1887. Museums of Ethnology and Their Classification. *Science* 9(229): 612–14.

———. 1891. Report of the Director. In *Seventh Annual Report of the Bureau of Ethnology to the Secretary of the Smithsonian Institution for 1885–1886,* pp. i–xxxv. Washington, D.C.: GPO.

Powell, Lawrence C. 1964. Erna Fergusson: First Lady of New Mexican Letters. In *The Little Package* by Lawrence Powell, pp. 140–45. Cleveland: World Publishing.

Powskey, Malinda, Lucille J. Watahomigie, and Akira Yamamoto. 1980. Language Use: Exploration in Language and Meaning. In *Proceedings of the 1979 Hokan Languages Workshop,* ed. James E. Redden, pp. 60–67. Occasional Papers on Linguistics No. 7. Carbondale: Southern Illinois University.

Price, D. J. 1965. Networks of Scientific Papers. *Science* 149:510–15.

———. 1971. *Science before Babylon.* New Haven, Conn.: Yale University Press.

Provinse, John, and Solon Kimball. 1942. Navajo Social Organization in Land Use Planning. *Applied Anthropology* 1:18–25.

Rabinow, Paul. 1977. *Reflections of Fieldwork in Morocco.* Berkeley: University of California Press.

Ransom, Michael R. 1989. Gender Segregation by Field in the Academic Labor Market. Mimeo. Provo, Utah: Brigham Young University.

Redfield, Robert. 1971. Art and Icon. In *Anthropology and Art: Readings in Cross-Cultural Aesthetics,* ed. Charlotte M. Otten, pp. 39–65. Garden City, N.Y.: Natural History Press.

Redfield, Robert, and W. Lloyd Warner. 1940. Cultural Anthropology and Modern Agriculture. In *Farmers in a Changing World.* U.S. Department of Agriculture, Yearbook of Agriculture. Washington, D.C.: GPO.

Reh, Emma. 1939. *Navajo Consumption Habits (for District 1).* SCS Field Report. (Edited and Annotated by Terry R. Reynolds. Republished by The University Museum, New Mexico State University, Occasional Papers No. 9. Las Cruces: New Mexico State University, 1983.)

Reiber, Linda K., and Jane de Hart Mathews. 1984. Refocusing the Past: Women in American History. *History News* 34:40–41.

Reichard, Gladys. 1928. *Social Life of the Navajo Indians.* Columbia University Contributions to Anthropology Vol. 7. New York: Columbia University Press.

———. 1932. *Melanesian Design.* 2 vols. New York: Columbia University Press.

———. 1934a. *Spider Woman: A Story of Navajo Weavers and Chanters.* New York: Macmillan.

———. 1934b. Hogan School. Ms. on file, Reichard Papers, Museum of Northern Arizona, Flagstaff.

———. 1936. *Navajo Shepherd and Weaver.* New York: J. J. Augustin.

———. 1938a. Social Life. In *General Anthropology,* ed. Franz Boas, pp. 409–86. New York: Heath.

———. 1938b. Grammar of the Coeur d'Alene Language. *Handbook of American Indian Languages* No. 3:517–707. New York: J. J. Augustin.

———. 1939a. *Dezba: Woman of the Desert.* New York: J. J. Augustin.

———. 1939b. *Navajo Medicine Man: Sandpainting and Legends of Miguelito.* New York: J. J. Augustin.

———. 1942a. Review of *Language, Culture and Personality,* ed. Leslie Spier, A. Irving Hallowell, Stanley S. Newman. *American Anthropologist* 44(3): 503–7.

———. 1942b. The Translation of Two Navaho Chant Words. *American Anthropologist* 44(3): 421–25.

———. 1943. Elsie Clews Parsons. *Journal of American Folklore* 56:45–56, 136.

———. 1944. *Prayer: The Compulsive Word.* Monographs of the American Ethnological Society No. 7. New York: J. J. Augustin.

———. 1950. *Navaho Religion: A Study of Symbolism.* 2 vols. New York: Bollingen Foundation.

———. 1951. *Navaho Grammar,* ed. Marian Smith. Publications of the American Ethnological Society No. 21. New York: J. J. Augustin.

———. 1968. *Spider Woman: A Story of Navajo Weavers and Chanters.* Glorieta, N.M.: Rio Grande Press [1934].

———. 1974. *Navajo Religion: A Study in Symbolism.* Bollingen Series No. 17. Princeton: Princeton University Press.

———. 1986. *Navajo Shepherd and Weaver.* Glorieta, N.M.: Rio Grande Press.

———. n.d. Another Look at the Navajo. Ms. on file, Reichard Papers, Museum of Northern Arizona, Flagstaff.

Remley, David A. 1969. *Erna Fergusson.* Southwest Writers Series No. 24. Austin, Tex.: Steck-Vaughn.

Reyman, Jonathan E. 1992. Women in American Archaeology: Some Historical Notes and Comments. In *Rediscovering Our Past: Essays on the History of American Archaeology,* ed. Jonathan Reyman, pp. 69–80. Worldwide Archaeology Series No. 2. Avebury, U.K.: Aldershot.

Richards, Cara E. 1960. Cooperation between Anthropologists and Medical Personnel. *Human Organization* 19:64–67.

Riley, Glenda. 1984. *Women and Indians on the Frontier, 1825–1915.* Albuquerque: University of New Mexico Press.

Roberts, Don L. 1972. The Ethnomusicology of the Eastern Pueblos. In *New Perspectives on the Pueblos,* ed. Alfonso Ortiz, pp. 243–56. Santa Fe, N.M.: School of American Research.

Roberts, Helen. 1923. Chakwena Songs of Zuni and Laguna. *Journal of Anthropological Folklore* 36: 177–84.

———. 1936. Indian Music of the Southwest. *Natural History* 27:257–65.

Robinson, Lora H. 1973. Institutional Variation in the Status of Academic Women. In *Academic Women on the Move,* ed. Alice S. Rossi and Ann Calderwood, pp. 199–229. New York: Russell Sage Foundation.

Roby, Pamela. 1973. Institutional Barriers to Women Students in Higher Education. In *Academic Women on the Move,* ed. Alice S. Rossi and Ann Calderwell, pp. 37–56. New York: Russell Sage Foundation.

Rogers, E. M. 1962. *Diffusion of Innovations.* New York: Free Press of Glencoe.

Rosaldo, Michelle. 1974. Women, Culture, and Society: A Theoretical Overview. In *Women, Culture, and Society,* ed. Michelle Rosaldo and Louise Lamphere, pp. 17–42. Stanford, Calif.: Stanford University Press.

———. 1980. The Use and Abuse of Anthropology:

Reflections on Feminism and Cross Cultural Understanding. *SIGNS* 5(3): 389–417.

Rosenberg, Rosalind. 1982. *Beyond Separate Spheres: Intellectual Roots of Modern Feminism.* New Haven, Conn.: Yale University Press.

Rossi, Alice S. 1970. Status of Women in Graduate Departments of Sociology. *The American Sociologist* 5:1–12.

Rossiter, Margaret W. 1982. *Women Scientists in America: Struggles and Strategies to 1940.* Baltimore, Md.: The Johns Hopkins University Press.

Rowbotham, Sheila. 1973. *Hidden from History: Rediscovering Women in History from the 17th Century to the Present.* New York: Vintage Books.

Rudnick, Lois Palken. 1984. *Mabel Dodge Luhan: New Woman, New Worlds.* Albuquerque: University of New Mexico Press.

———. 1987. Re-Naming the Land: Anglo Expatriate Women in the Southwest. In *The Desert Is no Lady: Southwestern Landscapes in Women's Writing and Art,* ed. Vera Norwood and Janice Monk, pp. 10–26. New Haven, Conn.: Yale University Press.

Sacks, Karen B., and D. Remy, eds. 1984. *My Troubles Are Going to Have Trouble with Me: Everyday Trials and Triumphs of Women Workers.* New Brunswick, N.J.: Rutgers University Press.

Sampson, E. E. 1978. Scientific Paradigms and Social Values: Wanted—A Scientific Revolution. *Journal of Personality and Social Psychology* 36:1332–43.

———. 1981. Cognitive Psychology as Ideology. *American Psychologist* 36:730–43.

Sands, Kathleen M. 1983. Dynamics of a Yaqui Myth. *American Quarterly* 35:355–75.

———. 1984. Ruth M. Underhill: Setting the Standard in Literary Anthropology. Paper presented at Ruth Underhill Symposium, American Anthropological Association Meeting, Denver.

———. 1986. Comments, March 17. Daughters of the Desert Conference. Globe, Ariz.: Wenner-Gren Foundation for Anthropological Research.

———. 1988. Preface. In *People of Pascua,* by Edward H. Spicer, pp. xiii–xxi. Tucson: University of Arizona Press.

Sanjek, Roger. 1978. The Position of Women in the Major Departments of Anthropology, 1967–76. *American Anthropologist* 80(4):894–904.

———. 1982. The American Anthropological Association Resolution on the Employment of Women: Genesis, Implementation, Disavowal, and Resurrection. *SIGNS* (University of Chicago Press) 7:845–68.

———. 1990. A Vocabulary for Fieldnotes. In *Fieldnotes: The Makings of Anthropology,* ed. Roger Sanjek, pp. 92–121. Ithaca, N.Y.: Cornell University Press.

Sapir, Edward. 1921. *Language: An Introduction to the Study of Speech.* New York: Harcourt, Brace and Company.

———. 1927. The Unconscious Patterning of Behavior in Society. (Reprinted in *Selected Writings of Edward Sapir in Language, Culture, and Personality,* ed. David G. Mandelbaum, pp. 544–59. Berkeley: University of California Press, 1949.)

———. 1934. The Emergence of the Concepts of Personality in a Study of Cultures. (Reprinted in *Selected Writings of Edward Sapir in Language, Culture, and Personality,* ed. David G. Mandelbaum, pp. 590–97. Berkeley: University of California Press, 1949.)

———. 1936. Internal Linguistic Evidence Suggestive of the Northern Origin of the Navaho. *American Anthropologist* 38:224–35.

Sasaki, Tom. 1950. *Fruitland, New Mexico: A Navajo Community in Transition.* Ithaca, N.Y.: Cornell University Press.

Savala, Refugio. 1980. *Autobiography of a Yaqui Poet.* Tucson: University of Arizona Press.

Schevill, Margot Blum. 1989. Kate Peck Kent, 1914–1987: Anthropologist, Textile Expert, Teacher, Valued Colleague, Wife, and Mother. In The Legacy of Kate Peck Kent: Material Culture Study in the Southwest, ed. Brenda L. Shears and Elizabeth Welsh. *Museum Anthropology* 13(2): 3–6.

Schiff, Esther (see also Goldfrank, Esther S.). 1921. A Note on Twins. *American Anthropologist* 23(3): 387–88.

Schmidt, Delores B., and Earl R. Schmidt. 1976. The Invisible Woman: The Historian as Professional Magician. In *Liberating Women's History:*

Theoretical and Critical Essays, ed. Bernice A. Carroll, pp. 42–54. Urbana: University of Illinois Press.

Schoolcraft, Henry R. 1854. *Archives of Aboriginal Knowledge: Information Respecting the History, Condition and Prospects of the Indian Tribes of the United States.* Philadelphia: J. R. Lippincott.

Schuyler, Robert. 1976. Images of America: The Contribution of Historical Archaeology to National Identity. *Southwestern Lore* 42:27–39.

Schwarz, Judith. 1982. *Radical Feminists of Heterodoxy, Greenwich Village, 1912–1940.* Lebanon, Pa.: New Victoria.

Shapiro, Judith. 1981. Anthropology and the Study of Gender. In *A Feminist Perspective in the Academy,* ed. E. Langland and W. Gove, pp. 110–29. Chicago: University of Chicago Press.

Shapiro, Virginia. 1983. *The Political Integration of Women: Roles, Socialization, and Politics.* Urbana: University of Illinois Press.

Shepard, Anna O. 1938. Appendix VI: Ceramic Technology. In *The Jemez Pueblo of Unshagi, New Mexico,* pp. 205–11. School of American Research Monograph No. 5–6 and University of New Mexico Bulletin No. 327. Albuquerque: University of New Mexico Press.

———. 1939. Review of *Classification of Black Pottery and Paint Areas* by F. M. Hawley and F. G. Hawley. University of New Mexico Bulletin Anthropology Series 2(4). *American Antiquity* 4:367–70.

———. 1957. *Ceramics for the Archaeologist.* Carnegie Institution of Washington Publication No. 609. Washington, D.C.: Carnegie Institution.

Shepardson, Mary Thygeson. 1963. *Navajo Ways in Government.* Memoirs of the American Anthropological Association No. 96. Washington, D.C.: American Anthropological Association.

———. 1965. Problems of the Navajo Tribal Courts in Transition. *Human Organization* 24:250–53.

———. 1975. (Consultant) Assessment of Cumulative Sociocultural Impact of Proposed Plans for Development of Coal and Water Resources in the Northern N.M. Region by James R. Leonard Associates. Prepared for Bureau of Reclamation.

———. 1980. Foreword. In *A Voice in Her Own Tribe: A Navajo Woman's Story* by Irene Stewart. Socorro, N.M.: Ballena Press.

———. 1986a. *Fieldwork among the Navajo.* Palo Alto, Calif.: BAS Press.

———. 1986b. Interview (with Jennifer Fox) for the Daughters of the Desert Oral History Project. March 13, Tucson, Ariz. Audio Recording. New York: Wenner-Gren Foundation for Anthropological Research.

Shepardson, Mary, and Blodwen Hammond. 1970. *The Navajo Mountain Community: Social Organization and Kinship Terminology.* Berkeley: University of California Press.

Silverman, Sydel, ed. 1981. *Totems and Teachers: Perspectives on the History of Anthropology.* New York: Columbia University Press.

Simeone, Angela. 1987. *Academic Women: Working towards Equality.* South Hadley, Mass.: Bergin and Garvey.

Simmons, Leo W., ed. 1942. *Sun Chief: The Autobiography of a Hopi Indian.* New Haven, Conn.: Yale University Press.

Simmons, Marc. 1979. History of the Pueblos since 1921. In *Southwest,* vol. 9 of *Handbook of North American Indians,* ed. Alfonso Ortiz, pp. 206–23. Washington, D.C.: Smithsonian Institution Press.

Simms, Barbara Young. 1976. The Fabulous Fergussons. *El Palacio* 82(2):42–47.

Simon, Rita, Shirley Clark, and Kathleen Galeway. 1967. The Woman Ph.D.: A Recent Profile. *Social Problems* 15(2):221–36.

Slivac, Barbara. 1986. Biographical Chronology: Muriel Thayer Painter. Ms. on file, Arizona State Museum, University of Arizona, Tucson.

Smith, Anne M. 1966. *New Mexico Indians: Economic, Educational and Social Problems.* Museum of New Mexico Research Records No. 1. Santa Fe: Museum of New Mexico.

———. 1968a. *Indian Education in New Mexico.* Publication No. 77 of Division of Government Research, University of New Mexico. Albuquerque: University of New Mexico.

———. 1968b. Indian Headstart. *El Palacio* 17(4):12–20.

Smith, Duane A. 1988. *Mesa Verde National Park: Shadows of the Centuries.* Lawrence: University Press of Kansas.

Smith, Jack E. 1981. Pioneering Archaeology in Mesa Verde: The Nusbaum Years. *Mesa Verde Occasional Papers.* 1(2): 9–23.

Smith, Marian W. 1943. Centenary of the AES. *American Anthropologist* 45:181–84.

———. 1956. Gladys Amanda Reichard. *American Anthropologist* 58(5): 913–16.

Smith, Watson. 1985. Interview (with Jennifer Fox) for Daughters of the Desert Oral History Project. New York: Wenner-Gren Foundation for Anthropological Research.

Smith, Watson, and John M. Roberts. 1954. *Zuni Law: A Field of Values.* Papers of the Peabody Museum of American Archaeology and Ethnology 43(1). Cambridge, Mass.: Harvard University.

Smith-Rosenberg, Carroll. 1985. *Disorderly Conduct: Visions of Gender in Victorian America.* New York: Alfred A. Knopf.

Society for American Archeology. 1991. Archaeology . . . Is Gender Still an Issue? Special Issue. *Society for American Archaeology Bulletin* 9(1).

Solomon, Barbara Miller. 1985. *In the Company of Educated Women: A History of Women and Higher Education.* New Haven, Conn.: Yale University Press.

Spector, Janet. 1988. *The Minnesota Plan II.* Minneapolis: University of Minnesota.

Speizer, Jeanne J. 1981. Role Models, Mentors, and Sponsors: The Elusive Concepts. *SIGNS* 6(4): 692–712.

Spender, Dale. 1981. The Gatekeepers: A Feminist Critique of Academic Publishing. In *Doing Feminist Research,* ed. Helen Roberts, pp. 186–P;3202. London: Routledge and Kegan Paul.

Spengler, Oswald. 1929. *The Decline of the West.* New York: Alfred A. Knopf.

Sperber, Dan. 1985. *On Anthropological Knowledge: Three Essays.* New York: Cambridge University Press.

Speth, John D. 1984. Foreword. In *The Archaeology of the Sierra Blanca Region of Southeastern New Mexico* by Jane Holden Kelley, pp. xxi–xxxiii. Anthropological Papers, Museum of Anthropology, University of Michigan, No. 74. Ann Arbor: University of Michigan.

Spicer, Edward H. 1940. *Pascua: A Yaqui Village in Arizona.* University of Chicago Publications in Anthropology, Ethnological Series. (Reprinted, Tucson: University of Arizona Press, 1984.)

———. 1943. Linguistic Aspects of Yaqui Acculturation. *American Anthropologist* 45(3): 410–26.

———. 1946. The Use of Social Scientists by the War Relocation Authority. *Applied Anthropology* 5(1): 16–36.

———. 1948. Southwest Chronicle: Pueblo Ethnology. *Arizona Quarterly* (University of Arizona) 4(1): 78–88.

———. 1952. Sheepmen and Technicians. In *Human Problems in Technological Change,* ed. Edward H. Spicer, pp. 185–207. New York: Russell Sage Foundation.

———. 1953. People of Pascua. Unpublished ms. Arizona State Museum Archives.

———. 1954. *Potam: A Yaqui Village in Sonora.* Memoirs of the American Anthropological Association No. 77. Menasha, Wis.: American Anthropological Association.

———. 1976. Beyond Analysis and Explanation? The Life and Times of the Society of Applied Anthropology. *Human Organization* 35:335–43.

———. 1988. *People of Pascua.* Tucson: University of Arizona Press.

Spicer, Rosamond Brown. 1938. The Easter Fiesta of the Yaqui Indians of Pascua, Arizona. Master's thesis, Department of Anthropology, University of Chicago.

———. 1985. Interview (with Jennifer Fox) for the Daughters of the Desert Oral History Project. August 20, Tucson, Ariz. Audio Recording. New York: Wenner-Gren Foundation for Anthropological Research.

———. 1986. Interview with Kathleen Sands. Tucson, Arizona.

———. 1988. Living in Pascua: Looking back Fifty Years. In *People of Pascua,* by Edward H. Spicer. pp. xxiii–xlvi. Tucson: University of Arizona Press.

———. 1990. A Full Life Well Lived: A Brief Account of the Life of Edward H. Spicer. *Journal of the Southwest* 32(1): 3–17.

Spier, Leslie. 1943. Elsie Clews Parsons. *American Anthropologist* 45:244–51.

———. 1959. Some Central Elements in the Legacy. In *The Anthropology of Franz Boas,* ed. Walter Goldschmidt, pp. 146–55. American Anthropological Association Memoir 89. Washington, D.C.: American Anthropological Association.

Stanislawski, Michael B. 1978. If Pots Were Mortal. In *Explorations in Ethnoarchaeology.* Albuquerque: University of New Mexico Press.

Starbuck, Alma J. 1986. *The Complete Irish Wolfhound.* 3d ed. New York: Howell Book House.

Stark, Miriam. 1991. A Perspective on Women's Status in American Archaeology. In *The Archaeology of Gender,* ed. Dale Walde and Noreen D. Willows, pp. 187–94. Proceedings of the 22d Annual Conference of the Archaeological Association of the University of Calgary. Calgary: The University of Calgary Archaeological Association.

———. 1992. Where the Money Goes: Current Trends in Archeological Funding. In *Quandaries and Quests: Visions of Archaeology's Future,* ed. LuAnn Wandsnider, pp. 41–58. Center for Archaeological Investigations Occasional Paper No. 20. Carbondale: Southern Illinois University.

Stevenson, James. 1883a. Illustrated Catalogue of the Collections Obtained from the Indians of New Mexico and Arizona in 1879. In *Second Annual Report of the Bureau of Ethnology for 1880–1881,* pp. 307–442. Washington, D.C.: GPO.

———. 1883b. Illustrated Catalogue of the Collections Obtained from the Indians of New Mexico in 1880. In *Second Annual Report of the Bureau of Ethnology for 1880–1881,* pp. 423–65. Washington, D.C.: GPO.

———. 1884a. Illustrated Catalogue of the Collections of 1881. In *Third Annual Report of the Bureau of Ethnology for 1881–1882,* pp. 519–

94. Washington, D.C.: GPO.

———. 1884b. Illustrated Catalogue of the Collections Obtained from the Pueblos of Zuni, New Mexico, and Walpi, Arizona, in 1881. *Third Annual Report of the Bureau of American Ethnology,* pp. 511–14. Washington, D.C.: GPO.

Stevenson, Matilda Coxe. 1881a. *Zuni and the Zunians.* Washington, D.C.: Privately printed.

———. 1881b. *Zuni Pottery.* Report of the Davenport Academy of Science.

———. 1883. The Cliff-Dwellers of the New Mexican Canyons. *Kansas City Review* 6(11): 636–39.

———. 1887. Religious Life of the Zuni Child. In *Fifth Annual Report of the Bureau of Ethnology for 1883–1884,* pp. 533–55. Washington, D.C.: GPO.

———. 1888. Zuni Religion. *Science* 11(268): 136–37.

———. 1893a. Tusayan Legends of the Snake and Flute People. *Proceedings, American Association for the Advancement of Science,* vol. 41, pp. 258–70.

———. 1893b. A Chapter in Zuni Mythology. In *Memoirs of the International Congress of Anthropology,* pp. 312–19. Chicago.

———. 1894a. *The Sia.* In *11th Annual Report of the Bureau of Ethnology for 1889–1890,* pp. 3–157. Washington, D.C.: GPO.

———. 1894b. The Zuni Scalp Ceremonial. In *The Congress of Women,* ed. Mary Kavanaugh O. Eagle, pp. 484–87. Chicago: American Publishing House. (Reprinted New York: Arno Press, 1974.)

———. 1898. Zuni Ancestral Gods and Masks. *American Anthropologist* 11(o.s.): 33–40.

———. 1903. Zuni Games. *American Anthropologist* 5(n.s.): 468–97.

———. 1904. The Zuni Indians: Their Mythology, Esoteric Fraternities, and Ceremonies. In *23rd Annual Report of the Bureau of American Ethnology for 1901–1902,* pp. 1–608. Washington, D.C.: GPO.

———. 1913a. Strange Rites of the Tewa Indians. *Smithsonian Miscellaneous Collections* 63(8): 73–80.

———. 1913b. Studies of the Tewa Indians of the Rio Grande Valley. *Smithsonian Miscellaneous Collections* 60:35–41.

———. 1915a. Ethnobotany of the Zuni Indians. In *30th Annual Report of the Bureau of American Ethnology for 1908–1909*, pp. 3–102. Washington, D.C.: GPO.

———. 1915b. The Sun and Ice People among the Tewa Indians of New Mexico. *Smithsonian Miscellaneous Collections* 65(6): 73–78.

———. 1987. Dress and Adornment of the Pueblo Indians, ed. Richard V. N. Ahlstrom and Nancy J. Parezo. *The Kiva* 52(4): 257–312.

Stewart, Irene. 1980. *A Voice in Her Own Tribe: A Navajo Woman's Story.* Socorro, N.M.: Ballena Press.

Stocking, George W., Jr. 1968. *Race, Culture, and Evolution.* New York: The Free Press.

———. 1974. Ruth Fulton Benedict. In *Dictionary of American Biography: Supplement for 1946–1950*, ed. John A. Garraty and Edward T. James, pp. 70–73. New York: Scribners.

———. 1976. Ideas and Institutions in American Anthropology: Thoughts toward a History of the Interwar Years. In *Selected Papers from the American Anthropologist, 1921–1945*, ed. George W. Stocking, pp. 1–53. Washington, D.C.: American Anthropological Association.

———. 1982. The Santa Fe Style in American Anthropology: Regional Interest, Academic Initiative, and Philanthropic Policy in the First Two Decades of the Laboratory of Anthropology. *Journal of the History of Behavioral Sciences* 18:3–19.

———. 1983. The Ethnographer's Magic: Fieldwork in British Anthropology from Tylor to Malinowski. In *Observers Observed: Essays on Ethnographic Fieldwork,* ed. George Stocking, pp. 70–120. Madison: University of Wisconsin Press.

Stocking, George W., Jr., ed. 1985. *Objects and Others: Essays on Museums and Material Culture*, vol. 3 of *History of Anthropology*. Madison: University of Wisconsin Press.

———. 1976. *Selected Papers from the American Anthropologist, 1921–1945.* Washington, D.C.: American Anthropological Association.

Storer, Norman W. 1966. *The Social System of Science.* New York: Holt, Rinehart and Winston.

Strathern, Marilyn. 1984. Kinship and Economy Constitutive Orders of a Provisional Kind. *American Ethnologist* 12(2): 191–209.

Sturtevant, William C. 1969. Does Anthropology Need Museums? *Proceedings of the Biological Society of Washington* 182:619–49.

———. 1977. *Guide to Field Collecting of Ethnographic Specimens.* 2d ed. Smithsonian Information Leaflet 503. Washington, D.C.: Smithsonian Institution Press.

Taft, Jesse. 1916. *The Woman's Movement from the Point of View of Social Consciousness.* Chicago: University of Chicago Press.

Tannen, Deborah. 1986. *That's Not What I Meant! How Conversational Style Makes or Breaks Your Relations with Others.* New York: William Morrow.

Tanner, Clara Lee Fraps. 1968. *Southwest Indian Craft Arts.* Tucson: University of Arizona Press.

———. 1976. *Prehistoric Southwestern Craft Arts.* Tucson: University of Arizona Press.

———. 1983. *Indian Baskets of the Southwest.* Tucson: University of Arizona Press.

———. 1985. Interview (with Jennifer Fox) for Daughters of the Desert Oral History Project. November 24, Santa Fe, N.M. Audio and Video Recording. New York: Wenner-Gren Foundation for Anthropological Research.

Thomas, Chester A. 1969. Jean McWhirt Pinkley 1910–1969. *American Antiquity* 34:471–73.

Thomas, D. H. 1978. *The Southwestern Indian Detours.* Phoenix: The Hunter Publishing Co.

Thomas, Dorothy. 1933. Exploring the Museum Field. *Independent Woman* 12(7): 238–39, 260.

Thomas, Dorothy S., and R. S. Nishimoto. 1946. *The Spoilage.* Berkeley: University of California Press.

Thompson, Laura Maud. 1940. *Fijian Frontier.* Honolulu: The American Council of the Institute of Pacific Relations.

———. 1941. *Guam and Its People: A Study of Culture Change and Colonial Education.* Honolulu: The American Council of the Institute of Pacific Relations.

———. 1945. Logico-Aesthetic Integration in Hopi Culture. *American Anthropologist* 47:540–53.

———. 1950. *Culture in Crisis: A Study of the Hopi Indians.* New York: Harper.

———. 1950–51. Personality and Government. *Americana Indigena* 10 (1–4) and 11 (1–2).

———. 1951. Personality and Government: Findings and Recommendations of the Indian Administration Research. Mexico, D.F.: Inter-America Indian Institute.

———. 1970. Exploring American Indian Communities in Depth. In *Women in the Field: Anthropological Experiences,* ed. Peggy Golde, pp. 47–64. Chicago: Aldine.

———. 1985. Interview (with Jennifer Fox) for Daughters of the Desert Oral History Project. November 18 & 19, Santa Fe, N.M. Audio and video Recording. New York: Wenner-Gren Foundation for Anthropological Research.

Thompson, Laura, and Alice Joseph. 1944. *The Hopi Way.* Chicago: University of Chicago Press.

Thompson, Raymond H. 1991. Shepard, Kidder and Carnegie. In *The Ceramic Legacy of Anna O. Shepard,* ed. Ronald L. Bishop and Frederick W. Lange, pp. 1–41. Boulder: University Press of Colorado.

Thompson, Raymond H., and Nancy J. Parezo. 1989. A Historical Survey of Material Culture Studies in Anthropology. In *Perspectives on Anthropological Collections from the American Southwest,* ed. Ann Hedlund, pp. 3–65. Anthropological Research Papers No. 40. Tempe: Arizona State University.

Thorndike, Edward L. 1914. *Mental Work and Fatigue, and Individual Differences and Their Causes,* vol. 3 of *Educational Psychology.* New York: Teacher's College, Columbia University.

Tidball, M. Elizabeth. 1974. The Search for Talented Women. *Change* 6(4): 51–52, 62.

Tjerandson, Carl. 1980. *Education for Citizenship.* Chicago: Emil Schwarzhaupt Foundation.

Trager, Felicia H. 1971. Some Aspects of 'Time' at Picuris Pueblo. *Anthropologists Linguistics* 13: 331–38.

Trager, George L., and Felicia H. Trager. 1970. The Cardinal Directions at Taos and Picuris. *Anthropological Linguistics* 12: 31–37.

Trigger, Bruce G. 1980. Archaeology and the Image of the American Indian. *American Antiquity* 45: 662–76.

Tyler, Stephen A. 1986. Post-Modern Ethnography: From Document of the Occult to Occult Document. In *Writing Culture: The Poetics and Politics of Ethnography,* ed. James Clifford and George Marcus, pp. 122–40. Berkeley: University of California Press.

Tylor, Edward B. 1884. How the Problems of American Anthropology Present Themselves to the English Mind. *Science* 4: 545–51.

Underhill, Ruth M. 1934. *Southwestern Indians: An Outline and Ceremonial Organization.* Washington, D.C.: Bureau of Indian Affairs.

———. 1936. *The Autobiography of a Papago Woman.* Memoirs of the American Anthropological Association No. 46. Menasha, Wis.: American Anthropological Association. (Reprinted as *Papago Woman.* New York: Holt, Rinehart and Winston, 1979.)

———. 1938. *Singing for Power: The Song Magic of the Papago Indians of Southern Arizona.* Berkeley: University of California Press.

———. 1939. *Social Organization of the Papago Indians.* Columbia University Contributions to Anthropology No. 30. New York: Columbia University Press.

———. 1941. *The Papago Indians of Arizona and Their Relatives, The Pima.* Lawrence, Kans.: U.S. Department of Interior, Bureau of Indian Affairs.

———. 1944a. *Navaho Weaving,* ed. W. Beatty. Washington, D.C.: U.S. Department of Interior, Bureau of Indian Affairs.

———. 1944b. *Pueblo Crafts.* Washington, D.C.: U.S. Department of Interior, Bureau of Indian Affairs.

———. 1946a. *Papago Indian Religion.* Columbia University Contributions to Anthropology No. 33. New York: Columbia University Press.

———. 1946b. *Work a Day Life of the Pueblos.* Phoenix: Education Division, Bureau of Indian Affairs.

———. 1948. *Ceremonial Patterns in the Greater Southwest.* American Ethnological Society Monographs No. 13. New York: J. J. Augustin.

———. 1951. *People of the Crimson Evening.* Indian Life and Customs Pamphlet No. 7. Riverside, Calif.: Indian Service.

———. 1953a. *Here Comes the Navaho!* Lawrence, Kans.: U.S. Department of the Interior, Bureau of Indian Affairs.

———. 1953b. *Red Man's America: A History of Indians in the United States.* Chicago: University of Chicago Press.

———. 1956. *The Navahos.* Norman: University of Oklahoma.

———. 1965. *Red Man's Religion: Beliefs and Practices of the Indians North of Mexico.* Chicago: University of Chicago Press.

———. 1979. *Papago Woman.* New York: Holt, Rinehart and Winston.

U.S. Department of the Interior. 1980. San Juan Regional Uranium Study. Washington, D.C.: GPO.

Vance, Carole. 1970. Sexism in Anthropology? The Status of Women in Departments of Anthropology: Highlights of the Guide Tabulation. *Anthropology Newsletter* 11(9): 5–6.

Van der Eerden, Sister Mary Lucia. 1948. *Maternity Care in a Spanish American Community of New Mexico.* Catholic University of America, Anthropological Series No. 13. Washington, D.C.: Catholic University Press.

Van Willigen, John. 1976. Applied Anthropology and Community Development Administration: A Critical Assessment. In *Do Applied Anthropologists Apply Anthropology?* ed. Michael Angrosino, pp. 81–91. Southern Anthropological Society Proceedings No. 10. Athens: University of Georgia Press.

———. 1980. Anthropology in Use: A Bibliographical Chronology of the Development of Applied Anthropology. Applied Anthropology Documentation Project, University of Kentucky.

Vetter, Betty M. 1987. Women's Progress. *Mosaic* 18(1): 2–9.

Vetter, Betty, and E. Babco. 1978. *Professional Women and Minorities.* Washington, D.C.: Scientific Manpower Commission.

Voget, Fred W. 1975. *A History of Ethnology.* New York: Holt, Rinehart and Winston.

Vogt, Evon Z., and Ethel M. Albert, eds. 1966. *People of Rimrock: A Study of Values in Five Cultures.* Cambridge, Mass.: Harvard University Press.

Wagner, Roy. 1975. *The Invention of Culture.* Chicago: University of Chicago Press.

Walde, Dale, and Noreen Willows, eds. 1991. *The Archaeology of Gender: Proceedings of the 22nd Annual Chacmool Conference.* Calgary: The Archaeological Association of the University of Calgary.

Wandersee, Winifred D. 1988. *On the Move: American Women in the 1970s.* Boston: Twayne Publishers.

Ware, John A. 1986. The Museum of Indian Arts and Culture: New Directions for The Laboratory of Anthropology. *El Palacio* 92(2): 12–17.

Ware, Naomi. 1970. Survival and Change in Pima Indian Music. *Ethnomusicology* 14: 100–13.

Warner, John Anson. n.d. The Individual in American Art: A Sociological View. Unpublished ms. in possession of Hardin.

Warren, Carol A. B. 1988. *Gender Issues in Field Research.* Newbury Park, Calif.: Sage Publications.

Warren, Carol A. B., and P. K. Rasmussen. 1977. Sex and Gender in Fieldwork Research. *Urban Life* 6(3): 359–69.

Watahomigie, Lucille. 1967. *Hualapai Dictionary.* Peach Springs, Ariz.: Hualapai Bilingual Program.

Watahomigie, Lucille J., Jorgine Bender, and Akira Yamamoto. 1982. *Hualapai Reference Grammar.* American Indian Studies Center. Los Angeles: University of California.

Waters, Frank. 1942. *The Man Who Killed Deer.* Denver: Sage.

Watson, Lawrence. 1976. Understanding a Life History as a Subjective Document: Hermeneutical and Phenominological Perspectives. *Ethos* 4(1): 95–131.

Watson, Patty Jo. 1979. The Idea of Ethnoarchaeology: Notes and Comments. In *Ethnoarchaeology: The Implications of Ethnography for Archaeology,* ed. Carol Kramer, pp. 277–88. New York: Columbia University Press.

Weal, L. 1970. Fact Sheet on Sex Discrimination in Universities and Colleges. In Discrimination against Women, Hearings before the Special Subcommittee on Education of the Committee on Education and Labor, House of Representatives. 91st Cong., 2nd Sess., on Section 805 of HR 16098, pp. 310–12. Washington, D.C.: GPO.

Weigle, Marta. 1989. From Desert to Display: The Santa Fe Railway and the Fred Harvey Company Display the Indian Southwest. *Journal of Anthropological Research* 45:115–37.

Weigle, Marta, ed. 1975. *Hispanic Villages of Northern New Mexico: A Reprint of Volume 2 of the 1935 Tewa Basin Study, with Supplementary Materials.* Santa Fe, N.M.: The Lightning Tree.

Weigle, Marta, and Kyle Fiore. 1982. *Santa Fe and Taos: The Writer's Era, 1916–1941.* Santa Fe, N.M.: Ancient City Press.

Weigle, Marta, and Peter White, eds. 1982. *New Mexico Artists and Writers: A Celebration, 1940.* Santa Fe, N.M.: Ancient City Press.

Wheat, Joe Ben. 1989. Discussion. In The Legacy of Kate Peck Kent: Material Culture Study in the Southwest, ed. Brenda Shears and Elizabeth Welsh. *Museum Anthropology* 13(2): 29–30.

Wheelwright, Mary Cabot. 1942. *The Navajo Creation Myth: The Story of Emergence by Hasteen Klah.* Santa Fe, N.M.: Museum of Navajo Ceremonial Art.

———. 1955. Journey towards Understanding. Ms. on file, Wheelwright Museum Archives, Santa Fe, N.M.

Wheelwright Museum of the American Indian. 1979. Mission Statement. Wheelwright Museum Archives, Santa Fe, N.M.

———. 1992. Mission Statement. Wheelwright Museum Archives, Santa Fe, N.M.

White, Leslie A. 1973. Parsons, Elsie Worthington Clews. In *Dictionary of American Biography, Supplement 3, 1941–1945,* ed. Edward T. James, pp. 581–82. New York: Charles Scribner's Sons.

White, Martha S. 1970. Psychological and Social Barriers to Women in Science. *Science* 170(3956): 413–16.

Whiteford, Andrew Hunter. 1988. Kate Peck Kent (1914–1987). Obituaries. *American Anthropologist* 90(4): 956.

Whitehead, Tony L., and Mary Ellen Conaway. 1986. Introduction. In *Self, Sex, and Gender in Cross-Cultural Fieldwork,* ed. T. L. Whitehead and

M. E. Conaway, pp. 1–14. Urbana: University of Illinois Press.

Whitehill, Walter Muir. 1962. Museum of Navajo Ceremonial Art. In *Independent Historical Societies* by Walter Muir Whitehill, pp. 407–14. Boston: Boston Athenaeum, distributed by Harvard University Press.

Whorf, Benjamin L. 1935. The Comparative Linguistics of Uto-Aztecan. *American Anthropologist* 37:600–8.

Wildesen, Leslie E. 1980. The Status of Women in Archaeology: Results of a Preliminary Survey. *Anthropology Newsletter* 21(5): 5–8.

Wilke, A. S., ed. 1979. *The Hidden Professorate: Credentialism, Professionalism and the Tenure Crisis.* Westport, Conn.: Greenwood.

Willey, Gordon Randolph. 1988. *Portraits in American Archaeology: Remembrances of Some Distinguished Americanist.* Albuquerque: University of New Mexico Press.

Willey, Gordon R., and Jeremy A. Sabloff. 1980. *A History of American Archaeology.* 2d ed. San Francisco: W. H. Freeman and Company.

Williams, Barbara. 1981. *Breakthrough: Women in Archaeology.* New York: Walker and Walker.

Wilson, Edmund. 1956. *Red, Black, Blond, and Olive. Studies in Four Civilizations: Zuni, Haiti, Soviet Russia, Israel.* New York: Oxford University Press.

Winkler, K. J. 1981. Women Historians Have Greater Access to Some Jobs but Remain Concentrated in Underpaid Ranks. *Chronicle of Higher Education* Jan 12:18.

Wissler, Clark. 1914. Material Cultures of the North American Indians. *American Anthropologist* 16(3): 447–505.

———. 1947. Review of Esther S. Goldfrank's *Changing Configuration of the Social Organization of the Blackfoot Tribe during the Reserve Period. Journal of American Folklore* 60(237): 308–09.

Witherspoon, Gary. 1977. *Language and Art in the Navajo Universe.* Ann Arbor: University of Michigan Press.

———. 1980. Language in Culture and Culture in Language. *International Journal of American Linguistics* 46(1): 1–13.

Wittfogel, Karl A., and Esther S. Goldfrank. 1943. Some Aspects of Pueblo Mythology and Society. *Journal of American Folklore* 56(219): 17–30.

Woodall, J. Ned, and Philip J. Perricone. 1981. The Archaeologist as Cowboy: The Consequence of Professional Stereotype. *Journal of Field Archaeology* 8: 506–8.

Woodbury, Nathalie Ferris Sampson. 1985. Interview (with Jennifer Fox) for Daughters of the Desert Oral History Project. July 7, Shutesbury, Mass. Audio Recording. New York: Wenner-Gren Foundation for Anthropological Research.

———. 1986. Tilly's Trials: Past Is Present. *Anthropology Newsletter* 27(3): 3–4.

———. 1987. Past Is Present: Amplification: The Death of Henrietta Schmerler. *Anthropology Newsletter* January: 3–4.

Woodbury, Nathalie F. S., and Richard B. Woodbury. 1988. Women of Visions and Wealth: Their Impact on Southwestern Anthropology. In *Reflections: Papers on Southwestern Culture History in Honor of Charles H. Lange,* ed. Anne V. Poore, pp. 45–56. Santa Fe: Ancient City Press for the Archaeological Society of New Mexico.

Woolf, Virginia. 1931. *The Waves.* New York: Harcourt, Brace.

———. 1938. *Three Guineas.* New York: Harcourt, Brace.

Wormington, H. Marie. 1947. *Prehistoric Indians of the Southwest.* 1st ed. Denver Museum of Natural History, Popular Series No. 7. Denver: Denver Museum of Natural History.

———. 1957. *Ancient Man in North America.* Denver Museum of Natural History, Popular Series No. 4. Denver: Denver Museum of Natural History.

———. 1985. Interview (with Jennifer Fox) for Daughters of the Desert Oral History Project. August 10, Denver. Audio Recording. New York: Wenner-Gren Foundation for Anthropological Research.

Wylie, Alison. 1991. Workplace Issues for Women in Archaeology: The Chilly Climate. Paper presented at Australian National University.

———. 1992. The Interplay of Evidential Constraints and Political Interests: Recent Archaeological Research on Gender. *American Antiquity* 57(1): 15–35.

Wyman, Leland C. 1951. Review of *Navaho Religion* by Gladys A. Reichard. *American Anthropologist* 52(4): 524–26.

Wyman, Leland C., and Clyde Kluckhohn. 1938. *Navaho Classification of their Song Ceremonials.* American Anthropological Association Memoir No. 50. Menasha, Wis.: American Anthropological Association.

Yellen, John E. 1983. Women, Archeology and the National Science Foundation. In *The Socio-Politics of Archaeology,* ed. Joan Gero, David Lacy, and Michael L. Blakey, pp. 59–65. Anthropological Research Report No. 23. Amherst: University of Massachusetts.

———. 1991. Women, Archaeology and the National Science Foundation: An Analysis of Fiscal Year 1989 Data. In *The Archaeology of Gender,* ed. Dale Walde and Noreen D. Willows, pp. 201–10. *Proceedings of the 22d Annual Conference of the Archaeological Association of the University of Calgary.* Calgary: The University of Calgary Archaeological Association.

Young, Robert, and William Morgan. 1943. *The Navajo Language.* Phoenix: Education Division, United States Indian Service.

Zuckerman, Harriet. 1967. Nobel Laureates in Science: Patterns of Productivity, Collaboration and Authorship. *American Sociological Review* 32: 391–403.

ABOUT THE AUTHORS

BARBARA BABCOCK is professor of English and comparative literature at the University of Arizona. She is especially interested in women's studies, Native American cultures and the American Southwest. One of the originators of the Daughters of the Desert Project she authored *Daughters of the Desert* (with Nancy Parezo, 1988), as well as *The Pueblo Storyteller* (with Doris and Guy Monthan, 1986), edited a collection of essays by Elsie Clews Parsons entitled *Pueblo Mothers and Children* (1991). She is currently working on a bibliography of Helen Cordero.

LINDA CORDELL formerly chair of the Department of Anthropology and Associate Dean at the University of New Mexico, is presently Irvine Curator of Archaeology at the Academy of Sciences, San Francisco where she is a specialist on the Northern Rio Grande. She has authored numerous works on southwestern archaeology including *Dynamics of Southwest Prehistory* (with George Gummerman, 1989) and her most definitive work *The Prehistory of the Southwest* (1984).

JENNIFER FOX is a doctoral candidate in anthropology and folklore at the University of Texas at Austin. Her dissertation is on poetic inspiration and affect in the *cantoria* tradition of northeastern Brazil. While doing fieldwork in Brazil she also apprenticed with a psychic healer.

DEBORAH GORDON, a recent graduate of the University of Santa Cruz History of Consciousness program, currently holds a post-doctoral fellowship at Stanford. She is interested in post modern structuralism, women's studies, literary criticism, and ethnographic writing.

KATHERINE SPENCER HALPERN is professor emerita at American University and Research As-

sociate at the Wheelwright Museum. A specialist in medical anthropology, applied anthropology, religion and mythology, her many southwestern fieldwork projects have been concerned with Navajo health and welfare. Author of *Mythology and Values: An Analysis of Navaho Chantway Myths* (1957) and "Navajo Health and Welfare Aides: A Field Study" (*Social Science Review*, 1971), she is currently working on a book on Washington Matthews with Susan McGreevy.

MARGARET HARDIN is Curator of Anthropology of the Los Angeles County Museum of Natural History where she is a specialist in material culture, especially Zuni ceramics and jewelry, as well as linguistics. She has worked among the Zapotec in Oaxaca, Mexico, and the Zuni of New Mexico. Her research at Zuni resulted in the publication of *Gifts of Mother Earth* (1983). She is currently working on new Southwestern ethnographic exhibits.

LOUIS A. HIEB is Head Librarian, Special Collections at the University of Arizona Library. A graduate of Princeton University he wrote his dissertation on Hopi clowning. He has written extensively on topics relating to Native American religion, symbolic systems, and architecture. Most recently he has compiled three bibliographical works on mystery writer Tony Hillerman and the work of early researchers at Hopi.

LEANNE HINTON is a professor of Linguistics at the University of California at Berkeley and has worked with the Havasupai for many years, first as an undergraduate student, then as a researcher and consultant for the tribe. Her numerous studies have included anthropology and ethnomusicology. She has also studied Hualapai and La

Huerta Diegueno. Her numerous publications include *Spirit Mountain: An Anthology of Yuman Story and Song* (with Lucille Watahomigie, 1984); *Havasupai Songs: A Linguistic Perspective* (1984); and *Havasupai Dictionary* (1984).

LOUISE LAMPHERE is professor of Anthropology at the University of New Mexico, a specialist on Navajo social organization, especially kinship and gender; women's studies; and women's work in the contemporary U.S. She is also editor of *Frontiers: A Journal of Women Studies*, past president of the American Ethnological Society and author of *To Run After Them* (1977). She has also published extensively on women and labor issues.

CHARLES LANGE is professor emeritus at Northern Illinois University. An archaeologist and cultural anthropologist, he has focused on the Rio Grande region. Author of *Cochiti: A New Mexico Pueblo, Past and Present* (1959, 1968, 1990); editor of W. W. Hills's *An Ethnography of Santa Clara Pueblo, New Mexico* (1982); and co-editor (with Carroll L. Riley and Elizabeth M. Lange) of *The Southwestern Journals of Adolph F. Bandelier, 1880–1892* (four volumes: 1966, 1970, 1975, 1984). He continues to teach at New Mexico Highlands University and to work on archival projects.

SUSAN BROWN MCGREEVY was director of the Wheelwright Museum from 1978–1982, and currently is a Research Associate with that institution. She is presently working on a biography of the Museum's founder, Mary Cabot Wheelwright. In addition she continues her research concerning art and culture change among the Navajo and Paiute. She authored *Anii Anaadaalyaa'igii: Recent Trends in Navajo Art* (with Bruce Bernstein, 1988) and *Translating Tradition: Basketry Arts of the San Juan Paiutes* (with Andrew Hunter Whiteford, 1985). She is presently collaborating with Katherine Spencer Halpern in a publication about Washington Matthews's work among the Navajos.

NANCY PAREZO is Curator of Ethnology at the Arizona State Museum and Associate Research Professor in the Department of Anthropology, University of Arizona. A former program officer at the National Science Foundation and university administrator she has authored *Navajo Sandpaintings: From Religious Art to Commercial Art* (1983); *The Fine Art of Federal Grantsmanship for Museums* (1988); *Native American Arts and Crafts: A Resource Guide* (with Ruth Perry and Rebecca Allen, 1991); and *Daughters of the Desert* (with Barbara Babcock, 1988). She is currently working on another book on Navajo sandpaintings and one on anthropological museum exhibits.

KATHLEEN MULLEN SANDS is professor of English and adjunct faculty in the Department of Anthropology at Arizona State University. A specialist in folklore and American Indian literatures she is the co-author (with Gretchen Bataille) of *American Indian Women Telling Their Lives* (1984) and *American Indian Women: A Guide to Research* (1991). She is editor of *Circle of Motion: Arizona Anthology of Contemporary Indian Literature* (1990), senior editor of *People of Pascua* by Edward H. Spicer (1988), and editor-interpreter of *Autobiography of a Yaqui Poet* by Refugio Savala (1980), as well as numerous articles on American Indian literature and folklore.

SHELBY TISDALE is a doctoral candidate at the University of Arizona and an adjunct faculty member in the Department of Social Sciences at Pima Community College. Her dissertation examines the affects of changing land tenure on the economy of the Raramuri household in the Sierra Madre Region of Chihuahua, Mexico. She is currently editing a collection of papers presented in a symposium entitled "The Commoditization of Indigenous Arts and Crafts in the Greater Southwest," and is writing articles on three southwestern Pueblos, Isleta, Nambe, and Tesuque for inclusion in *Encyclopedia of Native Americans of the Twentieth Century* (Garland Press, forthcoming).

INDEX